Routledge Handbook of International Political Economy (IPE)

This handbook gives an overview of the range and scope of International Political Economy (IPE) scholarship by mapping the different regional schools of IPE and noting the distinctive way IPE is practiced and conceptualized around the world. It is intended to serve as a critical survey of, not just the field of IPE in terms of its theories and results, but of those claims about the field made by IPE scholars themselves.

Providing a clear and coherent structure, the book is split into four parts:

- Part I: North American IPE
- Part II: British IPE
- Part III: IPE in Asia
- Part IV: IPE elsewhere—exemptions, exclusions, and extensions

These sections map out the contending approaches and key concerns that exist within each regional school and include chapters tackling key areas of IPE scholarship such as trade and development, finance, and global governance/globalization. Each chapter is an attempt to understand IPE by seeing how differently placed IPE scholars, by virtue of geography, intellectual history, personal training, and socialization, talk about the IPE and think about their subject.

With over twenty contributors from a wide range of countries, the *Routledge Handbook of International Political Economy* is an essential resource for all those with an interest in this complex and rapidly evolving field of study.

Mark Blyth is Associate Professor of Political Science at Johns Hopkins University.

Routledge Handbook of International Political Economy (IPE)

IPE as a global conversation

Edited by
Mark Blyth

Routledge
Taylor & Francis Group

LONDON AND NEW YORK

First published 2009
by Routledge
2 Park Square, Milton Park, Abingdon, Oxon, OX14 4RN

Simultaneously published in the USA and Canada
by Routledge
270 Madison Avenue, New York, NY 10016

Routledge is an imprint of the Taylor & Francis Group, an informa business

Typeset in Bembo by
Taylor & Francis Books
Printed and bound in Great Britain by
MPG Books Ltd, Bodmin

British Library Cataloguing in Publication Data
A catalogue record for this book is available from the British Library

Library of Congress Cataloging in Publication Data
Routledge handbook of international political economy (IPE) : IPE as a
  global conversation / edited by Mark Blyth.
    p. cm.
  International economic relations. 2. Economics. I. Blyth, Mark, 1967–
  HF1359.R69 2009
337–dc22   2008036955

ISBN 978-0-415-77126-9 (hbk)
ISBN 978-0-203-88156-9 (ebk)

Contents

Tables

Contributors

Rawi Abdelal is the Joseph C. Wilson Professor of Business Administration at the Harvard Business School, USA.

Giovanni Arrighi is Professor of Sociology at the Johns Hopkins University, USA.

Walden Bello is senior analyst at Focus on the Global South, President of the Freedom from Debt Coalition, a fellow of the Transnational Institute, and Professor of Sociology at the University of the Philippines, Diliman.

Angus Cameron is a Lecturer in Human Geography at the University of Leicester, UK.

John L. Campbell is the Class of 1925 Professor of Sociology at Dartmouth College, USA and Professor of Political Economy, Copenhagen Business School, Denmark.

Philip G. Cerny is Professor of Global Political Economy in the Division of Global Affairs and the Department of Political Science at Rutgers University-Newark, USA.

Ben Clift is Senior Lecturer in International Political Economy in the Department of Politics and International Studies at the University of Warwick, UK.

Benjamin J. Cohen is the Louis G. Lancaster Professor of International Political Economy in the Department of Political Science at the University of California, Santa Barbara, USA.

Alexander Cooley is Associate Professor in the Department of Political Science at Barnard College, Columbia University, USA.

Randall Germain is Professor of Political Science at Carleton University, Canada.

John M. Hobson is Professor of Politics and International Relations at Sheffield University, UK.

Nicolas Jabko is Research Director at SciencePo, France.

Jonathan Kirshner is Professor of Government at Cornell University, USA.

Paul Langley is Senior Lecturer in International Politics at Northumbria University, UK.

Michael J. Oliver is Professor of Economics at the ESC Rennes School of Business, France.

Ronen Palan is Professor of International Political Economy at the University of Birmingham, UK.

José Gabriel Palma is Senior Lecturer in Economics at the University of Cambridge, UK.

Ben Rosamond is Professor of Politics and International Studies at the University of Warwick, UK.

Leonard Seabrooke is Professor in International Political Economy in the Department of Politics and International Studies, and Director of the Centre for the Study of Globalisation and Regionalisation, at the University of Warwick, UK.

J. C. Sharman is Associate Professor in the Centre for Governance and Public Policy and Queen Elizabeth II Fellow at Griffith University, Australia.

Henry Wai-Chung Yeung is Professor of Geography at the National University of Singapore, Singapore.

Acknowledgments

I never thought I would edit a textbook, and I am glad that I still haven't. Taking Craig Fowlie's idea of doing an IPE textbook and turning it into something completely different; a global tour of IPE has, like most global tours, been both taxing and exciting. It has also been a long time coming. In that regard I would like to thank all the contributors to this volume not only for their copy, but for their patience. The result of this collective endeavor is a volume that I hope will serve as a useful orienting point of reference for the field for some time to come. Needless to say some readers will object that certain positions and perspectives are missed out. I can only say in my defense that many more people were asked to contribute than actually did, so if something isn't here and you think that it should be, I can tell you who to blame. In the meantime, I hope that you enjoy the conversation.

Mark Blyth
Baltimore, August 2008

Introduction

International political economy as a global conversation

Mark Blyth

Introduction

What you hold in your hands is not a textbook. Or, at the very least, it's a rather unusual textbook. Most textbooks start off with a declarative. That such-and-such field of study is defined by parameters A and B, which is in turn best studied by methods P and Q. In this way boundaries are set, and what is "in" and what is "out" of the field of study in question, in terms of theories, topics, etc., is established. International Political Economy (IPE) textbooks have from the field's inception attempted to do something similar; to define what IPE is and hence how it should be studied. For example, in many ways the original textbook of IPE, at least in the United States, was Robert Gilpin's magisterial *The Political Economy of International Relations* (1987). In this work Gilpin defines IPE as "a set of questions to be examined by means of an eclectic mixture of analytic methods and theoretical perspectives" (1987: 9). Thirteen years later Jeffrey Frieden and David Lake (eds.), in their *International Political Economy: Perspectives on Global Power and Wealth* (2000: 1); define IPE as "the interplay of economics and politics in the world arena." However, these seemingly quite open statements of intent belie what became a rather uniform way of answering these questions.

Gilpin's 1987 volume established a specific way of learning IPE as a field, which was to see it as composed of three rival approaches: realism, liberalism, and Marxism. These three "ideologies" were set up as the alternative foci though which one "studied" the IPE. Most textbooks continue to use this "holy troika" approach as a template to this day. Even a self-consciously different approach, that of John Ravenhill's (ed.) *Global Political Economy* (2005), takes much the same line of attack. However, rather than ditch Gilpin's triptych, Ravenhill uses it to question its continuing applicability to a field that is undeniably changing, which is good; but changing in what way? And is setting up "how to know" the IPE as choosing between these three supposedly separate perspectives still useful some twenty years later, even as critique?

Some scholars seem to think that it has served its purpose. For example, a recent survey of IPE by Jeffrey Frieden and Lisa Martin argues that despite these three different starting points the field has approached a "consensus on theories, methods, analytical frameworks, and important questions," at least for "North American scholarship" (2003: 19). Moreover, given the (neo)liberal bent of this apparent "consensus" you might be tempted to think that realism and Marxism have had their day and liberalism reigns triumphant as the only game in town. As we shall see in the contributions to this handbook, however, if only it were that simple.[1]

Such a view of settled boundaries, plug-and-play perspectives, and methodological uniformity is hard to square with the increasing pluralism of approaches we see in IPE today as the field continues to flourish, especially outside of the United States. Take for example, Hettne (1995), who along with scholars such as Robert Cox and Stephen Gill, have applied a Polanyian/Gramscian perspective to questions of IPE. Another set of scholars, anticipating Ravenhill's preference for a "Global Political Economy," bring to our attention concerns drawn from sociology, gender studies, and postcolonial studies (Palan ed. 2000). Still others seek a broader engagement with a post-structural politics of biopolitics, performativity, and even a "libidinal IPE" (de Goede 2006). Given such developments, the claim that the field is, by agreement and results, in the midst of a methodological narrowing at the same time as this undeniable theoretical broadening is going on seems hard to square. This leaves one with two choices. To either adjudicate a "true" version of IPE given some hierarchy of approaches and checklist of what constitutes valid knowledge, or to accept that there are *multiple versions of the field of IPE*. This latter stance is the one taken in this handbook. There are indeed multiple versions of IPE, and accepting this ought to be the starting point of understanding the field itself.

What this handbook is and what it is not

This handbook is intended to serve as a critical survey of not just the field of IPE in terms of its theories and results, but of those claims about the field made by IPE scholars themselves. As the Scottish poet Robert Burns once put it, "O wad some Power the giftie gie us. To see oursels as ithers see us!"[2] It is an attempt to understand IPE by seeing how differently placed IPE scholars, by virtue of geography, intellectual history, personal training and socialization, talk about the IPE and think about their subject. One way of doing this would be a book of interviews, but interviews with almost twenty academics would probably try the patience of a saint who worked part-time as an actuary in a morgue. Rather, the approach applied here was to ask each of these distinguished scholars to write about substance; what they think the core concerns of IPE are from where they sit in the world, and in doing so reflect upon what they think adds to our collective knowledge.

The result is this handbook. But this handbook, I hasten to add, is not a textbook in any normal sense. It does not line up a bunch of "top" authors and get them each to write thirty odd pages on some topic of importance for the study of the IPE; trade, finance, inequality, etc., as somehow canonical. Such volumes are oftentimes outdated by the time they hit the bookstore and usually end up simply adding to the dozens of such volumes that are already devouring library budgets and taking up valuable shelf-space.[3] Engaging with textbooks is not the only way to learn about the field of IPE.

It is also not a textbook insofar as it does not, apropos the discussion above, define IPE as being about one singular thing, field, area or approach. It is not an attempt to circle the methodological wagons and keep out some set of heretical Indians. It does not, in short, set boundaries in order to lift one versions of IPE up above the others. Rather, it seeks to understand and explore the different version of IPE we see around the world in order to strengthen what we know through a recognition of what particular perspectives unavoidably miss. Finally, it is not a textbook insofar as it does not presume IPE to be a settled and established body of knowledge that one studies in an "introductory" textbook, moving onto another more "advanced" textbook, and then, having mastered a variety of techniques, going off to engage in original research. Such textbooks exist in engineering and mathematics. The study of the IPE; an open, dynamic, evolutionary, complex adaptive system, populated by learning subjects, can admit no such pretensions. But, I hasten to add, this does not mean that one cannot learn "IPE." That is, engage with the field as it is actually constituted and in doing so learn about the international political economy as it exists. That, after all, is what this handbook is for.

Who this handbook is for and how to engage with it

This handbook is designed for three groups; undergraduate students in specialist IPE courses, graduate students embarking on the same intellectual journey, and scholars who want to "get a handle on" this complex and rapidly evolving field of study. And apropos the discussion above, rather than seek to convince the reader that the "IPE as subject" is "X" rather than "Y" or "Z," this volume takes a different track. It starts from the not unreasonable premise that, as Peter Gourevitch once said, "what people want depends on where they sit" (Gourevitch 1986: 56). I modify that here to say, "what people think and study depends on where they sit." Taking this as our starting point, this handbook suggests (perhaps against the wishes of some of its contributing authors) that IPE is composed of what one might call "multiple traditions," both *between schools* and *within schools*. For example, one can easily acquire the impression that scholars in the United States tend to see their version of IPE as, to a large extent, the only game in town. They see themselves, to paraphrase Burns, as owning particular understanding of how the field has evolved (as part of the subfield of political science called international relations), in a particular moment (in the late 1970s at the conjunction of the oil crisis, stagflation, the rise of Japan, and the perception of US decline).

Such a view is far from incorrect, especially from the point of view of US scholars. But the problem here is that by defining these moments as the founding moment for IPE in the US these events are sometimes read as the founding moment for IPE as a field of scholarship per se across the world.[4] Such a position has two consequences. First, it ignores the actual diversity of approaches to what the IPE is *within the United States*. Second, it ignores not just "contributions" from outside the US, but leads us to sideline other rather different versions of IPE generated elsewhere in the world from wholly different disciplinary origins.

British scholars, for example, have developed a rather different version of IPE in terms of what it is and how to study it. Rather than seeing a "consensus on theories, methods, analytical frameworks, and important questions," à la Frieden and Martin (2003: 19) as a good thing, British scholars tend to view pluralism and intellectual diversity as a good thing (Higgott and Watson 2008). Being less wedded to what Benjamin Cohen (in this volume and elsewhere) has usefully identified as the twin American cannons of "positivism and empiricism—the twin pillars of the hard science model" allied to a commitment to testing facts against data (Cohen 2008b: 176), British scholars have developed a way of studying the IPE and contesting its boundaries, rather than constituting and policing them as American scholars are seen, by British scholars, to seek to do.[5]

But let us return to this "where you sit determines what you think about IPE" notion of understanding IPE. Move IPE scholarship out of the US and UK to Asia and the picture of what IPE is changes once again. For example, what American scholars cele-brate as hegemony as leadership (Gilpin 1987; Mandelbaum 2005) and British (and Canadian) scholars question as hegemony à la Gramsci (Cox 1987; Morton 2006), Asian scholars tend to simply see as (neo) imperialism (Bello 2005). Consequently, IPE scho-larship produced in this different place is different again, focusing on similar concerns, but concerns refracted from where such scholars sit in the IPE itself and subject to the self-understandings such subject-positions produce. Similarly, as we continue through this volume we will tackle why there is no distinctively "European" version of IPE, why the Latin American tradition of IPE, which arguably predated both the American and British schools, died out, and what sociologists and economic historians, who have arguably been doing IPE for a long time without being so labeled, think about the project of IPE itself and their contributions to it.

In sum, given that the IPE itself is always evolving, usually in quite unexpected ways, the idea that IPE either can be, or indeed is constituted by a set of "true in all times and places" postulates that will narrow over time to produce "consensus on theories, meth-ods, analytical frameworks, and important questions," seems a naive hope at best and an exercise in intellectual exclusion at worst.[6] But, again, that does not mean one cannot learn IPE. One can, and this handbook aims to do so by treating the different ways in which IPE is studied around the world as constitutive of a global conversation about what the IPE is, and from there, what we know about it.

Why a global conversation?

The short answer to this question is because IPE, far from being wholly an offshoot of the American subfield of political science called international relations, is rapidly becoming an interdisciplinary field in its own right; at least elsewhere in the world. As such, this handbook seeks extend to a conversation usefully begun by Benjamin Cohen in his 2007 *Review of International Political Economy* essay, "The transatlantic divide: why are British and American IPE so different?" (Cohen 2007) and in his subsequent 2008 book *International Political Economy: An Intellectual History*. Cohen's 2007 article and 2008 book (in brief) made the following argument.

There is no singular IPE. Rather, there is a distinct "British school" of IPE and a dis-tinct "American school" of IPE, "and between the two is a deep divide" (Cohen 2007: 198). Cohen argues that Americans are state-centric positivists who think that if you can't taste it, touch it, or drop it on your foot, and then give a clear causal (and pre-ferably reductionist) explanation as to how that happened (usually quantitatively), then it doesn't matter/exist (Cohen 2007: 199–200; 201–7). Meanwhile the British are, by and large, a bunch of post-positivists who argue that such scientific pretension is misplaced and that the real issue is not to measure minutiae, but to ask who benefits from the order that is the IPE from whatever methodological standpoint works. In contrast to the Americans then, British IPE is not afraid to take on, front and center, the normative questions lurking behind the ostensibly positivist ones (Cohen 2007: 207–16).[7] However, Cohen opines, the gap has grown so large between these schools that "whereas the American School values 'normal science,' the British school identifies with critical theo-ry's oppositional frame of mind" to the point that partisans in each camp increasingly ignore, rather than learn from each other (Cohen 2008b: 176–77). Cohen is hopeful that such intransigence can be overcome, as am I. It is in this spirit that we begin this global conversation as a way of building upon the opening he has made, to further the trans-atlantic dialog and to broaden it past the "American versus British" divide and encourage a truly global conversation.[8]

IPE as a global conversation

American IPE

The first thing worth noticing about this handbook is its geographic layout; North America, Britain, Asia and Australia, are grouped together as separate schools while the rest of the world is discussed under "extensions, exclusions and exemptions." There is a method to such madness. Allowing for the notion that the American school of IPE identified by Cohen is the "biggest kid on the block" we begin there. The point of this first section of the handbook is not to canonize the American school as the hegemonic monolith it is sometimes seen to be. Rather, the point is to recognize the difference and diversity that exists within North American scholarship.[9] Appropriately then we begin with an essay by Benjamin Cohen, building upon his earlier interventions, who sets up the idea of the "multiple traditions of American IPE." That is, while agreement on a normal science model and strong links to political science/international relations as the "parent discipline" are common among American IPE scholars, "the American school rarely speaks with one voice" (Cohen, this volume: p. 23). As such, the notion of a singular "American school" masks great variation within the IPE research community in North America.

Cohen begins our global conversation by reviewing the evolution of the American school. He notes its emergence in the context of the economic turbulence of the 1970s, the abdication of American economists of this time from analyzing the political issues that drove those economic dislocations, and how this created a vacuum for putative IPE scholars to fill. According to Cohen, this emergent field found coherence around certain key individuals, critical topics, and problem areas, all of which were tied to real-world questions of political economy. Cohen traces how the American school evolved from Keohane and Nye's notion of complex interdependence as a challenge to realism; how this in turn evolved into a decade long battle between hegemonic stability theory/regime theory/neoliberal institutionalism and neo-realism in the 1980s (Baldwin 1993), and how this in turn narrowed to the point that these ostensibly different positions collapsed into one another in what Ruggie refers to as the "neo-utilitarian" synthesis (Ruggie 1999: 215).

Given this narrowing of the field in the US, Cohen notes how other approaches began to come to the fore.[10] Once dormant traditions of cognitive and ideational ana-lyses found a new lease of life at this juncture, and eventually even the constructivist analyses that had revolutionized security studies in the 1990s began to filter into Amer-ican IPE, creating new pathways for research. However, as Cohen notes, there is a trend running counter to this new broadening-out of American IPE; the "imitative scientism" of economics appearing as the sine qua non of "serious" IPE research in some of the top US journals, to the relative exclusion of other perspectives. In short, as this introduction has already noted, both within the US and outside of it, there is a "narrowing" of some aspects of IPE, methodologically and epistemologically, at the same time as there is a broadening theoretically and thematically. These two counter-trends very much engender each other and drive IPE in North America forward.

The chapters following Cohen's overview, by Kirshner, Cooley, and Abdelal, delineate what one might call the core American traditions of IPE in more detail. Kirshner's
contribution is to highlight both the legacy and continuing relevance of a realist perspective in contemporary IPE. Far from vanishing from the field in the 1990s at the end
of the Cold War, Kirshner reminds us of what the realist tradition of IPE is, how realism
has contributed to the study of IPE through its focus on relative gains, and why it
remains well poised to tackle contemporary questions such as the relationship between
globalization and relative power, questions that other approaches tend to ignore.

Realism does however, Kirshner suggests, need modification to maintain its relevance.
First, it needs to be more attentive to change rather than continuity in the IPE. Phenomena such as globalization should not be seen as "complex interdependence *part two*"
but as a change in the nature of the system that alters the capacity of all states. Similarly,
he notes that "to explain world politics … in the coming years, it is necessary [for realists]
to appeal to a host of other factors [apart from power as capability], including domestic
politics, history, ideology, and perceptions of legitimacy" (Kirshner, this volume: p. 43).
If realism is not renewed in this way, Kirshner warns, the sterile structuralism of "offensive realism" will be all that remains of realism's rich tradition, which would be extremely
narrowing for IPE as a whole.

Following Kirshner, Cooley's chapter guides us through what is in many ways the
dominant American school of IPE: the rationalist approach to understanding international
institutions. However, far from presenting this school as a unified "bloc" of "rational
choice theory as applied to IPE," Cooley notes how very different approaches come
together in what he terms a variety of "contractualist" approaches to the IPE. While these
approaches certainly do share the basic rationalist precepts of methodological individualism, utility maximization, a focus on agents' interests as primary, etc., where they differ
lies in the core concepts operationalized in each variant.

Cooley highlights three positions within the American rationalist school. First, he discusses
the neoliberal institutionalist approach highlighted by Cohen and its evolution into the project on rationalist institutional design, with its focus on the design of rules in the IPE and
the distributional consequences thereof. He next discusses the contribution of IPE scholars
who have built upon Oliver Williamson's work on hierarchy and control within frameworks
of relational contracting. The third strand of work Cooley examines are those IPE scholars
who stress the generic problem of credible commitments in institutional design, in particular,
and cooperation in general. Taken together, Cooley argues that these three contractualist
approaches provide a powerful set of tools for understanding the contemporary IPE.

In this regard what is especially significant about Cooley's contribution, beyond
showing the diversity that lies within this seemingly single approach, is his injunction that
contractualist approaches, which have often been criticized for their analogical basis (X
situation is modeled "as if" it's a contract, when in fact it is not) have actually become an
ever more appropriate tool of study over time for IPE scholars as more and more of the
IPE has become de jure as well as de facto contractualized. Large areas of sovereign
rights, from defense to foreign aid, to trade, have become the province of private contracts between states and non-state actors. As such, the reach of contractualism has grown
as a function of its appropriateness, which may also go some way to explaining why it
has (arguably) become the dominant school in the US.

Abdelal's chapter, in contrast, brings into relief the development of constructivist approaches into American IPE hinted at by Cohen at the end of his chapter. Despite the perception among some US scholars that this body of scholarship is at best underdeveloped,

Abdelal shows it to be a rich, and again, diverse position within (and outside of) the American school. Abdelal begins in a similar vein to Kirshner's critique of the structuralism of realist approaches, with the contention that neither interests nor actions can be simply "read-off" the material structure of the IPE as rationalist approaches tend to assume. Consequently, Abdelal views the rise of constructivism in the IPE as simply "the accumulation of explanations for how the world economy works" from a non-materialist basis (Abdelal, this volume: p. 63).

Abdelal first introduces us to what constructivism is through the revolution it wrought in security studies, and bit-by-bit in political economy, through the 1980s and 1990s via the work of scholars such as Ruggie (1982) and Katzenstein (1985), McNamara (1998) and Abdelal (2001). Although more pronounced as an established position in the literature outside of the US, Abdelal nonetheless shows how constructivist analyses have appeared in a variety of issues areas traditionally seen as the bastions of rationalist American IPE such as exchange rate politics (Best 2005), regime choice (Hall 2003), and financial globalization (Abdelal 2007). What is especially useful about Abdelal's contribution is how, drawing on forthcoming work with Mark Blyth and Craig Parsons, he identifies four varieties of constructivism in IPE research: meaning-oriented, cognitive, uncertainty, and subjectivity-based constructivisms. He details each position and highlights its specific strengths and logic of inquiry. Once again, given Abdelal's analysis, the American school of IPE appears much more diverse than a quick glance admits; if not more so than some of its protagonists would have us believe.

Rounding out Part I we have a chapter by Randall Germain. The difference that Germain's chapter makes to our overall story is to remind us that borders do matter for identity, insofar as being a Canadian scholar may make one part of North American IPE, but it does not necessarily make one a member of the American school. Indeed, according to Germain, what is germane about IPE in Canada is how, despite its proximity to the US, it has evolved along quite different lines from the multiple traditions evident within the US-based IPE community.

Germain sees the development of IPE in Canada as particularly affected by one scholar: Robert Cox. The difference that Cox made was that due to his influence "IPE in Canada ... paid less attention to the neo-classical synthesis and ... rational choice, in favor of ... Marx, Karl Polanyi and other ... theorists that were rapidly becoming marginalized in US academia" (Germain, this volume: p. 80). Echoing Cohen's assessment, Germain notes that while historical materialist approaches (qua Marxist) never really took off in the US, with the result that realism and liberalism held court until very recently, in Canada, such "critical" perspectives were constitutive of a very different type of mainstream of research where concepts such as "hegemony" were held to have had a very different meaning than typically was deployed in the American school. What is distinctive about Canadian IPE then is this attempt to craft an non-reductionist historical materialist approach that "in many ways [acts as] exactly the kind of transatlantic bridge" Cohen calls for between the British and American schools (Germain, this volume: p. 10). IPE in Canada then further complicates the notion of a monolithic North American IPE by adding another strong and vibrant research tradition to our picture of what IPE in North America is all about.

What can the reader take from all of this?

I would hope that the reader gets three things out of reading this section as a whole. First is an idea of the diversity of approaches within the broad North American school (including Canada). Second, in reading these essays I would hope that the reader will derive a basic working knowledge of what these positions—realist IPE, contractualist IPE, constructivist IPE, and critical/historical materialist IPE—actually entail and argue. That is, the reader should consider these essays to be partly a theoretical primer as well as an historical exploration of the field. Third, I hope that reader can use the knowledge of these different research traditions in North America to evaluate and compare them with what comes next, the very different approach to studying the IPE taken by British scholars.

British IPE

In Part II we pull together four chapters that not only set out a different way of "doing" IPE, but also establish a different history of how (British) IPE came about. Putting the British school of IPE in its historical context is the first chapter in this section, by Ben Rosamond and Ben Clift. Rosamond and Clift begin with a brief re-examination of Cohen's division of IPE into our two schools; one American and positivist, one British and post-positivist. While Rosamond and Clift accept this division on one level they seek to contest it along some other dimensions. The point of doing so is not to cast Cohen as "wrong" so much as to recast *why* British IPE is "different."

According to Rosamond and Clift, Cohen's division of the field into American and British schools rests upon a reading of the evolution of IPE everywhere as being driven by certain key individuals: Robert Cox in Canada, Susan Strange in the UK, Robert Gilpin, Charles Kindleberger, Steven Krasner, Peter Katzenstein and Robert Keohane in the US, and certain precipitating events, namely the economic volatility of the early 1970s. For Rosamond and Clift, this is a problematic way to cast British IPE for three reasons. First of all, British IPE has a far longer lineage than can be ascribed to Susan Strange and the economic dislocations of the early 1970s. Second, Rosamond and Clift maintain that there never has been a "parent discipline" for British IPE; it has always been a multidisciplinary exercise. Third, and similar to what Germain noted in the Canadian context, Marxist approaches have a long pedigree in UK scholarship that has allowed the development of understandings of the IPE far removed from the realist-liberal duopoly of the American school.

How then can we understand the different origins and consequent concerns of British IPE? For while it certainly is different as Cohen maintains, if those differences are not attributable to Susan Strange and the 1970s, what has brought about such an intellectual divergence from the American school? Clift and Rosamond identity four "drivers" of the study of British IPE that precede the US variant and give substance to its differences in foci and temperament. First, there is a long tradition of scholarship dealing with the political economy of British imperialism, which has given much of British social science a particular historicist cast. Second, there is the post-war literature on decolonization and the global role of sterling in that period. Third, there is the enormous literature on the UK's (relative) economic decline, especially the international determinants thereof, which makes the boundary cast in the US between international political economy and comparative political economy much more permeable in the UK. Fourth, there has been a continuing concern with the centrality of the state in both domestic and international economic relations.

As a result of these very different lineages of scholarship, Rosamond and Clift argue that for British IPE, "the presiding question has been less to do with problems [such as the] domestic preference formation [of states] ... but rather the degree to which the historical resolution of social and economic struggles have become inscribed upon the state and predispose it to certain types of action" (Rosamond and Clift, this volume: p. 107). This view of British IPE gives a greater understanding of not just *how*, but *why* it differs from US-based scholarship. In short, lacking the concerns that animated American scholarship, and grappling with its own particulars, British IPE has become more historically focused and more open to a variety of perspectives than its American counterpart.

The next chapter, by Angus Cameron and Ronen Palan, builds upon Rosamond and Clift's opening by taking issue with another aspect of Cohen's critique. Once again, the purpose is not to show Cohen wrong, but to explain along another metric *why* British IPE is different. Cameron and Palan are sympathetic to Cohen's charge that "the British School may be fairly criticized for its less rigorous approach to theory building and testing, which makes generalization difficult and accumulation of knowledge virtually impossible" (Cohen 2008b: 64). But nonetheless they wish to push back a little on Cohen's analysis. For these authors, while it may be the case that British IPE does not look like American IPE, nor does it necessarily believe in trans-historical cumulative knowledge building, etc., that does not mean that it is "less rigorous" nor, crucially, less *empirical*. As such, the challenge for these authors is not to "be more American," but to ask "how does one go about constructing reflexive and heterodox empirically-rich theories and methodologies in a complex world?" (Cameron and Palan, this volume: p. 113).

Cameron and Palan take the mainstream social sciences' (qua US IPE's) view of empiricism as corresponding to Hume's constant conjunctions of observable events. As such, what you see is what you measure, and hence what you get. The world is therefore different in kind from our words about it since, for American scholars, it exists irrespective of our inferences about it. Cameron and Palan, however, point out that *empiricism* has a much richer meaning than such a surface reading of Hume supposes. In particular, a standard Humean reading of causation qua empiricism ignores how even Humean causation is based upon a prior associational logic that is independent of the events themselves. That is, we only know things as being "X" or "Y" through their grouping into categories that precede the events. As such, "belief systems are not simply refracted expressions derived from ... observations, they also contribute to the shaping of the observed—they help constitute the subject" (Cameron and Palan, this volume: p. 116).[11]

In this sense, the concepts that delineate, for example, "the IPE," are themselves social products that are inextricably part of the analysis. In such a world, the constants and conjunctures assumed by the naive-Humean version of empiricism become impossible to sustain and a burden on actual research. Cameron and Palan argue instead for an empiricist and observational methodology, but one that takes seriously the reflexive and constructed nature of the world. This means rather than positing a given ontology as non-problematic and moving on from there, where, for example, "states are the primary actors in world politics" or "firms maximize revenues," a more open ontology is assumed such that the nature of the subject "is immanent to the subject of inquiry rather than logically prior to it" (Cameron and Palan, this volume: p. 119). This is not to say that the world can simply be imagined as being any way the scholar chooses, far from it. But recognizing reality as always mediated and associational allows scholarship *to question claims to empirical validity even more deeply*. This pushes Cameron and Palan to find a place between the American school where "data and observation are so unproblematic we can accept them as real" and the British school where "data and observation are so problematic that we can dispense with them altogether" (Cameron and Palan, this volume:

p. 123). That is, a deeper empiricism that does not allow for "anything goes," but moves beyond the temptation to see surface appearances as really all that matters.

Our third "British" chapter, from Paul Langley, takes our discussion of British IPE in a direction that makes the dynamics of this school seem more similar rather than more different to the American school. Just as Cohen noted the "as yet" marginal influence of constructivist approaches in the American school (a point contested by Abdelal in his chapter) so Langley puzzles over the "as yet" marginal influence of post-structuralist theorizing on British IPE. And in contrast to Clift and Rosamond, who see the figure of Susan Strange as far less than central to the origins and direction of British IPE than Cohen, Langley places Strange front and center to explain this so-far limited incursion.

Langley's version of Strange's influence on British IPE hews close to the line Cohen lays out, as perhaps *the* driving figure in the development of British IPE, but Langley's version of events problematizes Strange's influence in that the key concepts she bequeathed to British IPE, particularly her version of "power and knowledge," have led the British version of IPE down a peculiar evolutionary path. Strange's own work was based around a question and two concepts. *Qui bono?* (who benefits?) was the animating question, with "structural power" and the "relational power" being the key concepts deployed to tackle this question. For Strange, structural power was not reducible to material capability or dominance. Rather, it was "decentered … [operating] … through the four main structures in the global political economy—security, production, finance, and knowledge" (Langley, this volume: p. 129). In this way, Strange sought to move beyond simple notions of "who has power?" to ask "how is power generated and for whom?"

In doing so however, while broadening British IPE's conception of power in one way, Langley argues that Strange helped narrow it in another. Critical in the production of power for Strange was "the knowledge structure"; "what is believed … what is known and perceived as understood" (Strange 1994b: 119, quoted in Langley, this volume: p. 131). In so problematizing "knowledge as power" Strange could have opened up British IPE theorizing to the rich post-structuralist analysis of power then emerging on the continent, but she did not. As Langley puts it, "Strange at once opened-up and closed-down the possibility that thinking anew about power and knowledge could form the core of British IPE" (Langley, this volume: p. 133). Langley goes on to highlight, against the relief of the exclusion Strange created, critical post-structuralist contributions to IPE, and how these interventions can perhaps more fully realize Strange's vision of a new analysis of power in the IPE that more positively builds upon Strange's legacy.

Finally, putting some flesh on the bones of this more historical and reflexive approach to IPE theorizing is Cerny's chapter.[12] Picking up once again on Cohen's characterization of the two schools as real, Cerny makes the case for a transatlantic bridge built around the notion of a structurational approach to studying the IPE (Giddens 1985; Cerny 1990). Rather than find fault with Cohen's version of British IPE's lineages, for Cerny the real and deeper problem lies beyond diverging methodologies in the underlying philosophies of social science that underpin both schools, which suggests a radical incommensurability between the two positions.

Despite coming to this conclusion, and far from chucking his lot in with one or other of the schools by way of easy resolution, Cerny homes in on a quintessential British school concern, the relationship between structure and agency, and uses this opening to overcome the ontological "either/or" offered by the two schools via the theory of structuration. Doing so, Cerny argues, obviates the classic "levels of analysis problem" of IPE research by allowing one to focus on what he terms a multi-actor, multi-nodal, global politics. By focusing on processes of structuration (how agents respond to and innovate within specific structural environments), agents as different as states, firms, and NGOs can be accommodated within the same analytic framework. Though only suggestive of a broader project, such a common framework could, Cerny argues, allow analysts in both schools to attack problems from a variety of methodological and theoretical stances, thereby effectively bypassing the ontological issues that separate the schools at their base. This bold attempt at synthesis may not be to the taste of all scholars from either camp, but it does represent a progressive attempt to overcome the "either/or" choices presented by the two schools' protagonists.

What can the reader take from all of this?

I hope that the reader gets three things out of reading this section. First, that the reader engages with the key issues each chapter brings up in its attempt to contrast British IPE and its concerns with those of the American school. For Rosamond and Clift, *lineages matter*. British IPE has wholly different multidisciplinary roots to the American school. As such, holding them as competing schools is somewhat misplaced. For Cameron and Palan, *reflexivity matters*. British IPE foregrounds how knowledge of the IPE is constitutive of the IPE itself such that empirical research cannot get at "the real" as American IPE is wont to assume. However, this does not mean "anything goes." Rather, it signals how in a complex and socially constructed world, a deeper and richer empiricism is warranted for both schools. For Langley, *power matters*. In the opinion of British scholars at least, British IPE has always had a more sophisticated conception of power than American IPE; its own understandings have become somewhat "hamstrung" under the influence of Strange's dichotomy between structural and relational power. Exploiting this opening are very empirically oriented post-structuralist scholars who are making this new understanding of power the centerpiece of their research. In doing so, however, they are perhaps pulling the British and American schools ever further apart. Finally, for Cerny, *process matters*. How agents and structures reciprocally produce possibilities for either system reproduction or transformation becomes key to resolving the "transatlantic divide."

Second, I would hope the arguments made by British scholars get past the "MEGO" (My Eyes Glaze Over) reading of British scholarship they are sometimes charged with (Cohen 2008b: 141). Indeed, it is the case that the British do like their philosophers more than the pragmatic Americans. And yes, reading accounts of Deleuze, Hume, and Foucault is challenging. But British IPE is probably onto something very significant with the insistence on immanent ontologies, emergent causes, and reflexivity in complex adaptive systems like the IPE. Whether engagement with such "high theory" is the correct way to deal with such issues is an open question, but at least to their credit British scholars try to incorporate such understandings into their work. The result is a very different, but equally important, type of IPE.

Asian and Australian IPE

But there is more to life, and IPE, than simply the "special relationship" that exists between scholars in the US and the UK. The schools on either side of the transatlantic divide may be the two biggest IPE communities in the world, but they are far from alone. As IPE spreads around the world, and as scholars from outside of the US and UK take the training they acquire in these "core" countries "back home," so the concerns and models of IPE change again to suit local circumstances and concerns. However, and arguably more important in this case, are those IPE theories developed endogenously in these parts of the world, and/or through the study of these areas. Nowhere is this clearer than in Asian (and Australian) scholarship. Here we group another four chapters that together constitute another version of IPE and its concerns.

The first chapter in Part III comes from Giovanni Arrighi. Arrighi is a sociologist and a scholar of East Asia, rather than an East Asian scholar of IPE. As a consequence of which, Arrighi has developed a very different type of IPE that both geographically and intel-lectually de-centers the West and highlights the differences encountered when IPE is seen from an Asian perspective. Arrighi's point of entry is to consider how most Western—(especially American-) generated IPE tends, when it considers the interplay of economic and security concerns, to have as its underpinning a particular reading of European state-formation. That is, one based upon continual warfare and the con-comitant development of state fiscal capacity as key determinants in Europe's seemingly unique "rise." In this reading a Hobbesian anarchy encourages war-fighting, the rise of the nation state, and the attendant balance of power that mitigates otherwise continual warfare from around 1600–1914 (Waltz 1979; Tilly 1990; cf. Hobson 2004). This model of European state formation and behavior is then held to be a general theory of state behavior all around the world.

Arrighi points out that not only is this a rather narrow reading of European history on which to rest a series of universalist claims about state behavior, it also singularly fails to explain how states evolved and behaved in Asia at the time when Asia was the center of the world economy from 500–1500 AD and Europe was the sleepy backwater (Hobson 2004; Arrighi 2007). Rather than taking as his starting point the "realist" Hobbes' view of life as "nasty, brutish, and short," Arrighi notes Hobbes' less well known contention that "Riches joined with Liberality is power, because it procureth friends, and servants: Without liberality, not so; because in this case they defend not but expose men to Envy, as Prey" (Hobbes 1968: 150, quoted in Arrighi, this volume: p. 171). Engaging this very different Hobbes allows Arrighi to explain China's current rise to prominence in the IPE from a wholly different standpoint to that assumed in Eurocentric IPE literatures.

Noting the lack of warfare in the Chinese imperial period, that fact that it has always had an intensive rather than extensive growth model, and the dependent nature of China's capitalist class, both historically and today, allows Arrighi to re-center IPE and to see East Asia as "a hybrid political-economic formation that theories of international relations based exclusively on the Western experience are utterly incapable of compre-hending" (Arrighi, this volume: p. 166). IPE in Asia then emerges not merely as a part of the world that IPE scholars study, but as a generative type of IPE itself; with a very dif-ferent set of actors, institutions, and processes that simply do not correspond to the categories and labels Western scholarship tends to rely on.

If Arrighi gives us the "macro" picture of a non-Western-centered IPE, Walden Bello supplies the meso-level account of what that alternative IPE looks like in terms of con-temporary research. For Bello, although a variety of Western models have been applied to explain the particularities of the Asian IPE, the distinctive contribution that scholarship "in and about" the region has added to IPE is the literature on the developmental state. That is, a literature developed in and about East Asia that focuses on the state as an active agent in economic development per contra the "states as billiard-balls" model common in realist IPE. Bello's starting point is to note that "[I]f the evolution of IPE in the West ... reflected ... the market being liberated from the state ... the East Asian context could not but mirror opposite reality of … [the state] … harnessing the market for development" (Bello, this volume: p. 180). Moreover, there was, argues Bello, a strong normative edge to such scholarship as "developmental state" scholars argued "for" states in development against the "pro-market" inclination of much Western scholarship. As such, from its inception, these models were set up as a challenge to scholarship that sees universalist processes stemming from the Western experience.

Tracking the developmental state literature from its beginnings in Chalmers Johnson's work on Japan (1982), Amsden on Taiwan (1989), Wade on Korea (1990), to the latest work today, Bello argues for this literature's distinctive focus upon the state as being able to open up issues that Western IPE approaches miss due to their relegation of such processes to "domestic politics." As such, the economically positive "legacy-effects" of colonialism, the role of labor repression (and the lack of democracy) in state-led industrialization efforts, the importance of land reform and how the politics of firm–state relations changed over time given the success of these efforts, all come into focus. By tying the actual developmental history of the East Asian states into the story of the evolution of East Asian/developmental state scholarship, Bello puts more contemporary flesh on the bones of Arrighi's non-Western-centered IPE.

Our third essay by Henry Yeung adds the micro level to Bello's meso level focus on institutions and states-as-agents in developmental projects. Building upon Bello's discussion, Yeung investigates two things: the extent to which the East Asian developmental experience differs fundamentally from the Western one (and hence brings into question the universalist aspirations of *any* version of IPE), and how, below the level of the developmental state and its institutional supports, we find networked actors who add another layer of institutional complexity and difference to the Asian understanding of the IPE.

For Yeung, while the developmental state model is indeed a singular contribution of East Asian scholarship to IPE, that scholarship has inherent limits insofar as it can explain the rapid "catch-up" of Asian firms in the period 1960–80, but not their contemporary activities as global players. However, as Yeung reports, recent work on global production networks, qua networks of firms, suppliers and financiers, has gone beyond the developmental state approach to view the IPE of East Asia as being perhaps more fundamentally different from Western capitalism than hitherto assumed. Echoing Cerny's call for a multi-nodal, multi-actor politics, Yeung sees in this new literature a "multi-scalar" IPE that is "about diverse political-economic transformations spearheaded by actors and forces transcending the political realm" and that operates across levels of analysis (Yeung, this volume: p. 205). Specifically, Yeung argues that transnationalized "business systems" and their attendant networks of suppliers and contractors, above and below the level of the state, are the critical agents whose actions produce an IPE that is far removed from the one described in the Western literature.

What this in turn demonstrates, argues Yeung, is how the context-specific theories generated in Western scholarship are themselves as time and geography bound as the Asian scholarship it mirrors. However, where mainstream Western scholarship, especially in the American school, seeks invariant generalizations across as many cases as possible, the Asian view of IPE treats such ambitions as inherently flawed. Rather, IPE in Asia seeks not to generalize beyond the area in which the theory was generated; or to do so only with great care. As Yeung puts it, while we "need to theorize the international political economy beyond and below the nation state" to get a full picture of its generators and operations, the IPE generated in and about East Asia should not be used to generalize without end. Rather, the point of such scholarship is to "theorize back" upon American and British approaches in order to show their limits and expose their self-understandings.

Rounding out Part III is a final contribution from Jason Sharman, an Australian IPE scholar, who argues that being neither "in Asia nor America," and having a colonial heritage all of its own in terms of ties to the UK, Australian IPE emerges with a set of concerns that span, arguably, all of the different camps discussed so far. For Sharman, Australian IPE is a mixture of different traditions and positions drawn from all over the world. Given its geographical position and (until recently) cultural and political predisposition, one might expect the study of the IPE to hew close to the American school, and in one way it does. IPE is generally taught within departments of political science and/or international relations, thus having the "parent discipline" angle that the British school does not. Yet in another way Australian IPE is much closer to the British school in terms of, as Sharman reports, methodological approach, publication outlets, and Ph.D. training. Is Australian IPE then the transpacific rather than transatlantic bridge some scholars of IPE seek, perhaps even incorporating some of the Asian scholarship? Sharman gives a guarded "maybe" in reply.

Although methodologically homogeneous, Australian IPE scholarship covers a set of topics that reflect a tendency to import theories developed elsewhere, rather than, as we saw in Asia, provide us with endogenously generated theory. Sharman demonstrates how topics such as globalization and regionalism, the study of the IPE of Asia, development and inequality, and international institutions in the IPE are the common fare of Australian IPE, but how they are employed and investigated falls within a narrow band. As Sharman puts it "[r]esearch in Australia tends to center on critical theory, feminist, constructivist, or institutionalist approaches" (Sharman, this volume: p. 226). As such, the narrowness detected in the American school by British scholars is perhaps somewhat ironically replicated at the other end of the epistemological and methodological spectrum by Australian scholars. In contrast to Asian IPE scholarship then, Australia's position as a geographical part of Asia provides little temptation to theorize from that basis. Although Australia is increasingly integrated into Asian circuits of capital, it has not, as yet, integrated into its intellectual circuits.

What can the reader take from all of this?

I would hope that the reader can take three things from this section on IPE in Asia and Australia. First of all and once again, we see how where you sit, intellectually as well as physically, determines the IPE you both see and investigate. One does not have to be an American to be in the American school, or Asian to be part of the literature on the developmental state. But the concerns one brings to scholarship in part constitutes what is, and what is not, the IPE. For American scholars economic decline, the stagflation of the 1970s, and the Cold War constituted a particular IPE. Then later, neoliberalism, the Washington consensus, and the rise of China, constituted another. For British scholars, economic decline, their very different view of the state, and the end of empire, all combined to produce and IPE that is different again. And so it is with Asian scholarship. Whether seen from the *longue durée* of Arrighi's chapter, or the shorter time frames of Bello and Yeung, the Asian post-war experience gave rise to a particular type of IPE based around notions of developmental states and global production networks that are different in kind from how the IPE is envisioned in the West. Second, I would hope that the reader gets a basic understanding of why these scholars see the IPE in Asia as a very different entity, and how the body of scholarship this has generated challenges both American and British IPE.[13] Finally, I would hope that, especially regarding Sharman's chapter, we see how disciplinary legacies and disciplinary politics can also shape the IPE we see. It is in this regard that we turn now to the absence of IPE as a body of scholarship in other parts of the world, and track the disciplinary and extra-academic mechanisms that make such absences possible.

Exemptions, exclusions, and extensions

The final section of this handbook, Part IV, groups together essays that can be considered our "outlier" cases. And just like statistics, sometimes the most significant story about the trend-line can be seen in the analysis of the outliers. The IPE is not only constituted by what its differentially located partisans think it is. It is also constituted by its absences. In this regard the last section of this handbook groups together some exemptions: why is there no strong alternate versions of IPE in either Continental Europe or Latin America; explains some exclusions: the work of sociologists and economic historians in similar topic areas; and notes one major extension: the "everyday IPE" scholarship that is emerging at the moment.

Turning first to the lack of IPE in continental Europe, particularly France, Nicolas Jabko provides us with an explanation of this absence. Despite having a rich tradition of producing political economists—the names Cournot and Walras spring to mind immediately, and the continuing contributions of "Regulation school" economists to the study of the political economy of Europe—"when it comes to studying the politics of international economic relations, French scholarship is incredibly sparse" (Jabko, this volume: p. 231). Given such a heritage, why is this the case?

Jabko highlights three main reasons why IPE remains "underdeveloped" in France, and by extension continental Europe. First of all, heterodox economists, rather than political scientists, tend to define what "political economy" is, and is not, in the French context. Particularly important here is the work of the economists of the aforementioned "regulation school." The thrust of this work, grounded in a discussion of how particular domestic institutional complexes (regimes of accumulation) produce economic outcomes, and embedded within a macro-history of the historic shift from "Fordism" to "Post-Fordism," tends to concentrate on the internal (usually national) dynamics of capitalist economies. As such, both politics, and the notion of the "international" as a distinct sphere of action, are underplayed.

Second, there is in France, according to Jabko, a bias against importing mainstream, especially US scholarship, in preference to endogenously generated theories, thus showing a dynamic similar to the Asia case, but without the acknowledgment of the link to IPE. Third, and most importantly, we see in the French case something similar, but also very different, to what we saw in the British case. While both countries have long-standing legacies of Marxist scholarship, there was in the post-war period in France a general flight from Marxism in economics and political science rather than the embrace of it that we saw in the British case; except in the field of political economy, which became "a scholarly preserve for Marxists" (Jabko, this volume: p. 235). As such, France has certainly produced a lot of political economy, but not IPE as we know it elsewhere in the world. IPE in France, and in Europe in general, remains, as Jabko puts it, "underdeveloped."

Underdevelopment as a concept has, of course, a long pedigree in IPE scholarship, particularly in Latin America, where the "structuralist" and "dependency" analyses of the world economy developed there in the 1950s–1970s constituted its own school of IPE. Our second chapter in Part IV, by Gabriel Palma, addresses the puzzle of why, given this "glorious tradition" of IPE scholarship, endogenously developed IPE theory in Latin America disappeared almost completely over the last decade and a half.

For Palma the answer to this question stems from a whole different set of causes than those that explain the absence noted in Jabko's essay. Whereas for Jabko the reasons for the underdevelopment of IPE in France are primarily institutional and disciplinary, for Palma the reasons for the disappearance of the "critical tradition" in Latin America marks the IPE not as a field of study in which we observe the politics, but as a field of political writing and political action in and of itself. As such, what can and should be done by governments in Latin America is reflected in and altered by writings about the IPE and Latin America's place therein. In Latin America, argues Palma, we see, coming to the fore, the politics of writing about the IPE as a political act.

After introducing us to the old Latin American critical tradition of structuralism and dependency analysis, Palma notes how these progressive literatures turned pathological when, over time, the fit between the facts generated by the world economy and the theory diverged so much that the goal of dependency theorists became saving the theory at the expense of reality. Saving the world that the theory portrayed, one of socialist transformation, became more important than examining and explaining the reality that the world economy was actually producing. The really interesting outcome of this was, however, that the scholars who produced dependency theory rapidly became some of the best "true believers" in the neoliberal model of capitalist transformation; itself the exact opposite of dependency analysis, marking very much the abandonment of IPE for orthodoxy.

The reasons for theoretical denouement were multifarious, but three stand out: the pressure put on left wing movements during the transitions to democracy in Latin America not to alter the allocation of resources, the availability of the Washington consensus as an alternative "faith" for policy elites once dependency analysis had been constructed as a failure, and the shift to a managerial rather than a transformative democratic politics throughout all Latin America. As such, the absence of a Latin American IPE, despite its heritage, becomes understandable; becomes an act of politics; a deliberate forgetting by policy elites and intellectuals, rather than something generated only inside the academy.

Turning from our two exemptions, we turn toward two exclusions; IPE as practiced by sociologists and economic historians. After all, one consequence of not being able to "bound" IPE is that one is bound to run into other academics who are doing essentially the same thing, but not calling what they do IPE. So the obvious question becomes to what extent is this "the same wine in a different bottle" or a wholly different way of "doing" IPE? In an attempt to address this question, the next chapter by John Campbell takes two tracks: how sociologists think about and have contributed to the study of IPE, (usually) without calling it that, and what areas of sociology are particularly germane for IPE scholars to know about.

Campbell notes that sociologists have always been interested in processes that have, until recently, seemed marginal to the concerns of IPE scholars and more germane to the work of comparative political economists and political scientists. Campbell walks us through how sociologists have studied the diffusion of norms on an international level, how neoliberalism as a particular set of institutions and ideas has been transmitted around the world, how the international division of labor and the distributional politics therein is structured and why, and how the comparative economic performance of different states is explainable by regime type. All of these literatures are relevant for IPE scholarship, but are, Campbell argues, under-employed by IPE scholars.

Campbell also rings a cautionary bell regarding the potential for crossover between sociology and IPE, at least in the US. If the American school becomes more formal, quantitative, and rationalist, as Cohen has argued, then the types of variables employed by sociologists may become less, rather than more attractive to some IPE scholars since they are harder to fit into reductionist methodologies. As Campbell puts it, "sociologists have been more inclined to accept the importance of ideas (i.e., norms, values, cognitive frames) without a fight" with the result that it has developed along a different track from much American IPE scholarship (Campbell, this volume: p. 279). However, as the essays by the other authors in our American IPE section remind us, there is much more to American IPE than just this one strand of work. Consequently, the links between the type of scholarship Campbell surveys and the constructivist literature in IPE discussed by Abdelal (and as we shall see, the "everyday IPE" literature discussed below) suggests instead a growing set of connections between this strand of IPE and sociology.

Michael Oliver provides us with our second exclusion; the IPE as studied by economic historians. After all, if there is any group of scholars who have been examining the intersection of the "international," the "political," and the "economic," it is decidedly this group. But how does economic history as a discipline relate to the idea of IPE as a discipline, as opposed to it being simply "the field of study of economic history"? Oliver notes that economic historians tend to differ from IPE scholars in two regards. First of all, most economic historians do not seek, per contra some of the American school, to "provide an account of events which is grounded either in axiomatic theory or the discovery of empirical laws" (Britton 2002: 106, quoted in Oliver, this volume: p. 282). Second, they generally accept that the study of phenomena such as the IPE cannot be studied "within a narrow methodological perspective" (Oliver, this volume: p. 282), and subsequently see methodological pluralism as a good thing.

Given this, Oliver argues that there are two main points of contact between economic history and IPE as a field. First, some of the biggest names in IPE are "economic historian(s) in the broadest sense of the term" (Oliver, this volume: p. 282) so there is a natural overlap. Second, most of the work produced by IPE scholars is by its nature historical, whether in the form of numbers or words. However, where IPE scholars do fall short lies in the failure to recognize the importance of archives for historical work, the sine qua non of "doing" history. For IPE to be truly historical, and therefore more than a retelling of taken for granted second-hand stories, it needs to do more archival work since "it is precisely the close reading of the circumstances (via archives), which is required to challenge or illuminate *a priori* views of what leads states to cooperate or not" (Oliver, this volume, p. 288). As such, Oliver's advice for the field is, "[R]ather than becoming inductive econometricians or smart economists, if IPE scholars intend to do historical work then they should think more like historians" (Oliver, this volume: p. 289) and reduce their theoretical ambitions. But if one does so, what is there to differentiate IPE from allied fields such as economic history and sociology? This dilemma is particularly acute in the extension of IPE we examine in conclusion; the emerging "inter-discipline" of "Everyday International Political Economy" (EIPE).

In our final chapter Hobson and Seabrooke introduce "Everyday IPE" (EIPE) to us by contrasting it with "Regulatory IPE" (RIPE). RIPE is pretty much all other schools of

IPE, defined not by methods or epistemological position, but by what they think the key questions IPE should be asking are and who the key agents are presumed to be. While constructivist and contactualist approaches may be miles apart on many issues, according to Hobson and Seabrooke, they actually start from very similar premises. For all other schools "who governs?" is ultimately the core question of IPE and the answer is usually "some sort of set of *elite* actors." Thus in all other versions of IPE, the few at the top dictate the terms for the many at the bottom. Hobson and Seabrooke stress that EIPE does not reject such a stance entirely, but it does question if such a position is the only way of understanding the IPE. For everyday IPE scholars however, non–elite actors, the masses not the elites, their patterns of consumption and production, and crucially their ability to confer legitimacy on or withhold it from elite actions, all come to the fore as explanatory factors in the world economy.

Hobson and Seabrooke note two distinct approaches within the everyday IPE camp; a "logic of discipline" and a "logic of action" approach. The former draws on post-structuralist scholarship, detailing how projects of transformation in the IPE depend upon transformations in identity at a much more micro level. As such, how disciplinary practices and discourses produce particular subject positions upon which larger projects of transformation depend becomes the point of investigation. The logic of action approach, in contrast, derives from a more sociological tradition that focuses upon how the individual actions of everyday actors can collectively impact economic outcomes at macro levels of aggregation through mechanisms such as defiance of dominant norms, mimetic challenges to the prevailing order, and through other forms of covert resistance. These two approaches, though rival, are close enough together to make comparison meaningful, and there is more than enough work in both camps to talk about a new and emergent school of IPE. That school of IPE has engaged issues as diverse as pension reform (Langley 2008), the relationship between housing finance and global financial power (Seabrooke 2006), and the ability of microstate tax havens to persist despite OECD efforts to shut them down (Sharman 2006), from this interdisciplinary "bottom-up" rather than "top-down" perspective.

We close this introductory chapter with this discussion of EIPE, just as we close the handbook with it, since it takes us back to where we started: the divisions between schools. On the one hand we have made the case that these differences are exaggerated insofar as, for example, the American school is not as uniform as is often portrayed, scholarship outside the US is not devoid of theoretical rigor, and even the scholarship on Asia generalizes a bit. Seen in this way EIPE represents merely a welcome further broadening of IPE to encompass new actors and concerns. But on the other hand EIPE also seems to mark something else; the move toward an truly interdisciplinary way of studying political economy on a global level that moves far beyond the confines of much existing scholarship. The extent to which such scholarship represents a progressive extension of IPE or a deviation into sociology to the point that it dissolves within that discipline depends upon how one wishes to draw boundaries. Since the point of this handbook has been to contest rather than construct those boundaries, I leave that judgment, along with all the others, to the reader.

What can the reader take from all of this?

What I hope the reader gets from the final section of this handbook is the following. First of all, the essays that tackle the two exclusions—why no IPE in continental Europe and Latin America—tell us two very interesting things about IPE. First, IPE is an object of study, but how academies and intellectual traditions are constituted on a national level can create more or less space for a field to flourish. All countries have discovered physics; not everyone has felt the need to discover IPE, and some have even de-invented it. As such, IPE's claims to the status of a scientific field of study must be somewhat held in check by the fact that some parts of the world see no need for it.

Second, as a political subject in its own right, there is a politics of writing about the IPE that also throws IPE's claims about itself, à la the Robert Burns quote we opened with, into question. As the Latin American chapter showed most clearly, writing about the IPE underpins and can become part of the self-understanding of politics and strategy for elites in the IPE. Writing one way enables a particular politics; denying that writing, another. IPE is then not merely the study of the politics of the international economy, it is itself, in some cases, a political act in its own right.

Third, the perspectives on IPE drawn from sociology and economic history remind us that IPE is by necessity an interdisciplinary exercise. Sociologists and economic historians study similar things to IPE scholars, but the strength of IPE lies in its hybridity; in its ability to beg, borrow, and steal from other disciplines in order to create a useful synthesis for understanding a highly complex phenomenon. But there is also a risk in doing so. As the EIPE chapter shows, there is a danger in becoming so much an "interdiscipline" in its own right that it risks reproducing work done elsewhere without acknowledging this, or even knowing that it is indeed doing so.[14]

In sum, IPE is by necessity a broad and evolving global conversation. But it does not follow from that fact that IPE can and should be whatever we want it to be. Breaking down boundaries is a noble objective. But boundaries are a bit like borders. Once they are dissolved the first casualty is identity; who "we" are, and what "we" are for comes into question, which in IPE quickly becomes *"what then is IPE and what is it for?"* This handbook has taken the approach that answering this latter question is a bit like engaging the politics of identity; the acknowledgement of difference is the first step to understanding, but where one goes with that understanding depends on the map you have. I hope this handbook serves as a good map for IPE scholars, regardless of the direction their interests take them.

Notes

1 For a view that does make the case that after twenty years of scholarship liberalism is the last man standing, but mainly as an artifact of survey coding, see Malinaik and Tierney's (2007) quantitative analysis of the American School of IPE.

2 Author's translation: "you would learn a lot about yourself if you could see yourself as others see you." Original can be found at www.worldburnsclub.com/poems/translations/552.htm accessed August 3, 2008, 11:48 a.m. EST.

3 Not all of them are such a waste of space, although many are. For a particularly useful and well written exception that I use in class myself see Ravenhill (2005, 2008a).

4 Even in the hands of scholars as sensitive as Benjamin Cohen assertions such as "globally, the dominant (we might even say hegemonic version) [of IPE] is the one that has developed in the US" are deployed without any metric as to establish the worth of this claim (Cohen 2007: 198).

5 See the exchange between Richard Higgot and Matthew Watson, John Ravenhill and Benjamin Cohen in this regard in the *Review of International Political Economy* 15(1) (2008).

6 To see why this is the case in the related field of comparative politics see Blyth (2006).

7 As Cohen notes, one does not need to be in Britain to be part of the British school; but it does help in terms of having colleagues to talk to.

8 I put forward this agreement with Cohen with the following caveat. While I normatively like the idea of building a bridge between these two schools, I am not sure what such a bridge can be built out of (although see Cerny in this volume for such an attempt). Cohen argues that "[T]he American school could learn much from the British side's broad multi-disciplinarity ... [while] ... U.S. style IPE could benefit from a little more ambition ... The British school ... [in contrast] ... could ... learn much from the American side's more rigorous methodologies ... [while] ... British-style IPE could benefit from a little less ambition" Cohen (2008b: 177). However, if it is the case that British scholars are largely skeptical about the possibility of a scientific understanding of social phenomena, and American scholars are similarly dubious about "critical theory," then how they can really benefit from one another in a synthesis of views is doubtful. What is not in doubt, however, is that they can benefit from dialog with each other to learn the limits of both approaches, and to accept that there is no one way of approaching the IPE; a process that this handbook aims to further.

9 Geography does not square completely with intellectual affiliation entirely, however. As well as Canadians in the British school, one can find non-Americans, such as the editor of this handbook, who identify with the American school.

10 One could also note how the non-trivial event of the end of the Cold War delegitimated both neoliberal institutionalism and neorealism since neither school saw the bi-polar Cold War order, which was the predicate of their understanding, coming to an end. See Kratochwil (1993) for a discussion of this issue.

11 A simple example of this phenomenon is what constitutes terrorism. Once defined in a certain way, it becomes meaningful to speak of, for example, an incidence of terror, and hence terrorism as a distinct object.

12 Cerny, as an American who taught for many years in the UK and who only recently moved back to the US, is perhaps the only person who could write such a bridge-building chapter.

13 I would add here that much of what has been written about the developmental state does have an American lineage. However, this scholarship owes its lineage to comparative politics and comparative political economy much more than it does American (or British) IPE. See Blyth (2009) for a discussion.

14 For example, while the EIPE work on pensions and risk is itself extremely valuable, it tends to ignore the contributions of other scholars from outside IPE to these vary same areas. Compare Langley (2008) and Brooks (forthcoming), for example.

Part I

North American IPE

1

The multiple traditions of American IPE

Benjamin J. Cohen

International Political Economy (IPE) came late to the United States. Although astute observers had long acknowledged the obvious linkage of economics and politics in global affairs, it was just a few short decades ago that IPE began to emerge as a formal, recognized field of scholarly inquiry with its own standards, concerns, and career opportunities. The birth of American IPE is generally dated from the late 1960s or early 1970s—the result of a conscious campaign to marry the academic specialties of international economics and international relations (IR). What emerged from those early years was by no means a monolithic orthodoxy. From the start American IPE has been characterized by multiple intellectual traditions, reflecting the hybrid nature of the field itself.

Commonalities exist, of course. In the United States, IPE has become essentially a sub-specialty of the study of IR—in effect, a branch of political science. Most scholars working in the American style take for granted that, first and foremost, IPE is about sovereign states and their interactions, as in IR more generally. In the words of one popular textbook, IPE is about "the relationship of the world economy to the power politics among nations" (Lairson and Skidmore 2003: 6). National governments are the core actors. Public policymaking is the main concern. Analysis is directed largely to understanding the sources and implications of state behavior.

Further, most scholarship in the United States tends to hew close to the norms of conventional social science. Priority is given to scientific method—what might be called a pure or hard science model. Analysis is typically based on the twin principles of positivism and empiricism, which hold that knowledge is best accumulated through an appeal to objective observation and the systematic evaluation of evidence. Normative concerns are downplayed and grand theorizing is generally eschewed. Instead, most emphasis is placed on mid-level theory, concentrating on key relationships isolated within a broader structure whose characteristics are unquestioned and assumed, normally, to be given and unchanging. All these commonalities are distinctive enough to warrant designation of a unique "American school" of IPE, in contrast to alternative styles of inquiry that have arisen elsewhere (Cohen 2008b).

Yet for all that is shared in common, the American school rarely speaks with one voice. Within the US-based research community diverse camps have emerged over time, making for lively debate and a fruitful cross-fertilization of ideas. The earliest divide stemmed from natural differences between economics and political science, American IPE's two parent disciplines. The pioneers of the field in the United States were international economists or students of IR. Though the political scientists, as it turned out, largely predominated in shaping the US version of IPE, the economics profession has always remained influential, particularly in matters of methodology. Additional divides reflect paradigmatic differences, particularly among political scientists.

The aim of this essay is to explore the origins and interactions of American IPE's multiple traditions. Three themes are stressed: the early capture of the field by political scientists, who took custody of a terrain largely abdicated by economists; the subsequent emergence of the US community's diverse camps in an ongoing dialectical process of intellectual development; and, most recently, at the level of methodology, the gradual recapture of a good part of American IPE by the research techniques of economics. The field may be young in chronological terms. But it already has a rich and diverse history.

Capture

The origins of the American school go back, first and foremost, to the pioneering efforts of a remarkable generation of political scientists, led by the likes of Robert Keohane and Joseph Nye (1972, 1977), Robert Gilpin (1972, 1975a), Peter Katzenstein (1976, 1978), and Stephen Krasner (1976, 1983). The historical circumstances that triggered a systematic interest in IPE are not difficult to understand. More puzzling is why economists, by and large, so conspicuously absented themselves while the field was being built.

Historical circumstances

The birth of a new field of study does not take place in a vacuum. Particularly in the social sciences, intellectual developments tend to be tied to historical context—to new events and trends that make old ways of thinking inadequate. And so it was with American IPE. Fundamental changes were occurring in the world. Both the politics and the economics of global affairs were mutating, calling for new understandings of how things work and how they might be studied.

Most striking was the remarkable recovery of the European and Japanese economies after the devastation of World War II. By the 1960s, a decisive shift seemed to be taking place in the balance of economic power among industrialized nations. At mid-century, the United States had bestrode the world economy like a colossus. But with its growth rate slowing and its balance of payments mired in deficits, America now looked to be on the brink of decline. Continental Europe and Japan, meanwhile, were roaring back, once again forces to be reckoned with. America's moment of economic dominance appeared to be just about over. Meanwhile, postwar decolonization had brought new attention to the challenges and dilemmas of economic development. Pressures were mounting for a New International Economic Order that would fundamentally transform the rules governing relations between the wealthy North and the poverty-stricken South.

Behind these changes was a growing interdependence of national economies, which seemed to threaten the ability of governments to manage economic affairs. Year by year, world trade was growing more rapidly than output, bringing greater openness and mutual dependence. And soon financial flows began to accelerate as well with the growth

24

of offshore currency markets—the so-called euro-currency markets—from the late 1950s onwards. By the end of the 1960s it was evident that the spread of international economic activity had reached a critical juncture, soon to be manifest in a breakdown of the Bretton Woods monetary order, rising protectionism, oil shocks, and stagflation. Power now seemed to be slipping from states, limiting their ability to attain critical goals. Yet mainstream economics seemed incapable of providing effective solutions.

Conversely, the salience of national security concerns now appeared in abeyance. This was because of a growing détente between the United States and the Soviet Union, the two nuclear superpowers. For years, the Cold War had held center stage, reaching a dramatic peak in the brinkmanship of the 1962 Cuban Missile Crisis. But by the late 1960s, despite the distractions of the protracted Vietnam conflict, the competing Western and Soviet blocs seemed to be entering a new era of decreased tensions. Détente did not mean that the high politics of war and peace had suddenly lost all relevance; indeed, in the 1980s the Cold War was to intensify once again, as Ronald Reagan declared battle on the "Evil Empire." But for the time being at least, it provided an opening to political scientists. Students of world politics could now safely divert some of their attention elsewhere—for example, to the politics of the global economy.

Abdication

The new field did absorb elements of international economics, of course. But for Keohane and Nye and others of their generation, IPE seemed most naturally a logical extension of their interest in IR. As one colleague has suggested to me in private correspondence, Keohane and Nye "opened the door for scholars with an IR framework to think systematically about international economic relations." Soon every self-respecting political science department began to reserve a faculty slot or two for specialists. Every political science curriculum began to feature one if not several IPE courses. Textbooks in the field—once a trickle, now a veritable flood—were targeted directly at students of political science. Effectively, American IPE was captured by political scientists.

The critical question is: Why didn't economists fight harder for "ownership" of the field? Economists were there at the creation, after all. In fact, most of the field's earliest work in the United States was by economists, before the political scientists took over. One example, dating back to 1948, was Jacob Viner, who sought to explore the relationship between "power" and "plenty" as objectives of foreign policy. Twenty years later Richard Cooper (1968) published *The Economics of Interdependence*, highlighting the political challenges posed by the growing connections between national economies. In 1970, there was *Power and Money*, a short book by Charles Kindleberger (1970) on the growing tension between economic and political activity in an increasingly interdependent world. And in 1971 came Raymond Vernon's memorable *Sovereignty at Bay* (1971), which heralded the arrival of the multinational corporation as a key political actor on the global stage. The period also saw the reissue of a long-neglected study by Albert Hirschman, *National Power and the Structure of Foreign Trade* (1969 [1945]), now rightly regarded as a classic.

Yet once the political scientists arrived on the scene, economists for the most part abdicated. Since the early 1970s, IPE has been a preoccupation only at the fringes of the economics profession. On the conservative right are scholars like Thomas Willett (1988; Willett and Vaubel 1991) who extend so-called public-choice theory to the international arena, following the early lead of Swiss economist Bruno Frey (1984). Public choice is the study of politics using the tools of economic theory; its focus is on implications that can be drawn from the underlying motivations of individuals in the political process. Both members of the general public and government leaders are analyzed as rational, self-interested actors striving to maximize some objective utility function, in a manner analogous to the behavior of individuals and firms in the marketplace. The insights of public choice make a valuable contribution in helping us to evaluate policy outcomes in terms of standard efficiency criteria. But it is also a limited contribution since it makes little serious attempt to incorporate the insights or intuitions of political science into the equation. With its methodological individualism, along with its emphasis on formal modeling, public-choice IPE amounts to little more than an application of traditional economic concepts to decision-making in the global economy. It might best be labeled the microeconomics of international relations.

Conversely, on the radical left are scholars of a more critical persuasion, best represented by the Union for Radical Political Economics (URPE), founded in 1968. URPE's origins lay in the New Left politics of the turbulent 1960s, driven especially by a revulsion with the war in Vietnam. The group's aim was to promote a new inter-disciplinary approach to political economy, a fresh look at the connections between economics and politics, with particular emphasis on the dynamics and evolution of global capitalism. According to the group's website, URPE "presents constructive critical ana-lyses of the capitalist system and supports debate and discussion on alternative left visions of a socialist society" (URPE). The value of such an approach lies in its emphasis on the broader historical structures within which political and economic activity takes place. But with its self-conscious iconoclasm and its Marxist overtones, URPE has never managed to exercise much influence on the mainstream of the US economics profession.

Indeed, despite the dramatic changes in the international environment that were evident when American IPE was first getting started, the mainstream of the economics profession remained largely indifferent. The reasons were three-fold: ideological, ontological, and epistemological.

First, there was the chilling effect of postwar anti-communism. Political economy tended to be equated unthinkingly with Marxism or other unacceptable leftist doctrines. By the late 1960s détente may have been melting the ice of the Cold War, reducing tensions between the nuclear superpowers. But even so, the battle to defend the market system went on—a battle in which economists inevitably found themselves on the front lines. Political scientists might be called upon to defend the virtues of democracy, but not capitalism. Economists, on the other hand, could not avoid being drawn into the ongo-ing contest between Marxism and market liberalism. Apart from the youthful founders of URPE, few American economists at the time had much taste for ideas or arguments that might smack of anti-capitalist sentiment. In any attempt to integrate economic and political analysis, most of the profession saw ideological bias.

Second was a kind of intellectual myopia in the prevailing ontology of economics. Ontology, from the Greek for things that exist, is about investigating reality: the nature, essential properties, and relations of being. In other contexts, ontology is used as syno-nym for metaphysics or cosmology. In social science, it is used as a synonym for studying the world in which we actually live. What are the basic units of interest and what are their key relationships? Most economists preferred to concentrate their attention on the private sphere, mainly addressing considerations of technical efficiency and economic welfare. They were simply not trained to think in terms of the public sphere—the issues of authority and conflict that are inherent in processes of governmental decision-making.

Nor were they comfortable when confronted with the very political question of distribution—how the economic pie gets divvied up.

This created two blind spots. First, the importance of institutions was discounted. In the *timeless* analytical framework favored by mainstream of the profession, political structures, if considered at all, were introduced only as a constraint on economic activity, with underlying power relationships taken more or less for granted. Conventional economics at the time discouraged any interest in questions concerning how rules or norms are created or how over time they might support or undermine different patterns of economic activity. And second, attention was traditionally directed to the outcomes of policy rather than to its inputs. The aim of theory was to *evaluate* policy, not *explain* its origins in the give and take of distributional conflict. An old adage has it that politics is like sausage making: You really don't want to know what goes into it. Economists took that advice seriously.

Finally, there was resistance to IPE on epistemological grounds. Epistemology, from the Greek for knowledge, has to do with the methods and grounds of knowing. What methodologies do we use to study the world? What kinds of analysis will enhance our understanding? Mainstream economists were understandably hesitant to take up issues that could not be addressed comfortably using the standard toolkit of conventional economics. For a century, especially in the United States, the discipline had been growing increasingly abstract, relying ever more on deductive logic and parsimonious formal models to pare messy reality down to its bare essentials. The style was reductionist. The aim was to uncover core relationships—"to predict something large from something small," as economist Harry Johnson once put it (1971: 9).

In effect, mainstream economics presumes that social phenomena are amenable to scientific explanation in essentially the same manner as are natural phenomena. Hence the same principles of positivism and empiricism that are employed to isolate causal mechanisms in the physical sciences can be applied to the study of social relations as well. Universal truths are out there, just waiting to be discovered. John Kenneth Galbraith (1970: 8) derisively labeled the approach "imitative scientism"—a replication of the methods of the natural sciences "which is carried further in economics than in any other [social-science] discipline." Highest rank in what Galbraith called the "prestige system of economics" goes to those who best mimic the reductionist epistemology of the physical sciences.

In this context, political economy seemed to fit like a square peg in a round hole. How was formal analysis to account for the uncertainties of the political process? How could theory model the exigencies of war and peace? How could existing empirical methods cope with seemingly vague notions like power or dependency? Questions like these ran against the grain of the discipline's methodological standards. Thus mainstream economists could be excused for demurring. As one economist colleague said to me back when American IPE was first getting started: "If I can't quantify it, I'm not interested." His remark was only partially in jest.

Debates

While economists abdicated, political scientists debated. Students of IR may have agreed that IPE should be a sub-specialty of their own discipline. But they disagreed on virtually everything else, reflecting the broader dialogue that has gone on among IR theorists over the last several decades. The result is a multiplicity of intellectual traditions that can all claim a degree of legitimacy in the field as it is understood in the United States.

From realism to complex interdependence

The starting point for American IPE was the classic state-centric paradigm of world politics that had long dominated the study of IR in the United States. For decades, US-based scholars had been taught to think as realists. States were seen as the only significant actors on the global stage, conceived for analytical purposes as purposive, rational, and unitary actors. Moreover, states were assumed to be motivated largely by issues of power and security and to be preoccupied, above all, with the danger of military conflict. In US academic circles, realism ruled.

And then came Keohane and Nye, two young scholars whose collaborative efforts, beginning at the end of the 1960s, laid the earliest foundations for the American version of IPE. For Keohane and Nye, the realist paradigm had now become dated. World politics was being transformed. Just look around, they suggested. Who could fail to notice the seeming breakdown of order in the global economy? Disputes and tensions were on the rise; arguments over everything from tariffs and exchange-rate policy to management of the oceans were becoming more and more politicized. For Keohane and Nye, the radical change of atmosphere was pivotal. The safe certainties of the earlier postwar period had seemingly vanished into thin air.

The key, they contended, lay in the increasing fragmentation and diffusion of power in economic affairs stemming from the growing interdependence of national economies. States might still be central actors in international affairs. But with the expansion of the global marketplace they could no longer claim sole authority to determine outcomes. Liberalization of trade and finance was widening the range of *transnational* relations, adding new cross-border contacts, coalitions, and interactions beyond those controlled by the foreign-policy organs of government. Interdependence was spawning a growing swarm of transnational actors—individuals and entities whose control of resources and access to channels of communication enabled them, too, to participate meaningfully in political relationships across state lines. Hence, Keohane and Nye maintained, a new way of thinking was needed: a broader paradigm that would explicitly admit the full panoply of relevant actors. Their effort to conceive a new vision of international relations began with an edited volume entitled *Transnational Relations and World Politics*, published in 1972, and culminated five years later in their landmark study, *Power and Interdependence* (1977). In *Power and Interdependence* they even gave their vision a name: "complex interdependence."

Complex interdependence was defined by three main characteristics—multiple channels of communication, an absence of hierarchy among issues, and a diminished role for military force. Looking back later, Keohane and Nye (1987) expressed a degree of modesty over what they had wrought. Their purpose in developing their new vision, they claimed, simply had been to provide an alternative *ideal type* for analytical purposes. Their goal was not to discredit realism but, rather, to supplement it—to highlight dimensions of the picture that realism had overlooked. In their words,

> we regarded the two as necessary complements to one another. ... The key point was not that interdependence made power obsolete—far from it—but that patterns of interdependence and patterns of potential power resources in a given issue-area are closely related—indeed, two sides of a single coin.
>
> (1987: 728, 730)

The concept of complex interdependence itself, they insisted, was "underdeveloped" (1987: 733). "We did not pursue complex interdependence as a theory, but as a thought experiment about what politics might look like if the basic assumptions of realism were reversed. We therefore did not draw upon … theory as fully as we might have" (1987: 737).

Their modesty, however, is misplaced. It is true that realism was not discredited. Complex interdependence was indeed best conceived as a complement to realism, not a substitute. It is also true that the new paradigm failed to make the grade as a formal theory. A theory is best defined as a set of general statements combining the features of logical truth and predictive accuracy. Logical truth means that some of the statements (the assumptions or premises) logically imply the other statements (the theorems). Predictive accuracy means that the statements can be cast in the form of falsifiable propositions about the real world. Clearly, complex interdependence did neither. It could not be used directly to explain state behavior or bargaining outcomes.

Yet the accomplishment was undeniable. In ontological terms, the idea clearly broke new ground. Here was a wholly different alternative to IR's then prevailing paradigm— a fresh vision of the world that contrasted sharply with the realist model of purposive states single-mindedly preoccupied with the high politics of war and peace. National governments were still at the center of analysis. But no longer could they be conceived as uniquely worthy of scholarly attention, nor could they be assumed to be preoccupied above all with the danger of military conflict. This was real value added. Keohane and Nye made scholars look at the world anew. In so doing, they facilitated the birth of a new field of study

Today American IPE takes for granted that interdependence in the world economy can be analyzed in political terms, not just as an economic phenomenon. Specialists also take for granted that patterns of interdependence can be examined by separate issue areas. Implicitly or explicitly, the US version of the field is built on the ontology bequeathed by Keohane and Nye—a sense that the three characteristics of complex interdependence define the essential nature of the international system today. Without this inter-subjective understanding, systematic study of the low politics of trade and finance would have been more difficult, if not impossible. With it, researchers had a whole new insight into how things work. The term "complex interdependence" itself may no longer be particularly fashionable in the literature; many scholars have forgotten it completely. But the Weltanschauung it represents is now undeniably a part of the collective unconscious of the field.

Realism vs. liberalism

Reinforcing the insights of Keohane and Nye was Katzenstein, a comparativist by training, who directly challenged the unitary part of realism's characterization of states. The realist paradigm has frequently been described as a kind of billiard-ball model of international relations, with states conceived as closed "black boxes" driven solely by abstract calculations of national interest and power. Keohane and Nye began the process of opening the black box by adding the growing crowd of transnational actors to the picture. Katzenstein pushed the process further by emphasizing the purely domestic sources of foreign economic policy. In a memorable article (1976) and subsequently in a pathbreaking edited volume entitled *Between Power and Plenty* (1978), Katzenstein demonstrated the direct salience of the political and institutional basis at home for policy preferences abroad. In effect, the notion of complex interdependence was further expanded to encompass even strictly domestic actors, whether inside or outside government, as well as the institutional settings through which diverse interests were mediated and converted into policy. Yet more dimensions were highlighted that had been overlooked by realism.

None of this went uncontested, of course. Even as Keohane and Nye promoted their new vision of complex interdependence, others sought to defend the older realist tradition. Chief among them was Gilpin—"the dean of realist international political economy in the United States," as one source puts it (Murphy 2000: 798). In a key contribution to *Transnational Relations and World Politics* (Gilpin 1972), as well as in his subsequent classic, *US Power and the Multinational Corporation* (Gilpin 1975a), Gilpin explicitly confronted the issues raised by Keohane and Nye.

The emergence of transnationalism, he acknowledged, could not be denied. But that did not mean that realist theory had thus become obsolete. Quite the contrary, in fact. In insisting that a fundamental transformation was occurring in world politics, Gilpin argued in *Transnational Relations and World Politics*, Keohane and Nye were guilty of hyperbole. Transnationalism could only be understood within the context of the traditional state system, dating back to the Peace of Westphalia of 1648. For Gilpin, states were still the primary actors of interest and security concerns remained the crucial determinants of economic relations. In his words, "politics determines the framework of economic activity and channels it in directions which tend to serve ... political objectives" (1972: 54). Where Keohane and Nye went astray, he felt, was in failing to recognize the extent to which transnational actors and processes, ultimately, remain unavoidably dependent upon the pattern of interstate relations.

At issue was the nature of the underlying connection between economic and political activity, an age-old question that had long divided scholars of political economy. Does economics drive politics, or vice versa? Three schools of thought could be identified, Gilpin suggested, all drawn from traditional IR theory—liberalism, Marxism, and realism—each offering students of IPE its own distinct "model of the future." Liberals and Marxists shared a belief that economics was bound to dominate politics, though of course they differed enormously on whether this was a good or bad thing. Realists, by contrast, retained faith in the power of political relations to shape economic systems. Keohane and Nye, with their paradigm of complex interdependence, could be understood as the latest heirs of liberalism. Their approach, widely seen as a new variation on an old theme, was soon given the label "neoliberal institutionalism"; one source, emphasizing the pair's early Harvard connections, called it simply the "Harvard school of liberal international theory" (Long 1995). Gilpin, of course, was a barely reconstructed realist.

In *US Power and the Multinational Corporation* (1975a), Gilpin sought to respond to the new concept of transnationalism by carefully spelling out the strengths and weaknesses of each of the three approaches. His aim was to facilitate clearer and more consistent theorizing about the implications of interdependence. In so doing, he also provided a convenient template for future scholarship—an "intellectual edifice," as one friend describes it in private correspondence, that stands as perhaps his most lasting contribution to the construction of the infant field. In IPE textbooks today, Gilpin's three models—also referred to as paradigms or perspectives—are still regarded as the logical starting point for most serious discussion, even if then amended or combined in various ways. Few sources even bother any more to credit Gilpin for the taxonomy. Like the notion of complex interdependence, it has simply become an unexamined part of every specialist's toolkit.

For the next two decades, the development of American IPE was dominated by the dueling traditions of realism (later neorealism) and neoliberal institutionalism. (The Marxist model, though influential elsewhere, has never made much headway among mainstream political scientists in the United States, for the same ideological reasons that deterred economists.) Perhaps most illustrative was the prolonged debate between realists and liberals over the issue of systemic governance, sparked by the growing threat posed by economic interdependence to the political authority of sovereign states—the widening "control gap," as Keohane and Nye (1972: xxiii) put it, between state aspirations and state capabilities. The essence of governance lies in the power to define and enforce norms for the allocation of values in a collectivity. If national governments were losing control, who then would make the rules for the global economy and how would compliance with those rules be assured?

For a realist like Gilpin, the answer lay in power politics—specifically, in a concentration of capabilities in a single state sufficient to bring stability to the system as a whole. In a Westphalian world, economic relations could be successfully managed only by one dominant power, a "hegemon," such as the United States after World War II. Later labeled hegemonic stability theory (HST) by Keohane (1980), the idea was first broached by Gilpin in his contribution to *Transnational Relations and World Power* in 1972 and, more fully, in *US Power and the Multinational Corporation* in 1975; it was also echoed in an influential article by Krasner in 1976 (Krasner 1976). By 1987, in Gilpin's magisterial *The Political Economy of International Relations*, the theme had become grounds for an intense pessimism about the future of the global economy. America's dominance in the post-World War II period may have been self-serving, Gilpin conceded, but it had also served the world well, suppressing protectionism and managing financial crisis. Now, however, the times were changing. By the 1980s, he averred,

> American hegemonic leadership and the favorable political environment that it had provided for the liberal world economy had greatly eroded. … One must ask who or what would replace American leadership of the liberal economic order. Would it be … a collapse of the liberal world economy?
>
> (1987: 345, 363)

The outlook, he suggested, was exceedingly gloomy.

For liberals like Keohane and Nye, by contrast, there was more reason for optimism. America's postwar dominance may have eroded, they conceded. But hegemony was not the only possible source of stabilizing governance. Alternatively, the system could be managed cooperatively through the creation of international "regimes," embodying implicit or explicit understandings about the rules of the game in specific issue areas. The new notion of regimes could be understood as a particular form of international institution—hence the tongue-twisting sobriquet "neoliberal institutionalism." *Power and Interdependence* (1977) was first to put regimes at the center of analysis. Regime theory was then given further impetus by a landmark collection of essays on *International Regimes* edited by Krasner (1983) and reached its apogee with Keohane's monumental *After Hegemony*, published in 1984 (Keohane 1984). There is nothing in the logic of IR theory, Keohane declared in *After Hegemony*, that limits leadership in world politics to a single state. In principle, systemic stability could also be provided jointly through the framework of regimes, created and managed collectively. The issue was not the distribution of power but rather what conditions might best facilitate stabilizing leadership, whether by one state or several.

Effectively, the debate over HST was brought to a close by David Lake in a notable paper published in 1993 (Lake 1993). Reviewing two decades of dialogue, Lake offered a useful distinction between two different strands of HST. One was *leadership theory*, building on the logic of collective action and focused on the production of a framework for stability, redefined as the "international economic infrastructure." The other was *hegemony theory*, which seeks to explain patterns of international economic openness by focusing on national policy preferences. Both pointed to the salience of the global economy's political foundations—to the critical role that politics can play in overall system governance. Power mattered not because it might be concentrated, but rather because it is relevant to the management of economic affairs.

Rationalism vs. cognitive analysis

By the 1990s, debate in IR had begun to move on. Today, Gilpin's emphasis on the role of power politics in IPE lives on in what might be termed the "new realism" of such scholars as Joanne Gowa (1994), Jonathan Kirshner (1995), and David Andrews (2006). But gradually the differences between liberalism and realism came to be seen as less crucial than their similarities—in particular, their effective convergence around what John Ruggie (1999: 215) called "neo-utilitarian precepts and premises." Both traditions shared a preference for a rationalist and materialist ontology. Actors, whether states or non-state entities, were assumed to act in pursuit of clearly defined interests, usually expressed in terms of material preferences and goals. Identities were well established and unchanging. Outcomes were the result of a careful balancing of costs and benefits of alternative paths of behavior.

The debate now was between neo-utilitarianism of any kind, on the one hand, and on the other hand so-called cognitive analysis, which focuses on the base of ideas and con-sensual knowledge that motivate actor behavior. As originally conceived, cognitive ana-lysis was largely based in psychology and concerned strictly with the individual. What is in a person's mind? What is the independent influence of personal values and beliefs? Critical in bringing the insights of psychology to IR was Robert Jervis (1976), who emphasized the role that perceptions and misperceptions can play in shaping the mindsets of key decision-makers. Today, the tradition is best represented in the work of Rose McDermott (2004). However, in more recent years, the cognitive approach has also spawned a second track under the label of constructivism, following the pioneering efforts of such scholars as Nicholas Onuf (1989), Alexander Wendt (1992), and Martha Finnemore (1996a). The constructivist track is rather more sociological in nature, con-cerned more with connections between individuals—with learning, inter-subjectivity, and social knowledge. How did what is in a person's mind get there, and how do values and beliefs change over time? The spotlight of constructivism is on the independent effect of norms on behavior. "In the 1990s some of the major points of contestation [in IR] shifted," wrote Katzenstein et al. (1999: 43) in a definitive survey published at the end of the decade, stressing in particular the new prominence of the divide between rationalism and cognitive analysis.

Strikingly, to date the new debate has had only a limited impact on IPE in the United States. As Katzenstein et al. (1999: 9) conceded in their survey: "In the field of national security the discussion between rationalism (in its realist and liberal variants) and [cognitive analysis] has been more fully joined than in the field of IPE." First buds of a cognitive tradition are beginning to emerge in American IPE but are still far from a full flowering.

The reason is not difficult to fathom. Ideational factors sit uneasily in a hard science model. Like economists back when IPE was first born, US specialists in the field today instinctively resist a theoretical approach that runs against the grain of accepted methodological standards. How can formal analysis account for the inherent uncertainties of the human mind? How can existing empirical methods cope with the vagueness of notions like socialization and social facts? Here too, mainstream scholars have preferred to ignore what cannot be objectively observed or systematically tested.

Not that ideational factors were ever entirely excluded in American IPE. As early as 1979, John Odell was stressing the role of policy beliefs and subjective perceptions in the shaping of US monetary behavior. "In analyses of policy change," he argued, "beliefs should be elevated to an equal theoretical level" (1979: 80). Odell's focus was on the individual policymaker, representative of the psychological track of cognitive analysis. His aim was to demonstrate the degree to which state behavior could be traced to the mind set of senior officials. As he expanded in a subsequent book, "behavior depends not on reality but on how reality is perceived and interpreted … Substantive ideas held by top policy makers and advisers [are] decisive or necessary elements of explanation" (1982: 58). Ideas were also at the center of Judith Goldstein's pathmark study of US trade policy (1993).

Contributions like these, however, were few and far between, failing to inspire much emulation. Even scarcer were efforts to take the sociological track, highlighting processes of social construction and the constitutive role of norms. The major exception was Ruggie, who long wandered in the desert preaching the cause of constructivism even before the movement had a name. Most memorable was a well known chapter he contributed to Krasner's *International Regimes* volume (1983), addressing the origins of the postwar economic order. Central to his analysis was the notion of a normative framework, understood as an "intersubjective framework of meaning" (1983: 196). Regimes, he argued, are social institutions. "We know international regimes not simply by some descriptive inventory of their concrete elements, but by their generative grammar, the underlying principles of order and meaning that shape the manner of their formation and transformation" (1983: 196).

Only in the most recent years have studies of ideational factors begun to blossom in the American version of the field. Leading the way on the psychological track, once again, is Odell. In a thoughtful exploration of international economic negotiations (2000), Odell built on the insights of his earlier work to highlight the role of negotiators' beliefs as an independent influence on bargaining strategies and outcomes. The critical issue, he suggested, is what Nobel-prize winning economist Herbert Simon called "bounded rationality"—a variant of "rational choice that takes into account the cognitive limitations of the decision maker, limitations of both knowledge and computational capacity" (Simon 1997: 291). Given the constraints of bounded rationality, negotiators typically make use of cognitive shortcuts, convenient heuristics that rely heavily on subjective beliefs to guide their behavior. To understand economic diplomacy, therefore, it is vital to understand the ideas of the diplomats. In Odell's words (2000: 3): "If the real world is one of bounded rationality, identifying such key beliefs and their effects becomes a productive way to advance knowledge about, and the practice of, economic bargaining." Along similar lines, Mark Blyth (2002) has clearly demonstrated the critical role that ideas played in shaping institutional change in the world economy over the course of the twentieth century.

Systematic studies have also begun to appear on the sociological track, albeit still at a modest pace—mostly, as it happens, on monetary or financial matters where issues of reputation and perception are obviously critical. As Jacqueline Best (2004: 404) has observed: "Financial stability depends on confidence, and confidence is a matter of faith—not simply in the efficiency of institutions, but also in the robustness and legitimacy of the norms that inform them." One example comes from Kathleen McNamara (1998), who has carefully explored the "currency of ideas" as a driving force in the process of monetary integration in Europe. The key to understanding the evolution of European monetary politics in the 1970s and 1980s, McNamara suggests, lay in a new "neoliberal" policy consensus that took hold among policy elites, redefining state interests. A second example comes from Jeffrey Chwieroth (2007) in a constructivist study of financial liberalization in emerging market economies in the 1980s and 1990s. Capital markets were opened, Chwieroth contends, because of a new set of neoliberal norms that were diffused through a network of knowledge-based experts once they came to positions of political authority. Other constructivist research has highlighted the social sources of financial power and monetary leadership in the global community (Barkin 2003; Seabrooke 2006).

How successful all these efforts at cognitive analysis will turn out to be remains an open question. But it is clear that the field is now increasingly open to ideational factors in addition to the more traditional neo-utilitarian approaches. American IPE may still privilege the state as the basic unit of analysis. But the field has definitely come a long way from the narrow state-centric paradigm of early realism.

Recapture

One counter-trend should be noted, however. Even as American IPE has produced a multiplicity of traditions, a striking degree of standardization has gradually taken hold at the level of methodology. Political scientists may have dominated the field from the start, setting the agenda for research. But in terms of research technique, the economics profession has been making a steady comeback. Increasingly, the style of scholarship in much of American IPE has come to resemble the reductionist approach favored by economists, featuring the same penchant for positivist analysis, formal modeling, and, where possible, systematic collection and evaluation of empirical data. More and more, what gets published in the United States—particularly in such prestigious journals as *International Organization* or the *American Political Science Review*—features the same sorts of mathematical and statistical techniques that we have come to expect in economics journals. The trend is not universal, of course. Much valuable work continues to appear that is institutional, historical, or interpretive in tone. But it would not be inaccurate to say that in epistemological terms, a good part of the field today has been recaptured by economists.

Why is this? Puzzling over the trend, which has been evident for years, the economist Vernon once suggested that it might have something to do with the deceptive accessibility of the reductionist style. "The ideas that appear to travel most easily between the social sciences are the simpler, more inclusive ideas; and when gauged by the criteria of simplicity and inclusiveness, neoclassical propositions have had a decisive edge" (1989: 443). But there may also be an element of envy involved. Political scientists have an inferiority complex when it comes to economics. Even such notables as Katzenstein et al. (1999: 23) bow their heads, describing economics as "the reigning king of the social sciences." Whether the title is deserved or not, it is certainly true that the "imitative scientism" of economics now appears to set the standard for what passes for professionalism among social scientists in the United States. If today the most highly rated work in American IPE seeks to mimic the economist's demanding hard-science model, it may be simply be to demonstrate that the field, for all the uncertainties of the political process, is no less capable of formal rigor. Specialists in IPE want respect, too.

An enthusiasm for the methodology of economics is understandable, offering as it does both technical sophistication and intellectual elegance. Who wouldn't like to be able to predict something large from something small? But it is also undeniable that reductionism comes at a price in terms of descriptive reality and practical credibility. On the one hand, the full flavor of life is sacrificed for what one critic calls a "tasteless pottage of mathematical models" (DeLong 2005: 128), often wholly unintelligible to a wider public. On the other hand, the true character of life is often caricatured by the implausible assumptions that parsimony demands. The increasing standardization of IPE methods in the United States is by no means costless.

2

Realist political economy

Traditional themes and contemporary challenges

Jonathan Kirshner

Realist political economy rests upon three foundations: the state, pursuing the national interest, in an environment defined by anarchy. Each of these three attributes distinguishes realism from other approaches to the study of the politics of international economic relations, such as liberalism and varieties of Marxism (cf. Gilpin 1975b: 37–60). These attributes are interrelated. Realists see an autonomous state—that is, a state that is neither the sum of individual interests à la liberalism nor the implicit or explicit representative of certain privileged interests within society anticipated by Marxism. And that state pursues the national interest—which, again, is distinct from a pluralist vision that derives the national interest from the summation of individual interests, or from the radical charge that the national interest is a cloak for the advancement of particular interests (cf. Morgenthau 1951; Kennan 1951; Krasner 1978).

Much of the distinctness of the national interest comes from the existence of anarchy—the lack of an ultimate international authority, and thus the absence of any guarantee that the nation will not be invaded, overrun, conquered, and pillaged. Security is a public good; public goods tend to be underprovided by private actors; the state is responsible for the provision of security. Realists do not presume the imminence or ubiquity of war (nor do non-realists presume that war is impossible), but rather realists assume that states must be alert to the possibility that war could occur and are sensitive to the potentially catastrophic consequences of defeat. Thus the state will cast a judicious eye on international economic relations. Some mutually beneficial transactions might nevertheless leave the state less secure—compared to other perspectives realism tends to emphasize this tension between the national interest and economic interests—leading to the expectation that states will make departures from those policies that maximize wealth and short-run economic growth in the name of national security (Viner 1948: 10; Gilpin 1971: 403–4, 409–10; Mastanduno 1998: 827, 842–43, 848). Following this, and more generally, realists argue that international politics are an essential and formative influence on the pattern of international economic relations. As E. H. Carr wrote, "the science of economics presupposes a given political order, and cannot be profitably studied in isolation from politics" (Carr 1951: 117; cf. Strange 1970b: 304–15; Viner 1929: 408–51; Feis 1930; Spiro 1999).

Realists also have a distinct perspective with regard to how they contextualize the economic sphere of human relations, a perspective rooted in assumptions about the nature of mankind. Liberalism and Marxism share an inherently economistic perspective: individuals are motivated by desire to maximize their personal wealth; they want more stuff; and individual behavior is best described, explained, and predicted by the rational pursuit of more stuff. In his most intimate memoir, John Maynard Keynes skewered this "Benthamite calculus, based on an over-valuation of the economic criterion," and "the final reductio ad absurdum of Benthamism known as Marxism" (Keynes 1949: 97). Realist expectations of human behavior, in contrast, are first informed by politics and also by anthropology and sociology. This perspective does not dismiss the considerable significance of material incentives and ambitions, but it places the influence of those tangibles in the context of a mindset captured by the title of Stanley Kubrick's first film, *Fear and Desire*. Virtually all realists share the view that fear—alertness to the dangers of the world—is a primal motive of behavior, and that security is a principal and urgent desire. Beyond this—in those settings when physical security appears secure (often), realists vary with regard to their expectations regarding additional desires: here the approach is indeterminate. However, those desires, which will almost certainly include material comforts and luxuries, are not at bottom motivated by maximizing wealth, but rather with security, prestige, primacy, and even domination—as ends in themselves.

In a phrase, "realists aren't in it for the money." That is, actors behaving as realists would expect them to (though not necessarily realist scholars!), will often, without regret, trade wealth for power (or, when secure, status). Thus, while radical scholars would describe the use of power to hold in place a system of international capitalism that enforces economic exploitation, the realist view commonly reverses this relationship. This process was first described by Albert Hirschman, in his study of German inter-war trading relations. Germany cultivated a series of asymmetric trading relationships with the small states of Southeastern Europe as part of its pre-World War II grand strategy to secure needed raw materials and increase German leverage there. Although inefficient from an economic perspective, redirecting trade to contiguous regions enhanced Germany's autonomy. Focusing on small states increased Germany's political leverage there by making exit more costly for others (given their relative stakes in the relationship), and therefore threats to end or to interrupt the relationship, both explicit and implicit, provide power to the larger state (Hirschmann 1980 [1945]; cf. Krasner 1976: 320; Kirshner 1995: ch. 4).

This asymmetry, plus the relatively sweet deals offered by Germany, exerted, as Hirschman noted, "a powerful influence in favor of a 'friendly' attitude towards the state to the imports of which they owe their interests" (Hirschmann 1980: 29). Thus not only was Germany able to purchase greater autonomy and coercive leverage over its neighbors, it was also able to enhance its political influence with those states. As *National Interest* shows more generally, behind the headlines and with little fanfare, the pattern of international economic relations affects domestic politics, which in turn shapes foreign policy. This can have a profound effect on the international behavior of small states in asymmetric relations. Realists anticipate that large states will routinely make economic sacrifices in an effort to enhance their political influence in this fashion (Hirschmann 1980: 18, 28–29, 34–37).[1]

Continuity in the realist perspective over time

Realist political economy has, not surprisingly, evolved over time, in response to intellectual challenges and historical events. But there is also a notable continuity in its

underlying philosophy, from its intellectual roots in classical mercantilism, its more intimate association with nineteenth-century neo-mercantilism, and its development alongside the tumultuous world politics and emergence of the discipline of international
relations in the twentieth century.

Classical mercantilism, with its emphasis on the zero sum nature of international trade
and the need to accumulate precious metals, was subject to withering and in many
aspects irretrievable criticism in 1776 by Adam Smith in his millennial articulation of
liberalism (Smith 1976 [1776]: vol. I: 450–73, 496–502, 513–24, vol. II: 3–10, 103–57).
With regard to its implications for international relations, Smith established that wealth
derived from productive capacity, not precious metals; that the economic effects of trade
were positive sum, not zero sum; and that, consequentially, the balance of trade was not
usually a crucial determinant of economic well being. Each of these changes represented
an important departure from mercantilist thought.[2]

At the same time, there were important continuities between the classical mercantilists
and their liberal challengers. In particular, each school of thought sought to maximize
both power and plenty (witness Smith's famous support for the protectionist navigation
acts and for subsidies to defense-related industries), and each saw a long run harmony
between those goals (Smith 1976 [1776]: vol. I: 484–85, vol. II: 28).[3] The achievements
of the nineteenth-century neo-mercantilists, then, such as Alexander Hamilton, Fredrich
List, and Gustav Schmoller, were not to defend mercantilism from Smith's devastating
critiques, but rather were the result of integrating the advances in economic thought
produced by the liberal school with realist (rather than liberal) assumptions about politics.
Realists followed liberals by branching off, not chopping down. Hamilton's famous
"Report on manufactures" was heavily influenced by Smith; as for List, his classic com-
ment, "the power of producing wealth is ... infinitely more important than wealth itself"
could just as easily have appeared in *The Wealth of Nations* (Hamilton 1928 in Cole 1928:
248; cf. Bourne 1894: 329–48).[4]

Thus liberals and realists share the view that both power and plenty are crucial and
complementary aims of state action, and further that power flows from productive capability and productive capability from economic growth. The realist dissent is with
liberal politics, not liberal economics (cf. Morgenthau 1978: 126; Knorr 1975; Gilpin
1987: 328–36). "Adam Smith's Doctrine," List argued, "presupposes the existence of a
state of perpetual peace and of universal union." But of course, this is not the case. Thus
while List recognized the benefits of free trade, he argued that the "influence of war"
required states to deviate from some of the policy prescriptions of liberalism (List 1885:
316, 347).[5]

Similarly, in their political conception of the state, realists parted company with the
liberals. This central theme emerged unscathed in the transition from mercantilism to
neomercantilism, and remains a foundation of realist thought. According to Heckscher,
"The state stood at the centre of mercantilist endeavors developed historically: the state
was both the subject and the object of mercantilist economic policy." In fact, more than
half of Heckscher's massive study is devoted to the explication of mercantilism as a state-
building enterprise, and the emergence of the state as a powerful actor with interests
distinct from other groups within society (Heckscher 1935: 21, cf. 273, part 1). This
remained a central theme for the neomercantilists, most visibly Schmoller, for whom
"mercantilism in its innermost kernel is nothing but state making" and who argued
"What was at stake was the creation of real political economies as unified organisms"
(Schmoller 1897: 49–50).

States, as autonomous actors with their own interests, will often find those interests in conflict with the interests and preferences of other groups in society. Mun and other mercantilists called attention to the potential incompatibility of public and private interests; List reemphasized this theme, repeatedly insisting that "the interest of individuals and the interest of the commerce of a whole nation are widely different things" (Mun 1949: 25–26; cf. Viner 1948: 19; Heckscher 1935: vol. II: 317; List 1885: 269). Again, this is particularly likely to be the case when the state, due to its greater sensitivity to security concerns or its tendency to have a longer time horizon than individuals, is more willing to accept short term economic sacrifices in order to reap greater long run rewards. "The nation," List insisted, "must renounce present advantages with a view to securing future ones." As J. B. Condliffe has argued, List sees "the state as an end in itself and the major end of policy, rather than as an instrument for the promotion of individual welfare" (Silberner 1946: 278; Condliffe 1950: 278).

As with the discipline of international relations more generally, realist political economy was forged by the experiences of the world wars and the Cold War.[6] Two principal questions recurred, regarding the consequences of interdependence and the prospects for international cooperation, debates about which were influenced by major historical events. The First World War, in particular, confirmed realist skepticism that economic interdependence would assure peace, as liberals anticipated. For realists, states are more likely to chafe from the frictions and encroachments that interdependence will present, rather than be soothed by its multilayered embrace (cf. Carr 1951: 60; Gilpin 1971; Waltz 1970).[7]

Realists again part company with liberals over the question of cooperation. For liberals, market failure often prevents states from reaching mutually beneficial transactions and agreements; for realists, the existence of mutually beneficial transactions is not sufficient to assure international cooperation. Rather, states have to be concerned about the consequences of those interactions for national security. Would trade erode defense autonomy? Would specialization create new vulnerabilities? As with nineteenth-century neo-mercantilists, twentieth-century realists did not question that international trade would leave both participants wealthier; rather, the question was one of the composition of trade and the distribution of the gains. Thus, for liberals, the remarkable growth of the international economy after the Second World War is attributable to the leadership of the US, which provided international public goods, and the international regimes it founded, which produced the information, expectations, and mechanisms that reduced market failure. For realists, however, the same outcome is attributable to the dominance of the US vis-à-vis its allies, and the stable bipolar nature of the Cold War. These two (exceptional) factors, in combination, created the conditions under which the US concluded that its self-interest was best served by setting aside concerns about relative gains and encouraging the superior economic performance of its allies (Gilpin 1981; Kindleberger 1981: 242–54; Gowa 1984; Keohane 1984).

The emphasis on relative gains is something of a poster-boy for realist political economy, with a pedigree that can, again, be traced back to the classical mercantilists and followed through to the present day. In 1684, P. W. von Hörnigk stated that the wealth and might of a nation depends "principally on whether its neighbors possess more or less of it. For power and riches have become a relative matter." A decade earlier, the English mercantilist Coke wrote "if our treasure were more than our Neighboring nations, I did not care whether we had one-fifth part of the treasure we now have" (von Hörnigk and Coke in Heckscher 1935: Vol. II 22; cf. 24, 26, 239; Gilpin 1975b: 33; Grieco 1988:

485–507). Nevertheless, the voluminous academic debate on this issue has to some extent obscured the first principles at stake.[8] What ultimately distinguishes realism is not the pursuit of relative gains, but the motives behind that pursuit: as Joe Grieco argues, "states in anarchy must fear that others may seek to destroy or enslave them" (Grieco 1990: 217). But actors, in the absence of anarchy and concerns for security, routinely seek relative, not just absolute gains in their interactions. Moreover, in practice, analytically distinguishing between behaviors motivated by economic gain rather than by security will prove difficult.[9]

In sum, these are not settled research questions—nor are they likely to present opportunities for definitive settlement. But they illustrate the enduring themes of realist political economy that will inform realist analyses in the twenty-first century: a skepticism regarding the possibility that interdependence will significantly decrease the prospects for war, the assumption that international politics will crucially shape the pattern of international economic relations, and an expectation that states will monitor their engagement with the international economy with an eye toward mediating the dangers that derive from anarchy.

Realist political economy in the twenty-first century: issues and controversies

Realist political economy has struggled with the transition from the Cold-War international order to the post-Cold War international environment. Globalization, especially but not exclusively in the financial realm, has encroached on state autonomy without (as of yet, at least) generating a reassertion of state authority that realists would naturally anticipate. Similarly, the emergence of a more discriminatory (if still relatively porous) regionalism, a common realist expectation, has not emerged.[10] And the United States is increasingly and intimately economically enmeshed with China, the state widely anticipated to assume the mantle of its principal strategic rival—and moreover US policy has evidenced little remorse, or even much wariness, regarding the strategic consequences of its permissive posture in this regard.

But these problems, I argue, are not *disconfirming* of the realist perspective for contemporary politics; rather they flow from two old habits that realism should (and can) shed. Realist scholars have stumbled on the question of globalization, failing to recognize the distinction between it and that old realist whipping boy, interdependence; and realists have also hitched their analytical wagons to a structuralist albatross. These have led to false steps both with regard to analysis and prediction. A reformed and revitalized realism, true to the foundational principles of the approach described at the start of this essay, can move past these problems and provide great analytical insight into twenty-first century matters.

Globalization for realists

The realist instinct—and indeed the reaction of leading realist scholars—was to be skeptical of the significance of globalization (cf. Waltz 1999; Gilpin 2001: 326–76; Mearsheimer 2001: 370–72). This instinct was rooted in three foundations: first, the tendency for realism to stress continuity, rather than change, in the basic nature of world politics; second, the anticipation of realists that states will seek, to the extent that it is feasible and not self-defeating, to enhance and protect their autonomy; third, a visceral skepticism regarding the *commercial peace*, or the idea that interdependence between states is an important factor in inhibiting war. At times one suspects that the categorical dismissal of the significance of interdependence, with reference to World War I as the definitive falsification, is written prominently on the back of membership cards to the realist club.

But globalization is not interdependence, and it is disregarded at great peril. While globalization has been defined in a number of ways, it can be understood as an array of phenomena that derive from unorganized and stateless forces but that generate pressures that are felt by states. Globalization is manifested in a number of ways in contemporary international politics: through the intensification of economic exchange—including the fragmentation of production and the astonishing ascension of finance; dramatic changes in the nature of information flows resulting from a confluence of innovations including satellites and cellphones, faxes and the internet; and "marketization"—pressures that encourage the expansion of the set of social relations governed by market forces (Kirshner 2006).

These processes are distinct, they are mutually reinforcing, and, importantly, they are not *interdependence*. Interdependence relates to relations between two states, which can be more or less interdependent depending on the level and nature of economic exchange between them. Globalization is a condition. Intense economic interdependence between states can take place in the absence of globalization; and relations between two states with limited economic relations can be significantly affected by the condition of globalization.

Even while retaining realist foundations—a state-centric perspective, national security traditionally and even narrowly defined, and continuity regarding states' motivations (the pursuit of security and other manifestations of the national interest)—globalization matters for world politics and national security. Failure to account for the influence of globalization will make it increasingly difficult to understand changes in the balance of power, prospects for war, and strategic choices embraced by states.[11]

Globalization affects traditional national security issues in three principal ways. Globalization affects state capacity and autonomy, and thus reshapes the relative power of the state vis-à-vis non-state actors, social forces and market pressures. This does not of necessity suggest that the state will be weakened across the board; in some areas relative state power can be enhanced, for example in the area of surveillance.

Globalization also affects the balance of power between states, because due to the changes brought about to state autonomy and state capacity—no matter what the nature of those changes are, and even in the case where every state finds itself absolutely less able to advance its interests—there will be a reshuffling of relative capabilities. That is, even if, in the limiting case, that all states as actors are left less capacious, some will be weakened to a lesser extent, and all will probably be affected in distinct ways. Thus globalization will reshape the relative distribution of capabilities and vulnerabilities between states. Finally, globalization influences the nature and axes of conflict. Unlike interdependence theory, globalization does not imply more peaceful relations between all states. Rather, globalization likely reinforces already powerful incentives for peaceful relations between advanced industrial states—but at the same time, the disruptive effects of globalization in much of the world will likely contribute to new sources of conflict; and the weakening of the very weak will likely create an environment conducive to insurgency and civil war, and empower transnational criminal networks and terrorist organizations, creating distinct opportunities and incentives for political violence.[12]

Realist political economy can integrate the influence of globalization, if with certain caveats, and, always, with an emphasis on the primary role of politics in shaping both globalization and its consequences. From a realist perspective, globalization is not necessarily novel, irreversible, or irresistible. But to observe that it is snowing very heavily and steadily at the moment is not to deny that there have been blizzards in the past, or that it may subsequently stop snowing entirely—rather it is simply to argue that the blizzard matters right now and therefore it is important to understand the consequences of the snow. No claim of novelty or irreversibility is necessary to hold the conclusion that globalization significantly affects national security. Similarly, while many of the pressures brought about by globalization are quite powerful, globalization is not an irresistible force, nor an arbiter of unbending laws. Rather, processes of globalization reshape the costs, benefits, and consequences of pursuing different policy choices. Choices made by self-interested states pursuing national goals will be affected by those changing incentives.[13]

At all times, a realist perspective on globalization emphasizes its political foundations and political consequences, which are not neutral. American unipolarity has contributed to an environment more conducive to the advance of globalization than would have likely occurred had the Cold War's bipolar order endured, or if an illiberal state, rather than the US, were the world's preponderant power. And as the biggest fish in a more open pond, the US often finds itself advantaged by globalization, given its economic power and international political capacities. Yet in some other ways, the US is politically disadvantaged by its implication in a variety of globalization's consequences, attracting new forms and sources of resistance to its political objectives. In sum, realist political economy can and should, and while retaining fidelity to its first principles, generate hypotheses about the consequences of globalization for contemporary world politics.

Putting structure in its place

For several decades, realist analysis has been profoundly shaped by the influence of neorealism, that approach to realism most closely associated with Kenneth Waltz, and his book, *Theory of International Politics*. Neorealism has much to offer the study of world politics, but its influence, as well as its emphasis, if not insistence, on the systemic level of analysis has skewed, unhelpfully, realist analysis. The limitations of Waltzian neorealism—a consideration of states as like units differentiated only by their relative capabilities—are particularly notable for twenty-first century realist political economy.

To begin with, even at the systemic level, as Robert Gilpin has argued, the "most important factor" for understanding world politics is not the static distribution of power, but "dynamics of power relations over time." Gilpin's *War and Change in World Politics* (1981), a product of the same era, is the dynamic realist companion to Waltz's static approach. *War and Change* is the exemplar of those approaches that stress the importance of equilibrium in the international system. From this perspective, changes in relative power, which ultimately derive from changes in economic growth over time, are the mainspring of great power conflict. At moments of "equilibrium," the given distribution of power is such that no state sees benefits from challenging the prevailing order. Economic change, however, redistributes relative power over time, creating a natural tendency for the system as a whole to drift away from equilibrium. The resulting divergence between power and privilege encourages rising revisionist states to challenge the status quo. A central problem in international relations is addressing these changes to the balance of power, which is very commonly resolved by war (Gilpin 1981: 93; cf. Liska 1957; Organski 1968: 364–67).

Beyond this question of statics versus dynamics at the systemic level, the triumph of neorealism more generally, and its insistence on structural analysis, has rendered vanishingly small the perceived applicability of *realism* to practical problems. This need not be. Waltz is indeed dismissive of an appeal to variables at other levels of analysis—"it is not possible to understand world politics simply by looking inside of states," Waltz insists, "The behavior of states and statesmen ... is indeterminate" (Waltz 1979: 65, 68). This may be true. However, the elephant in the neorealist room is that this is also true for the system. Certainly, realists cannot dispense with close attention to the distribution of power and changes in the distribution of power over time, because, at bottom, in the context of anarchy and the possibility of war, these variables condition states' fears and expectations, and influence the pattern of interactions between them. Nevertheless, it is not possible to understand world politics simply by looking outside of states. The implications of systemic forces are inherently and irretrievably indeterminate.

Not surprisingly, since the microeconomic analogy was always explicit, the international system does indeed impose constraints on the states which constitute it in a way analogous to the way in which the range of choices presented to consumers and firms is expressed by market forces that derive from the collective behavior of all participants but which are beyond the control of any particular actor. But the analogy is imperfect and strained. Even assuming an idealized abstract market, with similar firms seeking singular goals (maximizing profits or market share), the deterministic implications of systemic market pressure are dependent on very strict assumptions of perfect competition—a very large set of small actors that have no market power but instead are price takers. As the idealized assumption of perfect competition is relaxed, market forces remain vital but individual choices—idiosyncratic choices—become increasingly central to explaining behavior. In particular, large firms in oligopolistic settings, while certainly not unconstrained by market forces, nevertheless enjoy considerable discretion as to how they will pursue their goals.[14]

States in world politics are much more like large oligopolists than small firms under perfect competition. This is especially true for great powers, even though, with unintentional analytical irony, it is the very greatest powers that neorealism is most interested in: "A general theory of international politics is necessarily based on the great powers" (Waltz 1979: 73). Further, despite their common attributes, states are less similar to each other than are firms of the same industry, and despite a common desire for survival, as realists have observed in the past states pursue a broad range of goals (certainly more diverse than goals of firms), the content of which will very likely vary from state to state (Wolfers 1962). And even in pursuit of that most narrow, common goal—survival—states are still less predictable than firms, because they typically have more latitude—firms are selected out of the system with much greater frequency than are states.

Structure thus informs importantly the environment in which all states act, but in that context, all states, and especially great powers, enjoy considerable discretion with regard to how they will pursue their goals and what sacrifices they will make in the face of constraints. It is thus impossible to understand and anticipate the behavior of states by looking solely at structural variables and constraints. Structural realists are trying to understand world politics with at least one hand tied behind their back. To explain world politics, and especially to address questions of political economy from a realist perspective in the coming years, it is necessary to appeal to a host of other factors, including domestic politics, history, ideology, and perceptions of legitimacy.

There is an inaccurate if commonly held assumption that "realists can't do that." This misunderstanding predates *Theory of International Politics*, and probably derives from the fact traditional realist analyses do not expect norms to prevent states from pursuing radically dangerous foreign policies, and in their unwillingness to label actions as *good* or *bad*, realists have placed less emphasis on the importance of variables like regime type. E. H. Carr, for example, went out of his way to stress that there was no moral difference between revisionist and status quo aims; George F. Kennan and Hans Morgenthau have also expressed considerable caution regarding the appeal to morality in foreign policy, and each chastised the US for its episodic emphasis on idealism in foreign policy (Carr 1951: 91; Morgenthau 1960: 10). But the desire of realist scholars to study world politics *scientifically*—that is, without reference to good and bad or right and wrong, the way one would study the causes and consequences of earthquakes or volcanic eruptions, does not mean that domestic politics, or history, or ideas are irrelevant for realists. There may be no *moral* difference, according to realists, between states that prefer the status quo to those that pursue revisionist strategies, but those states will nevertheless behave differently; similarly, norms may not stop states from engaging in acts of barbaric aggression, but history and perceptions of legitimacy nevertheless condition the way in which states interpret the meaning of each others' actions.

Realists can—and have—deployed and taken seriously these types of variables. In contrast to Waltz, for example, Gilpin's contemporaneous work has consistently included an important role for non-structural explanatory variables, from his earliest writings that helped establish the basis of contemporary realist political economy, and in his subsequent contributions that followed. In "The politics of transnational relations" Gilpin distinguished realism from liberalism and Marxism by noting the distinct realist emphasis on "national sentiment" and "political values"; and in "Economics and national security in historical perspective" Gilpin places emphasis on "the decay of bourgeoisie middle class work ethic" in explaining state behavior, a theme developed further in *War and Change in World Politics* (Gilpin in Knorr and Trager 1977: 59; Gilpin 1971: 401–3; Gilpin 1981; 154, 159).

What is realism? Realists see states, pursuing interests, in an anarchic setting where the real possibility of war, and with it the prospect of subjugation or annihilation, must be accounted for. Realists see humans as actors with political instincts, who organize into groups that are discriminatory and typically conflictual. (Realists, more so than liberal-materialists, for example, would be more likely to see nationalism as an important influence on state behavior (cf. Abdelal 2001).) Finally, it should be noted that realists seem to share a certain pessimistic view of humanity and of the prospects for fundamental progress or transformation in the nature of human behavior. But beyond an acute sensitivity to the balance of power, none of these tenets require structuralism; non-structural realism is possible and indeed necessary to better understand twenty-first century international politics and political economy.

Real realism on China

Central questions that will demand the attention of realist political economy now and in the coming decades involve China, and American foreign policy towards China. China is rising and is an emerging great power; it borders other major powers and is implicated in a host of security issues; its demand for energy is a potential source of political friction with other states; its participation in any international political conventions related to the environment is essential; and, most notably, it is at the same time an important strategic rival of, and intimately enmeshed economically with, the United States. China benefits immensely from its ability to access the American market; and its massive dollar holdings are a key pillar of support for the stability of the US dollar, which in the eyes of many observers rests upon otherwise shaky foundations.

From a realist perspective, this is not a pretty picture. It is a common assumption of realists that "as the power of a state increases, it seeks to extend … its political influence, and/or its domination of the international economy" (Gilpin 1981: 106; cf. Kahler 1988: 451). At a minimum changes in the balance of power are inherently destabilizing. Realists tend to expect that due to collective action problems, the security dilemma, and, importantly, opposing interests, international cooperation will be hard to establish and maintain; and they are skeptical that economic interdependence will have an important ameliorating effect on tensions that arise in world politics. Thus, regarding the consequences of China's rise, the default setting is pessimistic: China will become more ambitious, challenging the interests of other states; China's participation in international agreements will be increasingly necessary for those agreements to have meaning, but cooperation between strategic rivals will be brittle; China's interdependence with the United States will not inhibit political conflict, or even war, from breaking out between them.

Realists are therefore pessimistic about and wary of a rising China. But what does this suggest for policy? Here the pathologies of an over-reliance on structuralism become apparent. The exemplar of this is John Mearsheimer's brand of structural realism, "offensive realism" (Mearsheimer 2001). According to Mearsheimer, states, motivated to ensure their own security, recognize that the safest position in the system is one of regional hegemony. Only a regional hegemon is secure in the knowledge that it will not be conquered by others. Thus, given the anarchic nature of the international system, states that can plausibly make bids for regional hegemony will do so, as a matter of their own assessment of their best chances for survival.

Applying this to China, Mearsheimer assumes that "it is certainly in China's interest to be the hegemon in Northeast Asia," and therefore, once it is wealthy enough, it will embark upon a bid for hegemony. The current US policy of engaging China is "misguided," because "a wealthy China would not be a status quo power but an aggressive state determined to achieve regional hegemony." Thus, Mearsheimer argues, the US should "reverse course and do what it can to slow the rise of China" (Mearsheimer 2001: 401–2).

This analysis illustrates the limits of structuralism, and it also violates several core assumptions of realism. While non-structural realism is pessimistic regarding the consequences of China's rise, its tenets lead to the conclusion that engaging China is indeed the wisest strategy, in the only context that ever matters to realist analysis—that strategy compared to the likely consequences of other options. Offensive realism stumbles badly here for the reasons that should be expected—its insistence upon the absence of history and the irrelevance of domestic politics—and for one surprising reason: its embrace of idealism. The results are policy prescriptions that are naive, misguided, and not really *realist*.

Only a power with a complete ignorance of history would be quick to embark upon a bid for hegemony. For while it may be true that to be a regional hegemon is to be secure, getting there—to bid for hegemony—is to invite ruin, and for good realist reasons. Most states in history that have bid for hegemony have antagonized their neighbors and eventually elicited an encircling coalition that conquered them. Because, as realists expect, major powers and great powers prefer not to be threatened and pushed around— and China is in a crowded neighborhood, which includes Japan, Russia, India, and even Vietnam and Korea. If China pushes too hard, these states will likely push back. Thus, yes, a rising China will almost certainly be more ambitious and assertive. It may even ultimately blunder into a disastrous bid for hegemony. But its future foreign policy trajectory is uncertain, at least in the eyes of a number of realists—China hands and Asian security specialists—who have considered this question (cf. Friedberg 2005: 7–45; Goldstein 2005; Christensen 2006: 81–126).

One important determinant of those foreign policy choices will be the evolution of domestic politics within China. Interdependence may not assure peace, but China's continued and internationally oriented economic growth will empower those within China who, however ambitious, prefer relatively friendly relationships with the outside world. On the other hand, economic distress within China would likely create a legitimacy crisis for the ruling Chinese Communist Party, which might then resort to a virulent nationalism in order to cling to power. At that point, the misguided bid for hegemony becomes more plausible.

Is this what the US should want? At best the "offensive realist" approach is a self-fulfilling prophecy. At worst, and likely, it is dangerously unfeasible as well. Realists throughout history have universally criticized the idealism and even utopianism of others, who see the world as they would like to see it, rather than respecting the realities of power. But this sort of idealism is exactly what Mearsheimer is advocating: facing the rise of China's power, the US should "make sure that China does not become a peer competitor" (Mearsheimer 2001: 400). This is utopia, not reality—the world as the US wants it, not the world as it is. (Could Britain in the nineteenth century have *made sure* that the US would not emerge as a great power?) The US can delay and make more difficult China's rise, but it cannot likely stop it. The real realist approach would be to acknowledge this, and try to manage it as best as possible. Structure is indeterminate. China's foreign policy future remains unwritten. Wary and pessimistic as they approach the table, and expecting the worst to come from changes in the balance of power, realists nevertheless place hedged bets on engagement.

Contemporary realist political economy thus remains as it has traditionally been, focused on the state, pursuing the national interest, in an environment defined by anarchy. For realists, politics remains primal: international politics are an essential and formative influence on the pattern of international economic relations, and states will be sensitive to the political consequences of their economic engagements abroad, and be especially alert to the potential dangers that might result from them. As a consequence, realists expect that states will prefer, when possible, to enhance their relative economic autonomy, and remain skeptical that interdependence will inhibit conflict between states.

These foundational principles remain cogent and applicable. Nevertheless, realist political economy has been sluggish in engaging some of the prominent phenomena of the early twenty-first century. Part of this is due to the conservative (analytical) disposition of realism, with its emphasis on continuity over change. But it is also due to that fact that realism has indeed stumbled on the question of globalization, failing to recognize it as a condition in which states dwell, rather than as a rebranding of interdependence, which applies more narrowly to the relations between specific states. And ironically, while essentially blind to globalization, realists have also been considerably addled by an otherwise myopic attention to aspects of the structure of the system—that is, to the distribution of power—at the expense of other important variables. This has left realism with a diminished voice, and to some extent singing a one-note tune at a time when a much broader range is essential. But this need not be. Realism, still true to its roots, can easily bring globalization on board, and, crucially, inform its analyses—as it has for centuries—with appeals to domestic politics, history, ideology, and perceptions of legitimacy. As such, realism will continue to generate a productive and insightful research agenda regarding questions of contemporary political economy.

Notes

1 An attempt to elaborate and illustrate this mechanism can be found in Abdelal and Kirshner 1999–2000.

2 Late mercantilist James Stewart argued: "foreign trade, well conducted, has the necessary effect of drawing wealth from all other nations" (Stewart 1966 [1767]: 283, 363). On the conception of trade as zero-sum, according to Heckscher: "Scarcely any other element in mercantilist philosophy contributed more to the shaping of economic policy, and even of foreign policy as a whole" (Heckscher 1935: vol. II, 24). The balance of trade was of great concern to many prominent mercantilists, including Thomas Mun (1949 [1664]), indeed, the subtitle of the book is "Or, the Ballance of our Forraign Trade is the Rule of our Treasure" (cf. Mun 1949 [1664]: 83–86). Famed German mercantilist Johann Joachim Becher wrote "it is always better to sell goods to others than to buy goods from others, for the former brings a certain advantage and the latter inevitable damage" (Heckscher 1935: vol. II, 116). Heckscher argues that "this attitude became crystallized in a demand for an export surplus, a demand which was expressed in every possible way."

3 The classic statement of the mercantilist conception of harmony between economic and political goals is Jacob Viner (1948). While compelling, this paper dramatically overstates the extent to which Heckscher argued that mercantilists were willing to sacrifice wealth in their pursuit of power. Heckscher was aware of the underlying harmony, and his discussion of power is a small part of a large book (cf. Heckscher 1935: 25–26, 29).

4 Note that Hamilton's mercantilist themes are nevertheless longstanding (cf. Hamilton 1966 [1775]; List 1885: 133, 308–14, 351; Schmoller 1897).

5 These sentiments are stressed throughout the work. On p. 120, for example, List, in reference to Smith, states: "Although here and there he speaks of wars, this occurs only incidentally. The idea of a perpetual state of peace forms the foundation of all his arguments."

6 The Cold War, it should be noted, also had something of a stifling effect, as most discussions of the economic roots of politics was shouted down in the 1950s and 1960s as Marxist, and even as this became untenable, in the 1970s and 1980s the bipolar nature of the Cold War (and Soviet communism) allowed for the separation of political economy and security studies (Mastanduno 1998: 826; Kirshner 1998).

7 On the prominent role of interdependence for liberal theories of war and peace see Keohane and Nye (1977); Moravcsik (1997: 520–21, 528–30).

8 For an entrée into this enormous literature see Baldwin (1993).

9 The collective bargaining agreement of the National Basketball Association, for example, acknowledges a fight over relative, not absolute gains; it sets player's salaries at 48.04 percent of Basketball Related Income (BRI). On difficulties in distinguishing underlying motives see Mastanduno (1991: 73–113). For an example of how difficult it is to distinguish these behaviors in settings where security concerns should be salient, see Liberman (1996: 147–75).

10 Cf. Gilpin, which anticipates a system of "loose regional blocs" (1987: 395, 397).

11 This passage draws on Kirshner in Kirshner (2006).

12 On the heterogeneous effects of globalization on the prospects for war: cf. Brooks (2005); Kirshner (2007). On new conflicts see Kaldor (2001); Hoffmann (2002); Kurth Cronin (2003).

13 Indeed, realists would note that much of contemporary globalization was encouraged by states that made the calculation that such changes would advance the national interest (cf. Helleiner 1994).

14 For a good discussion some of these issues see Nye (1988: 235, 242, 245).

3

Contested contracts

Rationalist theories of institutions in American IPE

Alexander Cooley

Introduction

Across the US academy rationalist approaches dominate the study of international political economy. Rationalism assumes that economic actors act instrumentally in pursuit of their ranked preferences. US-based rationalists have examined how a variety of international actors such as governments, states, firms, factor endowment interest groups, economic sectors, and political parties, respond to the pressures of the world economy (Gilpin 1975, Krasner 1976, Olson 1982, Milner 1988, Rogowski 1989, Gowa 1994, Frieden 1991, Shafer 1994, Garrett 1998, and Hiscox 2001). These studies theorize the political reactions of these economic agents to the distributional consequences of new international economic pressures such as changing price signals or the internationalization of trade and investment. Economic actors demand new political arrangements to capture these benefits and attempt to insulate themselves from their costs. The rapid rise and legalization of these new international governance arrangements has led US IPE scholars to increasingly turn their attention to the study of the formation, dynamics and consequences of institutions.

Over recent years, the main way in which rationalism has been operationalized for the study of international institutions has been through contractarianism. As with all rationalist approaches, contractualists assume that international actors like states and firms are purposeful and consistent, however, they are often adversely influenced by the uncertainty of their contracting environment. Accordingly, contractualists have focused on the conditions that allow cooperative agreements, as transactions, to be reached, maintained and enforced within the international economy, as well as the evolution of various organizational forms within international relations, more broadly. The literature borrows heavily from economic approaches to the study of institutions, transactions and contracting environments.

This chapter examines the origins and evolution of U.S.-based contractualist approaches to the study of IPE and global governance more broadly. Overall, I argue that contractualist approaches have become more methodologically appropriate as the international economy and its governing institutions have become more integrated and complex. Yet, at the same time, some of the ontological assumptions of the early rationalist literature, especially the focus on states and the notion of international regimes as solutions to market failures, no longer adequately reflect the architecture of many contemporary global economic institutions.

In reviewing these trends this essay proceeds thematically and, for the most part, chronologically. The first section examines the origins and emergence of neoliberal institutionalist approaches to IPE and their exploration of how the international contracting environment could help or hinder cooperation among states. Following the work of Robert Keohane, rationalist institutionalism and its focus on transaction costs rapidly became the dominant theory in American IPE. This work was followed by the rational design of institutions project, which sought to examine the instrumental logic behind why purposive states adopt certain institutional forms over others. Together, these approaches continue to explore how rational contracting states use and design the rules of international institutions in order to further their interests.

The second part of the essay looks at the literature on relational contracting and international organization. Rooted in the work of Oliver Williamson, this work has sought to incorporate the importance of power, hierarchy, and even authority within the contractualist paradigm, focusing on the reasons why contracting parties adopt different organizational forms. Relational contracting has also been employed beyond the realm of IPE to the study of many different areas of international hierarchical relations and systemic change. The third section of this essay examines the now burgeoning literature on the credible commitments problem within IPE. This body of work explains why international actors fail to reach or maintain international agreements and identifies the characteristics that lend states greater credibility in their international transactions.

In the fourth and final part of this essay I explore an emerging paradox about the study of contracting in IPE. Even as contractual approaches have been critiqued as too restrictive and ahistorical, the use of contracting as a governing mechanism has dramatically increased in practice. As a result, contracting theory offers us a set of theoretical tools to gain fresh insights in areas not traditionally studied by IPE scholars. Accordingly, contractualist approaches continue to remain theoretically fruitful, but perhaps in different areas of study than those initially examined by American contractualists.

Contractualism and cooperation: the role of international institutions

The origins and influence of neo-liberal institutionalism

Every intellectual tradition, to some extent, reflects the events of its times. The rise of neo-liberal institutionalism or "regime theory" is no exception. Formulated in the early 1980s at the height of the "new Cold War," the literature in American international relations had taken a hard turn towards realist positions, following the publication in 1979 of Kenneth Waltz's *Theory of International Politics* and in 1981 Robert Gilpin's *War and Change in International Politics*. The international economic disorder of the 1970s had seemingly discredited claims that increasing interdependence in the world economy would have benign effects on world order. Instead, the collapse of the Bretton Woods monetary regime, the twin oil shocks and third world debt crisis seemed to validate the perceptions of Charles Kindleberger (1973) and other "stability" theorists that only a dominant or hegemonic power with an interest in stabilizing the international economy could hold together the international institutions that were necessary for economic cooperation.

Within this theoretical and political context, Robert Keohane (1983 and 1984) developed a theory of the importance of international institutions based on how institutions help to mitigate adverse contracting environments. Differentiating himself from previous liberal or "idealist" analysts who stressed the formally legal importance of international institutions, Keohane accepted the realist assumption that states operate in a condition of international anarchy and seek to maximize their national interests. Unlike realists, however, Keohane argued that cooperation, the mutual coordination or adjustment of state policies, could be facilitated by international regimes, defined as "sets of implicit or explicit principles, norms, rules and decision-making procedures around which actors' expectations converge" (Keohane 1984: 57; Krasner 1983: 2).

In this functionalist logic, international institutions allow states to reach cooperative solutions by improving the contracting environment or reducing the transaction costs of exchange. By providing information, standardizing and routinizing procedures, establishing reputation, increasing interactions, and offering a forum in which to link various issue areas and offer side payments, international institutions help states overcome the uncertainty generated by international anarchy and advance their mutual interests in an orderly fashion. In a widely cited parallel volume edited by Stephen Krasner (1983), Keohane and Krasner argued that international institutions could alleviate the "market failures" caused by international anarchy. Drawing on the work of Robert Axelrod (1984) on reciprocity strategies as a means to overcome the Prisoner's Dilemma, Keohane also reasoned that international regimes could continue to operate even after the initial power (usually, the hegemonic actor) that had established the regime had gone into decline (1984: 100–103). Separating the issue of institutional formation from institutional persistence was a key analytic contribution of the neo-liberal institutionalist literature.

Throughout the 1980s, the rational institutionalist paradigm became dominant within American IPE, not least because as the decade progressed we witnessed significantly more international economic governance and coordination than predicted by pessimistic realist accounts of hegemonic decline. Kenneth Oye's (1986) related volume further explored the functionalist logics of regimes—particularly increasing iteration and decreasing the number of players—and their effects on interstate cooperation. Essays by IPE theorists applied the framework to various instances of economic affairs including Charles Lipson's (1986) influential analysis of the collective action problems faced by the Paris Club in the wake of the international debt crisis. Another offshoot of this work came from Lisa Martin (1993), who further explored how institutions promoted issue linkage, especially in facilitating the imposition of economic sanctions. By improving the contracting environment and facilitating exchange, international institutions allowed states to pursue their interests, even within the strict assumptions of anarchy and rationality proposed by neorealists.

In the American academy, with the important exception of John Ruggie's (1982) work on "embedded liberalism" and Susan Strange's (1983) critique of the "wooliness" of regime theory, the theoretical backlash to regime theory came more from realists than from social constructivists. The functionalist or new institutionalist logic, according to realists, was no better than the optimistic liberalism of old. Some realists accused neoliberals, with their emphasis on the contractual environment, of fundamentally mis-construing the realist project (Grieco 1988 and 1990). The fundamental problem generated by anarchy, they argued, was not the problem of defection, but rather concerns about distributional consequences from cooperation. Thus, even though regimes might facilitate cooperation and generate more absolute gains, states would be more concerned about the relative gains emerging from their cooperative endeavors (Mearsheimer 1994).

These neorealist and neoliberal positions were collected and presented in the landmark volume edited by David Baldwin (1993). In retrospect, many of the contributions now seem to highlight both the intractability of the two sides as well as the narrow range of issues that they actually considered, just as the structure of international politics and the international economy were undergoing dramatic shifts. The post-Cold War expansion of the global economy and its dramatic deepening quickly rendered the neorealist-neoliberal debate, though still important in the study of international security, less compelling for the study of IPE.

The project on rational institutional design

In a 2001 special issue of the journal *International Organization*, Barbara Koremenos, Duncan Snidal, and Charles Lipson (KSL) sought to update and reinvigorate the contractualist approach to international governance and institutions. Having established that institutions facilitated cooperation among states, KSL turned their analytical attention to the design of international institutions and explanations for the diversity of their forms.

Like regime theory, the KSL project was contractualist and presumed that, "states construct and shape institutions to advance their goals. The most direct implication is that design differences are not random. They are the result of rational, purposive interactions among states and other international actors to solve specific problems" (Koremenos, Lipson and Snidal 2001: 762). Specifically, international actors purposefully negotiate and design membership rules, the scope of issues covered, the centralization of tasks, rules for governing the institution and the flexibility of these arrangements. As independent variables, KSL examined the potential impact of distributional concerns, the number of actors, enforcement and various types of uncertainty on these elements of institutional design. Cross-tabulating these relationships produced 16 "conjectures," such as "institutional centralization increases with the severity of the enforcement problem" and "flexibility increases with the severity of the distribution problem" (Koremenos, Lipson and Snidal 2001: 793). Ambitiously, KSL suggested that these relationships should hold, regardless of the exact form of the institution or its policy or issue domain.

Several of the immediate empirical applications of the KSL model were creative and significant contributions in their own right, not least because they examined international institutions that had received relatively scant attention in the US literature. For example, Andrew Kydd (2001) applied the insights about uncertainty and restrictive membership, to explain the dynamics of NATO's expansion and the organization's internal evolution. For Kydd, the uncertainty and mistrust generated by NATO's potential expansion, especially for Russia, could only be overcome by adopting a number of strict and enforced conditions for new applicants. Thus, prospective NATO members would have to fulfill a long list of domestic obligations and democratic institutional reforms before being granted membership. Although a wave of literature on the purpose and effects EU and NATO conditionality would soon follow Kydd's article (Jacoby 2004; Vachudova 2005), the article was an innovative application of the KSL model to a new and contemporary topic.

Similarly, Walter Mattli's (2001) essay on the institutional design of international arbitration arrangements also focused on a relatively new institutional venue within the globalizing economy. The increasing turn to private arbitration and away from national judicial systems by commercial entities to resolve contractual disputes, Mettle argued, pointed to the premium on establishing flexible institutions to cope with and speedily resolve transnational disputes in newly developing and technical issue areas. As a private form of contractual adjudication and enforcement, international private arbitration, from a functionalist perspective, is a superior venue for international businesses than traditional, more cumbersome state alternatives. The use of private arbitration is now the norm for resolving international contractual claims among private commercial actors and, even between states and international corporations if they are parties to an investment treaty or adjudication clause.[1]

Unlike the first wave of rational institutionalist literature, the critique of the rational institutional design project has been more pronounced from social constructivists. Critics challenge the assumption of fixed, ranked preferences and argue that international institutions, in their social relations, can also alter, transfer and construct the preferences of members (Johnston 2001). Institutions may be designed for functional or instrumental purposes, but then again, they may be designed with other goals in mind, such as universality of membership, the pursuit of shared ideals and normative commitments or the actual availability of ideas about institutional design (Wendt 2001). Particular ideas about the appropriateness of an economic grouping may spur regional cooperation and integration (Parsons 2003). International organizations may themselves absorb and then codify prevailing international norms such as the belief in the importance of international capital mobility (Abdelal 2007). Moreover, the state-centric assumptions of the contractualist perspective also discounts the importance of endogenous sources of IO behavior, especially the organizational cultures and resulting pathologies that inform the staffs and governing bureaucracies of international organizations such as the World Bank or IMF (Barnett and Fennimore 2004).

In sum, contractualist approaches, with their emphasis on understanding the environment in which actors cooperate, have pervaded American IPE's study of the role and significance of international economic institutions. From early regime theory and its transaction costs underpinnings, to newer efforts to explain the rational design of institutions, contractualists have sought to explain how purposeful states create institutions to advance their interests.

But in its persistent privileging of states as the principal contracting actors, the rationalist institutionalist approach increasingly risks missing some of the institutional innovations and new mechanisms that now govern the world economy. As we approach the year 2010, the institutional and legal architecture of the global economy is strikingly different from that of 30 years ago. States may face enduring barriers to cooperation, but it is not clear anymore that this is *the* major governance issue confronting the global economy. In fact, the rise of a thick international regulatory network of private and public institutions suggests that the traditional American IR assumption of anarchy may no longer be a helpful characterization of large cross-sections of global economic activity. This is not to say that problems of interstate contracting and coordination don't persist – they do, and they remain acute and challenging. Rather, it is to point out that a central issue facing international economic actors, public and private, is how to best choose and manage among the various overlapping venues designed to guarantee economic transactions and enforce contractual disputes.

Relational contracting: when do economic actors integrate?

Over the last two decades, a related strand of contractualism also has made its way into the American IPE and IR literatures. Like rational institutionalism, relational contracting is grounded in the economic literature that explores the instrumental logic behind international negotiations and institutional outcomes. However, the focus of relational contracting rests on the actual interaction and bargaining power between two contracting actors, rather than their resulting regimes.

The relational contracting approach is rooted in the now classic observations of Oliver Williamson (1975 and 1985) about when firms should contract using the market and when they should produce the input in-house or under hierarchy. The key to the Williamsonian perspective lies in the type of exchange conducted among firms and, more specifically, the types of assets that are transacted. In most asset classes, standard market contracting will suffice. However, in situations where transactions are frequent over specific assets—assets that are idiosyncratic and not readily substitutable—the possibility that one side will behave opportunistically or hold-up the transaction is ever-present. Without market alternatives, a contracting firm will be vulnerable to the relational power of a supplier of specific assets. As a result, Williamson recommends that firms requiring specific assets adopted unified governance or hierarchy in such situations to avoid potential hold-ups.

Over the last 20 years, the relational contracting approach has been used to explain variations in international organizational forms and modes of international economic integration. By analogy, the key challenge to states in designing international institutions is to constrain opportunistic behavior. Thus, hierarchical forms of international organization, as opposed to bilateral agreements, are most likely to emerge when states can realize substantial cooperative gains, but the assets that they transact in are relationally specific. For example, Beth and Robert Yarbrough have employed this reasoning to explain variations in the design of enforcement mechanisms and the dispute settlement bodies within trade regimes across different regional agreements (Yarbrough and Yarbrough 1992). Interestingly, the now formalized dispute settlement body of the WTO not only contrasts with the consensual norms of dispute resolution of the earlier GATT, but also provides an example of an international governance form that regularly rules against the interests and preferences of powerful state actors (Drezner 2007).

Relational contacting has also been employed to explain the dynamics of other forms of broader hierarchical order and semi-sovereign international relations. The study of imperialism is one example. In a now widely cited article, Jeffry Frieden (1994) reasoned that Williamsonian logic could potentially recast how we understand the historical relationship between international investment and colonialism. Frieden argued that formal colonial governance was more necessary to secure metropolitan investments in peripheries with site-specific assets, such as oil wells, mines, and plantations. Conversely, formal colonialism was less helpful to guarantee the metropole's investments in more mobile production plants or portfolio investment. Hendrik Spruyt (2005) used the same logic to argue that heavy investments by a metropole in peripheral specific assets delayed the process of decolonization. Similarly, David Lake's (1997) analytical focus on the prospects of renewed Eurasian integration focused on the importance of relationally specific assets in Russia's relationship with its former republican satellites, including pipelines, large-scale military-industrial complexes and defense installations.

Lake's work especially expanded the relational contracting approach to more broadly recast the issues of authority, governance and order in international relations (1996 and 1999). Emphasizing the anarchy/hierarchy continuum as contrasting governing logics of international relations, Lake's *Entangling Relations* examines why the United States established varying institutional arrangements in its foreign policy history, including informal empire in Europe and formal empire in the Pacific islands, and how these changes in institutional forms were determined by changes in US governance costs and fears of peripheral defection and opportunism. Lake's most recent work (2007) finds much more hierarchy than anarchy in international relations, and continues to explore the relational logics between core and weaker states in the international system. Under relations of hierarchy, powerful states provide public goods such as security guarantees to weaker states in exchange for deference to their authority.

At the same time, scholars have realized that the mere adoption of hierarchical arrangements may not necessarily guarantee authority or control over a contracting partner. Cooley's (2005) examination of varying forms of international hierarchy showed how both functional (unitary forms) and territorial forms (multidivisional forms) of hierarchical organization suffer from different types of opportunism: departmentalism in the U-form and principal-agent problems in the M-form. Indeed, by applying principal-agent models across a broad range of governance issues, including international organizations and private actors responsible for international standard settings, IPE scholars are now explicitly examining the different types of control problems that arise in delegated relationships within different international orders (Buthe and Mattli 2005; Hawkins, Lake, Nielson and Tierney 2006).

Incomplete contracting: jurisdictional expansion and renegotiation

Another variant of relational contracting focuses more explicitly on the political consequences of the incompleteness of contracts and the dynamics of their renegotiations. This strand is rooted in the modifications to the Williamsonian framework brought by economist Oliver Hart (1995) in his work on the determinants of the organizational boundaries of the firm. Like Williamson, Hart accepts the logic of the hold-up problem that is faced by contracting parties over relationally specific assets. However, Hart is also concerned with the downstream distributional consequences of contracts beyond their original specification and duration. Because contracting parties cannot possibly anticipate the full array of contingencies that might arise during the contract, they must necessarily leave aspects of the agreement incomplete, subject to later renegotiation. The key finding is that at a contractual renegotiation, the party with residual rights of control—ie. the rights to use an asset outside of what was specified in the original contract—will hold the bargaining power in the negotiation and dictate the revised contract's new terms (Hart 1995: 30–31).

The incomplete contracting framework is now being employed to explain the institutional evolution of a number of sovereign transfers among states, both bilaterally and to third parties such as supranational institutions. The dynamics of EU expansion, especially how EU supranational institutions have come to define the jurisdictional spaces created by broad framing agreements post hoc, has been a particularly fruitful area of study (Hix 2002; Farrell and Heritiér 2006). Cooley and Spruyt (2009) have examined how originally imbalanced agreements signed between colonial powers and peripheries over site specific economic assets and military bases, many of which helped to facilitate decolonization, were subsequently renegotiated by newly independent states on more favorable terms as they gained in their relational power. And Barbara Koremenos (2005) has argued that, contrary to standard IR assumptions, states strategically limit the duration of international agreements in issue areas characterized by high uncertainty about future distributional consequences. Strikingly, Koremonos finds that economic issue agreements (including exchange-rate, finance, investment, and trade agreements) exhibit a much higher rate of contracts of finite duration that are subject to renegotiation, than other issue areas such as the environment, security and human rights. In sum, relational contracting adopts many of the assumptions regarding rationality and instrumentality as rational institutionalism, but focuses squarely on the relative power, bargaining dynamic and resulting organizational forms among contracting actors. The approach has been employed across a number of issue areas in international relations, including the study of both international political economy and international security.

As with rational institutionalism, the relational contracting approach has been criticized on both ontological and methodological grounds. Ontologically, some have claimed that international hierarchical relations such as imperialism can hardly be analyzed in the voluntary language of contractarianism. Of course, in the more extreme cases of complete military occupation and coercion this would be true. But, even imperial relations were founded upon certain bargains between core powers and ruling intermediaries within colonial peripheries (Nexon and Wright 2007). Moreover, such criticisms miss the more fundamental point that asymmetric power relations also characterize most contractual relations in both the international and domestic spheres, including, for example, labor contracts.

Methodologically, some social constructivists may also object to the attempt to explain semi-sovereign forms without reference to the particular identities and social orders that are invoked to justify and legitimize authority in such a relationship (Hall 1999; Reus-Smit 1999). On this point we have more of a methodological stalemate or circle: for while constructivists can distinguish the unique identities and social orders underpinning individual hierarchies, they have much greater difficulty accounting for the many similarities in institutional design of hierarchies across different regions, eras and cultures (Cooley 2005: 34–36).

Contracting and the importance of credibility

Both the contractual institutionalist and relational contracting literatures underscore the problem of securing "credible commitments" within international transactions, a final area of contractualist theory that, as of late, has spawned a virtual cottage industry. For US-based rationalist scholars of international political economy, international security and international law alike, the question of how states maintain their credibility has become central. The origins of credibility problems differ somewhat across these theoretical approaches. For rational institutionalists and game theorists the commitment problem tends to arise from the environment of anarchy and the lack of central enforcement. Without a central governing authority, states cannot guarantee that their contracting partners will adhere to their commitments and signed agreements. In relational contracting the credibility problem lies within the vulnerability of one party making investments within a relationally specific asset or transaction with another. Still others argue that certain types of domestic institutions tend to affect a state's credibility (Lipson 2003; Martin 2000).

The credibility of commitment argument has been deployed to explain the interaction dynamics between international organizations and states, especially the capacity of organizations to enforce compliance. International organizations may be influential, but they are also, ultimately, subject to the preferences and international concerns of powerful states, especially the United States (Wade 2002). Accordingly, for scholars like Randall Stone (2002 and 2004), the failure of the IMF to enact basic institutional reform lies not in the content of its conditions, but rather its inability to actually enforce them in a consistent and universal fashion. In areas of prominent IMF activity such as Africa and the post-Communist states, geopolitical priorities have led major donors to pressure the IMF to relax standards in certain special cases, such as dealing with Russia in the 1990s. Donor interference also has undermined the organization's credibility and subsequent authority in its other lending interactions. On a broader level, a special issue of *International Organization* in 2000 explains the growing formal legalization of world politics, in part, as an attempt by states to lend greater credibility to their economic reform efforts (Goldstein et al. 2000). For example, Frederick Abbott (2000) observes that Mexico's willingness to formally codify regional trade via NAFTA, with its binding arbitration clauses, was intended to reassure foreign investors about its commitment to liberalizing reforms.

Another group of scholars has examined the internal features of states that make them more credible contracting partners. Some have sought to explain superior economic outcomes in democratic states from those in non-democratic ones by arguing that democratic institutions lend more credibility (Cowey 1993). The process of ratification by a legislature sends a strong signal that a particular international agreement or treaty has been democratically sanctioned and will endure beyond the regime that signed it (Martin 2000). Another strand of theorizing focuses on the "audience costs" or the electoral price a democratic leader pays from backing down from an international dispute or bargaining position (Fearon 1994). Still others point to the need for sufficient institutional autonomy from capricious political interference as a determinant of credibility, an argument that is frequently made by advocates of central bank independence (Maxfield 1997).[2] As such, democracies should be viewed as particularly "reliable partners," which can credibly maintain their promises and obligations to other international actors (Lipson 2003). Consequently, according to Nathan Jensen (2006), democracies (particularly democratic federations) attract significantly more FDI than authoritarian counterparts because they are more likely to guarantee the property rights of foreign investors and multinational companies.

Credibility issues

As with the bulk of the contracting literature, arguments about the precise role of credibility are often difficult to evaluate, especially after the fact. The potentially circular nature of this logic places high demands on empirical explication, which often is not adequately demonstrated or tested with basic counterfactuals. All too often, contracting actors maintain their credibility of commitment until they actually fail to do so. Moreover, social factors such as reputation and ideas about appropriate institutional design also inform perceptions about credibility. For example, is the credibility of independent central banks enhanced by their actual autonomy, or by the widespread belief by monetary economists and that such institutional arrangements are superior (Berman and McNamara 1998)? Moreover, from an organizational perspective the rapid diffusion and widespread adoption of certain institutional forms such as Central Banks may be less a function of their superior credibility, and more the result of institutional isomorphism and emulation in a high-information, globalized world where perceived successes easily spreads across competitive states. Explaining the actual adoption of institutional forms retrospectively as a result of their superior credibility may be possible, but it is methodologically perilous.

The domestic democratic credibility arguments also suffer from some empirical issues. Although both the democratic institutions and the elite "audience costs" arguments make a good deal of sense, the overall democratic experience of a country, and its potential impact on the status of international contracts, varies a good deal more than is captured within the standard democracy/autocracy distinction. In fact, there are compelling reasons to believe that actual periods of democratic transitions or democratizing environments may actually undermine a country's commitment to a pre-existing agreement (Cooley 2008). The key here is not so much credibility, but broader issues of regime change and contractual legitimacy. International contracts signed with non-democratic regimes, especially over fixed assets such as oil concessions, mines, and power plants, are especially prone to demands for renegotiation by democratizing states on the grounds that they were signed by an authoritarian regime and their terms have not been sanctioned by a nationally accountable body. For example, Louis Wells and Fariq Ahmed (2006) have shown how even international property rights protections, such as arbitration clauses, were insufficient to guarantee the sanctity of power plant deals in Indonesia during the post-Suharto era of democratic transition. The entry into the Indonesian political scene of new political actors such as NGOs, competitive political parties, an independent media, and local authorities with new decentralized powers all delegitimized contracts that had been signed by the previous ruling regime. So while new democratic governments that sign deals are likely to be credible from that point forward, they may not be as committed to adhering to previous deals.

New contractual settings: outsourcing international governance

Finally, it is important to note that although contractualist approaches are robustly represented within American IPE and IR scholarship, they are curiously absent from the emerging study of global governance, even though transnational actors are increasingly being linked by actual formal project contracts. Social constructivist and legal scholars traditionally have dominated the study of global governance, yet its current evolution would seem to make it an ideal area to apply many of the insights of contracting theories.

The rise of contracting within global governance

The rise of the use of contracting in the international arena has mirrored its widespread growth domestically. Over the last 20 years, governing priorities have shifted away from promoting state planning towards empowering markets and networks of individuals and non-state organizations as centers of economic and political activity. At the same time, pressures for increased accountability, transparency and efficiency has also pushed international actors to outsource services to supposedly more competitive providers.

This new contracting or outsourcing of state functions has opened a vast new range of issue areas for specialization for NGOs and for-profit corporations (Verkuil 2007; Feigenbaum et al. 1998). Internationally, the number of private actors involved in domestic and global affairs has risen almost exponentially as both states and international organizations have turned to these new actors to implement projects, thereby disaggregating traditional hierarchical structures of governance (Slaughter 2004). International domains such as the humanitarian aid regime, post-conflict reconstruction, development, the provision of healthcare and basic social services, and international educational programs are all increasingly governed by project contracts, granted by states and international organizations to international NGOs and private actors (Mills 1998; Berrios 2000; Cooley and Ron 2002). Even traditional areas of state monopoly such as the provision of security have been affected by the outsourcing trend, as the international market for private security has exploded since the end of the Cold War (Singer 2001; Avant 2005).

Potential consequences: organizational priorities, accountability, and trust

The political consequences of this contractualization of governance are potentially profound, yet rationalists and global governance scholars alike have been slow to fully grasp them. Rationalists have examined some of these governance issues through the lens of delegation dynamics and principal-agent problems more broadly, where global governance theorists have been reluctant to abandon their assumptions regarding the normative sources of the behavior of NGOs and other non-state actors.[3] The resulting omission is unfortunate, as the spread of actual contracting practices throughout global governance potentially has profound transformative effects on global actors, including on their organizational priorities, their accountability and their inter-organizational trust.

Over time, contracting is likely to change the behaviors and priorities of both a donor and a contracting agent. Organizations that depend on transnational contracts, such as certain humanitarian organizations or technical assistance consultants, are more likely to aggressively compete with each other for what is a finite number of global projects. Elsewhere, James Ron and I have suggested that the marketization of NGO activities promotes cutthroat competition and organizational insecurity among NGOs dependent on external contracts for their fiscal survival (Cooley and Ron 2002). Competition is most intense in the wake of disasters or complex emergencies, when scores of humanitarian NGOs descend and "scramble" in search of relief work. This tends to cluster NGOs and donors into just a few global humanitarian hotspots. For example, in 2004 six countries – Iraq, Sudan, Palestine, Ethiopia, Afghanistan and the DRC – received about half of all humanitarian contracts from Development Assistance Committee (DAC) countries (Walker and Pepper 2007: 3). Moreover, the increased bilateralization of aid since the late 1990s has seen many states directly contract NGOs and corporations for international services and bypass the UN system and multilateral providers altogether (Barnett 2005). Of course, this has raised concerns about political interference in NGO work as well as the supposed autonomy of contracted agents, regardless of their pre-existing social commitments.

The broader turn to contracting has also redefined the internal missions and structure of certain international organizations. These shifts have been especially dramatic in the humanitarian sphere. IOs such as the European Union's ECHO and UNHCR traditionally retained broad discretion over how best to allocate funds and respond to humanitarian crises, including housing a staff of policy experts and practitioners. However, changes in funding practices have transformed these IOs now into overseers of multiple outsourced projects. For example in 2000, ECHO spent 67% of its funds on NGO contracts, more than double the figure of 27% in 1990. Similarly, by 1999, only 20% of contributions to UNHCR were not earmarked (Macrae 2002: 16). Overall, then, the proliferation of contracting and aid bilateralization is transforming the internal organizational structures and priorities of NGOs and their multilateral donors.

The rise of contracting also raises issues of accountability and contractual governance. Unlike the domestic sphere where a breach of contract can be resolved in a routine fashion, or private arbitration clauses for international commercial disputes, many international contracting domains simply lack any mechanisms of direct sanctioning. In extreme cases, such as post-conflict environments, the relationship between states and contractors has been an uneasy one, as contractors have seemingly not delivered on their promises or have done so at exorbitant cost. For example, the scandals involving US contractors in Iraq highlight how the use of cost-plus contracts—a contract by which profits are a function of outlaid expenses—prompted contractors to waste money with relative impunity (Miller 2006).

Moreover, the split between project design and implementation potentially allows for the dispersal of accountability across donor and contractor. Contracting allows for a "plausible deniability," as donors can take credit for relatively successful projects, but can blame less successful outcomes on the contractor's poor execution or local circumstances. *Ex post* investigations into accusations of wrongdoing or misappropriation once funds have been dispersed are burdensome for all parties and rarely, if ever, undertaken. On the other hand, in some settings collusion among donors, contractors, and project targets seems to be systematically tolerated (Cooley and Ron 2002: 25–31; Lischer 2005).

Finally, the extensive use of contracting may actually redefine social ties among previously networked transnational actors. Specifically, in addition to encouraging competition among potential contractors, formal contracting may erode trust among donors and contractors. Introducing formal contracts into situations where actors have been previously networked exclusively through their common values or informal ties may change the way governors perceive each other's motives. In a fascinating and theoretically instructive experimental study, management scholars Deepak Malhotra and J. Keith Murningham (2002) compare and contrast the effects of formal (or binding) contracts with those of non-binding (or informal) contracts on the development of trust among players in an iterated game. The authors find a trade-off between the mitigation of risk and the development of trust. In post-game surveys and interviews, participants in the game with binding contracts attributed the plays of others to their contractual terms and constraints, rather than to their disposition, even if they had been previously deemed trustworthy.

As a result, the introduction of binding contracts into existing networks of global governance may have profound implications for governance relations. Even if we accept the constructivist assumption that transnational networks bound together by actors that share common values about certain global issues, introducing formal contractual relations into these networks may actually erode these ties by changing the dispositional relationship to a contractually situational one. And there is a good deal of literature across varied international issue areas including the humanitarian sector, public health, and post-conflict reconstruction to suggest that contracting may be fundamentally contributing to a growing mistrust among these international actors.

Although global governance theorists like to regard NGOs and IOs as more normatively driven actors than commercial entities or states, the widespread use of contracting may actually be rationalizing their organizational behavior in relatively predictable and similar ways. Certainly, the widespread use of the project contract across many issue areas suggests that contractualist approaches may be particularly fruitful for studying these emerging relationships.

Conclusions: theorizing our contractual world?

Ultimately the persuasiveness of the American contractualist approach to IPE will depend upon a scholar's pre-existing epistemological predilections. Those of the rationalist orientation are more likely to view the contractualist research agenda as important and fruitful, whereas those critical of rationalist IPE will be skeptical of both the analytical insights and appropriateness of such instrumentalist theories. But such disagreements should be separated from debates about whether we are studying the appropriate types of economic actors in the international system. Certainly, the state-centered focus of rationalist institutionalism, whatever its initial contributions, seems to be less relevant today as an over-arching theory of international cooperation. Other strands of contracting theory, however, retain considerable promise.

In fact, the rapid globalization and diffusion of various contractual practices and related institutions would seemingly blunt some of the ontological criticisms made by skeptical scholars of the appropriateness of contractual approaches to IPE. For example, contractualism has been criticized for assuming a sense of community and legal order that may not be characteristic of the international sphere. As a leading critic of rationalist approaches to international institutions wrote in 1994, "contractual solutions to the problem of authority have either to assume the existence of a well-established community, or they have to rely on a *deus ex machina*, i.e. 'territoriality', in order to delineate the 'members'" (Kratochwil 1994: 466).

Yet, fifteen years later, the world economy is composed of a much more dense set of relationships and integrated practices by various economic actors. The international contracting community, while still imperfect and uneven in certain regions, has in fact developed on a global scale. Global trade has been legally codified by an international organization with considerable enforcement powers. Outsourcing and intrafirm trade create dense webs of subcontracts and hybrid organizational forms that cross international boundaries (Friedman 2005).[4] International marketization continues to expand the boundaries of what goods and services are permissible for international exchange (Barber 2001; Bhagwati 2004). Private entities such as credit rating agencies or international arbitrators regulate an increasing portion of international debt issues and contracts (Sinclair 2005; Van Harten 2007). In the meantime, states continue to pursue deeper integration in the areas of trade, finance, and investment. Contracts abound within the actual practice of international political economy. Their impact upon the relational ties of the global economic community may well be more important, and even transformative, than we might care to admit.

This does not mean that contractualism as established in the American academy, or rationalist approaches more broadly, should be the only or even the most appropriate way to study the politics of international economic relations. But it does suggest that some of the long-standing methodological objections harbored against American contractual approaches may require fundamental rethinking or, at least, a renegotiated calibration.

Notes

1 Unfortunately, despite Mattli's important essay, little follow-up work has been conducted within American IPE on the importance of private international commercial arbitration. On the growth of investment treaties among states, see Elkins, Guzman, and Simmons (2006); and Van Harten (2007).
2 For a critique of the Central Bank independence approach, see Johnson (2000).
3 Although, see Hawkins, Lake, Nielson, and Tierney (2006).
4 But also see Ghemawat (2007).

4

Constructivism as an approach to international political economy

Rawi Abdelal

Introduction

Politics decisively influences the fate of the world economy. Government choices lead to cooperation and discord among countries; economic integration and disintegration; and openness and closure to cross-border flows of persons, goods and services, and capital. International markets have, therefore, political foundations. Since the emergence of the modern world economy during the mid-nineteenth century, politics made one era of globalization, circa 1870–1914, and then unmade it with two world wars, beggar-thy-neighbor economic policies, and failed efforts at international cooperation. The early post-war years witnessed the renaissance of cooperation, which in turn allowed trade in goods and services to expand. During the 1980s, governments laid the institutional foundations for truly international financial markets. Soon thereafter, policy makers acknowledged that we lived in a new era of globalization, an era made possible by profound political transformations and which resulted in far-reaching economic and social changes.

Although many scholars had crossed the disciplinary boundaries of economics, history, sociology, and politics in narrating stability and change in the world economy, international political economy (IPE), recognized as part of the field of international relations (IR) within departments of political science, is new. Among many others, scholars such as Charles Kindleberger, Karl Polanyi, and Susan Strange laid intellectual foundations on which we are still building (Polanyi 1944; Strange 1971, 1988; Kindleberger 1989a, 1989b; Cohen 2008b).

IPE, the study of political economy—that is, the interactions among governments and markets across countries—is composed of theoretical traditions that are parallel to those of IR more generally. The traditions of realism, liberalism, and Marxism have informed several generations' worth of analysis of the politics of the world economy. Because much of the best scholarship in IPE is puzzle-driven, focused on explaining patterns of politics and economics that are empirically surprising or theoretically curious, it is possible to judge the progress of the field by the number of questions that have been effectively and convincingly answered. By that standard, IPE made great progress with theoretical tools that have been essentially rationalist insofar as the agents—governments, market participants, and classes—make decisions primarily by trading off the costs and benefits of their actions. Those tools have also been materialist—in the sense that the incentive structures faced by agents are composed primarily of the material facts of the world, those facts that exist irrespective of our interpretation of them.

Yet there is so much more to the politics of the world economy than this. Material incentives, the struggle for more power and wealth, and distributional conflict among groups, including classes, within societies obviously influence the world economy. Applying the same standard of progress—the resolving of puzzles, the answering of questions—IPE was, however, for many years without some essential theoretical tools; namely constructivist tools. However, during the past decade, constructivist theorizing about the influence of social identities, norms, and other collectively shared ideas and beliefs has become a central part of the IPE canon. Constructivism is analytical language composed primarily of the social facts of the world, those facts that exist only because they are collectively shared ideas (cf. Searle 1995). Such social facts influence patterns of political economy directly as socially constructed coordination devices; they also influence how agents interpret the material reality around them.

In this essay, I highlight the substantive, empirical contributions of IPE scholarship that, over the past decade or so, has been informed by constructivist theory. At the risk of doing some violence to the epistemological stance of some constructivist scholars, I emphasize both the causal arguments that have been made and those that can, in my view, be discerned in this scholarly literature. In other words, I narrate the rise of constructivist IPE as the accumulation of explanations for how the world economy works. Those explanations are, in some cases, necessary complements to rationalist and materialist scholarship; in other cases, constructivist explanations are simply more convincing, fitting the empirical record better. It is equally common for surveys of constructivism to categorize the agenda according to epistemology, and for overviews of IPE to dismiss the constructivist research agenda as not positivist enough to warrant consideration among mainstream, "consensus" views (Frieden and Martin 2003). My approach is different: I aim to characterize constructivist-informed IPE as essential to the explanatory mainstream. In doing so, I also offer a categorization of constructivist IPE according to the logics of argumentation that scholars have adopted. That categorization is based on joint work with Mark Blyth and Craig Parsons (Abdelal et al. forthcoming).

I begin, however, with the rise of constructivism in the other sub-field of IR: security studies, which is where, at least within political science, the research agenda first made its mark, and indeed was soon recognized as essential to the mainstream scholarly endeavor. As IPE scholars engaged increasingly with constructivist theory, they also, as their colleagues in security studies had done, took aim at the central, seemingly immutable and *meaning-free* nature of the world they studied. Whereas the constructivist agenda in security studies undermined the standard realist argument that many meaningful hypotheses about state behavior could be deduced from the fact of anarchy, in IPE it was the global market that was found to be theoretically problematic. Although internationalization—the collection of liberal practices and rules that underpin the freedom of trade and financial flows—had by the 1990s seemed both inevitable and inexorable to many observers, a new generation of constructivist scholarship demonstrated that very little about the world economy could really be deduced from the putatively material facts of cross-border economic activity.

As Max Weber had tasked the social sciences, the basic constructivist stance is that with so much possibility, we must explain why things are "historically *so* and not *otherwise*" (Weber 1979). Both the practices and the rules of international markets, constructivists have shown, were social constructs that could have been otherwise, and which have indeterminate effects on politics until mediated by domestic organizations and institutions (see, for example, Hay and Marsh 1999). As Karl Polanyi (1944) wrote of an earlier era "There was nothing natural about laissez-faire." Instead, "free markets could never have come into being merely by allowing things to take their course." Sixty-odd years after Polanyi wrote those words, the disembedded, internationalized markets of the contemporary world have become so because of politics with profound constitutive consequences—and not because they are the natural, asocial context for choice.

Why a constructivist approach to IPE?

The construction of security and insecurity

The questions of war and peace have long tended to push scholars and policymakers toward acceptance of the seemingly inexorable, often materially based, ways of the world. The putative naivety of idealism was, tough-minded critics argued, laid bare by the destruction of the two world wars of the early twentieth century. The realist reaction, as articulated by scholars such as E. H. Carr (1951) and Hans Morgenthau (1960) emphasized the Hobbesian characteristics of international political life. As the realist canon evolved toward greater scientism, Kenneth Waltz (1979) proposed to derive a "neo-realism" from first principles—particularly the absence of a single world government—an entire theoretical apparatus to explain patterns of world politics. Realism became both the dominant theoretical tradition and the source of baseline explanations for international relations, explanations against which others would be judged.

Although many scholars had criticized realist and neo-realist approaches to analyzing politics for their problematic assumptions and sometimes sloppy history (Keohane 1986), the work of Alexander Wendt sought to undermine the entire theoretical apparatus by making problematic the first principle—anarchy—itself (1987, 1992, 1994, 1999). Arguing that anarchy could not by itself lead to self-help and unmanageable enmity, Wendt demonstrated that the identities and preferences of the agents involved, states, would lead to different patterns of international politics if they varied. By making endogenous that which realists tended to assume as exogenous and given, constructivist-informed scholarship showed how variation in identities, social norms, and state preferences could answer questions that would otherwise present intractable puzzles for realist theory.

Indeed, as a result of this constructivist turn, during the 1990s the field of security studies was well nigh revolutionized by an outpouring of scholarship that explained a diverse and impressive range of empirical puzzles. Martha Finnemore showed how international norms shaped state identities across a variety of policy domains, including how beliefs about the legitimate purposes of force and violence changed dramatically over several hundred years of world politics (1996a, 2003). A number of other scholars demonstrated how systemic norms of appropriate behavior had transformed, and often shrunk, the range of legitimate state practices, including: the decline of racist apartheid (Klotz 1995); the unacceptability of using chemical (Price 1995) and nuclear (Tannenwald 1999) weapons; and the responsible treatment of immigrants (Gurowitz 1999).

In addition to the transformation of systemic norms, constructivist scholars also showed how the policy practices of specific states—states whose importance in international politics ensured that their policies would be constitutive of systemic outcomes—were derived from domestic cultural norms and national identities. In addition to American grand strategy itself (Ruggie 1996), scholars showed that explanations informed by constructivism were necessary to make sense of the policies of the Soviet Union (Herman 1996), post-Soviet Russia (Hopf 2002), China (Johnston 1995, 1996, 2008), Germany (Katzenstein 1997), Japan (Katzenstein 1996a), interwar France (Kier 1996, 1997), and the countries that compose the Middle East (Barnett 1998).

Evidence accumulated. By the end of the 1990s, constructivist approaches to security studies had become part of the mainstream. Realist accounts of international politics would be convincing only to the extent that scholars could demonstrate that the empirical record was more consistent with their rationalist and materialist reconstruction of policy makers' choices. It was time, it seemed, to take stock of the constructivist turn in American IR (Adler 1997; Checkel 1998; Price and Reus-Smit 1998). More than a decade hence, the mainstream of American IPE has, however, remained surprisingly resistant to the accumulation of insights and evidence that social facts are as important to production and exchange as they are to guns and wars. The market, scholars have shown, is, like anarchy, an inadequate description of the context of policy choice. How constructivist scholars have opened up the study of the IPE by problematizing the market shows this trend clearly.

Undermining the market as materially given: a prehistory of constructivism

From embedded liberalism to globalization

With war still raging and the economic chaos of the interwar years fresh in mind, an extraordinary consensus emerged among policy makers in the early 1940s with regard to the post-war international economic system. The new order would be founded on fixed exchange rates, capital regulation, and government involvement in the economy—not to undermine capitalism but, rather, to rescue it. Policy makers shared a common vision and a common goal: the creation of a new order that could avoid the financial crises, disrupted commerce, wild exchange-rate movements, and political instability of the previous quarter century. The system, they hoped, would avoid the political consequences of the unsustainable "disembedding" of markets from social life (Polanyi 1944).

Compromises among the competing logics of economics and politics cohered into a world view about the prospects for growth, stability, and international cooperation. John Maynard Keynes called it "the middle way" (Kirshner 1999, 2003). Avoiding the narrow autarky of the interwar years, the "embedded liberal compromise," John Gerard Ruggie observed, "would be multilateral in character; unlike the liberalism of the gold standard and free trade, its multilateralism would be predicated on domestic interventionism" (Ruggie 1982). Polanyi, Keynes, and Ruggie all offered quintessentially constructivist interpretations of the social meanings, coordination devices, and cognitive world views of the historical processes through which markets were extracted from and then reintroduced to national societies.

The policy practices of the new, embedded liberalism privileged governmental autonomy from market forces: fixed exchange rates (Nurkse 1944); regulated capital flows (Helleiner 1994); monetary policy focused as much on maintaining full employment as on an inflation target (Kirshner 1999); trade policy oriented toward the promotion of growth and employment; and domestic welfare states to spread the risks and costs of adjustment to international market forces (Katzenstein 1985). Domestic stability was seen to be a necessary precondition for a flourishing international economy.

In the early 1980s, as Ruggie narrated the evolution the post-war order, the system itself was seen to be on the verge of a profound dislocation. At the time, observers worried that many countries in the world were about to turn inward and undermine the progress toward openness that had been achieved since 1945. Then, the new protectionism seemed to be tearing apart the world economy. Yet, as Ruggie noted, in many ways this "new" protectionism was simply a manifestation of the priorities societies and their governments accorded domestic stability, at the expense, when necessary, of international harmony and coordination. A real discontinuity within the post-war order was emerging, however. Protectionism was not it. Rather, Ruggie, writing as the agendas of Ronald Reagan and Margaret Thatcher were unfolding, recognized the "resurgent ethos of liberal capitalism" (1982: 413).

The new, *neo-* it would later be called, liberalism represented the ideological embrace of markets in a way that departed from the compromise of embedded liberalism. Markets, in this way of thinking, derived their legitimacy not from their enactment of social purposes. Instead, this new liberalism imparted even to markets, disembedded and otherwise, a standard of immutable rightness and inexorability of their own (cf. Fourcade-Gourinchas and Babb 2002; Denzau et al. 2007). Ruggie was right: in 1982 the world was not on the verge of protectionism, regulation, and autarky. Instead, encouraged in part by this ideological turn, the world economy was on the verge of a second great era of globalization. The decline and fall of embedded liberalism as a meaningful political compromise was the inevitable result (Blyth 2002).

It is this transformation that, in my view, has animated a new generation of constructivist scholarship. Just as the realist, and later neo-realist, tradition in security studies gave pride of place to anarchy, by the late 1980s and early 1990s, the liberal, and then neo-liberal, tradition in IPE tended to treat as the market as the central, enduring fact of the world economy. The market, however, is one of the world's most compelling social, not natural, facts. The markets for capital, goods, services, and people constitute the relevant reality in which governments and policymakers found themselves. One of the most powerful conclusions of fifteen years' worth of scholarship informed by constructivist theorizing is that this globalized world of empowered markets, retreating governments, and embattled, skeptical societies could have been, sociologically, otherwise. The ideas could have been different; so, too, could the practices. We know because they were before. As this era of globalization was made by a revolution in doctrines and practices, however, the compromise of embedded liberalism was unraveled. One set of social constructions replaced another.

Deconstructing the welfare state and the developmental state

During the 1940s and 1950s, advanced industrial states managed to produce an extraordinary, historically unique social compact. A concordance of world views made it possible. The Keynesian revolution in macroeconomics legitimated the systematic intervention of policymakers in interest rates, tax rates, social insurance, and government spending to maintain domestic stability amidst flourishing international markets. Many policy makers, those influenced by Keynes and others, recognized that societies' commitments to free, internationalized markets were tenuous and impermanent. The classic, developed-country welfare state was, in part, a result of various bargaining arrangements that underpinned the post-war order.

Decades later, the economic rise of a handful—and a small one at that—of Asian countries, which made the transition from poor and middle-income to rich, gave hope that some political arrangements could produce rapid economic growth and development. Through a combination of governmental activism, generally high levels of sovereign and corporate debt, and extremely low interest rates, the "developmental state" helped, many political scientists have suggested, transform emerging markets in Asia (Woo-Cumings 1999; Wade 2003).

Those institutional arrangements did not last, however, in part because they were unmade by politics and rendered illegitimate by a transformation in policy discourse. Essentially, the domestic foundations of embedded liberalism were purposefully destroyed (Blyth 1997, 2001, 2002). Perhaps the first piece to fall was "Keynesianism"—understood as activist macroeconomic management—itself, giving way as it did to a kind of "monetarism" (Hall 1989; Widmaier 2003, 2004). In Europe, the social democratic policies that had underpinned the welfare state changed dramatically (Berman 1998, 2006). Indeed, the European discourse on the crisis of the welfare state transformed what were seen as the boundaries of possible policy choice (Cox 2001; Schmidt 2003).

In the developing world, though the developmental state hardly represented "embedded liberalism" in the Polanyian sense, the departures from what were understood to be development orthodoxy—departures such as industrial policy, financial repression, capital regulations, selective protectionism—were also called into question by the narration of the financial crises that began in Asia in 1997. The Asian development model was, as Rodney Bruce Hall (2003) notes, discursively demolished. The Asian model was partly replaced with a renewed emphasis on "policy credibility," which, as Ilene Grabel (2000) and Jonathan Kirshner (2000) have argued, is endogenous to the beliefs of market participants. In this way of seeing the relationship between markets and governments, the content of the prevailing orthodoxy is much more powerful than the size of the financial markets themselves. And this new, resurgent liberal content certainly became so, but it could have been otherwise, were it not for the decisions and practices of firms, governments, and international organizations (Clift and Tomlinson 2004; Sinclair 2005; Fourcade 2006; Woods 2006).

Depoliticizing money and inflation

Whereas the welfare state implied by the compromise of embedded liberalism rested upon a combination of social insurance and active fiscal management, monetary policy making was generally understood as a critical, but supporting collection of practices. The basic logic of the post-war order was to fix exchange rates and limit capital mobility in order to reserve for domestic central bankers the opportunity to prioritize the domestic economy when setting interest rates. Those central bankers, it was generally understood, would work in coordination with—though often legally independent of—finance ministers and policy planners. As with the other policy practices supportive of embedded liberalism, domestic stability, understood as high employment with a modest, but politically acceptable inflation rate, was the goal. Whereas rampant inflation—say, above 20 percent—might undermine the economy and reduce the real obligations of debtors, deflation or even overly restrictive monetary policy would also imply distributional trade-offs (Kirshner 2000, 2003). The balance was to be struck by central bankers who played important roles in the overall system.

By the middle of the 1980s, however, following the disappointments of the stagflation of the 1970s and persistent inflationary expectations, central bankers began to take aim at different targets. In part this was because of institutional challenges, particularly the rise of central bank independence as the dominant mode of organization (McNamara 2002; Widmaier 2003; Epstein 2005, 2006; Polillo and Guillén 2005; Hall forthcoming). The purpose of this change, after all, was to liberate central bankers from political obligations that might undermine their vigilance in combating inflation. The international system evolved to continue to empower central bankers (Pauly 1997; Blyth 2007a). Within Europe, newly independent central bankers began to aim primarily at inflation reduction, rather than balancing employment and inflation; their efforts, based on concordant, liberal world views, helped to maintain domestic price and exchange-rate stability as European countries integrated their financial systems and, ultimately, their national monies (McNamara 1998; Parsons 2003; Jabko 1999, 2006, 2007).

More recently, the rise of inflation-targeting as the dominant practice of central bankers around the world has reproduced the very fetters that were supposed to have been thrown off when the gold standard collapsed for good during the early 1930s. It is clear, therefore, that these monetary practices are inescapably contingent (Kirshner 2003; cf. Maxfield 1997; Watson 2002). Regardless of the historical narration that undermined early policy norms, by the late 1990s the international monetary system was dominated by a handful of independent central banks, including the US Federal Reserve and the European Central Bank, committed primarily to targeting, and generally minimizing, inflation. Central banks could set alternate targets. They used to do, after all.

Internationalizing (disembedding) markets for capital

The regulation of cross-border capital movements was another critical part of the institutional architecture of embedded liberalism (Goodman and Pauly 1993; Helleiner 1994; Kirshner 1999). Although *productive*, long-term capital movements were to be encouraged, *speculative* short-term financial flows that undermined governmental autonomy were to be both regulated and explicitly discouraged. Capital controls were thus essential to the original vision of embedded liberalism. Unrestricted capital mobility, it was assumed, would introduce a deflationary bias in the international monetary system, and the 1920s represented the touchstone experience. Particularly amidst fixed exchange rates, without capital controls governments would be obliged to raise and lower interest rates in response to financial outflows and inflows.

As governments liberalized cross-border capital movements, they thereby created the possibility that ever-larger international financial markets would restrict their room to move. Whether the markets actually would restrict the options of policy makers depended in part on the preferences and beliefs of the market participants themselves (Mosley 2003; Watson 2002; Bell 2005). Capital regulations and liberalizations are signals interpreted by financial markets. Market participants, in this way of thinking, infer meanings from policies. Capital liberalizations are interpreted as positive signals, while capital controls are negative signals (Bertolini and Drazen 1997; Garrett 2000; Eichengreen 2002; Simmons and Elkins 2004). If these market expectations and inferences could be treated exclusively as fixed parameters, we might not need to delve further into the social environment of the financial markets.

These expectations and inferences are not parametric, however. In, say, 1958 capital controls signaled neither heresy nor even unfriendliness to financial markets. By 1998, however, capital controls apparently signaled poor international financial citizenship. The capital account regulations themselves were objectively identical during the 1950s and 1990s, and yet international organizations, ministries of finance, credit rating agencies, financial journalists, bankers, and managers drew different inferences from their implementation (Grabel 1997, 2000; Cohen 2002, 2003; Abdelal 2007).

International organizations affect the international financial system through mechanisms that are at once regulative (rationalist) and constitutive (constructivist or sociological). Once the norm of capital mobility was codified in Europe and the OECD, those organizations monitored the compliance of members, thereby helping to regulate and constrain their behavior (see Keohane 1984; Martin and Simmons 1998). International organizations also influenced the social context of the international financial system by fixing the meanings of capital controls as policy tools, defining for their members the range of legitimate policies, and disseminating the new orthodoxy of freedom of movement for capital (cf. Ruggie 1998; Johnston 2001; Barnett and Finnemore 2004; Abdelal 2007; Chwieroth 2007). The liberal rules of the EU and OECD define the economic policy "scripts" members were supposed to follow (cf. Dobbin 2004b).

Thus, changes in financial orthodoxy—a phenomenon that surely is generally recognized as a social construct—have powerfully influenced both policy practices and the institutional foundations of embedded liberalism. The newly liberal orthodoxy of the 1990s represented a sharp break with the recent post-war past, and many governments around the world adjusted accordingly. But if the orthodoxy had not changed, governments would have faced a very different set of putative obligations and market-created constraints. Again the social facts of the current era of globalization seemed to be as important as any abstract notion of "the market" or its dicta. All three aspects of the phenomena—capital liberalization, the codification of the norm of capital mobility, and the resultant delegitmation of capital controls—were contingent on politics, expectations, and beliefs. None of this was inevitable or inexorable.

Internationalizing (disembedding) markets for goods and services

The internationalization of markets for goods and services has been, from the perspective of the compromise of embedded liberalism, comparatively prosaic. That is, those markets have not produced constitutive consequences for states and policies in the same ways that the other transformations in welfare state management, monetary policy making, and capital deregulation have. Still, trade policy making, when understood as part of the collection of practices that defined embedded liberalism, implied a standard of legitimacy for deviating from linear progress toward market integration. That is, the expansion of markets for goods and services was premised upon, and in a deeply political sense was made possible by, domestic stability. And parts of the welfare state were supposed to balance the risks and costs of trade-induced dislocation with the benefits that, most observers recognized, were on net positive.

The international institutional architecture for trade has changed both quantitatively and qualitatively. Trade itself has increased, and impressively so. More meaningfully, however, that very internationalization has transformed employment relationships and created greater pressures for governments' management of the trade-off between increases in output and its distributional costs (Rodrik 2000). Systemically, WTO rules and the collection of regional trade agreements that, as Francesco Duina observes, codify "cognitive guidebooks" for policy makers have undermined deviations from free trade as legitimate (2004, 2006; cf. Skonieczny 2001; Golob 2003). Thus, the expansion of international trade might have been accompanied by a greater recognition that progress toward integration relied on the social legitimacy of the endeavor. Governments that are unwilling or normatively unable to justify the need to balance stability and international market integration may make for great liberalizers, but they risk the very sustainability of the system. As with these other changes, such a policy stance is hardly implied or required by internationalized markets. A collection of choices and practices helped to shape the norms, which became extraordinarily liberal, but could have remained more fundamentally embedded in national societies without undermining the project of expanding trade in goods and services.

Internationalization and globalization

As a result of these changes, internationalization became globalization, to use Peter Katzenstein's convincing and useful distinction. Internationalization, he writes, is "a process that refers to territorially based exchanges across borders." Internationalization refers to continuity in the system, changes in size of the flows of goods, services, and capital, for example—the intensity of economic interdependence. Globalization, in contrast, "is a process that transcends space and compresses time. It has novel transformative effects on world politics." In this way of thinking, globalization is transformative in a sociological sense, pushing toward the convergence of institutions and practices (Katzenstein 2005: 13).

During the late 1980s and early 1990s, mere internationalization, an increase in the degree of cross-border market integration, became the much more profound globalization, a collection of social constructions that delegitimated many of the policy practices that had constituted the compromise of embedded liberalism. And this process, the making of globalization, was neither the inevitable result of rapidly increasing economic flows, nor can it be separated from the formal and informal institutional foundations that continue to support it. Sociological accounts of globalization thus help us to characterize what is new about this era (Guillén 2001; Campbell 2004, this volume: Chapter 16).

Finally, international economic orders evolve in part because of underlying material changes; the United States overtakes the United Kingdom as the most powerful economy, for example. Those orders also change because the practices that constitute them become more or less socially legitimate and politically sustainable. As the delegitimation of embedded liberalism helped to turn internationalization into globalization, a variety of societal reactions to the instabilities of the current era have helped to cultivate a new crisis of legitimacy. This time it is not the legitimacy of interventionism of various sorts—monetary, fiscal, regulatory—that is at stake. Rather, the legitimacy of indifference, of the new laissez-faire, is being questioned both within countries and amidst the bureaucracies of international organizations (Abdelal and Segal 2007). Remarkably, these societal reactions are not for tearing down internationalization; few argue for autarky. Some hope, instead, to retreat from the pressures toward the convergence of practices and institutions, to find a way to have flourishing international markets without undermining domestic stability. We have seen such calls before, and the ability of policy makers to manage them will determine whether the current crisis of legitimacy leads toward the failure of a system primed for a major financial crisis, or whether, instead, national and international policy mechanisms can be put in place to save markets from their own excesses.

Logics of constructivist political economy

Given such a sweeping drama one might be tempted to think of constructivism as the *new and improved* theory of everything. Yet this would be a mistake, for the one thing constructivists have learned from the weaknesses of other approaches is that a single theory of political economy, constructivist or otherwise, is neither possible nor desirable. Such a theory is impossible, in the first instance, because constructivism is neither a theoretical apparatus nor a research program. As an analytical language, constructivism emphasizes "identities, norms, knowledge, and interests," whereas rationalist language employs "preferences, information, strategies, and common knowledge" (Katzenstein et al. 1998: 38). By drawing attention to the powerful constitutive effects of collectively held ideas, particularly how such ideas connect to self-understandings, the bounds of legitimate practice, the accumulation and interpretation of experience, and the material trade-offs of choices, constructivism offers a way to describe patterns of political economy that are simply not amenable to rationalism. Building on a language that has long been used by economic sociologists to describe and explain empirical puzzles that are often quite different from those of IPE, constructivist theories of IPE clearly owe a large debt to the groundwork laid by those scholars (Granovetter 1985; DiMaggio and Powell 1991; Granovetter and Swedberg 1992; Beckert 1996; Fligstein 1990, 2001; Dobbin 1993, 1994, 2004a, 2004b; Smelser and Swedberg 1994, 2005).

Employing constructivist insights to the study of the IPE thus leads to a series of distinctions with rationalist approaches—both liberalism and realism—that are, arguably at least, common to the variety of constructivisms (Abdelal 2001). First, a conception of the state is generally considered essential to any theory of international relations. For liberal theory, the state is generally considered regulatory and pluralist. Realists tend to assume a self-interested, rational state. In constructivist theories of IPE, by contrast, the state is understood as purposive, in the sense that political authority is derived not from power itself, but from the ends to which power is legitimately used.

Second, theories of IPE must also connect the state, as a collection of institutions and relationships, to the government, as an agent. In liberal theories of IPE government preferences are determined by domestic political struggles. Realist theories assume government preferences (or, since they often fail to distinguish between states and governments, state preferences), deducing from the fact of anarchy and the implication of self-help. Constructivism as an approach to IPE begins necessarily with the recognition that government preferences vary and may be endogenous to interaction with domestic societies, other governments, and international norms of appropriate practice. Perhaps the hallmark of all constructivist approaches to politics is that rather than deducing or assuming preferences, scholars problematize them and recognize the effects of their variation over time and across societies.

Third, rationalist and constructivist theories tend to differ in their locating the sources of behaviors and practices. Liberal theories generally emphasize material incentives, while realist theories are based on differences in relative power and the search for security, both unmediated by interpretation. In contrast to both, constructivism as an approach to IPE emphasizes that policy practices may result from international institutions, international norms (which specify the practices associated with a particular state identity), domestic cultural norms, and national identities. Beyond these basic similarities among constructivist theories of IPE—and attendant differences with both materialist versions of liberalism and realism—the range of such sociologically influenced approaches has been both broad and rich. Mark Blyth, Craig Parsons, and I (forthcoming) discerned four distinct logics that have formed the basis for constructivist explanations of empirical puzzles: meaning; cognition; uncertainty; and subjectivity. The following subsections reprise our joint approach to understanding how constructivism works.

Meaning as the basis for construction

The most common, and indeed most intuitive, logic by which social constructions influence political economy is through the meanings with which the material facts of the world are endowed (Ruggie 1992: 1998). In contrast to rationalist approaches to political econ-omy, which tend to assume that market participants, policymakers, and even whole societies unproblematically recognize the material incentives around them and act accordingly, one constructivist insight into patterns of IPE is that such agents endow the economies in which they are embedded with social purposes. Those social purposes may be domestic in origin, arising from cultural norms and national identities, or they may derive from the relationship between state identities and international norms.

The shared ideas of national societies, for example, endow production and exchange with purposes. What societies want, in this way of thinking, depends on who they think they are (Abdelal 2001; Helleiner and Pickel 2005; Abdelal et al. 2006). Societies' col-lective identities and cultural norms lead them to their own interpretations of the pur-poses of economic activity, the legitimacy of certain economic institutions, and the meaning of their economic interdependence with others. Collective identities thus influence how societies and governments interpret their place in the world economy. These sui generis social facts define the reasons for engaging in some types of economic activity, and not others. Collectively shared national purposes also can engender generational sacrifices, in terms of effort, material hardship, and foregone consumption. In that sense, these iden-tities may lengthen the time horizons of policy makers, much as contested, or unclear national purposes could promote decadence, not unlike the contemporary United States and its low rate of national savings, enormous current account deficit, and collapsing work ethic. The inherent directionality of these identities and norms implies as well that societies and governments tend to narrate their dependence on other countries' produc-tion and resources in specific, rather than general, terms. Much as post-Soviet Lithuania interpreted economic dependence on Russia as a security threat, while dependence on the European Union was an opportunity; today, the United States views foreign capital inflows from Europe as welcome financing of the current account deficit, while inflows from China and the Arab world are treated with much greater skepticism.

National identities differ from state identities. States are political institutions. Putative nations refer to societies. State identities are informed by international norms, which specify how certain categories of states (for example, civilized states, European states, welfare states) are both regulated and constituted by the practical content of international society. National identities are informed by domestic societies, whose identities refer to the population of a state rather than to the state itself.

With regard to these norms, then, an alternate, more international and institutional constructivist approach finds that meanings, as well as the boundaries of legitimate policy-making, vary for states of different types. In this sense, international norms define the boundaries of choice. International organizations play an important role in fixing the meanings, thereby constituting the legitimate boundaries of policymaking (Keck and Sikkink 1998; Bukovansky 2002; Finnemore 2003; Hall 2003; Barnett and Finnemore 2004; Jabko 2006; Abdelal 2007; Chwieroth 2007).

Thus, this constructivist departure from the rationalist mainstream of IPE does not mean that power and economic incentives are unimportant; the material facts of the world economy are still powerful elements in constructivist approaches. What is different is that these facts by themselves are indeterminate: norms, cultures, and identities give meaning to material facts so that governments and other actors in the IPE can interpret and react to them. In addition, constructivist approaches assume that the world economy consists of both material facts and social facts.

Cognition as the basis for construction

Collectively shared ideas, in addition to providing meanings so that material facts may be interpreted, may consist of explanations of how the world works and descriptions of the social reality of the group (Brubaker et al. 2004; Abdelal et al. 2006). Whereas meaning is about how agents interpret the world, cognition describes how they understand and narrate material changes (Denzau and North 1994).Yoshiko Herrera (2005), in a masterly book on the political economy of Russia, offers one of the most compelling accounts of how cognitive schema led different communities to understand a range of material changes, such as price increases, through frames that imply a shared causal model. The inter-subjective models of the economy in the communities of Sverdlovsk and Samara implied stances about the desirability of regional autonomy independent of the putatively objective material conditions of those local economies.

Such cognitive constructions are most powerful when they are taken for granted. As Wesley Widmaier (2007) has argued, the historical moment during the 1970s when the standard schema for explaining persistent inflation was the wage-pushing of unions led many Americans to conclude that the power of the United Auto Workers had increased. Some years later, inflation is more often narrated as the result of central bankers who have been insufficiently vigilant in their inflation-targeting (Denzau and Roy 2007). Thus, these days, when such cognitive schema are shared among financial market participants, Ilene Grabel has argued, the effects on policy options of governments can be profound. The inter-subjective construction of *unsustainable* and *credible* policies is self-fulfilling. Orthodoxy, almost regardless of its intellectual rightness, affects what governments can and cannot do (Kirshner 2000; Grabel 2000, 2003).

Other patterns in the world economy have been explained this way. Francesco Duina's account of the constitutive consequences of codifying the role of, for example, women in the work place, the dairy industry, and labor rights, demonstrates that cognitive schema can be disseminated through the legal architectures of free trade agreements. Keith Darden's work on the international trajectories of post-Soviet states emphasizes the influence of three alternate cognitive models of the economy on their governments' decisions to embrace either the World Trade Organization (WTO) or the regional Eurasian customs union, or instead to turn the economy inward and pursue autarky (2008).

Uncertainty as the basis of construction

Another compelling argument about the influence of social constructs on political and market outcomes finds that the pervasive uncertainty facing agents and groups leads them to adopt heuristics, rules of thumb, and other devices to guide their decisions. Here scholars emphasize what is sometimes referred to as "Knightian uncertainty," building on the classic work of economist Frank Knight: *Risk, Uncertainty, and Profit* (1921). Whereas rationalist models tend to simplify uncertainty as a collection of probabilities, or perhaps risk combined with incomplete information, Knightian uncertainty holds when agents cannot even estimate the probabilities of various outcomes. In such situations, social construction is at a premium since the ideas deployed by agents to diagnose the uncertainty they face, and the institutions they build to instantiate those ideas, produce the stability that makes political and economic transactions possible. This kind of theorizing in economic sociology has enjoyed a renaissance, following the work of Jens Beckert (1996, 2007).

IPE scholars have argued that inter-subjective ideas are essential to an account of both policy making and market outcomes because agents and communities use them to deal with their uncertainty (Schmidt 2002; Blyth 2002; Hay 2004a; Widmaier 2004; Best 2005; Seabrooke 2006, 2007a, 2007b). An important insight of this strand of constructivist theorizing is that the world economy, and most importantly, its underlying causes, change over time. Such a stance is intuitively attractive because knowledge accumulates, fashions change, expectations shift, and individuals holding policy and managerial roles turn over. Indeed, it would be a profound surprise to find that despite our progress, linear and otherwise, our economic history is a reliable guide to our economic future. The causes of market booms and busts, of successful and failed trade negotiations, of inflation, of many outcomes, are inconstant and, evidently, unpredictable. Thus, agents and communities construct their own senses of stability by adopting institutions, norms, and conventions (March and Olsen 1984; Biernacki 1995; Blyth 2006).

Subjectivity as the basis of construction

I have deliberately avoided a detailed discussion of the problem of epistemology in constructivist IPE. In part this is because philosophy of science is, apparently, something of a hobby for many scholars enamored with constructivism. Paradoxically, perhaps, constructivist scholars' sophisticated views on social science and the nature of explanation have made them less appealing to mainstream IPE scholars, whose generally unexplored positivism frames most of the debates in leading journals. By engaging difficult questions of how we know and explain the world, constructivist scholarship can problematize what most political scientists prefer to take for granted.

In part because my own work has sometimes been described as, alternatively, too constructivist or not constructivist enough, my general feeling is that both communities are making different errors. When constructivists casually dismiss the naive positivism of mainstream IPE, they erroneously imply that they are engaged in an altogether different social scientific enterprise—that is, that they do not intend to illuminate why the world is so and not otherwise in quite the same way as those who write in Greek symbols or run regressions. For their part, mainstream rationalist scholars who believe that they can continue to ignore the findings of constructivist IPE simply because of its over-use of words like *ontology* and *constitute*, as well as its under-use of words like *variable* and *cause*, they are depriving themselves of the insights of a now rich literature. For IPE to make progress, by whatever metric, both the social and the material facts of the world will have to play a part.

This need for engagement is even more important regarding the work of critical, or post-modern constructivists, whose scholarship has come to be seen by much of the mainstream of IPE as being much too far removed to be taken seriously; especially from scholars who have sought to combine constructivist theory with essentially positivist epistemologies. Yet, I would argue, this is a mistake since this post-modern IPE scholarship has also produced some important and useful insights into how the world economy works.

While the other three constructivist logics—meaning, cognition, and uncertainty—emphasize the social constructs that inform agents and the communities of which they are a part, post-modern IPE scholarship is primarily concerned with *subjects*, rather than *agents*; thereby stressing the constraining and structural role of discourses as opposed to the agential quality of constructivist scholarship that stresses ideas. This style of analysis makes discourse central to its narration of political economy, and the position a subject takes within that discourse then defines the subject's identity. Consider norms. For rationalists, norms are regulative; for many constructivists, norms are constitutive; but for post-modern constructivists, norms are objects of power that determine the boundaries of possible speech and action and operate by exclusion of alternatives as much as by constitution of identities. In this way of approaching scholarship, the context—the structure, or the discourse within which agents are situated—is decisively influential for the very "thinkability" of options (de Goede 2005; Epstein 2008b).

This kind of explanation recognizes the influence of ideas on practices in a deep sense. The mandate of many American schools of business and management is, for example, to influence what practitioners do through the dissemination of new scholarly ideas. But if the process is successful, then market participants will change what they do in part in response to theories originally designed to explain how markets work. Such agents (holders of MBAs) are *subjects* positioned with a discourse (of, for example, efficient markets) that they reproduce by acting within the terms of that discourse. But in doing so, they reproduce that discursive structure. The work of Donald MacKenzie is especially interesting in this regard. MacKenzie finds that the very financial models that were constructed to present a stylized view of financial markets were, once internalized by the market participants themselves, self-fulfilling. In MacKenzie's analysis, the theory was "an engine" for change, not a "camera" for recording market practices (2003a, 2003b, 2005, 2006; also MacKenzie et al. 2007). Similarly, if the regular reading of Samuel Huntington's *Clash of Civilizations* (1996) at American military educational institutions, as it is, makes it more likely that American policy will treat Muslim-majority countries differently, then the theory has not been proven right; the theory has been self-actualized. And then the data we derive from the world are evidence not of the logic Huntington has proposed, but rather evidence of the discursive structure his work helped to construct.

Conclusions: constructivism and the IPE

The last thing the field of IPE needs is yet another grand debate, wherein proponents of discrete theoretical traditions vie for analytical superiority and empirical primacy. The last such struggle, between liberalism and neo-liberalism, led to claims of incommensurability of arguments, vacuous and abstract analyses of opposing traditions' assumptions, and, amidst a convergence of analytical tools, claims by both perspectives to subsume the other (Baldwin 1993). Meanwhile, very little progress was made, particularly regarding the basic task of all of us: explaining how the politics and economics of the world economy inter-relate. I do not argue, therefore, that constructivism is the newer, better answer, or that the effort to identify the winner of the rationalist–constructivist debate should guide IPE scholarship. To the contrary, the field requires engagement most of all, across these two analytical languages. Rationalist and constructivist arguments should be taken seriously. They should be combined when useful in an analytically eclectic way (Katzenstein and Sil 2008; cf. Spiro 1999; Kirshner 2000 and 2003; Jabko 2006; and Culpepper 2008).

What is clear, however, is that the status quo of American IPE during the late 1990s, a situation in which the world economy was understood to be both straightforward and knowable with exclusively rationalist and materialist theoretical tools, has changed. The world economy is full of all manner of fascinating, important social constructs, identities, norms, and collectively held beliefs, and they should be incorporated into our explanations along with the obviously important material facts of the world. As Peter Katzenstein, Robert Keohane, and Stephen Krasner have written,

> The core of the constructivist project is to explicate variations in preferences, available strategies, and the nature of the players, across space and time. The core of the rationalist project is to explain strategies, given preferences, information, and common knowledge. Neither project can be complete without the other.
>
> (1998: 42)

Constructivism is not *the* answer. But as an analytical language and general theoretical orientation, it has led scholars to many essential answers, which should be understood just as much a baseline explanation as any other standard narrative in IPE scholarship.

5

Of margins, traditions, and engagements

A brief disciplinary history of IPE in Canada

Randall Germain

Introduction[1]

Canada is a giant country on the periphery of the world. It is famous for frozen winters, vast stretches of uninhabited land, and rugged terrain. It is also a magnet for immigration, and was built largely on the backs of northern European and Chinese laborers. It sits alongside the twentieth century's pre-eminent military and economic superpower, but has itself only a miniscule military capability honed through participation in both world wars and a mostly honorable record of involvement in UN peacekeeping operations. Its economy is powered by commodities and driven almost entirely by developments in its wealthy southern neighbor, yet it has been able to develop leading-edge technologies with global aspirations, such as the ubiquitous Blackberry. Is international political economy (IPE) even possible in such a place?

The answer must be a resounding yes. By virtue of its position next to the United States (US), its rich heritage of diverse intellectual traditions, and a strategic interest in the issues and themes that resonate at the heart of IPE, Canada has been a fertile place out of which a robust engagement with the discipline has developed. IPE in Canada engages with a large array of concerns that animate its study around the world, including issue-based subjects such as globalization, development, inequality, inter-governmental coop-eration and multilateralism, as well as thematic subjects such as great power rivalry, class formation, governance and inter-paradigmatic debates. Yet, what perhaps sets IPE in Canada apart from elsewhere is the way in which its close proximity to the US and its deep engagement with theoretical approaches that are critical of dominant American paradigms works out in practice. Proximity to the US presents to Canadian IPE scholars the sharp edge of how to deal with power in all its manifestations, while theoretical diversity ensures that IPE in Canada is not monolithic in its intellectual composition. The result is a vibrant disciplinary formation that engages with IPE on a global scale.

This chapter explores IPE in Canada in terms of its context, its diverse intellectual traditions, and its subject matter. A short chapter cannot do justice to the entirety of a discipline as it is practiced across the country's forty or so major universities.[2] Instead, it will use the career and work of one scholar—Robert W. Cox—to highlight how IPE has evolved in Canada and engaged with the world. Cox, a Canadian by birth and academic training, returned to Canada in 1977 after spending nearly a quarter of a century as an international civil servant in Geneva with the International Labor Organization, and several years as Professor of International Organization at Columbia University in New York. The impact of his work within the disciplines of IPE and international relations (IR) is ongoing and powerful, thereby providing a useful lens through which to read the development of IPE in Canada (Smith 1996). We can use his work to trace both how strongly influenced IPE in Canada has been by developments in the US, and yet how it has been able to escape the singular reading of the global political economy so prevalent within American academe. Canadian IPE is not synonymous with the work of Robert Cox, of course, but he has been the anchor around which much of the research done within Canadian universities is organized, and in part through which it has engaged with the world.

Margins: the context and organization of IPE in Canada

The modern day resurgence of IPE across the industrialized world can be traced to the period leading up to and following the end of the Bretton Woods era. During this time, both political scientists and economists began to question the technocratic ethos behind the organization of the world's political economy, raising questions about power and the changing distribution of wealth within and between nations. While there may have been no consensus on what power meant or how it could be measured, there was broad agreement that the constitution of power and its balance or arrangement was undergoing fundamental change as the turbulent 1970s gave way to the ideologically charged 1980s (Strange 1970b; Murphy and Tooze 1991b; Katzenstein et al. 1998; Murphy and Nelson 2001).

Up until the 1970s Canada profited nicely from its easy insertion into the post-war US-dominated global economy. Against the prescriptions of the Bretton Woods system Canada ran a floating exchange rate regime, and it also exercised moderate control over foreign (mostly American) investment into its manufacturing and resource extraction industries. As well, Canada departed significantly from American patterns of political economy, especially during the high-growth 1960s when it began to nurture socialized medicine and a relatively generous welfare system. In short, despite "sleeping beside an elephant," as a former prime minister once described it, Canada fit quite nicely into the international political economy as it was organized during the Bretton Woods era.

The breakdown of the Bretton Woods order, however, brought into sharp relief the vulnerability of Canada's position. It had of course no empire to fall back on, and no huge internal market or population to develop and/or exploit. Instead, Canada's economy in the 1970s suddenly found itself an open target of the turn towards a new form of mercantilism, with its welfare system, currency, investment controls, and budget all coming under pressure. Against this backdrop, IPE scholarship in Canada grew rapidly during this period. It built upon a tradition of classical political economy that was influenced by its long association with English intellectual currents, by the persistent dilemmas thrown up by developing within the orbit of a larger American economy, and by a sharp awareness of the impacts of global capital, labor and commodity markets on a relatively young but resource-rich country.

Historically, political economy in Canada had been organized around a peculiar accommodation between British and American disciplinary trajectories. During the late nineteenth and early twentieth centuries, it was subjected to the traditions of classical political economy and the tensions arising from the marginalist revolution and the neo-classical reformulation at work in English and American universities. Canadian political economy did not, however, succumb completely to the neo-classical synthesis; rather, a continued interest in classical political economy—and especially economic history—remained an important avenue through which Canada's economic development and its place in the world political order was understood.

This accommodation can be seen in the histories of political economy at work in some of the major Canadian universities of the time. At McGill, Toronto, and Queen's universities, small departments of political economy formed from the mid-decades of the nineteenth century, and all three universities witnessed persistent struggles to expand these departments and develop their curricula in this area. Moreover, they adhered to the classical conception of political economy well into the middle years of the twentieth century, and only abandoned this view once political science and economics irrevocably settled into separate disciplinary trajectories.[3] During this time, however, faculty were drawn from Canada and Britain, and most received their graduate training either at the great bastions of political economy in the US (especially Chicago and Harvard) or Britain (especially Edinburgh, Glasgow, Oxford, and Cambridge). Led by the contributions of such faculty as Harold Innis at Toronto, O. D. Skelton at Queen's, and Stephen Leacock at McGill, political economy in Canada developed through the early and middle decades of the twentieth century by deepening scholarly knowledge of fundamental structural aspects of Canada's economic development, and contributing practically to its growing role in the world by participating in public and governmental deliberation (Creighton 1957; Ferguson 1993).[4]

This accommodation can also be seen in the early development and career of Robert Cox, who received his master's degree in history from McGill University in 1946. Cox studied history from an interpretive disposition, which led him to engage with a number of what might be called *organic* conservative historians and intellectuals such as Arnold Toynbee, Oswald Spencer, Edmund Burke, and especially the Oxford philosopher R. G. Collingwood (Cox 1996, 2002). These engagements prompted Cox to inculcate an appreciation of the role of social context in apprehending political trajectories, and above all an awareness of how mind and consciousness in their collective manifestation form the necessary precursor to understanding the embeddedness of individual agency and popular social articulation. From these studies Cox moved into the world of international organization, where over the subsequent twenty-five years he rose to occupy senior positions in the bureaucracy of the International Labor Organization (ILO), including *chef de cabinet* to Director-General David Morse, chief of the ILO's Program and Planning Division, and ultimately becoming the first director of the Institute of Labor Studies. It is out of this experience that Cox came to his critical studies of international organization and political economy.

In this sense Cox's position at the confluence of critical historical reflection and world historical developments casts him as a kind of cipher for IPE in Canada. For almost uniquely among senior level international bureaucrats during this period, he also moved in the world of academia, and his position and interests allowed him to play a significant role in the early study of international organization (Kratochwil and Ruggie 1986). He became involved in particular with a large international research team composed of American and British scholars—including Susan Strange and Cox's long-time collaborator, Harold K. Jacobson—who authored one of the most widely cited early volumes on international organization (Cox and Jacobson 1973). He was for many years on the editorial board of the influential journal *International Organization*, and contributed several leading articles to it, including a pathbreaking article on the ILO and American power (Cox 1977). During this time (roughly from the early 1960s until the mid-1970s), Cox first incorporated behavioral social science methods into his research, and then progressively abandoned them in favor of a return to the more critical historical forms of reasoning that he inculcated at McGill. This increasingly placed him outside of mainstream American thinking about IPE, but at the same time opened up for him a critical space to reflect on the changes in production, class relations and institutional configurations that transformed the world over the 1970s and 1980s.

It was most importantly the series of publications from 1981 to 1987 that cemented Cox's place within IPE both internationally and in Canada. These publications—two articles and a monograph (Cox 1981, 1983, 1987)—enabled one institution to claim for itself the mantle of Canada's *national* school of IPE. This was York University, where Cox taught from 1977 until his retirement in 1992. From the early 1980s onwards all other universities in Canada positioned themselves with or against York. Interestingly, it was the recruitment of Stephen R. Gill from the UK which cemented York as the home of radical or critical international and comparative political economy in Canada, as his move to York University in 1991 built on the recent arrival of Leo Panitch and Reg Whittaker from Carleton University. The regular hiring of faculty from Britain, Canada and the US among most (but not all) Canadian universities contrasts starkly with the hiring hierarchy of top American universities, where it is rare for faculty trained outside of the upper tranche of that hierarchy to gain access to posts in the best departments.

Like elsewhere, IPE in Canada grew rapidly in stature and importance from the early 1980s, and York University and Cox in particular articulated the broad themes that were to dominate much of this resurgent discipline. These themes were catholic in their scope and animated by a search for theoretical templates which ranged much wider than the set of conceptual assumptions guiding most American scholarship. Whereas this period in the US was marked by a sharp concern for the decline of American power and the resulting question of how to facilitate international cooperation "after hegemony" (Keohane 1984), Canadian or Canadian-based scholars tackled themes associated not with American decline per se, but rather with social transformation and the tug of war underway between public and private authority within and across state/society complexes. Inter-state issues and themes were not completely ignored, but they were placed into a wider context that, like Cox's work itself, approached questions of state power and national economic issues through the lens of internationalization and class relations. IPE in Canada thus offered an engagement with theoretical traditions that paid less attention to the neo-classical synthesis, behavioralism and rational choice, in favor of a continued reading of Marx, Karl Polanyi, and other more historically informed theorists who were rapidly becoming marginalized in US academia.

Traditions: disciplinary trajectories and engagements

While Canadian scholars have made significant contributions to our understanding of particular issues and subjects across the social sciences, there has yet to emerge a theoretical tradition of inquiry that is distinctly Canadian. In terms of traditions of scholarship, the social sciences in Canada are importers of intellectual traditions, and IPE is no exception to this trend. Scholars across the country have traditionally tended to fall into one of three paradigmatic categories: variants of liberalism and neo-liberal institutionalism; variants of realism and neo-realism; and variants of historical materialism. Recently more up-to-date articulations of these categories have been offered, depending on the preferences of the assigning scholars, including rationalism, constructivism, postmodernism, post-structuralism and of course feminism. This penchant for reclassifying basic theoretical orientations reflects many factors, including new forays into methodology, epistemology, and ontology by IPE (and IR) scholars, along with the usual refinements to existing traditions which seem to occur more or less cyclically. Nevertheless, the basic point remains, namely that theoretical debates in Canada for the most part reflect rather than lead debates elsewhere in the academic world, and especially in America.[5]

The usual suspects: liberals and realists

During the period during and immediately following the breakdown of the Bretton Woods system, IPE in the US paid close attention to two principal intellectual traditions: the classical liberal tradition of political economy—including its Keynesian offshoot—and the state-centric or nationalist tradition of political economy that came within political science to be closely identified with neo-realism. Both traditions have deep roots in American scholarly history. Classical liberalism-cum-Keynesianism dominated departments of economics and produced political economists who used these analytical tools to understand the development of the US economy and its position in the world. Richard N. Cooper (1968) and Raymond Vernon (1971), for example, used traditional liberal assumptions and presuppositions concerning the relationship between the state and the market to explore the parallel developments of the internationalization of the American economy and its biggest corporations (now cleverly renamed *multinational* corporations) and the increasing interdependence between national economies that was the obvious empirical result. These themes were then picked up and extended by political scientists looking at the shift from international to transnational relations, which eventually produced a program of research oriented around the theoretical frameworks of "complex interdependence" and "international regimes" (Keohane and Nye 1972, 1977; Krasner 1983; Keohane 1984; Rosecrance 1986).

Within Canada this broadly liberal tradition received much attention. Important here were attempts to understand Canada's place in the new world of transnational relations, and to consider the affects of a decline in American power for international regimes and ultimately international institutions. David Leyton-Brown, who trained at Harvard under Joseph S. Nye, Jr. and Stanley Hoffman, considered Canadian–American relations within this liberal context, emphasizing the powerful pressure of continental market integration on Canadian foreign policy (Brown 1985). Mark W. Zacher published widely on international regimes, using liberal themes to examine ongoing institutional developments in transportation and communications (Zacher and Sutton 1996). As well, there have been scholars who have used the methodological tools of liberalism and its associated version of institutionalism to analyze free trade in North America (Winham 1986; Cameron 1993; Cameron and Tomlin 2000). Even Cox (1972), just beginning to emerge from his behaviorally oriented phase, has engaged with this tradition, through a chapter written for the volume on transnational relations edited by Robert O. Keohane and Joseph S. Nye, Jr.

Of course, in the US a powerful response to the liberal tradition took shape during the 1970s, led in the first instance by a group of scholars who were unconvinced by the claims of their more liberal brethren (they were almost all men) both in terms of the triumph-alism of markets and their associated integrationist pressures, and especially by the implied corollary of the decline of the state (if not the American state). Led by Robert Gilpin (1975a) and Stephen D. Krasner (1976), and memorably extended and buttressed from Britain by Susan Strange (1988, 1996),[6] these scholars developed what came to be identified as a neo-realist theoretical stance in IPE, arguing that states were central to the construction of markets and that political power was a pervasive material component within the operational logic of a global economy. In time this response produced several debates within the US, including the neo-liberal/neo-realist debate (Baldwin 1993; Grieco 1990), the debate over the decline of American power (Krasner 1978; Keohane 1984), and a further subsequent debate over the precise nature of American power (Nau 1990; Nye 1990). Although it has taken new twists, the engagement between liberal and realist perspectives in IPE continues to dominate American scholarship (Katzenstein et al. 1998).

In Canada, this realist-inspired theoretical influence has been significant, although not direct or unilinear. Among the most prominent IPE scholars in Canada whose work engages with some version of this framework are Michael C. Webb, Louis W. Pauly, and Mark R. Brawley. All received their training at top-ranked American schools asso-ciated with these debates, and all have made the tensions and trade-offs produced by the intersection of political interests pursued through state institutions and the protection of commercial advantage organized through market interactions a principal focus of their research. Webb (1995, 2004) has examined macro-economic cooperation and interna-tional tax competition, arguing that the realist/state-centric paradigm needs to take much more seriously the manner in which non-state actor preferences are worked into what are nominally statist interests. Pauly (1988, 1997; Doremus et al. 1998) has argued that market trends in fact reflect political choices about how power is to be shared, that a changing distribution of systemic power challenges the legitimacy and effectiveness of existing international institutions, and that the behavior of prominent market actors such as multinational corporations strongly reflects their national political roots. Both Webb and Pauly refuse to allow globalization to be named as the culprit in the regressive shift in taxation and in the redistribution of financial costs and rewards within the con-temporary global political economy; in this they have upheld a central tenet of realist political economy that holds the state—and the political classes in control of states more generally—to account. Brawley (1993; 1999) further supports these arguments through his close examination of domestic institutional constraints on foreign-policy making. He is one of very few IPE scholars in Canada to graft a form of public choice analysis onto realist assumptions, in a similar vein to much rationalist-oriented American scholarship. These scholars carry on in Canada a welcome engagement with debates unfolding in American IPE.[7]

Beyond the usual suspects: historical materialists

As important as liberal and realist variants of IPE in Canada have been, it is possible to argue that the most distinctive and influential tradition of IPE scholarship in Canada has been what should loosely be understood as historical materialism, that form of critical inquiry which takes its inspiration from the Marxist tradition in its most fulsome incarnation. And here the work of Robert Cox has been foundational for two reasons. First, his work has articulated within IPE a form of historical materialism that crucially integrates into its method the insights of Antonio Gramsci, an Italian Marxist who was imprisoned under Mussolini, thus providing scholars with a suggestive set of concepts to organize their research. Crucial here are the concepts of hegemony, historical bloc, and passive revolution. These concepts have captured the intellectual imagination of an entire cohort of scholars, allowing them to explore aspects of the contemporary global political economy that would not have been considered appropriate a generation ago.

Second, his work has inspired a renewed engagement with and within the Marxist tradition, both in Canada and internationally, principally because it offers such an idiosyncratic and in some respects challenging reading of historical materialism. Cox's work has pushed scholars to use Marxism at the global level in a way that tries to steer clear of overly determinist and excessively structuralist readings of global capitalism. Precisely because Cox's version of historical materialism reaches outside of the Marxist tradition itself—to embrace insights from theorists as diverse as Giambattista Vico, Ibn Khaldun, R. G. Collingood, E. H. Carr, and Fernand Braudel—he has challenged scholars from within the Marxist tradition to consider how ideational and inter-subjective *mentalities* must necessarily be incorporated into their work by adopting a more historicist-oriented epistemological position. Out of critiques of Cox's work (for example, by Burnham 1991; Panitch 1994; and Germain and Kenny 1998), a debate has developed that has taken historical materialist analysis firmly onto the terrain of global order.

Spurred on by these engagements, IPE scholars in Canada have tackled an array of topics associated with global transformation. Perhaps the best known of these is Stephen R. Gill, whose work on the Trilateral Commission and the new constitutionalism both employs the critical ethos pioneered by Cox, even as he extends this work in new and important ways. Gill's exploration of how the Trilateral Commission became implicated in the new arrangements of governance that followed the breakdown of Bretton Woods—and in fact was a crucial element of the emerging power structure of transnational neo-liberalism—provides a novel and powerful way of explaining a crucial element of the transformation of world order (Gill 1991). His allied concepts of "market civilization," "global panopticon" and "new constitutionalism" (Gill 2002) add further insights to Cox's framework of historical structures, especially where it draws out a Foucauldian element that directly addresses the organization of power within particular social formations. Gill also organized one of the earliest and most powerful contributions to the debate over the use of Gramsci in IPE (Gill 1993).

Gill himself arrived at York University just as his book on the Trilateral Commission was being published, and as Cox retired from active teaching. Indeed, he was recruited by Cox to be the main pillar of the next generation of critical IPE scholars at York. And between Cox and Gill, they have supervised a number of students who have gone on to make solid contributions to scholarship from within this broad, *critical* framework.[8] Working initially under the supervision of Gill, for example, Timothy J. Sinclair (2005) and Adam Harmes (2001a) both explore the mostly unseen power wielded within the global political economy respectively by credit rating agencies and mutual funds. Although in quite different ways, they each deploy elements of a critical political economy approach to unpack and illuminate the role of private authority and its relationship to state-sanctioned authority within the constitution and organization of global capitalism. Other York graduates, working more under Cox's influence, explore topics as diverse as migration, communication, and foreign policy, but always from perspectives which embed a critical historical materialist framework into a broader concern to examine the social underpinnings of state policy (Comor 1998; Pellerin 1999; Persaud 2001). The hallmark of their scholarship is a supple and critical historical materialism.

As influential as the York school has been in the development of IPE in Canada, it does not speak for all those within the country who either deploy an historical materialist framework or work within a framework that is sympathetic to historical materialism's core elements. For example, A. Claire Cutler (2003) uses an historical materialist analysis to consider the legal dimensions within the global political economy, and especially the way in which the increasing privatization of authority is serving to redistribute power among an increasingly transnational elite. Tony Porter (1993, 2005) and Robert O'Brien (O'Brien et al. 2000) have each examined governance arrangements at the global level—in finance and labor respectively—that utilize insights from a critical Coxian perspective but allied to post-modern and feminist sensibilities. Deborah Stienstra (1994) and Sandra Whitworth (1994) have similarly extended a Coxian critical ethos into feminist analyses of global institutions, while Eric N. Helleiner (1997) and Randall D. Germain (1996) have harnessed Cox's interest in Fernand Braudel (1958/1980) and the *longue dureé* to explore the historical development of globalization and global finance.

Research into IPE in Canada, however, does more than simply extend Cox's framework within a critical vein. There are some—such as Manfred Beinefeld (2000) and Suzanne Soederberg (2004)—who develop more orthodox forms of Marxist historical materialism in their assessment of recent developments in global capitalism. Others are more concerned to engage with recent theoretical developments in IPE in the US and elsewhere. Here, scholars such as Jacqueline Best (2005) have explored—through a constructivist lens—the normative and ideational basis upon which narratives of global finance have been constructed, while others such as Rob Aitken (2007) have turned to post-structural conceptual frameworks to help them map the unconscious but no less influential dispositions and sensibilities that encourage *popular* finance. Care must of course be taken not to distance analyses like those of Best and Aitken too categorically from those like Harmes and Sinclair, since all work within a broad critical framework that responds—albeit in different ways—to the initial critical ethos provided by Cox.

In theoretical terms, then, the disciplinary history of IPE in Canada displays a diversity that reflects its intellectual heritage at the crossroads of transatlantic scholarly exchange. This means of course that it sits uneasily with the more singular or monochromatic conditions at work in the US. In American academia, perhaps because of the hierarchical organization of research universities and departments together with the particular methods of career advancement, a kind of herd mentality is often at work with respect to intellectual trajectories and fashions.[9] This herd movement has been on full display over the past decade, with a determined attempt by leading theorists to recast the principal theoretical axis of debate along a rationalist/constructivist discourse in place of the older liberal/realist/Marxist one (e.g. Adler 1997; Katzenstein et al. 1998).[10] But because a larger ratio of scholars in Canada do not organize their research along these lines (indeed, much work in historical materialist political economy proceeds without reference to these newer theoretical developments), and because the Canadian academic hierarchy is not as strictly centralized, a richer and more historically attuned debate is underway. It is unfortunate, then, that this debate does not always exploit its own comparative advantages by confronting mainstream American scholarship over central issues within IPE, including the future of multilateralism, the drivers of globalization and globalizing governance, and the nature of order and power in the global political economy.

Engagements: Canadian peculiarities

Aside from hockey, poutine,[11] and perhaps multiculturalism, there are few uniquely Canadian gifts to the world. Nevertheless, within the rarefied world of IPE, Canadians do seem to spend a disproportionate amount of their energies concentrating on a few key themes: money and finance; multilateralism, international institutions, and global governance; and the thicket of issues at the confluence of development and regionalism. Of these, the most perplexing question must be why so many Canadians are drawn to investigate money and finance. After all, the Canadian financial system is incredibly stable and irrevocably tied into the American financial system. Its currency has been closely linked to the US dollar for well over a century now, and shows no signs of harboring any pretensions towards international reserve currency status. And its financial institutions are minnows in world market terms. Of course, Canada was in at the creation of the IMF, it is a G7 member, and its nationals seem rather well represented at senior levels of international financial institutions.[12] Nevertheless, with so little at stake in material terms, one wonders why so many Canadian scholars make the political economy of money and finance their bread and butter.

And many do just this in fact. From the West to the East Coast, but with a special concentration in Ontario, Canadian scholars are in the vanguard of enterprising and innovative interpretations of the globalization of finance. The IMF, for example, has attracted the attention of Canadian academics spanning theoretical divides, such as Louis Pauly (1997), Jacqueline Best (2005), Bessma Momani (2004), and Suzanne Soederberg (2004). Broader trajectories in global finance have also occupied the energies of Tony Porter (2005), Eric Helleiner (1994, 2003), Randall Germain (1997) and Geoffrey R. D. Underhill (1997), the latter included here as a Canadian trained in Britain but who now teaches at the University of Amsterdam (after stints at McMaster University in Canada and the University of Warwick in England). Even central banks do not escape the scrutiny of Canadians or Canadian-based scholars (Johnson 2000; King 2005; Helleiner 2006). When you add to this number those economists who were Canadian yet who taught at US universities from the middle years of the twentieth century onward—such as Robert Mundell, Ronald Mackinnon and Harry Johnson—the sheer weight of Canadian scholars fascinated by money and finance defies explanation.[13]

More understandable are those scholars interested in the provocative issues posed by multilateralism, international institutions, and more recently global governance. Canadians are understandably concerned with the erosion of multilateralism as a core principle of international relations, and as a material basis of international institutions. It will be recalled, for example, that international organizations have been a persistent and central concern of Robert Cox throughout his career. Indeed, he directed a large international research team into the changing basis of multilateralism after his retirement from York University (Cox 1992, 1997). Beyond this, there has been a strong Canadian interest in the regimes and institutions of international trade (Winham 1986; Zacher 1992; Wolfe 1998; Lanoszka 2001; Goff 2007), as well as an ongoing concern with the pressures that globalization places on maintaining a viable welfare state (Mahon 2002; McBride 2005) and of course international financial institutions such as the IMF and World Bank. And one cannot ignore the seminal work of John Gerrard Ruggie, a post-war immigrant to Canada who received his early education at McMaster University before going on to doctoral work at Berkeley under Ernst Haas. Ruggie's pioneering work on international institutions and regimes not only bequeathed to us the term "embedded liberalism," but has provided to IPE and IR more generally an idiosyncratic and provocative version of "constructivism" (Ruggie 1998).

85

Canadians have also ploughed their energies more recently into that intellectual woolly mammoth known as global governance. Indeed, in a country not generally known for philanthropic funding of social science research, generous (in the Canadian context) endowments from the private sector have recently helped to launch three research centers largely devoted to understanding the dynamics and tensions of global governance, and a number of scholars attached to them that have made this subject their top research priority (Bernstein 2001; Cooper 2004, 2008; Byers 2007).[14]

The final area that has attracted the attention of Canadian IPE scholars spans the thematic concerns of development and regionalism. Interest in both themes is not hard to explain. Canada has spent much of its colonial and post-independence history *developing*; thus a concern with the political economy of development is a logical extension of much of the earlier work done by Harold Innis and other pioneers in political economy.[15] Fittingly, however, given Canada's position as an intellectual crossroad, much of this work is focused on development outside Canada. Africa has long been a concern of IPE scholarship in Canada, with Timothy M. Shaw (1993), David R. Black (Black and Swatuk 1997) and Linda Freeman (1997) devoting much of their careers to explicating the links between global capitalism and national development. Latin America, Central America, and the Caribbean have also held pride of interest, with scholars such as Laura Macdonald (1997), Judith Adler Hellman (1999), and Cristina Rojas (2002) exploring the pressures faced by this region in a world marked by global capitalism and a resurgent American neo-imperialism. And finally, NAFTA and the complex global politics confronting Canada has drawn the attention of many Canadian IPE scholars (Laxer 1987; O'Brien 1997; Drache 2001; Hülsemeyer 2004).

This short excursion into the themes and concerns explored by IPE scholars in Canada is of course incomplete. No mention has been made of research into substantive issues such as the environment (Paterson 1996; Clapp 2001; Hall 2002; Andrée 2007) or Europe (Verdun and Jones 2005); or into thematic concerns such as the continuing vitality of nationalism (Helleiner and Pickel 2005). Absent also is an extended discussion of the work of Jonathan Nitzan, who has developed an idiosyncratic reading of power anchored in a political economy analysis that is critical not only of mainstream liberal and realist presuppositions but of many Marxist ones as well (e.g. Nitzan 1998). It must also be acknowledged that the question of gender and political economy has found a ready number of scholars determined to explore its theoretical and empirical parameters (Gabriel and Macdonald 1994; Brodie 1995; Bakker and Gill 2003). And finally, there has been only limited discussion of the research of a number of new faculty recently appointed across Canada's universities over the past five years, as their research has yet to become firmly established. Nevertheless, the outlines of the kind of research done within IPE in Canada should be clear: it is often directed toward global institutions, especially those concerned with finance, trade, and development; it is cognizant of changing social transformations; and it is concerned with the interface between the material factors affecting the evolution of markets and the political, ideological, and increasingly environmental factors required to support them.

Canadian IPE: reflections on a future assessment

As the twenty-first century firmly takes root, how should we gauge the vitality of IPE in Canada? One set of criteria could parallel Benjamin J. Cohen's recent assessment of

American and British IPE, examining the career possibilities and institutionalized networks through which IPE scholars in Canada engage with their counterparts elsewhere. If this set of criteria is used, the assessment would be quite positive, since in fact IPE scholarship in Canada constitutes in many ways exactly the kind of transatlantic "bridge" he calls for (Cohen 2007). This set of criteria also echoes Schmidt's conception of "disciplinary history," wherein the robustness of the internal conversation among practitioners is a crucial benchmark for assessing the vitality of a discipline and its trajectory (Schmidt 1998: 37–42).

Such a criterion, however, has less to say about two important aspects of any assessment concerning the future direction of a discipline. First, such an internally oriented set of criteria is relatively silent on the question of what a discipline actually has to say about the world it investigates. In other words, is IPE in Canada focusing on the important issues and/or themes that animate today's global political economy? Does it have interesting and important things to say about the world we inhabit? Second, Cohen's criteria leave little room for consideration of new substantive directions, for a call to turn attention to novel and perhaps different theoretical and/or empirical problems. Yet these are precisely the kind of criteria we need to deploy if we are to reflect on the future of IPE in Canada. In the last part of this chapter, therefore, I shall amend slightly Schmidt's disciplinary ethos by using Robert Cox's legacy for IPE in Canada to reflect on its future vitality.[16]

Cox's writings have made a substantial impact on the development of IPE worldwide; indeed, any number of disciplinary reviews have placed his work without question at the forefront of scholarship (Murphy and Tooze 1991b; Katzenstein et al. 1998; Murphy and Nelson 2001; Cohen 2007).[17] His contributions can be said to fall into three areas: methodological, epistemological, and ontological. The most important of these has been the methodological impact of his work, primarily through the very positive reception of his framework for understanding historical totalities, which essentially provides scholars with a method of apprehending transformations in the broad structure of world order. Whether approached through his diachronically related double triptych of ideas/material capabilities/institutions plus social forces/world orders/forms of states (Cox 1981), or through his Gramscian-inspired reading of historical blocs (Cox 1983), much of the work infused by a Coxian sensibility focuses on deploying the methodology he developed during the 1980s to ask (in many different ways) one crucial question: are we moving into a period of structural transformation, most importantly in terms of the decline or resurgence of a world hegemonic order?

Unsurprisingly, there are many nuances to how this question can be answered. Cox himself considers the world to be entering a moment dominated by a retreat from hegemony on the part of the US (Cox 2004). Gill also considers the present moment to be non-hegemonic, since he identifies the collective neo-liberal strategy to achieve world order as one of "supremacy" rather than hegemony (Gill 1991, 2002). Harmes further reinforces this view, noting that this push for dominance is producing tensions and contradictions that will in turn undermine capitalism's capacity to contain social strife, thus making the world ripe for a Polanyian "double movement" (Harmes 2001b; see also Ruggie 1998).

Yet, as interesting as this debate is, there are elements of Cox's heuristic framework that are not unproblematic. Materially, it is interesting that the framework of historical structures has great difficulty in ascertaining challenges to the status quo that come from outside the prevailing institutional configuration of social forces. For example, in his own

87

work, Cox was as surprised as other scholars by the implosion of the Soviet Union and the end of the Cold War, and by the sudden rise of China and the eclipse of Japan as the next major challenger to world order. The entire phenomenon of East Asian development and where and how it fits into the depiction of the organization of social forces in the global economy has in important ways challenged historical materialist analyses of the motor forces of historical development, which in some respects remain glued to an earlier historical template. Indeed, we now need to ask to what extent analyses that remain true to an orthodox and classically inspired Marxist reading of historical materialism are capable of grasping the new and historic wellsprings of the contemporary transformation of world order.

It is at this point that Cox's second contribution to IPE becomes significant, for Cox's historicist epistemology provides an avenue through which new wellsprings of transformation may be grasped. For Cox, the only suitable epistemological position for the critical scholar to hold is rooted in a radical form of historical reasoning that contains strong idealist overtones. Here Cox returns to his early training as an historian—influenced by the work of Collingwood and Vico in particular—to consider forms of consciousness (mind) as the key to enabling a connection between past with present to be made. Only such a formulation provides an understanding of the present that admits the human mind into the formation and evolution of historical institutions (Cox 1981). In other words, a theory of knowledge for Cox is nothing but a philosophy of history, which directs our attention to changes in inter-subjective *mentalités* as the key to understanding why the world changes as it does. Following this logic to its conclusion has taken Cox from a concern with international organizations (Cox and Jacobson 1973) to examining state–society complexes as they are embedded within world order formations (Cox 1987) to now exploring the ethos of civilizational orders and their multiple encounters (Cox 2002). Each advance in his thinking has been led by the search for the particular articulation of inter-subjective *mentalités* with material capabilities under specific historical conditions, and toward a progressive re-engagement with the more historically oriented scholars of his early education, such as Collingwood, Spengler, and Toynbee, but leavened by his further study of the work of Vico, Khaldun, Carr, Georges Sorel, and of course Antonio Gramsci.

This concern with epistemology connects directly with Cox's third contribution to IPE in Canada and abroad, namely a concern to advance an ontology anchored in the changing inter-subjective *mentalité* that allows particular configurations of social forces to acquire voice and act collectively through their material circumstances. Cox has long been a critic of agent-centered analysis, preferring instead a more structurally attuned history analogous to what Fernand Braudel (1958/1980) identifies as the *longue durée*. At the same time, however, he has not abjured analysis of agents in history; rather, the question for him always has been what are the (collective) agents of history, how are they changing and what forces are bringing them into being and/or undermining them? For Cox, agents are not given by history, they are made through history; thus what passes for the primary building blocks of the historical process change over time. We must in this reading of ontology be open to new forms of agency arising out of specific historical junctures. And on this basis he has argued that new forms of agency are now emerging, and this requires of scholars a renewed appreciation of changing historical forms.[18]

However, Cox's epistemological and ontological commitments are almost wholly out of tune with contemporary political economy in Canada. The reason for this is the very ambiguous relationship Cox's epistemology and ontology have with many strands of Marxism more generally and historical materialism in particular, not to mention with more mainstream accounts of social science (cf. Murphy and Nelson 2001). While Cox shares many of the concerns that Marxist and historical materialist critiques level at liberal and neo-realist analyses, his radical historical idealism and its associated historicism parts company with these critiques insofar as he refuses to privilege the forms of agency so central to their conception of the motor force of history. For Cox, there is and can be no single motor force: history has produced many motor forces, and the job facing today's scholar is to canvas the historical terrain and ask how new agents are being formed and/ or making themselves.

Thus the peculiar conclusion of this chapter that much of IPE in Canada, despite its rich intellectual history and vibrant publication record, remains wedded to a kind or type of analysis which refuses to consider new agential forms and alternative structural evolutions within political economy broadly construed. To the extent that IPE in Canada continues to be inspired by a Coxian framework of analysis, it is one that privileges his methodological framework but without taking on board the full implications of its historicist epistemological and ontological supports. The result is an attempt to quantify and measure the material decline or resurgence of hegemony, rather than the *fit* between the material structure of world order and its prevailing mental framework. It as if critical IPE in Canada has forgotten one of Cox's first insights about hegemony: "Hegemony is invisible, a latent force that can only be seized intellectually" (Cox 1996: 364). This demands a return to the ideational and historicist focus that Cox has championed more recently in his scholarship.

As this chapter has indicated, though, not all IPE in Canada is fixated by the analysis offered by Cox during the 1980s. Liberal and neo-realist traditions of inquiry continue to command attention, and newer (and older) traditions are also active among the research community. In this sense, the diverse intellectual history of political economy in Canada is alive and well. The material conditions facing Canada, at one level, will not change radically in the foreseeable future, as Canada will continue to be strongly affected by economic, political, social, and ideological developments in its southern neighbor. At another level, however, Canada—along with the rest of the world—is entering a new world marked by change on a planetary scale. Reaching a sustainable environmental accord with the economy, preserving a suitable biosphere, accommodating the rise of Asia and its billions, and searching for a new military balance between old superpowers and newer challengers: these are the concerns that should compel the attention of scholars of IPE, just as they will concentrate the minds of policymakers, political and economic leaders and everyday citizens alike over the coming years. Will IPE in Canada continue to engage with *this* world through its scholarship and teaching? My bet is yes, although it would be a more robust and vital IPE if it were to engage more centrally with the ontological and epistemological directions first charted by Robert W. Cox.

Notes

1 I would like to thank for his research help Bart Paudyn, whose bibliography of scholars active in international and comparative political economy research in Canada was enormously helpful. Lou Pauly, Eric Helleiner, and Mike Webb provided frank and insightful feedback on an initial draft; they are nevertheless absolved of responsibility for the final product, as is Mark Blyth, who cast the

sharp eyes of an editor over the chapter. Finally, the author's personal stake in this review must be acknowledged: he is a former student of Robert W. Cox who graduated from York University in 1993 and spent a decade teaching in Britain before returning to Canada.

2 The constraints on such a short chapter are almost too numerous to mention, but two in particular stand out. First, the rich history of political economy in Canada must be radically truncated, and although I will set up the historical context, the main focus in this chapter will be on the post-Bretton Woods period, when IPE became reconstituted as a disciplinary field. Second, although the roots of IPE in classical political economy and international/development economics is acknowledged, the principal emphasis of the chapter shall be on what can be termed "disciplinary IPE," in other words the field as it has come to be constituted through its institutional organization and internal conversations. I am here following the ethos of "disciplinary history" advocated by Brian Schmidt (1998). A final caveat is in order: although every effort has been made to be thorough and complete, some themes and/or scholars within IPE in Canada will have been undoubtedly missed. No slight is intended.

3 At Queen's the original Department of Political and Economic Sciences begat five separate departments between 1960 and 1969, with the departments of Political Studies and Economics being created in 1964. McGill's Department of Political Economy split into separate departments of Political Science and Economics in 1969, while Toronto's Department of Political Economy only formalized its separate constituent units in 1982. My thanks to Kim Nossal and Chris Ragan for help on this one.

4 Interestingly, all three of these scholars were educated at Chicago, and were heavily influenced by the work of Thorstein Veblen and his historical form of sociology and political economy (Ferguson 1993).

5 Categorizing and classifying theories and scholars in this way can be a nefarious exercise. Both the categories and the classifications can be challenged on several grounds, including the question of how to classify those who are unclassifiable (of which they are always some), the problem of identifying unalloyed exemplars in practice (which are exceedingly rare), and the thorny issue of accurately identifying the theoretical persuasion of individual scholars. Pedagogically, however, such typologies can be useful, and in this case they are used to illustrate the broad trends at work in how IPE scholars in Canada engage substantively with their work.

6 The impact of Susan Strange on the development of IPE in Canada cannot be overstated. Not only did she teach several prominent scholars (e.g. Louis Pauly and Eric Helleiner), but also her work continues to inspire and be used by many, including Robert Cox—a long-time friend and colleague—and Stephen Gill.

7 In this respect it is noteworthy that what is often considered to be the leading journal in the discipline—*International Organization*—moved to the University of Toronto in 2007 under the editorial team of Louis Pauly and Emanuel Adler. This is the first time its editorial office has been outside of the US.

8 Among the scholars mentioned below, Hélène Pellerin, Adam Harmes, and Edward Comor teach in Canada, while Randolph Persaud and Timothy J. Sinclair teach abroad. Additionally, other students of Cox who now teach in Canada would include Randall D. Germain, Eric N. Helleiner, Laura Macdonald and Robert O'Brien.

9 For different assessments of how this mentality operates, see Strange (1995), Cox (1996) and Wæver (1998).

10 Oddly, Adler labels Cox a constructivist, thus assimilating him into the new configuration of theoretical debates.

11 Poutine is a concoction of French fries covered in cheese curd and smothered in gravy that is very popular in Québec.

12 Canadians have for example, recently led the Organization for Economic Cooperation and Development, the Bank for International Settlements, and the G20 group of finance ministers and central bank governors.

13 I would like to thank Eric Helleiner for this point.

14 The three centers are the Munk Centre for International Studies at the University of Toronto, the Center for International Governance Innovation in Waterloo, an independent institute linked to Wilfrid Laurier and Waterloo universities and known more popularly by its acronym, CIGI, and the Liu Institute for Global Studies at the University of British Columbia. The Munk Centre is housed in a building refurbished with money given by one of Canada's richest mining entrepreneurs, while

CIGI was established with an unprecedented endowment from one of the founders of the firm that brought the world the Blackberry. The Liu Institute was established in part from an endowment from the Liu Foundation and businessman Dr. Jieh Jow Liou in 2000. Although these are not the only centers of research into IPE in Canada (others exist at Carleton University and Simon Fraser University, for example), they clearly constitute Canada's best known research centers into IPE and international relations.

15 And indeed, there is a rich seam of work in the political economy tradition in Canada that easily blends into themes also commonly associated with IPE. See for example the work of Stephen Clarkson (2002) and Wallace Clement (Clement and Myles 1994).

16 This adaptation thus rebalances Schmidt's framework slightly by devoting more attention than he does to what a discipline says about the world it inhabits, rather than to what it says about itself.

17 Cox is also the only non-American to have made the journal *Foreign Policy*'s list of most influential IR scholars in recent years (Peterson et al. 2005). In the recent Canadian version of that survey, he ranked fourth overall in Canada versus twenty-fourth in the US table (Lipson et al. 2007). For a sympathetic consideration of his work, see Mittelman (1998) together with the collection of essays in Gill and Mittelman (1997); for an inventory of critical engagements with Cox's work, see Schechter (2002).

18 Thus his analysis of the changing nature of class, the new importance of civilizations in history, and the renewed importance of the state and classical international relations (Cox 1987, 1999, 2004). It is not just that these are material developments; more critically, they are the material responses which collective forms of agency have produced as a result of changing forms of mind and consciousness. In other words, for Cox, a fusion of the material and the ideal is at the heart of changing forms of agency. This in a nutshell is his radical historical idealism, an idealism which places materialism at its core but in a way that respects how human beings apprehend and shape their world.

Part II
British IPE

6

Lineages of a British international political economy

Ben Clift and Ben Rosamond

Introduction

International political economy—like all academic fields—tells stories about its evolution. This is not just the business of IPE's intellectual historians. Such narratives are routine to the everyday practice of the field. A sense of how we got here, where we started from and where we might be going are arguably essential to any coordination of scholarly activity within the present. Moreover, as sociologists of knowledge and critical disciplinary historians have noted, the capacity of a particular narrative of a field's evolution to prevail over others is not necessarily either benign or banal. Indeed control over knowledge about the disciplinary past is one of the primary means through which particular moves in the disciplinary present are justified and legitimized.

We begin by outlining two prevailing propositions within IPE's storytelling which we reject. We go on to demonstrate why we find that these do a disservice to the richness and diversity of *British* IPE scholarship, by highlighting certain particularities of the British intellectual climate in which its political economy tradition developed in the postwar world. We go on to explore some of the implications—ontological, methodological, and epistemological—of this distinctive genetic material out of which British IPE grew.

What British IPE is not ...

Within IPE's story telling something of a convention has emerged around two propositions, both of which we will seek to deconstruct and challenge via a discussion of political economy scholarship in Britain. The first is a view of IPE as a field of relatively recent vintage, dating most conspicuously from the foundational moment in 1970 when Susan Strange published her seminal paper on the problem of "mutual neglect" between scholars of international relations (IR) and international economics (Strange 1970b).[1] The *1970 as year zero* thesis we feel must be resisted. This is in no way to deny the significance of Strange as a colossus of British IPE, but it is to problematize the notion of her as *the* foundational scholar of British international political economy, writing *the* foundational text in 1970. This chapter charts the relation of British IPE to longer and broader traditions of political economy analysis. These longer ancestries help account for the spirit and dynamism of British IPE, which emulates, at its best, *pre-disciplinary* or *classical* political economy (Gamble 1995; Watson 2005, 2008).

Seeing 1970 as year zero has the effect of imagining IPE as first and foremost an *international studies* project. This would seem to be a somewhat obvious thing to do, given the conspicuous presence of the *I* in IPE. So, by and large, IPE is talked about as if it were a subfield of IR that is both (a) located under the IR heading within a sub-disciplinary organization of the political sciences, yet (b) defined in several key ways by its departure from many of the main traditional thematic concerns of IR. IPE's conventional disciplinary geography is reinforced by its institutionalization as a thematic section of the International Studies Association (ISA) in the US and as a working group within the British International Studies Association.[2] IPE's evolution—again traceable to the year zero moment of the early 1970s has even been tied to the history of a particular journal—*International Organization* (*IO*). As one prominent intellectual history of the field puts it: "we use the term *IPE* when we refer to the subfield of work, centered in *IO* since 1971, that evolved from the study of international political economy to analyze a variety of aspects of world politics" (Katzenstein et al. 1998: 645). The presumed youth of IPE is, we suggest, in part a reflection of the fact that political economy as a set of intellectual tools has only recently been assimilated into the IR mainstream.

In contexts where there is a very clear and disciplined ordering of political science into component subfields (as in the US, where pedagogy and scholarship are conventionally subdivided into political theory, American politics, comparative politics and IR), legitimate dominion for any newer area of enquiry is secured though absorption into one of the legitimately designated sub-areas. As such, standard intellectual histories of IPE are constructed in ways that (a) proceed uncritically via a retrospective teleology that treats the early 1970s as a formal foundational moment; (b) search for—and occasionally find—prophetic scholarship (the likes of Charles Kindleberger, Fred Hirsch, Susan Strange) that was, as it were, doing IPE before IPE came into being; (c) seek out only IR antecedents of contemporary IPE;[3] and—most seriously—(d) privilege work conducted under the banner of *IPE as IR subfield* as the only admissible or relevant IPE work and thus treat work conducted in the present as necessarily further along a linear course of knowledge advancement (Gunnell 2005).

What British IPE is (partially) constituted by ...

The second proposition is that IPE is characterized by a relatively clear-cut transatlantic divide, with so-called "American" and "British" schools often invoked as divergent epistemological and methodological wings of the IPE movement (Cohen 2007, 2008a, 2008b; Denemark and O'Brien 1997; Dickins 2006; Higgott and Watson 2008; Murphy and Nelson 2001; Watson 2008). It is not our intention to completely discredit the notion that work conducted under the rubric of IPE is characterized by different approaches to the very business of scholarship. Indeed, there is something to be said for thinking through these differences in terms of the territorial geography of disciplines.

The utilization of territorial categories like "British" or "American" is not and should not be a bland descriptive exercise. Nor should it confuse the epistemological with the political, as seems to be the case with Cohen's assertion that some British IPE is motivated by a barely concealed anti-Americanism (2007: 213). Rather, such categorizations are only helpful when they are used as proxies to denote differences in knowledge production regimes (Wæver 1998). What follows is a recognition that national disciplinary communities tend to institutionalize in distinct ways at least four aspects of academic enquiry: (a) what is considered to be acceptable or admissible work in a given field, (b) how work should be conducted and how and where its results should be presented, (c) where the legitimate boundaries of the field might reside, and (d) "external relations" or the nature of engagement with/interaction between (and potentially the "othering" of) cognate disciplines. Indeed, the capacity to define propriety within these four components (admissibility, conduct, borders, and external relations) is reflective of power structures within disciplines (Rosamond 2007). The character of work in IPE is likely to differ across intellectual communities (which are to some extent national, although the boundaries are somewhat porous) because of different societal negotiations regarding admissibility, conduct, borders, and external relations with other disciplines.

In relation to admissibility and conduct, the epistemological contrast between British and US IPE is arresting. "As the American school has become standardized," Cohen observes,

> it has come to resemble nothing so much as the methodology of neoclassical economics, featuring the same penchant for positivism [and] formal modeling ... more and more, what gets published in the US features the same sorts of mathematical and statistical techniques that we have come to expect in economics journals.
>
> (2007: 206)

He notes that "the methodology of economics now appears to set the standard for what passes for professionalism among social scientists in the US" (Cohen 2007: 207). The ready acceptance of greater epistemological diversity within British IPE is, we argue below, both a considerable strength and a marked contrast to the norms of disciplinarity conduct and admissibility bound up in the US academy's conception of "professionalism."

At the same time, of course, these negotiations and contests are not purely national. Indeed if disciplines are thought of as transnational enterprises, then the most significant aspect of intra-disciplinary politics is the struggle over the terms of scholarly enquiry. As such the tendency to divide the field into rival "British" and "American" camps has the merit of bringing to the fore two alternative ideal typical modes of inquiry which articulate distinctive positions vis-à-vis admissibility, conduct, borders, and external relations. These are intellectual as much as geographical differentiations.[4]

As this indicates, the two camps metaphor needs to be deployed with caution. For example Cohen, following a "great scholars make intellectual traditions" approach, identifies Robert Cox as central to British IPE, such that "Cox defines the core *problematique* of the British school" (2007: 211). We do not deny Cox is a great and very influential scholar, but he is not a summation of the entire tradition. Here, we are concerned with thinking in more nuanced terms about the construction of the "British" school. A further illustration is the disciplinary location and characterization of IPE noted above. Here Cohen notes, "beyond an interest in marrying international economics and IR, there is no consensus at all on what, precisely, IPE is about" (2007: 198). It is worse than that. The distance between the British and American "two separate branches of a common research community" (Cohen 2007: 198) is larger than Cohen recognizes. For Cohen "the story" is "the interaction of economics and politics in international relations" (2007: 216), yet this assertion of an agreed core of IPE could be received by some British IPE scholars as smelling of US intellectual imperialism. That disciplinary location is at least debatable in the British IPE context. Not all see IR as a necessary, or necessarily helpful, point of departure for analyzing the global political economy (though, of course, many do).

What British IPE is, and why it got that way ...

A good deal of the discussion surrounding what divides British and American IPE has tended to revolve around matters of *conduct* (questions of approach and method, the legitimacy or otherwise of normative modes of enquiry in academic work) and to some extent around *borders* and *external relations* (questions of singular or multidisciplinarity). In a UK context where *external relations* between academic disciplines (and subdisciplines) have never been characterized by a "billiard ball" world view, but by more porous, neo-medievalist understandings of overlapping allegiances within social sciences, a particular kind of IPE can develop and flourish. British IPE has been able to exploit the potentialities of loose disciplinarity, grazing on the sunlit uplands of (to name but a few) Marxist sociology, economic sociology, economic history, and heterodox applied, institutional and evolutionary economics, in addition to political studies. Unlike the development of the intellectual tradition of IPE in the US, there has never been a pervasive sense of a *parent discipline* (or disciplines) of which British IPE is a subfield. There is no requirement to choose between a comparative politics or IR pathway in UK universities, and doctoral research is not defined in strictly delineated subdisciplinary terms. It is this relatively relaxed disciplinarity within the British academic environment that makes possible work that scavenges more readily across the social scientific spectrum (both historical and contemporary) for inspiration. Thus the pervasive US notion of IPE as a subfield of IR brings with it intellectual baggage which have largely been spared British IPE scholars. Here we want to raise issues of *admissibility*—to re-describe a rich tradition of work as elemental to what IPE scholarship should be about—and to broaden the question of *borders* and *external relations* to question the usefulness of the conventional temporal and (sub)disciplinary boundaries of modern IPE.

At this point it makes sense to engage with the sociology of British political economy and British social science more generally. If we are interested in understanding the distinctive quality of British (I)PE then we need to know something about the intellectual conditions in which it has developed and its feeder influences (and in turn the intellectual conditions within which they developed). Cohen rightly emphasizes the importance of intellectual culture, and the difference between US and UK international political economy in intellectual cultural terms (2007: 199–200), but—understandably—he does not explore all the contours of the British academic culture. British IPE evolved in intellectual conditions characterized by a *loose disciplinarity* and *multidisciplinarity* which shaped the norms of conduct, admissibility, borders, and external relations. One reflection of, and focus for, this loose disciplinarity and multidisciplinarity was a wide-ranging acceptance of and engagement with historical materialist approaches to social scientific enquiry.

Loose disciplinarity meant that the British variant of (I)PE did/does not suffer from those strictures of disciplinarity that have been so apparent in the US. We should not underestimate, for example, the relative longevity of "applied" traditions of economic science to the fashioning of British (I)PE (Comim 2000; Dow et al. 2000). Second, a lot of the key work emerged from beyond the formal walls of the academy, from government advisors and former civil servants from economic ministries (such as Alec Cairncross), or journalists (such as Susan Strange, Andrew Shonfield, and Samuel Brittan). This gives much of it a more (policy) problem-driven, rather than theory-driven quality, but this work effortlessly transcends the mooted Coxian divide.[5]

Multidisciplinarity pertains to the lack of an iron grip of a political science orthodoxy. The behavioral revolution never took hold within British political science as it did in the US, and this meant a different kind of borrowing of method from economics was possible, one not necessarily rooted in the methodology and underlying assumptions of neo-classical economics (Caporaso and Levine 1992: ch. 6). So, in Britain, "political science" was a disputed term, many preferring "studies"—because what has been accepted as orthodox methodology (built on particular ontological and epistemological assumptions) in the United States is but one possible methodology in British political studies, and by no means the dominant one (Kavanagh 2003; Kenny 2007). Such an intellectual context for the study of politics allowed for dialogue between different disciplinary discourses, for example on the political economy of decline, and also permitted the survival of multidisciplinary styles of enquiry such as Marxism.

Cohen's perhaps playful depiction of Marxists as "outside the 'respectable' mainstream of Western scholarship" (2007: 197) betrays a profound difference between British and North American academe. Marxism was a much more influential intellectual tradition right across the UK social sciences than was the case in the US. Scholars working in history, politics, sociology, and economics departments (who may not have all *been* Marxists) were exposed to the interconnections of the political and the economic inherent within a conception of capital as a set of social relations of production (a conception, incidentally, which was as familiar to Adam Smith as it was to Karl Marx). The degree of commonality of approach, though by no means necessarily of ideological position, within a wide range of social scientific disciplines helped in dissolving the "borders" and fostering cross-fertilization of political economy analysis. "External relations" were thus characterized by relatively close interdependence.

Internal and external stimuli

Many accounts of the evolution of IPE identify *real world* stimuli as the basis of an intellectual revolution that kicked off the field in the early 1970s. Susan Strange herself was, of course, an advocate of this "externalist" position, where intellectual evolution is explained in terms of reactions to changes in the object of study. Witness "Wake up Krasner, the world has changed" (Strange 1994a). O'Brien (1995) sees the emergence of modern IPE as rooted in the changes to the global political economy that became evident in the 1960s and the 1970s: tensions within the Bretton Woods regime as the 1960s progressed, the *Nixon shock* that ended Bretton Woods in 1971–72, OPEC price rises and a perception of declining US hegemony as exemplified by the military failure in Vietnam.

As critical disciplinary historians and sociologists of knowledge are keen to point out, this "externalist" position has obvious merits in explaining shifts in the general substantive orientation of a field. But it cannot account for the particular character that academic work takes at any given time. This needs to be understood within an "internalist" analysis that understands how the real world external divers are intercepted and adjudicated within academic communities (cf. Blyth 2006). "Internalist" dynamics refer to the range of norms and practices that together help to constitute questions of admissibility, conduct, borders and external relations within a field. In other words, part of the explanation for the distinctiveness of British IPE is precisely that the internalist dynamics are different and more tolerant of pluralism in terms of admissibility, conduct, and borders. We will come to this in due course. But we also want to suggest a more complicated understanding of externalism as it applies to the British political economy tradition. After all, the selection of the list above as the key external determinants of the consolidation of IPE reflects a particular set of priorities. If these are selected as *the* key external drivers of IPE, then British work might look thin on the ground. Table 6.1 (below) is a simple exercise to show that parallel but quite distinct external policy imperatives have acted as drivers of political economy scholarship within Britain. This is not simply to say that there is more to British IPE than meets the eye, but also to suggest that mainstream IPE should treat such work seriously and not deem it to lie external to its self-defined borders.

These elements of contextualization of the intellectual biographies of UK-based international political economy scholars help explain some of the particularities of British IPE. All in all this was a fertile ground conducive to analysis which, whilst often explicitly national in focus, nevertheless engaged with themes and issues which were, after the 1970s, to be claimed by IPE. In part because none of these political economy undertakings were self-consciously disciplinary exercises, this organized the mental furniture of UK-based scholars in a particular way.

Therefore, in broad terms, the external stimuli for contemporary British political economy scholarship are rooted in the changing relationship of the British state and its currency to evolutions in the wider global political economy. This brought home to British political economy scholars how advanced industrial states are both architects and subjects of the world economy. This prepared the ground for an appreciation of the core international political economy point that the dichotomy between the national and the global is false. Capitalism is simultaneously national and global, and sterling was/is simultaneously a national and a world currency. Nations are constitutive of the global, and are woven into the global political economy. The twentieth century as a whole, and post-war era in particular, saw for Britain an unpicking of the stitches, and a casting about for a new pattern. The character of internal drivers is perhaps best revealed by the emergence of a self-conscious *new* political economy school in the 1990s. Gamble's influential account of this "new political economy" (1995; cf. Payne and Gamble 1996) was a clarion call for a generation of scholars. It did much to revitalize political economy analysis in Britain toward the end of the twentieth century, heralding, the following year, a new journal of the same name (Gamble et al. 1996). Gamble situates "new" political economy within traditions of critique, and intellectual discourses, under the headings of state theory and government–industry relations. More specifically, British political economy analysis has generated, since the mid-1950s, a series of overlapping literatures, which include the politics of economic policy (Brittan 1964; Cairncross 1986, 1995; Conan 1952, 1961, 1966; Hirsch 1965; Manser 1971; Shonfield 1958; Strange 1971; Tomlinson 1990; Winch 1969), the relationship between the state and industry (in relation to planning, corporatism etc.) (Budd 1978; Crouch 1977; Grant 1982, 1985; Marquand 1988; Middlemas 1986, 1990, 1991; Shonfield 1969), the political economy of decline (cf. Anderson, 1964, 1987; Barnett 1972; Coates and Hillard 1986; Hobsbawm 1969; Kenny and English 2000; Nairn 1964, 1976, 1981a, 1981b; Pollard 1982; Rubinstein 1993), the political economy of Thatcherism (Gamble 1986, 1988; Jessop et al. 1988; Thompson 1986, 1990), industrial sociology (Goldthorpe et al. 1968; MacInnes 1987), evolutionary, organizational, and institutional economics (Hodgson 1993, 2001), the Cambridge school of economics (Robinson 1971; Robinson and Eatwell 1973), the British tradition of *applied* economics (Comim 2000; Dow et al. 2000), the state as an object of analysis (particularly, but not exclusively, for those inspired by Marxian political economy leading to regulation theory) (Crouch 1979; Gamble 1974; Jessop 1974, 1982, 1990, 2002; Leys 1983; Miliband 1969), and a tradition of thinking about philosophies of political economy and the history of political economic thought (Barber 1991; Backhouse 2002; Blaug 1990, 1992; 1997; Fine 1980; Hutchison 1994; Robinson 1962; Steedman 1977; Tabb 1999; Thompson 1999). None of these required (or had) IR as a starting point. This series of overlapping literatures formed the gene pool out of which the British IPE tradition evolved.

In the remainder of this chapter, we flesh these points out with reference to four literatures with a view to showing how the mixture of external drivers and internalist dynamics has yielded a rich formative tradition for contemporary IPE that is largely forgotten in the narration of IPE's history. The four overlapping literatures we examine are those distinctively British contributions to the political economy of imperialism, post-colonialism and economic policy, the political economy of decline, and the state.

Driver number 1: the political economy of British imperialism

Britain as an imperial power and nineteenth-century hegemon is a mainstay of IPE textbooks written for both US and non-US courses. It is also a major preoccupation of some of the great works in IPE (Cox 1987; Polanyi 1944). A standard periodization of IPE, however, would render inadmissible one of the seminal IPE texts dealing with the topic. Imperialism and decolonization were the central policy preoccupations of Britain's external economic and political relations for large parts of the twentieth century. Nowhere was the political economy of those relations better explored than in J. A. Hobson's *Imperialism*, first published in 1902. Hobson[6] was a self-confessed "economic heretic" (1988 [1938a]: 29), whose ontological position refuted the separation of politics and economics (Freeden 1988: 154). He endorsed, for example, Ruskin's "main charge against the current [neo-classical, marginalist] political economy" namely "that it had deliberately and systematically degraded the true and formerly accepted meaning of such terms as 'wealth', 'value', and 'profit' by putting them to the narrow services of business mentality" (Hobson 1988 [1938a]: 29). Ruskin's moral economic distinction between "wealth" and "illth" aligns with Hobson's own "human interpretation of cost and utility, and economic value" which "brings economic values into close organic relations with other human values" (Hobson 1988 [1938a]: 31). This, in turn, for Hobson, has profound ontological implications; "such intricate interactions evidently preclude much of the specialism and separatism which economic, political, and other social theorists have been prone to." Resisting this, Hobson laments

> the whole trend of orthodox economics has been to safeguard economic practices from submission to such a general survey of human values ... to keep economics within the limits of quantitative measures of markets, and to prevent the intrusion of ethical considerations into its field.
>
> (Hobson 1988 [1938a]: 32)

Hobson's conception of what political economy analysis should entail is a far cry from contemporary conceptions of professionalized political science that utilize the methods

101

of neo-classical economics. Hobson's critique of an earlier "new political economy," that of Mill, Jevons, and Marshall, was that its scope and method had not been "humanized." It fails to provide a framework through which to address "the Social Question," because it remains a "commercial science," "the Manchester framework still survives, but in a rickety condition" (Hobson 1988 [1901]: 34–39). The lifeblood of classical political economy is coursing through these veins. These are the perennial political economy insights which Strange "rediscovered," or rather re-emphasized, in 1970.

Hobson's insightful engagements with the interaction of the political and the economic, the domestic and the international were in evidence when arguing against protectionist tariffs against Germany in *The New Protectionism* (1988 [1916]: 168–72). It is Hobson's analysis of imperialism, however, which best illustrates his contribution to British IPE seventy years before it supposedly began. The political and foreign policy consequences of the advent of "the machine economy" generates "the economic condition of affairs that forms the taproot of Imperialism" (1988 [1938b]: 80–81). American "spread-eaglism" (imperialism) of his day was rooted in "the unprecedented rapidity of the industrial revolution in the United States from the eighties onwards" (1988 [1938b]: 74). The "economic nature of the new Imperialism" (1988 [1938b]: 71), Hobson argued, brought together "trusts", "combines" (what the Marxists termed monopoly capitalism) and an inability to find outlets for all the new capital, compounded by a crisis of over-production.

> it becomes more difficult for … manufacturers, merchants and financiers to dispose profitably of the economic resources, and they are tempted more and more to use their Governments in order to secure for their particular use some distant underdeveloped country by annexation and protection.
>
> (Hobson 1988 [1938b]: 80–81)

Imperialism amounted to "the endeavour of the great controllers of industry to broaden the channel for flow of their surplus wealth by seeking foreign markets and foreign investments to take off the goods and capital they cannot sell or use at home" (Hobson

Table 6.1 Externalist drivers of IPE research focus

	World order	Crisis	National money and the international system	Backdrop; framing	Problem(s)
US	US hegemony and the onset of *Pax Americana*	Vietnam	Role of the dollar under Bretton Woods: the Triffin dilemma	Cold War; economic performance compared to Japan, Germany.	The costs of hegemony; the US payments position
UK	Gold standard; empire; the end of *Pax Britannica*	Suez	Role of sterling under Bretton Woods: the sterling area, the sterling balances, devaluation	Decolonization; economic performance compared to France, Germany, US; decline and the British state; Thatcherism; labourism	Post-war reconstruction; the peculiar character of the British state; economic policymaking.

1988 [1938b]: 85). This dovetailed with Hobson's under-consumptionist account of a crisis of demand (and calls for domestic redistribution) as an alternative to imperialist policy (1988 [1938b]: 86). These dynamics also drove imperial policy in Great Britain, Germany, Holland, and France (1988 [1938b]: 79–81), generating enormous profits for "industrial and finance magnates" (1988 [1938b]: 78). Hobson's political objective was to change policy, and plot a different course for the British political economy. In the process he sought to dispel "the delusion that expansion of foreign trade, and therefore empire, is a necessity of national life" (1988 [1938b]: 91). That delusion, however, was very slow to be dispelled.

Driver number 2: the international politics of post-colonialism and British economic policy

British political economic debates throughout the twentieth century grappled with losing an empire, finding a role, and the place of the British economy generally, and sterling specifically, within that process. Although parochial in inspiration, such political economy became internationalized as a result of the world role of sterling and its political economic implications in the post-war world, a key focus of Brittan (1964, 1969), Conan (1952, 1961, 1966), Hirsch (1965) Manser (1971), Shonfield (1958), and Strange (1971) to name but a few British scholars writing in the 1950s and 1960s. The resultant international/domestic policy trade-offs and constraints became the central debates of the *proto-IPE* of British economic policymaking. This situated the domestic in the explicit context of the global political economy, and assumed the intimate interweaving of the political and the economic.

Perhaps the most significant policy-oriented work explored Britain's post-war overseas investment position and policies, and the resultant domestic policy constraints arising from international political economic pretensions. Despite Keynes' warning of Britain's "Financial Dunkirk" (Keynes 1979/1945: 374, 410), to an extraordinary extent given the "austerity" of these times, Britain in the late 1940s rebuilt its overseas investments, while simultaneously spending very large sums on international military and strategic goals (Cairncross 1986; Tomlinson 1996). Increasingly in the post-war era, capital mobility was recognized by the government to be a problem, because of the frequent foreign exchange crises, driven predominantly by short-term capital flows, not the current account (Hirsch 1965: 47–48).

Public criticism of the dominant analysis, and the underlying assumptions about the appropriateness of the UK's international payments situation, emerged from the 1950s. Authors such as Shonfield (1958), supported later by Hirsch (1965) and Strange (1971), argued that Britain was over-reaching itself internationally. Excessive government spending overseas, excessive overseas investment, but above all policies of defense of the role of sterling and adherence to the sterling area led to too much focus on financial confidence at the expense of domestic policy goals. These critics interpreted Britain's recurrent balance of payments problems as a result not of a lack of competitiveness, but of post-imperial "overstretch" of British resources. This "delusion of grandeur" (1958: 97), Shonfield argued, led to military and strategic decisions taken "with a deliberate disregard of their economic cost" (1958: 98).

The overstretch thesis saw Britain as adhering hubristically to an unsustainable status for sterling. Shonfield identified "a national attitude based on a historic view of Britain's role in the world, which leads to a succession of political decisions of an extremely costly character ... a deliberate decision to live beyond one's means" (1958: 91). Britain's post-imperial military and strategic reach exceeded its post-war fiscal grasp, a problem exacerbated by pretensions to international leadership in the economic sphere, the international role of sterling, and the "responsibilities that go with the headship of the sterling area" (Shonfield 1958: 103–4). This account gained plausibility in a global political economic context of increased capital mobility as sterling was progressively freed from controls in the 1950s.

Capital mobility meant that the authorities had to have increasing concern for the consequences of domestic policy for financial confidence. The UK government's response to this problem was to focus on trying to increase the current account surplus in order to build up the reserves and provide a bigger buffer against losses of confidence (Radcliffe 1958: para. 62). The export of capital on a large scale and high levels of government overseas expenditure were treated as "givens" in public policy pronouncements, so the issue was how these could be financed (Schenk 1994: 89–93; Tiratsoo and Tomlinson 1998: 24). Military expenditure abroad (as well as colonial grants and subsidies to foreign countries) and excessive foreign investment generated balance of payments strains (Shonfield 1958: 105–6), thus "converting a thoroughly healthy balance of payments into a kind of national anxiety neurosis" (Shonfield 1958: 123). The "displacement" of attention from the capital to the current account treated the latter as a "problem" even though it was in substantial surplus (Middleton 2002: 105–7; cf. Paish 1956). The substantial domestic economic policy strain this entailed could only be relieved, Shonfield argued, if those delusions of grandeur surrounding Britain's international leadership "pretensions" could be surrendered (1958: 107).

The exemplar of Britain's international financial role constraining its domestic economic policymaking was the sterling area. This complex web of networks, institutions, undertakings and obligations inherited from Britain's nineteenth-century world central banker role made Britain a "gentleman banker much reduced in circumstances, with clients who continue to deposit their money with the firm largely because of tradition and habit, [who] has to keep up appearances by handing out a certain amount of largesse each year" (Shonfield 1958: 128). In the 1950s, the sterling area involved an "ever open door for capital movements out of London" into the sterling area, and the right of sterling area governments to borrow on the London capital market. Both were "integral to the system" of the sterling area (Shonfield 1958: 123–26), thus "one of the conditions of for British leadership is that Britain shall continue to supply the bulk of the foreign capital required by these [sterling commonwealth] countries" (Shonfield 1958: 135). The capital export required to keep the sterling area afloat, Shonfield argued, had a deleterious effect on British productive investment, as well as putting a strain on the balance of payments (Shonfield 1958: 123–30; Conan 1961: 29).

Challenging the rationale of the sterling area, Shonfield argues "Britain staggers along holding a heavy umbrella over someone else's head" (1958: 150). The sterling area as "the focal point of British financial policy" was rooted in "the obsession with the status of sterling as an international currency", starving British industry of investment to keep the flow of capital into (the richer) sterling area countries (1958: 155–60). The enduring governmental and official attachment to sterling as an international currency, Shonfield concludes, entails "a number of activities, which render [Britain's] economic life intolerably exposed to international pressures" (1958: 160). Conan also questioned the assumption of enduring "dominant policy objectives" of "the maintenance of confidence in sterling and the creation of an adequate external surplus" (1961: 15). The burdens of the sterling system on the British economy, and London's role as international banker and investor, Conan argued, meant that "the reserve crises encountered by the United Kingdom in post-war years could be attributed to its responsibilities as the focal point of the sterling area" (Conan 1961: 25). For Conan as for Shonfield, muddled thinking about Britain's place within world order was at the root of a range of economic policy constraints, international (or post-colonial) in origin but primarily national in implication (Conan 1961: 1–2, 11, 30).[7]

Driver number 3: the political economy of decline

The debate about British decline provides a good (perhaps even the primary) example of how a diversity of political economy scholarship emerged from grounded engagement with a policy debate that became louder as the twentieth century progressed. At its height—from the late 1950s through to the late 1980s—the question of decline was elemental to the discourse of public intellectuals in Britain (Gamble 2000: 1) and became a matter of adversarial contest within inter- and intra-party politics (Coates and Hillard 1986). The preoccupation with decline reflected an anxiety, voiced across the political spectrum, that various elements of the British political economy were in crisis or that, along a range of indices, Britain was falling behind its established and emerging competitors (Crafts 1997; Pollard 1982). Various locations along the political spectrum brought with them alternative understandings of decline and competing diagnoses of its causes. Conservative imperialists would bemoan Britain's fall from world power status, neo-liberals would perceive a political system atrophied by the power of organized labor, and social democrats would despair at the dominance of the City of London and financial interests at a time when British manufacturing industry was in urgent need of modernization and investment.

These political debates in Britain concentrated on identifying various symptoms of decline together with pinpointing appropriate or critiquing inappropriate policy choices. The trajectory of the equally divisive academic debates moved from discussing symptoms to thinking through a range of long-term secular trends and institutional path dependencies that accounted for British decline. Although more obviously academic contributions were by no means immune from diagnosing moments of incorrect policy choice by specific governments at specific junctures, one of the striking characteristics of such work was its widespread tendency to focus on the pathologies of the British state as background explanations for crises in the present.

Take Marquand's famous thesis which links economic underperformance to the absence of a "developmental state" in Britain (1988). For Marquand the lack of directive and strategic public authority is not a simple matter of irrational or erroneous policy-making, but rather an indication of a deep-set ethos within the institutions of government that offers no space for notions such as "public intervention" and the "public realm" (1988: 11). Such work understands the solution to economic underperformance as resting not with the application of particular forms of doctrinaire politics, but rather with a program of constitutional reform that attacks the short-termism, majoritarianism, and dissensus that prevent a more developmental ethos from emerging (cf. Hutton 1995).

The arguments of historians like Barnett (1972) and Wiener (1981) look within the nineteenth-century British state to discover an anti-scientific and un-technocratic institutional culture. This, in turn, yielded amongst the elite a backward-looking ambivalence—bordering on cultural hostility—toward enterprise and the pragmatic modernization

105

imperatives of industrial capitalism. Wiener's point is that to understand contemporary "underperformance", we need to understand the historic success of the British state in containing the "cultural revolution of industrialism" (1981: 158). Barnett's (1972) argument is more expansive, focusing for example on the paradoxes of an educational system that trained the political elite in private institutions ("public schools," inherently suspicious of industrialism and bourgeois values) while failing to deliver practical, technical training for the emerging managerial classes. This latter problem was exacerbated by the widespread discourse of the "practical man" in industry itself—a view that preferred the educational value of on-the-job experience over formal technical training. Barnett's work sought to show—to some extent like Marquand—that the British state from the nineteenth century was empty of any impulse to think strategically how best to secure national competitiveness. Instead it was quite good at foreign policy and imperialist adventurism. For Barnett this was never better illustrated than in the aftermath of World War II, when Britain was well placed to re-ascend to a position of industrial leadership, at least in Europe. Barnett's view is that the opportunity, augmented by American credit, was wasted because the elite opted to engage in a politics of idealism rather than a politics of strategic pragmatism (1986).[8]

Perhaps the earliest and most systematic attempt to bring these themes together took place within the pages of *New Left Review* from the early 1960s as a group of Marxist historians sought to explore in depth the character of British capitalism. The so-called Nairn-Anderson thesis (Anderson 1964, 1987; Nairn 1964, 1976, 1981a, 1981b) held that Britain did not achieve a full or complete bourgeois revolution. This school understands the turbulent period in the seventeenth century between the Civil War in the 1640s and the establishment of the Hanoverian monarchy and the Glorious Revolution (1688) as Britain's moment of transition from feudalism. As Nairn puts it, the culmination was "a primitive capitalist state, frankly oligarchic and patrician in character" (1981a: 38). Anderson's exhaustive analysis (1964, 1987) posits that this state, while removing the institutional, practical, and normative obstacles to the development of capitalist relations of production, was nevertheless founded on a bizarre fusion of bourgeois and landed interests. This left significant residues of pre-democracy within the British constitution and facilitated Britain's historic allegiance to circulating/financial rather than manufacturing/industrial capital (see also Glyn and Sutcliffe 1972). In terms reminiscent of Hobson (1988 [1938b]), Hobsbawm argued (1969: 162) that late nineteenth-century Britain was developing into a "parasitic rather than a competitive economy," living off its imperialist accumulation strategies and acting as an exchange house for global flows of capital rather than as a productive source of capital itself.

This (more or less) academic literature reached its zenith in the 1970s and 1980s and emerged independently of any explicit moves toward IPE in the US disciplinary mainstream. Its prominence at this time was evidently connected to the furious debate amongst the British political class over decline, a debate which peaked in the early years of Thatcherism (Coates and Hillard 1986). But the academic peak of the decline debate—in all of its historical, comparative, and international finery—was, as Gamble (2000) notes, the progeny of a century-long series of controversies that date from anxieties about the rise of newly industrializing countries (Germany and the US mostly) which pre-occupied Hobson in 1902, through attempts to think through the implications of the altering international balance of power in the inter-war period, to the beginnings of projects to modernize the British political economy in the early 1960s. The rich scholarship on these debates produces results that are all too familiar to students of contemporary debates about globalization. For example, Friedberg's (1988) detailed analysis of the policy dilemmas at the turn of the twentieth century reveals a political elite seeking to grapple with the related problems of relative economic decline and imperial overstretch, while constrained by (a) the ideational frames of the day (free trade versus protectionism), (b) their limited ability to measure the extent of Britain's power or of its decline, and (c) a powerful concern about the domestic social costs/legitimacy of securing international competitiveness.

It is difficult to classify the main academic contributions to the decline debate in terms of precise disciplinary locations. They are used, cited, and taught in a variety of fields. This type of work corresponds to a definition of political economy that insists upon the analytical inseparability of social, political, and economic relations. The need for deep historical analysis is also more than apparent and it is no accident that much of the debate sketched here was driven by historians. The fact that these debates concentrate upon the British case might be thought of as excessively idiographic and driven by parochial policy problems rather than by a quest for general theory building. But it is important not to mistake historicism for thick description and in any case this work, because of its atten- tiveness to *relative* economic decline, is inherently and necessarily comparative. It is also profoundly international, woven into an account of the global political economy, as noted above, through the role of sterling, which fostered the widespread recognition that questions of economic performance are a function of a state's intersection with the dynamics of global capitalism.

Driver number 4: there never was a need to "bring the state back in"

As the discussion of the decline debate shows, a good deal of British political economy scholarship was centrally concerned with the character of the British state and the deri- vative hypothesis that economic underperformance was in some way related to that state's peculiarities. Decline was thus posed as (a) a classic political economy problem, (b) a matter to be resolved through historical analysis, and (c) an issue that could be better understood via an unpacking of the very qualities of stateness itself. The difference from much mainstream American IR-variant IPE is obvious. The latter, in its neoliberal and neorealist versions, has tended to treat the state as a rational agent navigating the struc- tural condition of anarchy and being exposed to respective logics of absolute or relative gains (Keohane 1984; Powell 1991; Waltz 2001). Of course, the literature on British decline has not at all been disinterested in the rationality (or irrationality) of state action, but its method has been to unpack the sociological, historical, and cultural sources of that (ir)rationality. The presiding question has been less to do with problems of domestic preference formation or the deduction of interest in light of geopolitical imperatives, but rather the degree to which the historical resolution of social and economic struggles has become inscribed upon the state and predisposes it to certain types of action. This is a political economy premised on an organizational view of the state (Burnham 1994). To understand this distinctive quality of analyses of the state within the British intellectual context, we need to attend to two important contextual factors: the distinctive quality of British political science/studies as it evolved in the first half of the twentieth century and the prominence of a vibrant historical materialist scholarly tradition.

On the first of these, the British study of politics is often thought of in terms of an evolutionary pathway that is quite distinct from that found in the US. In particular, the British version of political science is frequently characterized as lacking the disciplinary zeal of its American cousin (Hayward et al. 1999; for a more nuanced view cf. Kenny 2004). This had two implications. The first was that for many of its practitioners in Britain, the study of politics could not and should not be separated from the analysis of history, law, and philosophy (Kavanagh 2003: 598). The study of politics or political theory as it took shape in British universities by the 1950s might be seen in terms of a neo-Aristotelian project of classifying different government types via the analysis of either legal texts or philosophical treatises (Adcock and Bevir 2007: 211). The second implication was that British political studies was much less affected by what Bevir (2006) calls the "modernist empiricist" tendencies that produced movements like behavioralism in the US academy during the 1950s and early 1960s. Such tendencies, described by Bartelson (2001) as attempts to "excommunicate" the state from political analysis, barely took hold in Britain. Kavanagh (2003: 69) suggests that much of what enabled the founders of political studies in Britain to find common cause was a generalized discomfort with the nineteenth-century Whiggish view of state neutrality. In other words, even if some approaches to the state in Britain were overly historical-descriptive in character, the British state was never discounted as a serious object of study and there were no successful attempts to displace the project of "successive attempts to locate new data and new concerns in relation to the Westminster model" (Bevir 2006: 590). There was no need—as was the case in US-based comparative political economy in the 1980s—to proselytize on behalf of *Bringing the State Back In* (Evans et al. 1985) because it had never really gone away (cf. Cammack 1989).

The second tradition that ensured a key place for the state was the space allowed within British social science for a lively Marxist tradition. If by the 1950s, some forms of historical materialism worked with a heavily reductionist conception of the state, the same could not be said of the lively currents of anti-Stalinist Anglo-Marxism that emerged as part of the "New Left" in the mid-1950s (Kenny 1995). Drawing its inspiration from a diverse range of thinkers such as Luxemburg, Trotsky, Gramsci, Lukács, and the Frankfurt Sschool and finding expression in the *New Left Review* (*NLR*—founded in 1960), the New Left became a major source of thinking about the nature of the state, whilst—as one of the founding figures put it—looking to remedy the "native deficiency" of pre-existing British historical materialism (Anderson 1976: viii). The Marxist tradition as practiced in journals like the *NLR* and *The Socialist Register* (founded 1964) was also heavily informed by the ongoing work of a very notable group of leftist/communist historians such as Eric Hobsbawm, E. P. Thompson, Christopher Hill, and Raphael Samuel. In other words, the discussion of the state that emerged in the work of Anderson and Nairn on decline (see above) and in influential book-length arguments such as Ralph Miliband's *The State in Capitalist Society* (Miliband 1969) was not located in fixed disciplinary coordinates and in so far as it was obviously *political* analysis, then it was also informed by a powerful historicism. Part of this, as Kenny suggests, meant that Anglo-Marxist scholarship on the state shared similar subject matter (albeit radically different conclusions) to mainstream British political studies: "the unitary state, institutional continuity, class compromise, bureaucratic neutrality, and ministerial responsibility" (Kenny 2007: 177).

The legacy of these two strands of thinking about the British state was a political economy tradition that produced work through the 1970s and 1980s by scholars (Gamble 1974; Jessop 1974; Leys 1983) whose later style of critical IPE owed much more to a grounding in the critical historical materialist debate and studies of British politics than any encounter with US IR-variant IPE (e.g. Gamble and Payne 1996; Jessop 2002; Leys 2001). The heated exchange between Miliband and Nicos Poulantzas on the capitalist state (Miliband 1970; Poulantzas 1969) brought to light the contrast between two quite distinct Marxist conceptions of the state—instrumentalist and stucturalist (Hay 1999: 164–67). Miliband's sociological approach to capitalist biases within the state almost certainly owed a good deal to the formative influence of Harold Laski (Newman 2006). Laski's analysis evolved from a defense of pluralism and an Aristotelian pragmatic theory of the state (Laski 1919) toward an encounter with a fully "political economy" understanding of the socio-economic foundations of state action and an allied defense of radical socialist change being enacted via the electoral seizure of the state machinery (Laski 1938). The Miliband–Poulantzas debate has also been the springboard for significant British contributions to political science. For example, Jessop's prolonged encounter with Poulantzas and regulation theory has yielded his strategic relational approach to the state (Jessop 2002).

Conclusions

The ways in which one reads the history of a field, far from being an insignificant or neutral exercise, are critical to the nature of, and the conditions of possibility for, that field in the present. By disturbing the conventional temporal border of IPE (1970 as year zero), we have been able to re-inspect and (re)admit significant scholarship from the (British) political economy tradition with distinctive epistemological characteristics and a tradition of engagement with a succession of economic policy problems. Treating British IPE primarily as a subfield of IR is, we have argued, problematic, because it cuts off discussion of the complex intellectual lineage of work that emerges within the British intellectual context. This tendency is reinforced, we suggest, by taking the early 1970s as the key foundational moment of IPE. This account has offered a broad, historicized, genealogy of British IPE, demonstrating a direct lineage back across two centuries to the classical political economy tradition. More explicitly, we have shown how the development of political economy analysis within Britain in the twentieth century fed into and nourished a British IPE approach. Both these overlapping timeframes depart from conventional approaches to describing the origins of IPE as a discipline.

We have sketched out the contours of the British academic culture in the social sciences. British IPE evolved in intellectual conditions of loose disciplinarity, multidisciplinarity, and a wide-ranging acceptance of and engagement with historical materialist approaches. These factors shaped the norms of conduct, admissibility, borders, and external relations of British IPE. The ready acceptance of greater epistemological diversity within British IPE is, we argue, both a considerable strength and a marked contrast to the norms of disciplinarity conduct and admissibility of US IR-variant IPE. British political economy has been driven by a set of distinctive (indigenous) external drivers, and these have combined with an equally distinctive set of internalist drivers to fashion a rich intellectual tradition.

The perceived relative economic decline of the British model of capitalism was perhaps *the* central policy preoccupation of political economy scholars in Britain in the post-war era. Although much of this scholarship was parochial in inspiration, rooted in delusions of grandeur about Britain's rightful place at the helm of world affairs, its ineluctably comparative character countered the tendency to parochialism, with Shonfield being perhaps its best example. Such British IPE comes at questions from the perspective of a political economist's interest in the international (global). It does what it says on the tin, looking at the changing IPE in part in terms of its relationship to (and implications for) the UK political economy. Debates surrounding the role of sterling, the Bretton Woods order, the international trading system and relations with Europe are couched in these terms. Empire, decolonization, relative economic performance, sterling's role in international politics, and the peculiarities of the British state and its analysis have shaped the concerns and focus of British proto-IPE, and these sets of debates left their legacy for how contemporary British IPE gets done.

Our tracing of some of the lineages of British IPE does not claim to map out British IPE in its totality. We do not seek to set in stone the limits of the possible for British IPE, or erect borders of our own regarding what is admissible. That, as we have argued, would be counter to the spirit and pluralism of the British IPE tradition. Nevertheless, substantial parts of the body of contemporary British IPE scholarship can helpfully be situated in relation to the themes and antecedents we have outlined above. Thus, for example, the domestic policy implications of sterling's international role as mediated through the British balance of payments position (and its interpretation) have recently been re-examined by Clift and Tomlinson (2008). A focus on the politics of economic policymaking, and the place of Britain and sterling within the world order (rooted in a historical materialist conception of the British state) have been a feature of Burnham's work on Britain and the Bretton Woods order (1990, 2003; cf. Gamble 1985; Kettell 2004).

The state continues to be a central object of analysis within British IPE scholarship, and the distinctive quality of British IPE's analyzing of and theorizing about the state endures. The state, inscribed with the historical resolution of social and economic struggles, continues to be analyzed in terms of the sociological, historical, and cultural sources of its pathologies and particularities. Contemporary British IPE is arguably less parochial than its forbears; analysis of the British state coexists with comparative analysis of other state/ society complexes (Baker 1999; Breslin 2007: ch. 2; Clift 2003; Hay and Watson 2003; Hay et al. 2006; Jessop 2002; Pirie 2005, 2008; Thompson H. 1997, 2006).

The decline debates have to some extent dissipated, but this avenue of enquiry has evolved the late twentieth and early twenty-first century. We have seen a reinvigoration of many of the themes of the political economy of British decline in a more explicitly comparative framework, belatedly emulating the spirit of Shonfield's classic 1960s analysis. Thus comparative capitalisms has been a recurring theme of contemporary British IPE scholarship, analyzed with a conception of admissibility, conduct, borders, and external relations which departs in some respects from the dominant US *Varieties of Capitalism* approach (Hall and Soskice 2001b). The conception of the state at the heart of this political economy analysis echoes the approach to the state within British IPE outlined above, and this contrasts with the somewhat marginal place of the state within *Varieties of Capitalism*. Epistemologically, there is greater pluralism and less emphasis on formal modeling, and methodologically, there is no insistence upon microfoundations resembling neo-classical economics (Coates 2000, 2005; Clift 2007; Crouch 2003; Gamble 2003, 2004; Hay 2004b; Perraton and Clift 2004; Radice 2004; Thatcher 2007; Thatcher et al. 2007; Thompson, G. 2004; Watson 2003).

British imperialism per se is not, for understandable reasons, a central focus of contemporary British IPE, but analysis which evokes aspects of that intellectual tradition continues to shape parts of the British IPE research agenda in two ways. First, in the form of meditation upon Britain's post-imperial relation to and place within world order, albeit now framed in terms, not of imperialism, but "after empire" (Gamble 2003:

77–82, 220–25; cf. Burnham 2003). Second, exploration of the political economy of American power and its significance and impact within world order has been a theme of contemporary British IPE analysis (Bromley 1991, 2008; Thompson G. 2004; Thompson H. 2007), just as the exploration of British power within the world order in the nineteenth and early twentieth centuries was central to the earlier British proto-IPE outlined above.

Our central thesis is that by claiming 1970 as the temporal boundary of IPE and IR as its intellectual homeland, conventional accounts of the field miss not only the complex intellectual lineages that feed into the subject, but also open up (and more importantly close down) possibilities for the field in the present. Our problematization of an identifiable tendency in IPE's self-narration has as its goal not just to disturb that narrative, but to disturb some of the implications in the present for admissibility, conduct, borders, and external relations within British IPE. This re-evaluation of the past and the origins of British IPE permits a re-describing of its present, to include works which might be overlooked were it to be conceived in narrow 1970-as-year-zero or IPE-as-subfield-of-IR terms. The above rereading of the intellectual history of British IPE has been designed in part to readmit valuable, neglected elements into British IPE's big tent.

Notes

1 Some identify 1971, when she founded the IPEG group of BISA, as the key creational moment.
2 IPEG—the International Political Economy Group—was founded in 1971, a full three years prior to the formal constitution of BISA.
3 For example, Cohen's odd and empirically unsustainable claim that "British" IPE has its partial roots in the English School tradition of IR (Cohen 2007: 212; 2008b: 60).
4 Indeed, arguably such a conception of "British" IPE could claim ownership of fellow travelers such as Immanuel Wallerstein, and other historical materialist US-based scholars who do not situate themselves explicitly within IPE, and certainly not within "American IPE".
5 Cammack has recently argued that the ironically uncritical "me-clever-you-stupid" (Smith 2000: 379) acceptance of the Coxian distinction between critical and problem-solving IPE has allowed British IPE "to be hegemonized by '"US' IPE" (2007: 2, 3–7). We would certainly agree with him that much great and valuable political economy scholarship is motivated by (policy) problems, but that in no sense makes it not critical (in a Coxian *or* a commonsense understanding of the term).
6 For general treatments of Hobson see Freeden (1988), Clarke (1978: ch. 7), Thompson (1988: 262–66; 1994).
7 Manser's political economy was also concerned with dichotomies of domestic and international, state and market. He explored the appropriate role for the public and the private sectors in Britain's international transactions (1971). Manser emphasized a dichotomy between the international transactions of the private sector (which earned a surplus), and those of the government (which generated a deficit). His central thesis was clear: "if there were no Government spending, there would be no deficit, and no balance of payments problem." (1971: 30). Manser's argument of government extravagance obscuring the success of the private sector was stimulated by the recurrent balance of payments crises of the 1960s, culminating in the traumas surrounding devaluation in 1967.
8 Some economic historians have even asked whether Britain was ever a proper industrial manufacturing economy. This is the argument of Rubinstein (1993), who suggests instead that British capitalism was always more commercially and financially oriented. In a sense the educational–cultural pathologies identified by Wiener and Barnett were actually functional fits for this type of economy.

7

Empiricism and objectivity

Reflexive theory construction in a complex world

Angus Cameron and Ronen Palan

Introduction

In what promises to be an influential anthology of the discipline of international political economy, Benjamin Cohen identifies two competing perspectives, or schools of IPE: the American and the British (Cohen 2008c; and in this volume, Chapter 1). Interestingly, perhaps the most significant difference between the two schools for Cohen comes down to their divergent perspective on theory and theory construction. The American school of IPE is closely associated with American political science and as such is often regarded (usually critically) as sharing that discipline's inclination toward positivist empiricism. American IPE has a clear and unambiguous concept of theory construction as an accumulated process of knowledge. It thus imports the rather optimistic notion at the heart of any conventional scientific endeavor, that knowledge is incremental and slowly but surely approximates some universal truth. In Cohen's words:

> In the "American school," priority is given to scientific method—what might be called a pure or hard science model. Analysis is based on the twin principles of positivism and empiricism, which hold that knowledge is best accumulated through an appeal to objective observation and systematic testing.
>
> (2008c: 7)

The British school, by contrast, is far more eclectic, critical, and passionate. Cohen is rather fond of this strand of IPE because it never forgets the big questions. But, he adds, "The British school may be fairly criticized for its less rigorous approach to theory building and testing, which makes generalization difficult and accumulation of knowledge virtually impossible" (2008c: 16). Cohen's suggestion that British school IPE lacks rigor is perhaps borne out by the recent experiences even of some of its members. One of the more innovative contemporary thinkers in this tradition, Jonathan Nitzan, recalls an encounter he had at one Marxist conference:

> I criticized one of the presenters on my panel for dealing with pseudo-facts. She provided a theory for why neoliberalism has made the world more unstable yet

without first demonstrating that the world *indeed* has grown more unstable, or at least that our senses tell us that it has. I used several charts with fairly simple indicators for unemployment, growth rates, and the stock market to show that the neoliberal period of the 1980s and 1990s was neither more nor less unstable than the earlier postwar years. My statistical intervention was not challenged. Instead, it was deemed irrelevant: "What are facts?!" lashed back the flabbergasted theorist (yes, in these very words). Facts were time consuming, problematic, and ambiguous. Worse still, they were merely "constructed" by rulers to impose their power, so why bother?

(Nitzan and Bichler 2006: 3)

One of us (Palan) had a similar encounter at another conference where members of the panel were discussing the merits of constructivism. When they were challenged over their rather cavalier application of Lacanian and other psychological theories of the subject to such psyche-free entities as states, the brusque response was that such questions were out of order. "Constructivism," the discussant on that panel insisted "was whatever you wanted it to be." It is this kind of anything-goes approach that has, in our view, done much to undermine the credibility of the British school. This rather facile adoption of extreme relativism (in the name of anti-essentialism) leads to much critical theoretical work being dismissed—often with ample justification—for its obscurantism, indeterminacy, voluntaristic idealism and/or ahistoricism.

The incidents cited above are probably the exception rather than the rule, but nevertheless demonstrate precisely the less rigorous approach to theory and theory construction identified by Cohen. Since this debate is taking place within the so-called British school itself, however, Cohen's blanket assertion is not entirely accurate. This raises some important questions. First, if the rather cavalier approach to theory Cohen identifies is not in fact endemic to the British school, how is theory being developed in more positive and rigorous ways within the tradition? Second, since this more rigorous work is clearly not moving in the direction of American political science, what implications does it have for the nature of IPE? Third, does it therefore offer the possibility of an IPE that is simultaneously critical and rigorous both in theoretical and methodological terms? If so, and clearly we think this to be the case, why is it still so easy to characterize British IPE as a kind of plucky amateurism against the allegedly more rigorous scholarship of the American positivist tradition?

The answers to all these questions, we believe, center on some profound misunderstandings on all sides concerning the nature of empiricism. Despite its routine depiction as anti-empiricist by promoters and critics alike, the heterodox British tradition is, unlike its American counterpart, at heart solidly empiricist. Unlike American IPE which starts from an essentially positivist empiricism, the British, or, more appropriately, the British and European schools of IPE, adopt the fundamentally different and much more skeptical perspective that theories and the processes of their construction are themselves empirical objects. Far from being marginal, contradictory or cavalier, this mode of theorizing, which we might dub *critical empiricism*, is conceptually rich, rigorous (albeit in a different form to its counterparts), and has a long, sometimes rather surprising, heritage. Our aim in this chapter is, therefore, to take Cohen's criticism seriously and ask, how does one go about constructing reflexive and heterodox empirically rich theories and methodologies in a complex world?

Empiricism revisited: Hume and Deleuze

The real and the empirical

Notwithstanding the routine rejection of empiricism by those promoting post-positivism in general, certain strands of empiricism can be traced back to the early work of a scholar commonly associated with the more extreme ends of post-structural thought—Gilles Deleuze. Far from being hostile to empiricism, an examination of Deleuze's early writing reveals a close and critical engagement with earlier philosophers over its meaning and continued relevance. Deleuze's *Empiricism and Subjectivity*, first published in French in 1953, is an analysis of Hume's theory of human nature (Deleuze 1991). It proved to be extremely influential in the context of the development of French philosophy and post-structuralism in general. Deleuze retrieves from Hume an important strand of empiricist thought and method which was subordinated by nineteenth-century positivism, and which has been further obscured by more recent manifestations of naive anti-positivism. Deleuze's reading of empiricism is equally salient in interpreting other schools of thought, all of which are at the heart of contemporary heterodox IPE.

In conventional interpretations, empiricism is taken to be a form of social scientific enquiry that takes experience (the empirical) as the only legitimate subject-matter of social investigation. Humean empiricism is conventionally interpreted as implying that all knowledge must be based on sensory experience alone—understandable since throughout his work Hume relies on examples of the interaction of purely physical objects. Translated uncritically into the social sciences, Hume's physicalist empiricism is populated by institutions and processes treated as though their existence were entirely unproblematic—states, markets, firms, trades unions etc, are all regarded as *real*.

The problem is, of course, that sensory experience cannot identify those structural forces, habits of thought, deep socializations, and other intangibles that appear to determine a good portion of our individual and collective lives. Understood in this restricted and positivistic way, social scientific empiricism is often criticized for taking appearances at face value and failing to appreciate underlying properties that generate surface effects. By confining knowledge to pre-theoretical facts, positivist empiricism excludes entire categories of real events and dynamics. Although there is a long-standing debate in the philosophy of the social sciences from Kant to contemporary critical realism concerning the role of non-observable yet real structures and forces, positivism cannot account for the determining effects of such intangibles as emotion, fear, superstition, desire, greed, and so on.

Conflating the real with the empirical

Such criticisms, it has to be said, can be laid fairly and squarely at the door of American IPE. Despite intense concern with the finer points of methodology—i.e. how we go about enumerating and evaluating various pre-theoretical things—American IPE often displays a breathtaking lack of reflection on many of the key socio-cultural drivers of state form, power distribution, socio-economic structures, and so on. Observation is considered in and of itself an unproblematic proposition. Hence, the observed phenomena of IPE are treated as discrete, unproblematic and fundamentally knowable as unambiguously real.[1] The theories (which are in fact simple statements) that states are power-maximizing unitary actors or that individuals and corporations are utility-maximizing monads, are considered as self-evident truths—as empirical facts. Actors, from this perspective, whether individual, corporate or state, are not supposed to undergo any fundamental changes during the course of their interaction. Rather, they begin and end essentially the same, but modifying their behavior instrumentally when confronted by a superior opponent. From this point of view it does not seem to matter that the nature of stateness for the USA, Britain or Burma, say, has undergone important changes in the past 200 years—they remain states, and we already know what they are like. Similarly, there is little apparent appreciation that contemporary capitalism may be very different from the prevalent economic systems (global, national, regional) of say, the seventeenth or nineteenth centuries, or that the meaning of "economy" might be historically or spatially specific (cf. Mitchell 1998; Poovey 1998). It is perhaps because of this that the notion of structure is by and large absent from such accounts of the world. There are no theories of structural power, structural determinacy or structural change. Occasionally we hear of the concept of a system (such as the state system, the financial system the market and so on), but even then, these are conceived of from a methodological individualist perspective as a product of interaction of isolated actors.

Whilst it is easy enough to be critical of the absences from this essentially functionalist version of IPE, our purpose here is not simply to reverse Cohen's criticism to demonstrate that American IPE is not really empirical either. To do so, in addition to being rather pointless, would be to risk throwing the empiricist baby out with the positivist bathwater. A more searching exploration of empiricism reveals that neither IPE school has any claim to a monopoly of empirical rectitude. Similar observations, indeed, were precisely the point of Deleuze's engagement with the supposed source of this crude empiricism—David Hume.

Like Hume, Deleuze takes experience as the starting point for knowledge of the world and the meaning of the knowing subject within it, however this is not merely the experience of the senses. Indeed, Deleuze argues, Hume himself deploys "experience" in a way that certainly includes sensory perception, but which cannot be reduced to it. As he puts it:

> [E]xperience for the empiricist, and for Hume in particular, does not have this univocal and constitutive aspect that we give it. Experience has two senses, which are rigorously defined by Hume, and in neither of these senses is it constitutive. According to the first, if we call "experience" a collection of distinct perceptions, we should then recognize that relations are not derived from experience. They are the effect of principles of association … And if we use the word in the second sense, in order to denote various conjunctions of past objects, we should again recognize that principles do not come from experience, since, on the contrary, experience itself must be understood as a principle.
>
> (Deleuze 1991: 107–8)

While Deleuzean empiricism recognizes the importance of experience and observation in social investigation, it roundly rejects the confusion between experience and explanation. For the genuine empiricist like Hume, the method of observation and experience is not to be confused with the assumption that observation and experience are unmediated. There is always another important element in the production of knowledge: the sphere (or indeed, spheres) of mediation that must be taken account of in the relationship between the observer and the observed. Deleuze considers himself an empiricist in the sense that he gives priority to observation and experience, but also because he pays equal attention to the mediating processes (language, concepts, habits, historical institutions, etc.) that allow us to reconstruct not only that phenomena exist, but how they come to exist in the form that they do and how we (as observers, analysts or simply people) participate in that existence.

The real and the empirical as mediated constructs

The critical difference between a natural and social scientific empiricism is that all processes of knowledge-mediation are double-edged. Belief systems are not simply refracted expressions derived from neutral and passive observations, they also contribute to the shaping of the observed—they help constitute the subject. For example, the fact of a divine being has served humanity as a key explanatory concept for many observed phenomena—rain, sun, day, night, death, life, and so on—for many millennia. It still does for many people in many parts of the world. Although not itself directly observable, and therefore, in positivist empirical terms, theoretical, divine beings continue to have tremendous real effects on human history. George W. Bush's presence in the White House (at the time of writing) and the efforts of his many opponents in places such as Afghanistan, Iraq, Iran, Pakistan, and so on, are all in part attributable to the material effects of the belief in divine beings. Similarly, and of more immediate interest perhaps, it is easy to reject such ambiguous ideas as "nation," "working class," "utility maximization," "culture," or "masculinity" for the artificial human constructions they undoubtedly are. However, for all their artificiality each of these categories has in one way or another profoundly affected human behavior and is, therefore, in one sense, real. The social world, in other words, is fundamentally reflexive—it is influenced by belief systems and any empirical work must take account of the power of concepts in shaping the observed. How can an empiricism that takes no account of this reflexivity be considered empirical?

To return to Deleuze and Hume, despite the former's insistence to the contrary, in our view Hume does prioritize sensory experience in the ontology of human understanding he develops. Even when he does venture into the consideration of the social, his analogies are those of billiard balls, marble slabs, stones, pieces of metal, and so on. Whilst for critics of positivism this is more than enough to condemn Humean empiricism, they miss the point that even within his underlying materialism, Hume's ontology is profoundly associational and relational.

The idea of an associational ontology was brought into sharp relief by Martin Heidegger's analysis of the emergence of Newtonian physics. Heidegger demonstrated that the key to Newton's revolution in science was not a new theory but a new ontology: that of *every body*. Armed with this new ontology, "the distinction between earthly and celestial bodies has become obsolete. The universe is no longer divided into two well-separated realms ... all natural bodies are essentially of the same kind" (1993: 286). Only when all bodies were considered to have a uniform mode of existence within a common, abstract space could Newton contemplate the possibility of *general* laws of physics. Regarding the empirical content of Newton's physics, this is a subtle but important point. Newton did not possess superior powers of observation; there was nothing that he was able to see that was in principle unavailable to his predecessors. It was not any change in sensory experience that made possible the movement toward experimental physics, but a new association of ideas.

In a similar vein, the reality of an economy is only identifiable because various economic things (some of which are not things in the material sense at all) are brought together—are explicitly associated—in the complex concept "economy," again situated in an homogeneous abstract space (Lefebvre 1991a). Such associational concepts are never self-evident, but emerge at particular times and places and evolve over time. It is for this reason that historical and evolutionary institutionalism holds that the social field is heterogeneous or layered, consisting of an array of institutions and institutional arrangements with only a degree of coherency among them. The clear implication of this is that to be properly empirical a theory of economics must be critical and historical and not universal (cf. Palan 2008). Again, associational ontology is the key to the subsequent empirical theories that emerge.

Of these, the idea of relationality is central because, as Hume goes to great lengths to explain, whilst knowledge may have its origins in sensory experience, "all ideas" are connected through three relational principles of "Resemblance, Contiguity and Causation" (Hume 1999). Whilst these relational principles also constitute the foundations of natural scientific analytical techniques, for Hume they are as applicable to poetry and history as they are to the physical world. Indeed, Hume is very clear as to the significance of a reflexive relationality in order that ideas may not "resemble more the ravings of a madman, than the sober efforts of genius and learning." He continues:

> As this rule admits of no exception, it follows, that, in narrative compositions, the events or actions, which the writer relates, must be connected together, by some bond or tye [sic.]. They must be related to each other in the imagination, and form a kind of *Unity*, which may bring them under one plan or view, and which may be the object or end of the writer in his first undertaking.
>
> (Hume 1999: 102)

The fundamental reflexivity which Hume insists upon with respect to the comprehension and production of knowledge is strikingly different from the caricature of empiricism that later finds expression in logical positivism. Hume, places the relational function of the imagination squarely at the heart of empiricist knowledge.

There are indeed some good empirical reasons to take a somewhat skeptical view of our methods of theory construction. Some of our very basic concepts in the social sciences, many of which we take for granted, including the notion of experience that empiricists are so fond of, are in fact learned ideas, appropriated by one field of study as a metaphor from another. The development of the field of anatomy, for instance, was crucial in shaping modern epistemology.

Early political treatieses in the sixteenth and seventeenth century often used anatomical or anthropomorphic imagery: e.g. William Petty's 1691 *The Political Anatomy of Ireland*. Such metaphors are not neutral, but are culturally rich concepts, heavily imbued with significations, shaping perceptions of the subject at hand. Anatomical metaphors have also shaped our concept of money and the financial *system*. Money and finance were conceived in the sixteenth century to be analogous to the circulation of blood in the human body. Indeed, we still talk today of monetary "circulation" and "liquidity" (Lowry 1974; Neocleous 2004) and of money and taxes as the "sinews of power" (Brewer 1989). The best known and most influential expression of this came in Hobbes' anthropomorphic image of the state as analogous to a "natural man"—the *Leviathan* (1968).

Whether these inherited and firmly ingrained anatomical metaphors are accurate or appropriate is a matter of debate. However, there is no escaping the influence they have had on thinking about the corporeal nature of political economies and we need,

117

therefore, to maintain a critical attitude not only to the subject of investigation, but also to the concepts, ideas, categories, and metaphors that shape our thinking about the world *out there*. A critical empiricism therefore advocates skepticism as a mode of investigation and not merely a means of deconstruction.

Deleuze sums up the philosophical position of empiricism in full agreement with Hume: "In fact, empiricism is a philosophy of the imagination and not a philosophy of the senses" (1991: 110). Indeed, he goes further, flatly contradicting the conventional reading of empiricism, by declaring: "We will call 'nonempiricist' every theory according to which, *in one way or another*, relations are derived from the nature of things." (1991: 109). This is a critical point, capturing the very heart of the epistemological debate between positivist and critical empiricist methods.

Imagined political economies

Reality and fiction

The idea that empiricism is a philosophy of the imagination and not of the senses may appear counter-intuitive, but it is fundamental to the meaning and efficacy of heterodox social science. It is empiricist in the sense that it is still based on an observational methodology, but that which is observed is a *constructed* world emanating from the human imagination. Most important is the central importance of language and narrative to the constitution of what is described as social reality.

The unity that appears to us in thought is conferred by language; it is a product of the thinking subject, not to be confused with the subject of thinking. Humans act and behave within some notion of a totality, or an image of a world in which parts seem to fit together into some sort of a comprehensive picture, or a whole, a totality. Nelson Goodman's account of "worldmaking" may serve to illustrate the point:

> For the man-in-the-street, most versions [of the "real" world] from science, art, and perception depart in some ways from the familiar serviceable world he has jerry-built from fragments of scientific and artistic tradition and from his own struggle for survival. This world, indeed, is the one most often taken as real; for reality in a world, like realism in a picture, is largely a matter of habit.
>
> (1978: 20)

In this spirit, the message from Humean empiricism to naive positivism is not to confuse a reality lived and perceived with, as it were, the real thing. We know, through direct sensory experience, that when we watch TV we are watching nothing more than dots of light. However, what we know is not what we see because our mind cannot help but connect the dots up into a picture, and the successive pictures into a story. While positivism stubbornly refuses to see anything but dots, for a Humean empiricist both dots *and* story are valid empirical objects.

It is for this reason (rather confusingly for some) that the heterodox tradition treats the rise to dominance of rational choice theories as itself an important empirical fact. Many rationalists are infuriated and frustrated by the apparent unwillingness of their critics to play fair and use the rules of rational thought to argue for or against their methodology. For the heterodox school, however, bodies of theory are also products of historical times and places, and thus tell us something important because the *common sense* perceptions and habits of thought they invoke and/or create constitute the substrate of *real* power relationships.

The symbolic, the imaginary, and the real

Having established that empiricism need not be reductive or reactionary, we now turn to the issue that ultimately divides American IPE from its British counterpart—ontology. This is not necessarily to suggest that American IPE's ontological foundations are necessarily wrong or false.[2] Nor is it the case, following Hume and Deleuze, that all ontology, by making positive claims about the nature of the real, is therefore essentialist.[3] Rather, what we are confronted with in these two quite distinct traditions are very different ontological orders reflecting both their differing philosophical traditions and, perhaps more importantly, their different relationships to the state.

The traditions that believe we investigate the world of things assumes that we inhabit an essentially two-dimensional world: the world of the real and the world of reflection about the real (theory). The former necessarily takes priority, hence the appeal to empiricism. The latter is detached from the real, its role is limited to describing and/or exploring the real from a respectful distance with scientific tools. As American IPE appears to subscribe to such assumptions, it inherits from the so-called realist tradition of IR a cast of characters whose existence is not in need of critical enquiry. In fact, theory construction often means, in practice, taking for granted the nature of these characters— states and firms are utility maximizers analogous to the *homo oeconomicus* of orthodox economics, meaning both that they are all essentially alike and that they will behave in identifiable and predictable ways in particular circumstances.

The British critical empiricist tradition does not start from an assumed ontology but, rather, from the perspective that ontology is something to be explained and questioned. Where rigor is applied in this tradition, therefore, is not in enumerating pre-established categories to develop predictive behavioral theories, but in establishing the ontological ground appropriate to the problem at hand. This presupposes a more complex approach to ontology whereby it is regarded as immanent to the subject of enquiry rather than logically prior to it. To understand this apparently rather obscure point, and beyond it why heterodox IPE has the annoying tendency to pay attention to soft things such as imagination, social construction and discourse, we need to dwell briefly on another set of social theories, unavailable to Hume, but which has its origins with Freudian thought.

Within this tradition, the external world—the ontological—is apprehended only through a complex set of processes, mediating between observer and observed. The influential French psychoanalyst Jacques Lacan postulated three realms of apprehension, the *symbolic*, the *imaginary* and the *real* (cf. Wilden 1972). The symbolic is, among other things, language. We can only understand the world through language because we are incapable of experiencing the world directly. However immediately they may be produced, even inside our own perceptions, words, phrases, pictures, metaphors, and so on, are always representations of something. Language and communication, in other words, constitute a filtering process through which raw data is systematized and given meaning—meaning itself not being a feature of the object, but a feature of our associational perception of it. Since in order to function at all language must be a complete system, with rules of syntax, grammar, iconography, symbology, and so on, the world around us is perceived and apprehended through the medium of a symbolic order.

The Symbolic itself is constituted in another realm: the Imaginary. At this level of everyday discourse, the subject's relationship to the Symbolic is fundamentally mis-recognized—the order of the Symbolic is accepted as entirely transparent. In other words, the subject believes language (verbal and visual) to be a neutral instrument for the simple description of the Real, and not a symbolically dense and constraining system of comprehension. Thus it is, for example, that we can happily accept money tokens (coins, notes, etc.) as money itself, despite the fact that money in a credit-based capitalist system is intrinsically virtual (Maurer 2006). Even confronted with symbols that are no more than representations of other symbols, we routinely acknowledge their carefully con-trived materiality as constitutive of value because it seems to be *more real*. We even make our coinages look like gold, silver and copper/bronze to underpin their fictive materiality even though we know they contain no precious metals at all. The unreality of the Symbolic is not therefore recognized. Thus the Imaginary is both the primary site of comprehension of the Real and, simultaneously, a domain of illusion in which the Symbolic substitutes for the Real. As this implies, what we take to be reality at any given time or place is both emergent and fundamentally contestable. This does not, however, mean that reality has no empirical meaning.

For Lacan and others, although our way of existing in the world prevents us from knowing about the Real in any unmediated way, reality is nevertheless a necessary hypoth-esis without which we cannot function. We live our social, political and economic lives, indeed our physical existence, *as if* there is a real world *out there* and, whilst we may be able to reflect upon the contingent nature of this reality, cannot do otherwise. We may know that the housing market is a social construct rather than a product of the laws of economics, this is to say, but even the most ardent post-structuralists take out mortgages and are as annoyed as the rest of us when interest rates go up.

Whether one can ever arrive at a final definition of the real is a matter for intense philo-sophical debate. In pragmatic philosophy, which underpins much of heterodox thought, the real is fundamentally indeterminate, being actively remade by knowing and acting subject in the course of their daily lives. For others (such as the critical realists), whilst the real does not have the absolute character of a positivist empiricism, it is nevertheless present as an important element in the constraint of possibilities and the *construal* of outcomes (Sayer 1995, 2004). For the latter groups, the anything–goes approach of some of the more extreme ends of post-structuralism is ultimately defeated by a fundamental physical and social materiality which, however complex its mode of comprehension, cannot be reduced simply to imagineering and cannot be, therefore, be anything you want it to be.

The imaginary in neo-classical economics

At this point it might seem that we have fallen into precisely the same clever scholasti-cism that Cohen reproves for its lack of rigor. Even if there is a link between Hume and the early Deleuze over the question of empiricism, any appeal to Lacanian theories of the imaginary is likely to be dismissed for veering dangerously, or perhaps just irritatingly, far into the anything-goes camp. Yet, on reflection, even within the more sober and sci-entific end of the social sciences, the imaginary and the symbolic are of central concern. Indeed, it may come as somewhat disconcerting to the American branch of IPE to dis-cover that their own model of rigorous social-scientific endeavor, economic modeling within what is often described as the neo-classical tradition, operates within a mediated and associational environment.

Consider the important transformation that took place in economic thought in the late nineteenth century. Specifically, the transition from classical to neo-classical economics, despite the appearance of continuity, involved the adoption of what is essentially a post-structural ontology and a post-modern sensibility (cf. Ruccio and Amariglio 2003 for a much fuller account of this). We tend to think of neo-classical economics (or more appropriately, today's mainstream economics) as the logical continuation and development of classical economics—hence the prefix neo-. However, if we look beyond the super-ficialities of ascribed disciplinary inheritance, a more fundamental difference between the two appears with the adoption by neo-classical economists of an emergent and very different empirical foundation to that of their predecessors.

Classical economics, of which Marxist economics is an important strand, sought to anchor the central issue of economic thought and practice—its theory of value—in the real. Marx, for whom value was ultimately derived from real labor, adopted Ricardo's labor theory of value which grounded the entire economic system in concrete relations of production. Neo-classical economics, by contrast, significantly loosened this con-ceptual anchoring of the economic system to the real. The theory of marginal utility, for example, explicitly distances value from concrete factors of production, arguing that value is a product of complex (associational and relational) exchange relations mediated through the market. Marginal utility theory effectively tells us that however important real eco-nomic relations might be, the value of commodities or services is produced in the rela-tionship between availability and desirability articulated through the price mechanism. Value is a product of the expression, manipulation, and interpretation of human desire. This can be seen most clearly in the emergence (again in the late nineteenth century) of a whole set of service industries whose sole function was the generation and channeling of this desire: advertising, public relations, brand consultancy, market research, product design, and so on. It is for this reason that in contemporary business control of intellectual property—brand image, logo, software, trademark, trade name, website address, internet domain name, and so on—has gradually come to be more important (i.e. profitable) than control of the physical product—protected through the patent (May 2007).

Understood in this way, markets can be seen as having developed into complex media for the communication of human desire. This does not mean that the neo-classical conception of the market is imaginary in the sense of not being real, but that the reality of markets is one that articulates the central role of the imaginary in economic life. That these essentially fictional products and services are made real through the mathematics and algorithms of the hard science of economics does not, therefore, signify a progressive and problematic virtualization of the real economy (as some fear the internet has done; cf. Tanzi 2000)), but simply reveals the already and necessarily virtualized nature of capitalism. These ideas are taken to the very extreme by Lyotard (1993) whose arch-post-modernist theories of *Libidinal Economy*, with outrageous-sounding chapters like "Use me," "Nicomachean erotics," "Institutive prostitution," "Coitus reservatus," and so on, may seem light years away from the familiar and secure ground of economics. Lyo-tard in fact, is making the point, albeit in the most provocative manner possible, that economics is not a separate sphere of life in which we participate from time to time, but an intimate aspect of our daily life. Our behavior as consumers or producers of modern artifacts is, from an evolutionary psychological perspective, complex, often contradictory, and extremely demanding, contributing to various psychoses, including narcissism and schizophrenia. There is much more to the economy than conventional economics is capable of recognizing: lust, Lyotard is saying, is orthodox economics' dirty little secret.

121

Problems with the British school of IPE

To sum up what we have argued so far, British IPE is based in a profoundly different understanding of the nature of empiricism from that of American IPE, and this understanding has shaped the thinking of heterodox traditions in the social sciences. The British school of IPE is inherently and necessarily heterodox in its approach to theory construction. As such, all British school approaches draw on the traditions of critical empiricism which are founded on two central propositions:

(a) Heterodox theories of causality are necessarily associational, they begin from the *whole* social context of any subject of analysis: they are fundamentally holistic;
(b) They are, therefore, critically empiricist (at least in aspiration).

At this point we would suggest, and partly in agreement with Cohen, that while the British school can be regarded as essentially and properly empiricist, empiricism itself is scarcely understood, let alone debated within the school—at least not explicitly. This is despite the fact, as noted above, that key contributors to the development of the school—scholars such as Cox and Strange—have long described themselves as empiricist. At the very least we can say that the British school is intuitively empiricist in the sense described above—albeit often in a manner that is rather confused (indeed, claiming to be anti-empiricist) and therefore advanced with an apparent lack of rigor. The British school is thus marked by a fundamental lack of agreement over how the two primary aspects of empiricism—the nature and role of theory and the associational nature of knowledge— are to be incorporated into academic praxis. We will treat each in turn.

First, those writing within the tradition give primacy to the development of theory as integral to analysis of a subjective world over a priori theoretical constructs. Again, the difference from American IPE illustrates the point. American IPE tends to begin with a puzzle; the world *out there* somehow fails to behave as theory predicts (theory here understood to be objective because based on analysis of prior realities). For instance, according to neo-classical trade theory, free trade is assumed to generate a general good in the form of long-term equilibrium and is hence considered to be a rational policy. Why, then, do utility-maximizing states fail or refuse to adopt free trade policies? Approaches such as two-level game theory (Milner 1997; Putnam 1988) or Rogowski's (1989) rendering of collective action seek to answer this conundrum by employing the same rationalist model. The new theories are considered to constitute an advance because they somehow manage to resolve the puzzle by using (extending and/or adapting) existing theories. The assumption of rationalism is not in question—merely the data used to inform and/or explain rational behavior.

The British school, by contrast, rarely puzzles over the failure of theory to correspond to the world out there because theoretical constructs are not separate. We rarely encounter work, for instance, that seeks to validate empirically the neo-Gramscian concept of the hegemonic bloc. Even Susan Strange, despite her avowed empiricism, never provided conceptual tools for investigating the truth-claims of her theory of structural power. Nor do we find any developed validation (empirical, conceptual, analytical) of Cox's claims about the nature and functioning of international organizations. Cox's argument about the relationship between international organizations and overall power structures is certainly interesting and persuasive, but similar behavior and policies of the same organizations can be interpreted persuasively by different theories. Jason

Sharman's (2006) recent study of the OECD's and IMF's treatment of tax havens is a case in point.

There can be two interpretations of this lack of reflexivity in the (allegedly reflexive) British school. A negative reading is that far from being empiricist, critical or not, the British school gives primacy to theory over description and is, as a consequence, overly theoretical and abstract without adequate empirical (in the positivist sense) foundation. In the above-cited case of the neo-Gramscian hegemonic bloc, one typical treatment is to assume the existence of the bloc, the role of theory being to reinterpret the behavior and policies of states as a product of it. The empirical work, therefore, often seems to consist of no more than highly selective reading and data-collation in order to prove some a priori assumptions; namely, that there are social classes, they are in competition with each other, and that they are organized into hegemonic blocs. One can find similar theoretical circularities in relation to the concepts such as *neoliberalism, crisis* (cf. Cameron 2008) and so on, which are used liberally and without specification.[4] Any attempt at definition, let alone quantification of such concepts is treated, as Nitzan found out above, with disdain.

A more positive reading would say that at heart, the British school prefers to puzzle over the world *out there* as itself in part a product of theory, rather than some imputed and arbitrary relationship between world and theory presented as separate. On this reading, the starting point is contextual and critical observation, not pure theory. Free trade is not assumed to be innately good, but as a normative and power-laden discourse the meaning and impact of which differs in various regions of the world and over time. A number of British school writers have therefore developed much more historically and geographically nuanced explanations of the reorientation of many states' policy discourses and practices to be more "business-friendly" (cf. Cameron and Palan 2004,). They describe these changes in terms of the emergence of the "competition state" (Cerny 1990), the "Postnational Schumpeterian Workfare State" (Jessop 2002), and so on. These are theoretical generalizations born out of empirical observations—the questions asked being: what effect does partial internationalization/globalization of, say, finance and investment practices have on state form? What are the likely effects of new state forms on the meaning and nature of such concepts as society or citizenship, whose established meanings are rooted in other, older configurations of political economy? As such questions imply, there is no escaping the need to generalize, the difference being that these are derived from a holistic and empiricist "Critical Political Economy" (Jessop and Sum 2001) rather than a priori assumptions.

We agree with the above, but returning to Hume and Deleuze we would also argue that a critical empiricism gives priority to observation and experience. Data may be complex, and open to many interpretations, but there are no substitutes for data and observation even if we make them more complex. Unless this is recognized we find ourselves caught between two untenable positions, both of which we take to be non-empiricist. One (the American) is that data and observation are so unproblematic we can accept them as real; the other (the un-rigorous British) that data and observation are so problematic that we must dispense with them altogether.

A more careful critical empiricism can avoid these pitfalls by accepting that the concepts we use are both descriptive and heuristic; they do not assume to represent an unmediated real, hence, their value is historical and conjunctural; they are considered to be the best available until proved otherwise. For instance, one set of theories may describe the manner in which individuals adapt to their environment by the term *socialization*, another as *normalization* (Foucault), third as *habituation* (Veblen, Bourdieu). These concepts do not possess absolute but only relative value, operating within a grid that includes other, overlapping and contradictory, concepts. How do we evaluate the relative merits of these concepts? Critical empiricists of the Humean/Deleuzean type employ the old-fashioned method of reasoned assessment in light of observed evidence, but without assuming that the issue of theory is or can be finally settled: i.e. can be proved correct.

To give another example, Alain Lipietz (1987) maintains that dependency theory captured an important dimension of the relationship between advanced and developing regions between the 1930s and the 1970s. The concept of dependency is an excellent concept, according to him, in capturing the dynamics of the division of labor during that period. The mistake dependency theorists made, however, was to generalize this pattern and believe it was a theory of capitalism. In other words, dependency theory assumed that such relationships are endemic to capitalism, whereas empirical work could demonstrate otherwise: namely, that the pattern of relationships has changed quite dramatically since the 1970s. This is a classical case of employing the old-fashion method of rational assessment in light of observed evidence.

As argued above, this different construction of the nature of the empirical object of analysis is related to a second dimension of critical empiricism: the associational and relational nature of the real. The concept of US hegemony, for instance, has no innate value in and of itself. The concept attains value within a wider context of normative constructions of capitalism, modernity, power, imperialism, gender, and so on. We cannot validate empirically the reality of a US hegemony without also knowing the theoretical context out of which the concept is produced. US hegemony cannot be taken, therefore, as fact, but as a theory whose value is purely relational, emerging within the context of a theory. The role of theory in the heterodox tradition is, therefore, profoundly practical, which means, for instance, that the neo-Gramsican theory of hegemonic bloc must be argued and debated and shown to be of practical use. Its value lies in that it offers ways seeing and explaining social objects and their interrelationships. But it must be subject to the same type of empirical and rational valuation and assessment.

Conclusion

Due to these ambiguities and a general lack of proper understanding of its empiricist heritage, the record of British IPE is very mixed and we find both its negative and positive dimensions even within the same books and articles. That is why the British school can appear, even to its own insiders, as infuriatingly good and bad, full of innovation but still carrying too much disciplinary baggage, blessed with extraordinary insight but weighed down by facile anything-goes pronouncements. To that extent we, along with many others, share Cohen's frustration. However, and as suggested above, the point here is not that one version of IPE is right and the other wrong. Rather, it is but that the conception of the real to which they each appeal is fundamentally different and incommensurate. If we choose to pursue the richer explanatory potential of critical empiricism, this is because we regard the world *out there* as fundamentally emergent and incomplete and thus in need of both explanation and intervention. Embracing experience, belief systems, habits of thought and so on as empirical objects, therefore, is not just about producing a better (i.e. more complete) descriptive picture of the world. Empiricism in this sense is also a political choice.

Whilst this suggestion clearly echoes Marx's oft-quoted assertion that the role of the philosopher is to change rather than merely describe the world (something we both profoundly agree with), this does not lead inexorably into either orthodox Marxism (which has little or nothing to do with Marx) or to the often naive voluntarisms of extreme constructivist/activist IPE and/or social theory. And if this sounds an overly harsh on some of our British school colleagues, it is equally true of the American school. It too, as argued above, is thoroughly voluntarist—it really wants to believe that the world is, or at least can be, more like its theoretical models. To propose a critical empiricism as a political intervention seems odd at first hearing, but less so in light of all this wishful thinking. As we have argued elsewhere (Cameron and Palan 2004) politics is not just about what should be done, but what can be done—it is about the art of the possible. Whilst any judgment about the possible is necessarily subjective, it is less so to the extent that our analysis is rooted in some form of critical empiricism. We may not start from or ever finally reach any unambiguous truth, but we do at least engage thoroughly and enthusiastically in the messy complexity and contingency of that which constitutes the real.

Notes

1 The one exception to this perhaps is the state, which does receive a limited airing from time to time.
2 The classic case of such an accusation was Susan Strange's article "Wake up, Krasner!" (1994a).
3 Ironically, the routine dismissal of essentialism by many post-positivists itself constitutes an essentialism. Declaring that there is no secure basis for ontological claims is every bit as essentialist (and unhelpful) as declaring that the only basis for such claims is sensory experience.
4 As has been pointed out recently the term *neoliberalism* is hardly, if ever, used by those to whom its theorization and practice is attributed (particularly the Chicago school). Rather, it is a term mobilized by critics to categorize such disparate practices as Reaganomics, privatization, globalization, and so on, as though they were part of some grand design or conspiracy. As we have argued elsewhere with respect to globalization, neoliberalism is a monster reified in the imagination only of its opponents (Cameron and Palan 2004). On neoliberalism see Peck (2008).

8

Power-knowledge estranged

From Susan Strange to poststructuralism in British IPE

Paul Langley

If we are to consider the academic and intellectual consolidation of the field of international political economy (IPE) in Britain, then the contribution of Susan Strange is certainly worthy of specific attention. Strange came to academia after a successful career as a journalist, having been White House correspondent for the *Observer* newspaper at just twenty-three years of age, and a reporter for the *Economist* magazine. Whilst a senior research fellow at Chatham House, Strange co-founded the British International Studies Association (BISA) in 1974/5, and was the inaugural convenor of BISA's International Political Economy Group (IPEG). Aside from this institutional input and legacy, Strange's presence and personality also loomed large in IPE in Britain for three decades. As a doctoral student presenting my work at annual BISA conferences and IPEG workshops in the latter half of 1990s, I soon learned that it was *what Susan thought* that seemed to matter most. On her comments and questions appeared to hinge whether a conference paper or thesis would hold up. Indeed, on a personal note, I can recall my dismay following her remark at a panel session at the BISA conference in 1997 that she "could not make head nor tail of the Langley paper!" In the words of Strange's long-time collaborator Roger Tooze, IPE was "a subject that she made her own, at least in the UK if not in the USA" (1999: 280).

Strange's capacity to make IPE in Britain her own did not result solely from her enthusiasm for her chosen academic subject, and the considerable energies that she devoted to its institutional development. Susan Strange was also a remarkable writer who, through an extensive array of books, articles, and papers (May 2002), shaped the intellectual trajectory of IPE in Britain. And, for Strange, IPE in Britain had to be different from, and should seek to define itself against, the modes of IPE inquiry predominantly practiced in the United States. As Tooze suggests, it is possible to read Strange's work as a series of contributions that were "critical and dialectical interventions in the dominant practice of American IPE" (1999: 281). Strange's over-riding motivations in making such interventions were political. Her distaste for American IPE arose, first and foremost, from the ways in which she regarded it to produce knowledge in the service of the power of the United States and its foreign economic policy. Strange, in contrast, wanted to call the US to account for what she saw to be its misguided abuse of the privileged place that it occupied at the apex of the global political economy. In her terms, "our priority problematic as students of international political economy for as far ahead as it is possible to see … is to see how to persuade people and politicians in the United States to use the hegemonic, structural power they still have in a more enlightened and consistent way" (Strange 1990: 274).

For Strange, the American IPE that she often characterized, after the title of Joan Spero's (1977) book, as "the politics of international economic relations," was necessarily unfit for the political and transformative task that she had in mind. It was too narrow and closed, failing both to look beyond mainstream international relations (IR) and liberal economics for conceptual inspiration, and to question the associated hierarchical privileging of issues of trade and money. If Strange (1991) had her way, IPE was to be eclectic in conceptual terms. Such eclecticism was only possible if IPE was "open to the concerns and insights of a variety of disciplines and professions," and eschewed the "dialogue of the deaf" that was created by those in America IPE who slavishly followed IR's three main paradigms (1991: 33–34). Her peers in British IPE were in broad agreement. For example, the initial editorial statements of two journals launched in Britain the mid-1990s—*The Review of International Political Economy* and *New Political Economy*—called for heterodoxy and a broad-based renewal of political economy. Furthermore, for Strange (1986, 1990, 1998), recognizing and responding to the power of the United States required that an eclectic bag of conceptual tools was brought to bear, in particular, on the contemporary financial dominance of the United States. While she set a definition for IPE that seemingly ruled very little out of its empirical remit, it was nonetheless the "finance structure" that Strange felt should primarily occupy the attention of contemporary IPE scholars.

My aim in this chapter is not to trace the many ways in which the research and writings of Susan Strange came to frame the intellectual trajectory of British IPE. Commentaries on Strange's work from the mid-1990s (Cox 1996: 174–88; May 1996), and those that followed her death in 1998, aged seventy-five, successfully capture the rich and wide-ranging elements of her intellectual legacy (Brown 1999; Lawton et al. 2000; Leander 2001; Palan 1999; Tooze 1999). Rather, I want to concentrate on what many of these commentaries identify as the kernel of Strange's contribution—her focus on, and conception of, power and knowledge. I am interested, specifically, in the consequences that Strange's work on power and knowledge had for the engagements of British IPE scholars with a diverse body of philosophical and interdisciplinary work that I will label *poststructuralism*. In contrast to other fields in British academia such as sociology and geography, the engagement with poststructuralism in British IPE has been somewhat limited and slow to take hold. As Marieke de Goede has it, "It is possible to say that IPE has been particularly resistant to poststructural intervention" (2006: 1). Indeed, as Ronen Palan remarks, "many believe that political economy, including its international variant, stands as a bulwark against the ephemeral, fashion conscious, if not reactionary tendencies of the 'post-ies' in the social sciences" (2000: 215). For many scholars of British IPE, poststructuralism is alien, unfamiliar, and perhaps too unsettling and dangerous to contemplate.

I want, then, to make a two-fold argument here. First, as I will suggest in the opening section of the chapter, the limited and resistant engagement with poststructuralism in British IPE during the 1990s in particular can in part be understood to be a consequence of the grip of Susan Strange's intellectual interventions and, specifically, of her pioneering work on what she termed "structural power" and the "knowledge structure." Strange's work on power and knowledge was pivotal to her attempt to set the coordinates for a

British IPE that could be clearly differentiated from American IPE. Yet, Strange's writing on power and knowledge was somewhat paradoxical. On the one hand, Strange broke new ground, opening up previously settled conceptions of power to critical scrutiny, and raising questions about the significance of knowledge in the materialization of the global political economy. On the other hand, however, Strange's work re-settled the categories of power and knowledge in British IPE. She thus contributed to the insulation or estrangement of the field from debates about power taking place across the social sciences, debates in which poststructuralism and Michel Foucault's (1980) work on "power-knowledge" loomed large.

Second, I want to argue that recent moves to engage with poststructuralism are, somewhat ironically, carrying forward the spirit of Strange's vision of a British IPE that demarcates itself from its largely uncritical American other by exploring the relation of categories of power and knowledge. As such, the second section of the chapter sets out how Strange's vision of British IPE is beginning to thrive, albeit in a very different form to that which she would have recognized and, no doubt, approved. I focus on several poststructural interventions in British IPE that, despite their diversity, can be read as broadly united by a concern to place questions of power-knowledge at the core of the field on this side of the Atlantic. Thus, not only do these interventions push the critical scrutiny of relations of power in the global political economy in new and highly significant directions, they also signal the continued revitalization of British IPE.

Strange power, strange knowledge

Reading across commentaries on Susan Strange's intellectual contribution to the field of IPE in Britain and beyond, her work on questions of power is commonly identified as especially noteworthy. For instance, in drawing out five key themes that "dominate Strange's approach to the analysis of international political economy," her long-time friend and sparring partner Robert Keohane suggests, first up, that "For her, structural power was more fundamental than either bargaining [between collective agents] or agenda setting through international regimes" (2000: x). Not dissimilarly, for Roger Tooze, there are three "elements of Strange's approach and substantive analysis of IPE" and, again, first up, is the suggestion that power was not only "the core of political economy" for Strange, but that "Power can be exercised in many ways, particularly in structures rather than in direct relations with entities" (1999: 282). It is no surprise, then, that the title *Strange Power* was given to perhaps the single most significant volume that brings together discussions of Susan Strange's intellectual legacy (Lawton et al. 2000).

There can be little doubt that, for Strange, "the end result" in the "study and analysis of international political economy" hinged on "giving explicit or implicit answers" to the "fundamental questions about how power has been used to shape political economy" (1988/1994b: 24). She was frustrated by "answers" that only took into account "relational power," that is, "as conventionally described by realist writers of textbooks of international relations" as "the power of A to get B to do something they would otherwise not do" (1988/1994b: 24, original emphasis). Relational understandings of power are, of course, not only found in realism and IR, but have a standing in political science that arises, in this formulation at least, from the work of Robert Dahl (1976). Yet, it was the consequences of thinking only in terms of relational power when addressing the "fundamental questions" of IPE that most concerned Strange and which, over time and through empirical investigations, led her to elaborate on what she came to call "structural power." For Strange, structural power is "the power to choose and to shape the structures of the global political economy within which states, their political institutions, their economic enterprises, and (not least) their professional people have to operate" (1987: 565). "In short [it] confers the power to decide how things shall be done, the power to shape frameworks within which states relate to each other, relate to people, or relate to corporate enterprises" (Strange 1988/1994b: 24–25).

Moving beyond realist IR's preoccupation with power as military capabilities and the Marxist privileging of the social relations of production, Strange saw structural power as operating, in a somewhat decentered manner, across and through four main structures in the global political economy—security, production, finance, and knowledge. Each of these four structures is accorded equal ontological status and, at a particular point in time, may make a specific contribution to the power of the actor being analyzed, whether state, corporation, private authority, or international organization (e.g. Stopford and Strange 1991; Strange 1996). The distribution of power within each structure is likely to be quite different, and none of the four structures are necessarily and always primary overall.

While Strange (1988/1994b) later presented the analysis of structural power as a significant advance in the study of the global political economy in general, her initial motivations in elaborating on structural power clearly lay in enabling her corrective intervention in debates over the apparent decline of US hegemony (Strange 1987). For Strange, debates about the seeming relative decline of the US in the face of an ascendant Japanese economy missed the point about US power. As she summarized in the article that perhaps most clearly distills her thoughts on the matter: "there is a big difference between the financial power exercised by the United States and that exercised by Japan ... this difference is a rather good illustration of the difference between structural and relational power" (Strange 1990: 259). Japan is shown to exercise relational power in finance as a consequence of its position as the world's major creditor economy and aid donor. Meanwhile, the United States—by virtue of the standing of the dollar as "top currency," and the sophistication of the information and communication technologies controlled and utilized by its top banks—is shown to enjoy unrivaled structural power. Thus, perhaps the main political message that Strange (1986, 1998) iterated and reiterated in her writings on finance was that the self-interested actions of the US state in particular had unleashed a speculative wave in the markets that harmed productive economies and societies everywhere, including in the USA. Writing at the end of the 1980s, she seemed convinced that "it is logical to conclude that it is they—US Presidents and Congress—who have the power if anyone has to reverse the process and tip the balance of power back again from market to state" (Strange 1990: 266). A decade on, however, and what Strange (1996) termed "The retreat of the state" in the face of global markets and private authorities seemed to impacting on all states, even the United States: "these days, no single hegemonic leader is strong or rich enough to fill the role unaided. ... we may have to pin our hopes to the chances of a collective leadership as a substitute for a national hegemon" (Strange 1998: 55).

As Keohane highlights, although she stressed structural as opposed to relational power, Strange nonetheless "emphasized the role of self-interested agents, seeking control over valued outcomes such as security, wealth, the freedom to choose, justice, protection from risk" (2000: x; Strange 1988/1994b: 18). Strange would, throughout her work, and confronted by all manner of situations in the global political economy, ask *Cui bono?* or

Who benefits? Pivotal to the nature of such outcomes and who benefited from them was the extent to which states, and agents of authority more broadly, enabled or restricted market forces. The balance between authority and markets was key, for example, in determining the extent to which freedom was prioritized over justice. As Strange (1986) illustrated through her own research into the contemporary financial structure of "casino capitalism," it becomes possible following her method to identify the significance of key decisions in the emergence of a particular authority–market nexus. That the United States, as principal agent, took what Strange termed the key "non-decisions" to free-up and integrate formerly constrained and separated financial markets was, for her, very revealing as to who was benefiting from the resultant speculation and cross-border flows of capital.

From Keohane's (2000) American IPE perspective, the significance that Strange attributed to self-interested and powerful actors was something that she got right. While the category of structural power challenged the work of Keohane and others on international regimes, Strange's emphasis on self-interested agents also provided an avenue through which her "enlightening results" (Keohane 2000: xi) could, with a little theoretical tinkering, be situated within the confines of a neo-realist-neo-liberal American IPE. American IPE was, after all, also beginning to tentatively question an exclusive focus on state–state economic relations, and to explore the importance of systemic and institutional constraints and incentives. It is no surprise, therefore, that parallels emerged between Strange's analysis of the global political economy and that offered by some in American IPE. For instance, Guzzini (2000) notes the similarities between Strange's account of US structural power, and Joseph Nye's (1990) work on "soft power."

It is here, then, that we begin to get a sense of the somewhat paradoxical quality of Susan Strange's work on the question of power and, ultimately, her contribution to the direction taken by British IPE. On the one hand, Strange seemed to rip up the rule book that framed thinking on power in IPE by drawing on insights from beyond IR, thereby shaping the trajectory of British IPE and seemingly securing its identity against an American IPE other. British IPE was different because it was multidisciplinary (Strange 1996: xv), and recognized the importance of structural power in general, and the structural power of the United States in finance in particular. On the other hand, however, structural power for Susan Strange was always largely *hard* and *soft* material resources controlled and wielded in a restrictive manner by collective agents rationally seeking a particular outcome. In her terms, asking "who has power" was accompanied by the question of "what is the source of power" (Strange 1988/1994b: 23). The structural power that Strange sought to understand was, for the most part, the power of one agent to set the agenda for their interactions with others. Seen in this light, as May (1996) reminds us, Strange's conception of structural power resonated strongly with the thesis on power advanced by Steven Lukes (1974/2005) in the context of social scientific debates provoked by the rise of Gramsci's notion of hegemony. Just as for Lukes there is a third and most significant dimension of power—that is, how a prevailing agent sets agendas in broadly ideological terms and thereby keeps potential issues unaddressed—so for Susan Strange there is structural power.

As Chris May (1996) initially argued over a decade ago, then, how Susan Strange conceived of what she calls the "knowledge structure" is pivotal to her theory of structural power, and thus to the framework that she set out for British IPE inquiry more broadly. By giving ontological status to the knowledge structure, Strange certainly pushed British IPE to consider that which tended to be "overlooked and underrated"

(1988/1994b: 119). She also forcibly argued that there were solid empirical grounds for addressing the contemporary importance of the knowledge structure as she described it, especially developments in information and communication technologies (Strange 1990; 1991). As such, "the production, possession, control, communication and, above all, the legitimization of knowledge" (Tooze 2000: 187) found a place on the burgeoning research agenda of British IPE. But, in marking out her conception of knowledge as an objectively identifiable structure, Strange also set a particular course for inquiries into structural power that did not give ontological primacy to knowledge.

For Strange, the knowledge structure combines "what is believed (and the moral conclusions and principles derived from those beliefs); what is known and perceived as understood; and the channels by which beliefs, ideas, and knowledge are communicated—including some people and excluding others" (Strange 1988/1994b: 119). In May's terms, Strange makes a distinction between "action informed by belief, and action informed by information," typically uses "'knowledge' and 'information' as interchangeable terms," and, as a consequence, is able to escape from "unresolved debates over the nature of knowledge itself" (1996: 182–84). The knowledge structure is relevant to questions of structural power for Strange because, like the security, production and financial structures, it contains informational material resources that confer power on those able to command those resources. To borrow terms from Stefano Guzzini, Strange was "the champion of a power-materialist discipline of IPE" (2000: 216). As such, Strange (1988/1994b: 136–38) was, in the first instance, concerned with the ways in which competition and asymmetries between states increasingly turned on their relative standing in information–intensive economies (cf. Mytelka 2000). As Ronen Palan suggests of Susan Strange, "her concept of the 'knowledge structure' probably owes much more to the work of the New Trade theorists than to a sociological conception of knowledge" (1999: 127). It follows that she "did not engage properly with the various power theorists" (1999: 128).

Now, it certainly cannot be said that Strange was unaware of the questions and debates that her work was beginning to confront. For example, the concluding section of the chapter on the knowledge structure in *States and Markets* features a paragraph where she notes that:

> I have made no reference in the course of this brief survey … to the active debates conducted by philosophers, especially in Europe, on the nature of knowledge, or the relation between power and communication systems or on the role of ideology in defining the goals of knowledge and thus determining in some degree the findings of "social science."
>
> (Strange 1988/1994b: 136)

The paragraph also mentions and references the contributions made to these "active debates" by Jürgen Habermas, Michel Foucault, Karl Popper, and Georg Lukács. Strange, it would seem, recognized that to "engage properly with the various power theorists" would necessitate a significant transformation in the conception of structural power that she wanted to work with. This, is turn, would have transformed the agenda that she set out for British IPE. As May summarizes: "If the control of knowledge is the way agendas are set, and agenda-setting is a central role of structural power, then knowledge issues must be prior. This is not the direction in which Strange wishes to move" (1996: 184).

At the very time that Strange directed British IPE in particular to set aside philosophical debates about power and the sociology of knowledge, much of the social sciences was doing precisely the opposite. Strange's frustration with American IPE, and her view that the knowledge it produced was in the service of US power, rested on the foundational and rationalist epistemological assumption that power corrupted *the truth*. Strange's agenda, for her own work, and for British IPE, was to respond to this situation by revealing *the truth* about US power through reason. Although Strange was certainly not a simple empiricist, much of her philosophical and conceptual reflection about power and knowledge in particular lay somewhere in the background or alongside her analysis (Cox 1996; Palan 1999; Tooze 1999). Yet, beyond British IPE, foundationalism was being questioned, and social order was coming to be understood to hinge upon the creation and recreation of meanings in social practices through knowledge, discourse, and representation. Consider, for example, the imprint created by this questioning on the literature in IR from the late 1980s onwards (e.g. Campbell 1993; DerDerian and Shapiro 1989; George 1994).

Michel Foucault's (1980) category of "power-knowledge" was particularly influential in suggesting that relations of power turn on the reproduction of certain meanings and "truths" and militate against others. Relations of power thus produce "conditions of possibility" in which subjectivities are forged and expressed in practice. From this perspective, power—as sets of "relations, a more-or-less organised, co-ordinated hierarchical cluster of relations" (Foucault 1980: 198)—has decentralized, incoherent and capillary-like qualities. The apparent rationality of a social order and the seemingly rational utility-maximizing agents that inhabit it are, for example, something to be explained. So, while for Strange, knowledge (largely as informational resource) is power that is wielded in a constraining manner by rational agents, for Foucault, the statement that "knowledge is power" is misleading. The formulation "power-knowledge" is made precisely to question their relation in different settings, and to highlight the extent to which power does not emanate from a central source or from a collective agent.

As Chris May's (1996) commentary on Susan Strange illustrates, many in British IPE were well aware of the ways in which her work set aside power-knowledge. When May sets out an alternative agenda to that of Strange, he frames this in implicitly Foucauldian terms, calling for inquiry that asks *"why certain 'truths' are accepted as known, while others are not, and how this agenda of 'truth' is set and contested within the knowledge structure"* (1996: 185, original emphasis). That this call did not gain traction in British IPE was a reflection of Strange's grip on the field, and also the manner in which her conception of structural power also chimed in during something of a Gramscian-inspired moment. In the same year that *States and Markets* was published, Gill and Law's (1988) *Global Political Economy* provided British IPE with the first textbook that drew largely on Gramsci and the reception of his work by Robert Cox and others in Canadian IPE (see Chapter 5 in this volume). Although Gill and Law were primarily concerned with the power of capital as opposed to the power of states, their definition of structural power largely mirrored that of Strange. So, while the knowledge structure could not be given ontological priority by Strange over and above the structures of finance, production, and security, Gramscian-inspired work in British IPE regarded knowledge as largely the ideological legitimation of material power arising from the social relations of production. Ultimately, then, as Palan has it, it would seem to be the case that Strange's "rather off-hand treatment of the concept of structural power represents a wasted opportunity to challenge international relations theory at its very core" (1999: 128).

Poststructural interventions

It is the context described above that confronted those in British IPE who attempted to draw on poststructuralism during the 1990s in particular. The work of Susan Strange on power and knowledge contributed to setting boundaries for inquiry in British IPE, to establishing borderlines that made engagements with poststructuralism and a concern with power-knowledge seem illegitimate and unnecessary. A range of disparate, sporadic but significant interventions have, however, been made in the last decade or so. A notable feature of these interventions is that, in important ways, they echo the very concerns with questions of power and knowledge that Strange herself stressed. Strange at once opened up and closed down the possibility that thinking anew about power and knowledge could form the core of British IPE. Recent interventions in British IPE that draw on poststructuralism have, in effect, revisited that possibility. This is not to suggest that those engaging with poststructuralism in British IPE explicitly or implicitly view their contributions as following from or supporting the vision that Strange set out for IPE, far from it. Strange often appears as an author who those drawing on poststructuralism in British IPE choose to critique, and her work would also seem likely to be invoked as part of "a disciplinary politics that seeks to regulate IPE's agenda of study" (de Goede 2006: 1–2). Rather, what we see is something of an irony: engagements with poststructuralism are carrying forward Strange's vision of a British IPE in which the categories of power and knowledge (and especially their relation) are significant in demarcating it from its largely uncritical American other.

Before discussing several key poststructural interventions in British IPE below, it is important to stress both the great diversity and broad unity of the work to which I am referring. There is a danger that labeling this work under the single banner of post-structuralism leads to the impression that a singular poststructural IPE is emerging in Britain. This is not the case, and it is also highly problematic. While commonly acknowledged to be derived from the break with structuralism in linguistic theory, poststructuralism itself is a highly contested concept that does not capture the sharp disagreements between those French philosophers—Deleuze, Derrida, Foucault, Lyotard—to whom it is typically used to refer. We would seem to be left only with characterizations of poststructuralism, such as that offered by Michael Peters, as not reducible to "a set of shared assumptions, a method, a theory, or even a school," but as "a *movement of thought*—a complex series of refrains— embodying different forms of critical practice and influenced in its different trajectories through the appropriation of a range of different sources" (2000: 2, original emphasis). Such characterizations have, indeed, figured in attempts to demarcate poststructural inter-ventions in IR and, as de Goede (2006) suggests, can provide a basis for understanding what it means to group together a body of work as "poststructural" in IPE. In de Goede's terms, following David Campbell, poststructuralism becomes an "interpretative analytic" that "invites us to reconsider and destabilize not just the conceptual categories that IPE deploys (the state, the firm, the financial system, the economic actor, capitalism), but also the way knowledge is produced and legitimized in this disciplinary practice" (2006: 5).

However, if we also accept that, in large part, "poststructuralism inaugurates and reg-isters the French reception of Nietzsche" (Peters 2000: 3), then we can begin to capture more specifically how poststructuralism manifests itself in an impact upon British IPE which coalesces around questions of power-knowledge. As Peters has it,

Nietzsche's texts provided poststructuralists with the intellectual resources not only to go beyond Marx and Freud by combining the registers of power and desire without privileging one over the other, but they also enabled these French thinkers to conceive of power as a set of forces somehow larger than Man, beyond the individual, whether they be economic, libidinal, linguistic, or ecological.

(2000: 5–6)

It is far from a coincidence, then, that although the poststructural interventions in British IPE that I discuss below are diverse, they nonetheless can be seen to share a broad concern with power as a *set of forces* that are *somehow larger* than that which tends to form the focus of American and much of British IPE. Strange's vision for British IPE is beginning to thrive, albeit in a very different form to that which she would have recognized and, no doubt, approved.

The first poststructural intervention by British IPE scholars that I wish to highlight is made by Ash Amin and Ronen Palan (2000). Amin and Palan are concerned with the ways in which IPE has confronted "indeterminacy" and "non-linear evolution" in the global political economy with "ontological perturbation" that "has stopped short of abandonment of assumptions about the centrality of rational, calculating actors, or rule-driven allocation mechanisms" (2000: 559–60). They call upon "a lineage of thought that does not take a rationalist ontology as given," and suggest that "it offers the basis of an IPE capable of grasping the orderings of practices that are intersubjective, historicized, socially embedded, and non-cognitive" (2000: 560). Central to Amin and Palan's "non-rationalist international political economy" is, then, a challenge to the narrow and misleading assumptions of rational and instrumental collective agency present in both the relational power of American IPE, and the structural power of Susan Strange. As they put it, "a long-standing aspect of anti-rationalist thought has been its critique of conceptions of the subject as an intrinsically rational actor," and "it is through inculcation" that utility-maximizing and calculative subjects are forged (2000: 564).

Moving toward a non-rationalist IPE is, for Amin and Palan, at once an ontological and epistemological move. For them, claims to "the truth" are "always entangled in systems of belief, and structures and institutions," and the "temporal, discursive, and contingent" nature of truth claims thereby ensures that the "knowledge systems" that generate them "must be systems of power grounded in particular sets of social relations" (2000: 565). In this respect, Amin and Palan bring a Foucauldian conception of power to the front and center of their project, where power is not "domination or capability," but "a constitutive dimension of social life, imbricated in and expressed through knowledge" (2000: 565). Specifically, they draw attention to the significance of categories, calculations and technologies of classification for power-knowledge and the naturalization of social truths, and to the rooting of rationalities in "collective institutions such as laws, rules, habits, conventions, norms" (2000: 565).

The various implications that such epistemological moves hold out for IPE become especially clear when Amin and Palan, towards the end of their intervention, offer a concrete example of "global firm-state relations" (2000: 570–73). The selection of this example is itself particularly telling in the light of my suggestion that poststructural interventions in British IPE tend to coalesce around placing questions of power-knowledge at the core of the field. If the intellectual legacy of Susan Strange for British IPE was ultimately to close off consideration of power-knowledge, then Amin and Palan want, in effect, to open up the field in a manner that brings power-knowledge to front and center. Thus, they differentiate their *new approach* from those who would offer a *rationalist treatment* of relations between transnational corporations (TNCs) and states. The latter is "based on two sets of utility-maximizing actors interacting with each other," and "shows that power has shifted from states to TNCs, or is shared between TNCs and the most powerful states" (2000: 570). For Amin and Palan, however, neither states nor TNCs can be understood to be "driven by an *a priori* maximizing rationality," whether that be the search for power or profit (2000: 570–71). Rather, attention to "discursive practices," "scripts," "histories," and "techno-structures" ensures that "both states and TNCs lose their identities as rational subjects" (2000: 571). What it means to be a firm or state is in continual and dynamic transformation. Indeed, as Amoore (2004) suggests, the typical representation of firms and states as "rivals" (e.g. Stopford and Strange 1991) is especially problematic when both draw heavily on the calculative devices and technologies of risk provided by management consultancy. Ultimately, from this vantage point, as Amin and Palan conclude, the global political economy is no longer "a 'powerful states versus big capital' drama." It cannot be read off on the basis of analysis of the material-informational resources of firms and states, and assumptions about their rational power-wielding behavior. Instead, the focus is "on the constructed nature of power" (2000: 573).

A concern to bring "the constructed nature of power" into view is also the principal motivation in the second poststructural intervention in British IPE that I wish to draw attention to. Writing in the academic journal of BISA fifteen years after the publication of *States and Markets*, Marieke de Goede (2003) would seem quite justified in suggesting that "critical IPE has not yet examined how the politics of representation and practices of discourse analysis have a bearing on its field of study." Her call is for an IPE that does not separate "the realm of the ideal and the realm of the real," and she uses "the label 'economism' for IPE approaches which assume such a prediscursive economic materiality" (2003: 80). What interests de Goede is contributing to an IPE that, for example, views "practices of capital and labour" as "shaped, regulated and *brought into being* through historically grounded discourses of money and work" (2003: 81, original emphasis). Her argument, reflecting her wider research interests, is that "understanding the politics of modern finance … starts with a consideration [of] how current discourses of financial rectitude and economic necessity have taken shape at the expense of other possible financial representations" (de Goede 2005: 81). What is on the agenda for British IPE here, then, is inquiry into power-knowledge and the materialization of capital, and not the reification of capital as a powerful predatory agent and system.

In order to contrast to her own poststructural intervention, de Goede marks out what she regards to be the three principal "strands within IPE literature [that] have fruitfully integrated the study of ideas and ideology into their analysis" (2005: 85). These are: first, the epistemic communities approach that "seems to offer a way to integrate questions of valuation and meaning-making into the study of IPE" (2005: 86; e.g. Haas 1992); second, the "avenue for the inclusion of ideas and information into the study of IPE … provided by the work Susan Strange has done on the knowledge structure" (2005: 87); and, third, the conception of ideology brought to IPE by Robert Cox's (1996: 124–43) reading of Antonio Gramsci (e.g. Gill 1993). De Goede offers a careful analysis of the three strands, and argues that each, in different ways, is guilty of economism and the artificial separation of the political and the economic. That is, theses strands within the IPE literature posit the economy as "a prepolitical domain" that has an "indisputable materiality" (2003: 90). For de Goede, in contrast, "Moving beyond economism requires the recognition that neither the politics/economics distinction, nor the idealism/realism distinction, exist beyond their historical articulation" (2003: 91). Such distinctions and their materiality are, in short, produced through historical and political relations of power-knowledge.

Drawing on the actor-network theory of Bruno Latour (1987), and broadly in common with Amin and Palan (2000), de Goede highlights the place and political significance of "centres of calculation" and scientific devices of classification in the creation of dichotomies between the ideal and the material, the economic and the political (2003: 93). She is thus able to begin to illustrate one of the significant pathways for research in the global political economy that is opened up by an IPE which coalesces around a core concern with power-knowledge. Finance capital is no longer an all-powerful agent or overwhelming systemic logic replete with the resources of ideological legitimation, but a dynamic, contingent, performative, and contested set of networks that can be unpicked through careful analysis of calculative and classificatory devices and practices (cf. Aitken 2007; de Goede 2005; Langley 2008; MacKenzie 2006). As de Goede underlines, the primary motivation in following such a pathway in IPE research is to (re)politicize finance capital in the face of its de-politicized constitution through scientific discourses, representations, and calculations. This is because, as she puts it, "these particular discourses of financial knowledge and rationality make *real* material distributions and effects possible: they channel credit access and they create and distribute financial resources" (2003: 95, original emphasis). Such "distributions and effects" often may operate through liberal discourses of rights and responsibilities, for example, and through processes of identification.

By way of illustration, consider the materialization of economies of "mass investment" in contemporary US and UK society. From Adam Harmes' (2001c) neo-Gramscian perspective, changes in occupational and personal pensions and the rise of mutual funds (unit trusts in the UK) are a direct consequence of the material and ideological hegemony of finance capital. As I have stressed in my own research, however, the transformations of Anglo-American saving are not imposed from "the outside," but are embedded and embodied on "the inside" through the contingent assembly of financial networks and everyday investor subjects (Langley 2008). The shift from defined-benefit ("final salary") to defined-contribution ("money purchase") in occupational pension networks has, for example, entailed the displacement of the calculative devices of collective insurance by those of asset management and investment. The making of regular contributions to a defined-benefit scheme, in return for a pension guaranteed by the employer and based upon salary at retirement, no longer appears to be the most rational form of saving for retirement. Instead, the individual seeks to maximize their own returns through the equity-based mutual fund investment of a defined-contribution plan, as taking greater risk is assumed to realize greater returns. The individual, summoned up as an investor across a range of contemporary liberal programs of government, is thus responsible for their own freedom and security in retirement and embraces the risk/ return of the financial markets. Those who do not invest for their own retirement cannot expect the state to provide much more than a minimal safety net.

An emphasis on liberal government also marks the final poststructural intervention in British IPE that I wish to subject to a close reading. Ian Douglas (1999) begins his intervention by noting the teleological and liberal institutionalist representation of "global governance" offered by the Commission on Global Governance, and "the actions and values sanctioned and affirmed" through that representation (1995: 135). What is at stake here, for Douglas, is "a monologue of reason that has concealed the intervention of power, transformed so many real lives—real people—and given dignity, if not legitimacy, to the violence of a kind of disciplinary governance that has become our destiny and destination" (1999: 135). Aiming to "disturb" this "monologue of reason," Douglas draws broadly on Foucault's principal works which, taken together, reveal a great deal about the constitution of modern society. Across these principal works, as Douglas notes, "*Power* … is seen as *productive*; inscribed in knowledge, revealed as truth, operative at the level of the everyday mundane" (1999: 135, original emphasis). Again, then, the relations of power-knowledge are to the fore in this poststructural intervention in British IPE.

Douglas takes particular inspiration from Foucault's (1991) later work on "governmentality," that is, the type of power that has come to dominate over all other forms (e.g. sovereignty, discipline) in the modern liberal societies of the West (cf. Barry et al. 1996; Burchell et al. 1991; Dean 1999; Rose 1999). It is, in Foucault's terms:

> The ensemble formed by institutions, procedures, analyses and reflections, the calculations and tactics that allow the exercise of this very specific albeit complex form of power, which has as its target population, as its principal form of knowledge political economy, and its essential technical means apparatuses of security.
>
> (1991: 102)

For those taking up the notion of governmentality, a key focus thus becomes the government of the self by the self, the points "where programmes for the administration of others intersect with techniques for the administration of ourselves" (Rose 1999: 5). So, for Douglas, the ascendance of a discourse of "global governance" does not spell the end of modern liberal government, far from it. Rather, "Maintaining this focus on government while trying to describe the parameters of governance is indeed essential as both emerge from the same political reason (the targeting of populations by power)" (1999: 138).

Drawing on Foucault, Douglas turns on its head the common sense representation, shared by policymakers and many in IPE, which casts the diffusion of authority implied by the rise of global governance as the antithesis of the centralized and territorial state. Individuals, as, for example, "consumers" or "investors" in global markets that appear to lie beyond the control of the state, are not free from political authority. As Douglas has it, "authority, at least from the eighteenth century onward *specifically targeted individuals to become the vectors of their own processes of transformation*" (1999: 151, original emphasis). It follows that "the disappearance of the state has run parallel with the ascendance of new modalities of governance based on the positive constitution of individuals themselves" (1999: 152). In exploring the relations of power-knowledge in the contemporary global political economy, Douglas thus maps a course for inquiry that decenters modern power and questions the apparent conceptual and institutional fixing points of "state" and "market."

Furthermore, as I have argued in my own research, such analysis of relations of power-knowledge in the global political economy also has implications for how we might understand those practices that IPE scholars tend to conceptually fix through the category of "global civil society" (GCS) (Amoore and Langley 2004). Once defined in unambiguous terms as an identifiable public sphere of voluntary association that is distinct from both state and market, GCS is filled with meaning and political potential. Yet, once we begin to consider the production of GCS and the practices that are licensed in its name, then the conceptual and political ambiguities of GCS begin to come into view. Rather than a bounded "non-governmental" space, GCS is precisely a means of making global politics governable in particular ways. GCS is not simply a realm of

137

empowerment leading to political transformation, then, but is shot through with the relations of power, tensions and contradictions which lie at the heart of transformative politics.

Concluding remarks

I have sought in this chapter to make a two-fold argument. First, that the relatively minimal and somewhat unwilling engagement with poststructuralism in British IPE during the 1990s in particular was in part a consequence of the grip of Susan Strange's intellectual interventions and, specifically, of her pioneering work on what she termed "structural power" and the "knowledge structure." Second, that Strange's vision of a British IPE that demarcates itself from its largely uncritical American other by exploring the relation of categories of power and knowledge is now, somewhat ironically, being taken forward by those who draw on poststructuralism. As poststructural interventions thus move an agenda for a British IPE that coalesces around questions of power-knowledge, debates are currently ensuing over whether it is possible to address such questions within the confines of a broadly defined historical materialism.

Marieke de Goede's (2003) intervention discussed above, for example, provoked a sharp rebuke from Mark Laffey (2004) that is illustrative of the tensions that are now emerging in British IPE over the future direction of the field. To borrow terms from Laffey, the issue is whether IPE (and for that matter IR) is to conceive of itself as "after Marx" or "instead of Marx" (cf. Jessop and Sum 2001). For some, such as Adam Morton (2006), any form of "critical" IPE that does not privilege class identity and struggle, and situate IPE scholarship in the "materialist structure of ideology," is condemned as merely and necessarily "liberal pluralist analysis." It is, in short, simply "instead of Marx" and is therefore and certainly wrong (cf. Germain 2007). For Laffey, meanwhile, although he would broadly welcome a "return to historical materialism in IR/IPE," if this "is primarily a return to classical models" then it "ironically reinforces an impoverished disciplinary discussion of contemporary Marxisms" (2004: 465). For Laffey, the issue is not whether poststructural interventions "are just wrong" (2004: 468). Rather, and more subtly, the danger is that the field, "bereft of the resources made available by the long and distinguished tradition of Marxist scholarship" (2004: 460), may lose sight of the "real political effects" of its analyses (2004: 461). The main charge—quite familiar for at least a decade to those elsewhere in the social sciences who have taken poststructuralism seriously in their work (e.g. Gibson-Graham 1996, 2006)—is expressed by Laffey as follows:

> In a world increasingly subject to the workings of an informational and multinational mode of capitalism, characterised by flux and instability, hybridity and fragmentation, it is also hard not see the poststructuralist dismantling of the subject ... as unintentionally complicit in the world.
>
> (2004: 468)

There is a need, then, for poststructuralists to "think a bit more carefully about the politics and the locations of ... [their] representations" (2004: 468). Such a charge would indeed be fair if it were the case that poststructural interventions in British IPE, or elsewhere, amounted only to a concern with subjectivity and processes of identification. This, however, is not the case. As I have argued here, a reading of poststructural interventions in British IPE in the wake of the intellectual legacy of Susan Strange can, with some considerable irony, reveal an agenda for the field that coalesces around core questions of power-knowledge. The asking of such questions certainly includes, but is not reducible to, the dismantling of the subject. It also ensures that, as the interventions discussed in the second section of this chapter attest, those working in British IPE are, in the spirit of Susan Strange, acutely and radically aware of the political significance of their work.

9

Bridging the transatlantic divide?

Toward a structurational approach to international political economy

Philip G. Cerny

Introduction: structuring international political economy

The contrast drawn by Cohen between "American" and "British" international political economy (Cohen 2007) is based on a partially false dichotomy. On the one hand, these discrepancies are not specific to IPE, nor are they merely transatlantic, as Cohen observes in this volume. They reflect deep, ever-present paradigmatic divergences within the social sciences in general, and political science in particular. The social sciences have never been dominated by the kind of hegemonic paradigms Kuhn found in the natural sciences. The philosophy of social science, like political philosophy, is characterized by multiple, competing paradigms (Kuhn 1962; Wolin 1968). On the other hand, however, the re-emergence of these divergences within IPE reflects not merely old philosophical and methodological disputes but also the special role of the core subject-matter of international political economy in the twenty-first century. At one level, IPE today represents the latest instantiation of old divergences. Yet the consequences are exceptionally significant because of the increasingly high profile IPE is taking within the social sciences as the result of its claim to offer unique insights into the most significant transformation taking place in the world today—globalization.

Although these fundamental paradigmatic conflicts cut across both quasi-geographical camps, for specific historical reasons, what were then called behavioralist approaches to political science never became dominant in the United Kingdom in the way they did in the American academy. However, in the 1960s and 1970s, such scientific approaches to political science fell on hard times in the United States as well. These developments had several taproots.[1] More recently, American graduate schools have reinvented behavioralism. This development is reflected not only in the renascence of quantitative analysis but also in the more recent paradigmatic influence of rational choice theory, spilling over from the late-twentieth-century hegemony of neoclassical and neoliberal economic theory.[2] Therefore it is no surprise that these divergences have been reproduced in the development of IPE more generally as a transdisciplinary field of analysis across different parts of the world. These variations reflect contrasting approaches at four levels: (a) methodology, especially between quantitative and formal approaches, on the one hand,

and qualitative, discursive, process-tracing approaches on the other; (b) underlying philosophies of social science, in particular whether the social sciences can indeed ever be scientific in the first place, at least in the sense of emulating models derived from natural science (Blyth 2006; Taleb 2007); (c) the role of political philosophy and values as pre-methodological framing variables, sometimes crudely expressed in terms of a left–right spectrum but usually far deeper and more complex; and (d), in consequence, what sort of empirical variables are the most appropriate and reliable to study, in particular the relationship between structure and agency (Cerny 1990).

What I intend to do here is focus on one aspect of divergence—the relationship between structure and agency—in order to open the way for a third approach that may partially bridge the paradigmatic divide. This approach is rooted in the concept of structuration (Giddens 1979) and the rediscovery of a political process methodology in both political science and IPE (McFarland 2004), in contrast to both the materialist (or structuralist) and constructivist camps that currently dominate. This chapter surveys a range of political aspects of IPE, globalization in particular, and argues that they involve independent variables promoting, accelerating, and shaping change in ways neither exogenous social and economic factors alone nor an overly ideological or ideational constructivist approach alone can explain. In these conditions, *political structuration* is the primary process linking two relatively independent variables—structure and agency—and therefore both driving and shaping not only globalization as such but also the analytical *path* taken by IPE. The analysis of political structuration is methodologically as well as paradigmatically pluralistic and necessitates combining elements of quantitative and formal analysis with qualitative, discursive, and process-tracing methods in creative, synergistic ways.

The concept of structuration is rooted in the capacity of political actors to act not only as political and institutional entrepreneurs but also as mixed-motive participants in an evolving, widening political process that has spread across borders to the international, transnational, and translocal levels. In contrast to the traditional levels-of-analysis distinction between domestic and international politics (Hollis and Smith 1990), I argue that a new transnational political process is emerging and crystallizing—what I here call *multi-nodal politics*. This complex process involves: (a) the opening up of a range of new opportunities for political action as the result of underlying structural changes in the international political economy; (b) the growth and proliferation of transnationally linked interest groups and social movements, the strategic activity of political entrepreneurs, and the restructuring of social and political coalitions, with significant transnational linkages, resources, and goals; and (c) the reorganization of policy spaces, decision-making processes, and institutional superstructures through a process of institutional bricolage.

Taken together, these three inextricably intertwined dimensions have the effect of ratcheting up globalization, altering the rules and norms governing political behavior, and further entrenching the globalization process itself—analogous to what Hendrik Spruyt has called "institutional selection" (Spruyt 1994). However, this process is not linear; rather it is characterized by significant indeterminacies and is therefore open in important ways to the strategies and tactics chosen by relatively autonomous actors. Its development is still in its early stages. Certain aspects are as yet highly amorphous, making formal and quantitative analysis—especially the choice of proxy variables—unusually problematic. In particular, the shape of longer-term institutional outcomes is still unclear. However, these changes open up a range of future possibilities and developmental pathways that did not exist previously. Today previous patterns of path dependency are being disrupted. Political actors in our unevenly globalizing world are faced with everyday choices that reflect the existence of medium-to-long term *multiple equilibria*. In other words, the same causal variables can lead to different outcomes depending on the contingent juxtaposition of those variables—in essence, the unpredictable element of conjuncture or even historical accident—and the relatively autonomous decisions of key actors in those circumstances. What actors choose today will therefore influence and shape deep structural outcomes tomorrow. In this context, disputes within the social sciences and IPE today reflect the fluidity and indeterminacy of this underlying situation. Careful attention to these disputes, a willingness to be self-critical and to understand the drawbacks of each approach, are crucial to our evolving understanding of the possibilities that lie ahead. As academic practitioners of IPE we also are responsible for shaping wider understandings of these potential transformations. It is our ethical duty to be both as analytically sophisticated and as philosophically critical as we are able, while attempting creatively to reconcile the two. IPE professors are actors too.

In the second section, international political economy and globalization are situated the wider context of historical political change. The third section looks at a range of transformations in the underlying structure of public/private goods and at how these structural changes are impacting the constraints and opportunities faced by agents in the globalization process, especially the ongoing transformation of the state from the national industrial welfare state to the competition state. The fourth section focuses on strategically situated actors who may have the potential to become institutional entrepreneurs in the political globalization process. In developing the concept of multi-nodal politics, I will argue that the complexities of the processes involved require an eclectic and pluralistic approach that includes, in different circumstances and depending on the specific issue-area involved, *both* quasi-scientific methodologies—especially where clear and reliable quantitative data are available—*and* qualitative, discursive, process-tracing methods. At one level, a synergistic combination of the two approaches is desirable. Nevertheless, I argue, quantitative and formal methodologies are only as good as the qualitative and discursive assumptions, hypotheses and narratives they are built around. The former therefore need to be firmly embedded in and subordinated to the latter.

Eroding the inside/outside distinction

Traditional international political economy was concerned primarily with economic relations among states in the international system—i.e. with foreign economic policy, with trade relations, with the international monetary system, and with political aspects of the internationalization of production. To the extent that there was a distinctive way of looking at and understanding the subject matter of IPE, it tended to be an uneven mixture of interstate relations of a realist kind, on the one hand, and domestic bureaucratic and pressure group politics, on the other. Such a view of the IPE sat well with the notion of the nation-state as the dominant structured field of action for both domestic and international politics (Cerny 1990). Despite its long gestation and organizational durability, however, the modern nation-state as we have known it represents only one particular kind of governance structure among many theoretical possibilities. Only in the Second Industrial Revolution did the modern nation-state develop the range of socio-economic functions we are accustomed to seeing today, when mass production and modern industrial enterprises (Chandler 1990; Rupert 1995), the Weberian bureaucratic revolution in both public and private sectors, and mass politics that brought together a range of structural elements conducive to the development of the industrial welfare state of the mid-twentieth century (Cerny 1995).

Whereas these alternative orders have long been debated in theory and practice, it is only when the state itself can no longer effectively carry out its dual institutional role as arena of collective action and source of credible commitments that such possibilities have any chance of being realized in practice. In this context, the prospect of significant transformation opened up in the second half of the twentieth century through what has been called globalization. Globalization is not an end state; rather, it is a process (or a complex set of processes) made up of the addition or cumulative results of denser relations among states (internationalization), denser relations cutting across states (transnationalization), and relations at a distance between and among local and regional areas ("translocalizaton": Spruyt 1994). More important than any one of these levels, however, are the interaction effects among them. It is these interaction effects that destabilize the structural equilibrium underpinning the levels of analysis distinction, thereby undermining the path dependency of the international system as we have known it.

In other words, rather than continuing path dependency, these effects generate multiple equilibria, creating the possibility of new branching points and therefore the reconstruction of the system itself. It is crucial to identify these structural faults and explore the potential constraints and opportunities that actors may face in attempts to manipulate and reshape the structure of the system. This evolving relationship between structure and agency involves the strategic action of individuals and groups across both public and private domains, not only for more concrete competitive advantages in the world marketplace but also for reshaping social and political processes and institutions to reflect new distributions of power and resources ("distributional changes") and new ways of looking at the world ("social epistemologies": Ruggie 1993). Future structural developments will be the product of an increasingly transnational, cross-cutting process of micro- and meso-interdependencies, partially mediated through the state but with their own autonomous dynamics too. In the long run, political actors will adapt their own strategies to perceived global realities, while other kinds of actors, economic and social, will play key roles too in restructuring the political arena.

Processes of structuration

Theories of globalization have privileged structural explanations of change. The prevalent image is that of a shrinking world. In this context, changes in exogenous conditions are seen in turn to alter human behavior in ways that are broadly predictable because their patterns are determined by the material or ideational morphology of those exogenous conditions per se.[3] Nevertheless, attempts to extrapolate future world orders from such structural changes always border on science fiction. They never really capture the range of possibilities, possibilities which are shaped by actors. At the same time, many agency-centered approaches, including those of some constructivists, have shied away from grappling with globalization. Constructivists' overemphasis on the potential autonomy of ideas and institutions have paradoxically turned the attention of scholars away from broad paradigmatic change and focused discussion on limited debates about the ideational character of existing institutions, incremental changes within the existing states system, and/or the possibilities for resistance within the current world order, although analysts like Blyth have stressed the dynamic character of constructivism (Blyth 2003). Nevertheless, too much of today's constructivism in international relations, far from reflecting the transformational epistemological vision of Berger and Luckmann's (1966) critique of functionalist social theory, seems content to challenge the hard structuralist character of neorealism (Waltz 1979) with a soft classical realism of a more historical and ideational type (Wendt 1992)—although allowing national actors greater scope for international regime-building within that context (Finnemore 1996a). In addition, postmodernism and post-positivism, while taking a more critical stance, have nevertheless had little to say about the globalization process except as a potential negation of modernism and positivism.

In contrast to both the determinism of structuralism and the indeterminacy of constructivism, this chapter starts from the structurationist view that structure and agency are mutually constituted in an ongoing process that simultaneously both (a) consolidates and yet fractures structures and (b) constrains and yet empowers agents, in a reciprocal, interactive process over time. Thus agents can only be conceived of as acting within (unevenly) structured sets of constraints and opportunities—Crozier and Friedberg's (1977) concept of "structured fields of action"—while at the same time those sets of constraints and opportunities can, in turn, only be conceived of as the cumulative products of agency in an ongoing interactive process. Structures, whether static or changing, can be either uneven and loosely held together, or tightly woven and homogeneous. Agents, in turn, can act either in structure-bound or merely adaptive ways, or in entrepreneurial and potentially transformational ways. In this sense, I would suggest a stylized heuristic typology of ideal-type or polar-type structuration processes (Table 9.1).

Where structure-bound actors are situated within a tightly woven structural context (Type 1), the interaction between structure and agency would tend to be of a fairly static, *routine* kind, predominantly leading to passive *adjustment* to exogenous structural changes; such change should be robustly predictable from knowledge of its exogenous sources. Where structure-bound actors are situated within a loosely articulated structure (Type 2), a form of *incremental adaptation* analogous to certain kinds of traditional Darwinian random selection might be anticipated; however, actors would be likely to have some limited opportunities (wiggle room) for creative adaptation and institutional bricolage. Where change-oriented or transformational actors—those whose understandings, visions and knowledge enable them to transcend existing structural constraints in developing their strategies and tactics—are situated within a tightly woven structure (Type 3), one might expect an uneven structuration process where both exogenous and endogenous pressures for change would build up over time and lead to *punctuated equilibria*—e.g. to unpredictable conjunctural upheavals, the outcomes of which can take a variety of different forms from re-equilibration to structural degradation to revolutionary change. Stanley Hoffmann (1974) has referred to this process as "homeorhetic change." And where change-oriented actors are situated within a loosely held together structure (Type 4),

Table 9.1 Structuration processes

Actor orientation	Structural coherence	
	Loose	Tight
Structure bound	Type 1: Routine adjustment	Type 2: Incremental adaptation
Transformational	Type 3: Punctuated equilibrium	Type 4: Articulated restructuring

possibilities for actor-orchestrated *articulated restructuring* would be greater—accompanied, however, by increased uncertainty about how controllable different component parts of the structure might be (especially under strong exogenous structural pressures). With the partial exception of Type 1 structuration, therefore, even the tightest exogenously-led processes of structural change generate multiple equilibriums that actors can to some extent manipulate or reshape. Globalization generates *permissive conditions* for change, not restrictive ones, despite increasing uncertainty.

Structural change, public goods, and the role of the state

The power structure of a globalizing world therefore inevitably becomes increasingly complex and diffuse, diffracted through a prismatic structure of socio-economic forces and levels of governance (Riggs 1964); from the global interaction of transnational social movements, interest/pressure groupings, and multinational corporations, financial markets, to the re-emergence of subnational and cross-national ethnic, religious and policy-oriented coalitions and conflicts of the type familiar in domestic-level political sociology. World politics, that is, both domestic politics and international relations, is being transformed into a *polycentric* or *multinucleated* global political system operating within the same geographical space and/or overlapping spaces. In these conditions, it becomes harder to maintain the boundaries which are necessary for the efficient packaging of public or collective goods. Indeed, it becomes harder to determine what collective goods are demanded or required in the first place, that is, even to measure what is the "preferred state of affairs" (Ostrom et al. 1961; Cerny 1999a). State actors themselves, although they continue to have a range of significant economic, financial, political, and bureaucratic resources at their disposal and are still crucial actors in regulating particular economic and social activities, paradoxically act in routine fashion to undermine traditional state sovereignty. The result is a growing "privatization of the public sphere," not only by selling off or contracting out public services and functions, but in the deeper sense of reducing society itself to competing "associations of consumers" in which administrators are little more than buyers in competing corporations (Ostrom et al. 1961: 839).[4]

This combination of structural trends triggers a reassessment of the conception of public or collective goods in a globalizing world. Collective goods in theory are those from the enjoyment or use of which *insiders* cannot be excluded, requiring authoritative mechanisms for identifying and excluding *outsiders* (Ostrom et al. 1961; Olson 1965; Ostrom and Ostrom 1977)—a classic task of hierarchical governments (states). Many of what were thought to constitute collective goods at the time of the Second Industrial Revolution are either no longer controllable by the state because they have become transnational in structure and/or constitute private goods in a wider world marketplace. For example, oligopolistic and mass production industrial sectors that have been incorporated into state-led and/or neocorporatist structures must become internationally competitive; technological changes diffuse quickly across borders; defense industries and other strategic sectors are no longer immune from foreign competition while macroeconomic policy is increasingly vulnerable to cross-border shifts in demand, supply, and financial flows (Cerny 1990, 1995 and 2000d). Thus the nature of the political debate changes in fundamental ways. In theoretical terms, the idea of what is public is essentially normative. For example, in the economic theory of collective goods (e.g. Olson 1965), rooted in concepts of economic efficiency rather than social or political values, the main issue is indivisibility, on two levels: the structure of production and the structure of consumption. Goods are truly public when both the structure of production and the structure of consumption lead to conditions of indivisibility.

The first condition, concerning the structure of production, is referred to as *jointness of supply*, or the indivisibility of the production process. This concerns the extent to which technological economies of scale in production plus the structure of transactions costs mean that large factories, long production runs, etc., make collective provision through hierarchical management structures (usually seen in political terms as involving an exist-ing governmental structure, i.e. municipal, regional, or national) more efficient than private or free-market provision—as is said to be the case with so-called natural mono-polies. In a globalizing world, however, such calculations become more complex. In some industries, goods that once may have been most efficiently produced on a collec-tive basis (especially on a national scale) may nowadays be more efficiently organized along lines which imply larger, *trans*national optimal economies of scale, making tradi-tional public provision unacceptably costly and uncompetitive. In other cases, technolo-gical change and/or flexible production may actually reduce optimal economies of scale, turning such goods effectively into private goods, which also are increasingly produced and traded in a global rather than a national marketplace. The fates of traditional Fordist mass production industries such as steel in the 1980s "Rust Belt" are emblematic (Reich 1983; Zysman and Tyson 1983).

With regard to consumption, economists refer to the criterion of excludability, or the indivisibility of the consumption process. Public goods are by definition non-excludable, which means that collective provision has to be organized to prevent non-paying users (so-called free riders) from making the provision of the good too expensive for the rest, that is, such goods must be financed through forced payments (taxes). Again, in a glo-balizing world it has become increasingly difficult to exclude non-paying users (free riders) from both inside and outside national boundaries from benefiting from nationally provided collective goods in ways that appear costly in terms of domestic politics and public policy, as shown in contemporary debates on immigration and free trade agreements. The rapid growth of transnational private regulation (Mügge 2006), transnational network forms of organization, both private and public (Slaughter 2004), and legal convergence and extraterritoriality are again symptomatic. Thus with regard to both production and consumption, it is becoming more and more difficult to maintain the sort of public or collective boundaries necessary for efficient state provision of public or collective goods.

Different categories of collective goods have different kinds of normative and eco-nomic characteristics. I refer elsewhere to four such categories: regulatory, productive, distributive, and redistributive collective goods (Cerny 1999a, where I adapt the cate-gories developed by Lowi 1964). Each of these categories has been transformed by the structural changes associated with globalization and the other economic and political trends that are inextricably intertwined with globalization. With regard to regulatory public goods, in a world of relatively open trade, financial deregulation, and the increasing impact of information technology, property rights and other basic rules are increasingly complex for states to establish and maintain. In this context, the ability of firms, market actors, and competing parts of the national state apparatus itself to defend and expand their economic and political turf through activities such as transnational policy networking and regulatory arbitrage, has both undermined the control span of the state from without and fragmented it from within. With regard to productive collective goods, the advent of flexible manufacturing systems and competing low-cost sources of supply—especially from firms operating multinationally—has been particularly important in undermining state-owned and parapublic firms, for example in the crisis of public ownership and the wave of privatization of the 1980s and 1990s. Competitiveness counts for far more than maintaining an autonomous, self-sufficient national economy, in both the developed and developing worlds (Haggard 1990; Harris 1986). The same can be said for more traditional forms of industrial policy, such as state subsidies to industry, public procurement of nationally produced goods and services, or trade protectionism.

In contrast to productive collective goods, distributive collective goods are characterized less by their technical indivisibility—economies of scale and transactions cost economies deriving from *hard* production systems—and more by potential *soft* scale and transactions cost economies deriving from their management structures, on the one hand, and from the collective characteristics of their consumers rather than their producers, on the other. Policy-oriented economists have come to consider a much larger range of such goods as being appropriate for market or quasi-market provision. Many of the basic public services and functions such as the provision of public health, education, garbage collection, police protection, certain kinds of transport or energy infrastructure, etc., which have been at the bureaucratic heart of the modern industrial welfare state, are being disaggregated and commodified in a range of ways (Osborne and Gaebler 1992; Dunleavy 1994). Redistributive collective goods are even more fundamentally political, with their public and collective character deriving typically from political decisions about justice and fairness rather than from the economic efficiency (or inefficiency) of those public allocation mechanisms which they engender. Today, for example, neocorporatist bargaining and employment policies are under challenge everywhere in the face of international pressures for wage restraint and flexible working practices. Although developed states have generally not found it possible to reduce the overall weight of the welfare state significantly as a proportion of GDP, there has been a significant transformation in the balance of how welfare funds are spent—from the maintenance of free-standing social and public services to the provision of unemployment compensation and other "entitlement" programs, and from maintaining public bureaucracies to devolving and privatizing their delivery (Clayton and Pontusson 1998). And the most salient new sector of redistributive public goods, environmental protection, is particularly transnational in character; pollution and the rape of natural resources do not respect borders. These changes not only increase actors' options but also prioritize strategic and tactical flexibility, increasing overall openness to change.

New roles for the state

In terms of policy transformation, several types and levels of government activity are affected by the globalization process, opening new avenues for actors to transform political and policymaking processes and their outcomes. The interaction of transnationalization, internationalization, and domestic restructuring has pushed four specific types of policy change to the top of the political agenda. First, there has been a shift from macroeconomic to microeconomic interventionism, as reflected in both deregulation and industrial policy. Second, the focus of that interventionism has shifted from the development and maintenance of a range of *strategic* or *basic* economic activities to one of flexible response to competitive conditions in a range of diversified and rapidly evolving international marketplaces, i.e. the pursuit of dynamic *competitive advantage* as distinct from the more static *comparative advantage*. Third, policymakers have increasingly emphasized the control of inflation and neoliberal monetarism—supposedly translating into non-inflationary growth—as the touchstone of state economic management and interventionism. Fourth, the focal point of party and governmental politics has moved away from general maximization of welfare within a nation (full employment, redistributive transfer payments and social service provision) to the promotion of enterprise, innovation, and profitability in *both* private and public sectors. In this context, there have been some striking similarities as well as major differences among both developed and developing countries (Soederberg et al. 2005). Trade policy, monetary and fiscal policy, industrial policy, and regulatory policy are all changing (Cerny 2000c).

Under pressure from recessionary conditions in a relatively open world economy, first in the 1970s and then in the early 1990s, the problems faced by all capitalist industrial states have given rise to certain similarities of response—in particular, the shift from the welfare state model, nurtured by the long boom from the 1950s to the oil crisis of 1973–74, to a more differentiated repertoire of state responses to the imperatives of growth and competitiveness (Cerny 2008). In this context, states are less and less able to act as "developmental" or "strategic" states (Johnson 1982; Zysman 1983), and are more and more "splintered states" or "disaggregated states" (Machin and Wright 1985; Slaughter 2004). State actors and their different agencies are increasingly intertwined with "transgovernmental networks"—systematic linkages between state actors and agencies overseeing particular jurisdictions and sectors, but cutting across different countries and including a heterogeneous collection of private actors and groups in interlocking policy communities, especially those involving regulators, legislators, and the legal system (Slaughter 2004) as well as what have been called "epistemic communities" of experts and policymakers in a range of technical issue-areas (Haas 1992; Stone 1996).

Complex globalization therefore has to be seen as a structure involving (at least) *three-level games*, with third-level—transnational—games including not only "firm–firm diplomacy" but also transgovernmental networks, transnational policy communities, internationalized market structures, transnational pressure and interest groups and many other linked and interpenetrated markets, hierarchies, and networks (Cerny 2003). These changes increase the opportunities actors face in reacting to such changes, manipulating the possibilities inherent in the multiple equilibria that result, to restructure coalitions, develop strategies for change, and transform institutional structures. In particular, contrary to the popular image of deregulation, the growth of competing authorities with overlapping jurisdictions does not reduce interventionism. Rather, it expands the range of possibilities for splintered governments and competing groups of actors to challenge old fiefdoms and attempt to develop new patterns of influence and power domestically and transnationally.

Constructing a new world order?

Debates about globalization and internationalization are essentially debates about the nature of ongoing structuration in the international system. They address three fundamental questions. First, how vulnerable is the existing system in structural terms? Second, do the various exogenous processes of social, economic and political change which have been identified in the international system in recent decades add up to a wider, cumulative process of structural change, often called globalization? And finally, what kind of choices might agents be able to make that potentially could shape those processes of change in the future? I argue that the development of a range of *transnational opportunity structures* provides vital structural space for key agents to act in potentially transformative ways, in turn increasing the vulnerability of the system in feedback fashion. At the same time, however, such changes also give rise to adaptive as well as transformative modes of behavior. The particular shape a transformed international system is likely to take will be determined primarily by which sets of actors are best to most effectively exploit the manifest and latent structural resources or political opportunity structures available to them in a period of flux. A key variable in explaining actor-led change is thus the presence of *strategically situated actors* in a flawed and/or fluid structural context. Their presence constitutes a necessary but not a sufficient condition of structural change (Blyth 2003).

Of course, where what is perceived to be a highly constraining organizational pattern has been deeply embedded over a long period of time, most actors, even strategically situated ones, will take that pattern for granted and work within it rather than trying to change it. There is thus a strong tendency toward inertia built into most social structures most of the time. However, there are two ways in which strategically situated actors can in fact effect change. Either they believe (à la constructivist analyses) that the combination of their preferences and objectives, along with a perceptive understanding of the fault lines and gaps in the existing structure, will bring about change, and therefore they systematically and consciously act in a rational fashion to pursue that outcome. Or they interact with others in such a way that the pursuit of their preferences puts strain on the structure itself in contingent fashion, opens up existing gaps, and creates new possibilities for forms of coalition-building and power-seeking that alter existing resource distributions and ultimately force de facto changes in fundamental, system-sustaining rules or resource distributions. Judging the state of that balance of forces is a risky business both intellectually and practically. But in either case, the durability, fungibility, and ultimately the evolving morphology of the system are, in the last analysis, the product of actors' actions, and not directly the product of structural preconditions.

Within this context, key sets of agents who in the past have been closely bound up with the territorial nation-state are increasingly experimenting with new forms of quasi-private regulation of their activities. Businesses and business pressure groups, for example, are more and more divided between those seeking old-fashioned government protection, but whose economic base is often declining, and those more active in transnational markets, seeking deregulation and liberalization (Milner 1988; Frieden 1991). Furthermore, the securitization and transnational integration of financial markets have undermined traditional state–bank–industry relationships of finance capital (Chernow 1997). Labor movements, too, which were such a crucial element in the consolidation of the welfare state, are being eroded from both above and below, as their relationships with state actors and agencies become increasingly ineffectual in achieving their collective demands, leading to a strengthening of "free-riding" tendencies (Olson 1965; Evans 2007). And state actors themselves, once said to be "captured" by large, well organized domestic constituencies, are increasingly captured instead by transnationally linked sectors which set state agencies against each other in the desire to "level the playing field" for their domestic clients in the wider world—a process called "regulatory arbitrage."

In this context, although specific changes may take place, whether change overall is fundamental and far-reaching enough to be transformative change, will depend upon the balance of forces between sets of agents whose actions continue to reinforce existing structural forms and practices, and those whose actions generate and reinforce new forms and practices. Fundamental change, however, is more likely to depend upon the way potentially transformative agents actually act in practice; although they might be expected to act in ways which challenge the structure, they also may for various reasons—

including cultural and ideological reasons as well as calculations of short-term gains—not be able, or even not choose, to act in such ways. Adaptive behavior, attempting to maintain the essentials of the status quo, may in the end be the preferred course of action for many strategically situated actors. And finally, those alternative structural forms—the potential but contingent outcomes (multiple equilibria) which may in theory be possible—may prove either too ambitious, on the one hand, or too amorphous and fragmented, on the other, to form an effective foundation for those agents' strategic or tactical calculations. *Thus alternative equilibria may also be too flawed and/or fluid to be a ground for effective action.* In this context, I will identify three stylized sets of agents—economic, political, and social—and attempt to generate some broad hypotheses about when each set is likely to act as transformative agents and when as adaptive agents.

Economic agents: workers, managers, financiers

Most of the literature on globalization asserts that the key category of agents in terms of developing transnational linkages which have structurally transformative potential involves economic agents, mainly because globalization is most often seen as primarily an economic process. The modern division of the international economy into relatively or partially insulated national economies is widely seen to be flawed, although the opposite notion of a "borderless" or "flat" world has been widely debunked (Florida 2005; Aronica and Randoo 2006). In this context, economic agents are identified as driving change, although there is a hierarchy of groups with some having more autonomous influence than others in this process.

Of these groups, the least likely to take on the role of institutional entrepreneur is the labor movement. The labor movement could only grow and succeed in the twentieth century because of the permissive conditions embodied in the consolidation of the nation-state as the hegemonic structural arena of both political and economic action, an arena which was structurally suited to the large-scale mass politics of the Second Industrial Revolution and created the conditions for a de facto alliance between trade unions, national-reformist or social democratic political parties, and national capital. Today, given the increasing significance of flexible manufacturing processes for large firms and the growing resort to flexible contracting and subcontracting among both large and small firms, including transnational strategic alliances, and other management practices, the potential collective power of labor has been greatly reduced. Nevertheless, the possibility of labor movements shifting their focus from collective industrial action of a Second Industrial Revolution type to more widespread (if more fragmented) forms of social action in alliance with transnational social movements may provide more potential for labor to participate in a transformative fashion in transnational structural change (Evans 2007). In such cases, labor movements would overlap between the categories of economic agents and social agents (see below).

Another set of strategically situated economic agents includes owners and managers of multinational corporations. Whether at a localized, regionalized or genuinely transnational level, for example, owners and managers of high technology firms large and small are often seen as taking on a collectively transformative role—but only the major executives of the larger firms, such as Bill Gates of Microsoft, are seen as credible potential institutional entrepreneurs. Nevertheless, such agents are generally still dependent upon states and the states system for providing basic public goods, enforcing property rights, etc. In other words, the capacity of even the most cutting-edge multinational corporations, widely seen as the main carriers of transnational capitalism since the 1970s, to live up to their structural potential is probably fairly limited at a strategic level. These limits are reinforced by "enduring national differences" in corporate organizational forms (Pauly and Reich 1997) and "state-societal arrangements" (Hart 1992). At the same time, however, they are drawn into transnational opportunity structures in extensive, if tactical, ways on an ever-increasing scale. One of those ways involves the increasing participation of both large and small firms in transnational financial markets, participation which could well give leading-edge firms in high-tech fields a strong competitive advantage in those markets themselves.

Probably the main group of economic agents that is most often seen as having the potential to become institutional entrepreneurs on a wider scale are participants in global financial markets. Their (mainly indirect) ability to constrain macroeconomic and microeconomic policy and their close links with certain government agencies which play an enforcement role, such as central banks (Maxfield 1997; Pauly 1997), mean that the immediate transnational impact of their actions is evident both to them and to other groups, including mass publics. Recent turmoil in various financial markets, from Asia in 1997 to the subprime mortgage crisis in the United States ten years later, and the impact that this is having on the ability of middle-income developing countries to expand their role and influence in international markets, has highlighted the capacity of international finance.

In terms of economic agents, then, despite their central and widespread interaction with the latent and manifest transnational opportunity structures existing in both political and economic terms, it is unlikely that the more powerful among them will seek to promote a fundamental shift in the broader transnational structuration process—although they may inadvertently drive *other* actors to attempt to effect more far-reaching structural change to counteract perceived negative political, economic and social consequences of economic transnationalization. To be successful, such counter-action, blocked for the most part at domestic level, will need to be played out on the international and transnational fields. Economic agents themselves, however, are most likely to continue to adopt adaptive forms of behavior in structurational terms, e.g. promoting a dialectic of regulatory competition and cooperation in the financial market sector, supporting the continuing reduction of trade barriers and the consolidation of international regimes such as the World Trade Organization and fora like the G7, etc.

The main direct influence of economic transnationalization in terms of agent behavior will be felt in two ways. First, we can identify the spread of an ideology of market globalization through the mass media, the teaching of management in business schools, popular business literature (the "airport bookshop" approach to globalization), and the like. Second, economic transnationalization has had a wide-ranging impact on other categories of agent—in particular, on political agents attempting to reconfigure forms of political authority to meet the potential challenge of transnationally rooted market failures and the demands of popular constituencies for the reassertion of political values such as the public interest in the face of the economic, social, and indirect political power of economic agents. In the last analysis, it will be networks which cut across the crude economic–political–social boundaries examined here that will determine the shape of change.

Political agents: politicians and bureaucrats

In this context, pressures on political agents to act as institutional entrepreneurs are likely to grow. Nevertheless, their actual capacity to act is likely to increase in some ways and decline in others. Such patterns of opportunity and constraint are distinct in several ways from the patterns described above with regard to economic agents, however. In the first place, politicians and bureaucrats are to a great extent *expected* to act as institutional entrepreneurs in the modern world, a role which they generally attempted to fulfil in the world of the nation-state and states system. Their authority and legitimacy depend upon their role as upholders (and to some extent, designers) of constitutions and institutional systems, their capacity to use "non-economic coercion" (Holloway and Picciotto 1978) to protect and further the "national interest." Political agents are expected to combine carrots and sticks in the pursuit of, ideally, collective goals (or at least the goals of dominant groups), to blend "voice" and "loyalty" (in different combinations) while minimizing threats of "exit" or "free-riding." At the same time, that very authority and legitimacy are inextricably intertwined with the *multifunctionality* of their authority (Cerny 1995), and that multifunctionality is generally only made possible by limiting their power to the domestic arena (and/or to the traditional international strategic/diplomatic arena).

The capacity of state actors, in particular, to act as institutional entrepreneurs is extremely uneven. At one level, of course, they can engage in institutional bricolage. Most of the time, however, such agents are relatively bound by existing structural constraints, especially given the embeddedness of state institutions, which remain the main sources of legitimate political power despite trends of disaggregation and policy innovation. At the same time, however, they suffer from a growing disillusionment with governments, politicians, and bureaucrats generally. In this context, too, traditional domestic pressure and interest groups, especially sectional pressure groups, are perceived less and less as parts of a positive-sum, pluralistic process of negotiating satisfactory compromises within the national political arena, and more and more as special interests, acting against the public interest or free-riding on the collective actions of others. With the splintering of the state and the crystallization of more and more complex transnational opportunity structures, many domestically oriented interest and pressure groups are increasingly "out of the loop," condemned to pursue politically problematic goals such as protectionism, and open to marginalization as obsolete representatives of the old Left or the populist Right. Transnationally linked interest groups, on the other hand, are better able to use their influence at a number of different domestic and transnational levels at the same time, even playing state actors off against each other in their desire to "level the playing field" in a politically as well as economically competitive world (Cerny 2006a).

It is at this level where political agents can play a key entrepreneurial role, by acting as intermediaries between (a) transnational pressures and interests and domestic pressures and interest, (b) a complex *transnational public sector* and *transnational private sector*, and (c) producer groups and social movements. A more limited power triad of this type has been identified as the core of contemporary neopluralist political processes in the United States (McFarland 2004: 48 and *infra*), and its extrapolation to the transnational arena creates the potential for new and complex cross-border, "three-level-game" patterns— what I have elsewhere called "golden [or flexible] pentangles" (Cerny 2001). However, no longer having the capacity to systematically privilege the domestic over the transnational, the new political consensus which enables political agents to become institutional entrepreneurs is one which identifies international competitiveness and other broader goals as the main criterion for policy success. Therefore, in terms of both discourse and coalition behavior, this state of affairs privileges those actors who are systematically linked to other transnationally connected actors and who are able to mobilize resources across borders.

Political agents, especially state actors, by identifying international competitiveness as the chief totem of political discourse, put themselves in a position where they require of themselves—and evoke expectations in others, whether businessmen or mass publics—that they must attack not only domestic protectionism but also the state-enforced decommodification of socially deleterious economic activities and practices in the name of leveling the international playing field and, indeed, that they must provide domestic economic agents with greater competitive advantages in a more open world. However, it is not at this obvious level, but in the day-to-day transformation of state intervention by politicians and bureaucrats in their interaction with transnationalizing pressures and interests that the state itself becomes a major collective agent in the structuration process, in turn creating through ongoing bricolage a complex new set of transnational opportunity structures. Paradoxically, political agents are potentially among the main institutional entrepreneurs of the transnationalization process simply because they must attempt to manage key developments in that process through participating in and attempting to manipulate transgovernmental networks and transnational policy communities.

At the same time, however, the capacity of political agents to act is still inextricably intertwined with the maintenance of state institutions and national discourses. Political agents are not about to try to deconstruct the state itself and design overtly transnational constitutional processes to replace it. On the one hand, the very structural strength of state institutions and political processes inhibits the development of effective, autonomous institutions and processes via international regimes and global governance (Lake 1999; Kahler and Lake 2008). On the other hand, in paradoxical fashion, the weight of state interventionism overall tends to increase—often significantly—as states undertake enforcement functions on behalf of (especially) transnationally linked economic agents, functions which transnational structures are unable or unwilling to undertake. The state may be becoming the main terrain of political conflict and coalition-building between forces favoring globalization and those seeking to resist it, but political agents will not be willing to undermine the state itself as the central institutionalized political arena, and thereby undermine the most significant single source of their own power. Thus the state may be dramatically altered through a wide range of adaptive behaviors on the part of political agents, but it will not itself be fundamentally left behind.

Social agents: social movements, interest groups, ordinary people

Social agents are in a complex position with regard to their capacity to reinforce and generate transnational structural change. The depth of politically imposed national identities in the developed world enabled nation-states and the states system during most of the twentieth century to spawn two world wars and the Cold War as well as to dominate processes of political development in the postcolonial era. Nevertheless, especially in the last two decades of the century, increasing tensions over the distribution of economic and political goods, and a proliferating set of demands by diverse social actors cutting across both global and domestic arenas throughout the world, have fueled endemic dissatisfaction with existing institutions and processes of governance. The uncertain and destabilizing processes of democratic transition, globalization, and the rapid formation of new collective identities have created tremendous social as well as political volatility and inspired popular pressure both for new kinds of control and accountability and for specific policy remedies. As with the other two categories of agents discussed earlier, there are three aspects to consider: the population of agents; the changing structured action field in which they operate; and the potential for their action to direct or shape structural change.

In the first place, there is emerging a new range of pressures from below. The proliferation of social agents on the international and transnational levels has been widely noted. These numbers and activities of such groups have grown in range, scale, and scope. Some are more like traditional pressure or interest groups (Willetts 1982), adjusting the scale of their organization to conform to the scale of problems facing particular categories of people in a global setting. Probably the least represented at this level have been what the traditional pressure group literature called "sectional groups." However, more emphasis is placed today on the recent growth of what the traditional group literature called "cause groups" (Key 1953) or what at global level are now called "transnational advocacy coalitions [or networks]" (Keck and Sikkink 1998), "social movements" in issue-areas like environmental activism, women's rights, population policy, socioeconomic development, and even military policy, as in, for example, the campaign for an international treaty banning the use of landmines. These advocacy groups do not merely mimic domestic cause groups for three reasons.

In the first place, they target issues which are international and/or transnational in scope. In particular, they pursue objectives which either are not being responded to or cannot be effectively responded to at national level because of the structural linkages among different levels and spaces (both territorial and virtual). Another reason is that they can bring together a range of coalition partners who would not normally be prepared to work closely with each other in a national setting for a variety of structural and historical reasons. For example, rainforest campaigns in Latin America can bring together displaced workers and peasants, women, quasi-elite groups concerned with environmental degradation per se, indigenous groups and organizations concerned with Third Word economic development and the like, and that is just *within* the developing state or states involved in the action. Furthermore, each of these indigenous groups will have links with external, often First World-based organizations (non-governmental organizations—NGOs) concerned with directing campaigns in the international and national media in the developed world, not to mention links with other kinds of elite and mass networks, including various scientists and experts ("epistemic communities"), in developed countries. These broad (but shifting) coalitions usually either have established relationships, through transnational policy networks and policy communities, with international (intergovernmental) regimes and with state actors in particular agencies in the richer countries too, or else they are in the process of developing those links through new activities. Finally, the internet and other new communications and information technologies give these coalitions great reach and flexibility in the ways they can target different agents in states, international institutions, academics, the media, and the like. In this sense, the narrower pressure group model overlaps more and more with the NGO model, which in turn overlaps considerably with broader egalitarian New Social Movements (Murphy 1998) creating a potential virtuous circle of action.[5]

Second, these groups of social agents also benefit from the changing structured field of action, or what Krieger and Murphy (1998) have called the "Transnational Opportunity Structure." The TOS refers to what in the traditional public policy and pressure group literature were called "points of access"; structural openings in political and bureaucratic institutions where pressure groups can influence particular interlocutors within the state apparatus, whether individual state actors, specific agencies, or so-called "iron triangles" of the policy network type. Whereas the traditional pressure group and social movement literature focuses on the more embedded institutional points of access of the state, commentators on NSMs and NGOs are increasingly pointing to opportunities at the international and transnational levels.[6] Indeed, transnational cause groups can strategically "whipsaw" policymakers at local, national, and international levels, going back and forth between applying traditional pressure group tactics to government officials, organizing local resistance, and pursuing international or transnational media and other campaigns, as shown by a case study of the Clayoquot and Great Bear rainforest campaigns in Canada (Krajnc 1999).

In this context, then, social agents involved in the processes just described are increasingly strategically situated in a changing global order. Their influence is still heavily constrained by the regularized allocation of resources and the public goods decisions faced on a routine basis by states and state actors. Nevertheless, it can also be argued that transnational opportunity structures, unlike national ones, are not configured primarily by hierarchical state structures, but by multilayered, quasi-anarchical, overlapping and cross-cutting—transnational—political processes, including not only states-in-flux but also transnational economic and transgovernmental linkages. In such conditions, it is at least conceivable that the standard wisdom may be stood on its head, and that transnational social movements may nurture the growing influence of sets of social agents which themselves will impose new structural forms on the transnational field. At one level, then, social agents, in the form of NGOs and NSMs, may be the most strategically situated agents of all and have the greatest potential leeway to imagine and to construct new forms of transnational structuration. However, the embeddedness of existing state and governmental institutions continues to constitute a major constraint. Whether their diverse bases of support and complex areas of involvement and expertise would permit them to develop an overall structural impact of a kind that could transform the international system itself is somewhat more problematic. As with economic and political agents, of course, the key will not be the action of social agents taken in isolation. Rather it lies in the way that social agents can alter the shape of cross-cutting networks linking all three categories of agent in a globalizing world.

The three categories of actors discussed in this section are pulled and pushed between adaptive and transformative forms of behavior. In the final analysis, however, both kinds of behavior are likely to reinforce and entrench the globalization process, although outcomes are likely to take different forms in different circumstances. The result is a transnational political process that resembles even more complex sets of political opportunities, potential strategies, and forms of political action and interaction across multiple levels than even domestic neopluralism as theorized by McFarland and others in the "research sequence" he describes (McFarland 2004: 2ff.). Like his neopluralist process, multi-nodal politics can be seen as creating new forms of feedback, path dependency, and the ratcheting up of global politics. Indeed, we may be seeing the emergence of what Stone has called a "global *agora*"—"a growing global public space of fluid, dynamic, and intermeshed relations of politics, markets, culture and society ... [characterized by] multiple publics and plural institutions ... a social and political space—generated by globalization—rather than a physical place" (Stone 2008: 21).

Conclusion: scenarios of change

This chapter has focused on both sides of the global structuration process. What kind of outcomes might be hypothesized with regard to the ongoing process of transnational structuration, given the increasing openness of the system, will depend on the way strategically situated agents of all kinds consciously or unwittingly shape that process. Taking our cue from Murphy (1994), we could look at the recent era of rapid marketization and the relative "retreat of the state" (Strange 1996) as merely a stage in the development of a wider social-liberal "world order" or more transnationalized "embedded neoliberalism" (Cerny 2008). Transnational social movements, in this context, might be seen to have not only the widest *scope* for potential action—in order to succeed, they must, in a sense, target the world—but also the greatest *range* or scale of potential action. That is, they can pick and choose their issue-areas to reflect the qualitatively *global* issues they most value and which they are best at pushing—even when those issues appear *local* in purely territorial terms (Sassen 2007). Such movements will likely play a vital role in creating new forms of identity in a more transnationally structured international system, and may indirectly cause new lines of conflict and coalition-building.

A first scenario might suggest that the structural developments outlined above do *not* entail a fundamental shift in the international system. From this perspective, globalizing pressures merely trigger a range of adaptive behaviors on the part of strategically situated actors in each of the categories developed above who are still significantly constrained in their capacity to form effective transformative networks cutting across those categories. In such circumstances, it is likely that the key to understanding structural change (however limited) is most likely to rest with traditional political agents. Such agents, enmeshed deeply in the embedded nation-states system, would react to pressures for change by increasing the adaptive capacity of, for example, traditional forms of international cooperation, especially intergovernmental regimes, along with pressure on domestic actors to adapt as well.

A second alternative scenario might be based on the predominance of transnational social movements and their ability to shape the agendas of other actors both within and cutting across states. Two linked hypotheses can be raised again here: on the one hand, the development of a global civil society, based on common transnational norms and values; and on the other, the emergence of a cross-cutting pluralism (or "plurilateralism": Cerny 1993). Held (1995), for example, has suggested some mixture of analogous developments might well lead to the emergence of a transnational "cosmopolitan democracy." It might especially be the case that, should transnational social movements prove to be the predominant institutional entrepreneurs of the transnational structuration process, then a more complex, supranational process of "mainstreaming" might well provide the glue for some form of de facto democratization-without-the-state. However, this remains a rosy scenario, an idealized state of affairs which it might be unwise to expect.

Nevertheless, the dominant image of transnationalization and globalization today, as suggested earlier, is still that of economic and business globalization. Economic agents, through the transnational expansion of both markets and hierarchical (firm) structures and institutions, increasingly shape a range of key outcomes in terms of the allocation of both resources and values. Neoliberal ideology presents such developments as inevitable; in Mrs. Thatcher's famous phrase: "There is no alternative" (TINA). Should transnational social movements prove more peripheral to the structuration process than a Polanyian "double movement" might suggest, and should political actors and the state continue to act as promoters of globalization and enforcement, then the governance structures of the twenty-first century international system will be likely to reflect in a more direct and instrumental way the priorities of international capital. Without a world government or set of effective *inter-national* (cooperative/interstate) governance mechanisms, private economic regimes such as internationalized financial markets and associations of transnationally active firms, large and small, are likely to shape the international system through their ability to channel investment flows and set cross-border prices for both capital and physical assets as well (Cerny 2000a). In this sense, the shape of the governance structures of such a system will merely mimic the structures of capital itself.

This raises a number of issues. In the first place, it has been suggested that capital cannot directly control society. Capitalists are concerned first and foremost with competing with each other, not with policing the system (which can eat up profits); and there is no collective mechanism, no "ideal collective capitalist" to regulate the system in the interests of capital as a whole, other than the state (Holloway and Picciotto 1978). Nevertheless, indirect forms of control, for example through Gramscian cultural hegemony, may be more important than the state per se (especially in its limited guise as a nation-state). Gill (1990, 2003), for example, sees the Trilateral Commission, the World Economic Forum (Davos) and other formal and informal networks among transnationally linked businessmen and their social and political allies as bearers of such hegemony. In this sense, then, it may be possible to hypothesize that, should transnational capital take a relatively holistic hegemonic form, then the international system of the twenty-first century will represent a truly liberal (or neoliberal) capitalist society in a way that no capitalist state has ever been able to. Private sector-based mechanisms of control at a transnational level may indeed replace the state as a "committee of the whole bourgeoisie." However, the crystallization of other forms of international capital can also be envisaged, reflecting an unequal distribution of power or representation, for example among different economic sectors. For example, in the 1970s what essentially were cartels of multinational corporations were thought by many on both sides of the political divide to be the form that international capital would take in the future. But in the twenty-first century world of dramatic international capital movements, it is more often the financial markets which might be seen as exercising a "sectoral hegemony" over the international system (Cerny 1994a, 1994b and 1996). In either case, however, any significant transfer of power or system control from political agents (via states) to economic agents would represent a fundamental change.

A final scenario, which I have explored elsewhere (Cerny 1998, 2000b), is that exogenous pressures on the nation-state/states system, interacting with and exacerbating the tensions within that system, will cause that system to erode and weaken in key ways, but *without providing enough in the way of structural resources to any category of agents (or combination of categories) to effectively shape the transnational structuration process.* In other words, no group or group of groups will be at the steering wheel of change in the international system, and competition between different groups will in turn undermine the capacity of any one of them to exercise such control. In such circumstances, the outcome might be what has been called "neomedievalism": a fluid, multilayered structure of overlapping and competing institutions, cultural flux, multiple and shifting identities and loyalties, with different "niches" at different levels for groups to focus their energies on. As Minc (1993) has argued, the medieval world was not a world of chaos; it was a world of "durable disorder." Unless some coherent group of institutional entrepreneurs emerges to control and direct the process of transnational structuration, the medieval analogy may provide a better guide to understanding the international system in the twenty-first century than previous models involving states and the states system, both domestically and internationally. There is no reason in principle, after all, why "governance" in this broad sense has to be tidy and logically coherent. The nation-state as such, and in particular the national industrial welfare state of the Second Industrial Revolution, may well be caught

157

up in such wider, more complex webs, leading to increased uncertainty and possible disorder. At the same time, however, crosscutting networks of economic, political and social agents would lead to an increase in the influence and power wielded by transnationally linked institutional entrepreneurs, some of whom will certainly attempt to transcend the limits of adaptive behavior and develop new institutional strategies for transforming and reconstructing the political in this fluid, globalizing world.

In each of these scenarios, nevertheless, we can see either an incremental or a much more rapid feedback process, based on actors' evolving strategies, behaviors, and discourses, leading to a ratcheting up of the globalization process itself. However, the shape that process takes will differ depending on which actors—and coalitions of actors—develop the most influence and power to manipulate and mold particular outcomes within and across a range of critical issue-areas. Moreover, it should be obvious by now that the kind of analytical methodology most appropriate to defining, unraveling, explaining, and understanding the emergence and increasing paradigmatic predominance of multi-nodal politics is one of qualitative, discursive, historically informed process-tracing, informed by the competition among alternative paradigms suggested by Wolin (1968). Quantitative methods may permit the testing of certain hypotheses where clear and unambiguous data are available, and formal methods may assist in the development of logical connections, but both need to be clearly framed and operationalized within wider and more complex theoretical and historical parameters.

The continuing development of international political economy as a transdisciplinary field is absolutely essential to our understanding of what is happening in the world today. We are faced with significant structural changes, but their import is uncertain (Blyth 2003). Structural changes by themselves not only emerge from earlier processes of structuration, but are also ambiguous and amorphous in their ramifications for short-term events as well as for long-term transformation; they can lead to a range of alternative outcomes. The ideas and interests of a wide range of significant actors inevitably mediate and shape not only day-to-day developments but also fundamental transformations—the chief of which today is globalization. IPE has been and will continue to be at the forefront of expanding our understanding of this process. Therefore it is crucial that we analyze globalization through competing paradigms, narratives, and discourses. Unlike Darwinist evolution, globalization is not a random process of selection. Nor can it be reduced pseudo-scientifically to predictable indicators by applying Ockham's razor to a data set, formula, equation, or large-n study. It involves conscious actors, whether individuals or groups, who can interpret structural changes, alternative pathways and opportunities creatively; change and refine their strategies; negotiate, bargain, build coalitions, and mobilize their power resources in ongoing interactions with other actors; and—both in winning and losing—affect and shape medium-term and long-term outcomes. Multi-nodal politics is a complex phenomenon that must be analyzed and understood in its historical, structural, and conjunctural complexity. However, by restoring political action and process to center stage, it may provide a way to begin to bridge the transatlantic divide.

Notes

1 Not limited to the impact of the Civil Rights Movement and of radical protests against the Vietnam War, this reaction notably included the influence of the conservative, anti-behavioralist followers of political philosopher Leo Strauss (Storing 1962) as well as the renascence of Marxist and neo-Marxist

approaches throughout the social sciences; the revival of interest in the state as an analytical concept in both comparative politics and international relations; and the development of new postmodernist, poststructuralist and post-positivist approaches in literary criticism, cultural studies and social theory, spilling over into political science and IR theory and analysis.

2 It must be emphasized, however, that proponents of non-quantitative, non-rational choice approaches have remained a vocal minority in the American academy, as represented in particular by the recent perestroika movement in the American Political Science Association. In turn, the establishment of the International Political Economy Society in the United States in 2006 represents, in part, a counter-reaction by supporters of quantitative and formalistic approaches—sparking off the transatlantic divide controversy as expressed by Cohen at that society's inaugural meeting, where some of the arguments made in this chapter were offered in a formal response. Political science—and IPE—in Britain, Canada, Australia, Europe, and elsewhere, however, have not made this renewed scientific turn to the same extent as in the United States, although its supporters are, in a mirror image of the situation in America, in a strong minority in particular institutions and departments.

3 Exogenous structural variables include the infrastructure of travel and transportation, competitive imperatives facing the multinational corporation, the abstract and all-pervading character of international finance, the flexibility of post-Fordist production techniques, the innovation and spread of information and communications technology, a general speeding up of the tempo of life and consciousness, the cultural "global village," or the indivisible ecology of the planet.

4 Lake (1999) calls this the "privatization of governance."

5 Although the very diversity of such a process also can lead to overcomplexity and uncertainty.

6 These points of access include, of course, international regimes, particularly the United Nations, which has always been open to such groups in both formal and informal ways (Willetts 1982); particular state agencies with jurisdictional scope in the very issue-areas focused on by these coalitions (environmental agencies, etc.); wider epistemic communities of experts, think tanks, scientists and the like; the proliferation of new fora such as UN-sponsored conferences on social development, population, human settlements, women's health, climate change, and the like (Betsill 1999; Clark et al. 1999; Dodgson 1999); and private organizations in other spheres, particularly business.

Part III

IPE in Asia

10

Reading Hobbes in Beijing

Great power politics and the challenge of the peaceful ascent

Giovanni Arrighi

"Particularly in the social sciences," notes Benjamin Cohen, "intellectual developments tend to be tied ... to new events and trends that make old ways of thinking inadequate." The birth of IPE in US political science in the early 1970s was no exception, rooted as it was in the seeming decline of US power that ensued from remarkable recovery of the European and Japanese economies after the devastation of the Second World War on the one side, and the fundamental transformation of relations between the wealthy North and the poverty-stricken South entailed by postwar decolonization on the other. Partly cause and partly effect of these changes, a growing interdependence of national economies seemed to threaten the ability of governments to manage economic affairs, while a growing détente between the two nuclear superpowers seemed to undermine the salience of the traditional concern of students of world politics with national security. This was the historical context in which the pioneers of American IPE challenged the then dominant "realist model of purposive states singlemindedly preoccupied with the 'high politics' of war and peace" (Cohen, this volume, Chapter 1).

Thirty years later, the spectacular economic ascent of China has led to a resurgence of realist concerns with the high politics of war and peace to which IPE seems to have no easy answer. Thus, on the eve of 9/11, John Mearsheimer concluded *The Tragedy of Great Power Politics* with a call "for the United States to ... do what it can to slow the rise of China." He then went on to claim that "the structural imperatives of the international system, which are powerful, will probably force the United States to abandon its policy of constructive engagement in the near future. Indeed, there are signs that the new Bush administration has taken the first steps in this direction." In reiterating this position in a later interview, he suggested that the most effective strategy would be for the United States to put in place a political and military "balancing coalition" that included Japan, Vietnam, Korea, India, and Russia. The United States could then back Russia in a border dispute with China; it could back Japan in a dispute with China over sea lines of communication; or it could "go to war on behalf of Taiwan" (Mearsheimer 2001: 402; Kreisler 2002).

As it turns out, by getting bogged down in the Iraqi quagmire, the Bush administration has been forced to deepen rather than abandon the constructive engagement with

China. But the idea of containing China through a variety of strategies, including the kind of political and military "balancing coalition" envisaged by Mearsheimer, has continued to hold sway in US foreign policy circles. Thus, echoing Mearsheimer, Robert Kaplan has contended that the emergence of China as a great power inevitably clashes with US interests.

> Whenever great powers have emerged ... (Germany and Japan in the early decades of the twentieth century, to cite two recent examples), they have tended to be particularly assertive—and therefore have thrown international affairs into violent turmoil. China will be no exception.

The result "is likely to be the defining military conflict of the twenty-first century: if not a big war with China, then a series of Cold War-style standoffs that stretch out over years and decades" (Kaplan 2005: 50–51).

As a direct rebuttal of the idea of a "China threat" and as a charm offensive designed to counter the US strategy of encircling China with a system of military bases and security relationships, in 2003 the Chinese launched the doctrine of *heping jueqi* (literally "emerging precipitously in a peaceful way"). The central tenet of the doctrine is that China will avoid the aggressive stance of earlier rising powers. In the words of one of the framers of the doctrine, "China will not take the road of Germany in the first world war, or Germany and Japan in the second world war" (Leonard 2005). Rather, as another authority put it, "China aims to grow and advance without upsetting existing orders. We are trying to rise in a way that benefits our neighbors" (Funabashi 2003). Although the expression "peaceful rise" was later dropped in favor of "peaceful development" or "peaceful coexistence," the underlying doctrine has remained firmly in place, as witnessed by President Hu Jintao's 2004 proclamation of "four 'no's" ("no to hegemony, no to force, no to blocs, no to the arms race"), and "four 'yes's" (to "confidence building, reducing difficulties, developing cooperation, and avoiding confrontation") (Bulard 2005). Chinese officials see no contradiction between their doctrine of "peaceful development" and their determination to develop more capable armed forces, which they see as integral to China's development as well as a natural response to the humiliations from the Opium Wars of the mid-nineteenth century to the brutal Japanese invasion and occupation in 1931–45. "China's national defense policy is one of self-protection," claimed Prime Minister Wen Jiabao in April 2005. "Over the past 100 years, China has always been bullied by others. China has never sent a single soldier to occupy even an inch of another country's land" (Dickie et al. 2005).[1]

In a recent exchange with Zbigniew Brzezinski—who appeared to accept the possibility of a peaceful rise of China—Mearsheimer once again dismissed this possibility. If China's dramatic economic growth continues over the next few decades,

> the United States and China are likely to engage in an intense security competition with considerable potential for war. Most of China's neighbors, including India, Japan, Singapore, South Korea, Russia, and Vietnam, will likely join with the United States to contain China's power.

In order to realize this, he claimed, we must privilege theory over political reality. Whereas "we cannot know what political reality is going to look like in the year 2025," his theory of the rise of great powers has "a straightforward answer" on what to expect "when China has a much larger gross national product and a much more formidable military than it has today." China will "try to push the United States out of Asia, much the way the United States pushed the European great powers out of the Western Hemisphere"; and the United States "will seek to contain China and ultimately weaken it to the point where it is no longer capable of dominating Asia ... [behaving] toward China much the way it behaved toward the Soviet Union during the Cold War" (Brzezinski and Mearsheimer 2005: 2–3).

Brzezinski dismissed the claim that theory must be privileged over political reality on the ground that "theory—at least in international relations—is essentially retrospective. When something happens that does not fit the theory, it gets revised." In his view this will be the case with US–China relationships. Quite apart from the fact that nuclear weapons have altered power politics, how great powers behave is not predetermined. "If the Germans and the Japanese had not conducted themselves the way they did, their regimes might not have been destroyed." In this respect, "the Chinese leadership appears much more flexible and sophisticated than many previous aspirants to great power status" (Brzezinski and Mearsheimer 2005: 3).

It is true that what happens in the "short-run" of a decade or two is determined by a host of contingent and random events that in a longer perspective, as Mearsheimer put it, "get washed out of the equation" by more durable underlying trends. Unless we have a theory capable of identifying and explaining these more durable trends, we will be at a loss in figuring out what will happen when the "dust" of contingent and random events settles. To be of any use, however, a theory of relations between incumbent and emergent great powers must be grounded in the historical experiences that are most germane to the problem at hand and at the same time leave open the possibility of breaks with underlying trends. If the problem with Brzezinski's views is that they have no theoretical foundation, the problem with Mearsheimer's theory is that it is built on wholly inappropriate historical foundations.

For one thing, Mearsheimer downplays the role that markets and capital have played historically as instruments of power in their own right. In his scheme of things, only the conversion of economic power into the kind of military power that is now concentrated in the hands of the United States can transform China into a truly great power.

> If the Chinese are smart, they will. ... concentrate on building their economy to the point where it is bigger than the U.S. economy. Then they can translate that economic strength into military might and create a situation where they are in a position to dictate terms to states in the region and to give the United States all sorts of trouble.
>
> (Brzezinski and Mearsheimer 2005: 4)

The possibility that it might be *smarter* on the part of the Chinese to continue to use their rapidly expanding domestic market and national wealth as instruments of regional and global power (as they are already doing, while the allegedly all-powerful US military apparatus is bogged down in Iraq) is ruled out on specious historical grounds. In dismissing Brzezinski's contention that China's desire for continued economic growth makes conflict with the United States unlikely, Mearsheimer argues that "that logic should have applied to Germany before World War I and to Germany and Japan before World War II." And yet, despite their "impressive economic growth," Germany started both World Wars and Japan started conflict in Asia (Brzezinski and Mearsheimer 2005: 3). In reality, neither Germany before the First World War, nor Germany and Japan before the Second World War were all that successful economically. They were very

165

successful industrially, but in terms of national wealth they were barely narrowing the per capita income gap that separated them from Britain, and were falling behind the United States. Their resort to war can in fact be interpreted as an attempt to attain by military means the power they could not attain by economic means (Arrighi 1994: 268, 334).

The United States, in contrast, had no need to challenge Britain militarily in order to consolidate its growing economic power. In both World Wars, all it had to do was, one, let Britain and its challengers exhaust one another militarily and financially; two, enrich itself by supplying goods and credit to the wealthier contestant; and three, intervene in the war at a late stage so as to be in a position to dictate terms of the peace that facilitated the exercise of its own economic power. Today there are no emergent military powers with the inclination or the capacity to challenge the dominant power. Nevertheless, the dominant power is involved in an open-ended war which is exhausting it militarily, financially, and politically. Under these circumstances, could not China's optimal power strategy vis-à-vis the United States be a variant of the earlier US strategy vis-à-vis Britain? Would it not be in China's best interest, one, to let the United States exhaust itself further in an endless war on terror; two, to enrich itself by supplying goods and credit to the increasingly incoherent US superpower; and three, use its expanding national market and wealth to win over allies in the creation of a new world order centered on China, but not necessarily dominated militarily by China? A theory that does not even raise this question, and predicts that the United States and China are inevitably headed toward a military confrontation, may well be worse than no theory at all.

The problem arises in part from Mearsheimer's exclusive focus on instances of competitive rather than cooperative relations between incumbent and emerging great powers (such as Germany's relation to Britain in the late nineteenth and early twentieth century, or Japan's relation to the United States in the inter-war period, or US–Soviet relations after the Second World War), when in fact the comparison most relevant to today's US–Chinese relations may well be with relations between the incumbent hegemonic power of the late nineteenth and early twentieth centuries (the United Kingdom) and the economically most successful emergent power of the epoch (the United States). As Brad DeLong has noted with specific reference to possible future developments of current US–Chinese relations, this was a relationship that evolved from deep mutual hostility to increasingly close cooperation, precisely when the United States began challenging British hegemony both regionally and globally (Ip and King 2005).

The main problem with Mearsheimer's theory, however, is its complete disregard of the historical experience of the indigenous East Asian interstate system. The main purpose of this essay is to show that this system has been characterized by a long-term dynamic that contrasts sharply with the Western dynamic on which Mearsheimer's theory is based. The eventual incorporation of the East Asian system within the structures of the globalizing European system transformed this dynamic, but it contributed also to the transformation of the Western dynamic. The result has been a hybrid political-economic formation that theories of international relations based exclusively on the Western experience are utterly incapable of comprehending.

The five-hundred years' peace

Contrary to widespread belief, national states and their organization in an interstate system are not European inventions. Except for a few states that were the creation of European colonial powers (most notably, Indonesia, Malaysia, and the Philippines), the most important states of East Asia—from Japan, Korea, and China to Vietnam, Laos, Thailand, and Kampuchea—were national states long before any of their European counterparts. What's more, they had all been linked to one another, directly or through the Chinese center, by trade and diplomatic relations and held together by a shared understanding of the principles, norms, and rules that regulated their mutual interactions as a world among other worlds. As Japanese scholars specializing in the China-centered tribute trade system have shown, this system presented sufficient similarities with the European interstate system to make their comparison analytically meaningful (cf. Ikeda 1996).

Both systems consisted of a multiplicity of political jurisdictions that appealed to a common cultural heritage and traded extensively with one another. Although cross-border trade was more publicly regulated in East Asia than in Europe, since Song times (960–1276) private overseas trade had flourished and transformed the nature of tribute trade, the main purpose of which, in Takeshi Hamashita's words, "came to be the pursuit of profits through the unofficial trade that was ancillary to the official system." Analogies can also be detected in the interstate competition that characterized the two systems. The tribute trade system centered on China provided its separate domains with a symbolic framework of mutual interaction that nonetheless was loose enough to endow its peripheral components with considerable autonomy vis-à-vis the Chinese center. Thus, Japan and Vietnam were peripheral members of the system but also competitors with China in the exercise of the imperial title awarding function, Japan establishing a tributary-type relationship with the Ryukyu kingdom, and Vietnam with Laos (Hamashita 1993: 75–76, 1994: 92, 1997: 114–24). Kaoru Sugihara explicitly maintains that the diffusion of the best technology and organizational know-how within East Asia makes it "possible to think of the presence of an East Asian multi-centered political system … with many features analogous to the interstate system in Europe" (Sugihara 1996: 38).

These similarities make a comparison of the two systems analytically meaningful. But once we compare their dynamics, two fundamental differences become immediately evident. First, the dynamic of the European system was characterized by an incessant military competition among its national components and by a tendency toward the geographical expansion both of the system and of its shifting center (Arrighi 2007: ch. 8). Long periods of peace among European powers were the exception rather than the rule. Thus, the "hundred years' peace" (1815–1914) that followed the Napoleonic Wars was "a phenomenon unheard of in the annals of Western civilization (Polanyi 1957: 5)." Moreover, even during this 100 years' peace European states were involved in countless wars of conquest in the non-European world and in the escalating armament race that culminated in the industrialization of war. While initially these involvements resulted in a new wave of geographical expansion which dampened conflicts within the European system, they eventually led to a new round of wars among European powers (1914–45) of unprecedented destructiveness (cf. Arrighi 2007: chs. 5, 7).

In sharp contrast to this dynamic, the East Asian system of national states stood out for the near absence of intra-systemic military competition and extra-systemic geographical expansion. Thus, with the important exception of China's frontier wars to be discussed presently, prior to their subordinate incorporation in the European system the national states of the East Asian system were almost uninterruptedly at peace with one another, not for 100, but for 300 years. This 300 years' peace was bracketed by two Japanese invasions of Korea, both of which precipitated a war with China—the Sino–Japanese wars of 1592–98 and 1894–95. Between 1598 and 1894 there were only three brief wars that involved China—the 1659–60 and the 1767–71 wars with Burma, and the 1788–89 war with Vietnam, and two wars that did not involve China—the Siamese–Burmese Wars of 1607–18 and of 1660–62. Indeed, in so far as China is concerned, we should speak of a 500 years' peace, since in the 200 years preceding the 1592 Japanese invasion of Korea, China was at war against other East Asian states only during the invasion of Vietnam in 1406–28 to restore the Tran dynasty (Arrighi 2007: 316).

The infrequency of wars among East Asian states was associated with a second crucial difference between the East Asian and European systems: the absence of any tendency among East Asian states to build *overseas* empires in competition with one another and to engage in an armament race in any way comparable to the European powers. East Asian states did compete with one another; Sugihara, for example, detects a competitive rela-tion in the tendency of Tokugawa Japan (1600–1868) to create a tribute trade system centered on Japan instead of China and to absorb technological and organizational know-how in agriculture, mining, and manufacturing from Korea and China. Through these tendencies, as Heita Kawakatsu put it, "Japan was trying to become a mini-China both ideologically and materially" (Sugihara 1996: 37–38; Kawakatsu 1994: 6–7). This kind of competition, however, drove the East Asian developmental path toward state-and-national-economy-making rather than in the European direction of war-making and territorial expansion.

This contention may seem to be at odds with the long series of wars that China fought on its frontiers during the closing years of Ming rule and in the first 150 years of Qing rule. As Peter Perdue has noted, the history of the China-centered system appears in a different light when seen from a frontier perspective. The presence of nomadic horsemen who raided the borders and sometimes conquered the Chinese capital made military activity particularly prominent in the history of China's north and northwest frontier. Military activity became more prominent when northern conquerors in 1644 established the Qing dynasty and set out to ensure that other northern invaders would not do to them what they had done to the Ming. In the north and northwest, the Qing "could … claim to be the uncontested central pole of a tribute system focused on Beijing [only] after they had created military alliances with the Eastern Mongols, exterminated the rival Western Mongols, conquered Xinjiang, and secured formal suzerainty over Tibet" (Perdue 2003: 60, 65).

The territorial expansion that ensued and the military activities that sustained it were aimed primarily at transforming a hard-to-defend frontier into a pacified periphery and a buffer against raiders and conquerors from Inner Asia. Once the objective had been attained, as it was by the 1760s, territorial expansion ceased and military activities turned into police activities aimed at consolidating the monopoly of the Chinese state over the use of violence within the newly established boundaries. Although quite substantial, this territorial expansion paled in comparison with the successive waves of European expan-sion—the earlier Iberian expansion in the Americas and Southeast Asia; the con-temporary Russian expansion in North Asia and Dutch expansion in Southeast Asia; not to speak of the later expansion of Britain in South Asia and Africa and of its offspring in North America and Australia. Unlike these successive waves, the Qing expansion was strictly limited in space and time by its boundary-drawing objectives, rather than a link in an endless chain of connected expansions.

The difference was not just quantitative but qualitative as well. China's territorial expansion under the Qing was not part of the kind of self-reinforcing cycle through which the competing military apparatuses of European states sustained, and were sustained by, expansion at the expense of other peoples and polities of the earth (McNeill 1982: 143; Arrighi 2007; 266–72). No self-reinforcing cycle of this kind could be observed in East Asia. Qing China's territorial expansion was neither driven by, nor did it result in, competition with other states in extracting resources from overseas peripheries. The logic of political economy associated with this kind of competition had little in common with China's practices. "Rather than extract resources from peripheries, the Chinese state was more likely to invest in them. Political expansion to incorporate new frontiers committed the government to a shift of resources to the peripheries, not extraction from them" (Wong 1997: 148).

These different dynamics of the European and East Asian systems can be traced to two other differences—a difference in the distribution of power among the systems' units, and a difference in the degree to which the primary source of power was internal or external to the system. Even before what Fernand Braudel has called the "extended" sixteenth century in European history (1350–1650)—which corresponds almost exactly to the Ming era in East Asian history (1368–1643)—political, economic, and cultural power in East Asia was far more concentrated in its center (China) than in Europe, where a center proper was hard to identify. But the difference became sharper with the defeat in 1592–98 of Japan's attempt to challenge militarily Chinese centrality by conquest in Korea and with the institutionalization of the European balance of power by the Treaties of Westphalia in 1648.

The balanced power structure of the European system in itself contributed to the disposition of European states to wage war on one another. As Karl Polanyi has underscored, balance-of-power mechanisms—the mechanisms, that is, whereby "three or more units capable of exerting power … behave in such a way as to combine the power of the weaker units against any increase in power of the strongest"—were a key ingredient in the organization of the nineteenth-century 100 years' peace. Historically, however, balance-of-power mechanisms had always attained the objective of maintaining the independence of the participating units "only by continuous war between changing partners" (Polanyi 1957: 5–7). The main reason why in the nineteenth century those same mechanisms resulted in peace rather than war among European states is that political and economic power came to be so concentrated in the hands of Britain as to enable it to transform the balance of power, from a mechanism that no individual state controlled and functioned through wars, into an instrument of informal British rule that promoted peace.[2]

The nineteenth-century association between an increase in the imbalance of power and a decrease in the frequency of war among European states suggests that the imbalance of power typical of the East Asian system was a reason for the infrequency of wars among East Asian states. However, the previously noted fact that the nineteenth-century concentration of power in British hands was accompanied by an escalation of interstate competition both in the production of ever more destructive means of war and in the use of these means to gain access to extra-systemic resources, suggests that a greater imbalance of power cannot in itself explain the virtual absence of these two kinds of competition in the East Asian system. Some other ingredient had to be present in the European and absent in the East Asian mix to produce this divergent pattern of interstate competition. The most plausible candidate is the greater extroversion of the European developmental path in comparison with, and in relation to, the East Asian path.

Although trade within, between, and across political jurisdictions was essential to the operations of both systems, the economic and political weight of long-distance trade relative to short-distance trade was far greater in the European than in the East Asian system. International trade in general, and East–West trade in particular, was a far more important source of wealth and power for European than for East Asian states, especially China. It was this fundamental asymmetry that had made the fortunes of Venice and induced the Iberian states, instigated and assisted by Venice's Genoese rivals, to seek a direct link with the markets of the East (Arrighi 1994: ch. 2). It was this same asymmetry, as we shall see, that underlay the low returns, relative to costs, of Zheng He's fifteenth-century expeditions in the Indian Ocean. Were it not for this asymmetry, Zheng He might very well have sailed "around Africa and 'discover[ed]' Portugal several decades before Henry the Navigator's expeditions began earnestly to push south of Ceuta" (Kennedy 1987: 7).[3] Columbus' accidental discovery of the Americas, while seeking a shorter route to the wealth of Asia, changed the terms of the asymmetry by providing European states with new means to seek entry in Asian markets, as well as with a new source of wealth and power in the Atlantic. But even two centuries after the discovery, Charles Davenant still claimed that whoever controlled the Asian trade was in a position to "give law to all the commercial world" (Wolf 1982: 125).

This extroversion of the European power struggle was a major determinant of the peculiar combination of capitalism, militarism, and territorialism that propelled the globalization of the European system (Arrighi 2007: 234–49). The opposite dynamic of the East Asian system—in which a growing introversion of the power struggle generated a combination of political and economic forces that had no tendency towards *endless* territorial expansion—provides counterfactual evidence in support of this contention. But just as the emergence of the extroverted European path can only be understood in light of the diffusion of the strategies of power pioneered by the Italian city-states, so the emergence of the introverted East Asian path can only be understood in light of the success of Ming and Qing policies in developing by far the largest national market of their times.

Market economy and the antecedents of peaceful coexistence

As Adam Smith knew very well but Western social science later forgot, through the eighteenth century by far the largest national market was to be found not in Europe but in China (Arrighi 2007: ch. 2). This national market had long been in the making, but its eighteenth-century configuration originated in the state-making activities of the Ming and early Qing. During the Southern Song period (1127–1276) and under the Yuan (1277–1368), state support for private sea trade and migration to Southeast Asia led to the formation of overseas Chinese trading networks across the Southern Seas and the Indian Ocean as extensive as any contemporaneous European network. Under the Ming, however, this kind of development did not lead to interstate competition in overseas commercial and territorial expansion as it did in Europe, but was instead kept in check by policies that prioritized domestic trade. By moving the capital from Nanjing to Beijing in 1403 to protect more effectively the northern frontier from Mongolian invasions, the Ming extended to the north the circuits of market exchange that had formed in the south. And by repairing and extending the canal system that connected the rice growing southern regions to the northern political center in order to guarantee food supplies to the latter, they promoted the further growth of the market economy and "canal cities" in the lower Yangzi region (Arrighi et al. 2003: 269–71; Hung 2001a: 491–97).

While promoting the formation and expansion of a national market, the Ming sought to centralize control over revenues by imposing administrative restrictions on foreign trade and migration to Southeast Asia. Admiral Zheng He's seven great voyages to Southeast Asia and across the Indian Ocean between 1405 and 1433 were also meant to extend state control over foreign trade. The expeditions, however, turned out to be exceedingly expensive, and as the Ming became more preoccupied with military threats on the northern frontiers, they were discontinued. For more than a century thereafter the Ming regime continued to promote internal trade but circumscribed private maritime commerce, cracked down on unauthorized external trade, restricted the number of tributary missions, and even banned the building of seagoing ships (McNeill 1982: 47; Hui 1995: 34–38, 53; Wang 1998: 316–23).

Along with many others Janet Abu-Lughod has been puzzled by this withdrawal, which left "an enormous vacuum of power that Muslim merchantmen, unbacked by state sea power, were totally unprepared to fill, but which their European counterparts would be more than willing and able to—after a hiatus of some 70 years" (Abu-Lughod 1989: 321–22). The previously noted asymmetry between the pursuit of wealth and power in the East Asian and European contexts provides a simple solution to this puzzle. European rulers fought endless wars to establish an exclusive control over sea lanes linking West to East, because control over trade with the East was a critical resource in their pursuit of wealth and power. For the rulers of China, in contrast, control over these trade routes was far less important than peaceful relations with neighboring states and the integration of their populous domains into an agriculturally based national economy. It was therefore eminently reasonable for the Ming not to waste resources in trying to control East–West sea lanes and concentrate instead on developing the national market.

Indeed, even China's "tribute trade" had greater economic costs than benefits. Ever since the establishment of a unified taxation system under the Qin and Han dynasties more than 1,000 years earlier, tributary relations between the Chinese imperial court and vassal states did not involve the collection of a tax. On the contrary, especially after the Tang dynasty, and with the sole exception of the Yuan dynasty, vassal states offered the Chinese imperial court only symbolic gifts and received in return much more valuable gifts. Thus, what was nominally "tribute" was in fact a two-way transaction which enabled the Middle Kingdom to "buy" the allegiance of vassal states, and at the same time to control flows of people and commodities across its far flung frontiers (cf. Gao 1993: 1–78). World-historically, this practice provides the most important validation of Hobbes' contention that "Riches joyned with liberality is Power, because it procureth friends, and servants: Without liberality, not so; because in this case they defend not; but expose men to Envy, as a Prey" (Hobbes 1968: 150). As we shall see, "riches joyned with liberality" has become the main source of power also in the Western interstate system. But in this respect the West has been merely catching up with a practice that had been dominant for centuries in the China-centered tribute trade system.

The sustainability and efficacy of this practice depended on several conditions. The Chinese economy had to generate the resources necessary to buy the allegiance of the vassal states; the Chinese state had to be in a position to command these resources; and surrounding states had to be persuaded that attempts to seize resources from China by means that challenged the authority of the Chinese government (such as raids, conquest, war, and illegal trade) would not pay off. Despite, or possibly because of, their success in consolidating and expanding the national economy, by the early sixteenth century the Ming faced increasing difficulties in reproducing these conditions. Widespread corruption,

171

mounting inflation, and increasing fiscal shortfalls on the domestic front, were accompanied by growing external pressures from the expansion of the Jurchens in the north and from the expansion of illegal trade that bypassed Ming tax collectors along the Southeastern coast. Internal degradation and external pressures reinforced one another leading to explosive social disturbances, which the Ming sought to ease by substituting a single tax payable in silver for corvée labor and taxation in kind, and by abandoning the crippled paper currency in favor of a silver standard. Although Spanish shipments of much of their American silver to China via Manila temporarily eased the fiscal and social crisis, Ming financial difficulties skyrocketed owing to the costly war with Japan in the 1590s, the outbreak of full-fledged warfare with the Manchus in the 1610s, and mounting corruption at court and throughout the administration. Japan's imposition of restrictive trade policies in the 1630s, combined with a sharp decline in European silver supplies in the 1630s and 1640s, was the straw that broke the camel's back. By driving up the price of silver, it increased the burden of taxation on the peasantry and led to the resurgence of empire-wide unrest that culminated in the collapse of the Ming in 1644 (Wills 1979: 210–11; Wakeman 1985: ch. 1; Atwell 1986, 1998: 407–15; Elisonas 1991: 261–62; Tong 1991: 115–29; Flynn and Giraldez 1995; Hung 2001a: 498–500; 2001b: 12–18).

With the consolidation of Qing rule, the early Ming's policy privileging domestic over foreign trade resumed with greater vigor. Between 1661 and 1683, the Qing re-imposed the ban on private sea traffic and pursued a scorched earth policy that transformed China's southeast coast from a crucial link connecting the Chinese and the world markets into a no-man's-land that kept the two apart. The sea ban was lifted in 1683 but firearms on board were outlawed and restrictions on the size and weight of trading junks were imposed on the shipbuilding industry. Moreover, in 1717 Chinese subjects were once again forbidden to go privately overseas and in 1757 the designation of Guangzhou as the sole legal port for foreign trade sealed the fate of the whole southeast coastal region for nearly a century (Wills 1979; Skinner 1985: 278–79).

While foreign trade was discouraged, the incorporation of borderlands on all sides increased the scale of the national market and reduced protection costs throughout the empire—a reduction that Qing rulers passed on to their subjects in the form of low and stable taxes. Low and stable taxation was accompanied by vigorous state action aimed at stamping out bureaucratic corruption and tax evasion, through empire-wide land surveys, fiscal reforms, and more effective information-gathering systems. Equally important, in order to consolidate their power vis-à-vis Han landlords, the early Qing encouraged the ongoing partition of large estates into small plots and the conversion of indentured labor into tenants. At the same time, they launched land reclamation programs aimed at re-establishing the fiscal base without raising taxes (Jing 1982: 169–81; Huang 1985: 97–105; Perdue 1987: 78–79; Bartlett 1991; Hung 2004: 482–83). This double "democratization" of land tenure—through the breakup of large estates and through land reclamation—called forth massive state action to maintain and expand the hydraulic infrastructure. Equally important, while relying on market mechanisms to feed China's huge and expanding population probably more than any of its predecessors, the Qing government surpassed them all in protecting the population from the vicissitudes of the grain market through a system of granaries that enabled it to buy and store grain at times of abundance and low prices, and to sell the grain back at sub-market prices at times of scarcity and unusually high prices (Will and Wong 1991; Rowe 2001: 155–85).

The outcome of these policies was the remarkable peace, prosperity, and demographic growth which induced leading figures of the European Enlightenment to look to China "for moral instruction, guidance in institutional development, and supporting evidence for their advocacy of causes as varied as benevolent absolutism, meritocracy, and an agriculturally based national economy" (Adas 1989: 79; cf. Hung 2003). And yet, neither the Chinese rulers nor their European admirers realized that the extroverted European developmental path was re-making the world through a process of creative destruction that would soon overshadow all these achievements. "European ships"—in William McNeill's words—"had in effect turned Eurasia inside out. The sea frontier had super-seded the steppe frontier as the critical meeting point with strangers, and the autonomy of Asian states and peoples began to crumble" (McNeill 1998: 231).

Crucial in this respect was the capitalist character of Europe's developmental path. This character is determined, not by the mere presence of capitalist institutions and disposi-tions, but by the relation of state power to capital. Add as many capitalists as you like to a market economy, but unless the state has been subordinated to their class interest, the market economy remains non-capitalist (Arrighi 2007: chs. 3, 8). Braudel himself took imperial China as the example that "most opportunely supports [his] insistence on separating the *market economy* and *capitalism*." China did not just "have a solidly-established market economy." It also had communities of merchants and bankers comparable to the business communities that constituted the preeminent capitalist organizations of six-teenth-century Europe. And yet, the state's "unmistakable hostility to any individual making himself 'abnormally' rich" meant that "there could be no capitalism, except within certain clearly-defined groups, backed by the state, supervised by the state and always more or less at its mercy" (Braudel 1982: 153, 588–89, emphasis in the original).

Braudel exaggerates the extent to which under the Ming and the Qing—not to speak of earlier dynasties—capitalists were at the mercy of a hostile state. It remains nonetheless true that there is no parallel in East Asia for the *sequence* of ever more powerful states that in Europe identified themselves with capitalism—from the Italian city-states, through the Dutch proto-nation-state, to a state, Britain, in the process of becoming the center of a world-encircling maritime and territorial empire. It is this sequence more than anything else that marks the European developmental path as capitalist. And conversely, the absence of anything comparable to this sequence is the clearest sign that in the Ming and early Qing eras market-based development in China and throughout East Asia remained non-capitalist. Closely related to this was the absence of anything remotely resembling the incessant armament race and overseas territorial expansion typical of European states. As R. Bin Wong put it,

> Much European commercial wealth was tapped by needy governments anxious to expand their revenue bases to meet ever-escalating expenses of war. ... Both European merchants and their governments benefited from their complex rela-tionship. ... The late imperial Chinese state did not develop the same kind of mutual dependence on rich merchants. Lacking the scale of financial difficulties encountered in Europe between the sixteenth and eighteenth centuries, Chinese officials had less reason to imagine new forms of finance, huge merchant loans, and the concept of public as well as private debt.
>
> (1997: 146)

As a result, Chinese capitalists remained a subordinate social group with little capacity to subject the national interest to their own class interest. Indeed, the best chances for capitalism to develop in East Asia were not close to the centers but interstitially on the outer rims of the system's states. The most prominent embodiment of this development was the overseas Chinese diaspora, whose resilience and enduring economic importance has few parallels in world history. Despite governmental restrictions, periodic reverses and challenges from Muslims and other competitors, the overseas Chinese diaspora made extraordinary profits and provided a steady flow of revenue for local governments and of remittances to China's coastal regions. It was nonetheless incapable of preventing European states, companies and merchants from gradually filling the political void that the inward-looking policies of Qing China and Tokugawa Japan left in maritime East Asia (Wang 1991: 85–86, 1998: 320–23; Cushman 1993: 136; Hui 1995: 35–36, 79–80; Wills 1998: 333).

In short, the very success of China's self-centered development—which impressed even Europeans—prevented the Qing from detecting the new kind of power that the aggressive seaborne "barbarians" were bringing to the region. The absence in East Asia of the synergy typical of the European developmental path between militarism, industrialism and capitalism, which propelled, and was in turn sustained by, ceaseless overseas territorial expansion, meant that East Asian states were at peace for much longer periods than European states and that China could consolidate its position as the world's largest market economy. But the lack of involvement in overseas expansion and in a European-style armament race eventually made China and the entire East Asian system vulnerable to the military onslaught of the expanding European powers.

Incorporation and hybridization

The subordinate incorporation of East Asia within the European system was not primarily the result of the competitive edge of Western vis-à-vis East Asian, especially Chinese, economic enterprise. Outside of railways and mines, Western merchants and producers had a hard time competing with their Chinese counterparts, and throughout the first half of the nineteenth century opium was their only feasible entrée into the Chinese market (Feuerwerker 1970: 371–75; Esherick 1972: 10; Nathan 1972: 5; Chen 1984: 58–61; So 1986: 103–16; Kasaba 1993). In Britain's case opium was much more than that, because British sales of Indian opium to China were crucial in the transfer of tribute from India to London. As early as 1786, Lord Cornwallis, then governor-general of India, claimed that the expansion of the India–China trade was essential to the transfer the vast tribute of Bengal to England *without heavy losses through exchange depreciation.* When the India trade monopoly of the East India Company was abrogated in 1813, the company redoubled its efforts in promoting opium smuggling into China, and as shipments expanded rapidly, the soundness of Cornwallis' claim was fully vindicated (Greenberg 1951: ch. 2; Bagchi 1982: 96).

As competition in this lucrative branch of British commerce intensified, British merchants agitated for "the strong arm of England" to bring down the restrictions that the Chinese government imposed on the opium trade. Far from yielding to British pressures, the Chinese government moved to suppress a trade that was as baneful for China as it was beneficial for Britain. Having failed to persuade Britain to cooperate in the suppression of the traffic in the name of international law and common morality, the Chinese authorities proceeded to confiscate and destroy smuggled opium and to incarcerate some smugglers. This police operation on Chinese territory was denounced in the British Parliament as "a grievous sin—a wicked offence—an atrocious violation of justice,

174

for which England had the right, a strict and undeniable right," by "the law of God and man," "to demand reparation by force if refused peaceable applications" (Semmel 1970: 153). Evidently, two quite different views of international law and common morality held sway in Britain and China. But while the Chinese claimed a right to lay down and enforce the law only at home, the British claimed a right to lay down and enforce the law not just at home but in China as well. To paraphrase Marx, between equal rights force decides. China had no answer to the steam-powered warship that in a single day in February 1841 destroyed nine war junks, five forts, two military stations, and one shore battery (Parker 1989: 96).

After a disastrous war, an explosion of major rebellions, and a second, equally disastrous war with Britain (now joined by France), China became a subordinate and increasingly peripheral member of the global capitalist system. This loss of status and power was not just the direct result of defeat in the Opium Wars. It was also its indirect result because the Opium Wars, by revealing brutally the full implications of Western military superiority, awoke the ruling groups of China and Japan to the imperatives of accelerated military modernization and led to the "internalization" within the East Asian system of the armament race that had long been a feature of the European system (cf. Tsiang 1967: 144; Fairbank 1983: 197–98; So and Chiu 1995: 49–50).

For about twenty-five years after they were launched, industrialization efforts in China and Japan yielded similar economic results. Nevertheless, Japan's victory in the Sino–Japanese War of 1894 was symptomatic of a fundamental difference between the industrialization drive of the two countries. In China, the main agency of the drive were provincial authorities, whose power vis-à-vis the central government had increased considerably during the repression of the rebellions of the 1850s and who used industrialization to consolidate their autonomy. In Japan, in contrast, the industrialization drive was integral to the Meiji Restoration, which centralized power in the hands of the national government at the expense of provincial authorities (So and Chiu 1995: 53, 68–72).

The outcome of the Sino–Japanese war, in turn, deepened the underlying divergence in the trajectories of Japanese and Chinese industrialization. China's defeat further weakened an already fragile national cohesion, imposed further restrictions on sovereignty and crushing war indemnities, which led to the final collapse of the Qing regime and the growing autonomy of semi-sovereign warlords, followed by Japanese invasion, and recurrent civil wars between the forces of nationalism and communism. Victory over China in 1894, followed by victory over Russia in the war of 1904–5, in contrast, established Japan—to paraphrase Akira Iriye—as "a respectable participant in the game of imperialist politics" (Iriye 1970: 552). The acquisition of Chinese territory—most notably Taiwan in 1895, followed by the Liaodong peninsula and the securing of all Russian rights and privileges in South Manchuria in 1905, and culminating in China's recognition of Japanese suzerainty over Korea, annexed as a colony in 1910—provided Japan with valuable outposts from which to launch future attacks on China, as well as with secure overseas supplies of cheap food, raw materials, and markets. At the same time, Chinese indemnities amounting to more than one-third of Japan's national income helped Japan to finance the expansion of heavy industry and to put its currency on the gold standard. This, in turn, improved Japan's credit rating in London and its capacity to tap additional funds for industrial expansion at home and imperialist expansion overseas (Feis 1965: 422–23; Duus 1984: 143, 161–62; Peattie 1984: 16–18).

This bifurcation of the Japanese and Chinese developmental paths culminated in the eclipsing of Britain by Japan as the dominant power in the region. With the Japanese seizure of Manchuria in 1931, followed by the occupation of north China in 1935, full-scale invasion of China from 1937, and the subsequent conquest of parts of Inner Asia and much of Southeast Asia, Japan seemed to be succeeding in re-centering upon itself the East Asian region. Japan's bid for regional supremacy, however, could not be sustained. Stalemated in a fifteen-year war with China (1931–45) and facing the US-led juggernaut unleashed in response to Pearl Harbor, Japan succumbed in a classic example of imperial overreach. Once Japan had been defeated, the formation of the People's Republic of China would contest Western hegemonic drives in a struggle for centrality in East Asia that has shaped trends and events in the region ever since.

In the course of this struggle the process of hybridization of the Western and East Asian developmental paths changed direction. While in the late nineteenth and early twentieth century convergence was primarily from the East Asian toward the Western path, in the second half of the twentieth century it was the turn of the Western path to converge toward the East Asian. This little noticed convergence began with the establishment of the US Cold War regime. The US military occupation of Japan in 1945 and the division of the region in the aftermath of the Korean War into two antagonistic blocs created, in Bruce Cumings' words, a US "vertical regime solidified through bilateral defense treaties (with Japan, South Korea, Taiwan and the Philippines) and conducted by a State Department that towered over the foreign ministries of these four countries," all of which "became semisovereign states" (Cumings 1997: 155).

The militaristic nature of this US regime had no precedent in East Asia, with the partial exception of the Yuan regime in the late thirteenth and early fourteenth centuries and the aborted Japan-centered regime of the early twentieth century. Nevertheless, the US regime presented three important similarities with the China-centered tribute trade system. First, the domestic market of the central state was incomparably larger than that of the vassal states. Second, in order to receive regime legitimation and to gain access to the central state's domestic market, vassal states had to accept a relationship of political subordination to the central state. And third, in exchange for political subordination, vassal states were granted "gifts" and highly advantageous trade relations with the central state. This was the "magnanimous" early postwar trade and aid regime of Pax Americana, which contributed decisively to the take-off of the East Asian economic renaissance (Ozawa 1993: 130; Sugihara 2003: 81).

In light of these similarities, we may say that after the Second World War the United States turned the periphery of the former China-centered tribute trade system into the periphery of a US-centered tribute trade system. The US-centered system, however, was not only far more militaristic in structure and orientation than its China-centered predecessors; it also fostered a relationship of political exchange between the imperial and the vassal states that had no precedent in the old China-centered system. In this relationship, the United States specialized in the provision of protection and the pursuit of political power regionally and globally, while its East Asian vassal states specialized in trade and the pursuit of profit. This relationship of political exchange played a decisive role in promoting the spectacular Japanese economic expansion that initiated the regional renaissance. "Freed from the burden of defense spending, Japanese governments ... funneled all their resources and energies into an economic expansionism that ... brought affluence to Japan and [took] its business to the farthest reaches of the globe" (Schurmann 1974: 143).

Another important difference is that, unlike the earlier China-centered regimes, the US-centered Cold War regime in East Asia started breaking down soon after it was established. The Korean War had instituted the US-centric East Asian regime by excluding the PRC from normal commercial and diplomatic intercourse with the non-communist part of the region, through blockade and war threats backed by "an archipelago of American military installations" (Cumings 1997: 154–55). Defeat in the Vietnam War, in contrast, forced the United States to readmit China to normal commercial and diplomatic intercourse with the rest of East Asia. The scope of the region's economic integration and expansion was thereby broadened considerably, but the capacity of the United States to control the process was reduced correspondingly (Arrighi 1996; Selden 1997).

The crisis of the US militaristic regime and the contemporaneous expansion of the Japanese national market and business networks in the region, marked the re-emergence of a pattern of interstate relations that resembled more closely the indigenous (East Asian) pattern—in which centrality was determined primarily by the relative size and sophistication of the system's national economies—than the transplanted (Western) pattern—in which centrality had come to be determined primarily by the relative strength of the system's military-industrial complexes. While the defeat of the United States in Vietnam laid bare the limits of industrial militarism as a source of power, Japan's growing influence in world politics in the 1980s demonstrated the increasing effectiveness of economic relative to military sources of power.

The main foundation of Japan's growing economic power was not technological but organizational. As argued elsewhere, the worldwide proliferation of vertically integrated, multinational corporations intensified their mutual competition, forcing them to subcontract to small businesses activities previously carried out within their own organizations. The tendency toward the vertical integration and bureaucratization of business—which had made the fortunes of US capital since the 1870s—thus began to be superseded by a tendency toward informal networking and the subordinate revitalization of small business. This new tendency has been in evidence everywhere but nowhere has it been pursued more successfully than in East Asia, where Japanese big business relied heavily on the assistance of multiple layers of formally independent subcontractors. Starting in the early 1970s, the scale and scope of this multilayered subcontracting system increased rapidly through a spillover into a growing number of East Asian states (Okimoto and Rohlen 1988: 83–88; Arrighi et al. 1993: 55 ff; Arrighi 2007: ch. 6). Although Japanese capital was the leading agency of the spillover, the overseas Chinese were from the start the main intermediaries between Japanese and local business in most Southeast Asian countries, where the ethnic Chinese minority occupied a commanding position in local business networks (see Yeung, in this volume). The region-wide expansion of the Japanese multilayered subcontracting system was thus supported, not just by US political patronage from above, but also by Chinese commercial and financial patronage from below (Hui 1995; Irwan 1995).

Over time, however, patronage from above and below began to constrain the capacity of Japanese business to lead the process of regional economic expansion. Japanese dependence on US military protection was an advantage only as long as the "magnanimous" postwar US trade and aid regime was in place. But as "magnanimity" gave way to veritable extortions (such as the massive revaluation of the yen and the Voluntary Export Restrictions imposed on Japan in the 1980s, or the huge "protection payment" that the United States extracted from Japan to pay for the First Gulf War), the profitability of Japan's relation of political exchange with the United States began to wane (Arrighi 2007: ch. 9). Worse still, US business began restructuring itself to compete more effectively with Japanese business in the exploitation of East Asia's rich endowment of labor and entrepreneurial resources through all kinds of subcontracting arrangements in loosely integrated organizational structures. The more intense competition over East Asian low-cost and high-quality human resources became, the more the overseas Chinese emerged as one of the most powerful capitalist networks in the region, in many ways over-shadowing the networks of US and Japanese multinationals (Ong and Nonini 1997; Arrighi et al. 2003: 316).

The mobilization of East Asian subcontracting networks in the intensifying competitive struggle among the world's leading capitalist organizations thus resulted in the revival of another legacy of the East Asian developmental path: the overseas Chinese capitalist diaspora. As it turns out, this revival was only a prelude to the re-centering of the East Asian political economy on China. Decisive in this respect was the decision of the Chinese government under Deng Xiaoping to enter into an alliance with the diaspora aimed at the double objective of upgrading the economy of the PRC through its reintegration in regional and global markets and of promoting national reunification with Hong Kong, Macau and, eventually, Taiwan in accordance with the "One Nation, Two Systems" model. Although reunification with Taiwan is still up in the air, the re-centering of the regional political economy on China has proceeded much faster and more smoothly than anyone might have predicted.

Conclusions

If we now return to Mearsheimer's theory of great power politics, we may conclude that—quite apart from its misleading bias toward competitive rather than cooperative relations among incumbent and emergent powers—its bias toward military rather than economic sources of power flies in the face of two basic facts of great power politics, one concerning the East Asian and the other the Western historical experience. The Chinese doctrine of "peaceful coexistence" is no mere propaganda. It reflects the predominant experience of the East Asian interstate system in the five centuries preceding its subordinate incorporation within the structures of the globalizing Western system. Throughout this period the main foundations of Chinese power were not military but economic, and not wealth as such but, to paraphrase Hobbes, wealth combined with liberality.

The reproduction of these foundations of national power for a country of China's size was no easy task, and on two occasions they collapsed under the joint impact of external military pressure and internal social upheavals. On the first occasion, the collapse merely led to a dynastic change (from Ming to Qing) and to a reconstitution of Chinese power on similar foundations, albeit on a larger territorial scale, that reduced the risks of invasions from the steppe frontier. On the second occasion, however, the collapse led to a precipitous decline of Chinese power which lasted more than a century.

This precipitous decline was caused primarily by Chinese unpreparedness, not just for the shift of the main threat to national security from the steppe to the sea frontier, but especially for the combination of military and economic power that Western imperialism brought to the region. Military defeat in the Opium Wars and the consequent internalization of the armament race within East Asia resulted in a situation in which for a century China was indeed "bullied by others"—by the Western powers, of course, but most disastrously by neighboring Japan. As we have seen, this is the experience that Wen Jiabao has recently recalled to reconcile China's determination to strengthen and modernize its armed forces with the doctrine of "peaceful coexistence/development." In light of the historical experience sketched in this essay, we may reformulate this claim by saying that a continuing adherence to the East Asian tradition of peaceful coexistence does not rule out, nay, requires avoiding the kind of military unpreparedness that overwhelmed that tradition 150 years ago.

But does not this qualification support Mearsheimer's and all other arguments based exclusively on the Western tradition of great power politics? Has not this tradition buried once and for all the East Asian tradition of peaceful coexistence and thus become the only relevant historical foundation for a theory of great power politics? These questions might have to be answered in the affirmative were it not for a second basic fact of great power politics. This other basic fact is that the synergy of capitalism, militarism, and territorial expansion that underlay the Western dynamic has attained its limits, and nowhere have these limits been more evident than in East Asia.

To the extent that the latest and most powerful embodiment of the Western dynamic—the United States—could become hegemonic in the region it was through the adoption of the principle—which Hobbes theorized but China had successfully practiced for centuries—that "Riches joyned with liberality is Power, because it procureth friends, and servants." More important, US attempts to complement economic magnanimity with military force as a source of power in the region were only partially successful in Korea and failed miserably in Vietnam. Worse still, they contributed to the transfer of economic power from the United States to some of its vassals in the region—most notably Japan and to a lesser extent Taiwan—and forced it to readmit China to normal intercourse in the region. After a failed, US-supported, military adventure of its own against Vietnam, China was quick to learn the lesson of the limits of military might—later confirmed by the collapse of the USSR—and put its bets on the ongoing revival of the East Asian tradition of relying primarily on economic sources of power.

The wisdom of this choice has been fully borne out by the outcome of the opposite US bet in West Asia, where reliance on military might has plunged the United States in a quagmire which is undermining US economic and political power regionally and globally, creating a void that China has skillfully moved in to fill. Whether this tendency can eventually result in a resurgence on a global scale of the East Asian tradition of peaceful coexistence remains to be seen. But theories of great power politics that fail to consider this possibility are indeed worse than no theory at all, and IPE can revitalize itself only by focusing on the new understandings of the politics and economics of global affairs called for by the Chinese ascent.

Notes

1 Conveniently glossed over here are China's invasions of India in the early 1960s and Vietnam in the late 1970s. Nevertheless, as we shall see, the image of China being bullied by others fits well the historical record from the Opium Wars to the establishment of the PRC.

2 On the British transformation of the balance of power into an instrument of informal rule, cf. Arrighi and Silver 1999: 59–64.

3 With ships that probably displaced 1,500 tons, compared to the 300-ton flagship of Vasco Da Gama, China's seaborne capacity at this time had no peer (cf. McNeill 1982: 44).

11

States and markets, states versus markets

The developmental state debate as the distinctive East Asian contribution to international political economy

Walden Bello

Rather than try to discern whether or not there is a distinctly East Asian school of international political economy, it is probably more productive to approach the question of the development of IPE in East Asia by asking if there are approaches deployed by analysts, Asian or non-Asian, that have been uniquely associated with the study of the configurations and transformations of political and economic power in the region. Different paradigms have been harnessed to the effort to understand regional power realities, among them dependency theory, different varieties of the hegemony paradigm, realist balance-of-power approaches, and constructivist analysis. However, if there is one theory or approach that might be said to be uniquely associated with the region, it is the theory of the developmental state. Indeed, one can say that theoretical innovation and empirical work in IPE in East Asia has been largely driven by the developmental state debate.

This has not, however, been theoretical work done in a vacuum. If the evolution of IPE in the West, particularly in the Anglosphere, reflected the historical trajectory of the market being liberated from the state, in the East Asian context it could not but mirror the opposite reality of a hegemonic state harnessing the market for development and non-economic goals such as military security or political pacification. Not surprisingly, initial efforts to try to explain East Asian development through the prism of a Western IPE that was under the spell of neoclassical economics—especially its neoliberal version that correlated economic growth with economic freedom—simply fell flat, being out of touch with actual trends and processes.

Moreover, the IPE in East Asia was not divorced from policy preferences. Those preferring the prism of the market to interpret East Asian economic realities were often seeking not only to describe but to prescribe. Those for whom the role of an activist state provided greater explanatory power not only tried to reflect state-assisted capitalism but to justify it. It is its being embedded in policy and, indeed, in ideological politics, that made IPE in East Asia, much more than in the West, an object of struggle, contestation, and definition.

Another key factor influencing the trajectory of political economy was one's disciplinary perspective or paradigm. While economists found it difficult to accept a creative or constructive role for the state in the making of an economy, sociologists and political scientists who placed power at the center of their analysis found a paradigm that fundamentally saw the state as an obstacle to economic development as theoretically unhelpful, to say the least, and dangerous policy-wise.

The genesis of the developmental state concept

It was Chalmers Johnson who first introduced the concept of the developmental state in his path-breaking book *MITI and the Japanese Miracle* (Johnson 1982). According to Johnson, Japan's road to capitalism differed from that of the West, with the central role played by a state elite subordinating market forces to a strategic plan to force-march the country to industrialization. The private sector definitely had a role to play in this process but it was under the administrative guidance of the state bureaucracy, in particular the Ministry of Trade and Industry (MITI), which engaged in the task of picking winners. Much of the effectiveness of the state elite was its ability to legitimize its project and to mobilize people through its appeal to a commonly shared project, in the case of Japan, national economic development in the context of wartime defeat and post-war privation. Johnson went on to characterize the Japanese developmental elite as "revolutionary" or "quasi-revolutionary," but in contrast to Leninist elites, what "distinguishes these revolutionaries … is the insight that the market is a better mechanism for achieving their objectives than central planning" (Johnson 1999: 53).

Johnson's characterization of Japan as a developmental state provoked varied reactions, among them denials by both Japanese and Western Japan specialists that the state superseded the market. Probably to counter US government criticism that MITI's practices were anti-market in the charged trade relationship of the 1980s, a MITI-created foundation asserted that industrial policy simply meant government strategies "that are put in place to supplement the market mechanism only when and where necessary" (Johnson 1999: 45). Several American economists and political scientists, among them Kent Calder, reversed the argument, saying that, in fact, MITI and state objectives in the post-war period were in support of the market-driven private sector (Tresize 1983; McCall Rosenbluth 1989; Calder 1993). This drew Johnson's rejoinder that Calder "fails to understand that even his 'private' managers … are not American-style, short-term profit maximizers but engaged in a nationally sanctioned cooperative enterprise" (Johnson 1999: 45).

Over time, however, Johnson's characterization of Japan as a developmental state became the orthodox view. This is not to say that other analysts did not make contributions that nuanced Johnson's paradigm. Marie Anchorduguy, for instance, offered a more fleshed out description of the Japanese system as an "elite-managed, catch-up system with its focus on the maximization of producer welfare and the use of managed markets to promote political, social, and economic stability and overall national economic well being" (1997).

Bill Emmott conceded the leading role of the state, but claimed that the market did still play a role in the Japanese system. Emmott argued that "it is true that Japan does not practice pure laissez-faire, free market economic policies. … But the lack of a free-market ideology does not mean that the Japanese economy is immune to market forces" (1989: 209–10). For Emmott, bureaucratic power, cartels, and conspiracies acted as a "powerful drag," but this only meant that movements in prices had to be "grander in scale" to "overcome the drag" (1989: 209–10). And, surprisingly, given his being editor of the rabidly pro–market *Economist,* Emmott went on to say the despite the drag on the market, Japan's bureaucrat-led "system seems to work, even if it is a bit corrupt and prone to encourage cartels. Bureaucrats have run Japan remarkably well, certainly from the point of view of prosperity and economic development" (1989: 206).

The regional resonance of an idea

Even as the developmental state argument enlivened Japan studies, the impact of Johnson's concept went far beyond Japan. Alice Amsden radicalized the concept when she claimed that "[N]ot only has Korea not gotten relative prices right; it has deliberately gotten them 'wrong'" (1989: 139). Robert Wade made the same point with respect to Taiwan, though in more measured terms: "Almost certainly some of Taiwan's industries and some of its exports would not have been initially profitable without state encouragement ... The government pushed and pulled the structure of relative prices to secure a pattern of growth which it mapped out in advance in rolling plans" (1990: 302). And in the period before the economic ascent of the Southeast Asian countries in the late 1980s, specialists on the region came to see as their problematique the absence of a developmental state à la Taiwan or Korea.

Why did Johnson's idea have an immediate cross-border appeal? One answer was provided by Meredith Woo-Cumings:

> Johnson's *MITI and the Japanese Miracle* is a country-specific study without much reference to the external world, but it became more than an account of idiosyncratic practices analyzed in isolated splendor. It was an implicitly comparative account, containing within it a truth about East Asian developmental regimes and their outlook. This is why a whole generation of scholars in comparative politics can deploy any number of country cases ... and still not grasp the basic truth about the political economy of a single country, and why a single case study by an astute analyst can generate insights that are immediately recognizable as true for many different societies.
>
> (Woo-Cumings 2005: 95)

Why Korea and Taiwan? The Japanese connection

The developmental state provided a tool not only for comparing East Asian countries. It also offered a theoretical approach to understanding why the Northeast Asian countries, which came to be called NICs (newly industrializing countries) or "tiger economies," succeeded where other post-colonial states in Asia, Latin America, and Africa appeared to have failed. This led to a number of fruitful avenues of comparative research. One area of investigation had to do with the common origins of Korea and Taiwan as colonial states set up for social control and economic extraction by imperial Japan in the decades before the Second World War. Given the historical animosity between Japan and Korea, this was not an area that Korean scholars were comfortable in exploring. Not surprisingly then, perhaps the most emphatic assertion of the centrality of the Japanese colonial connection in the case of Korea was made by a non-Korean, Atul Kohli, in a comparative study of the development process in Korea, India, and Brazil:

[T]he highly cohesive and disciplining state that the Japanese helped to construct in colonial Korea turned out to be an efficacious economic actor. The state utilized its bureaucratic capacities to undertake numerous economic tasks: collecting more taxes, building infrastructure, and undertaking production directly.

More important, continued Kohli,

> this highly purposive state made increasing production one of its priorities and incorporated property-owning classes into production-oriented alliances. These propertied classes were variously rewarded—especially with handsome profits—for cooperating with the state in fulfilling this economic agenda. The state, in turn, utilized numerous means—including promotion of technology, control over credit, subsidies, capital accumulation, and even noneconomic exhortations—to ensure compliance from both Korean and Japanese landlords and businessmen. The result was an economy successful at exporting manufactured goods … This model of development—inspired by Meiji Japan and transformed in the colonial setting— eventually situated the state-directed economy with its state-capital alliance at the heart of the strategy of transformation.
>
> (2004: 56)

The point Kohli was making was not that post-war Korea inherited an industrial structure from the colonial regime, since much of Korea's industrial infrastructure, a major part of it located in the north, was, in fact, destroyed during the Korean War in 1950–53. Rather it was that "a war-destroyed economy with an experience in rapid industrialization behind it is quite different from a tradition-bound, stagnating, agrarian economy" since "in the institutions and practices of industrialization—the knowledge and ideas associated with industrialization—continue to live on" (Kohli 2004: 49).

The hegemonic web

A related thrust of research and analysis was to try to locate the determinants of industrialization in Korea, Taiwan, and Japan more broadly in the dynamics of the politico-military sphere of influence that the US established in the Western Pacific during the Cold War. Much like early modern Europe, this was a case of war and conflict being the mother of development and prosperity. Chalmers Johnson saw the Korean War as the "virtual equivalent of the Marshall Plan for Japan" (Johnson 1999: 55). The Vietnam War, in turn, proved to be a boon to both Taiwan and Korea. According to Thomas Gold, the war provided an "incalculable boost" to the Taiwanese economy in the form of US purchases of agricultural and industrial commodities, spending for "rest and recreation," and contract work for local firms in Vietnam (Gold 1986: 86–87). As for South Korea, most exports of its young capital-intensive industries in the 1960s were destined for Vietnam (Woo-Cumings 1991: 95–96). The export of services was even more stunning. By the end of the war in 1975, overseas work contracts had reached a total of $850 million, accounting for almost 20 percent of Korea's exports of goods and services. Given their start by the US military in Vietnam, Hyundai, Daewoo, and other Korean construction giants went on to conquer the Middle East in the late 1970s and early 1980s (McCormack 1978: 101). This was not just a case of demand stimulating supply, in this case the demands of war-making creating a market for Korean and Taiwanese products. The Vietnam War, noted one analyst:

> was not only a cornucopia of huge invisible earnings and immense US assistance, but an incubator of new industries before testing the fires of international competition. The phenomenon whereby a foreign market is turned into a laboratory for infant industries is, in other words, often political and, therefore, foreign to the assumptions underlying neoclassical trade theories. Nonetheless, it is one of the ways in which a mercantilist state engineers a movement upward in the industrial product cycle.
>
> (Woo-Cumings 1991: 97)

Industrialization in Japan, Korea, and Taiwan took place, in other words, in a US sphere of military influence within, one is tempted to say, a region-wide garrison state made up of about seven semi-sovereign Asia-Pacific countries, where economic decisions were profoundly influenced by political considerations. Not only did war-making provide a demand for the goods of nascent industries, but political considerations, meaning the overwhelming priority of the politico–military alliance against communism, gave the East Asian newly industrializing countries certain privileges that were quickly translated into opportunities by the Taiwanese and Korean states, among them access to the US market, while not being pushed to make reciprocal concessions, thus allowing them to pursue export-oriented production cum protected domestic markets. Bruce Cumings invokes an interesting metaphor in describing this regional economic configuration where the politics of national security and anti-communism impinged on the market at every turn:

> [T]he central experience of Northeast Asia in this century has not been a realm of independence where autonomy and equality reigned, but with the enmeshment in another web: the hegemonic web. This web had a spider: first England/America, then America/England, then war and defeat, then unilateral America, then and down to the present, hegemonic America. Japan, South Korea, and Taiwan industrialized mostly within this web. North Korea and China defined themselves outside the web, thus endowing the web with overriding significance—and so they structured their states to resist enmeshment. Japan, South Korea, and Taiwan have thus had states "strong" for the struggle to industrialize but "weak" because of their enmeshment: they are semisovereign states.
>
> (Cumings 1999: 92)

Subtext of a debate

The market-versus-state debate was more than an academic debate. Part of the reason it raged so fiercely was that it was, in a very real sense, a debate between disciplines. With the ascendancy of neoliberal thinking in the early 1980s, development economics had little use for the state except as an obstacle to the creative play of market forces. What came to be the neoclassical orthodoxy was expressed by Seiji Naya, who attributed the East Asian NICs' success to "a combination of more thorough and timely adoption of outward-looking, market-oriented policies and rapid improvement in human resource and institutional development" (Naya 1988: 93). While not denying that the state made some contribution to the development process, economists said that the East Asian states had behaved in a "market friendly fashion," the contrast being with Latin American and other developing states that had behaved in dirigiste, market-distorting ways. Some economists seemed to be arguing that, yes, these countries have high growth rates, but these would be even higher without state intervention. It was almost as if, contrary to the evidence of the senses, economists were seeking to make the state invisible in the development process.

Not surprisingly, this provoked political scientists or political economists like Robert Wade to ask rhetorically: "Can it be seriously argued that if the Governor of the Bank of Japan had got his way in the mid-1950s, and prevented a concentration on steel and automobiles on the grounds that Japan's comparative advantage lay in textiles, Japan would now be economically better off?" (Wade 1988: 151–52). Echoing Wade, one could also ask if Korea's Heavy and Chemical Industry Drive (HCI) in the 1970s, much criticized at the time by economists as wasteful, had little to do with the conquest of world markets by the Korean steel, automobile, and microelectronic industries in the 1990s?

Another reason for the polarized character of the debate was that theory was very much linked to policy. At a time when neoliberalism was on the rise and already sweeping Latin America, the question of which road to follow became a high-stakes game for countries in Southeast Asia, South Asia, Africa, and the Middle East. The multilateral institutions had been captured by neoliberalism, and in Southeast Asia, the Philippines had already been chosen as one of the guinea pigs for structural adjustment in the early 1980s. Yet, the record of the NICs was not in line with the expectations of the new hegemonic doctrine. Not surprisingly, for many academics, policymakers, and even civil society activists, what became known as "the Japanese path" or "Asian capitalism" began to emerge as an alternative to market-driven strategies. Indeed, in the late 1980s, before Japan blundered into its decade of stagnation, there were many calling on US policymakers to adopt Japanese-style industrial policy (Fallows 1994).

In a bid to become a key player in the development arena, Japan not only surpassed the US to become the world's largest aid donor; it also bankrolled a World Bank study to determine the causes of the success of the tiger economies. The results of the study, which came out as a book titled *The East Asian Miracle* in 1993, satisfied neither the neoclassicists nor the developmentalists. On the one hand, the study acknowledged that the "very rapid growth of the type experienced by Japan, the Four Tigers, and more recently the East Asian NIEs has at times benefited from careful policy interventions" (World Bank 1993: 24). On the other hand, it noted: "Whether these interventions contributed to the rapid growth made possible by good fundamentals or detracted from it is the most difficult question we have attempted to answer. It is much easier to show that the HPAES [High Performing Asian Economies] limited the costs and duration of inappropriately chosen interventions than to demonstrate conclusively that those interventions maintained for a long time accelerated growth" (World Bank 1993: 24).

The basic methodology of the study, however, was to put the burden of proof on the state and state-led initiatives rather than on the market and the private sector, so that its analytical and policy conclusions were, many ways, predetermined:

[T]he market-oriented aspects of East Asia's experience can be recommended with few reservations. More institutionally demanding strategies have often failed in other settings and they clearly are not compatible with economic environments where the fundamentals are not securely in place ... So the fact that interventions were an element of the success of some East Asian economies' success does not mean that they should be attempted everywhere, nor should it be taken as an excuse to postpone needed market-oriented reforms.

(World Bank 1993: 26)

Not surprisingly, the Japanese were said to be disappointed with the report's conclusions.

The politics of the state–market debate

The market-versus-state debate was not only a debate between disciplines. Nor was it merely a debate about development strategy. It was also a political debate, with those on the side of market-driven growth tending to be on the right or right-of-center while those supporting the developmental state position tended to be critical toward or ambivalent about capitalism and minimally regulated markets. One of the attractions of the Asian NICs to left-minded scholars was the relatively equal income distribution that had been created by state-sponsored land reform in Korea, Taiwan, and Japan, which expanded the domestic market and spurred industrialization. This was a feat that, whatever the motivations of its authors—and here depriving the communists of a peasant base loomed large—was in signal contrast to the failure of agrarian reform owing to resistance from agrarian elites in other developing countries. The beauty of the NICs' experience, from a progressive point of view, was the way it demonstrated how social justice and economic growth were complementary.

For many of the developmentalists, East Asian-style command capitalism was a mechanism for the achievement of economic sovereignty, and, with its preference for governing rather than eliminating the market, it promised a faster and more efficient route to development than socialism. This accounted for the ill-concealed admiration for the Korean strongman Park Chung-Hee among developmentalists who placed a premium on the loosening of the hegemony of center economies. He was repressive. He was pro-American. But he was able to use the opportunities and the space provided by American hegemony to lift the country from underdevelopment to industrial status through a state-led nationalist economic program that was effective in eventually raising standards of living for the majority. Given their fascination with what one analyst characterized as the "genius of the states in South Korea and Taiwan ... in transforming very real fears of war and instability into a remarkable developmental energy" (Woo-Cumings 2005: 116), it was not surprising that, notwithstanding their progressive predilections, the partisans of the developmental state tended to overlook or implicitly play down the downside of the high-speed growth in the East Asian NICs.

In contrast, growing inequality, the crisis of agriculture, environmental degradation, and political repression were the concerns of a number of scholars who were less impressed with the NICs' developmental energy and challenged what had become the stylized view of the developmental state. The key to the "Asian miracle" for these analysts was not a smart state elite able to turn the military alliance with the US into economic advantage, but a super-exploited working class, in large part female, that was constantly replenished by fresh cheap labor from the countryside and prevented by the state elite from enjoying the most elementary labor rights (see among others Choi 1983; Asia Monitor Resource Center 1987; Koo in Kim 1987; Hart-Landsberg 1993). These analysts disputed the alleged efficacy of the nationalist ideology of the national security state, preferring to see the development process as a forced march imposed on a working class whose attitudes verged on the insurrectionary. Neither Korea nor Taiwan resembled Japan when it came to social or national solidarity, they argued. Economic development was pursued by unpopular elites as a way of gaining domestic legitimacy, but while they did deliver development, they did not gain legitimacy. Labor–management relations, which in the case of Korea were patterned after the military hierarchy, were regarded as being so bad they were seen as likely to have negative implications for the future of the development process. As Stephanie Rosenfeld and I put it in *Dragons in Distress*:

> [P]recisely because labor and other groups had been so strongly repressed in the pursuit of high-speed development, political decompression did not lead to the creation of a new consensus around the traditional strategy of growth but to a politics of polarized struggle over the distribution of income, sectoral priorities, the trade-off between environmental and economic priorities, and the direction of development itself. Late industrialization, followed by late democratization, promoted not consensus but divergent views on economic priorities.
>
> (Bello and Rosenfeld 1991: 13)

Made in the dawn of democratization in Korea in the late 1980s, this projection was probably even more valid in the late 1990s, when the Asian financial crisis exposed to the world the panorama of two bitter nations in one country that had been created by repressive high-speed industrialization, with the warring parties disagreeing fundamentally not only on the future direction of Korean development but also on the past. That is, on whether that process had been a positive one in the first place.[1]

The Southeast Asian conundrum: security and land reform

In the late 1970s and early 1980s, at a time that Taiwan and Korea were drawing the attention of the world as high growth economies and before the massive flow of Japanese investment into Southeast Asia, the question of why they were able to pull away from the Southeast Asian countries was a source of intense academic speculation.

One line of thinking was security-related. The Southeast Asian countries were not on the frontlines of the Cold War in Asia, as Taiwan and Korea were. What this meant was that not only were foreign aid flows much smaller than what went to Korea and Taiwan, but the Americans were not as keen about pushing land reform and other asset reforms as they had been in Japan, Korea, and Taiwan. Land reform in Japan destroyed the rural strongholds of Japanese militarism and contributed to the focus on economic growth as the national goal, aside from expanding the domestic market by giving millions of peasants effective purchasing power. In Korea, to blunt the appeal of communism, the Americans, as they reconquered the south during the Korean War, let stand the land reform initiated by the North Koreans to prevent a civil war from engulfing their rear. In Taiwan, the US threw itself behind the Kuomintang's use of land reform to destroy the Taiwanese landed class as an alternative power center when they evacuated their forces to the island following the communist victory on the mainland in 1948–49. In both areas, redistribution significantly expanded rural demand that stimulated early industrialization and served as a key pillar of the continuing dynamic growth of the economy (Cumings and Putzel in Masina 2002: 163, 165).

In the Philippines, on the other hand, the US consolidated the Philippine rural elites into a national ruling class to serve as the basis of its colonial rule in the period 1898–1946. A communist insurgency did emerge as a threat in the post-war period, but it was relatively easily contained with a strategy of land resettlement cum counterinsurgency. Efforts at sustained industrial growth consistently came up against the limits of a small internal market (Rocamora and O'Connor 1977).

The curse of natural resources

Another explanation is what might be called "the curse of natural resources." According to those advancing this thesis, the notion that a country blessed with natural resources had a leg up in the economic development game, as asserted by economists such as Gerald Meier, Walter Rostow, Ann Krueger, and Bela Balassa (Rostow 1961; Belassa 1979: 121–56; Krueger 1980; Meier 1989), was questionable. In fact, an abundance of resource endowments might actually pose a major block to industrial development. One version of this view, which emphasized economic factors, was articulated by Seiji Naya:

> It is ironic that, to some degree, wealth in natural resources in labor-abundant countries, such as those in Southeast Asia, makes it more difficult to adopt policies that promote growth with equity through labor-absorption in an outward-looking manufacturing sector. Resource wealth (outside of agricultural crops) tends to have concentrated ownership as well as a requirement for capital-intensive technologies for development. The effect of natural resource booms on non-resource sectors capable of producing exports is often negative because of "Dutch Disease" effects. Often the sectors that are adversely affected are labor-intensive. Natural resource wealth may also encourage adoption of policies that lessen incentives to produce while providing subsidies to domestic consumers.
>
> (Naya 1988: 93–94)

On the other hand, the NICs "were forced by circumstances to adopt the policies they did. They lacked natural resource wealth and had little beyond abundant labor with which to begin their impressive modernization drive" (Naya 1988: 93–94). For Robin Broad, the preceding account, emphasizing economic factors, though in the right direction, was inadequate, since it failed to take into account historically developed class structures and political institutions that trapped capital and labor in the natural resource sectors and discouraged vigorous capital accumulation in industry. According to her, two factors interacted to produce this result: the existing insertion of the country into the international division of labor as a producer of natural resources and the post-colonial politico-economic system shaped partly by this insertion. Broad made it clear that she was not saying that natural resource abundance necessarily discouraged industrial capital accumulation. Her point, rather, was that, historically, owing to their integration into the world economy, natural resource abundance in some societies

> catalyzed interactions ... entwining the state with privileged groups. That state finds itself without relative autonomy to pursue policies that do not reflect the

short-term interests of the exploiters; parts of the state are not just politicized but are 'captured.' Such a state is not what has been called a 'strong state' or a 'developmental state'—that is, one able to formulate and implement policies independently of powerful groups.

(Broad 1995: 330–31)

Varieties of patrimonialism

This notion of a state captured by rent-seeking groups, which resulted in the channeling of resources away from relatively weak industrial capitalist interests dependent on domestic and international markets, is associated principally with Paul Hutchcroft. The post-World War II Philippine state was what he called a "patrimonial oligarchy," where a powerful economic elite extracted resources from and manipulated a weak and disorganized state bureaucracy, a configuration of power that was inherited from the American colonial period (Hutchcroft 1998). Superficially, the Marcos dictatorship (1972–86) might have seemed to be a strong state, but actually it was a system that "facilitated the capture of the state by new—and more centralized—regime interests" (Hutchcroft 1998: 111). Quoting Marcos' chief ideologue, Hutchcroft wrote that Marcos "believed he had a vision for society and could still loot it" (1998). What financial resources were generated by the economic system was siphoned via state mechanisms to the Marcos family, relatives, and cronies instead of being recycled into productive investment in a market-driven economy.

Inspired by Weber's classification of patterns of authority, Hutchcroft contrasted the Philippine state to the state in Indonesia and Thailand, which he described as a system of "administrative patrimonialism," where power was located in a class of office-holders who were the key beneficiaries of the extraction of rent from a weak and disorganized business class. While both were largely rent-seeking systems, the administrative patrimonial system was more likely to evolve in development-friendly ways. The key reason he gave for this was that the private interests that emerged as dependent groups in the shadow of a powerful authoritarian bureaucracy were more likely to become impatient with the uncertainties and caprice of the bureaucracy's demands for rent and see their interests as being served by impersonal legal-institutional regimes (Hutchcroft 1998: 45–64).

The second generation NICs: bringing the market back in?

Hutchcroft's differentiation between rentier regimes in terms of their receptivity to capital accumulation was a convoluted and, to many, unconvincing response to the fact that after the late 1980s the question to be explained was not Southeast Asia's lack of development but its vigorous growth. In fact, the debate on the relative merits of different rentier elites that were portrayed as derailing and privatizing wealth that would otherwise go to sustained capital accumulation and allowing at best a sickly industrialization, was superseded by the same market-versus-state debate that had been raging in Northeast Asia.

The World Bank's *East Asian Miracle*, written at the height of the Southeast Asian NICs' drive to development in the early 1990s, suggested that governments in Thailand, Indonesia, and Malaysia were much more market-friendly and much less interventionist than those in Northeast Asia (World Bank 1993: 310, 312), and implied that this was the reason for their high growth rates in the late 1980s. But while granting that the Southeast Asian NICs were less interventionist than their Northeast Asian brethren, partisans of the developmental state asserted that this did not mean that the interventions were insignificant or that the interventions had a negative impact on growth, as the study implied subtly at various points. In the case of Thailand, the 8–10 percent growth rates that dazzled the world coincided with a period when it was moving to a *second stage* of *import substitution*—the use of trade policy to create the space for the emergence of an intermediate goods sector—in the second half of the 1980s (cf. Akrasanee et al. 1991: 17; Sakasakul 1992: 19). The effective rate of protection for manufacturing stood at a high 52 percent in the mid-1980s in this supposedly market-friendly country. Given the evidence, claimed Jomo and his associates, "Despite the frequent political regime changes in Thailand, bureaucratic capacity and autonomy has facilitated modest, but fairly effective industrial policy by Southeast Asian standards, though often compromised by military and politicians' rentier activity" (Jomo et al. 1997: 20).

In the case of Malaysia, while it was true that some privatization and deregulation favoring private interests took place in the late 1980s, the developmentalists asserted that it would be a mistake to overestimate the impact of these policies, as the World Bank did on the basis of limited data (World Bank 1993: 311). A number of examples strongly suggested the central—and positive—role of state interventions. Petronas, the state oil company, was consistently rated among one of East Asia's best-run firms. And certainly, though it had its share of problems, one of the most innovative and successful enterprises in the whole region was a state-directed joint venture between a state-owned firm and a foreign automobile transnational corporation, Mitsubishi, which produced the so-called Malaysian car, the Proton Saga. The Proton Saga came to control two-thirds of the domestic market and turned a profit for its producers. Indeed, so threatened were the world's auto giants by its success and example for the rest of the developing world that they successfully pushed to get *local content* policies, requiring an escalating percentage of car components to be sourced locally, to be banned under the Trade Related Investment Measures Agreement (TRIMs) of the new World Trade Organization.

As for Indonesia, some change along market-oriented lines did take place in the 1980s and 1990s, but up to the end of the Suharto era in May 1998, the state continued to be a more important actor in the economy than the private sector. Hardly any of the big state enterprises passed to the private sector. State enterprises contributed about 30 percent of total GDP and close to 40 percent of non-agricultural GDP. Government production accounted for 50 percent of the mining sector, 24 percent of manufacturing GDP, 65 percent of banking and finance, and 50 percent of transport and communications. Indeed, in the last decade of the Suharto regime, there was a resurgence of statist policy in the form of trade policy, subsidies, and other mechanisms directed at the creation of a heavy-industry nucleus around which to center the economy, including an integrated steel complex, a shipbuilding complex, and an aircraft industry (see among other works Rosser 2002).

The second generation NICs: bringing the Japanese back in?

Export-oriented growth was the cutting edge of the Southeast Asian high-speed industrialization of the 1980s and 1990s. But, as Jomo and his associates pointed out, this policy itself was itself pushed by the state via a variety of incentives (Jomo et al. 1997: 17–18). This echoed the argument, made with respect to Taiwan and Korea, that the market alone was unlikely to turn entrepreneurs into exporters.[2] Moreover, export orientation did not conflict with industrial policy. Export-oriented growth was pursued alongside policies of strategic protectionism driven by the state, the objective of which was to deepen the industrial structure. Export orientation and protectionism, in turn, could not be separated from the rentier elites' drive to divert much of the profits of the resulting economic growth in their direction.

Yet the impact of domestic policy choices was likely to be much less significant than that produced by external forces. That is, it was very difficult to explain the surge in Southeast Asia's growth without reference to what can only be described as a tidal wave of Japanese direct investment. Owing to the historic Plaza Accord of 1985, which saw the Japanese cave in to American pressure to revalue the yen to solve the US trade deficit, production in Japan became prohibitive in terms of labor costs, forcing the Japanese to move their more labor-intensive operations to low-wage areas, in particular to China and Southeast Asia. At least $15 billion worth of Japanese direct investment flowed into Southeast Asia between 1985 and 1990, with Indonesia receiving $3.1 billion, Thailand $3.7 billion, and Malaysia $2.2 billion (Japan Ministry of Finance). The inflow of Japanese capital allowed the Asian NICs to escape the credit squeeze of the early 1980s brought on by the Third World debt crisis, surmount the global recession of the mid-1980s, and move on to a path of high-speed growth. The centrality of what came to be called the *endaka*, or currency revaluation, was reflected in the ratio of foreign direct investment inflows to gross capital formation, which leaped spectacularly in the late 1980s and 1990s in Indonesia, Malaysia, and Thailand (Jomo et al. 1997: 14).

The dynamics of foreign-investment-driven growth was best illustrated in Thailand. The country's technocrats, for instance, had no illusions about the source of their economy's dynamism. As one of them wrote,

> The current explanation of Thailand's accelerated growth was the 1985 appreciation of the value of the yen, rendering Japanese production more costly. Japanese multinational companies were forced to look for new lower-cost production locations. In 1987, Japanese investment approvals by Thailand's Board of Investments exceeded the cumulative Japanese investment for the preceding 20 years.
>
> (TDRI 1992: 2, 26)

If one included the investment flows from Taiwan and Korea that followed closely in the wake of the Japanese investment, one was talking about Thailand receiving East Asian investment coming to $24 billion in just five years, 1987 to 1991 (Yoshihara 1994: 49). Commenting on the magnitude of the investment wave, one research team claimed,

> The truth is that whatever might have been the Thai government's policy preference—protectionist, mercantilist, or market-oriented—the vast amounts of Japanese capital coming into Thailand could not but trigger growth. The same was true in the two other favored nations of Japanese investment, Malaysia and Indonesia.
>
> (Bello et al. 2004: 20)

It was, however, not just the scale of Japanese investment over a five-year period that mattered. It was the process as well. The Japanese government and *keiretsu*, or conglomerates, in fact, planned and cooperated closely in the transfer of corporate industrial facilities to Southeast Asia. One key dimension of this plan was to relocate not just the

191

big corporations like Toyota or Matsushita but also the small and medium enterprises that provided their inputs and components. Another was to integrate complementary manufacturing operations which were spread across the region in different countries. The aim was to create an Asia Pacific platform for re-export to Japan and export to third country markets. This was industrial policy and planning on a grand scale, managed jointly by the Japanese government and corporations and driven by the need to adjust to the post-Plaza Accord world. As one Japanese diplomat put it rather candidly, "Japan is creating an exclusive Japanese market in which Asia Pacific nations are incorporated into the so-called *keiretsu* [financial-industrial bloc] system" (Okazaki 1992: 18).

The Philippines: the anti-developmental state?

Though state strength was of less significance than external forces in Southeast Asia's industrialization in the 1980s, it did still matter in the last instance. This became evident when the record of the Southeast Asian NICs was compared to that of the Philippines, which came to be called "the sick man of Asia." Malaysia, Thailand, and Indonesia had formal structural adjustment programs, but, being stronger states, they were able to resist or blunt harsh adjustment such as that visited on the Philippines, which had been chosen as a guinea pig for the new development paradigm by the World Bank as early as 1980. This had fatal consequences for development. The political transition in the mid-1980s resulted in the new democratic government of President Corazon Aquino assuming the massive foreign debt of $26 billion contracted by the Marcos dictatorship. Aquino decided to assume what was known as the *model debtor strategy* and pay off the country's creditors on their terms. In return for World Bank and IMF loans that would go to repaying the debt to the commercial banks, the government agreed to carry out drastic liberalization measures.

The combination of adjustment and draconian debt repayment resulted in an average growth rate of 1.5 percent between 1983 and 1993. The reason was not hard to find. Government was by far the biggest investor in the Philippines, and debt repayment ate up funds that would otherwise have gone into capital expenditures that would stimulate economic activity. Very little could be spared for improving the country's physical, technical, and educational infrastructure. Obliged by an "automatic appropriations law" to cover the foreign debt falling due, the government allocated some 40–50 percent of the budget to debt repayment in the late 1980s (Business World 2003). A financial hemorrhage marked the later 1980s and early 1990s, with the net transfer of financial resources to external creditors coming to $1.3 billion a year on average between 1986 and 1991 (Freedom from Debt Coalition 1997).

Equally important, the impact of structural adjustment fed into the calculations of foreign investors. With poverty engulfing over a third of the population and inequality rising, the Philippines was a depressed market as far as Japanese investors were concerned with an unstable, violent polity, and they were not about to sink much money into it. Between 1987 and 1991, for instance, a paltry $797 million in Japanese investment entered the Philippines, while Thailand received $12 billion (Yoshihara 1994: 49). When one included Korean and Taiwanese investment, which tracked the Japanese, the gap was even greater. Thailand received $24 billion in investment during the same period, or fifteen times the amount invested in the Philippines, which came to $1.6 billion. "This difference in the flow of foreign investment from the three countries," Kunio Yoshihara rightly observed, "produced a significant disparity in growth performance of the two countries [Philippines and Thailand] during the period" (1994: 49).

The combination of harsh adjustment measures, a weak, compliant state that made debt servicing the national economic priority, and growing poverty combined to create in the case of the Philippines a vicious cycle of stagnation that contrasted with the virtuous circle of growth among its neighbors propelled by state activism, industrial policy, and massive Japanese direct investment.

In this connection, Paul Hutchcroft's portrayal of the Philippines as a patrimonial oligarchy, where a weak state was plundered by strong elites in civil society, was consistent with this picture. What he failed to take sufficient account of was that this weak state was manipulated as well by powerful external forces, a dimension that was stressed by students of the policies of the World Bank and International Monetary Fund (IMF) toward the country (cf. Bello et al. 1982; Broad 1985). Indeed, the local elite and international actors often worked in tandem, though perhaps not consciously, to create a weak, "anti-developmental" state (Bello 2005). This was particularly the case in the 1980s, when the local elites successfully emasculated state-led land reform, a key element in the industrial take-off of Korea and Taiwan, while the IMF and World Bank significantly altered the country's trade structure via structural adjustment and the imposition of debt servicing as *the* national economic priority.

Japan's stagnation and the crisis of the developmental state paradigm

The late 1980s saw the developmental state paradigm at the peak of its influence both as theory and policy prescription. Not surprisingly, this was also when it seemed that Japan was poised to overtake the United States as "number one." In fact, Japan sunk into fifteen miserable years of stagnation from which it has only recently and hesitatingly recovered. And, not surprisingly too, it was inevitable that Japan's long stagnation would diminish the luster of the developmental state since it was, after all, the developmental state par excellence.

In looking at Japan's crisis, analysts have divided on whether its causes are macro-economic or structural. The first perspective stresses the role of policy errors such as the adoption of tight monetary policies when recession threatened in the early 1990s or the impact of normal cyclical trends such as overinvestment in the stock market and real estate in the 1980s, leading to the stock market and property bubble that saw the shares of the Nippon Telegraph and Telephone Corporation priced at 300 times the company's earnings per share and the land in Tokyo occupied by the imperial palace and gardens attain a value more than the whole state of California (Emmott 1989: 112). In this view, a correction would come in the form of a bursting of the bubble, followed by a recession that would itself be corrected through the managed stimulation of demand.

But as the recession dragged on, with the economy registering an average growth of 1 percent of GDP during the dismal 1990s and proving resistant to a variety of Keynesian mechanisms to stimulate demand that merely left the country with a public debt three times the size of the gross domestic product, the macroeconomic explanation was increasingly challenged by the structuralist view. This view held that while Japan's brand of developmental state might have been positive in the period of its catching up with the West, it had become dysfunctional as the economy reached maturity.

There is something markedly missing, however, in both the macroeconomic and structuralist explanations for Japan's economic stagnation, and this was an effort to put it in the context of global economic trends. In fact, it is probably at the level of the global economy that much of the explanation of Japan's prolonged stagnation lies. According to an IMF analysis, the Japanese bubble was one moment in a broader and more protracted crisis of overinvestment that has wracked the global economy since the 1980s, the other moments being the Asian financial crisis of 1997 and the collapse of the dot com market that led to the US recession of 2001–2 (Rajan 2005).

What the IMF revealed but failed to give proper stress to is that the crisis of over-investment is a crisis created by *overinvestment in the financial sector*. This has its roots in the phenomenon of excess capacity or overproduction which stems from a growing gap between tremendous additions to global productive capacity and the slow growth of global demand. With profits meager from stagnant productive sectors, investments have increasingly been channeled to financial speculation, be it in real estate, stocks, bonds, and complex financial mechanisms such as derivatives. From this perspective, the collapse of the Japanese stock and property markets in the early 1990s was one of a series of spectacular collapses associated with the financialization of the process of capital accu-mulation. From this vantage point, locating the crisis in either the business cycle, as the macroeconomic explanation does, or in the obsolete configuration of the Japanese developmental state, as the structuralist perspective proposes, does not yield much of a credible explanation.

The Asian financial crisis—or how financial markets subverted the developmental state

It was not surprising that a version of the structuralist view of Japan's economic stagna-tion would also surface as an explanation for the Asian financial crisis of 1997. Then US Undersecretary of the Treasury Larry Summers was quick to point to "crony capitalism" as being "at the heart of the crisis" (1998). This was a remarkable volte-face, given the fact that under Summers as chief economist, the World Bank had come out with the famous *East Asian Miracle* that praised the very same economic regimes that Summers now labeled "crony capitalist" as efficient technocracies insulated from political pressures:

> In each HPAE [high performing Asian economy], a technocratic elite insulated to a degree from excessive political pressure supervised macroeconomic management. The insulation mechanism ranged from legislation, such as balanced budget laws in Indonesia, Singapore, and Thailand, to custom and practice in Japan and Korea. All protected essentially conservative macroeconomic policies by limiting the scope for politicians and interest groups to derail those policies.
>
> (World Bank 1993: 348–49)

But the claim that economies that had been registering growth rates of 6–10 percent a year—for over thirty years in the case of Korea—would be laid low overnight by the accumulation of the distortions or state interventionism or "crony capitalism" was hardly credible. Indeed, even more than the case of Japan's stagnation, external, global forces played a central role in the Asian financial crisis. And, contrary to the claim of the crony capitalist school, it was liberalization and deregulation, not interventionist distortions or corruption, that proved to be the precipitating factor. Financial liberalization was the key trend in Southeast Asia's economies in the early 1990s. The reasons for this were twofold.

First, strong pressure from the IMF and the US Treasury Department, which in turn were pressured by US financial groups that wanted a piece of the Asian miracle. Second, the desire of Asian technocrats to access alternative foreign funds to fuel the export machines they had built up since the mid-1980s as Japanese foreign direct investment began to taper down. With practically all capital controls lifted and investment rules liberalized, some $100 billion flowed into the key Asian economies between 1993 and 1997, with the money gravitating toward the areas of high and quick returns, like the stock market and real estate. Contrary to the notion that the "non-transparent" practices of crony capitalism conned foreign investors into coming in, the latter were eager and determined to get into Asian capital markets, whatever the "true" state of these markets was.[3]

With few controls on where the funds went, overinvestment soon swamped the stock and housing markets, causing prices to collapse and triggering follow-on dislocations in the exchange rate, the balance of payments, and the balance of trade. These were taken by foreign speculators as signs that it was time to leave and there resulted a rush to the exits as they scrambled to exchange baths or rupiahs or pesos for dollars before the long-awaited devaluation that would radically reduce the value of their investments. With both entry and exit rules liberalized, there was no way for governments, except for Malaysia, which defied the IMF and imposed capital controls, to stop the stampede, and the $100 billion that fled the region in a few short weeks in 1997 brought economic growth to a screeching halt from Korea down to Indonesia. As Stanley Fischer, the American deputy managing director of the IMF, admitted: "[M]arkets are not always right ... Sometimes inflows are excessive, and sometimes they may be sustained too long. Markets tend to react late; but they tend to react fast, sometimes excessively" (Fischer 1997).

That it was not state interventionism but, on the contrary, a retreat of the state that was at the heart of the crisis was clear in the case of Korea, the classic tiger economy. During the period of industrial ascent, the government used its control of credit to both encourage and discipline the *chaebol* or conglomerates. By the early 1990s, however, the credit demands of the conglomerates had become voracious. At the same time, foreign banks and foreign funds were eager to get into Korea and pressed Washington and the IMF, in turn, to pressure the Koreans to open up their financial sector. Korea's entry into the OECD (Organization for Economic Cooperation and Development) in the early 1990s proved decisive, since membership in this circle of advanced economies required the liberalization of its capital account, financial sector, and foreign investment regime. Although the government formally adopted a gradualist liberalization strategy, the inflow of foreign funds was anything but gradual. In 1993, the government relaxed its controls over cross-border capital flows, allowing both conglomerates and newly created banks greater liberty to borrow abroad. As Ravi Palat has pointed out, the 1993 financial liberalization signified the weakening of the state as a buffer between the local economy and the international economy, on the one hand, and the rise of an uncontrolled private sector as the principal mediator between the two, on the other (Palat 1999: 25–26).

The results were disastrous. Korean banks plunged gleefully into the inter-bank market,

> taking advantage of lower interest rates overseas and passing the funds on to their domestic consumers ... [T]his was hardly prudent banking practice since it meant

195

that Korea Inc. was borrowing short term money abroad, money that had to be repaid in hard currency, and lending it long-term to the expansion-crazed *chaebol*.

(Blustein 2001: 125–26)

But, as always, it took two to tango, and "foreign banks rushed into this promising new market, led by the Europeans and the Japanese" (Blustein 2001: 126). The country's foreign debt promptly trebled, from $44 billion in 1993 to $120 billion in September 1997, and went on to reach $153 billion in February 1998 (Palat 1999: 52).

The high-profile collapse of some highly indebted *chaebol* early in 1997 and the financial panic in Southeast Asia that summer combined to make the Korean economy a sitting duck that fall. Speculators and banks began dumping the won and pulling out, the pullout turned to panic as in Southeast Asia, and only the looming threat of a bankruptcy by a strategic ally that would disrupt the global financial system compelled Washington to pressure bankers to roll over their loans to Korea, causing the bleeding to stop (Blustein 2001: 196–205). The Korean and Southeast Asian countries, it now is even clearer in retrospect, were victims of the global financial liberalization that picked up steam in the early 1980s and which, at the latest count, has produced some 100 financial crises in the last quarter of a century. Like Japan's fifteen-year recession, the principal cause or causes of the Asian financial crisis were located at the global level—that is, in the rapid and intense financialization that accompanied the overaccumulation, overcapacity, and overproduction that has gripped the global economy over the last three decades.

The death of the developmental state?

In a paper assessing trends in the decade following the Asian financial crisis, the economist Jayati Ghosh claimed that despite aggregate economic recovery in the affected countries, growth rates were lower, employment generation was inadequate, unemployment rates were rising, and the conditions of a large sector of the poor had not improved. More important, she claimed that "the project of the developmental state which was such an essential feature of economic progress in the region in the past, has effectively been abandoned" (Ghosh 2007). How valid is this claim?

It is true that the United States lost no time in taking advantage of the crisis to push for the dismantling of the trade, investment, and regulatory structures that had been able to withstand Washington's pressure in more prosperous times. In testimony before the US Congress, US Trade Representative Charlene Barshefsky told legislators that in Indonesia, Thailand, and Korea, the IMF had been able to impose programs of comprehensive liberalization that included privatization of strategic industries, the sweeping away for "market access impediments," the dismantling of local monopolies, and the elimination of industrial policy initiatives like Indonesia's national car project. All this would translate into "business opportunities for US firms" (US House of Representatives 1998). More strategically, noted Jeffrey Garten, undersecretary of commerce during President Bill Clinton's first term, "Most of these countries are going through a dark and deep tunnel ... But on the other end there is going to be a significantly different Asia in which American firms have achieved a much deeper market penetration, much greater access" (*New York Times*, February 1, 1998). Indeed, so intent was the US to take advantage of the crisis to dismantle the developmental state instead of assisting in the economic recovery that Chalmers Johnson could credibly claim that "having defeated the fascists and the communists, the United States now sought to defeat its last remaining rivals for global dominance: the nations of East Asia that had used the conditions of the Cold War to enrich themselves" (Johnson 2000: 206).

Did this US-IMF effort to dismantle the developmental state via neoliberal reforms succeed? The answer depends on which country we are talking about. Having evaded IMF surveillance by rejecting an IMF program, Malaysia's political economy seems to be the least changed. The momentum for neoliberal reform in Indonesia seems to have been lost, though many of the initial initiatives demanded by the IMF remain in place. Thailand froze the initial reforms, then threw out the IMF approach after the Thaksin government came to power in 2001. In Japan, the developmental state successfully resisted internal and external pressures for significant reform, to the dismay of market partisans. Korea, on the other hand, has witnessed fundamental transformation in a neoliberal direction. It is useful, in this regard, to compare the contrasting paths of Thailand and Korea.

In Thailand, the election of Thaksin Shinawatra as prime minister in 2001 was followed by his government's abandonment of the contractionary IMF policies followed by its predecessor governments after the Asian financial crisis and the adoption of Keynesian-style expansionary policies with a strong populist appeal, among them, a cash grant of one million baht to each district to invest in producing a commodity; a 30-baht (less than a dollar) per hospital visit universal health care program, and a moratorium on farmers' debt repayments. On July 31, 2003, Thaksin claimed that Thailand had paid off all its debts to the IMF and declared independence from it, vowing that Thailand would never again return to that institution for financial help.

Thaksin's other policies were not easy to categorize since they involved measures that opened up the Thai economy to transnational corporations while also expanding monopolistic privileges for domestic capitalist groupings, such as his own telecommunication empire, Shin Corporation, and business allies such as the Thai food transnational CP (Charoen Pokphand). Thaksin's model of governance, according to some observers, was drawn from the CP corporate model and amounted to a "CEO-ization" of government (Greenfield 2006).

Whatever its ideological coloration, this CEO-style of governance combined with Keynesian populist measures and an anti-IMF nationalistic populism translated not into a weakening of the developmental state but to its strengthening and transformation in Thailand. This process was not reversed by Thaksin's ouster by a military coup in September 2006, which brought to power policymakers who, if anything, were in favor of more state regulation of the market in the form of capital controls and resulted in the popularization of the king of Thailand's "sufficiency economy" economic paradigm, with its anti-globalization, anti-market overtones.

In Korea, in contrast, the government has faithfully followed the IMF's precepts, resulting in a truly neoliberal transformation of Korea's political economy. As a result, *chaebol* behavior has been drastically altered, with "Korean companies, like their counterparts in many countries around the world … driven by the need to increase shareholder wealth" (Breen 2007: 32). Domestic competition for the *chaebol* was spurred by the passage, at the height of the US Treasury-IMF surveillance of the landmark Foreign Investment Promotion Act in 1998, which opened 98.2 percent of all business sectors to foreign investment, about the same as other OECD economies (Kim and Lee 2005: 42). Also, an amendment to the Foreigners' Land Acquisition Act in May 1998 saw the complete removal of restrictions on foreign ownership of land, property, and houses.

The results have been sweeping. The amount of land owned by non-Koreans climbed 3.9 times to 148.5 million square meters from 1997 to 2003 (Wan-Soon and You-Il 2005: 42). Total foreign direct investment between 1998 and 2004 came to $79 billion, or three times the $25 billion that came in during the previous thirty-five years. Even more striking, the ratio of foreign-owned shares in the Korean stock market increased from 12.97 percent in 1996 to 40.02 percent in 2003 (Hyun-Chin and Jin-Ho 2006: 18). As the presence of transnational actors increased, the role of labor, which was already limited under the old regime, was eroded even further by neoliberal labor-market reforms.

As for the Korean state, it was, from the point of view of many analysts, propelled out of its old developmental role to a "regulatory role" wherein its key mission was to transform the "domestic structure in an 'investor-friendly' way and [integrate] it deeply into the global economy" (Hyun-Chin and Jin-Ho 2006: 18). At the level of social power, a new power bloc united by acceptance of neoliberal reform was in the making. For the old developmental regime, say Lim Hyun-Chin and Jang Jin-Ho, the handwriting is on the wall:

> The answer to whether or not the developmental state in the country of the "state-banks-*chaebols* nexus" can survive in the wake of globalization and neoliberal restructuring ... seems to be negative as of the present with the transformation of major institutional actors, their functions, and the relationships among them.
>
> (Lim and Jang 2006: 22)

Why the different directions taken by Thailand and Korea? There have undoubtedly been many factors at work. However, one cannot resist putting the emphasis, in the case of Korea, on the special relationship with the United States. Ironically, the same security-based relationship that the Park regime had taken advantage of to put Korea on the path of high-speed industrialization proved to be the factor that led to the undoing of the developmental state. In contrast to its posture in the other Asian countries hit by the financial crisis, the United States took a hands-on role in Korea, one that was even more prominent than the IMF's. The US simply could not allow the economic breakdown of a country that was not only a key trading partner but also a militarily strategic ally, and it was at Washington's direct request that the banks stopped the capital flight at the height of the crisis (Blustein 2001: 196–205). The quid pro quo, however, was a reform process that was directly supervised by the US Treasury Department and strictly implemented by the IMF, with the unstated threat of a ban from global capital markets should the government and parliament resist or stall.

But why Korea and not Japan, one may ask. True, Japan is perhaps equally important to Washington strategically. But while Japan may be pressured, as it has been since the 1980s, it is too big to be bullied, which is the appropriate term for Washington's behavior toward Korea. Korea was tied in myriad ways to the US, and it was not big enough to resist Washington's tightening of the strings. In the end, Korea's "semi-sovereign" status, to borrow Bruce Cumings' description, proved to be the Achilles heel of its capitalist developmental state.

Conclusion

The debate over the developmental state is what has driven innovation in international political economy in the Asia-Pacific region. This theoretical debate has not taken place in a vacuum, being inextricably linked to disciplinary paradigms, policy preferences, and, more broadly, political predilections.

Initially constructed by Chalmers Johnson as a paradigm to understand the workings of the Japanese economy, the theory of the developmental state also provided a lens that better captured the dynamics of economic development in Taiwan and Korea than the market paradigm. It led to research that located the emergence of these economies in the dynamics of the regional security system centered on the United States and in common structures inherited from the era of Japanese colonialism.

It was inevitable that scholars would ask the question why Southeast Asia did not produce developmental regimes such as those in Northeast Asia. In seeking to answer this question, analysts proposed various explanations, among them, the importance of being on the frontlines of the Cold War and Southeast Asia's being "cursed" with natural resources. Among the most useful tools to come out of this discussion was the neo-Weberian concept of a "patrimonial oligarchy" such as that in the Philippines that cornered resources through rent strategies and channeled them to consumption instead of investment.

By the early 1990s, however, what needed to be explained was not Southeast Asia's backwardness but its energetically following in the wake of the Northeast Asian tiger economies. The state-versus-market debate in Northeast Asia was now reproduced in Southeast Asia. While the role of the state in development was not as prominent as in Korea, Taiwan, and Japan, it was nevertheless significant. However, domestic policy choices, whether neoliberal or state-oriented, probably mattered much less than external factors, such as the deluge of Japanese foreign investment that hit Southeast Asia in the latter half of the 1980s. Southeast Asia's industrialization was, in many ways, a planned process instigated by the Japanese and the *keiretsu* as Japan sought to avoid the negative impacts of the yen appreciation brought about by the Plaza Accord in 1985.

Nevertheless, state strength was still important in the last instance, as shown by the case of the Philippines, which was skirted by Japanese investment owing to its having a depressed market that resulted from the inability of the state to resist the IMF's imposition of repayment of the foreign debt as the country's economic priority and the elite's emasculation of land reform, which could have created a class of consumers that could have stimulated industrial growth.

The long Japanese stagnation of the 1990s and the Asian financial crisis of 1997 renewed the state-versus-market debate, with some saying that the crises could be traced to the interventionist practices and structures of a developmental state that coddled vested interests. "Crony capitalism" was also said to be the prime cause of the Asia's unraveling in the fateful year of 1997. The crony capitalist thesis, however, enjoyed fleeting credibility, and what came to be seen as a more solid explanation as a cause of the crisis was capital account liberalization, which the Asian economies adopted partly at the urging of the US Treasury Department and the IMF. This exposed them to the gyrations of finance capital, the dynamics of which had become the main driver of the global capitalist system. Both the Japanese stagnation and the Asian unraveling more likely stem from financialization, which is a consequence of the crisis of overproduction, oveaccumulation, and overcapacity that has plagued the global economy over the last three decades.

The Asian financial crisis and its aftermath brought about the "death of the East Asian developmental state," say some analysts. Whether this is the case depends on the country being discussed. In Thailand, the developmental state is being transformed and being brought to new directions with politico-economic formulas that mix some economic liberalization with populism, more privileges for local conglomerates, greater executive control over the economy, renewed capital controls, anti–IMF nationalism, and anti-globalization initiatives. In Korea, on the other hand, there has been a rapid dismantling of protectionist trade, investment, and property structures, and there is in progress a transition from a developmental state regime to a regulatory neoliberal regime. Ironically, the special security relationship with the United States that the Park Chung Hee regime took advantage of to create the modern developmental state has become the source of Korea's undoing as Washington has taken a hands-on approach to Korea's economic transformation in a neoliberal direction.

Notes

1 With democratization in the late 1980s, the militant Korean Confederation of Trade Unions (KCTU) replaced the compliant Korean Federation of Trade Unions (KFTU) as the leading Korean labor federation. It pursued a confrontational strategy toward management and resisted the neo-liberal labor market reforms after the Asian financial crisis with street battles as well as strikes. The KCTU did not see the high-speed industrialization as having benefited Korean labor and Korean society as a whole.

2 As Song Byung-Nak, a technocrat under Park Chung-Hee, noted: "The export targets agreed upon between the government and individual firms were taken by businessmen as equivalent to com-pulsory orders. Firms that failed to achieve their export targets without a plausible excuse ran the risk of heavy administrative sanctions from the government." (Byung-Nak 1989: 126).

3 As Summers' superior, Treasury Secretary Robert Rubin, admitted a few months after the crisis:

> One of the things that has struck us most about the Asian crisis, is that after the problems began to develop and we spoke to institutions that had extended credit or invested in the region, so often we found these institutions had engaged in relatively little analysis and relatively little weighing of risks that were appropriate to the decisions.
> (Robert Rubin, remarks at the Sasin Institute of Business Administration, Chulalongkorn University, Bangkok, June 30, 1998)

12

The rise of East Asia

An emerging challenge to the study of international political economy

Henry Wai-Chung Yeung

Introduction

From the meteoric rise of Japan in the 1970s and the 1980s to the rapid industrialization of the four East Asian "tiger" economies and the recent ascendance of emerging giants such as China, the rise of East Asian economies poses a challenging analytical problem for the field of international political economy (IPE), understood as both a field of academic enquiry and a substantive issue area (see Gilpin 2001; Higgott 2007; Ravenhill 2008a).[1] Does this general rise of East Asia necessarily follow the pathways of North America and Western Europe? Or is the phenomenon made possible because of an era of hegemonic (in)stability as originally envisaged in Keohane (1984)? If so, the rise of East Asia can simply be read off and explained by existing IPE theories. The reality of East Asian IPE as a substantive issue, however, seems to be much more complicated than allowed for in mainstream IPE theories that emanate from the US-centric view of the international political economy (see Cohen 2007, 2008b; cf. Higgott and Watson 2008; Ravenhill 2008b). In his review of the subject matter, Higgott (2007: 170) noted that "IPE, in large part because of its twentieth-century location within IR scholarship, has tended to focus on the developed, the rich and powerful of the North at the expense of the developing and the poor of the South." Yet there is a contrary tendency in the East Asian "case"; its rapid ascendance cannot be read off as a straightforward outcome of power play among hegemonic nation-states in the global arena—a traditional focus and concern in mainstream IPE theories. East Asian economies have experienced such diverse developmental trajectories that cannot be easily captured in the form of changing inter-state relations within the context of an international or global economic order. Instead, the rise of East Asian economies reflects the complex interaction between states and non–state actors embedded in different spatial scales that range from the global economy to regional divisions of labor and local specificities.

   In this chapter, I seek to deal with this analytical challenge by revisiting some of the most significant substantive concerns and conceptual approaches to the study of the diverse development trajectories in East Asian economies. In unpacking this changing East Asian political economy, we need to go beyond the state-centric view in IPE to incorporate other important non-state actors (e.g. firms and networks) and social institutions (e.g. business systems). Seen in this broader perspective the rise of East Asia provides fertile research ground for us to "theorize back" at dominant IPE theories in the "North." I do so in three steps. First, I locate East Asia in the mainstream field of IPE enquiry, particularly the realist perspective on the global economic order. Here, I want to question the analytic purchase of this perspective for East Asian development. Second, I expound two alternative IPE approaches to the study of East Asia, namely the developmental states and varieties of capitalism approaches. In both cases, I provide some important correctives that theorize the role of global production networks in refiguring the developmental state and in hybridizing capitalism in East Asia. These revisions demonstrate the inadequacies of mainstream IPE theories in accounting for capitalist diversity and change in an East Asian context. Third, I conclude by offering some tentative remarks on the key question of this chapter: what kind of IPE theories for what kind of East Asian development? Taken together, this chapter aims to show how the complex unfolding of political economic forces in East Asian economies tells us something important about existing IPE theories and how such theories represent a collective effort to develop context-specific theories that allow us to challenge mainstream approaches in the social sciences (see Yeung and Lin 2003; Yeung 2007a).

East Asia in international political economy

To insert East Asia into the study of IPE, we must first start with Japan as the first serious post-war challenge from East Asia to American economic hegemony. Alternatively known as the "crisis of Fordism" during the mid-1970s and through the 1980s, an earlier wave of mass production methods and economies of scale could no longer provide a competitive edge to incumbent firms and corporations in advanced industrialized economies, particularly the US. Ezra Vogel's (1979) influential book *Japan as Number One* became widely circulated in major intellectual and policy circles. Coupled with the emergence of Asian newly industrialized economies and the 1973 oil crisis, the rise of Japan triggered what was later conceptualized as flexible specialization, post-Fordism, and globalization. Japan was also significantly featured in Piore and Sabel's (1990) *The Second Industrial Divide* and Womack et al.'s (1990) *The Machines That Changed the World*. Both MIT products have fundamentally shaped the subsequent debates about America's and, by extension, the world's industrial future in the international political economy.

The meteoric rise of Japan as a major economic challenge to the US and other OECD countries coincided with the perceived relative decline of US hegemony. This finding was so significant that Robert Gilpin, himself named by Benjamin Cohen (2007) as one of the four "pioneers" and "giants" of the American school of IPE, had to devote special attention to the rise of Japan in his 1987 magisterial work *The Political Economy of International Relations*, which offers a definitive realist view on the international political economy. As Gilpin put it, "I emphasize the meteoric rise of Japan and its challenge to the liberal international economic order. The remarkable shift in the locus of the centre of the world economy from the Atlantic to the Pacific in the closing decades of the twentieth century is given special attention" (Gilpin 1987: xiv). In this view, the "transfer of the full spectrum of Japanese competitive dynamism into the American market" (260) was both significant and conflict-laden because of the tendency of Japanese investments in circumventing trade barriers, the decline of European presence in the

US, and negative responses in the US to Japanese "takeovers" in the American economy (e.g. Sony's acquisition of Columbia Pictures). Gilpin (1987: 260) therefore concluded: "The outcome of these conflicting developments in the Nichibei economy will affect not only the future of the U.S. economy but also the shape of the international political economy." True enough, he noted in a later work that "the concerted effort to forge a Japanese-led Pacific Asian economy has continued and signifies Japan's increasing assertiveness and independent stance within the global economy" (Gilpin 2000: 12).

(Un)realism on Japan?

With hindsight, this realist view of the rise of Japan is inadequate. It not only ignores important domestic transformations in Japan and the wider regional context in which its production activities are embedded (see Hatch and Yamamura 1996; Katzenstein 2005). More importantly, it continues to advocate a zero-sum game view popular in IPE where the gains of Asian states such as Japan are theorized to have occurred at the expense of American power. According to Gilpin (1987: 13), realists

> stress the role of power in the rise of a market and the conflictual nature of inter-national economic relations. They argue that economic interdependence must have a political foundation and that it creates yet another arena of interstate conflict, increases national vulnerability, and constitutes a mechanism that one society can employ to dominate another.

In this realist interpretation of the international political economy,

> the process of uneven growth stimulates political conflict because it undermines the international political status quo. Shifts in the location of economic activities change the distribution of wealth and power among the states in the system. This redistribution of power and its effect on the standing and welfare of individual states accentuate the conflict between rising and declining states.
>
> (54–55)

In this conflict-laden and anarchic model of the international political economy, the rise of Japan became a paradox vis-à-vis American hegemony in the global economy (see Abegglen 1994; Katzenstein and Shiraishi 1996). On the one hand, the rise of Japan was "allowed for" in the context of US-driven Cold War geopolitical imperative or what Katzenstein (2005: 2) calls "the American imperium." The US willingly and uncondi-tionally opened its domestic market to Japanese exports, provided the necessary tech-nologies for Japan's industrialization to take off rapidly, and relieved Japan of the financial burden of national defense. On the other hand, a successful and competitive Japanese economy would pose a significant challenge to this American embrace. This realist-inspired fear of the rise of Japan, nevertheless, was a short-lived one. With the downturn of the Japanese "bubble" economy since the late 1980s and the early 1990s, as Dicken (2007: 44) aptly observed, the "United States' fear of the Japanese threat receded; the 'bash Japan' literature virtually disappeared."

The rise and fall (and rise again?) of Japan, both as an empirical phenomenon in the international political economy and as a research topic for debates in IPE, is clearly instructive in the context of this Handbook. It not only speaks volumes about the myopic tendency of mainstream (American) IPE theories, but also points to the analytical challenge identified in the opening section of this chapter. First, the failure of the realist perspective in predicting and explaining Japan's post-1990 economic stagnation has a lot to do with its reluctance to get out of its intellectual straight-jacket in the discipline of international relations that assumes inter-state rivalries and conflicts as its central analytical foci. The result of this imposition of a bargaining-cum-conflict realist framework in the case of Japan is clear. There is an inadequate attention in the requisite IPE literature to domestic transformations and intra-regional contexts that significantly impact Japan's economic competitiveness in the international political economy. This "force-fit" of Japan into existing hegemonic and well established theories of IPE has produced only a weak explanation of the rise of Japan (cf. the developmental state literature in the next section), let alone a dynamic theory of the subsequent decline and potential recovery of Japan in the past two decades.[2]

Second, the case of Japan illuminates the importance of moving away from the assumption that context-specific theories, such as those developed in the American school of IPE, are necessarily universally applicable. In other words, the rise of East Asia is clearly evident as a reality in the international political economy. And yet, we are still quite a distance away from developing the appropriate IPE theories to account for this phenomenon. If we are unable to tackle this analytical challenge, we might miss another "boat" of accounting for the rise of China in the global political economy. Indeed, even though Gilpin (1987: 294) claimed in the mid-1980s that "it is too soon to know what the effects of China's reentry into the world economy will be,"[3] we are already witnessing realist-inspired interpretations in the recent literature on the alleged rise of China as a threat to the international economic order (Goodhart and Xu 1996; Brown 2000; Gertz 2000; Breslin 2007; Cooney and Sato 2007; cf. Zweig 2002; McNally 2007; Zweig and Chen 2007). How else can we conceptualize the rapid emergence of the East Asian newly industrialized economies? What might these alternative conceptualizations tell us about the inadequacies of mainstream IPE theories? To answer these questions satisfactorily, I next revisit some non-US-centric approaches that are firmly grounded in the international political economy in East Asia.

International political economy in East Asia

While the above section situates East Asia in mainstream IPE theories, this section takes a rather different approach. Here, I survey two leading theoretical perspectives on East Asian development that focus on the changing international political economy in East Asia: developmental states and varieties of capitalism approaches. This focus necessarily draws upon contributions from multidisciplinary fields beyond the mainstream of IPE, such as development studies, economic sociology, economic geography, and regional studies. In both approaches, I present the theoretical ideas emanating from research grounded in the international political economy of East Asia. I then provide an update on how some of these ideas have been re-examined in the context of regional change and global transformation. More importantly, this detailed introspection of East Asian-specific theoretical perspectives demonstrates the inadequacies of realist IPE as an allegedly universal explanation of capitalist political-economic changes and dynamics. The diverse national trajectories within East Asia point to the importance of understanding these changes and dynamics at different spatial scales, not just at the international scale as often found in realist accounts of East Asian change. A conceptual clarification of the term "international political economy" is therefore critical here. The word "international" in an East Asian context does not necessarily and exclusively refer to the kind of transnational economic relations and international interdependence originally envisaged in the American school of IPE associated with such scholars as Keohane and Nye (1972, 1977) and Gilpin (1987). Rather, what might be counted as "international" in East Asia can encompass a much wider range of political-economic phenomena that go beyond the territorial confines of a single nation-state (e.g. development trajectories, economic organization, systemic and institutional changes, and so on). While the state remains a critical player in this approach, other non-state actors and institutions operating at different spatial scales can just be as important and influential.

In short, East Asian IPE is not just about inter-state bargaining and conflicts in search of wealth and power bounded within the Westphalian territorialized nation-states—an ontological foundation of the American school of IPE. It is about diverse political-economic transformations spearheaded by actors and forces transcending the domestic political realm. These actors and forces can be as globalizing as transnational corporations and international organizations, as regionalizing as production networks linking different territories and sub-national regions, and as localizing as social institutions and cultural foundations. This *multi-scalar* dimension of East Asian IPE differentiates it from a focus on what IPE reductively refers to as "domestic politics" and differentiates this approach from the dominant IPE theories in the "North." In such a conception of IPE, inter-*national* relations are only one aspect, albeit a highly important one, of these multi-scalar formations. As discussed below, the transformative role of globalizing forces and processes in recent decades has brought into sharp relief the role of deterritorialized actors and institutions that crosscut and span different state boundaries and spatial scales.

Developmental states, not "domestic politics"

As mentioned above, the rise of Japan as an economic challenger to the US by the 1980s was noted in the American school of IPE. But it was situated within the realist framework that assumed inherent conflicts and competition in the political economy of international relations. Unsatisfied with such an external (US-centric) interpretation of the Japanese "miracle," some political economists and political scientists began to search for an alternative answer from *within* Japan and, more broadly, East Asia. In doing so, they have developed the "developmental statist model" of economic organization that accounts for many aspects of the changing international political economy in East Asia. So how does the developmental state work exactly? Johnson (1982, 1995) and Wade (1990) have defined a developmental state as a state preoccupied with economic development through the establishment of elite economic bureaucracy to "guide" the market. A developmental state tends to engage numerous institutions for consultation and coordination with the private sector, and these consultations are an essential part of the process of policy formulation and implementation. While state bureaucrats "rule," politicians "reign." The latter's function is not to make policy, but to create economic and political space for the bureaucracy to maneuver. They also act as a "safety valve" by forcing the bureaucrats to respond to the needs of groups upon which the stability of the system rests; that is, to maintain the relative autonomy of the state while preserving political stability (Evans 1995).

Ironically, Johnson's (1982) idea of the developmental state was picked up by Gilpin (1987). But instead of acknowledging the role of the developmental state in fashioning a distinct pathway of development in Japan, he was rather dismissive of the burgeoning literature on the role of state capacity in governing the market:

> The record on the efficacy of structural adjustment policy (i.e., what is usually labeled industrial policy) is unclear; it is difficult, if not impossible, to reach any definitive conclusion. It is doubtful, for example, that the stunning success of Japan in one product area after another can be attributed primarily to the perspicacity of MITI [Ministry of International Trade and Industry] and Japan's economic managers. Indeed it is not even certain that MITI and its industrial policies have outperformed the market.
>
> (Gilpin 1987: 213)

This outright dismissal reflects a missed opportunity to engage with this East Asian-specific theoretical approach. Instead, Japan's phenomenal success by the 1980s was explained away as simply relating to "the changing conception of comparative advantage and to its implications for national policy, trade practices, and ultimately for economic theory" (Gilpin 1987: 214). The realist status quo theory of the international political economy is visible in this interpretation. In his sequel book, Gilpin (2001: ch. 7) has devoted much more attention to the role of the developmental state in Japan's post-war economic development. This important corrective, however, has come a little too late, as Japan has since the late 1980s gone into a prolonged period of economic stagnation.

The limits of the developmental state approach

While the developmental state literature can be credited for explaining the *early* success of Japan and three of the four East Asian tiger economies (Singapore, South Korea, and Taiwan) within the context of changing international political economy, it suffers from a kind of myopia the other way round. This time, domestic state structures are seen as largely deterministic in shaping economic development trajectories; other non–state actors and institutions are viewed as simply the "followers" of state-centric economic strategies and industrial policies. Reflecting on the "market versus state debate" in understanding economic development in Asia, Hobday (2001: 25) observed that

> because of the dominance of this debate, there are few studies which derive "bottom–up" policy conclusions from firm-level studies. The activities and strategies of firms in engaging with international production networks cannot be properly accounted for within theories of the developmental state, as latecomer firm behaviour tends to be treated (usually implicitly) as an automatic response to policy and economic circumstances, rather than as a shaping influence in its own right.
>
> (see also Doner et al. 2005)

Like the realist perspective that insists on viewing domestic adjustments as structural outcomes of conflict-ridden international relations, this developmentalist perspective often appears to be too inward-looking and ignorant of the emergent and multiple connections that over time link East Asian economies to each other and to the wider global economy. In more theoretical terms, while the developmental state might be instrumental in "getting prices wrong," to use Amsden's (1989) famous phrase, this market distortion approach to economic development will eventually become ineffective, as national champions and transnational corporations increasingly seek new ways of competing in the global, not just domestic, economy. The 1997/1998 Asian economic crisis has further discredited the developmental state approach (see Bello 1998; Haggard and MacIntyre 1998). Indeed, what we saw during the 1990s was a simultaneous process of *strategic dis-embedding* of these non-state actors from the developmental state and their *reembedding* in an organizational platform that transcends the nation-state—global production networks.

From developmental states to global production networks

This reorientation of previously domestic firms, including national champions and other non-state-sponsored entities, toward the global economy has spurred a new wave of research into the rise of East Asia. This more recent literature is particularly concerned with the strategic articulation of East Asian economies into production increasingly organized on a global scale. Instead of seeing East Asian development as a structural political-economic outcome of changing international relations (the realist perspective) or domestic state initiatives (the developmental state perspective), this non–state-centric view of the international political economy places its analytical attention on both firms and states in global competition through the dynamics of participation and incorporation in global production networks.

According to Henderson et al. (2002), the concept of a *global production network* (GPN) involves both business firms and national economies in organizationally complex and geographically extensive ways and provides a convenient conceptual point of entry to the changing international political economy in East Asia:

> Production networks—the nexus of interconnected functions and operations through which goods and services are produced, distributed and consumed—have become both organizationally more complex and also increasingly global in their geographic extent. Such networks not only integrate firms (and parts of firms) into structures which blur traditional organizational boundaries—through the development of diverse forms of equity and non-equity relationships—but also integrate national economies (or parts of such economies) in ways which have enormous implications for their well-being.
>
> (Henderson et al. 2002: 445–46)

In this view, a GPN is defined as one that is coordinated and controlled by a globally significant transnational corporation (TNC) and involves a vast network of their overseas affiliates, strategic partners, key customers, and non–firm institutions (see Dicken et al. 2001; Coe et al. 2004; Hess and Yeung 2006; Yeung 2007b). In a typical GPN a global lead firm coordinates its own R&D and manufacturing affiliates worldwide and has less than a dozen strategic partners located in different national economies. It also has to coordinate marketing activities with its key customers worldwide and to deal with non-firm institutions such as labor organizations and civil society organizations in different host countries. This diversity of firms and institutions in different countries explains why a GPN is organizationally complex and geographically extensive. It also points to a diversity of strategic modes through which any particular GPN is governed (see Gereffi 2005; Gereffi et al. 2005).

In the East Asian context, different groups of researchers have worked on several related concepts such as global commodity chains (Gereffi and Korzeniewicz 1994;

Gereffi 1996, 2005; Appelbaum, 2000; Appelbaum and Smith, 2001), regional produc-
tion networks (Hatch and Yamamura 1996; Tsui-Auch 1999; Hatch 2000; Yeung 2001;
Katzenstein 2005), international/global production networks (Borrus et al. 2000;
McKendrick et al. 2000; Hobday 2001; Doner et al. 2004; Ernst 2004; Yusuf et al. 2004;
Yang and Hsia 2007; Yeung forthcoming), and global value chains (Gereffi et al. 2005).
These interrelated concepts and approaches, while grounded in different theoretical
foundations, point to a common thread that asserts the central importance of using
"chains" and "networks" to analyze the changing global political economy (see also
Dicken et al. 2001; Hess and Yeung 2006). In contrast to both the realist framework and
the developmental state approach, these approaches tend to privilege neither the nation-
states nor non-state actors. Instead, they are brought together in a common analytical
framework ungrounded in any necessary territorial units (e.g. the state) and spatial scales
(e.g. national). This ontological accommodation of both territoriality and networks in
co-constituting the international political economy tends to work well in accounting for
the diverse political-economic trajectories experienced in East Asian economies.

To sum up, these "chains" and "networks" approaches in East Asian IPE have so far
produced some promising results that enable us to avoid the "territorial trap"; the theoretical bias in mainstream theories of the IPE that views the state as a container (Agnew
1994, 2005; see also Ruggie 1993; Taylor 1995, 1996, 2007). They have offered an
important corrective to the state-centric view of East Asian political economy in both realist
and developmental state approaches. Most importantly, these "chains" and "networks"
approaches have shed light on the changing spatial configurations of territorial development in East Asian economies and linked these dynamics to the changing organizing of
global production under the aegis of globalization. In fact, they have compelled us to
rethink the complex relationships between territorialization, deterritorialization, and reterri-
torialization in today's global political economy (see an example in Yeung forthcoming).

From varieties of capitalism to hybrid capitalisms

As the debate on the nature of the developmental state moved on during the late 1980s
and the early 1990s, a parallel effort in theorizing the international political economy
emerged in Europe. Here, crucial insights from earlier nationally specific IPE studies fed
into the wider debate on the nature and diversity of global capitalism(s), commonly
known as the "varieties of capitalism" (VoC) approach (Lazonick 1991; Berger and Dore
1996; Whitley and Kristensen 1996, 1997; Crouch and Streeck 1997; Whitley 1999;
Guillén 2001; Hall and Soskice 2001a; Lane and Myant 2007). In this fairly large body of
work closely related to the French regulation school[4] and its variants in the UK, theories
of capitalist states not only were made in continental Europe and now in East Asia, but
they also destabilized the conventional notion of Anglo–American capitalism often taken
for granted as the "default" form of global capitalism. A global mosaic of different varieties of capitalism was said to exist. Although this VoC literature shares with the realist
IPE a similar epistemological foundation in methodological nationalism, there is not
much cross-fertilization between these two schools of IPE. Indeed, the issue of VoC was
noted in Gilpin (1987: 16–17) when he argued that "Capitalism is too ambiguous a label
to be used as an analytical category. There are in fact many varieties of capitalism that
function differently." But he offered neither further explicit theorization nor empirical
elaboration on how these varieties of capitalism fit into his realist conception of the
international political economy. Instead, he continued his realist approach to IPE by

asserting that "The contemporary world is composed largely of mixed economies that at the international level are forced to compete with one another" (17).

In an important early formulation of this approach, Lazonick (1991; see also Chandler 1990; Whitley 1999), highlighted three varieties of capitalism in accordance with their variations in the *configurations of economic institutions and competitive strategies*: proprietary (e.g. the UK), managerial (e.g. the US), and collective (e.g. post-war Japan). Proprietary capitalism is dominated by vertically and horizontally specialized firms that coordinate their inputs and outputs through market contracting (see also Sako 1992). These firms have little distinctive organizational capacity to pursue innovative strategies and typically delegate control over labor processes to skilled workers who are managed through piecework-based reward systems. Managerial capitalism, in contrast, is dominated by large vertically integrated and often horizontally diversified firms run by salaried managers organized into authority hierarchies (Chandler 1977, 1990; cf. Best 1990; Sabel and Zeitlin 1996). During much of the early twentieth century, these firms developed their own innovation capabilities through establishing R&D laboratories and competed through innovation-based strategies for mass markets. They also tended to exert strong managerial control over work processes through formal rules and procedures and mechanization. Finally, collective capitalism exhibits even higher levels of organizational integration of economic activities through extensive long-term collaboration between firms in business groups and networks, both within sectors and across them. Additionally, integration within firms is greater in this form of capitalism because loyalty and commitment between employer and employee extend further down the hierarchy than in either of the other two types. This investment in manual workers is crucial to the development of innovative organizations since it encourages employees to improve products and processes on a continuing basis.

Whether labeled proprietary, managerial or collective, different varieties of capitalism or "business systems" constitute distinctive and enduring ways of structuring market economies that are both wide-ranging and long-term in nature. Once established in particular institutional contexts, these national business systems may develop considerable cohesion and become resistant to major changes (Whitley 1998; Hall and Soskice 2001b). These institutional structures form established systems of economic coordination and control in specific market and non-market economies. They inherently shape the logics governing economic decision-making, and the market processes through establishing and enforcing the so-called "rules of the game."[5] How then do these different configurations of capitalism shape the organization of economic coordination and control systems? This diverse institutional structuring of organization systems is evident in the substantial variations in ownership patterns, business formation and coordination, management processes, and work and employment relations across countries and/or regions. For example, the ways in which industrial capitalism developed in the US, Germany, and Japan differ significantly as a result of variations in their political systems and the institutions governing production and distribution. To a large extent, the structure and practices of state agencies, financial organizations, and labor-market actors in these countries continue to diverge and to reproduce distinctive forms of economic organization (Whitley 1992, 1999). Pauly and Reich (1997) and Doremus et al. (1998) thus provide a succinct analysis of the embeddedness of business firms in their national political-economic structures in the US, Germany, and Japan (see also Gilpin 2001: ch. 7). Taken together, all of this strongly suggests that business firms embedded within and constitutive of different capitalist economies tend to behave differently in their organizational and strategic action.

This VoC/business systems approach, nevertheless, has been criticized for its methodological nationalism and a tendency toward a latent institutional functionalism, a charge not too dissimilar to that leveled at the realist perspective in IPE. For example, researchers in East Asia have begun to question whether different capitalist formations and their allegedly distinctive business systems (e.g. Japanese and Chinese) can be as stable and enduring in today's context of accelerated globalization. By grounding varieties of capitalism in different East Asian national and sub-national economies, this new research frontier offers a much more geographically nuanced understanding of not just different forms of nationally based capitalisms in the global economy. It thereby helps one both understand and transcend the limits of methodological nationalism common in other approaches to the IPE. It shows how these different capitalist forms can intermesh and morph into a new form of *hybrid capitalism* at different spatial scales. In particular, it allows us to recognize and interrogate transborder flows of economic activity among East Asian economies that are critical to the process of hybridizing capitalism (see Yeung 2000, 2004; Yang 2007). Before I conclude, it is useful to discuss in the next subsection one such example of political-economic formation that is both transborder and multi-scalar in nature.

A multi-scalar phenomenon in the East Asian IPE: ethnic Chinese capitalism

In contemporary East Asia, one of the most pervasive business systems outside Japan is the "overseas Chinese" capitalism.[6] This historically and geographically specific form of economic organization or, in Katzenstein's (2005) terminology, "regional order," refers to the social organization and political economy of ethnic Chinese living outside mainland China, particularly in East Asian economies such as Hong Kong, Macau, Taiwan, Singapore, Indonesia, Malaysia, the Philippines, Thailand, and Vietnam. This form of ethnic Chinese capitalism is a dominant mode of economic organization in East and Southeast Asia because of not only its economic significance in the host economies, but also its complex and, yet, intricate social organization and authority systems (see Redding 1990; Orrù et al. 1997; Yeung 2004; Hamilton 2006). By dropping below the level of the nation-state, it becomes common for researchers in East Asian IPE to argue that there are distinctive ways of organizing economic institutions in different parts of East Asia. This stability in capitalist organizations and patterns of economic relationships often persists in the face of rapid political-economic change external to the societies concerned. Together, these patterns of social and organizational structuring form different business systems. Their evolutionary trajectories are seen as dependent on pre-existing configurations of domestic social, economic, and political institutions (see also Whitley and Kristensen 1996, 1997; Guillén 2001; Hall and Soskice 2001a). This business–systems perspective is particularly relevant in analyzing the political economies of the Asia-Pacific region where business systems are socially and institutionally embedded.

More recently, a multi-scalar approach to capitalist diversity and change adheres to a transformative view of globalization (see Held et al. 1999; Peck and Yeung 2003; Dicken 2007), which defines globalization as a set of dialectical processes that simultaneously create a functionally interdependent world economy and accentuate the importance of all kinds of differences in societies and space. These processes include global flows of materials (e.g. people, goods) and intangibles (e.g. capital, technology, information, and services). The core argument of such an approach is that it is important to distinguish between business systems as enduring *structures* of capitalism, and key social actors in these systems as *agents* of change. The lack of explicit attention to actors and their strategies/ behavior as agents of organizational and system change is a major lacuna in most strands of IPE literature discussed above. As argued by Hall and Soskice (2001b: 5), such strategic interactions are "central to economic and political outcomes, the most important institutions distinguishing one political economy from another will be those conditioning such interaction, and it is these that we seek to capture in this analysis."

In the case of East Asian IPE, this multi-scalar approach specifies how globalization tendencies can transform the dynamics of phenomena such as ethnic Chinese capitalism and, subsequently, its nature and organization toward a form of hybrid capitalism (Yeung 2000, 2004). It brings together key capitalist actors such as firms and states and political-economic structures such as institutionally embedded business systems. It champions the importance of different spatial scales, from the personal (entrepreneurs) and the national (states) to the regional (production networks) and the global (changing international divisions of labor). Clearly the realist idea of a single spatial scale of the international fails to analyze and capture the rich diversity and multiplicity in such a dynamic form of transborder phenomenon in the East Asian international political economy. The changing nature and organization of ethnic Chinese capitalism cannot be read off as a passive outcome of structural interdependence in the international political economy (cf. Keohane and Nye 1977; Gilpin 2001). No doubt this context of interdependence at the international scale is important, for it provides a window of opportunity for ethnic Chinese and their home economies in East Asia to emerge as a major group of political-economic players in the global economy. Still, this mono-scalar approach dominant in mainstream IPE fails to account for the dynamic and emergent forces internal to the East Asian regional political economy. Ethnic Chinese capitalism must be conceived as an "open" system and subject to dynamic changes from within, that is, at the level of actors themselves. These complex interactions between actor-networks in ethnic Chinese capitalism and dynamic business systems occur in the context of contemporary globalization. Operating on such a multi-scalar platform, we are better able to transcend the analytical limits of methodological nationalism inherent in both realist and VoC approaches. By challenging the necessary role of the US as a hegemon in East Asian development, this transformative approach to hybrid capitalism also disrupts the ontological assumption of hegemonic stability so entrenched in the realist account of international political economy.

Conclusion: toward an East Asian IPE?

This chapter has critically examined the changing international political economy in which the rise of East Asia is situated. Grounded in a *realist framework* derived mainly from the American school of IPE, previous analysis of the rise of East Asia, particularly Japan, has been shown to be fraught with analytical problems. In particular, the assumption of inter-state conflicts over wealth and power and zero-sum games in the mainstream realist framework has produced an analytical bias by seeing the rise of Japan as a challenge and threat to American economic hegemony in the global economy. This American-centric view of the international political economy fails to understand the changing political economy of East Asian economies in their own right. Drawing upon two parallel theoretical developments in what might be branded an East Asian IPE, I have shown how the *developmental state approach*, originating from the study of Japan and

211

later South Korea and Taiwan, has been useful in illustrating the initial political-economic transformations in East Asian states that in turn created favorable conditions for rapid industrialization and economic development. As East Asian economies have become much more integrated into the global economy, we begin to witness the important role and operation of trans-state actors and processes at work that are best analyzed within a *global production networks framework*. Collectively, this latter literature has demonstrated how increasingly complex global production networks are spanning different states and regions in East Asia, drawing them together like overlapping spider webs with distinct nodes and centers. Couched in these terms, the changing international political economy in East Asia cannot be simply understood as a structural outcome of inter-state politics and relations. Through their embedded links and multi-scalar connections, non-state actors and their networks are contributing as much to this changing international political economy.

One particular dimension of this changing international political economy in East Asia is the dynamic transformation of the nature and organization of capitalist systems of individual East Asian economies. This brings us to the second theoretical development, parallel to the realist IPE literature, which refers to the deeper analysis of the institutional structuring of East Asian capitalisms. In this *varieties of capitalism approach*, East Asian economies are analyzed in relation to their distinctive business systems resulting from the institutional structuring of different historical political-economic processes and socio-cultural change. To some scholars, these business systems are enduring structures that are highly resistant to change even under the condition of contemporary globalization. They condition the strategic behavior of business firms emerging from these systems and limit the cross-national economic coordination of activity. Still, this VoC-inspired approach to business systems has not been accepted wholesale without immanent critique and challenge. Drawing on my own work on the international political economy of ethnic Chinese capitalism in East Asian economies, I have offered a revisionist approach to the VoC literature and demonstrated how globalization tendencies and key actors (state and non-state) in East Asia are interacting in such ways that fundamentally reshape the institutional structuring of ethnic Chinese capitalism. This interactive process at multiple spatial scales, from the global to the regional and the local, has produced a form of *hybrid capitalism* that prevails in many East Asian economies today. Conceived as such, ethnic Chinese capitalism has a certain degree of systemic endurance and, yet, is subject to dynamic transformations over time through its agents of change. At any given time, this hybrid form of capitalism evolves through the strategic interactions of key actors with globalizing forces—its hybridism represents the outcomes of these complex interactions in globalizing actor-networks.

How do these theoretically sophisticated analyses of East Asian economies matter in "theorizing back" at the mainstream IPE studies? Before I tackle this final issue in this concluding section, I must acknowledge that the mainstream IPE in the "North" might have produced the "right" kind of theories emanating from context-specific cases, issues, and geopolitical concerns in their countries of origin, albeit most likely the US. It remains unclear if these context-specific theories and concepts can be construed as "universal principles" that are equally and necessarily applicable to other more marginal regions in the global economy. Still, this inherent limit to context-specific theories does not stop mainstream IPE from venturing beyond its own epistemological and empirical contexts. In doing so, it clearly fails to heed Appadurai's (1999: 230) telling warning— issued in the context of area studies—that "the more marginal regions of the world are not simply producers of data for the theory mills of the North." In the East Asian context, there is clearly a need to establish such "theory mills" that can process and create value from the "raw" data uniquely produced within East Asia. This epistemological reorientation brings me to the crucial question for this chapter: what kind of IPE theories for what kind of rising East Asia? I think there are at least three elements to this East Asian approach to the international political economy.

First, it might be seen as a passé for me to argue for the need to move away from state-centric analysis in the study of East Asian IPE. As confessed by Strange (1994a: 218) over a decade ago, "It becomes much more interesting to teach, to research and to write about when you drop the idea that states are the units of analysis" (see also Stopford and Strange 1991; Strange 1994b; Cerny 1995; 2006b). Even the quintessential realist, Robert Gilpin (2001: 15), admitted in his revision of the 1987 work that state-centric realism "is a philosophical position and an analytic perspective; it is not necessarily a moral commitment to the nation-state." Whatever one's theoretical predisposition (realist, Marxist, liberal, poststructuralist, and so on), the reality of East Asia is constituted by a messy and complex intermingling of actors and processes in global networks that "touch down" and embed in specific territories not limited exclusively to the spatial scale of the nation-state. The developmental state approach represents a good starting point in theorizing the comparative developmental trajectories of East Asian economies. But it still fails to get out of the shadow of a state-centric analysis of the international political economy in East Asia.

To destabilize this state-centrism in IPE, we need to theorize the international political economy *beyond* and *below* the nation-state and its territoriality. Indeed, some anthropologists have argued for a new perspective on sovereignty in East Asia situated within a particular zone of the nation-state. Ong's (2000) idea of "graduated sovereignty" represents such an analytical lens of seeing the state as comprising different layers of graduated sovereignty, some of which are fairly well controlled by the existing state apparatus and others which are directly interacting with global actors and forces beyond the control of any nation-state (see also Wallerstein 1999). This idea is indeed similar to and further elaborated in the earlier perspective on global production networks. In this GPN approach, we need to consider both actors (state and non-state) and structures (GPNs and power relations) in fundamentally reshaping the global political economy. It not only encapsulates the kind of lateral inter-state analysis well performed by the realist approach, but also brings to the IPE field a new focus on globalizing actors whose political-economic activities crosscut different spatial scales in ways that cannot be captured by any realist analysis.

Second, this kind of *vertical* analysis of the international political economy, as promulgated in the global production networks and hybrid capitalism approaches, clearly brings *multi-scalar processes* back into our conceptual apparatus. As a site for these multi-scalar processes to work themselves through, East Asia provides a unique "laboratory" to develop context-specific theories of globalizing political economy that can "theorize back" at mainstream IPE. Let me give one example of this kind of "theorizing back." In understanding how global competition operates in East Asia, we are often tempted to adopt a kind of beggar-thy-neighbor approach that shows how different East Asian states are behaving as Cerny's (1997) "competition state" in ways that inevitably lead to a phenomenon of "race to the bottom." Such national competitiveness approach, inspired by Porter (1990), Reich (1991), Tyson (1993), and others (e.g. the World Economic Forum's *World Competitiveness Report*), has undoubtedly reinforced the realist notion that nation-states are directly competing against each other in the global economy. As Krugman (1994) has passionately argued, however, there is indeed no such thing as nations competing against each other in the economic realm. Indeed, such competition should be understood as only operating at the firm level (see also Stopford and Strange 1991).

Deploying a multi-scalar approach to intensified competition, the global production networks approach clearly demonstrates the role of lead firms and their networks of strategic partners and suppliers in spearheading global competition. As different regions and states are articulated into the global economy through diverse networks of local firms and their global lead firm partners, we expect inter-regional and inter-national competition to be significantly intensified. In the East Asian context, regions are competing directly with each other through their efforts in developing indigenous firms, facilitating their coupling with global lead firms, and attracting the direct presence of these lead firms in GPNs. For example, as the Taipei-Hsinchu region, the Yangtze River Delta, Penang, Rayong, and Singapore are competing fiercely in the global ICT industry, there is a misleading perception that these different regions and their states are in head-on collision with each other within the realist context of a zero-sum game. Indeed, the reality is far more complex and interdependent than the above casual observation. There are, for example, intricate and, often, complementary relationships between global lead firms, their strategic partners in Taiwan and Singapore, and production sites in the China's Yangtze River Delta, Malaysia's Penang, and Thailand's Rayong (see Yang and Hsia 2007; Yeung 2007b; forthcoming). This "inter-regional" and "inter-national" competition in East Asia should rather be theorized as intra- and inter-GPN competition. At the intra-GPN level, different strategic partners and service providers are competing against each other for the same lead firms that may originate from North America and Western Europe. At the inter-GPN level, lead firms and strategic partners belonging to different GPNs are competing for global market shares. Grounded in an East Asian IPE, this GPN approach enables us to "theorize back" at the dominant realist framework of inter-state competition and conflict.

Third, these complex lateral and vertical relationships simultaneously operating at and permeating the national scale not only compel us to rethink our existing conceptual apparatus through the process of "theorizing back," but also require a different suite of research methods. As I have argued elsewhere (Hess and Yeung 2006), there are significant methodological challenges to GPN research. It is clear that empirical testing in the guise of the rational choice paradigm of the mainstream American school of IPE will not easily work in East Asia. The tremendous heterogeneity between and within East Asian states and their highly differentiated processes of articulation into the global economy necessitate a multiple logics and rationalities approach. The fact that East Asian IPE is governed as much by political-economic imperatives as by other socio-cultural logics makes it all the more difficult to apply a plug-and-play rational choice approach. Putting together these multiple and yet overlapping logics and rationalities in East Asia within a dynamic context of global economic change produces an international political economy not readily amenable to simplistic causal statistical analysis. The rise of East Asia will remain as an enigma in the mainstream study of IPE if the latter's context-specific theories, assumptions, and methodological toolkits are used in a direct and unproblematic way (cf. Keohane 2001). This research challenge in the IPE study of East Asia can only be satisfactorily addressed if its changing dynamics are analyzed in ways grounded firmly in its material reality and discursive contexts.

Notes

1 To minimize confusion in terminology, this chapter uses IPE as an abbreviation for the multi-disciplinary field of academic enquiry and "international political economy" as a label for the substantive reality of political economic configurations in the global economy.

2 The case of Japan, however, is curiously not an isolated case of myopic interpretation in the American school of IPE. As Susan Strange (1994a: 209) once noted in her critique of Krasner's (1994) insistence on the use of realist international relations theories for the study of IPE,

> most—not all—of my colleagues who teach international relations theory tend to suffer from some degree of myopia when it comes to the world around them. They would rather fit the facts of life into [existing] international relations theories than question the validity of the theories to explain the nature, and the causes and consequences of change in the world.

3 China remains not much featured in his two books published in the new millennium (Gilpin 2000, 2001).

4 One of the key proponents of regulation theory, Robert Boyer, is heavily involved in the VoC literature (see Boyer and Drache 1996; Hollingsworth and Boyer 1997).

5 Interestingly, Gilpin (2001: 18) has deployed a similar idea of the "national system of political economy" and argued that "the interests and policies of states are determined by the governing political elite, the pressures of powerful groups within a national society, and the nature of the 'national system of political economy'".

6 The term "overseas Chinese" may be contentious to some scholars of ethnic Chinese who are living outside mainland China. The term is related to the Chinese term *huaqiao* (Chinese national abroad) that has been sharply criticized in Southeast Asia for its implications that ethnic Chinese born abroad with citizen-status in another nation are still Chinese nationals in essence (see Wang 2000). *Huaren* (ethnic Chinese) has become a more politically acceptable term. Throughout this chapter, I will refer to "ethnic Chinese" rather than "overseas Chinese" in my discussion. But references to the literature sometimes require the term "overseas Chinese" to be clear. In such cases, I will use inverted commas to illustrate my discomfort with the term.

13

Neither Asia nor America

IPE in Australia

J. C. Sharman

Since the early 1970s, Australia has directed its foreign security and economic policies toward the United States and Asia, alternating only between the relative emphasis placed on Asian export markets and the military relationship with Washington. In 1973 Britain had entered the European Common Market, sounding the death-knell for the system of imperial trade preferences that had underpinned a large proportion of Australia's foreign trade. Australia's foreign economic relations have undergone a halting realignment toward Asia; at first to Japan, and now by way of the Chinese-driven minerals boom. From time to time Australian governments have sought to match the close economic ties with Asia with closer security and cultural relations. Despite the launch of regional initiatives like Asia-Pacific Economic Co-operation (APEC), however, these efforts have borne little fruit. Under the conservative government that was in power from 1996 until late 2007, Australia emphasized its dependence on the United States. Australia contributed troops to wars in both Afghanistan and Iraq from 2001 and 2003 to the present. The government has been a consistent supporter of US diplomacy, rejecting the Kyoto protocol, studiously avoiding complaints about the treatment of its citizens in Guantanamo Bay, and concluding a preferential trade agreement with the United States in 2004.

Yet despite these links with the United States and Asia, this chapter argues that the study of international political economy in Australia is based on a much older connection: that with the United Kingdom, the former colonial mother country. Academia in Australia was founded on British lines, and remains set within this mold in terms of its institutions, graduate training, and nomenclature. The methodological and theoretical orientation of the field also shows a pronounced British, or perhaps more broadly European, influence. Rather than getting embroiled in the controversy over what counts as British IPE (Cohen 2007; Higgott and Watson 2008; Ravenhill 2008b), this is taken as a useful if crude simplification, supported by data indicating that international relations publications by Australians appear disproportionately in British rather than US outlets (and supported more generally by data provided by Maliniak and Tierney 2007). Thus although the subject matter of what is researched often follows the government's priorities, namely security and economic relations with the United States and Asia, the manner in which these relations are studied is not American, still less Asian, but shows some mixture of British and local characteristics. Despite Australia's isolation (around 20 hours flying time from both London and New York, 12 hours from Tokyo), it is perhaps surprising that international relations, and IPE, in the country continues to follow the British model so closely.

This chapter aims to survey the study of international political economy in Australia within the overall field of international relations. As such it largely excludes by fiat a great deal of high-quality research on political economy carried out in Australia under the auspices of economics, sociology, anthropology, geography, and other fields (Braithwaite and Drahos 2000 is an exception). The focus is restricted still further by a rough and impressionistic division between IPE and scholars analyzing the economic aspects of Australian foreign policy or comparative political economy (e.g. Bell 2005; Capling 2001). Relating to the latter, the sub-field of comparative politics is largely an alien concept in Australia (as distinct from area studies work, tending to focus on Asia), but there is a strong tradition of comparative public policy analysis (e.g. Considine 2005; Kane and Patapan 2006; Bell 1995; Weller and Xu 2004).

The structure of the chapter is as follows. The first section presents the general similarities in Australian and British universities that underpins the particular parallels between the practice of IPE in both countries. The next presents some descriptive statistics demonstrating the high profile of Australian IPE scholars in UK publication outlets compared with those publications based in the US. The third section highlights a sample of some of the IPE work done by Australians, which serves in part to give the flavor of the field. The chapter concludes by speculating about the potential for change.

Depending on one's definition, there are approximately 250 or at most 350 faculty in political science and international relations nationwide. International relations has usually been housed within political science departments. Although the number of such departments has increased as more universities have been founded in the 1980s and 1990s, the number of those employed in the larger established departments has tended to fall. International relations has, however, tended to gain a bigger slice of a shrinking pie (generally at the expense of the study of Australian politics), with increased student and policy interest in international politics broadly defined since the beginning of this decade. Reflecting this change, many political science and politics departments have added "international relations" or "international studies" to their names. From a foreign perspective, Australians have had a modest impact on the field of international relations. The only name that might appear on North American graduate syllabi could be Hedley Bull, author of *The Anarchical Society* and co-founder of the "English" school after leaving the Australian National University for Oxford. According to the 2007 Shanghai Jiao Tong index, there are three Australian universities in the top 104 for social sciences (the Australian National University, the University of Melbourne and the University of Queensland, all in the 77–104 bracket). This compares with 73 in the United States and three in Asia. Simon Hix's ranking of political science departments includes two in the top 100, ANU (with up to seven separate political science and international relations departments, depending on the counting system) at 19 and the University of Western Australia at ninety-eight. The United States provide 67 of this top 100, Asia none.

Domestically, given the tight state regulation of the university sector in Australia, changes of government and policy have had a significant and sharp impact throughout academia in a way that would be alien to readers in the United States, but much less so to those in Europe. Thus in the 1990s the government tied university funding to the number of publications produced, on a set 5:1 ratio for books to articles, but without any weighting for the quality or standing of the publisher or journal. In a consequence pre-dictable to all except the policymakers in question, the number of publications rose while the impact measured by citations fell. Thus between 1988 and 2003 Australian academics' publication rates rose rapidly (in excess of 25 percent), but alone among the OECD it was the only country that combined this upward trend in quantity with a substantial decline in the number of citations (Butler 2003: 145). Australian scholars have been publishing more than ever before while their output seems to be read less than ever before. Having woken up to this problem two decades later, the Australian government has instituted a reform emphasizing research quality and impact to remedy the effects of its earlier interference. Although its final form is undecided, this effort to re-balance the focus on quality over quantity is based closely on the British Research Assessment Exercise, renounced in its home country just as Australia moved to adopt it. Similar measures are employed in other Commonwealth countries like New Zealand, South Africa, Hong Kong, and Singapore. The advent of national research ratings has threa-tened to introduce market characteristics to the academic job market, and has prompted Australian universities to bid to attract and retain those seen as likely to improve an institution's score according to the government's metric.

Spurred on by government policy change, each field has had to segment and rank journals and publishers in order of prestige, impact, standing, and/or general regard. A survey of the frequency of publications would indicate to North American audiences the strength of Anglo-Australian ties. Thus the top tier for international relations journals comprises two British-based journals (*European Journal of International Relations* and *Review of International Studies*) and five from North America (*International Studies Quarterly, International Security, International Organization, Journal of Conflict Resolution,* and *World Politics*). The figures below present the location and relative frequency of publishing in the period from the beginning of 1998 to mid-2007 for scholars based at Australian universities (and therefore *Australian* for the purposes of these figures, regardless of their actual national-ities). No Australian-based scholar has published in *International Organization* or *World Politics* in this period. Only one co-authored piece has been placed in *International Studies Quarterly*. But 15.5 articles have been published in *Review of International Studies* and 9.5 in *EJIR* (with an additional eight in *International Affairs* and six in *Millennium*). Of course it could and has been said that American journals are dominated by American scholars, and thus the lack of Australian representation is no surprise (Wæver 1998). However, Australians do poorly in US journals even relative to British, Canadians, Germans, Scandi-navians, and Israelis, indicating that something more than simple American parochialism is at work (Sharman 2007a).

In part this performance reflects the greater emphasis placed on books rather than journal articles. Like the humanities of which they are intellectually a part, Australian international relations and IPE scholars place greater emphasis on book publications, and thus are reluctant to accept journal-based metrics (like ISI Impact Factors and citations) as giving a fair and accurate indication of the state of the field. Because there is no generally accepted metric incorporating books (both Wæver and Hix exclude book publications in their assessments) this complicates the picture. But again the demands of the new assess-ment exercise have given rise to a tier-ranking system of publishers. The apex of this hierarchy is comprised of the university presses of Cambridge, Chicago, Cornell, Har-vard, MIT, Oxford, Princeton, and Yale. Australian scholars have supplied one title of thirty-eight in the Princeton Studies in International History and Politics (Reus-Smit 1999), three monographs of ninety-two as part of the Cornell Studies in Political

Economy (Weiss 1998, Seabrooke 2006 and Sharman 2006) but seven of fifty-six since 1997 as part of the Cambridge Studies in International Relations (Reus-Smith 2004, Weiss 2003, Keal 2003, Rae 2002, Shapcott 2001, Bleiker 2000, Hobson 1997); Reus-Smith (unusually, American-trained) is now editor of the series. While it is not possible to provide hard numbers, anecdotal evidence suggests that many more of those working in IPE in Australia have been trained in the UK than the US, and certainly international career paths are much more likely to involve movement between Australia and Europe rather than Australia and the United States. A similarly tentative impression is that Australian IPE is much more balanced in gender terms, particularly at the level of graduate students and junior academics, than in the United States.

Aside from these descriptive statistics, some comments on the general cast of IPE scholarship in Australia are in order. Most strikingly perhaps for an outside observer is the scarcity of quantitative, rational choice, and formal modeling work. Even the soft rational choice using concepts so much in vogue in American IPE (credible commitment, transaction costs, veto players, etc.) are rare. While qualitative methods, constructivism, and critical approaches may be an embattled and marginalized minority in the United States, jointly they are dominant (hegemonic, one might say) in Australia. The lack of quantitative work may reflect the short graduate training period and the absence of doctoral course work (which also inhibits language training). There may not be any time to acquire a deep knowledge of statistical techniques, and no requirement to take any methods training. But more broadly, once expectations have become established in the field there is an obvious tendency to self-perpetuation. From a local perspective, the question is not why Australian IPE scholars do not produce quantitative or rational choice work, but why would they?

The sections below review a sample of some of the leading works in Australian IPE which also serve to provide an idea of the scope and nature of the sub-field. The review is divided thematically and includes a mix of senior and junior scholars. Of course, it does not seek to be exhaustive. The first theme considered is that of globalization, with reference to the work of first John Braithwaite and Peter Drahos, and second Linda Weiss. The next section looks at the Asian regional economy and in particular the causes and effects of the Asian financial crisis of the late 1990s as covered by John Ravenhill and Andrew MacIntyre. The Bretton Woods institutions have been a major focus for Australian IPE, and a review of some of this research concentrates on work by more junior academics, Andre Broome and Leonard Seabrooke, Susan Park, Penny Griffin, and Heloise Weber. The final theme considered is the interface between IPE and the environment, with reference to whaling (Charlotte Epstein) and the World Trade Organization (Robyn Eckerlsey).

Globalization

Given the explosion of interest concerning globalization in and beyond IPE, it is not surprising that many Australian scholars have also been captivated by this topic. John Braithwaite and Peter Drahos have presented one of, if not the most, exhaustively researched studies of the globalization of regulation ever written. In *The Myth of the Powerless State*, Weiss presents a compelling critique of maximalist accounts of globalization in emphasizing the still powerful role played by states in the economy (1998).

Braithwaite and Drahos' *Global Business Regulation* (2000) is truly a great work in terms of its size and scope, being based on over 500 interviews conducted by the authors all over the globe. It covers almost the whole range of business activity, including thirteen painstakingly researched and detailed case study chapters, ranging from property and contract, to food, to transport, to telecommunications, to finance. The sheer magnitude and strongly inductive cast make it a difficult book to summarize. There is no sound-bite sized encapsulation of the book's message, with seven concluding chapters of analysis. Almost every generalization about the book can be contradicted with a specific instance from one or more of the case studies. Each of these thirteen case study chapters is divided into sections covering the history of globalization in that area (starting from ancient times), the most important actors involved, and the key principles and mechanisms at play.

Although a great deal of coverage is devoted to the activities of international organizations, firms, and social movements in driving or responding to the globalization of regulation, the authors hold that states are (and look likely to remain) the most important class of actors. Yet in forsaking a simple globalization-as-corporate-power account or a "race to the bottom" metaphor (which Braithwaite and Drahos do see operating in a few of the areas examined), the book does not fall back on a simple state-centered schema either. The military and economic coercive resources of the state have been a vital mechanism in spreading global business regulation. But the single most important mechanism has been what is referred to as "modeling": "observational learning with a symbolic content ... based on conceptions of action portrayed in words and images" (2000: 580). More than unreflective copying, modeling explains the growing convergence in regulatory solutions across countries as it constitutes and changes interests and channels. Modeling is more important than coercion in fostering globalization because it is logically prior to coercion, but also because coercion is an expensive and inefficient way of reaching particular regulatory solutions. More broadly, the primacy of modeling as persuasion and learning gives a point of entry for social movements and non-governmental organizations looking to effect change. Braithwaite and Drahos make no secret of their admiration for (and participation in) such movements, and give a good deal of advice as to how such groups can have the maximum impact on the process of setting global regulations. Braithwaite subsequently founded the ANU Regulatory Institutions Network (RegNet) and is co-editor of the journal *Regulation and Governance*, published from 2007.

Weiss's 1998 book takes issue with globalization, or at least the maximalist version of globalization as markets and firms eclipsing states. Unlike earlier rounds of what Weiss terms "state denial," which rested on the theoretical orientation of social scientists, this time premature accounts of the death of the state as an economically meaningful unit are premised on empirical arguments. Trade and capital flows are greater than ever before, and in response states are forced to adopt similar economic solutions as the policy discretion of governments is stripped away or hollowed out. Weiss makes a strong case against such views in demonstrating the continued vitality of the state as an agent of economic management, and the continuing variety of responses adopted by states to achieve national development goals. Evidence is drawn from investigations of the newly industrialized states of East Asia, Sweden, Germany, and Japan. Instead of globalization and the end of the state, the recurrent themes are enduring state capacity in industrial policy and more general "governed interdependence." While a decade on the maximalist globalization accounts may seem rather quaint for IPE scholars (in large part thanks to the searching criticism of Weiss and others), it is worth noting the continued hold this view often has on the minds of policymaking elites and their anti-globalization opponents. More recently, together with Elizabeth Thurbon, Weiss has turned her attention to economic relations with the United States (Weiss and Thurbon 2006), including a scathing critique of the US–Australian preferential trade agreement (Weiss et al. 2004; cf. Capling 2005).

The study of Asian IPE

Andrew MacIntyre (from 1994 to 2003 based at the University of California San Diego and thus only intermittently Australian for the purposes of this chapter) has been one of the world's leading scholars researching the political economy of Southeast Asia (1995, 2001, 2002). In particular, he has provided an institutional explanation for the differing fortunes of those countries hit by the financial crisis of 1997–98. This explanation hinges on the distribution of veto power in political systems. If veto authority is too widely distributed this creates rigidity in policy decisions, but if it is too tightly concentrated this produces volatility. When governments are exposed to an economic crisis, either extreme tends to be bad for investors. MacIntyre focuses on the varying experiences of four countries: the Philippines, Malaysia, Thailand, and Indonesia. Veto power in Malaysia and especially Indonesia was concentrated, and thus these countries suffered economically (as measured by GDP growth, gross domestic investment, and new capital flows) in proportion to their institutional concentration of power. Thailand, however, had the opposite problem: an excessive dispersal of veto power, meaning it also was hard-hit by the crisis. Finally, because the Philippines was more toward the middle of the spectrum in terms of its institutional structures, it was able to avoid the worst effects of the crisis.

How is institutional structure linked to economic outcomes? Policy posture is the intervening variable, which from investors' point of view is policy risk. Although having a relatively majoritarian parliamentary constitutional structure, because the government was formed from a coalition of six, small fissiparous parties, there were at least six veto players within the Thai government. An initial resolute response proposed by the finance minister in early 1997 was rejected by coalition members, who instead insisted on continuing a policy of underwriting failing finance companies, crucially undermining investor confidence and allowing the crisis to gather pace. At the other end of the scale, Indonesia under Suharto was an authoritarian state, while Malaysia has been dominated since independence by the United Malays National Organization. Suharto, and therefore the Indonesian government, lurched from one extreme to the other: an orthodox, IMF-approved rescue package closely followed by a populist attempt to bail out troubled banks and corporations. In the Philippines the American-style division between Congress and presidency prevented both paralysis and wild oscillation, allowing moderate, consistent reforms that mitigated the effects of the regional crisis.

After earlier writing about the political economy of Africa, John Ravenhill has for the last decade switched focus to the Asian IPE, in particular looking at the decline of regionalism and the rise of bilateral economic deals (like MacIntyre, Ravenhill is an intermittent Australian, spending time as chair at the University of Edinburgh). Rather than focusing on Southeast Asia, Ravenhill has examined the hopes raised by APEC (Asia-Pacific Economic Co-operation) since its founding in 1989, and more particularly why these hopes have gone generally unfullfilled. APEC boosters are wont to reel off the list of statistics attesting to the potential of the group: its geographic span (from Peru to Korea to Australia); the power of its leading members (the United States, China, Japan, and Russia); the magnitude of economic activity within the region (almost half the world's trade); and the ambitiousness of its goals (full trade liberalization between all developed members by 2010 and developing by 2020). For all this potential, however, APEC has largely failed to deliver. APEC did nothing to prevent or respond to the Asian financial crisis. The free trade zone targets are clearly out of reach, all the more so as a "noodle bowl" of bilateral trade agreements increasingly criss-cross the region.

According to Ravenhill, these shortcomings can be ascribed in large part to internal disagreements about means and ends within APEC membership and a lack of engagement with civil society (indeed, the most recent APEC summit in Sydney saw most of the city barricaded off, with residents banned from entering). Additionally, there is no equivalent to the European Commission to consistently push for collective goals, with the secretariat kept deliberately small and powerless in line with some members' sensitivities concerning sovereignty. In assessing APEC, however, much depends on the point of comparison. The inevitable yardstick for regional economic groupings is the European Union, and just as inevitably other bodies fail to measure up. But compared with the Mercosur, the Association of Southeast Asian Nations (ASEAN) or the African Union, perhaps the comparison is much less damning.

Currently in the region there is a rush toward bilateral preferential trade agreements that has arisen in the wake of disillusionment with APEC (and ASEAN). Every country in the region bar Mongolia has signed at least one such agreement. Unlike other commentators, Ravenhill sees the drift toward trade bilateralism as depending at least in its early stages much more on regional forces than the flagging fortunes of the World Trade Organization (Ravenhill 2003: 301). This can be traced back to even before the abortive Millennium Round of trade talks fizzled in Seattle, let alone the current deadlock in the Doha Round. The moribund nature of APEC, and the decision to widen rather than deepen ASEAN (with the admission of Burma, Cambodia, Laos, and Viet Nam), meant that countries like Singapore and Thailand which were interested in further liberalization had few other options apart from bilateral deals. Those members reluctant to liberalize, or at least very keen to continue protecting politically powerful industries, have found it much easier to craft bilateral deals that obviate the sort of sacrifices necessitated by the broad-ranging GATT/WTO process or the sweeping APEC targets.

Development and the Bretton Woods institutions

Perhaps one of the fastest growing areas of study in Australian IPE is that of the role of international organizations in development and the global economy more generally. This ranges from a concentration on the Bretton Woods institutions, to non-governmental organizations and social movements. The tendency is to examine such institutions from a constructivist or critical theory standpoint, in contrast to the ideas of rational design or New Institutional Economics common in the United States.

Susan Park begins her study of the World Bank from the point that scholars like Martha Finnemore and Michael Barnett leave off: if international organizations teach or socialize states according to certain norms, how do international organizations come by these norms in the first place? Park takes the example of the World Bank and the norm of environmental sustainability. Until the late 1980s the World Bank had an unwavering focus on economic growth, and saw green issues as either irrelevant or someone else's problem. Over the last two decades, however, the World Bank has taken the cause of sustainable development to heart with a vengeance, proselytizing this norm among its members and borrowers. The bank maintains a huge public relations apparatus to manage relations with environmental and other NGOs. In tracing the change from then to now, Park investigates the complex process of socialization that took place. Socialization involved different strands and venues: the direct protests against the World Bank in Washington and developing countries, debates in the US Congress concerning what strings to attach in capitalizing the bank, discussion between pro-environmental executive directors and others, and finally internal lesson-drawing in response to policy failures associated with large infrastructure projects, most prominently dams.

Similarly focused on the World Bank is Penny Griffin's work. Griffin instead argues that gender is important for IPE, but that it has tended to be marginalized in most discussions of political economy (see also the work of Juanita Elias on this same topic, 2004). In noting this absence feminists are, according to Griffin, largely talking to themselves; few outsiders are listening (2007b: 720). What is mainstream IPE missing out on by not joining this conversation? Like its conversion to green norms, the World Bank has also developed an interest in gender, aiming to mainstream this as a priority across its work. But Griffin argues that because the World Bank is still so firmly rooted in its neo-liberal ideology, in line with this ideology it ends up essentializing differences between the genders which should properly be seen as contingent, variable, and constructed. The World Bank is part of but also contributes to broader neo-liberal belief structures that act to institutionalize an unquestioned and unquestionable common sense, and as such excludes and marginalizes alternatives as being unthinkable, or at the very least impractical and utopian. This common sense may relate to relatively technical questions (e.g. central bank independence), but may also relate to deeply personal and ostensibly uneconomic matters like gender and sexual orientation. Ideas like rational utility-maximizing individuals, efficient markets, and competition are far from being objective, somehow beyond cultural context, but instead represent and reproduce particular hierarchies of race, gender, and sexual orientation. "Doing Business" reports have men on the cover, reports on gender feature women with children (2007a: 233). Overall,

> The creation and perpetuation of homo economicus, and the gendered meanings that are predicated, pre/proscribed and (re)produced therein, depend upon regimes of power in which the masculinities and femininities that drive economics, trade, profit and production appear to follow naturally from the state of things; a kind of preordained economic reality prescribed by the discourse's own parameters of intelligibility.
>
> (2007a: 235)

Again relating to development, Heloise Weber has written on how the politics of international development are implicated in both the institutions of national sovereignty and global capitalism. By defining the problem of development in terms of state units, development discourse obscures the importance of capitalism as a system for producing global inequality. For example, despite all the attention given to globalization, rather than the "Third World" being defined socially, as impoverished people, it is defined territorially as poorer states. The solution is always conceived of in terms of neo-liberal modernization, naturalizing capitalism and excluding alternatives.

> Thus, through the way in which the discourses about development replay the co-ordinates of inequality/equality, underdevelopment/development through a spatial

223

cartography, they can be seen to function as a counter-discourse to displace what is generally also implicit in the dynamic of the "clash of globalisations": the problematisation of territoriality as a political principle.

(2004: 201)

Although World Bank–IMF Poverty-Reduction Growth Papers are aimed at enhancing the developing world's "ownership" of and participation in the determination of their economic destiny, in the way it operates this program is fundamentally similar to the structural adjustment program it replaced. Once again, Weber's analysis seeks to expose power relations inherent in the seemingly apolitical, technical concepts and frames we use to perceive and structure the social world. Like Griffin, Weber argues that methodological choices are also political choices, and explicitly aims for an emancipatory, progressive political impact.

Rounding out work on the Bretton Woods institutions is Broome and Seabrooke's work on "Seeing like the IMF" (2007), part of a larger on-going project. This work marks a change of focus and approach from the feminist and critical theory pieces. Substantively, the authors argue that the relationship between the IMF and its rich state members has been overlooked. They employ an institutionalist framework in comparing the significance of the IMF's advice on tax with reference to two co-ordinated market economies (Denmark and Sweden) and two liberal market economies (Australia and New Zealand). Despite the association of the IMF with conditional lending, the fund spends more of its time engaged in surveillance activities, monitoring member states' economic performance and offering advice. Even though there is no link with concessional credit, Broome and Seabrooke argue that the IMF's policy suggestions can be influential with reference to the small open economies they consider. First, policymakers and national officials recognize the IMF as a source of expertise and assistance in problem-solving, and as such they may be genuinely persuaded by the advice offered from Washington. Second, the advice may act as a signal to international audiences; negative reviews may embarrass national representatives before their peers, or damage the perception of the country among ratings agencies and in international financial markets. Finally, the IMF's pronouncements may be significant for domestic politics and policy, as governments trumpet praise they have received, or opposition parties seize on criticism of perceived failings. Drawing inspiration from James Scott's (1998) *Seeing Like a State*, Broome and Seabrooke argue that the IMF does not see reality in unmediated terms, but via "associational templates." The practical upshot of these templates, in contrast to much of the other literature on the international financial institutions, is that the IMF does *not* advocate one-size-fits-all solutions. Instead, it tailors its policy advice to fit regional circumstances, rather than (for example) trying to shoe-horn the Scandinavian countries into some liberal market ideal.

IPE and the environment

The final strand of Australian IPE work sampled is that looking at the intersection of international economic and environmental concerns (obviously relevant to Park and Braithwaite and Drahos' research also). Charlotte Epstein's book on whaling, *Producing Whales, Performing Power: A Study of Discourse in International Relations* (2008a), and Robyn Eckersley's analysis of the relations between international trade and environmental regimes (Eckersley 2004, 2007) provide excellent examples of this work. With regard to whaling, the very classification of the issue in many ways determines the policy outcomes; is whaling an IPE issue of effectively managing a scarce resource to ensure long-term exploitation, or an environmental question of safeguarding endangered fauna (cf. Heazle 2006)? Epstein details how the discourse about whaling shifted away from the former perspective over the decades to the extent that anti-whaling discourse has now become dominant. Discourse is defined as a syntax that regulates practice and thought on a particular topic and in so doing constitutes subject-positions. Environmental activists were able to introduce an anti-whaling discourse of resistance which subsequently fixed and reproduced the environmental groups themselves. Beyond the discourse, the context is also vital. Thus Epstein provides some very counter-intuitive findings concerning the changing profitability of whaling. Furthermore, she looks at the interaction of states and NGOs in and around the International Whaling Commission (IWC). Again the results are provocative: the "dirty tricks" like buying small countries' votes on the IWC for which environmental groups now criticize Japan and other pro-whaling countries were first employed by these same environmental groups as they entrenched the anti-whaling discourse. In this manner Epstein combines a highly sophisticated post-structural theoretical framework with a closely researched and fascinating historical study.

Eckersley may well herself eschew the label of being an IPE scholar at all, but has nevertheless produced a good deal of work on the intersection of the environment and political economy (1995), and in particular at the World Trade Organization (2004, 2007). According to Eckersley, the impact of the WTO as an organization, set of agreements and as a dispute resolution mechanism on environmental issues is neither as dire as many green critics would have it, nor as benign as the WTO itself claims. The bad news for environmentalists is the chilling effect that the WTO has on multilateral environmental negotiations and national policy (Eckerlsey 2004). Rather than directly ruling against environmental standards, the mere fact that the implementation of such standards might in the future be challenged in the WTO acts a brake. For on-going multilateral environmental negotiations, the shadow of WTO rules leads national delegations to self-censor with regard to the new measures proposed. Internally, the WTO's Committee on Trade and the Environment is deadlocked and seems unable to resolve the tensions in its remit. A more positive development is the potential for transnational public spheres to improve the WTO's environmental accountability, specifically the admission of NGOs to the dispute resolution process via *amicus curiae* briefs (Eckersley 2007). A recurring theme in criticism of the WTO has been the lack of access for outside civil society groups and the bias this is said to impart. Because NGOs have now on several important occasions been admitted to the dispute resolution and appellate bodies (cases concerning biotech approval within the European Union), this structural bias is ameliorated by the play of Habermasian critical reasoning brought to bear from the transnational public sphere. Although careful not to overstate her conclusions, Eckerlsey sees this as part of a broader tension "between weak or subaltern counterpublics seeking reflexive modernisation, on the one hand, and strong or hegemonic publics (in this instance, led by the US) seeking neoliberal globalisation, on the other" (2007: 331).

Common patterns and future trends

It bears emphasizing once more that the work presented above is only a sample of the high-quality IPE research published by Australian-based scholars. Particularly strong contributions have also been made in more specific areas, like the international energy policy (Xu 2004), or the automotive industry (Mikler 2005). What patterns, if any, can be extrapolated from the research summarized above to discover the nature and future direction of IPE in Australia? Although there is a considerable diversity of methods and approaches, the spectrum is somewhat truncated when compared to the United States. Research in Australia tends to center on critical theory, feminist, constructivist or insti-tutionalist approaches (e.g. varieties of capitalism). Notwithstanding the presence of some soft rational choice, there is very little use of quantitative techniques, formal modeling, spatial analysis or advanced rational choice. In this sense, IPE is representative of political science in Australia more generally (for some exceptions see Coram 2001, Goldsmith 2007; Pelizzo 2003). It would thus be common for not a single panel in the Australasian Political Studies Association annual meeting or Oceanic Conference on International Studies to have a quantitative inclination. Relatedly, Australian international relations scholars have a closer intellectual affiliation with the International Studies Association, the British International Studies Association and the European Consortium on Political Research IR conferences than those of the American Political Science Association or the newly formed International Political Economy Society.

The prospects for any change in this area look slight. Given that senior scholars in the field have advanced a program of qualitative research, the gatekeepers have no reason to enforce a change of methodological direction. Judging by dissertation topics and pub-lications of new scholars entering the field, the turn to the humanities looks set to con-tinue or even strengthen. Intellectual currents do not favor the taste for econometrics or micro-economic techniques that have come to characterize the field in the United States. Institutionally, there would seem to be little appetite to restructure the three-year, dissertation-only format of the doctoral degree, which limits the ability of students to master complex methodological techniques even if the desire was there. If there is not the diversity in methods present in the United States, however, Australia may have more diversity in terms of the proportion of academics trained outside the country. Whereas in the US it is common for foreign nationals to do their doctoral training in the country and then work their way into a tenured position, many more scholars relocate to Australia after having either trained abroad, or having begun their career elsewhere. Although dependent on factors outside Australia, again there seems little reason for this to change.

Where there may be a break with the past is in the area of publications. The drive to reverse the previous emphasis on quantity over quality may see Australian scholars aiming to publish less, but in higher-visibility journals and foreign university presses. To the extent that the new system relies on metrics (as opposed to peer review), in the future there may also be a tilt away from books over articles as the indicator of research success. But although there are many close parallels between the proposed successors to the Australian Research Quality Framework and the British Research Assessment Exercise, so far the Australian government has been much more ambivalent over how closely to tie funding to the results obtained. Most of the pressure exerted on universities would seem to be reputational, as they scramble to get as far up the various league tables as possible relative to their domestic competitors.

Finally, a tension that looks likely to grow in IR and IPE is the government's emphasis on policy-relevant research versus the field's turn toward increasingly abstract, theoretical approaches drawn from the humanities. The Australian federal government (which, to repeat, exerts a much tighter grip on the university sector than in the United States or Canada) has tended to see social science as something that is valuable to the extent that it can deliver direct and measurable benefits to the nation, preferably in dollars and cents terms. Thus from Canberra's perspective, IR and IPE should be helping the government to fight terrorism in tandem with the United States and assist Australia's export competitiveness, especially in Asia. On these terms, deconstructing performativity and meta-narratives does not help fight terrorism or generate export dollars, and thus is not useful. Because research funding is again an almost exclusively public affair (donations to educational institutions are not tax-deductible), there are definite pressures on scholars to take heed of these preferences when applying for grants from the Australian Research Council, the local equivalent of the National Science Foundation. With this tension in mind, it can be seen that IPE in Australia has a political economy all its own.

Acknowledgment

I would like to gratefully acknowledge the financial support of Australian Research Council Discovery Grant DP0771521.

Part IV

IPE elsewhere—exemptions, exclusions, and extensions

14

Why IPE is underdeveloped in continental Europe

A case study of France

Nicolas Jabko

Paris, he granted, was no longer what it used to be. Nevertheless he often quoted Balzac's statement that no event anywhere in the world was an event until it was observed, judged, and certified by Paris.[...] One could say that genius was still welcome in France. But very few intellectuals got high marks from Abe Ravelstein. He did not care for foolish anti-Americanism.

(Bellow 2001: 103)

In comparison to the United States and Britain, the study of international political economy is almost absent in continental Europe, and singularly in France. This is strange from two standpoints. First, and most obviously, the absence of a strong IPE is strange in a country where so many voices vilify neoliberalism and America's hegemony over the global economy. Since De Gaulle's policy of converting the Bank of France's dollar reserves, successive French governments have often been vocal critics of the American-led global economic order. Second, the weakness of IPE is puzzling in a country that has historically been an important breeding ground for political economy. From the Physiocrats to more contemporary schools of thought like the *Annales* historians or *Régulation* economists, distinctive French contributions to political economy have gained international recognition. Yet when it comes to studying the politics of international economic relations, French scholarship is incredibly sparse. A recent review of a French-language IPE textbook noted the existence of only a handful of books in this field in France (Woll 2008: 201–5). In 2005, the description of an IPE workshop organized by the Association Française de Science Politique noted apologetically that "one can only observe the dim awareness of this discipline in France" (Association Française de Science Politique 2005).

How can we explain this underdevelopment of IPE? In their surveys of international relations as an "American" or as a "not-so-global discipline," Stanley Hoffmann and Ole Wæver used similar categories to explain the peculiarly American flavor of the discipline (Hoffmann 1977: 41–60; Wæver 1998: 687–727). For Hoffmann, the explanation lies in "intellectual predispositions, political circumstances, and institutional opportunities." Using a sociology-of-science framework, Wæver stressed different "layers" of explanations—"society and polity," "social sciences," and "intellectual activities" in IR. While I think such typologies are useful, my understanding of the French case is that different factors interacted and reinforced each other to preclude the development of a French IPE. The crux of the matter, I argue, was the longstanding strength of Marxism in French academe. The influence of Marxist thought through the 1970s had enormous intellectual but also political and institutional consequences. It led to a flourishing of French political economy scholarship; but it also prevented the development of *international* political economy as an autonomous field of study. Since the 1980s, the decline of Marxism led to a general decline of French political economy. French scholars interested in studying the politics of the economy were somewhat caught in their history, and the politics of international economic relations has remained singularly under-studied. Although the French rejection of the (American-defined) mainstream is somewhat extreme, French scholars face a dilemma that is in a sense common to all European scholars.

IPE in France and Europe: a brief inventory

IPE in France—and in most of continental Europe—is not really a structured field of study. In part, this has to do with the underdevelopment of international relations, its parent field in America. The reasons for the underdevelopment of IR in Europe are complex and beyond the scope of this essay (cf. Hoffmann 1977; Wæver 1998). Suffice it to say here that the twentieth-century retreat of big European states from the status of great powers to that of middle powers under the protection of the US superpower certainly had an impact; international politics is interesting above all for countries that are able to play an active role in it—much less so for the spectators of dramas that are being acted out by others above their heads. Yet the American-ness of IR is not the whole explanation, since IPE also intersects with the broader and more ecumenical field of political economy—a field that has a distinctive European pedigree and continuing presence in continental Europe. In post-1945 France, political economy has been well represented amongst two groups of scholars: economic historians and heterodox economists. In order to understand the underdevelopment of IPE, we must first look at how political economy has been practiced by these two groups.

A first area where political economy has a distinguished pedigree in France is among historians. Here the key influence is the *Annales* school and especially Fernand Braudel, one of the most influential French scholars after World War II. In his major opus, *The Mediterranean and the Mediterranean World in the Age of Philip II*, Braudel argued in favor of a focus on the *longue durée*—the study of history not as a succession of events but with a focus on long-term trends and cycles (Braudel 1949).[1] Rather than analyze the actions of Philip II of Spain, Braudel's book is concerned with the economic and social evolution of the Mediterranean region as a whole. Braudel was the editor of the journal *Les Annales* and founded the Centre de la Recherche Historique, the predecessor to the Ecole des Hautes Etudes en Sciences Sociales, France's leading research institution in the social sciences. He was also appointed professor at the Collège de France, the most prestigious appointment in French academia.

The contrast is striking between Braudel's national and global recognition throughout his career and the lack of a strong tradition of Braudelian economic history scholarship in France after him. The study of the *longue durée* in world politics lives on, but for the most part not among French economic historians. Immanuel Wallerstein and world system theorists have built on these insights, but most of this work so far has been carried out in the United States (cf. example Wallerstein 2004). With the cultural turn among historians, Braudel's emphasis on economic and social history has become less central to the discipline. Braudel's macroscopic perspective and his rejection of event history also went against the grain of the prior (and continuing) diplomatic history tradition among historians of international relations. For political scientists interested in the analysis of contemporary as well as historical political economy, the *longue durée* is an interesting yet difficult concept to work with. The benefit of long historical hindsight is necessary in order to discern *longue durée* trends, which makes it almost impossible to research fine-grained political developments.

Perhaps the most direct heirs of the *Annales* historians in France are the economists known as the Regulation school—the second distinctively French contemporary contribution to the field of political economy. This group of heterodox economists who study political economy defines itself in reaction to the more orthodox view of most academic economists. Scholars who belong to this school of thought focus do not believe in the existence of a-temporal economic mechanisms or laws. Instead, they trace particular patterns of economic order (*modes de régulation*) back to historically situated and institutionalized regimes of capital accumulation (*régimes d'accumulation*) within modern capitalist economies (Boyer 1990, 2004). They achieved international recognition through their seminal studies of the 1970s recession (cf. Aglietta 1976, 2001; Boyer and Mistral 1978).[2] They identified "Fordism" as a matrix of capitalist organization premised on the "intensive" expansion of industry through productivity gains, and the development of a consumer society; industrial workers become both the main producers and the primary consumers of industrial goods, under the benign oversight of "state monopoly capitalism" (Aglietta 1976: 96–101, 323–26). In turn, the exhaustion of this Fordist regime and the retreat of the state as an underwriter of its social costs contribute to explain the crisis of the 1970s and the advent of new post-Fordist capitalist regimes.

The sociology of the Regulation school within the French economics profession is interesting and quite illuminating on their research interests. A majority of French economists, following the trend set by the Anglo-American world, study economics in a rather orthodox way. But in a country where professional sanctions and incentives within social science disciplines are not as clear as in the United States, a significant minority of heterodox economists were able to refuse the dominant paradigms of neoclassical or even neo-Keynesian economics. They have created a journal, the *Revue de la Régulation* (formerly *Année de la Régulation*), and a rather successful newsletter with a global circulation. Yet these scholars remain economists, despite their important differences with the mainstream of their profession. The primary focus of their work is the internal dynamic of capitalist institutions. They investigate the ways in which economic activities and transactions are organized and hold together as coherent accumulation regimes and modes of regulation. They recognize the importance of the state and political institutions, but politics is rarely a central motor of their explanations. Even when they analyze institutions such as money, they focus on mechanisms inherent to the existence of money and the "acquisitive violence" of market relations (Aglietta and Orléan 1982: 17, 20). They do not really investigate historically identifiable political decisions that transform the management of currencies or affect the nationality and international hierarchy of moneys, like the movement toward independent central banks or creation of the euro in recent years.

As a consequence, and despite the existence of strong traditions of political economy scholarship in France, there is little interest for international political economy defined as the *politics* of international economic relations. A possible objection to this diagnosis is that the definition of international political economy as a field separate from comparative political economy is somewhat artificial in the European context. After all, the EU is both a sphere of interactions among states and a very developed political and economic system in its own right. But even if we broaden the scope of the survey and consider French scholarship in CPE as well, we find very little systematic work that would resemble the kind of work that IPE and CPE scholars produce elsewhere. A few isolated individuals (including myself) do work in these areas, but there is nothing close to a French school of IPE. France is perhaps an extreme case, but even if we look across the border to Germany, the field of IPE remains rather sparse. European scholars who study political economy for the most part are interested in the comparative study of national models of capitalism. This has been the case especially of the Max-Planck Cologne group around Fritz Scharpf and Wolfgang Streeck in Germany. Yet it would be difficult to identify an indigenous French or even European school of IPE.

The French situation is especially revealing because there is a strong and overt reluctance to import the Anglo-American mainstream IPE perspective. French scholars often consider that most of what is done in the United States is fundamentally misguided—excessively state-centric and theoretically uninteresting (cf. Graz 1999: 105–11). This sort of critique in part reflects the intellectual perspective that is most prevalent in international relations in France—the French IR mainstream, so to speak. In stark contrast to the majority of American or British scholars, few IR scholars in France pay much attention to the actions of and interactions between states. Rejecting the state-centric perspective of their colleagues, they generally focus on transnational movements and civil society groups. More generally, a striking trait of contemporary French political science is its emphasis on micro-empirical issues—contrary to what may be expected in an Anglo-American world that has been a ravenous importer of French philosophical thought in the humanities.[3] French political scientists today are often reluctant to engage in grand or even mid-level theory, except in broad dilettante essays directed to the general public. Most of their production consists of monographic work at a micro level, with very few attempts to engage in historical or theoretical speculation.

Insofar as it touches international and especially comparative political economy topics, most of the work done by French political scientists is carried out in the field of *politiques publiques*. Although the name of this field sounds like "public policy," its practical and normative orientation is much less pronounced than in the United States (where public policy has been farmed out to specialized professional schools). French students of *politiques publiques* typically trace the decision-making processes that lead the state (or the EU, or local authorities) to conduct particular public policies in a variety of areas. The strength of this scholarship lies in its often very solid empirical grounding; there is little taste for abstract theorizing for the sake of theorizing. Its weakness is that French political scientists often face problems when challenged to draw broader lessons from their monographic studies. Although academic in orientation, *politiques publiques* scholarship in France lacks the structured disciplinary status and theoretical orientation of IPE in the United States—for better or for worse.

The longstanding legacy of Marxist political economy

How can we explain the peculiar flavor of political economy scholarship in France, and the absence of a clear bridge to Anglo-American IPE scholarship? A crucial factor, it seems to me, is the longstanding influence of Marxism in French academe. The subtitle of Marx's magnum opus, *Capital*, was *A critique of political economy*. Marx reacted against liberal political economists of his time in the name of science and historical materialism. The Marxist critique became very influential in the social sciences in continental Europe, especially after World War II. The situation contrasts with the United States, where Marxism never really took hold—in part because of active repression under McCarthyism—and where liberal political economy remained on a pedestal. Contrary to American political scientists who often have considerable respect for economics as a more scientific discipline, few French political scientists harbor any kind of inferiority complex vis-à-vis economists (quite on the contrary). The influence of Marxist thinking in France and arguably in continental Europe has clearly waned today, but it has produced major consequences for the secular direction of political economy and political science more broadly.

A first consequence of the Marxist critique was a flight of scholars away from the field of political economy. Largely in reaction to the Marxist critique, scholars interested in economic phenomena gave up on the notion of "*political* economy" often retreated into the new science of "economics" (*science économique*).[4] In France, this retreat was also institutional, as engineering schools rather than universities became the main breeding ground for economists. This evolution was foreshadowed by some of the leading French economists of the nineteenth century like Cournot or Walras, who introduced mathematics into economics and gave a precise focus for the study of economics in engineering schools. As a result, the separation of economics from other social sciences went much further than in Britain and the US, where economics and other social sciences were taught in the same universities' social science divisions. In France, the economists' retreat and the Marxist critique combined to produce a wholesale avoidance of market economics in other social sciences. Whereas Marxist scholars rejected the science of economics as the fig leaf of liberal economic ideology, non-Marxists stressed the autonomy of politics and society from economic trends and rejected economic categories of thought as simplistic materialism.

Ironically, then, the long-term effect of the Marxist critique was to turn the field of political economy into a scholarly preserve for Marxists. This is not peculiar to France, as a similar connotation of IPE as a Marxist field existed in Germany.[5] In France, political economy scholarship had an unmistakable Marxist flavor. In the two main schools cited above, there was an important Marxist heritage. The Annales School and the concept of *longue durée* did not come out of nowhere. Braudel's emphasis on socio-economic structures and his genealogy of capitalism as a historically situated mode of production were clearly influenced by Marxist historical thinking. Likewise, the Regulation school clearly owes some of its theoretical inspiration to Marx.[6] Although Regulation scholars have given up Marx's vision of capitalism as a uniform economic system at a particular stage of history, they have retained other key Marxist concepts. The Regulation school's cyclical understanding of the economy and its emphasis on regimes of capitalist accumulation such as Fordism are reminiscent of Marx's understanding of the economy as a system evolving by successive stages and crises. The notion that the economy functions as a coherent system inserted in history—even though the unit of analysis may be the national economy—is itself a Marxist legacy and a significant departure from liberal economic thinking about the economy as subject to natural *laws*.

A second, perhaps no less important consequence, was an increasing division of labor between theoretical (predominantly Marxist) and applied social sciences. Political science only slowly developed as a discipline and became mostly an applied science that never gained a strong foothold in universities, except as part of law faculties. During the Cold

War, the French state was never particularly inclined to favor the study of politics by scholars with a Marxist inclination. At the height of Marxism in the social sciences, the universities that housed them increasingly suffered from chronic under-funding as they were flooded by unprecedented numbers of students gaining access to higher education. This new population was at the core of the big movement of student protest in May 1968. Meanwhile, France's professional schools of higher education (*Grandes Ecoles*) became ever more important for the selection of the elite.[7] Two of these schools (Institut d'Etudes Politiques at the undergraduate level and Ecole Nationale d'Administration at the graduate level) specialized in the study of politics and administration. Yet their main function was to serve as what Bourdieu categorized as "schools of power" as opposed to "intellectual schools" (1990: appendix 1). As social science theory was suspected of being dangerously influenced by Marxism, these elite schools focused on empirical and practical knowledge.

Although many *Grandes Ecoles* today want to strengthen their research capacity, the legacy of that period is difficult to shed. In fields where a strong national scholarly tradition did not already exist before World War II, social science scholarship has not prospered. Political science is perhaps the best example. In France, there are only a handful of departments of political science. Most professional political scientists are employed as lone rangers in law departments. The exception is the nine *instituts d'études politiques*, of which the most prestigious is located in Paris and better known as Sciences Po. Sciences Po is not a school of political science, but of political sciences (plural), which means for the most part public and business administration, economics, and history—paradoxically leaving very little room for political science as an autonomous discipline. Discouraged from addressing politically sensitive questions of power and wealth, Sciences Po focused for most of the postwar period on vocational training for managerial positions in the public and the private sector, rather than academic research.

The difficult transition in political economy

With the decline of Marxism since the 1980s in France and continental Europe, the social science landscape has considerably changed, but the transition away from Marxism has been difficult for political economy scholars. Scholars influenced by Marxist thinking found themselves increasingly isolated, especially within a discipline of economics that increasingly converged with the global (i.e. Anglo-American) mainstream. The case of heterodox economists within the Regulation school is a good illustration of this difficult transition. In order to remain part of the global dialogue, the Regulation school has more systematically attempted to convert their insights into economic models and to apply the techniques of economic analysis.[8] The Regulation school's main concepts are being translated as variables such as "institutional complementarities" that enable a dialogue with these scholarly communities (cf. Amable 2003). Scholars have thus actively built bridges both toward comparative political economy scholars in political science (especially the Max Planck group around Wolfgang Streeck in Germany) and toward New Economic Institutionalism in economics.

But are these kinds of rapprochement likely to remedy the relative scarcity of IPE in France? On the one hand, institutionalism appears as a promising avenue of research for post-Marxist political economy. The analysis of institutions is interesting because it opens the way both for theoretical and for empirical contributions. It is not (or it should not be) possible to speak of institutions without specifying their theoretical status as causal factors. Conversely, it is not (or it should not be) possible to speak of institutions in a completely abstract sense. In addition, there is a rich history of institutionalist analysis in French social science, especially in sociology. Durkheim appears as an important milestone from this perspective, on which contemporary scholarship could build.[9] To hark back to this tradition seems like a good idea at a time when English-language scholarship is increasingly narrow in its methodological and theoretical focus. It is a good starting point for conceptualizing the state, the market, the law; the respective status of ideas and interests as motors of actions; etc.

On the other hand, there is a risk that institutionalist analysis may be re-imported from abroad in a rather shallow sense. Too often, French scholars invoke institutionalism, but they rarely engage at any deep level with its theoretical concepts. Even though many institutionalist insights were originally invented in France, they now appear as foreign and they are not truly re-appropriated. Thus, institutionalism has been a convenient theoretical label in order to justify a proliferation of case studies, especially in political science and *politiques publiques*. Many political scientists who study institutions (i.e. state or local government bodies) pay a sort of compulsory reverence to institutionalism, occasionally borrow a few institutionalist concepts like path dependence—but they do not really go much beyond that in their theoretical ambitions. Some of these studies are very interesting, but they stand no chance whatsoever of leaving their mark on major international scholarly conversations that are theory-intensive. Empirically anchored theory could be a very promising avenue of research for French social scientists. But at a time when scholarship is becoming increasingly global and in need of a common language that rises above local experiences and specificities, empiricism without theory is a scholarly dead end.

This risk of excessive empiricism seems due to the lingering identification of theory with Marxism. Marxism considered as a coherent ontology of the social sciences has practically disappeared, but this disappearance has not led to any real theoretical renewal so far. French scholars today produce very little theory because theoretical ambitions are still reminiscent of an obsolete and excessively abstract form of Marxism. The tendency for disciplinary retreat and for the ever-narrower definition of disciplinary fields is a logical consequence of the difficulty for scholars to address broad social science concerns across field boundaries. This narrowing of perspectives is also happening elsewhere, of course, and it is the subject of intense criticisms (Shapiro 2005). As political scientists who study political economy start to publish in economic journals, they clearly have to conform to the disciplinary norms of economics—and other political scientists find it increasingly difficult to understand what they are saying, unless they move in the same disciplinary direction. But in France the reason for narrowness is an excessive emphasis on empirical scholarship at the expense of grand theory, rather than a turn to abstract theorization and modeling techniques.

Another strange absence in France is that of a poststructuralist French IPE. Unlike Britain, France has no discernable tradition of poststructuralist IPE—despite being the home of Foucault and other luminaries of poststructuralism. Oddly, French poststructuralist thinkers have prospered in the Anglo-American world, but not in France. This is the case not only in IPE, but in French academe more generally. The reasons for this absence are complex and may be due in part to the relative conservatism of French academe.[10] But there is also a rather simple explanation as far as IPE is concerned—there is little poststructuralism because there is little structuralism left to react against in France, at this point. Poststructuralist IPE has prospered in the US (as a fringe phenomenon) and

237

in Britain (as a more central strand of IPE scholarship) because it makes sense as a form of contestation against a strong structuralist IPE mainstream.[11] In France, the tradition of liberal structuralist political economy disappeared a long time ago. Thus, the decline of structuralist political economy that accompanied the decline of Marxism has made post-structuralism ipso facto less meaningful.

In this context, the emergence of world-class IPE research in France will necessarily be a long march. To this day, few French political scientists have received a formal training in political science or have a precise idea of the way in which the field is structured elsewhere. The lack of a structured, coursework-intensive, multi-year graduate training means that the discipline is not nearly as strong. In this context, there is little awareness of the fact that political economy is an important area of political science scholarship in the Anglo-American world, especially within the fields of comparative politics and international relations.[12] Of course, there are certain advantages to the insulation of French political economy in particular and political science more generally. Since there are few disciplinary pressures, original scholarship is possible. But the drawbacks are equally clear. Absolute freedom carries a heavy toll and keeps French scholarship largely off the global map. For the time being, the production of coherent and cutting-edge disciplinary knowledge can only be accidental and localized.

France as one extreme pole of a European dilemma

The underdevelopment of French IPE is interesting in and of itself, but also as a symp-tom of a broader European dilemma—whether or not it makes sense to fully participate in a disciplinary discourse that primarily reflects the concerns of American scholars. This is a stark dilemma. Of course, European scholars can choose to overlook the American version of IPE. This is sometimes the case in the bigger European countries like France, but also Britain (albeit to a lesser extent). In such cases, the rejection of the American mainstream often plays an important role in justifying the total neglect of IPE—as I argued is the case with France—or, less radically, in defining IPE quite differently than in the United States—as may be exemplified by Britain (see Langley, this volume; Clift and Rosamond, this volume). But if they reject American IPE too strongly, they may cut themselves off from a global conversation that de facto is no longer centered on Europe. The structure of this volume and most other demonstrates that IPE *as defined by American scholars* is most often the starting point and has gained near-hegemonic status.[13] French scholars (and others) may or may not like this state of affairs. In a sense, this is completely irrelevant. If American IPE is to become any less of a universal reference, this can only be the result of a dialectical process that starts with a direct—albeit critical—dialogue with American IPE.

There is, in a sense, a second and probably easier option—to simply import IPE as it is defined and practiced in America. Some national academic communities that are histori-cally oriented toward America—namely in the Netherlands and Northern Europe—have largely chosen this path. It is often a question of size, since the political science com-munities in these countries are simply too small to foster a logic of internal development in their national languages.[14] This is particularly clear in the field of IR considered as a whole. Unlike their French colleagues, most Scandinavian and Dutch scholars and journals regularly publish in English, with many American references. Without going so far, it is also possible to adopt intermediate solutions that only import part of the American scientific discourse and categories. Germany, for example, can be analyzed in this way. On the one hand, it has a long and lively national tradition of scholarship in the social sciences and social theory, with Habermas playing a special role today.[15] This is especially clear in IR, as exemplified by the work of Thomas Risse and others (cf. for example Risse 2000: 1–39). A quick glance at the *Zeitschrift für Internationale Beziehungen* highlights the importance of themes such as argumentation, communication and deliberation in German IR. At the same time, German social science scholarship is markedly influenced by American social science, especially in political science. Historically, the discipline was actively encouraged by the United States after World War II as a guarantee of democratization and as a substitute for social-scientific fields like geopolitics that had Nazi connotations. The result today is that German political science sounds a bit American, as well as German. For example, there is an active *IPE* (*IPÖ*) group at the Deutsche Vereinigung für Politische Wissenschaft (around Christoph Scherrer, Stefan A. Schirm, Susanne Lütz, Andreas Busch, and Philipp Genschel)—which as we saw is not the case at all in France.

Yet none of these solutions to the European dilemma vis-à-vis American IPE is without problems. Tagging on the global—i.e. American—literature is clearly an option, but not necessarily optimal in all respects. Again, the sociology of science matters, and it has an impact on intellectual output. The existence of relatively fluid academic job markets in the Netherlands, Scandinavia, and Switzerland is certainly a good thing for the free market of ideas in Europe. Compared with France, there is certainly more competition and more openness to imports from the outside world. (Germany is once again an intermediate case.) Importation is not synonymous with creative emulation, however. One can understand the main character's impatience with French intellectuals' "foolish anti-Americanism" in Saul Bellow's novel *Ravelstein*; but uncritical pro-Americanism is not evidently any less foolish. While the increasing professionalization of European academe along the American model may be welcome, it also carries certain intellectual costs. Publications in English are beginning to matter, but quality is not always there. Again, the lack of structured and intellectually intensive doctoral programs in most of Europe certainly limits the ability of European scholars to really appropriate and build on a field of IPE that remains most developed in America.

The growth of indigenous bodies of European scholarship that genuinely contribute something original to the global scientific discourse on IPE is a difficult proposition. Perhaps this can take place not primarily within IPE per se but within other fields like (old-style) political economy and sociology that have distinct national lineages and arguably have a stronger foothold on the continent. In this respect, the countries with a long social science tradition—mostly France and Germany—have an advantage because they can work from that tradition. But this alone will not solve the problem. A long tradition can be a mixed blessing if scholars become trapped in it, as the case of France illustrates. Furthermore, it is difficult to speak to the global discourse on IPE from a different disciplinary position than political science. What Clift and Rosamond call its "neo-medievalist" relation to other social-scientific fields appears, in this respect, as an epistemological limitation as well as a source of intellectual richness. As John Campbell remarks in this volume, disciplinary barriers are quite high and difficult to surmount. European scholars can create all the schools of thought that they want. But for these schools to emerge powerfully on the global stage, they must demonstrate that they have something original to say and that they speak *directly* to issues of international disciplinary interest.

Although there is no easy and surefire recipe for this, it is not a priori impossible for continental European scholars to contribute something original to IPE—by focusing on phenomena and by developing theoretical approaches that are under-studied in American and even in British IPE. In the first place, it should be recognized that some phenomena are more interesting than others from a European perspective (and also perhaps beyond the borders of Europe). For example, it is not clear why continental Europeans would find it interesting to engage with American scholarship on "hegemony stability," a somewhat self-centered theory that grew out of a largely American concern about the (perceived) decline of US hegemony in the 1970s. Interestingly, only a few British scholars actively contributed to this American academic cottage industry at its height in the 1980s. Conversely, I would argue—at the risk of preaching for my own church—that it makes sense for continental European scholars to directly confront the American literature on regional integration, especially in Europe. Perhaps their knowledge of national histories of European membership and their insertion in continental political and scholarly cultures can help them develop perspectives on this phenomenon that will be creative and different to the bulk of American and even British scholarship on this topic.

Second, European scholars should recognize that the most promising theoretical approaches are not necessarily those that are all the rage in the United States. Today, conflicts of methods and theory are rife in American political science, and IPE (and political economy more broadly) is one of the key battlegrounds. After long neglecting the study of political economy, a number of scholars both in economics and political science are actively trying to redefine the field in rather narrow terms as "the methodology of economics applied to the analysis of political behavior and institutions" (Weingast and Wittman 2006: 3). This is not an innocent exercise. The authority to delimit what is and what is not science is a key resource in the academic world. Before they jump on this American bandwagon, European scholars need to ask themselves whether they will be able to contribute something original to a thus-redefined political economy. They also need to ask whether the new definition of political economy is really the wave of the future. Academic success can be ephemeral—even though some scholarly fads die hard. Witness behaviorism, a dominant framework in political science in the 1950s that quietly went away in the following decades—and it is not clear that Europe's failure to adopt it (by and large) was an impediment to scientific progress. And it is perhaps no coincidence that American scholars of political economy whom we would now call "historical institutionalist" turned to Europe as a source of inspiration in the 1970s and 1980s when they were busy elaborating their approach.

Although less optimistic than Ole Wæver's upbeat prediction of a "more global, less asymmetric discipline," my rather prudent assessment of the state of continental European and especially French IPE should not be construed as a prognosis of indefinite stagnation. There may be changes in the making. On a political level, French policymakers are now beginning to see the price of their longstanding lack of commitment to the social sciences. In global fora that are increasingly knowledge-intensive, the weaknesses of French scholarship and training in the social sciences diminishes France's capacity to offer credible alternatives to US (or even British) worldviews on politics and the economy. On an academic level, the global and European competition between universities is now affecting even the closed world of France's *Grandes Ecoles*. Sciences Po has officially decided to reinvent itself into a research university—and this may be a significant evolution for French political science as a whole, given the institutional centrality of Sciences Po within the discipline. In some growing fields like European studies, a knowledge of and confrontation with the English-language literature are unavoidable. Over time, this confrontation may produce a renewal and a consideration of topics that have been neglected in France. Already in the planning of the 2009 meeting of the Association Française de Science Politique, the theme of "economics and politics" is identified as one of the top eight priorities—even though this is not at all a vibrant area of research at this point.

In order for this renewal of French scholarship to take place, however, French political scientists will have to "surmount the 'Asterix complex', which hastily dismisses the emptiness of a fantasized Anglo-Saxon mainstream" (Association Française de Science Politique 2007). It is all too easy for French scholars to join the resistance against the Anglo-American invasion and to retrench on their own little turf behind the protection of linguistic barriers. If they want to be part of the global scholarly conversation, French scholars must directly confront and engage the English-language literature at the same level. And they must do this with both humility and self-confidence. France's scholarship in the social sciences is no longer the universal reference that it once was, but French scholars must not be shy to articulate their thoughts in the terms of the international debate. The future will tell whether French and other continental scholars are able to introduce new blood in the field of international political economy, and whether they are still able to produce work of international significance.

Notes

1 Braudel's book was translated and reprinted many times in English and other languages. For the original book in French: Fernand Braudel, *La Méditerranée et le monde méditerranéen à l'époque de Philippe II* (1949).
2 In America, for example, Michael Piore and Charles Sabel recognize their debt to the Regulation school. In Britain, the Regulation school was also a formative influence on "new political economy" (Piore and Sabel 1990: 309; Gamble 1995: 516–30).
3 On the empiricism of French scholarship in European studies and political science more broadly, cf. Irondelle (2006: 188–208).
4 Nineteenth-century economists often argued that the adjective "political" should be dropped from the name of "the economic science" (cf. Gernier 1852). For a critical appraisal of this evolution from the perspective of international relations, see Carr (1939: 114–20).
5 According to a recent survey of IPE, "In West Germany, the term IPE was for a long time a synonym of Marxism" (Scherrer 2005: 1387).
6 On the original Marxist inspiration of the Regulation school, see Boyer (2004: 4–5). For a state of the art of Regulation scholarship, see Boyer and Saillard (2002).
7 On the close relationship between *Grandes Ecoles* education and the occupation of elite positions in French society at the height of the system, see Suleiman (1974: 72–99).
8 For a survey of the new and more eclectic orientation of the Regulation school, see Boyer (2007).
9 For an insightful Durkheimian analysis of institutions by a contemporary British scholar, see Douglas (1986).
10 For a controversial statement of this argument, see Cusset (2008).
11 In the British case as described by Rosamond and Clift in this volume, poststructuralism seems to serve as a sort of professional retraining scheme for former Marxists who want to stay in the realm of radical theory. But even in this case, poststructuralism is meaningful perhaps because structuralist political economy of the liberal variety was never completely displaced by Marxism, and remains powerful to this day.
12 Part of the problem is that many French political scientists have a rather vague notion of comparative politics and international relations. In this context, the advocacy of political economy is often tantamount to preaching in the desert.
13 Even though British scholars might have claimed co-ownership of the field given the prominence of scholars like Susan Strange within it, they seem to accept the characterization of American IPE as

mainstream or orthodox: "American hegemony and the hegemony of [the American] school of IPE created opportunities for those who opposed either or both projects" (Murphy and Nelson 2001: 405). See Murphy and Nelson 2001: 393–412 (Cited by Cohen 2007: 197–219).

14 According to Danish political scientist Ole Wæver, "research in Scandinavia is often oriented toward the American mainstream" (cf. Wæver 1998: 725).

15 As Wæver again puts it: "One has a Habermas at hand in the original language" (cf. Wæver 1998: 705).

Why did the Latin American critical tradition in the social sciences become practically extinct?

José Gabriel Palma

Anyone who wants to move with the times is not allowed to be different. Psychological emptiness is itself only the result of the wrong kind of social absorption.

Today the appeal to newness, of no matter what kind, provided only that it is archaic enough, has become universal.

Newness only becomes mere evil in its totalitarian format, where all the tension between individual and society, that once gave rise to the category of the new, is dissipated.

Theodor Adorno (1951: 139, 238)

Introduction: the Latin American critical tradition in political economy

Discussing Say's Law, Keynes once said that Ricardo had conquered England as completely as the Holy Inquisition conquered Spain. Something similar has happened in Latin America (LA) today, where neo-liberalism has conquered the region, including most of its left-wing intelligentsia, just as completely (and just as fiercely) as the Holy Inquisition conquered Spain. In fact, this process has been so successful that it has actually had the effect of closing the imagination to conceptualizing real alternatives. As a result, not even the Latin American left that has so far resisted the neo-liberal tsunami has been able to generate a new tradition of critical thought; hence the neo-liberal slogan "there is no alternative" has become one of the most effective self-fullfilling prophecies ever.

LA is a region the critical social imagination of which has stalled, changing from a relatively prolific period during the 1950s and 1960s to an intellectually barren one since the 1982 debt crisis and the fall of the Berlin Wall. Of course, it could be argued that what happened in LA is not really different from what happened in the rest of the world. One could even argue that the recent demise of critical thinking has spread around the world almost as a pandemic—transforming critical thinkers into an endangered species. However, in LA the downswing of this cycle of critical thinking seems to have been more pronounced. These phenomena bring to light issues related to the sustainability of an intellectual tradition.

The emergence in LA after the Second World War of an intellectual tradition in the social sciences somehow runs against what one could call the "Iberian tradition." This tradition has been far more creative in painting, music, literature, and film than in its contributions to the social sciences. Basically, in the Iberian peninsula social sciences have suffered as a result of a lack of enlightenment beyond the arts and letters, and, more specifically, because of the lack of sophistication in the exercise of power by the state. Here the ideas of Foucault are crucial to an understanding of this issue.

One of Foucault's main points in this respect was that knowledge and power are inter-related, one presupposing the other. Aside from its philosophical dimension, Foucault's idea intended to show how the development of social sciences was interrelated with the deploy-ment of "modern" forms of power. These need to be exercised with a much more fine-grained knowledge of society and of forms of domination. The modern state required the development of the social sciences to find more sophisticated forms of "disciplining" individuals and groups; that is, more sophisticated forms of knowledge are required for more sophisticated technologies of power (cf. Foucault 1980, and Frangie 2008).

In the Iberian world, since states have often governed through un–modern means, and at times via crudely mediated forms, they have required a much lower level of devel-opment of social knowledge. And as these states have had either no real need for the advancement of this knowledge, or the capacity to develop the institutions that were necessary for acquiring it when it was required, social sciences have been relegated to a relatively marginalized academic enterprise.

In fact, a crucial input into the rapid development of LA's social (and natural) sciences after the Second World War was the impact of a non–Iberian European immigration. This immigration was in general different from previous ones in that it comprised a large number of intellectuals, including many Jewish academics escaping Nazi persecution. Another input was provided by the rise in many countries of a more endogenous *mestizo* class, struggling to transform white-Iberian dominated pre-capitalist societies. The writ-ings of Mariátegui probably best reflect this phenomenon (cf. Mariátegui 1928). His main message was that a socialist revolution should evolve organically on the basis of local conditions and practices, not as the result of mechanically applying European formulae. This, of course, is also extremely relevant to the issue of the sustainability of a regional intellectual tradition. As will be argued below, this lack of sufficiently strong endogenous roots in Latin American critical thinking explains in part why it moved so easily in tandem with ideological and political changes elsewhere, particularly in Western and Eastern Europe.

The emergence of structuralism and dependency analyses

After the Second World War the Latin American critical tradition revolved around two axes, structuralism and dependency. Although there was an important degree of diversity to them, one crucial characteristic of these intellectual traditions was that they were associated with a growing regional consciousness of under-development; i.e. a growing realization that, from an evolutionary point of view, LA was not progressing along a developmental path that would bring the countries of the region closer to the socio-political and economic structures of more industrialized countries. Instead, LA was get-ting increasingly trapped in a sort of evolutionary blind alley. What was needed then was a new (and vigorous) form of agency; for structuralists, a renewed leading economic role for the state, and for *dependentistas*, a more radical political leadership for the left.

Structuralism

The main root of Latin American structuralism was French economic structuralism (cf. Blankenburg et al. 2008). Perroux (1939), for example, who was the main intellectual influence in Furtado's early work, including his doctoral dissertation at the Sorbonne, defined structural economics as the science of the relations characteristic of an economic system (ensemble) situated in time and space. Central to this approach was the view that, over and above the givens of neoclassical theory (preferences, resources, and technology), the analysis of institutions and structures over time had to be at the heart of economic analysis. One of the innovative contributions of Perroux concerns his theory of domination, which became central to ECLAC's conception of economic systems: rather than being constituted by relationships between equal agents, the economic world is conceptualized in terms of hidden or explicit relationships of "force" and "power" between dominant and dominated entities.

From the very beginning ECLAC's analysis was structuralist in the sense that it viewed the world economy as a system within which the center and the periphery are intrinsically related, and that most economic problems of the periphery, such as slow growth, stop-go macroeconomics, inflation, and unemployment, are associated with the specific economic structure that emerged from that interaction. ECLAC's analysis was also structuralist in the sense that it tried to focus on underlying structures and relationships, as opposed to epiphenomena.

The hub on which the whole of ECLAC's analysis of underdevelopment turned was the idea that the structure of production in the center and in the periphery differed substantially. That of the center was seen as homogeneous and diversified; that of the periphery, in contrast, as heterogeneous and specialized. Heterogeneous because economic activities with significant productivity differences existed side by side, with the two extremes provided by a high productivity export sector, and a subsistence agriculture. Specialized because the export sector, which is concentrated upon a few primary products, represents a high proportion of GDP and has very limited linkages. It was this structural difference that lay behind the different function of each pole in the international division of labor; and within this framework there were few (if any) endogenous forces in the periphery leading its structure of production to become more homogeneous and diversified. Thus the interrelationship between center and periphery could not be understood in static terms since it is part of a single system, dynamic by its very nature.

The nucleus of ECLAC analysis was the critique of the conventional theory of international trade (as expressed in the Heckscher–Ohlin version of Ricardo's theory of comparative advantages). It aimed to show that the international division of labor which conventional theory claimed to be *naturally* produced by comparative advantages was of much greater benefit to the center (where manufacturing production is concentrated) than to the periphery (which was destined mainly to produce primary products); i.e. in these matters, the "invisible hand" was neither so invisible nor even-handed! From this starting point, ECLAC analyzes three tendencies which are considered inherent to the development of the periphery: structural unemployment; external disequilibrium; and the tendency to deterioration of the terms of trade (cf. Rodriguez 2006).

First, due to structural heterogeneity, full employment of the labor force could only be achieved if the rate of capital accumulation in the modern sector is sufficient not only to absorb the growth of the active population, but also to reabsorb labor displaced from the traditional sector. It is from this heavy burden on the modern sector that the structural tendency toward unemployment is deduced. Second, as the structure of production in the periphery is excessively specialized, a substantial proportion of the demand for manufactured products has to be oriented toward imports; and given their high income elasticity, imports tend to grow much faster than income. The opposite is the case in the center vis-à-vis its imports from the periphery, as these consist essentially of primary products, for which income elasticity is usually less than unity. Therefore, the growth of income in the periphery that is sustainable from its balance of payments point of view is one that is lower than that of the center in proportion to the degree of the disparity between the respective income elasticities of demand for imports. If the periphery attempts to surpass this limit, it will expose itself to external disequilibrium and stop-go macroeconomics. Thus, the only long-term alternative to an ever-increasing foreign debt will be a greater effort to satisfy the highly income-elastic demand for manufactured products with domestic production, and to try to diversify exports toward more income-elastic products. Only a proper process of industrialization, given these assumptions, can allow that and enable the periphery to enjoy a rate of growth of real income not so highly constrained by its higher income elasticities of demand for imports.

Third and finally, for ECLAC the tendency to deteriorating terms of trade, and the asymmetries in terms of gains from specialization which it brings with it, are a logical analytical deduction from the phenomena of specialization and heterogeneity. The basic problem is the effect of economic growth on the terms of trade. Following the issues discussed above, as the periphery grows both the consumption and the production paths of the periphery are biased toward trade (cf. Palma 2008a). That is, as incomes grow the proportion of importables in total consumption increases, and as output grows the proportion of exportables in domestic production also increases. As the consumption and production paths of the center are less biased for trade vis-à-vis the periphery, the combined effect would be an excess supply of primary products. Hence the tendency toward deterioration of the terms of trade of the periphery.

According to ECLAC (and as opposed to the current pessimism of the "resource curse hypothesis") commodity-rich countries could escape from these asymmetries through a process of transformation of their economic structure. The central element in this is the process of industrialization, which could provide a higher rate of accumulation, higher domestic production of income-elastic importables, and more income- (and price-) elastic exportables. But this process could not be expected to take place spontaneously, for it would be inhibited by the international division of labor which the center would attempt to impose, and by a series of structural obstacles internal to the peripheral economies. Consequently, what was needed was a process of vigorous state-led industrialization.

The limits of economic structuralism: the politics of uneven development

The dimensions of ECLAC's thought are based then not only upon its structuralist nature, but also upon its breadth and internal unity. Nevertheless, it is also this structuralist nature that the limitations of ECLA thought lie. ECLAC proposes an ideal model of sectoral growth designed in such a way that the three structural tendencies above would not be reproduced. From this are derived the necessary conditions of accumulation. However, this type of structuralist approach is insufficient for the analysis of the evolution of the system as a whole, as it clearly involves more than the transformation of the structure of production. The theories of ECLAC examine certain aspects of the development of the forces of production, but do not touch on relations of production or the nature of the state, nor, as a result, on the manner in which they interact.

Furthermore, the analysis of the asymmetries of development in the world economy cannot be carried out solely in terms of the unevenness of development of the forces of production; it is necessary also to bear in mind that they develop in the framework of a process of generation, appropriation, and utilization of the economic surplus, and that process, and the relations of exploitation upon which it is based, are not reproduced purely within each pole, but also between the two poles of the world economy.

It is not particularly surprising that ECLAC should have attracted its share of criticism. From the right the reaction was at times ferocious: ECLAC's policy recommendations were totally heretical, and threatened powerful domestic and foreign interests. It was also criticized from sectors of the left for failing to denounce sufficiently the mechanisms of exploitation within the capitalist system.

ECLAC analysis re-emerged in the 1980s in academic circles as an attempt to re-examine (and formalize) some of the traditional hypotheses from the perspective of modern economics (cf. Taylor 2004). Although this has made important contributions to macroeconomics and development economics, it has not succeeded in introducing structuralism as a new method of enquiry into modern economic analysis.

Dependency

Dependency theories emerged in the early 1960s as attempts radically to transform ECLAC-type structuralist and Comintern-type Marxist thinking about the obstacles facing capitalist development in the periphery. There can be little doubt that the Cuban Revolution was the turning point. This new approach argued mostly against the feasibility and necessity of capitalism in LA. Consequently, it also argued against the politics of the popular fronts, and in favor of an immediate transition toward socialism.

The pre-dependency, pre-Cuban Revolution Marxist approach saw capitalism as still historically progressive, but argued that the necessary bourgeois-democratic revolution was being inhibited by a new alliance between imperialism and the traditional elites. The bourgeois-democratic revolution was the revolt of the forces of production against the old pre-capitalist relations of production. The principal battle-line in this revolution would be between the bourgeoisie and the traditional oligarchies, between industry and land, capitalism and pre-capitalist forms of monopoly and privilege. Because it was the result of the pressure of a rising class whose path was being blocked in economic and political terms, this revolution would bring not only political emancipation but economic progress too.

Therefore, this pre-dependency Marxist approach identified imperialism as the main enemy. The principal target in the struggle was therefore unmistakable: North American imperialism. The allied camp for this fight comprised everyone, except those internal groups allied with imperialism. Thus, the anti-imperialist struggle was at the same time a struggle for capitalist development and industrialization. The local state and the national bourgeoisie appeared as the potential leading agents for capitalist development, which in turn was still viewed as a necessary stage toward socialism.

The post-Cuban Revolution Marxist analysis began to question the very essence of this approach, insisting that the local bourgeoisies no longer existed as a progressive social force but had become lumpen, incapable of rational accumulation and rational political activity, dilapidated by their consumerism and blind to their own long-term interest. It is within this framework that the main branch of dependency analysis appeared on the scene. At the same time, both inside and out of ECLAC there began to develop the other two major approaches to this analysis.

The analytics of dependency analyses

The general focus of all dependency analyses is the development of peripheral capitalism from the point of view of the interplay between internal and external structures. However, this interplay was analyzed in several different ways. With the necessary degree of simplification that every classification of intellectual tendencies entails, I would distinguish between three major approaches—not mutually exclusive from the point of view of intellectual history—in dependency analysis. First is the approach begun by Frank; its essential characteristic being that dependency was seen as causally linked to permanent capitalist underdevelopment (cf. Frank 1967). The second approach is associated with ECLAC's structuralist school. The third and final approach, trying explicitly to avoid the formulation of a mechanico-formal theories of underdevelopment based on its dependent character, concentrated on what was called the study of "concrete situations of dependency." In the words of Fernando Henrique Cardoso:

> The question which we should ask ourselves is why, it being obvious that the capitalist economy tends towards a growing internationalisation, that societies are divided into antagonistic classes, and that the particular is to a certain extent conditioned by the general, with those premises we have not gone beyond the partial—and therefore abstract in the Marxist sense—characterisation of the Latin American situation and historical process.
>
> (1974: 326–27, my translation)

Dependency as a theory of the inevitability of capitalist under-development

The father of this approach was Paul Baran. His principal contribution (1957) took up the approach of the Sixth Congress of the Comintern regarding the supposedly irresolvable nature of the contradictions between the economic and political needs of imperialism and those of the process of industrialization and development of the periphery. To defend its interests, international monopoly capital would form alliances with precapitalist domestic elites intended to block progressive capitalist transformation in order to have continuous easy access to peripheral resources; the traditional elites, in turn, would be able to maintain long-established modes of surplus extraction and monopoly on power. Within this context the possibilities for economic growth were extremely limited, as the surplus was largely expropriated by foreign capital, or otherwise squandered by traditional elites. The only way out was political. At a very premature stage, capitalism had become a fetter on the development of the productive forces and, therefore, its progressive historical role had already come to an early end.

Baran developed his ideas influenced both by the Frankfurt school's general pessimism regarding the nature of capitalist development and by Sweezy's proposition (following Habermas) that the rise of monopolies imparts to capitalism a tendency toward stagnation and decay. He also followed the main growth paradigm of his time, the Harrod–Domar theory, which held that the size of the investable surplus was the crucial determinant of growth (together with the efficiency with which it was used: the incremental capital/ output ratio; cf. Baran 1957).

Starting out with Baran's analysis, Frank attempted to prove the thesis that the only solution was a revolution of an immediately socialist character. For our purposes we may identify three levels of analysis in Frank's model of the "development of underdevelopment." In the first (arguing against "dualistic" models), he attempted to demonstrate that the periphery has been fully integrated into the world economy since colonial rule. In the second, he attempts to show that such incorporation has transformed them immediately into capitalist economies. Finally, Frank tries to prove that this integration was achieved through an interminable metropolis–satellite chain, through which the surplus generated at each stage was successfully siphoned off towards the center (cf. Frank 1967).

However, Frank never defines what he mean by capitalism; he simply affirms that, since the periphery was never "feudal" and has always been incorporated into the world capitalist system, then it must follow that it has been "capitalist" from the beginning of colonial times.[1] In turn, it is capitalism (and nothing else but capitalism), with its metropolis–satellite relations of exploitation, which has produced under-development. The choice was clear: socialist revolution or continuing endlessly to under-develop within capitalism. Therefore, "[t]o support the bourgeoisie in its already played-out role on the stage of history is treacherous …" (1967: xvii).

In my opinion, the real value of Frank's analysis is his critique of the supposedly dual structure of peripheral societies. Frank shows clearly that the different sectors of the economies in question are and have been, since very early in their colonial history, linked to the world economy. Moreover, he has correctly emphasized that this connection has not automatically brought about economic development, as would have been predicted by "optimistic" models (derived from Adam Smith), in which trade and the division of labor would necessarily bring about development. Nevertheless, Frank's error (shared by the whole tradition of which he is part, including Sweezy and Amin) lies in his attempt to explain this phenomenon by using the same economic deterministic framework of the model he purports to transcend. In fact, he merely turns it upside-down: the development of the "core" necessarily requires the underdevelopment of the periphery.[2]

Basically, I would argue that the theories of dependency examined here are mistaken not only because they do not fit the facts, but also because their mechanico-formal nature renders them both static and ahistorical. Their analytical focus has not been directed to the understanding of how new forms of capitalist development have been marked by a series of specific economic, political, and social contradictions. Instead they are directed only to asserting the claim that capitalism had lost, or never had, a historically progressive role in the periphery.

Now, if the argument is that the progressiveness of capitalism has manifested itself in the periphery differently than in advanced capitalist countries, or that it has benefited the elite almost exclusively, or that it has taken on a cyclical nature, then this argument does no more than affirm that the development of capitalism in the periphery has been characterized by its contradictory and exploitative nature. The specificity of peripheral capitalism stems precisely from the particular ways in which these contradictions have been manifested, the different ways in which many of these countries have faced and temporarily overcome them, the ways in which this process has created further contradictions, and so on. It is through this process that the specific dynamic of capitalist development in different peripheral countries has been generated.

249

Reading their political analysis, one is left with the impression that the whole question of what course the revolution should take in the periphery revolves solely around the problem of whether or not capitalist development is viable. Their conclusion seems to be that if one accepts that capitalist development is feasible on its own terms, one is automatically bound to adopt the political strategy of waiting and/or facilitating such development until its full productive powers have been exhausted, and only then to seek to move toward socialism. As it is precisely this option that these writers wish to reject, they have been obliged to make a forced march back toward a pure ideological position in order to deny any possibility of capitalist development in the periphery.

Dependency as a reformulation of ECLAC's structuralist analysis

Toward the middle of the 1960s the ECLAC approach suffered a gradual decline. The process of import-substituting industrialization seemed to have aggravated balance-of-payments problems, instead of alleviating them. Income distribution was worsening in several countries. The problem of unemployment was also growing more acute, in particular as a result of increased rural–urban migration. Industrial production was becoming increasingly concentrated in products typically consumed by the elites, and was not having much of a "ripple effect" upon other productive sectors, and few manufactures were exported (cf. Furtado 1970).

This apparently gloomy panorama led to substantial ideological changes in many influential ECLAC thinkers, and it strengthened the convictions of the dependency writers reviewed earlier. The former were faced with the problem of trying to explain some of the unexpected consequences of their policies; the latter tried to deny with the greatest possible vehemence the possibility of dependent capitalist development. Finally, by making a basically ethical distinction between growth and development, ECLAC's dependency analysis followed two separate lines, one concerned with the obstacles to economic growth, and the other concerned with the perverse character taken by local development. The fragility of this formulation lies in its inability to distinguish between a socialist critique of capitalism and the analysis of the actual obstacles to capitalist development.

Dependency as a methodology for the analysis of concrete situations of development

Briefly, this third approach can be summarized as follows. First, in common with the two other approaches, this one sees LA as an integral part of the world capitalist system, in the context of increasing internationalization of the system. It also argues that some of the central dynamics of that system lie outside the peripheral economies and that the options open to them are, to a certain extent, limited by the development of the system at the center. In this way the particular is in some way conditioned by the general. Therefore, a basic element for the analysis of these societies is given by the understanding of the general determinants of the world capitalist system, which is itself rapidly changing. The analysis therefore requires an understanding of the contemporary political and economic characteristics of the world capitalist system, and of the dynamics of its transformation.

Thus, for example, this approach was quick to grasp that the rise of the multinational corporations progressively transformed center–periphery relationships. As foreign capital became increasingly directed toward manufacturing industry in the periphery, the struggle for industrialization, which was previously seen as an anti-imperialist struggle, in some cases became the goal of foreign capital. Thus dependency and industrialization ceased to be necessarily contradictory processes, and a path of "dependent development" became at least possible.

Second, the third approach has tried to enrich the analysis of how developing societies are structured through unequal and antagonistic patterns of social organization, showing the asymmetries, their exploitative character, and their relationship with the socio-economic base. This approach has also given importance to the diversity of natural resources, geographic location and so on, thus also extending the analysis of the internal determinants of the development.

However—third—while these characteristics are important, the most significant feature of this approach is that it attempts to go beyond these elements, and insists that from the premises so far outlined one arrives only at a partial, abstract, and indeterminate characterization of the historical process in the periphery, which can only be overcome by understanding how the general and specific determinants interact in particular and concrete situations. It is only by understanding the specificity of movement in the peripheral societies as a dialectical unity of both these internal and external factors that one can explain the particularity of social, political and economic processes in these societies.

Only in this way can one explain how, for example, the same process of mercantile expansion could simultaneously produce systems of slave labor, systems based on other forms of exploitation of indigenous populations, and incipient forms of wage labor. What is important is not simply to show that mercantile expansion was the basis of the transformation of most of the periphery, and even less to deduce mechanically that that process made these countries immediately capitalist. Rather, this approach emphasizes the specificity of history and seeks to avoid vague, abstract concepts by demonstrating how, throughout the history of backward nations, different sectors of local classes allied or clashed with foreign interests, organized different forms of the state, sustained distinct ideologies or tried to implement various policies or defined alternative strategies to cope with imperialist challenges in diverse moments of history.

The study of the dynamic of dependent societies as a dialectical unity of internal and external factors implies that the conditioning effect of each on the development of these societies can be separated only by undertaking a static analysis. Equally, if the internal dynamic of the dependent society is a particular aspect of the general dynamic of the capitalist system, it does not imply that the latter produces concrete effects in the former, but only that it finds concrete expression in that internal dynamic. The system of external domination reappears as an internal phenomenon through the social practices of local groups and classes, who share the interests and values of external forces. Other internal groups and forces oppose this domination, and in the concrete development of these contradictions the specific dynamic of the society is generated. It is not a case of seeing one part of the world capitalist system as developing and another as under-developing, or of seeing imperialism and dependency as two sides of the same coin, with the dependent world reduced to a passive role (cf. Cardoso and Faletto 1979).

There are, of course, elements within the capitalist system that affect all developing economies, but it is precisely *the diversity within this unity* that characterizes historical processes. Thus the analytical focus should be oriented toward the elaboration of concepts capable of explaining how the general trends in capitalist expansion are transformed into specific relationships between individuals, classes, and states, how these specific relations in turn react back upon the general trends of the capitalist system, how internal and external processes of political domination reflect one another, both in their compatibilities and their contradictions, how the economies and polities of peripheral countries are articulated with those of the center, and how their specific dynamics are thus generated.

However, as is obvious, it is not at all clear why this third approach to the analysis of peripheral capitalism should be restricted to *dependency analyses*; so it has outlived them.

Whatever happened to the structuralists and the "dependentistas?"

Two characteristics of structuralist and dependency analyses that are relevant to the story of the subsequent downfall of Latin American critical thinking are the highly *economicist* nature and the increasingly *fundamentalist* character of a substantial part of their intellectual output (especially of the first, and politically most influential, approach to dependency analyses discussed above).[3]

The central proposition of my 1978 survey on dependency was that in most of these analyses the complex dialectical process of interaction between beliefs and reality kept breaking down. Although not an unusual phenomenon in the social sciences, this took rather extreme forms in most dependency studies. For example, while many *dependentistas* wrote on the non-viability of capitalist development in LA, the region was experiencing a rather dynamic period of growth, which had no precedent and has had no continuity since. In Brazil and Mexico, for example, productivity grew at about 4 percent per year between 1950 and 1980 (trebling during these three decades). However, a huge amount of the Amazon was deforested to keep up with publications analyzing why capitalism had become intrinsically unable to develop the productive forces of the region! Oddly enough, nowadays I would struggle to find sufficient publications that are really critical of capitalism in its neo-liberal reincarnation to justify a similar survey article, even though productivity in both countries (and in most of the region) has practically stagnated for the last three decades (cf. GGDC 2008).[4] And what critical literature does exist tends to concentrate mostly on important but rather specific issues, such as the urgent need to re-introduce some form of (market-friendly) trade and industrial policies, preventative capital account regulations, more growth-enhancing exchange rate and monetary policies, and increased investment in human capital and technological innovation and absorption.[5]

However, the problem with many *dependentistas* was not only related to how factual matters were revealing internal theoretical inconsistencies. It was also about the emotional energy that most of them began to invest in the idea that peripheral capitalism was about to collapse under its own (dead) weight, and the symbolic meaning that they began to attach to the almost "inevitable" arrival of socialism in the region. Even though political events in the following four decades may have proved them right in their "now or never" approach to the socialist revolution in the region, the question still remains: why did their analysis have to be fixated on trying to prove the economic non-viability of capitalism in LA in order to argue for this "now or never" hypothesis?

Since Picasso said that "every portrait also has to have elements of a caricature," perhaps I may be forgiven for one: a great deal of dependency analysis became like one of those cults that predict the end of the world—in this case, "the end of capitalism in the periphery is nigh!" The serious point I am making, of course, is that the problem with the members of those cults is: what are you supposed to do the day after the predicted doomsday date has passed? Especially when capitalism, far from of collapsing like a house of cards, gained instead a new and powerful lease of life as a result of rather remarkable international events and the neo-liberal reforms. The region's oligarchy in particular gained a new lease of political life characterized by a degree of political and ideological hegemonic control not seen in the region since before the First World War.

The notion that this new lease of life for capitalism in LA has so far not been particularly dynamic does not change the fact that capitalism did get a new lease of life when it was supposed to collapse. Basically, industrialists lost most of their political power to those associated with commodities, finance, and retail—making LA resemble what would have probably happened in the USA had the South won the Civil War. Accordingly, the logic of accumulation and policymaking switched from domestic industrialization to what could be called "plantation economics cum downwardly flexible labor markets and easy finance".[6] Not surprisingly, the new lease of life of Latin American capitalism has been characterized mostly by predatory and rentier forms of accumulation (by both domestic and foreign capital), which followed a rather extreme process of primitive accumulation especially through corrupt privatizations. And this faltering process of accumulation has brought not only *premature* de-industrialization, but also economies with little or no capacity to increase labor productivity (particularly when measured in per hour-worked terms, rather than per worker, with each worker working ever longer hours in an ever more downwardly flexible and precarious labor market). Still, the poor performance of most countries in LA does not change the fact that capitalism in LA was politically re-energized when it was supposed to disintegrate—sub-prime capitalism is still capitalism.

There is little doubt that many structuralists and some *dependentistas* did make substantial contributions to our understanding of how capitalism worked in the periphery. Dependency analysis also had a powerful impact on the anti-capitalist and anti-imperialist struggles in LA. It even had an impact on the anti-fascist struggles in Spain and Portugal. And, of course, many dependentistas were prepared to put their own lives on the line for their ideas. But as a whole, dependency analysis as an intellectual approach ended up being significantly constrained by its growing fundamentalism (and concept-worshipping) in which, as mentioned above, the purity of belief inevitably comes into conflict with the complexities of the real world.

The fear is that allowing new ideas or forms into one's system of belief might destroy the belief itself. An example of such an idea for many *dependentistas* would have been a real consideration of the possibility that the struggle for socialism in post–Cuban-Revolution LA may yet prove to be a rather long one. The dread of a collapse in one's system of belief can easily bring the destructive instinct into play; a fundamentalist system of belief needs constantly to purify the realm of ideas. There can be no such thing as the right of dissent. For example, in dependency analysis one clearly finds Britton's proposition of an inverse relationship between the expectation to understand the real world and the intolerance of dissent (cf. Britton 2002). This, of course, is not unique to dependency analysis. For example, when Gustavo Franco (Harvard Ph.D. and one-time heterodox economist), was asked as president of the Central Bank of Brazil during Cardoso's first term of office why he became neo-liberal, his answer was simply that in Brazil at the time: "[t]he choice was between being neo-liberal or neo-idiotic [neo-burro]" (*Veja*, November 15, 1996).[7]

However, even if a significant part of dependency analysis was eventually hijacked by fundamentalist beliefs, the post-war Latin American critical tradition did have a great deal of critical creativity, especially in the way in which it tried to articulate many of its inputs (French structuralism, the German historical school and Keynesian macroeconomics) with Latin American economic and political history.[8] Of course, part of the subsequent problem also came as an influence from abroad when in a great deal of dependency analysis this mix was eventually taken over by "global dogmatic Marxism," which characterized left-wing thinking in so much of the world at the time. And this phenomenon helps to explain why this critical tradition collapsed when the overall political climate changed for reasons that were pretty much unrelated to LA.

In sum, as an intellectual movement, the pre-1980 critical tradition in LA had many original inputs and creative thinkers, but no strong political and social base. However, a great deal of the movement was eventually seduced by fundamentalist beliefs, in part due to the above-mentioned influence of dogmatic "global" critical thinking of the time, and in part due to the fact that most of its analyses got stuck in analytical culs-de-sac. In the case of the structuralists this happened when it became obvious that the Latin American capitalist elite was quite happy to appropriate all the rents created by the state with their import-substituting industrialization policies, provided they did not come (as in East Asia) with performance-related conditionalities, or had to move to a meaningful process of regional integration (i.e. the Latin American capitalist elite only likes carrots that come with no sticks!). In the case of the Marxist left associated with the communist parties, this happened when it became obvious that broad anti-imperialist alliances did not work because the domestic bourgeoisies were anything but anti-imperialist. And in the insurgent left, this point was reached when it became obvious that the Cuban Revolution was not replicable in the rest of the region, even if the armed struggle was led by a figure such as Ernesto Guevara.

The election of Allende in Chile in 1970 gave all branches of dependency analysis a much needed boost (and many *dependentistas* held senior jobs in government), but with the deaths of Allende and the "Chilean road to socialism," dependency analysis entered what proved to be a terminal decline.

In sum, structuralist and dependency analyses were not only too economicist and (in the case of most the latter) increasingly fundamentalist, but also got themselves into analytical culs-de-sac, which in part explains not only why they were obliterated by later events, but also why it has proved to be so difficult to recover subsequently. That is, these culs-de-sac were so intractable that they seem to have led structuralists and *dependentistas* to fail in what Keynes calls (following his own efforts to break out from mainstream economics of the time) "the struggle of escape" (Keynes 2007: 9).

So, what needs to be discussed next is not only why the Latin American left lost its absolute certainties; it is also why, instead of moving from a position of absolute certainty to one of absolute doubt (or, ideally, to a more creative position based on uncomfortable uncertainties), it actually chose to move from one type of absolute beliefs to another type of absolute beliefs. That is, why an important part of the Latin American left was seduced by the next available religion: neo-liberalism of the type embodied in Mrs. Thatcher's favorite slogan: "There is no alternative!"

Switching from one form of "absolute belief" to another form of "absolute belief"

Even though much has been said regarding the ideological transformation of most of the Latin American left after the 1982 debt crisis and the fall of the Berlin Wall, the basic question remains: why has the mainstream of Latin American socialism mutated from a "dangerous" idea/movement to the capitalist elite's best friend?[9] One of the key problems for the left is the difficulty in implementing a progressive nationalist development agenda today. This agenda requires a sufficiently strong domestic constituency behind it so as to be able simultaneously to take on all the usual suspects (in the form of international and domestic forces) that are fiercely opposed to it. This constituency is required, for example, for the state to be able to impose East Asian-style discipline on capitalists (and sometimes on workers), and indeed to carry out other necessary social restructuring (like the modernization of the state and the appropriation of rents associated with natural resources). One of the main lessons of the economic and political history of the South is that these strategies seem to be feasible only if those at the top happen to face very limited internal opposition. That is, in most places apart from East Asia—which had a very peculiar history to do with Japanese colonialism—this has proved very difficult to organize politically (cf. Khan 2000).

The new left in LA is characterized by having come to the conclusion (a bit too eagerly) that, under the current domestic and international constraints, the construction of the necessary social constituencies for progressive agendas is off the political map. As a result they gave up their progressive agendas, abandoned the economy as the fundamental site of the struggle, and eventually conceded the whole terms of the debate. Why?

The first issue that it is necessary to understand is the political pressure put on left-wing parties by the transitions to democracy. Democratic governments became possible in LA during the 1980s and early 1990s in part due to controversial political settlements based on an agreement (partly explicit, partly implicit) that the new democratic forces when in power would not challenge existing structures of property rights and incentives. Probably the best way to summarize the nature of these transitions to democracy in LA is that implicit in these was the understanding that Latin Americans would get their much desired freedom of speech, provided that in practice they would not demand, and eventually they would not even think, what they had previously been forbidden to say.

Of course, the good governance agenda of the Washington Consensus helped in this direction, as in the small print it contains two additional items for ex-critical thinkers now in government (although really not in power): one is that the first thing they have to learn is how to govern their own critical tendencies. The other is that they have to do whatever is necessary to govern the critical tendencies of the rest of the left. The mechanism was simple enough: they had to dramatize to the extreme the economic risks associated with any progressive change (speculative attacks, exchange rate crises, possible stampedes by restless fund managers, inflationary pressures, fiscal collapses, and so on). This is not really difficult to achieve, since in the new model "openness," "liberalization," "deregulation," and "flexibility," particularly in the financial sphere, really mean increasing risk and heightening uncertainty, which leads to a situation in which one has to live permanently under the logic of a state of emergency (cf. Arantes 2007).

As progressive change came off the political agenda of the official left, the Latin American left separated into two camps: the managerial and the radical. The first, the huge majority, reinvented itself into a new political role in which the only progressive challenge ahead was to learn how to manage a new social-risk-hedging-state effectively. The radical camp tried to remain as a critical thinking force, but today is rapidly becoming an endangered species. The critical ideological trick of the managerial majority was to disguise the pro-business component of their new ideology in a fog of *new-look* pragmatism; and, in particular, never to say or do anything that could wake the socialist ghosts of the past. Eventually, for them to be or not to be left-wing became practically a biographical fact (a detail that needed to be played down in their résumé).[10] It also helped them to convince themselves and the rest of society that the dissident left-wing camp was just made up of pedantic doctrinaires.[11]

It would not be an exaggeration to suggest that perhaps there is an important similarity here between (best friends) Mrs. Thatcher and Pinochet. In a recent interview, the former British prime minister said that her greatest political achievement was "New Labour." Likewise, perhaps the greatest political achievement of Pinochet (and other military dictators of that time) is the Latin American "new-left," with its use of "newness" and its manic managerial defenses as disguises for its ideological retreat.

Another instrumental factor has been that within the Iberian tradition societies are often run by huge state apparatuses full of bureaucrats prepared to follow whatever ideology is the order of the day. This political weakness of (what Mushtaq Khan has called) "the administrative classes" has proved to be of great help for the new political agenda of the managerial left (Khan 2000).

However, the issue of why it was so difficult for socialist thinkers in LA to integrate markets with their previously held beliefs is a complex one. As Gramsci said, for an ideology to remain hegemonic it has to be able to absorb (in a creative sense) elements from alternative ideologies. But the bottom line is that in this case new ideas, instead of interacting creatively with existing ones, ended up shattering the previous system of belief; so, a new set of ideas and beliefs ended up simply replacing the preceding ones. This did not happen in Asia, at least nowhere to the same extent as in LA. For example, in many countries in Asia economic reform was implemented in a much more prag-matic, imaginative and diverse way, and all actors in favor of the reforms (including local capitalist elites and most ex-anti-capitalist intellectuals) were probably just too cynical to be charmed by fashionable new ideologies—especially if most of the "new" ideas were just recycled ones from the past. In short, they did not fall, as their Latin counterparts did, in the trap of "newness" (see Adorno's words quoted at the beginning of this chapter). At the same time, a critical tradition remained—as was the case, for example, in India.

Something similar to the new left phenomenon in LA happened to the ANC in South Africa. In its first fifteen years in office the ANC has not challenged the previous struc-ture of property rights and incentives—creating a black capitalist elite through the black empowerment program can hardly be called a challenge to that structure. In fact, it has actually strengthened the previous structure of property rights by, for example opening the capital account to legal capital flight by the white oligarchy—a right they never had under apartheid. Moreover, more than anyone else the ANC had the political con-stituency necessary to construct a feasible alternative progressive economic strategy. In LA, only Lula and the Workers' Party in 2002 had a political constituency that could resemble that of the ANC in 1994.

In sum, even if one were to agree with the majority of the new left that there was little option but to accept a political settlement of the kind found in LA and South Africa;[12] and even if it were possible to understand that part of the logic of this strategy was to tell "stories" to their base (to hide backroom agreements not to investigate cor-rupt privatizations and so on) and to tell "stories" to the capitalist elite and international financial markets (in order to conceal their initial reluctant acceptance of the neo-liberal model), what truly amazes me is how easily the "story-telling" convinced the story-tellers themselves. In fact, often the crucial factor in the credibility of the story being told ended up being whether the story-teller himself or herself truly believed in it.[13] For example, one of the crucial problems of the "new left" governments was that if they wanted to continue with the neo-liberal model, especially fully-open finance, they had to be "credible" with international and domestic financial markets. But how to sell cred-ibility if they had never previously believed in neo-liberal economics and politics

256

themselves? How to sell credibility after so many years of neo-liberal atheism? Surely their former hostilities did not make for the best business card! So to be credible and placate international and domestic financial markets there was little alternative but to become true born-again neo-liberals. Nothing less would do.[14]

In fact, I sometimes wonder whether the brand of neo-liberalism bought by the new left in LA is just shorthand for "nothing left to decide"—and, of course, "nothing left to think about critically"! Indeed, the new left's attitude to neo-liberal economics today resembles Lord Kelvin's attitude to physics at the end of the nineteenth century, when he declared that "[t]here is nothing new to be discovered in physics now. All that remains is more and more precise measurement" (Kelvin 1900).[15]

Is it appropriate to call the "new left" in LA neo-liberal? From structural adjustment to ideological adjustment

To begin with, there is a major question still to be considered here: what is neo-liberalism? Although this issue cannot possibly be tackled comprehensively in this chapter, from the perspective of what I am discussing here the key characteristic of neo-liberalism is that it emerged in opposition (in the form of an undertow) to the Keynesian consensus of the "Golden Age." In fact, and as opposed to what is often argued, its initial discourse of "prudent-macroeconomics-cum-smaller-states" (framed within the "politics of resent-ment") was just a tactical discursive strategy. What neo-liberalism was really about was capital attempting to regain its power and control through a more sophisticated form of legitimization and a more refined technology of power. That is, it was a sophisticated exercise by the "angry right" in restoration of class power. The mechanism for this was rather ingenious: the reintroduction of risk and the heightening uncertainty at the heart of a by then too self-confident *welfarized* population and too-autonomous state. In fact, it could be said that neo-liberalism is about a deliberate move from stable to unstable equilibria; that is, a movement from Keynesian attempts to manage risk and reduce uncertainty via national and international policy coordination, closed capital accounts, stable exchange rates, low and stable interest rates, low levels of unemployment and unemployment benefits for those out of work, the welfare state, and a state capable of some disciplining of the capitalist elite, to an intended movement in reverse.

In developing countries, capital was even more in need of a new and more sophisti-cated form of legitimacy and a more refined technology of power: in a post-Cold-War scenario, a Pinochet or two just would not do anymore.

In essence, capital could only regain the upper hand if the economic environment was switched to one that was permanently unstable and highly insecure, which could have the necessary debilitating effect on workers and the state—in the jungle, capital is king! The bottom line was how to reconstruct an economic and institutional scenario in which everybody knew that capital could pull the plug whenever it wanted to.

The paradox in this is that this new environment increases the likelihood that capit-alism would be even more crisis-ridden from within. That is, the wide-ranging trade and financial liberalization policies at a global level and those of liberalization, privatization, and deregulation at a local one favored by neo-liberalism have driven the self-destructive tendencies of capital (and not just financial capital) to their extreme. But as in this new environment the downturns are just too horrifying even to contemplate, when instability gets out of hand and becomes dysfunctional, capital, as in every good old western, can always count on the state to call in the cavalry in the nick of time.

According to Foucault, once capital has regained its legitimacy, as part of the new technology of power neo-liberalism also turns into a discursive strategy for a new form of governance; i.e. a new form of interaction between political power and the dynamics of unregulated markets (cf. Frangie, 2008). An important component of this is (yet again) the reversal of the Keynesian logic of this interaction, in which one of the principal roles of the state was to contain the rent-seeking practices of oligopolistic capital for the sake of competition. In the neo-liberal paradigm, instead, a fundamental role for the state is one of a *facilitator* of the rent-seeking practices of big business. As Foucault says, according to neo-liberalism what is needed is "[a] state under the surveillance of the market, rather than a market under the surveillance of the state" (2004: 120).

From this perspective, if for Smith and the Enlightenment the fundamental issue was that human beings can look after their own interests without the need of a king or a church to tell them what to do, for (neo-feudal?) neo-liberals unregulated markets are now the new king and the new church that tell people and the state what to do.

Finally, in LA (and many other DCs, including South Africa) the new process of legitimization of capital has been so remarkably successful that neo-liberalism has turned the tables on progressive forces and has become liberal democracy's best friend! Before the neo-liberal "restoration", capital always saw democracy in DCs as its main threat. Now, following the success of its new form of legitimization—and helped by the remarkably precarious life of most of the working population, and the weakness of a state mostly reduced to a "fire-fighting" role—low-intensity democracy (as opposed to popular or radical democracy) is a crucial part of capital's new technology of power to rule over the working population, and to restrain the state and to subject it to greater market accountability. From this perspective (including, of course, that of the "good governance" agenda of the World Bank), low-intensity democracy becomes an effective instrument to block any attempt to implement a progressive nationalist development agenda, or the exercise of a Keynesian or of more radical forms of state agency; it also becomes a valuable insurance against any significant challenge to the rent-seeking practices of big business, or the facing up to the new forms of "neo-colonial" attempts at country-subordination. So, after a first stage aiming just at the "downsizing" of the state, at the end of the 1980s the Washington Consensus entered a second stage of "good governance" aimed at "rightsizing" the state, or matching its interventions to its capabilities to facilitate unregulated markets.

In sum, democracy becomes part of a neo-liberal discursive strategy to guarantee that the exercise of state power will not deviate from the requirements of unregulated markets. In this respect, low-intensity liberal democracy replaces the role of military regimes as an effective form for oligopolistic capital to hedge against the risk that a new political elite (including, of course, the new left) might come to power and threaten their neo-liberal brand of rent-based capitalism. In fact, in the new framework even the legitimacy of the state is linked to the effectiveness with which it adheres to the logic of unregulated markets.

Regarding critical thinking and the emergence of neo-liberalism, when different left-wing ideologies hit a (falling) wall in Europe critical thinkers followed three different paths: some attempted to reconstruct their critical discourse of capitalism while retaining the economy as the fundamental site of the struggle; others, instead, began to ignore capitalism and the economy as their central problems, but still tried to continue thinking critically on other fronts; the rest decided simply to disembark and endorse capitalism in full. That is, one group of critical thinkers attempted to reconstruct their radical critique of capitalism while trying to continue along the lines of what Einstein (1949) (following Veblen) called the "real purpose of socialism", namely "to overcome and advance beyond the predatory phase of human development" (23). Another group, instead, shifted their analytical focus from the economy to other issues such as gender identity, radical democracy, and so on; i.e. while conceding defeat in the economic sphere, they were still able to continue to be organically attached to critical thinking in other fields. Although in these new critical traditions the economy disappeared as the fundamental ideological challenge, at least critical thinking could continue. Finally, another group took events in Eastern Europe and the rise of neo-liberalism everywhere as a proof of the defeat of their economic and political beliefs and (under many disguises, including the "Third Way") simply joined the neo-liberal mold.

However, it seems that in LA the second option discussed above (switching to critical thinking in other fronts) was not really available. Basically, in particular after the return to democracy, those who did not want to "disembark" did not seem to have had the two (intellectually more constructive) choices discussed above. That is, when the idea of the unremitting critique of the economy within dependency analyses got stuck, those within the dependency tradition who wanted to follow the second option (because their previous analyses had been based almost exclusively on an economicist critique of capitalism) found it almost impossible to shift to other critical discourses in an organic way. Basically, the left that wanted to abandon the economy as the fundamental site of the struggle, but still continue to think critically, found it very difficult to do so as it seems to have felt that it had lost not just some but *all* its progressive relevance.[16] So, in LA a much larger majority of the left simply ended up joining (at different pace, and with different disguises) the neo-liberal mold. And those few who tried to resist the neo-liberal tsunami by reconstructing their critique of capitalism have not been able to generate a new tradition of critical thought.

Thus, more than anywhere else, in LA mainstream socialism has mutated into an ideology that by exchanging pragmatism for opportunism, by always prioritizing contingency over necessity, has ended up seeing nothingness behind contingent-reality. So, not surprisingly, the new left in LA has substituted critical thinking for anything sounding *modern*; i.e. "newness" has become the best disguise for their ideological U-turn—in fact, the "modernization" of their economic discourse could best be summarized as transforming almost anything previously considered as virtue into vice, and vice-versa (cf. Sader 2005). Thus, what supposedly defines a mainstream socialist today ended up having a check-the-box quality to it, such as being pro-poor, pro-a bit more gender equality, pro-renewable energy resources, pro-good manners toward indigenous populations and so on.[17] That is, anything ahead of the curve would do as a raison d'être for an up-to-the-minute, cool, avant-garde, forward-looking, pop socialist ideology; provided that it is mostly empty rhetoric, that it excludes anything that would challenge the neo-liberal understanding of the market economy, that it would be irrelevant to power, or would require any form of proper critical thinking.

However, my contention here is not just that my neo-comrades have become neo-liberals simply in view of the remarkable degree to which they have transformed their ideology. Basically, what most characterizes my neo-comrades in political terms, and the reason why they have become proper neo-liberals, is that this new check-the-box pop socialist ideology is just a disguise for having gladly accepted to help capital to consolidate its new form of legitimization and to develop its more sophisticated technology of power. In LA, the new political settlement that the new left have happily accepted can be summarized in the following way: if they succeed in taming the dangerous classes into not defying the current heightened-risk logic of accumulation of the capitalist elite, they will be able to have the resources to deal with those that become redundant to that logic of accumulation.[18] Hence, the region's oligarchy has been able to gain a degree of political and ideological hegemonic control not seen in the region since before the First World War, while the *managerial* left has been able to make significant improvements in terms of extreme poverty reduction. So, in Chile, for example, half of the people who used to live below the poverty line are now above this important (albeit, for a high-middle income country, a remarkably unambitious) line; and in Brazil eleven million families receive today on average a subsidy of about fifty dollars a month. However, what is also remarkable is how little these programs of poverty reduction have cost, and how little else has been done to help continue improving the lot of those helped by these programs.[19]

If for the old right the poor had previously been the torturable classes, the disposable *homo sacer* of Giorgio Agamben, for the new right is now more effective for its latest form of legitimization and for it more sophisticated technology of power to go along with the managerial left's new perspective. In this, the poor, instead of playing their progressive historical role as the proletariat, are now reduced to a passive role of "poor-letariat." And what these poor-letariats need is only help in the form of (market-friendly) insurance to hedge them against the most unacceptable risks of unsteady open economies with downwardly flexible labor markets. That is, in the vision of my neo-comrades social justice has been metamorphosed into social charity, and the state into a solidarity-with-the-very-very-poor type of enterprise. Accordingly, workers have been transformed from proletarians into paupers, from citizens into patients. And, of course, *patients* are much more susceptible to pressures for clientelist political paybacks (cf. Arantes 2007).

In fact, the neo-liberal left may on the surface appear just as the champions of safety-nets and institutional "modernizations," but their political role is far more complex than that: they are the ones who have taken the responsibility to deliver the neo-liberal version of capitalism—one without excessive need for crude coercion—by engineering a frictionless-type of economy in which workers are kept on a tight rein, the capitalist elite is kept sweet (i.e., without having to struggle with "market compulsions"), and the masses that become redundant to the new logic of capitalist accumulation are kept at least partially hedged. Hence, when Cardoso was recently asked his opinion of Lula as president, his answer was brief and to the point: "He knows how to please the elite!"[20] At the same time, Lula's government, as that of the "Concertación" in Chile, are paraded by the World Bank the world over as best practice in poverty alleviation (*Economist*, 2/7/2008). Being perfect magicians, no one but they are supposed to know the necessary tricks for making conflict evaporate, coercion conceal itself, and military regimes become obsolete.

In a sense, they have been remarkably successful in political terms. In Chile the "Concertación" is in its fourth successive government (and the second led by a member of Allende's Socialist Party), and Lula was re-elected easily in 2006. However, in a Keynesian sense, they have failed in that they have helped to make it so cosy for the capitalist elite that they may in fact be partly responsible for the remarkably poor economic performance of the region. In fact, if one compares the share of national income appropriated by the top 10 percent with the share of private investment in GDP, LA appears now even more as an outlier: while in LA the income share of the top decile is approximately three times the GDP-share of private investment (roughly 45 percent and 15 percent, respectively), in India and China this ratio is about 1.5, in Malaysia and Thailand it is only slightly above 1, and in Korea, Taiwan, and Singapore the two shares are actually approximately the same. Perhaps few have contributed as effectively as the managerial left to make the "discreet charm" of the Latin American bourgeoisie so remarkably unique!

Moreover, by being able to convince so many in LA that any progressive alternative agenda today is just a suicide pact maybe the new left has actually become the most effective enemy of any true progressive struggle. In sum, it is not only that the new left has become neo-liberal, it is also that it has become so in a sub-prime, uncritical way. Now, for how long will the neo-liberal left be able to tame the dangerous classes? For how long will they be able to keep getting such a bang for the few bucks they give to the very poor? And for how long will they be able to keep subjective violence in check, while being the very agents of the structural violence that creates the conditions for this violence? (cf. Zizek 2008).

You've really got to hand it to the Latin American capitalist elite. In the 1950s and 1960s they convinced the progressive forces of the region (all the way up to the communist parties) that there was nothing more anti-imperialist than to provide them with vast rents via import-substituting industrialization; and that these huge rents, as opposed to what was happening in East Asia at the time, should be given to them without any form of performance-related conditionality. And now, in the new century, their process of legitimization has been so successful, and their new technologies of power so effective, that they have convinced the majority of the left not only of "TINA" ("there is no alternative"), and that "there is nothing left to decide"—and even less to think critically—but that they actually deserve every privilege and reward (and, of course, especially any rent) that they can get. That is, that the new political settlement (best described by Gore Vidal as "socialism for the rich and capitalism for the rest") is the best of all worlds not just for them but for everybody else as well!

Conclusions

As has often been the case, what is happening in LA today could be straight out of a García Márquez novel: the dominant classes are quite happy to let the dominated ones govern, provided that they do not forget who they are! The idea is that this is a win–win situation: the capitalist elite is able to accumulate with a minimal need for coercion and little "market compulsions," the managerial left is able to develop a relatively effective solidarity state, and military governments have become unfashionable. What is crucial here is that as the new left believes that it cannot get political power to implement its own progressive agenda, it then tries to gain power to implement what Chico de Oliveira has called "upside-down hegemony" (Oliveira 2006).

Perhaps this is partly the result of a post-doomsday date reaction to the fact that capitalism, far from of collapsing like a house of cards (as so often predicted in most dependency analyses), gained instead a new and powerful lease of life. The failure of the post-Cuban-Revolution *all or nothing*-type political struggle probably also played a part—if *all* was not possible, some ended up believing that maybe the only viable political alternative was safety-nets![21]

By now the new left does actually believe that "collaboration" in trying to deliver capitalism with minimal "friction," disguise coercion, a modern state administration and decent safety-nets is as good as it can possibly get. Their ideological passions have been diluted into managerial routines. As has been argued, it seems that LA has moved from the "Age of Extremes" into the "Age of Indistinction" between the new left and the new right (cf. Oliveira 2006). That is, the extremes have become indiscernible. People often say that in couples opposite poles often attract one another. Until now, this has rarely been the case with ideologies. And when two ideological poles are thinking alike, most likely only one is actually doing the thinking.

Perhaps the greatest sign of the intellectual amnesia of the neo-liberal left in LA is to have forgotten that "[t]he ideas of the ruling class are in every epoch the ruling ideas; i.e., the class which is the ruling material force of society is at the same time its ruling intellectual force" (Marx and Engels 1845). Manic managerial defences may be very useful for dealing temporarily with vital problems such as poverty alleviation and the modernization of the state, but they can hardly hope to become the ruling intellectual force of society. For example, it is no coincidence that these manic managerial defences have not led the neo-liberal left even into the temptation of questioning the conventional wisdom that in the current globalized world there is no role for human agency in the regulation of market forces. That would certainly be trespassing into a territory that is simply taboo for the ruling ideas.

An analogy with quantum mechanics could help to illustrate this point. Since its inception, the many counter-intuitive results of quantum mechanics have provoked strong philosophical debates—Einstein and many of the other greats seem particularly to have enjoyed this.[22] However, an influential school of thought within the subject argues that physicists should just get on with their work and not waste time with metaphysical issues; so they call themselves the "shut-up and calculate" school. When discussing the issues analyzed in this chapter with my managerial neo-comrades, their usual response could best be summarized as "Shut up and do something useful!"

Of course there is a *real* world down there, and the radical left is certainly not known for its capacity to construct practical alternatives. But why did the managerial left have to move all the way to a sub-prime neo-liberal understanding of the world in order to be able to construct a practical alternative? If the managerial left in LA was willing to concede the economy as the fundamental hub of the struggle, why were they not able to construct a practical alternative which at least contained a more liberal-progressive Keynesian understanding of economic life, and a more radical-democratic understanding of political life?[23] Why were they so desperately keen to concede the economy, the terms of the debate, and almost everything else? Why when events moved in the wrong direction did they lose the capacity to hold basic ideological principles in their minds in a thoughtful way? And why do they have to look at the past with such contempt?[24]

What we have today in LA is the combination of an insatiable capitalist elite, passive citizens, and a stalled social imagination. One could add that we also have a bunch of neo-comrades who are rather pleased with themselves. Only a few critical doctrinaires whine—particularly from their comfortable tenured positions in universities far away! Why can't the latter understand that life is so much simpler when one succeeds in transforming "delving deeply into the surface of things" into an art form? What is so wrong with making it one's basic tenet never to let one's ideology venture beyond ideas that can be googled?

Perhaps what is happening in LA in this respect can be better explained (as Arantes does) by restating Adorno. For Adorno "[i]ntelligence is a moral category" (1951: 197); maybe there are times when a lack of critical thinking is also a "moral category." In fact, for Arantes what has happened in LA is even worse: for him, LA shows that "stupidity" can also become a moral category (2007).[25]

In short, is Lula right when he suggests that the emergence of the new left in Brazil is just "[a] positive sign in the evolution of the human species," or is Francisco de Oliveira right when he claims that the new left in Brazil (and in the rest of LA) is like the platypus, a creature that violates evolutionary theories and yet still exists, and is likely to continue, despite the fact that it is at an evolutionary dead-end?[26]

When Keynes said, "[p]eople usually prefer to fail through conventional means rather than to succeed through unconventional ones," he could not have guessed just how accurately his remarks would define Latin American left-wing governments in office today. However, the intellectual poverty (and ideological self-satisfaction) of the neo-liberal left is unlikely to lead to its political death (as many have predicted).[27] In fact, what is likely to happen is almost the opposite, as this very poverty is what makes it so functional to the current system of domination and control.

Oscar Wilde famously said that "America is the only country that went from barbarism to decadence without civilization in between." Maybe now it is LA's turn to move from the barbarism of the military regimes straight into its current ideological neo-decadence without much civilization in between.

In 1915 Freud summarized his views on the effects of the outbreak of the First World War with the following statement: "We cannot but feel that no event has ever destroyed so much that is precious in the common possessions of humanity, confused so many of the clearest intelligences, or so thoroughly debased what is highest" (1957: 274).

I do not think it would be an exaggeration to say that no other event in peacetime LA has had such similar effects—especially in terms of confusing so many of its clearest intelligences—as the advent of an all-powerful and tyrannical neo-liberalism, with the same remarkable capabilities for heightening risk and insecurity for the majority of the population, as for generating personal and political rent-seeking opportunities for political leaders of the left (and those in their "intellectual periphery") who are prepared to acquiesce.

What happened in LA after 1980 shows (yet again) that intellectuals, particularly when working without a proper social and political base, can be fickle and can easily turn to the next set of beliefs on their horizon to continue their business of providing a world-view and a theoretical legitimacy to it.

Acknowledgments

Paulo Arantes, Stephanie Blankenburg, Ronald Britton, Samer Frangie, and Fiona Tregenna have greatly influenced this paper. Mark Blyth, Jonathan DiJohn, Daniel Hahn, Geoff Harcourt, Juliano Fiori, Otilia Fiori, Mushtaq Khan, and Carlota Pérez also made important suggestions. The usual caveats apply.

Notes

1 It is not surprising that this analysis leads Frank to displace class relations from the center of his analysis.
2 Although Frank did not go very far in his analysis of the world capitalist system as a whole, Wallerstein tackled this challenge in two remarkable books (1974 and 1980). For surveys of this literature cf. Palma (1978) and Kay (1989). The most thoroughgoing critiques have come from Laclau, Cardoso, Lall, Warren, Brenner, and Palma.
3 By fundamentalist I mean that the purity of belief increasingly came into conflict with the intricacies of the real world.
4 The basic difference between the two periods (pre- and post-1980) is that, during the former, the "engine" (manufacturing) was able to pull along the rest of the economy with it, while the new

post-1980 engine (commodity exports) has failed to do the same. In Brazil, for example, between 1950 and 1980 the real rates of growth of manufacturing and GDP were very similar (8.8 percent and 7.3 percent per year, respectively), while in the five years since Lula was first elected in 2002, the asymmetry between export and GDP growth could hardly be greater (13.3 percent and 3.5 percent respectively; see ECLAC's statistical database: www.eclac.org). In the Mexican case the stagnation of the country's average productivity took place in a context of both massive inflows of FDI and practically unrestricted market access to the US—the first two items on all DCs' growth agenda today—cf. Palma (2005a).

5 See for example the papers in Ocampo (2005). In this area, see the work of Díaz-Alejandro, Fajnzylber, Ffrench-Davis, Frenkel, Ocampo, and Taylor.

6 Consequently, manufacturing industry was decimated; for an analysis of this process of *premature de-industrialization*, see Palma (2005b) and (2008b).

7 For a similar attitude in dependency, see some of the papers in *Latin American Perspectives*, 1(1).

8 Cardoso once called this "the originality of the copy" (1977).

9 The two socialist parties in Chile and the Workers Party in Brazil are the paradigmatic cases. For example, when Fernando Flores (Allende's minister of finance and de facto chief of staff) returned to Chilean politics to run for a seat in the Senate, his close friend, Carlos Slim—one of the three richest persons on earth—took time off from his busy life to come to Chile to help in his campaign.

10 Lula has explained his revolutionary past as being down to his youth; however, now "[m]aturity has distanced me from the left" (cf. FOLHAONLINE 2/5/2008: www1.folha.uol.com.br/folha/brasil/ult96u87635.shtml).

11 Or, in the words of Cardoso, of "neo-bobos" ("neo-silly").

12 I firmly believe that democratic forces had much more room for maneuver than they acknowledged at the time

13 Adorno once said that a German is someone who cannot tell a lie without believing it himself (or herself); maybe my neo-comrades are now the ones that cannot tell a story without believing it themselves!

14 The Chilean finance minister between 2000 and 2006 (a member of one of the two socialist parties, and former member of the Communist Party; currently top executive at the IMF) is on record as saying that the reason why Chile performed so much better than the rest of LA is that "[i]n Chile, we truly believe in the neo-liberal model, while the rest of LA implemented this model only because they had no option but to do so."

15 Lord Kelvin was one of the most important physicists of the nineteenth century, who played key roles in the development of thermodynamics, electric lighting, and transatlantic telecommunication; he was buried next to Isaac Newton in Westminster Abbey.

16 In the Arab world, for example, secularism and the Palestinian issue provided those of the left who wanted to concede the economy with relevant issues with which to continue to think critically (cf. Frangie 2008).

17 In fact, why not also check the boxes of favoring macrobiotic diets, attacking-style football, and post-modern art!

18 As Adorno once said, domination is more effective if "[it] delegates the [...] violence on which it rests to the dominated" (1951: 182).

19 In Brazil, for example, in 2008 the whole "Bolsa Familia" subsidy described above has a total annual cost of about 0.5 percent of GDP (cf. Fiori 2008). And in Chile, in the unlikely event that all the proposals recently put forward by President Bachelet's Commission of Work and Equity were implemented, the total cost would also peak in 2015 at just about 0.5 percent of GDP.

20 Cardoso (Estado de São Paulo, 12/1/2008). A bit rich coming from a former president who in his first period in office bailed out private banks (with no questions asked) at the cost to the public sector of $43 billion (cf. Palma 2006).

21 Some people still think that in Venezuela something else is supposed to be happening, but so far there are more gesticulations than results (and a huge excess-supply of boligarchs)—this wasn't the way things were supposed to play out!

22 For example, in his autobiography John Wheeler writes that the existence of black holes "teaches us that space can be crumpled like a piece of paper into an infinitesimal dot, that time can be extinguished like a blown-out flame, and that the laws of physics that we regard as 'sacred', as immutable, are anything but." (2000)

23 Despite many promises of a radical democratic project and open government, the new left has been quite happy to continue with a low-intensity clientelist form of democracy. In Chile, for example,

after two decades of center-left governments, the electoral law left by Pinochet is still making it de facto impossible for the Communist Party and other left-wing groups to get any representation in Parliament—it seems that the new left, like any large corporation, only likes oligopolistic forms of competition!

24 The head of Brazil's central bank described President Cardoso's agenda as "[having] to undo forty years of stupidity" (*Veja*, 15/11/1996). For him, the fact that Brazil's previous "stupid" development strategy had prior to 1980 delivered one of the fastest growth rates in the world was probably a mere detail of history.

25 This reminds us of what Einstein once said: "Two things are infinite: the universe and human stupidity; and I'm not sure about the universe." President Cardoso once described his head of the central bank (quoted in text) as Brazil's Copernicus ...

26 For Lula's speech, see FOLHAONLINE (2/5/2008); and for Oliveira, see (2003). The platypus is a semi-aquatic mammal found in eastern Australia that still lays eggs.

27 Commenting on the intellectual poverty of the new left, Green states that "[in the 'São Paulo Forum people] were dismayed by the lack of ideas and imagination shown by the politicians" (1996: 121).

16

What do sociologists bring to international political economy?

John L. Campbell

International political economy (IPE) is a field that has been dominated by political scientists and economists. But sociologists have also been interested in IPE. Some of their work has managed to percolate into the mainstream literature. Some of it has not. This chapter takes stock of all this. It shows where the work of sociologists is most obviously related to the study of IPE. But it also shows that there are other areas of sociology to which conventional IPE scholars might pay attention with considerable benefit. This is particularly true insofar as IPE scholars and political and economic sociologists have turned their attention to economic globalization, by which I mean the increase since the mid-1970s in transnational trade, capital flows, and economic activity in general.

However, as some IPE scholars have recognized (e.g. Finnemore 1996b), many sociologists approach these things differently than do conventional IPE scholars. Sociologists often emphasize that norms and ideas of various sorts—as opposed to the pursuit of material interests—shape the behavior of actors. Of course, some sociologists take intellectual positions that are quite close to the materialist (or realist) view, which is common in conventional IPE scholarship. But one of sociology's most original contributions to the IPE literature is to offer normative and ideational rather than realist explanations. I begin by discussing areas where the normative approach of sociology is most obvious. This includes research on the international diffusion of norms and ideas and the rise of neoliberalism. I then move on to areas where sociologists are less inclined to favor normative explanations, but still have insights that diverge from mainstream IPE scholarship. There I discuss research on the international division of labor in the world system, socioeconomic performance as it is influenced by political-economic institutions and international networks, and welfare reform, particularly insofar as social class and family figure prominently in sociological accounts of reform. Two caveats are in order. First, IPE emerged from the traditional literature on international relations, which assumed that international relations was largely about states making war or peace (e.g. Hoffman 1965; Waltz 1959). That is, international relations was about states, security issues, and the politics that linked them (Holsti 2004: 3). IPE argued that international relations was to an increasing extent not just about states, diplomacy, security, and military power, but also about building national economies that could compete internationally—and thereby provide an economic base for state power in the diplomatic, security, and military domains (e.g. Gilpin 1987; Keohane 1984). As this is a volume on IPE, not international relations in this sense, I will not deal with the sociological literature that is of obvious importance for traditional international relations. This would include, for example, the work of Charles Tilly (1990), Anthony Giddens (1985), Gianfranco Poggi (1978), and Michael Mann (1993) on the relationship between war-making and state-building. Proper treatment of this literature would require a separate chapter.

Second, there has been a disciplinary separation between the fields of IPE and comparative political economy (CPE). On the one hand, traditional IPE scholars emphasize how *international* pressures operate on states and other international actors to constrain or drive their behavior. They view the structure and functioning of national political economies as being very much embedded in international processes, particularly as state power in the international arena has come to depend increasingly on economic power (e.g. Gilpin 1987). On the other hand, CPE scholars emphasize the study of *national* institutional differences in political economies. They recognize that international pressures impinge on national political economies, but their focus has been more on the different national responses to these pressures than on the pressures per se (e.g. Gourevitch 1986; Katzenstein 1978). To a degree, then, IPE and CPE study flip sides of the same coin. But especially since the oil crises and stagflation of the 1970s, and then the rise of economic globalization and concerns about how it affects national political economies, these two fields have moved much closer together and blurred (Weber 2001: 7). Indeed, there are now a fair number of people who do work that overlaps CPE and IPE (e.g. Garrett 1998; Keohane and Milner 1996; Kitschelt et al. 1999). Hence, this chapter does not draw a sharp distinction between IPE and CPE.

International diffusion

Nowhere are norms more prominent in sociological approaches to IPE than in the research on international diffusion. The typical argument is that normative principles and practices diffuse across nation-states in ways that lead to isomorphic—that is, homogeneous—outcomes. This can be because nation-states mimic the countries that appear to be doing the best; because they learn from experts and advisors from around the world; or because they are coerced by powerful external forces, such as the International Monetary Fund or World Bank. This work is inspired by a more general literature in organizational sociology that seeks to explain why organizations operating in a common environment tend to adopt similar practices (DiMaggio and Powell 1983). The point here is that conventional IPE scholars assume that diffusion is driven by coercive pressures, often exercised by hegemonic states or their allies. Sociologists do not. Hence, sociology offers new insights into the mechanisms underlying the diffusion process.

Representative of this genre is the work of John Meyer and his colleagues (e.g. Strang and Meyer 1993; Thomas et al. 1987) who studied the diffusion of many elements of modern world culture among nation-states. For instance, they showed that the diffusion of a modern ideology of childhood as a distinct stage in the life cycle precipitated the gradual world-wide development of constitutional provisions for the education of children and the regulation of child labor (Boli and Meyer 1987). Based on this and other studies they concluded that the practices of nation-states are enactments of broad-based cultural prescriptions operating at the global level (Meyer et al. 1987: 32). In this view, the driving force behind diffusion is the quest by nation-states to obtain legitimacy from their fellow nation-states in the world political community.

All of this has influenced IPE insofar as scholars have criticized conventional realist approaches for neglecting the importance of norms, culture, and identities for world politics (Kahler 1998). Martha Finnemore (1996b), in particular, has called for an integration of the ideas of Meyer and other sociological diffusionists into conventional approaches to world politics. And some IPE and international relations scholars have taken this call seriously, arguing, for instance, that the formation of national norms and identities actually precedes the definition of national interests—even in national security issues (Jepperson et al. 1996; Katzenstein 1996b; Risse et al. 1999).

But Meyer and his colleagues' work has been criticized for not specifying carefully enough the mechanisms by which world culture actually impacts the institutional structure and practices of nation-states and other organizations, and for ignoring how conflict and struggle are often involved in the diffusion process (Finnemore 1996b; Keck and Sikkink 1998: 33–35; Risse and Sikkink 1999). That is, it is not clear in their empirical work whether mimetic, normative, coercive, or other mechanisms cause nation-states to enact the principles associated with modern world culture (Boli and Thomas 1999b: 2). In an effort to address their critics, world culture theorists have tried recently to specify the mechanisms whereby world culture diffuses to nation-states through the activities of international nongovernmental organizations (INGOs) and other transnational actors like the United Nations (Boli and Thomas 1999a; Katzenstein 1996b; Meyer et al. 1997).

In this regard, and of particular note for IPE scholars, sociologists have argued recently that the transnational political-economic environment is increasingly governed by so-called *soft rules*, such as professional standards, technocratic blueprints and guidelines, auditing criteria, and a variety of norms and values. And these soft rules are often propagated by transnational organizational networks made up of INGOs, law firms, multinational corporations, and others. The emergence and diffusion of the New Public Management model is a case in point. Guidelines and standards for corporate bookkeeping is another. The point is twofold. On the one hand, the transnational arena is increasingly becoming what sociologists call a *field*—that is, a network of organizations that creates certain normative and cognitive meaning systems that govern the behavior of individual actors within the field. On the other hand, and this is very important for IPE scholarship, the transnational arena is no longer dominated by nation-states and firms, but now also includes to an increasing extent a variety of public and private organizations—many of them non-profit organizations—as well as transnational social movements whose influence is growing in terms of their ability to regulate and change the transnational environment (Djelic and Sahlin-Andersson 2006; Kay 2005; Keck and Sikkink 1998).

Specifying mechanisms such as these is an important step forward, although one that is still subject to criticism (e.g. Finnemore 1996b; Keck and Sikkink 1998: 33–35, 214; Risse and Sikkink 1999: 4). First, despite the fact that several diffusion mechanisms have been identified in the literature, few researchers have tested them against each other head-to-head to see which ones are most important in empirical cases of international diffusion (Dobbin et al. 2007). One exception is Tim Bartley (2007) who showed that the diffusion of transnational labor and environmental soft-rule certification programs occurred as a result of both the competitive self-interest of corporations and the normative pressure brought to bear on them by INGOs and others. But the point remains that much work needs to be done by sociologists and others to sort out the relative effects of different diffusion mechanisms.

Second, the discussion of diffusion generally ignores what happens when an institutional principle or practice arrives at an organization's door step and is prepared by that organization for adoption. Here the story often ends and it is assumed that the principle or practice is simply adopted uncritically and in toto. We are left, then, with a black box in which the mechanisms whereby new principles and practices are actually put into use and institutionalized on a case-by-case basis are left unspecified.

Let me provide another illustration. Meyer and colleagues (1997) argued that the development of a global scientific discourse, embracing the concept of a world ecosystem, caused many national governments to establish environmental ministries during the late twentieth century. To use the language from Meyer's earlier work, the new scientific discourse was enacted by national governments. The problem is that their argument omitted any discussion of the national-level political processes that were responsible for this enactment. Hence, they assumed apparently that these ministries were all basically the same. Similarly, Meyer's earlier work on the diffusion of constitutional provisions for childhood assumed that such provisions were enacted uniformly across countries.

Sociologists have examined through the use of fine-grained case studies how institutional diffusion occurs from the transnational to the national level (e.g. Duina 1999; Guillén 1994; Marjoribanks 2000). Case studies are more amenable to identifying precisely how diffusing principles are enacted—or *translated* into local practice—than most quantitative approaches, including Meyer's, that use large data sets with dozens or even hundreds of cases to track institutional change over time. By translation I mean the process by which exogenously given principles and practices, such as those diffusing from the transnational to the national level, are incorporated into endogenous or local ones. Case studies have shown that the concept of diffusion is under-theorized because diffusion studies fail typically to recognize that when institutional principles and practices travel from one site to another the recipients translate them in different ways, and to a greater or lesser extent. Several things affect how they are translated into practice.

First is the local institutional context. Actors must blend new ideas into local practice. This tends to ensure that implementation of a new idea rarely constitutes a total break with past practice. For instance, Yasemin Soysal (1994) showed how the global diffusion of a new postnational model of citizenship was translated into practice in locally distinct ways in Europe during the late twentieth century. Postnational citizenship is the normative idea that all residents within a nation-state, regardless of their historical or cultural ties to that state, ought to be guaranteed certain basic rights, notably the right to participate in the authority structures and public life of the polity and the right to have access to basic services, such as welfare, health care, and education. How this was done varied according to local political institutions. In Sweden, a country favoring corporatist institutions, guest workers and other immigrants are treated by the state like other corporate groups. The state helps organize immigrants in associations that represent their interests at national level negotiations over policy, budgets, and the like, just as it helps organize associations that represent the interests of labor, business, and other groups. In France, a country where the central state ensures the protection of citizens, the state spends a lot of money supporting social and cultural activities, housing, education, job training, and so on, specifically for immigrants. In Switzerland, a liberal country in the sense that the market is trusted to provide for its inhabitants, the federal government has little direct involvement in immigrant affairs per se, but provides significant resources for social workers, occupational training, and other services, primarily at the local level, to help everyone, including immigrants, obtain what they need in order to participate in the labor market. Thus, the principle of postnational citizenship was translated into Swedish, French, and Swiss practice in very different ways in order to fit it with local institutions.

Sociologists have also shown that political mobilization affects the translation process. Elsewhere I have shown that a neoliberal model of fiscal reform diffused from the West to postcommunist Poland, Hungary, and the Czech Republic after 1989 but was translated into practice differently and in varying degree in each country depending on the institutional clout of labor unions and political parties (Campbell 2001; see also Bönker 2006). Similarly, Francesco Duina (1999) showed that European Union directives on the environment and women's employment were translated into national practice in varying degrees depending on the politics involved. In some countries, this went smoothly as directives were translated into national law quickly and then enforced rigorously. But in other cases, where political resistance was greater, directives were translated into law slowly and with much struggle, and then enforced in a much more lackadaisical fashion. And Marie-Laure Djelic (1998) showed how diffusion of the so-called American model of political-economic organization diffused to France, West Germany, and Italy after the Second World War in different ways and with different outcomes depending on the prevailing national political and institutional conditions. France and West Germany experienced relatively radical shifts toward the American model, but change in Italy was much more modest.

The rise of neoliberalism

An important object of international diffusion that has drawn the attention of IPE and CPE scholars are economic ideas, such as Keynesianism (e.g. Hall 1989). More recently, however, sociologists have become interested in the diffusion of neoliberalism. By neoliberalism I mean the belief that lower taxes, less government intrusion into the economy through expenditures and regulation, and balanced state budgets are the best medicine for what ails national political economies. Much IPE and CPE has been concerned with how nation-states have reacted to the world-wide rise of neoliberal ideology and policy recommendations since the 1970s. As stagflation gripped the advanced capitalist countries, and as developing countries struggled with rampant inflation, debt crises, fiscal deficits, and the like, neoliberalism gained prominence and diffused internationally. Although a number of comparative political economists have examined the rise of neoliberalism (e.g., Blyth 2002; Hall 1992, 1993), sociologists have also shed light on how this happened.

Much of the sociological work pays close attention to how neoliberal ideas diffused internationally and were adopted locally. Hence, it reflects the translation approach to diffusion discussed above. Notably, Sarah Babb (2001) showed that Mexico's shift from leftist to neoliberal economic policy resulted from the movement of economists—often trained in the United States—into positions of influence in the government after 1970. The result was the emergence of a professional class of Mexican technocrats who essentially transported neoliberal theories and models from the United States back home and implemented them in ways that fit the political institutional conditions they found there. More recently, she and Marion Fourcade-Gourinchas (2002) expanded this analysis in comparative directions showing how the manner in which neoliberalism was adopted in particular countries varied considerably according to national state–society relations, political ideology, and the degree to which a country was susceptible to external economic pressures (see also Campbell and Pedersen 2001; Kjaer and Pedersen 2001; Prasad 2005). Once again, the sociological notion of translation comes to the fore.

Sociologists have made three additional insights regarding the rise of neoliberalism. First, as Babb's analysis of Mexico illustrates, neoliberalism did not diffuse internationally simply as a result of the coercive pressures of international financial organizations, such as the International Monetary Fund, or the United States, as some IPE scholars have intimated (e.g. Wade and Veneroso 1998). In addition, the internationalization of certain professions was integral to the process. In particular, private consultants, public technocrats, and scientific experts, many of whom were trained as professional economists, played important roles in spreading the word that neoliberalism was the appropriate approach to pursue. Indeed, central to all of this was the economics profession. This is because after the Second World War the economics profession in the United States rose to a place of international prominence. American economists as well as foreign economists who had been trained in the United States were often revered by political and business elites in other countries so their views carried considerable legitimacy and weight. And because their views were increasingly neoliberal after the early 1970s, this point of view gained considerable traction world-wide (Fourcade 2006). Indeed, the internationalization of professions has been central to the diffusion of a variety of norms and standards throughout the world during the late twentieth century (e.g. Halliday and Carruthers 2007). And the advent of conservative economists in the IMF was responsible for its neoliberal turn in the first place (Babb 2007).

Second, the rise of neoliberalism does not represent a sharp break with the past. Political scientists have been fond of invoking so-called punctuated equilibrium models to explain paradigmatic shifts in policymaking (Krasner 1984; Thelen 2003). In this view, exogenous shocks, such as deep recession or stagflation, undermine current policy models, disrupt the policy equilibrium, and trigger searches for new ones, which, when found, are institutionalized thereby creating a new policy equilibrium. But, pursuing a more evolutionary approach, sociologist Colin Hay (2001) argued that in Britain—the paramount neoliberal case—the Labour government began experimenting in marginal ways with some neoliberal ideas (i.e. monetarism) during the 1970s when they began to realize that conventional Keynesian policies were not adequate for resolving stagflation. When Margaret Thatcher and the Conservatives came to power they extended the neoliberal ideas with which the previous government had toyed. Thus, the rise of neoliberalism was a more continuous process than many scholars have recognized. A similar story can be told about postcommunist Europe (Campbell and Pedersen 1996). The broader point, however, is that sociologists, like political scientists, are now taking seriously the notion that policy and institutional change is often an evolutionary path-dependent process and that we need to learn more about the mechanisms whereby change occurs in an evolutionary rather than an abrupt, punctuated, or revolutionary fashion (e.g. Campbell 2004: ch. 3; Haydu 1998; Mahoney 2000).

The third insight is that the diffusion of neoliberalism is not a uniform process. As noted above, the degree to which welfare policy has shifted in neoliberal directions is quite variable *across* countries due to the politically contested and institutionally constrained nature of the process. The same is true for tax and regulatory policies (Campbell 2005, 2004: ch. 5; Ó Riain 2000). But there is also much variation *within* countries. For instance, since the breakdown of the Bretton Woods accord in 1971 there has been a tendency for governments to grant their central banks more autonomy to set interest rates and regulate the money supply in order to better control inflation and defend currencies in the face of increasingly mobile international capital and currency speculation— a trend that has removed monetary policy from national politics and made it more austere (Polillo and Guillén 2005). However, this has been matched with important changes in bankruptcy law. Governments eventually recognized that stringent monetary policy increased the possibilities of recession, business failure, and unemployment. So, out of concern for the political ramifications, many of them revised their bankruptcy laws in order to facilitate corporate reorganization rather than liquidation. In other words, neo-liberal deregulation in monetary policy was counterbalanced with non-neoliberal re-regulation in bankruptcy policy (Carruthers et al. 2001). The important notion here, and one to which we will return later, is that nation–states and national political economies are institutionally complex, multidimensional entities—a fact that is occasionally neglected by IPE, if not CPE, which tends to treat them as uniform and coherent wholes.

The international division of labor

Of all the work done by sociologists, perhaps that which is most obviously relevant for IPE comes from dependency and world system theorists. Dependency theory suggests that national economies are interdependent such that developing countries depend on more advanced ones for economic opportunities, finance, technology, and access to markets. This is due to the fact that dependent countries are often former colonies of more developed ones, but also because multinational corporations, based in developing countries, exploit the resources and opportunities in developing countries in ways that create situations of dependency (Cardoso and Faletto 1979; Evans 1979). In other words, there is an international division of labor based on the economic relations among countries.

Somewhat in reaction to dependency theory, which emphasized the importance of *economic* relations among countries, Immanuel Wallerstein (1974; 1980) and other world system theorists argued that *political* relations are just as important. That is, the world economic system is organized fundamentally by political units, most recently nation–states. Here sociologists embrace a realist view of the world similar to that of conventional IPE scholars. Nation–states absorb the costs and manage the social problems that arise from the world economy. In this view the world system includes three types of states. Core states, such as the United States, Germany, and Japan, have strong governmental structures that are rich and dominating within the system. Their ability to maintain a position in the core depends on their ability to maintain capital accumulation on a world-wide scale and keep the demands of the working class at bay. Peripheral states, such as those in Africa, are poor and economically dependent on core states for loans, military support, technical aid, and the like. Semi-peripheral states, such as Singapore and the Philippines, have moderately strong governmental structures that are somewhat dependent on core states.

These approaches are treated elsewhere in this volume (Chapter 10 by Arrighi) and need not concern us here at length. However, three points are worth mentioning. To begin with, the field of IPE has been influenced by this work to a considerable extent insofar as IPE scholars studying economic development have either adopted some of the concepts and arguments from these literatures or have developed their own theories and research agendas in reaction to it. In particular, IPE scholars have argued that the problem with dependency and world system theories is that they have difficulty explaining cross-national variation in levels of dependency and development, not to mention political systems, among the developing countries (e.g. Haggard and Kaufman 1992).

Furthermore, proponents of the world system view have engaged recent debates on globalization that are of concern to IPE scholars. In particular, Christopher Chase-Dunn and colleagues (2000) have argued that globalization is by no means a recent phenomenon. The density of international economic and political interactions has expanded and contracted repeatedly for centuries. And of special concern in this work has been the degree to which this pulsation is associated with the presence or absence of a world hegemonic power that can ensure peace, stability, and thus greater international interaction—something that ought to be of obvious interest to IPE scholars given their concern with hegemonic nation-states (e.g. Keohane 1984). Like traditional IPE scholarship, world system theorists like Chase-Dunn hold open the possibility that hegemonic actors facilitate international activity, such as trade, through the exercise of economic and military power. This includes the projection of international force, the implementation of free-trade treaties, and the encouragement of international capitalists from the hegemon and allied core powers to promote international investment. But Chase-Dunn acknowledges the very sociological possibility that hegemonic power may also operate by normative means—that the hegemon promotes international stability and activity by providing cultural and ideological leadership. To a degree, this argument resonates with the sociological research about how a world-wide normative culture influences the behavior of actors in it, including nation-states, and especially how certain nationally based professions (i.e. US economics) do the same.

Finally, many IPE, dependency, and world system scholars share a tendency to view the state as a unitary whole. They often fail to recognize that states are organizations consisting of diverse parts with elites that may have different interests and, therefore, be in conflict with one another. This is an insight that political sociologists have emphasized (e.g. Evans et al. 1985). It is important in this context because it raises the possibility that states may be more or less susceptible to dependency or other international influences depending on which branch of the state and which elites happen to be in charge. For instance, Babb (2001) showed how the degree to which Mexico was in a dependent relationship with other countries varied according to which elites were in charge of its economic policy. Thus, a more nuanced institutional account of the state, which sociologists tend to favor, is an important insight to which IPE scholars should be attentive.

Comparative socioeconomic performance

Another body of literature from sociology that overlaps with IPE comes from political and economic sociologists working closely to the CPE tradition. Several sociologists have examined factors affecting the socioeconomic performance of national political economies. This work is well illustrated by Alex Hicks and Lane Kenworthy (1997), who identified the institutional conditions most likely to affect economic growth during the globalization era. Using pooled time-series analysis of OECD data since 1960, they showed that various aspects of firm-level cooperation, such as cooperative purchaser–supplier relations, alliances among competing firms, and the presence of work teams and multi-divisional project teams within firms, tended to increase rates of national economic growth and investment. However, they also found that the presence of neocorporatist institutions, such as centralized business confederations, coordinated wage bargaining, and cohesive government-interest group interrelations, tended to increase the amount of government transfers, strengthen active labor market policies, and reduce unemployment rates. In other words, while some institutional arrangements affected economic performance, others affected the distribution and redistribution of economic resources within society.

Other sociologists have conducted comparative studies to identify, for example, the degree to which globalization has contributed in the OECD countries to deindustrialization (Alderson 1999), unemployment (Western 2001), and a convergence in national performance across a wide variety of economic and social indicators (Campbell 2003, 2005; Dore 2000; Kenworthy 1997). Sociologists have also examined the political, economic, and especially institutional conditions under which particular industries do better or worse in one country than another (e.g. Biggart and Guillén 1999; Campbell 1988).

Attention among sociologists is not just on the advanced capitalist countries. Some excellent comparative work has been done looking at the conditions under which developing countries tend to perform better or not and, therefore, compete successfully in international markets. Notably, Peter Evans (1995) showed that the character of institutional relations between key state agencies and firms was an important determinant of successful economic development and international competitiveness. At issue was the degree to which these agencies in Brazil, India, and South Korea enjoyed *embedded autonomy*—that is, a close enough relationship with firms to understand their problems and interests, but enough autonomy to nurture and regulate these firms without being captured by them. Too little autonomy, he argued, led to rent seeking by private actors and inefficient crony capitalism. Too much autonomy led to ineffective development policy due to the fact that policymakers were out of touch with the needs of business. More recently Evans has also shown that developing countries do better if they have states that resemble the classic Weberian type with, for instance, meritocratic recruitment and long career paths (Evans and Rauch 1999). Other sociologists have also investigated the institutional conditions affecting the performance of particular industries and national political economies in developing countries during the globalization era (e.g. de Soysa and Oneal 1999; Guillén 2001; Schrank 2005, 2004; Schrank and Kurtz 2005).

Much of this work on developed and developing countries cuts close to the turf of both IPE and CPE (e.g. Gilpin 2000; Haggard and Kaufman 1992; Kitschelt et al. 1999; Swank 2002). Yet four things stand out prominently in this sociological literature that ought to be of interest to IPE. First, in contrast to conventional IPE and CPE scholarship, sociologists are often at least as interested in the *social* effects of political-economic institutions as they are the *economic* effects. Hicks and Kenworthy, for instance, paid close attention to the distributive and redistributive effects of various institutional arrangements. And a variety of sociologists have studied inequality more generally within and across countries as it may or may not be affected by globalization and the increasingly integrated nature of the international political economy (e.g. Firebaugh 2006; Mann and Riley 2007; Nielsen 1994; Nielsen and Alderson 1995). For example, Kenworthy (2004) examined the alleged trade-off, stipulated by some economists, between policies that promote economic growth and those that promote relatively egalitarian income distributions. He found that such a trade-off is not inevitable if societies can maintain high levels of employment—even in an increasingly global economic environment. Similarly, otherwise conventional studies of unemployment and economic performance by sociologists tend to keep an eye on social aspects of the problem. Bruce Western and Katherine Beckett (1999), for instance, showed that during the 1990s although US unemployment rates were considerably lower than they were in Western Europe, much of the difference actually stemmed not from the American economy being more efficient or internationally competitive than the European ones, but from the United States incarcerating a much higher percentage of people who would otherwise likely be jobless (e.g. poor, uneducated, young, African-American males).

The second thing that stands out in the sociological literature on performance is that a considerable amount of the work by sociologists focuses on interorganizational or inter-personal *networks*. Those interested in neocorporatism, like Hicks and Kenworthy, are an example insofar as neocorporatism is all about the formal ties linking trade unions, firms, state agencies, and sometimes others. This, however, is also ground well trodden by IPE and CPE scholars. But beyond that sociologists have made additional contributions. For instance, Evans' notion of embedded autonomy is essentially shorthand for a particular (non-corporatist) type of network relationship linking actors in the state and private sectors. Similar arguments about such networks have been made by sociologists focusing on advanced capitalist societies (e.g. Ó Riain 2004). Moreover, sociologists who have studied the transformation of postcommunist European political economies have shown that previously existing interorganizational networks often constituted the basis for sub-sequent postcommunist corporate acquisitions and trading relationships (Stark and Bruszt 1998). And sociologists have shown that today's most internationally competitive firms are often embedded in networks of alliances and other interorganizational relationships that influence their behavior and performance. Indeed, a variety of network resources, such as access to material resources and perceptions of a firm's legitimacy in the eyes of other actors like investors and banks, stem from a firm's network position (Gulati 2007). Of course, many of these networks are increasingly international and take a variety of forms ranging from research collaborations (Powell et al. 1996), to parent–subsidiary relationships within multinational firms (Kristensen and Zeitlin 2005), to more traditional supply-chain arrangements (Gereffi 2005; Schrank 2004).

In addition to interorganizational networks, sociologists have studied interpersonal networks. For example, some have examined transnational migration networks and the effect that these have on national and local economies, which in some cases can be extensive. Financial remittances from relocated family members to relatives in their country of origin may run as high as $400 billion annually world-wide. In some coun-tries the sums exceed private and official capital inflows and are the primary source of foreign currency. As a result, some governments (i.e. Mexico, El Salvador, Guatemala) have implemented policies to encourage such remittances whereby the state agrees to match remittances to varying degrees. Some countries also use the promise of future remittances to demonstrate creditworthiness and secure loans for economic development from private, bilateral, and non-profit sources (Levitt and Jaworsky 2007). And, as is well known, immigration networks often provide a source of labor for countries as either guest workers of various sorts or illegal aliens. Such networks may also facilitate the development of niche markets in local economies (Sassen 1999).

The third thing that stands out in sociological accounts of socioeconomic performance is that there are often important *cultural* determinants of success, such as national identity and cultural homogeneity. In this case, for example, sociologists have argued that, all else being equal, countries exhibiting a higher degree of cultural homogeneity on ethnic, linguistic, and other politically salient lines tend to have competitive advantages compared to more hetero-geneous societies (Campbell and Hall 2006, 2007). This sort of argument was proposed per-haps most famously by Ernest Gellner (1983) and touched upon briefly by Peter Katzenstein (1985), who pointed to the importance of an ideology of social partnership in facilitating the sort of corporatist institution building required especially of small states trying to compete in international markets. But the sociological point is that countries that are culturally homo-geneous tend to have greater capacity for cooperation, sacrifice, flexibility, and concerted state action—all of which can enhance national competitiveness in international markets.

Finally, the fourth thing that sets sociologists apart from much IPE scholarship on socioeconomic performance is the argument that *institutional heterogeneity* may facilitate rather than inhibit success. Much IPE and CPE scholarship now embraces the notion that there are two ideal types of national political economies. In liberal market economies (LME), like the United States, economic activity is coordinated largely by markets and corporations such that they compete successfully on the basis of low costs and major product and technological innovation. In coordinated market economies (CME), like Germany, economic activity is coordinated more through non-market mechanisms, such as informal networks or corporatism, such that they compete successfully on the basis of high-quality products and innovations in production processes. It is argued that both types can perform successfully, but for different reasons. However, it is also argued that the more closely a country resembles either type, the more institutionally coherent it is and, therefore, the better it will perform. Conversely, the more a country consists of a heterogeneous mixture of elements from both types, the less institutionally coherent it is and, the worse it will perform (Hall and Gingerich 2004; Hall and Soskice 2001b).

Sociologists often disagree, noting that *all* national political economies are to a considerable degree a hybrid mixture of liberal and coordinated elements (Crouch 2005; Zeitlin 2003). As noted earlier, they appreciate the institutional complexity of national political economies. The counterbalancing of monetary with bankruptcy policy, mentioned earlier, illustrates the point. Indeed, even apparently archetypical coordinated market economies, such as the United States, are actually much more hybrid than often recognized (Campbell et al. 1991). Moreover, when subjected to quantitative analysis, Kenworthy (2006) found that there is very little relationship between the degree to which a country fits either the pure LME or CME type and its socioeconomic performance. This may be because institutional heterogeneity provides a wide range of institutional options with which to adjust to changes in the international political-economic environment, and because certain CME elements may compensate for the deficiency of LME elements and vice versa (Crouch 2005). In Denmark, for example, low levels of employment protection, typically found in LMEs, are combined with high levels of unemployment protection and labor market policy, typically found in CMEs. The result is a very flexible labor market with low unemployment due to the fact that employers do not hesitate to fire workers when necessary, but retraining and job relocation is readily available and workers frequently shift jobs voluntarily as new opportunities arise (Campbell and Pedersen 2007). In sum, flexibility in labor markets and other aspects of the political economy are often viewed by sociologists as an important ingredient for socioeconomic success in today's increasingly volatile and fast-paced global economy (Whitford 2005; Whitley 1999). Institutional heterogeneity may enhance rather than inhibit such flexibility.

Welfare state reform

Interest in the social effects of international political-economic forces points toward another sociological literature that should interest IPE. This concerns the development and transformation of welfare states. Sociologists have contributed some of the most influential research on the conditions under which different types of welfare states emerged in the advanced capitalist countries (e.g. Amenta et al. 2001; Hicks 1999; Skocpol 1995). Most famously, Gøsta Esping-Andersen (1990) showed that there are three distinct types of welfare states—liberal, corporatist, and social democratic—each one associated with a different type of advanced capitalism.

Recently, however, sociologists have turned their attention to how welfare states are being affected by globalization. Much has been written about this, especially with respect to the degree to which welfare states have been cut back in various ways in response to rising budget deficits and unemployment, increased globalization, the decline of Keynesianism, and the rise of neoliberalism. And there has been much debate about whether all of this has led to convergence in welfare state structures and policies (e.g. Korpi 2003). The conventional IPE/CPE literature on welfare state retrenchment argues that retrenchment has been minimal and, therefore, differences among types of welfare states have endured. Why? Because welfare states, once established, develop powerful constituencies that mobilize to defend against cut backs when policymakers propose them. Moreover, although globalization may create incentives that can lead to welfare state retrenchment, the more open economies are to international trade, the greater are the political incentives to protect their workers from the vicissitudes of the global economy (e.g. Cameron 1978; Garrett 1998; Ruggie 1982). Hence, despite pressures for retrenchment welfare states persist for the most part due to these and other path-dependent processes (e.g. Pierson 1994; Swank 2002).

Many sociologists have come to the same conclusions, although not always for the same reasons (e.g. Esping-Andersen 1999; Hicks 1999: ch. 7; Glatzer and Rueschemeyer 2005; Stephens et al. 1999). In particular, while the conventional IPE/CPE view discounts the importance of traditional class-based movements in favor of other factors as inhibitors of retrenchment (e.g. Pierson 1994), sociologists often argue that class-based movements are still very important (e.g. Hicks 1999; Korpi 2003). Notably, Walter Korpi (2006) argued that economically well endowed groups with relatively low risks are likely to favor locating distributive processes in markets. But groups with less economic resources and higher risks are likely to favor locating distributive process in welfare state programs. In other words, not only have the political manifestations of class conflict shaped welfare state policies in the past, they continue to do so in the late twentieth and early twenty-first centuries.

Some sociologists also focus on aspects of welfare state retrenchment that are virtually ignored by IPE and CPE researchers. For instance, Esping-Andersen (1999) argued that family structure, gender roles, and the household economy in general influence the sorts of pressures that today's welfare states are facing. Of course, as is widely known, low fertility rates stress the contributory foundation of many welfare state programs like public pensions. Beyond that, however, the postwar welfare states were built on the assumption that most families were of the traditional nuclear variety. But today women are less inclined to work in the family performing unpaid labor, such as caring for children and aging parents. They are entering the paid labor force at increasing rates, divorce rates are rising, and alternative family forms are emerging. These changes are hitting some countries harder than others. In the Nordic countries, where welfare states have long provided care for children and the elderly, the effects of these family changes have not been as great. But in southern European countries, where traditional Catholic family values obtain, and, as a result, the state does not absorb much of these responsibilities, changes in family life have generated tremendous pressure on welfare states as the family-based system of supports has started to crumble. In short, according to Esping-Andersen, it is not globalization but changes in the world of families that is causing the most problems for welfare states.

Sociologists have also shown that welfare retrenchment involves more than just social policy expenditures, although this is what receives almost all the attention in the IPE/ CPE literature. Hence, Korpi argues, among others, that contrary to the conventional wisdom, there *has* been much welfare state retrenchment in many countries since the mid-1970s. By retrenchment he means "policy changes involving or implying cuts in social rights in ways that are likely to increase inequality among citizens" (2003: 591). This is because many West European governments have abandoned full-employment policy—a cornerstone of the postwar European welfare state. As a result, they have experienced significantly rising unemployment rates during this period. The return of mass unemployment, he suggests, must be seen as a major retrenchment, even though this is not something that receives much attention in the conventional IPE/CPE literature. Mass unemployment has occurred for various reasons, including internationalization of the economy, changing relations between nation-states due to the end of the Cold War, and the political-economic integration of Europe. Specifically, international trade increased and, in turn, unemployment rates become more dependent on fluctuations in imports and exports. Small countries found it especially difficult to maintain full employment as cross-border capital controls were dismantled and economic integration advanced. Furthermore, the creation of the European Monetary Union precipitated institutional changes, such as minimum fiscal deficit requirements, that tended to depress overall demand and thus further exacerbated unemployment problems in member countries. In sum, for Korpi and others the abandonment of full-employment policy has been tantamount to a major reworking of the social contract established in Western Europe after the end of the Second World War.

According to some sociologists, the causal link between international political-economic affairs and the transformation of domestic social rights policies involves a normative explanation. For example, John Skrentny (1996, 1998) analyzed changing US civil rights policy—an episode in US history that involved not only the passage of the Civil Rights Act but also a burst of welfare-state building and expansion. According to Skrentny, during the late 1940s and early 1950s, international norms changed and increasingly favored democratic reform world-wide. This normative shift was led by the United States to help stop the international spread of communism after the Second World War. The change in international norms was a blessing for the US civil rights movement because it brought increasing international pressure on Washington for African-Americans to receive equal protection under the law. This made US policymakers more vulnerable on normative grounds to pressure from the civil rights movement and provided an important political opening that went a long way toward ensuring the movement's success in changing national civil rights law. In turn, as others have shown, this empowered African-Americans politically in ways that helped bolster a slew of new welfare programs (Piven and Cloward 1971). Of course, this line of research resonates not only with the sociological emphasis on norms, but also with the more general trend among IPE scholars to take seriously the importance of normative causes in international affairs (e.g. Katzenstein 1996b).

Conclusion

I have argued that a variety of sociological literatures are relevant for IPE. Some of them have received notice in the IPE and CPE literatures, but more often than not they have been relegated to the side-lines. This is unfortunate because the insights of sociology improve our understanding of the international political economy. These insights include the identification of normative and ideational determinants of political-economic phenomena and diffusion in addition to the material determinants typically favored in IPE. The influence of professions in the rise of neoliberalism is a case in point. Sociologists have also recognized the importance of translation as an integral part of the diffusion process. Furthermore, they have provided insights about the social outcomes of international political-economic activity as well as the economic outcomes upon which IPE tends to concentrate. And sociologists have explored the importance of networks and institutional heterogeneity in all of this. Moreover, sociologists have contributed to the debates about welfare state reform by showing—contrary to much IPE and CPE scholarship—that in certain respects retrenchment has been substantial and that class (and family) forces remain an important determinant of welfare policy during the recent globalization era.

Much of the sociological literature discussed here is from sociologists in the United States. Because much of the IPE literature has also been produced by US scholars (Gill and Law 1988: 7–8), it is especially curious that much of the relevant sociology—which has emerged in their own backyard—has been side-lined by most of them. Why has this happened?

The most obvious reason is that at least in US social science the professional boundaries separating academic disciplines and sub-disciplines are formidable. This is clear, for instance, in economics where institutional economics has long since been marginalized professionally by formal theorists, modelers, and neoclassicists (Yonay 1998). Certainly within sociology there is much less conversation between sub-disciplines, such as political and economic sociologists, than one might expect. Indeed, when people inside the American Sociological Association mobilized in the mid-1990s to establish a professional section on economic sociology within the organization, there was considerable concern among some other sections in the organization that this would threaten their memberships and compromise their professional standing. So, if this is what happens *within* disciplines, it is not surprising that meaningful conversation *across* disciplines should be rare, and that the conversation within IPE/CPE would often exclude the work of sociologists.

But there may be another reason why sociology has been side-lined. The lines of broad paradigmatic debate in IPE and CPE have been rather sharp. In particular, realist or rational choice views have been pitted against institutionalist views (e.g. Thelen and Steinmo 1992). And more recently a third theoretical position has emerged, which emphasizes the importance of ideas, belief systems, and discursive structures (e.g. Blyth 2002; Goldstein and Keohane 1993; Katzenstein 1996b). In sociology, these debates are not as pronounced. In particular, rational choice theory has not been as dominant an intellectual presence as it has in IPE and CPE. Hence, somewhat less attention has been spent by sociologists attacking it from various other perspectives. And sociologists have been more inclined to accept the importance of ideas (i.e. norms, values, cognitive frames) without a fight. In other words, the intellectual battle lines have been drawn differently in sociology. This makes it difficult for sociologists and IPE/CPE scholars to find much common theoretical ground upon which to build alliances and, in turn, recognize each other's work. Perhaps with a growing common interest in globalization this will change.

Acknowledgments

Thanks for comments go to Mark Blyth, John Hall, Alex Hicks, and Andrew Schrank.

17

Economic history and the international political economy

Michael J. Oliver

It is not a particularly original observation, but one nevertheless worth insisting on, that though economists are very well trained to specify and declare their assumptions when they embark on statistical calculations or algebraic expositions of economic theory, their boasted rigour and intellectual precision tends suddenly to desert them whenever they refer to some general concept or goal which, though it seems to fall broadly into the field of economics, is really highly political.

(Strange 1970a: 737)

This opening salvo from a review essay by Susan Strange in 1970 was one of a series of pleas for scholars to avoid academic apartheid which became the launching pad for international political economy (IPE) (Strange 1970b, 1971, 1972). Since the early 1970s, scholars have moved toward combining international economics and international organization and have taken the politics of the international economy far more seriously, although there is still a way to go before the IPE is truly interdisciplinary. Arguably, economic history and IPE share a lot of common ground, and the recent growth in historical IPE, with its strong links to monetary history, has meant that the IPE scholar has now truly invaded the monetary historian's turf. It is an invasion to be welcomed if it brings with it new ideas, methods, and approaches that further our knowledge and understanding of international monetary issues and move economic historians away from a strictly economic focus. There are signs, however, that some of the recent work in historical IPE is in danger of being dismissed by economic historians, just when IPE has undertaken a very positive step toward using archives.

To consider these issues, the chapter is divided into three sections. The first section explores the relationship between economic history and IPE. The second section examines three specific examples of recent work on the Bretton Woods period and some limitations with the work from the perspective of the economic historian. The third section considers how economic history and IPE can forge greater links for future research.

IPE and economic history: what are they all about?

In a volume focused on IPE, it might seem strange to begin defining what the subject is and reminding readers where it came from, but it is important for the discussion that

280

follows on economic history. According to Tooze (1984: 2), IPE is "an area of investigation, a particular range of questions and a series of assumptions about the nature of the international 'system' and how we understand this 'system.'" While the roots of IPE go back to the seventeenth and eighteenth centuries, its rebirth followed the crisis in the sub-field of international relations in the 1970s. The break-up of fixed exchange rates within the Bretton Woods system, instability in international finance, supply-side shocks and the rise of OPEC (to name but a few of the problems of the 1970s) were not able to be explained within traditional international relations theory. Moreover, economists who had previously examined international politics through institutional economics became less interested as the discipline moved towards statistical and mathematical models (Ravenhill 2008a). The lacuna was filled by IPE, concerned with the "politics of international economic relations" (Spero 1977; Strange 1988: 12) and the focus of IPE became "the manner in which the rise and fall of state power, the politics of national economic policymaking and international economic agreements impinge upon the exchange (i.e. trade) relations between national economies" (Langley 2002: 4).

The distinction that has blown up between orthodox and what is sometimes termed the "new IPE" over the last thirty years is worth dwelling on for the purpose of this chapter. As Langley's (2002: 4–7) brief survey has shown, orthodox IPE is derived from neo-liberal political economy, and in epistemological terms it tends to share with neo-liberalism a combination of empiricist epistemology and positivist methodology. Its specific areas of investigation have been world money and finance and in particular, how stable international monetary relations are created and maintained. In contrast, the new IPE, with its focus on global political economy, world economy, and world orders has examined social movements and social forces, inter alia. This new IPE challenges the traditional line of enquiry couched in neo-liberal terms. It questions the assumption that actors are rational and it expresses the view that stability and order should not be explained in terms of utility maximizing actors but rather by structurally contingent forms of alliances and identities.

As Gill and Law (1989: 475–76) have noted about the work of Robert Cox—a leading proponent of new IPE—the emphasis on social forces in his work "points to a more comprehensive and flexible approach to the question of structural change than that provided in various mechanistic 'modes of economism' in the literature." Subsequent developments in new IPE have led to what has been described as "Historical International Political Economy" with an approach that "is characterised by a concern with structured social practices, social change, social space, social time and social orders as the principal categories for inquiry" (Langley 2002: 10). However, as Cohen remarks about Cox's work in his excellent essay on the differences between what he terms American and British IPE:

> Because of the high degree of historical contingency in his approach, it is difficult to reduce his insights to a concise set of logical theorems. Because of the lengthy time perspective of his analysis, it is difficult to convert his conclusions into empirically falsifiable propositions. And because of his propensity to mix positivist observation and moral judgments, it is difficult even to assess the fundamental soundness of his reasoning. So rather than engage Cox directly, scholars in the US have found it easier simply to dismiss or ignore him.
>
> (Cohen 2007: 211)

Yet it is far harder to dismiss the key ingredient of IPE—history—without which "international relations (and IPE) cannot identify the kinds of patterns of which they are so fond" (Higgott 2007: 165). But what sort of history are we talking about?

Arguably we are talking about economic history. Economic historians examine themes ranging from trade, manufacturing, technology, transportation, industrial organization, labor, agriculture, servitude, demography, education, economic growth, the role of government and regulation, and money and banking. Unlike the majority of economists, economic historians "do not claim to provide an account of events which is grounded either in axiomatic theory or in the discovery of empirical laws" (Britton 2002: 106). Neither do they approach their subjects with a narrow methodological perspective, and before the recent demise of economic history departments in the UK, the emphasis of the subject in many universities from the 1960s was balanced between economic and social history. This was largely the result of E. P. Thompson's (1963) classic work, which thrust the importance of social history onto what had been the preserve of economic history. However, the more forward-looking purveyors of economic history had always eschewed a parochial approach to the discipline. Bland et al. (1931: v) noted "that economic history cannot be studied apart from constitutional and political history" and G. M. Trevelyan (1946: vii) bluntly stated that "without social history, economic history is barren and political history is unintelligible."

If cultural, political, social and economic perspectives are employed then the discipline allows a far wider and more rounded understanding of historical episodes. The economic historian can embrace qualitative or quantitative methods. To be sure, the emphasis given to the more mathematical methodology in economic history—known as cliometrics—is now an established part of the profession, but even if they had wanted to, the cliometricians cannot quash the other approaches (Lyons et al. 2007). For example, although the historiography of the Industrial Revolution has become steadily more quantitative since the work of Crafts (1985) and Harley (1982), it is impossible to imagine how a period of such profound economic and social transformation cannot be fully explored without recourse to a variety of methodological approaches.

The Industrial Revolution and many other areas besides hold little interest for IPE scholars. What concerns IPE are the international dimensions of issues surrounding money and finance, and to understand these, scholars have to use the work of financial and monetary historians. A brief survey of the citations in the IPE literature comes up with the names of the most prominent monetary and financial historians, which include Michael Bordo, Barry Eichengeen, Harold James, and Charles Kindleberger. Each of these authors writes as an economic historian in the broadest definition of the term. Whether they have been trained in neo-classical economics (Bordo) or international economics (Kindleberger), or even if they currently hold chairs in history (James) or political science (Eichengreen), each has a solid grounding in economic history. Moreover, the impact of the work by these authors on the economic history profession is simply impossible for IPE scholars to ignore.

Consider Kindleberger's (1973) work on the absence of a single dominant power (a leader) in the inter-war years. His original discussion, which related to a specific historical episode, has been applied to "virtually every setting in which nations interact" (Kirshner et al. 1997: 340) and has been very influential on work in IPE (Cohen 2008b). The gradual morphing of Kindleberger's initial argument through the writings of Gilpin (1975a) and Krasner (1976), until the presence of a single dominant power was labeled the theory of hegemonic stability by Keohane (1980), was perhaps unsurprising for political scientists seeking to raise (and answer!) the "big questions" in IPE. However, it would come as little surprise to economic historians if hegemonic stability "theory" failed to replicate in other settings. Moreover, when Keohane (1984) questioned the analytical underpinnings and empirical applicability of the thesis, Kindleberger (1986: 841) responded in a review of Keohane's book that he was "uncomfortable" with the theory. By then, however, hegemonic stability theory had led onto an investigation of institutions and their role in governing global economic relations, culminating in Krasner's (1983) book on regime theory, and the argument that a single powerful state (a hegemon) was required for the establishment and smooth operation of a stable international monetary system, had taken hold.

The economic historian, meanwhile, waited patiently until Barry Eichengreen produced two challenges to hegemonic stability theory based on his detailed historical work grounded in economic theory. The first was a challenge to the monetary implications of the theory. Eichengreen (1989: 267) argued that in the two most notable instances of hegemony—the UK in the second half of the nineteenth century and the US after World War II—the leading economic power influenced the form of the international monetary system but had been "incapable of dictating the form of the monetary system." In short, while hegemonic stability theory was helpful in understanding the "relatively smooth operation of the classical gold standard and the early Bretton Woods system, as well as some of the difficulties of the interwar years ... much of the evidence is difficult to reconcile with the hegemonic stability view" (Eichengreen 1989: 287). The second challenge took the argument directly back to Kindleberger's initial study. Eichengreen (1992) argued that inadequate cooperation, and historically specific imbalances in the global economy, were to blame for inter-war instability, and not the failure of hegemonic leadership.

As economic historians examine specific episodes in the past and are not necessarily looking for generalized laws across time and space, there might be a conflict between what IPE wants to do and how it does it, and what economic history wants to do and how it does it. However, the gulf between monetary history and IPE is not as wide as it is between a monetary economist and IPE. Consider the response of the monetary economist who reviewed Strange (1998): "it is always difficult for an economist to read and benefit from the writings of international political economy experts, because of the difference in conceptualisation between the disciplines" (Cobham 2000: F260).

Until recently, one of the most serious criticisms which an economic historian could level against work in IPE was that it was predominately based on secondary sources. If, as Bearce (2007: 32) notes, scholars of international monetary policy have to be aware of the gap between "words and deeds," archival documents are a valuable resource for providing insights that the secondary literature cannot always deliver. Arguably, this would help to address one of the most important criticisms that Lukauskas (1999: 263) has made of research in IPE, namely that "it is not explicit about which actors, private or public (and which groups among these), should be the analytical focus and what their policy preferences are." To be sure, archival work alone cannot fully address this or the two other criticisms that Lukauskas levels against IPE—that the links between security and financial and monetary policy are largely ignored and that scholars have not analyzed how the size and power of states affects the constraints imposed on them by growing financial integration. Nevertheless, new IPE has made some strides toward economic history and we now turn to examine a selection of this work.

Historical IPE and the international monetary system

The evolution of the international monetary system (IMS) has fascinated political scientists almost as much as it has economic historians. Yet even approaching the subject it is impossible not to stumble over semantics. Most economists and economic historians would be happy to define the IMS as a "set of arrangements, rules, practices and institutions" (Solomon 1977: 5). For political scientists, however, the word "regime" is frequently substituted for "system," hence Keohane's (1980: 132) definition of a regime as "the norms, rules and procedures that guide the behavior of states and other important actors." Elsewhere, I have been content to use system and regime interchangeably (e.g. Aldcroft and Oliver 1998; Oliver 2006) but would agree with Eichengreen that the phrase "international monetary regime" is a broader framework which embeds the rules

> within a set of implicit understandings about how economic policymakers will behave (promises to coordinate macroeconomic policies or to provide loans in times of convertibility crisis, for example) ... the international monetary regime may involve issues that impinge indirectly, such as trade policy or diplomatic action.
>
> (Eichengreen 1989: 289)

In any case, the three systems that have been studied are the Gold Standard era (lasting from roughly the 1870s until 1914); Bretton Woods (which most historians generally date as having existed between 1944 and the early 1970s); and the period of generalized floating since 1973.

It would probably be fair to say that of the three systems, Bretton Woods has attracted the most attention from political scientists. After all, it was from the work of Cooper (1968), Kindleberger (1970, 1973), and Strange (1971) on the politics of Bretton Woods which encouraged the development of IPE. This work was added to such that by the end of the 1990s, there was a significant number of monographs which focused on Bretton Woods (Block 1977; Ruggie 1982; Gowa 1983; Helleiner 1994; Kirshner 1995). However, the move to historical IPE with an emphasis on archival work has been a phenomenon during this decade. How well has it been done, and how has the economic history profession received it? Three particular episodes are considered below, two of which do use archives. Peter Burnham has re-examined the UK monetary authorities' decision not to float the pound in the early 1950s (known as Operation Robot) using an extensive range of archival material. By contrast, Jacqueline Best's recent book on financial governance under the Bretton Woods regime does not use archival work, but I want to use her work to highlight one area that IPE scholars might wish to consider in more detail. Finally, Francis Gavin's work on the US's relations with Western Europe between 1958 and 1971 does use archival documents, and attempts to link the politics of security and financial and monetary policy.

Operation Robot

The background to the discussions on floating the pound stemmed from sterling's devaluation in 1949. Initially, Britain's external economic position improved but by 1951 problems of external economic management had become severe. The balance of payments had swung sharply into deficit and by December 1951 the dollar reserves had dwindled to such a degree that they were lower than at any time since the war. Although sterling was technically inconvertible, and hence immune to shifts in hot money, a cheap sterling market had emerged. Overseas holders of sterling were becoming increasingly adept at bypassing exchange control restrictions and converting their sterling into dollars (TNA 1955). Although this trade did not directly dent the reserves, it did damage confidence in the currency, because of the disparity between the official and unofficial rates. The fact that the pound was officially inconvertible also posed a threat to sterling's international role, because it appeared that the sterling area was less prepared than the US to accept continued inconvertibility and consequently there was the risk that the area might unravel (TNA 1952).

This potential crisis for the UK, and by implication, the fledgling Bretton Woods agreement, called for urgent action, particularly as the Treasury had estimated that the reserves would fall to $1.4 billion by June 1952, the bedrock figure below which emergency action would have to be taken. On February 28, 1952, the Treasury and the Bank of England presented proposals to the Cabinet that the pound should be floated; however, they were narrowly rejected. A year later, a revised proposal was put to the Cabinet but this too was rejected.

Operation Robot has been examined in detail by two economic historians, Scott Newton (2004) and Sir Alec Cairncross (1985: 234–71), but for the political scientist there is great drama in this historical episode, both from an internal (British) perspective on the future of Britain in the international economy, and also because of the impact floating would have had on the entire international monetary system. Peter Burnham's (2003) account has mined the archives to an enormous extent but his arguments are controversial. He makes the argument that if the float had been adopted, the EEC would not have been formed and that for Britain, floating would have "encouraged structural adjustment and jettisoned the politicized form of economic management … which ensnared governments until the late 1970s" (Burnham 2003: 185). More broadly, if adopted, Operation Robot would have "transformed the international political economy" (Burnham 2003: 2). One of the problems with his approach is that it does not consider a well thought out counterfactual. Per contra, Bordo and Eichengreen have undertaken a counterfactual on what the world would have looked like if the Great Depression had not occurred (Bordo and Eichengreen 1998: 406). In this, they conclude that because of Britain's experience with floating in the 1920s, even in the absence of the Great Depression, policymakers would have been suspicious of floating after World War II and thus Robot would not have been adopted.

Moreover, the reviewer of Burnham's book in the *Economic History Review*—a respected economic historian of the 1950s—took issue with his suggestion that had the fixed rate been abandoned and floating undertaken, and had the destruction of the international political economy occurred, then Britain would have been re-established as a leading power in the world. The criticism is worth quoting in full:

> if I had been a Conservative minister who was presented with this argument in 1952, I would have wanted substantive answers to questions such as: was Britain really suffering "creeping paralysis" in the early 1950s? (It was certainly not suffering from "falling productivity" as Burnham states). Was the economic situation, both domestically and internationally, really so bad that a gamble on the scale of Robot, with the unknowns and uncertainties involved, was required? Were there not alternatives with regard to Britain's competitiveness? And perhaps most relevant of all, would I be re-elected if Robot was introduced?
>
> (Rollings 2004: 428)

285

Thus, the economic historian criticizes the political scientist for not giving the political dimension enough consideration!

Bretton Woods and the Gold Pool

By contrast, an IPE book which steers between the realist approach of Block (1977) and the constructivist approach of Ruggie (1982) and Helleiner (1994) has been written by Jacqueline Best (2005). Her book seeks to develop a theory of political-economy ambiguity in an account of the history of financial governance under the Bretton Woods regime. Unlike Burnham, she has not made use of any archival material. This is unfortunate because one area which she does not consider, the Gold Pool, is a rich area for IPE scholars to examine using archival material. The Gold Pool involves issues surrounding the collective interest versus the national interest, the limits of cooperation and coordination and the ever important question of power (the decline of the dollar and sterling).

Consider the history of the Gold Pool (TNA 1975; Eichengreen 2007: 43–52; Hamilton 2008). Gold was the anchor in the post-1944 Bretton Woods system, with the dollar pegged to gold and the currencies of other member countries pegged to the dollar. The price of gold had been fixed at $35 per ounce as far back as January 1934 and although the spot price of gold was market-determined (in London), its price was influenced by official intervention.

The difficulty that arose was that the London market price could rise relative to the official price, thereby creating an incentive for central banks to buy gold from the US at the lower price in exchange for dollar-denominated assets already in their possession and to sell it on the London market at the higher price. The worry was that the market price could rise to a level which could not be matched by the official price and would encourage central banks to buy gold from the US and sell it at a higher price in the market. The US might even be forced to raise the official price of gold or embargo official sales of gold if central banks began to convert their dollar reserves into gold.

From 1958 there was a constant fear that the ratio of dollar liabilities to gold would increase to a level that could cause a loss of confidence in the dollar and lead to a run on gold. In October 1960, there was a spike in the market price of gold to more than $40 an ounce, forcing the US to sell $350 million of gold to the Bank of England to stabilize the market. In 1961, a combination of political and economic uncertainty caused by the erection of the Berlin Wall and a widening US deficit encouraged further upward demand for gold.

The US suggested to its Western allies that rather than taking on the entire cost of stabilizing the official price of gold alone, the price of gold in the London market could be stabilized by the formation of a "Gold Pool." The Bank of England would act as the controller of an international reserve stock of gold, fed by the central banks of the US, France, Belgium, Germany, Italy, Britain, Switzerland, and the Netherlands. Between 1961 and 1965, the price of gold was low and the supply of gold outstripped the demand. In this phase, the consortium became a net buyer of gold. However, with the worries about the weakness of sterling from 1964 and then a change in attitude on behalf of the French who wished to restore the gold standard, confidence in the Gold Pool began to wane (Bordo et al. 1998). Increased speculation by private investors and an increasing demand for gold for commercial and industrial purposes pushed the price higher, so that the Gold Pool became a net seller. The price in the London market came dangerously near the upper limit of $35.20 per ounce and by the middle of 1967 rarely dropped below that figure. There was a scramble for gold in June 1967 at the time of the Six Day War and holders of sterling moved into gold after the devaluation of sterling in November. Further unease was caused on November 21, when *Le Monde* leaked the news that the French had withdrawn from the Gold Pool in June. Between November 1967 and March 1968, the pool sold $3 billion of gold (Eichengreen 2007: 56–71). Further selling was undertaken after the publication of the US balance of payments figures for 1967 in March 1968, which revealed a deficit of $3.6 billion (Gavin 2004: 173–80). On March 13 it was rumored that Italy had withdrawn from the pool and by the week ending March 14, $792 million had been sold to the market (TNA 1975: 27). The gold market was subsequently closed on March 14.

Is it the case that you can only be an economic historian to appreciate the significance of the Gold Pool? No, but it does require a more in-depth historical investigation which can go beyond the comfort zone of political scientists. If this is done, however, it becomes apparent that the operation of the Gold Pool reflected a classic case of collective interest versus the individual interest and, as such, would make a fascinating study for political economists (it could be a box in chapter 3 of the next edition of Ravenhill's (2008a) textbook). On the one hand, the collective interest was clearly defined: all countries participating in the Gold Pool wanted to maintain the dollar peg to gold, which anchored the international monetary system. For individual countries, however, it made sense for them to continue to exchange dollars for gold at the Federal Reserve before the US either raised the price of gold or closed the gold window.

The most fundamental problem was that the operation of the Gold Pool could not prevent the wider problem that was inherent in the Bretton Woods system, namely the increase in the ratio of dollars to gold, which grew ever larger as world trade expanded and with it, the demand for international reserves. As Eichengreen (2007: 63–68) has discussed, however, there were other reasons for the collapse of the pool. First, those taking part in the consortium did not share a common understanding of the problem they were trying to solve (compare the attitude of the French to that of the Americans); second, there was no enforcement mechanism to abide by a set of rules; third, there was a group of developing countries and Middle East oil producers outside the cartel who could both free ride and undermine the operation of the Gold Pool; and finally, there was an aura of secrecy surrounding the operations of the Gold Pool, and the implicit agreement by European central banks not to convert dollars into gold conflicted with the IMF's articles of agreement.

The break-up of Bretton Woods

The demise of the Gold Pool also marked the beginning of the end for the Bretton Woods system, and an account that has used archival work to examine this episode has been written by Gavin (2004). Gavin's book examines money and security issues and the US's relations with Western Europe from the late 1950s through 1971. The treatment by Gavin of the *politics* of international monetary relations has been praised by Eichengreen (2004) and it is refreshing to find an account which uses the archives to report what US policymakers were considering and the alternatives to the Bretton Woods. For instance, one of the more radical plans (known as "Plan X"), which the Federal Reserve had considered in 1966, was to use a sterling devaluation to abandon fixed exchange rates and dollar–gold convertibility (Gavin 2004: 169–71). Unfortunately, one of the limitations of Gavin's study is that because it only uses the US archives, it does not provide any comparisons to the decision making process in other countries. This omission is compounded because Gavin fails to consider the secret talks which the Federal Reserve and US Treasury set up with the UK and EEC countries on plans for a more flexible exchange rate system after the election of President Richard Nixon (Oliver and Hamilton 2007: 499–502), all of which would have been useful to consider in the power and privilege debate.

Indeed, it is precisely this sort of close reading of the circumstances of a specific historical context which is required to challenge or illuminate a priori views of what leads states to cooperate or not in international monetary policymaking (*pace* Lukauskas 1999: 268). The recent archival work by historians into British, French, and German policymaking after 1968 demonstrates the extent to which governments wrestled between adhering to their domestic objectives and stabilizing the exchange rate (Chivvis 2006; Gray 2007; Oliver and Hamilton 2007) and represents a serious challenge to "embedded liberalism," a concept which has never really found favor amongst economic historians.

Conclusion: a way forward for economic history and IPE?

Given the synergies that exist between IPE and economic history, where are the opportunities and pitfalls in greater collaboration? There are two problems with future alliances which need to be addressed, and two opportunities which could take IPE and economic history into new directions. The first stumbling block is language. A few years ago, one prominent British economist—who is not anti-political science and who is pro-economic history—remarked to the author that he found the language of political scientists "rather confusing." An economic historian who reviewed Cohen (1998) was quick to note that economists would soon become "exasperated" by the political science jargon in the book (White 2000: 951). Even a former APSA president has remarked that "if we are to engage in civic deliberation with our fellow citizens, we need to learn to speak ordinary English" (Putnam 2003: 252). Gilpin's (2001) magisterial book shows that a common language is possible and that both disciplines should be able to understand each other. However, some of Gilpin's criticisms of economics lead onto a second stumbling-block, namely, the political slant of new IPE. The number of historical IPE books that are critical about the capitalist system and the neo-liberal framework of the international monetary system dwarf any that are supportive. Economic historians such as Forrest Capie (2008) who reviewed Burn (2006); Catherine Schenk (1995) who reviewed Helleiner (1994), and Battilossi (2006) who reviewed Best (2005), all make the same point about the bias in each book they reviewed.

There is a golden opportunity for IPE to examine the failure of international financial markets and the assumption made by economists that markets are rational, when history clearly shows that they are not (Kirshner et al. 1997: 340–43). It is not that the efficient markets hypothesis is incorrect, but that the theory is incomplete. Thus the usual version of the efficient markets hypothesis, namely that investors cannot consistently outperform a market making use of existing available information, should be more accurately expressed as "investors cannot consistently outperform a market making use of existing available information without taking unacceptably high risk of loss, bearing in mind the way risk of loss can vary with the circumstances of an investor and the behaviour of a market" (Pepper and Oliver 2006: 71–72). This crucial caveat opens up the field of behavioral finance and economics to IPE, and as Elms (2008) has suggested, a fascinating research agenda awaits.

A second opportunity would be to focus more on the role of ideas. Although there have been attempts to do this, in particular by McNamara (1998) and Blyth (1997, 2002), there does seem to be a reluctance for IPE to leave the more traditional concerns with power. Yet, as Hugh Heclo (1974: 305–6) has remarked "Politics finds its sources not only in power but also in uncertainty—men collectively wondering what to do … Governments not only 'power' … they also puzzle. Policy-making is a form of collective puzzlement on society's behalf." Collective puzzlement—the role of ideas—needs more work by IPE scholars but it could be conducted in tandem with economic historians, enabling the nature of ideas to be examined within historically specific settings and where the archives can reveal more about policy debates and why certain policies were chosen and others rejected.

In any case, even if there is no interest within IPE or economic history for collaboration, as Maliniak and Tierney (2007) have shown, over the past fifteen years the prevalence of formal models and econometrics in IPE research has given political scientists the tools to act like economists. Eichengreen (1998: 1012) has urged scholars of international relations "to move in the direction of formulating parsimonious models and clearly refutable null hypotheses, and toward developing empirical techniques that will allow those hypotheses to be more directly confronted by the data."

The message for IPE in this chapter goes further. Rather than becoming inductive econometricians or smart economists, if IPE scholars intend to do historical work then they should think more like historians. Each of the three episodes which were examined above serves to reinforce this. With Operation Robot, Burnham has used an excellent range of archival sources but he lacks the historian's ability to sift through the material and to provide a more nuanced perspective. Conversely, with Gavin's account of the demise of Bretton Woods, we are only given the perspective from the US archives, which limits the scope of the study. Finally, as the example with the Gold Pool made clear, archival work can raise many interesting questions germane to IPE. Clearly, there is plenty of material from monetary and financial history which awaits the analysis of the IPE scholar, but for a considered understanding, it must be examined with the historian's hand.

18

Everyday international political economy

John M. Hobson and Leonard Seabrooke

In recent years a new perspective, which might be termed *everyday international political economy* (EIPE), has begun to emerge within the discipline of IPE. Still only in its formative phase, its central task is to map out the relationship between the actions of everyday actors and the global economy and, in effect, to bring the everyday into the study of IPE. This movement is overwhelmingly concerned with highlighting how change in the world economy requires practices to be engrained in the lives of non-elite actors, and that such agents have actual or potential agency in transforming their own political and economic environments. When aggregated, changes in the everyday then have knock-on effects that lead to change in the world economy. In this chapter we suggest that there are now emerging two variants of EIPE; what we call the *everyday life* and *everyday politics* approaches.

The former contains a strong emphasis on *disciplinary logics* while the latter is a more *action*-based approach. Overall, EIPE imports insights from the everyday literature that was pioneered outside of the discipline. As we explain, the disciplinary/everyday life approach draws from social theorists, such as Henri Lefebvre (1971, 1991b) and Michel Foucault (1980), while the actions-based/everyday politics approach draws more from the political-anthropological works of James Scott (1976, 1985), Benedict J. Tria Kerkvliet (1990, 2005) and others. But what unites these variants is that in seeking to bring the everyday actor into focus they issue different visions of the world economy to that provided by mainstream accounts.

As we explain in the first section, we see conventional IPE, or what we call *regulatory IPE* (RIPE from henceforth), as overly concerned with providing a purely top-down understanding of a *small number of big and important things* that exist within the world economy. These comprise principally trade and financial flows, as well as international economic regulatory institutions and hegemony. Focussing only on the elites of the world economy, states, regions, and hegemons, RIPE necessarily obscures the everyday lives of ordinary people from view. How the world economy is played out at the everyday level of ordinary people, and how such people might even impact the world economy is a lacuna that everyday political economists seek to fill.

EIPE also seeks, albeit to varying degrees, to bring into focus how the actions of everyday actors are important vehicles for issuing change in the world economy. We stress that exploring this territory does not simply provide new information on how elite actors can do what they do. To an important extent the approach focuses on *bottom-up* agency, though the extent to which structures of power are also factored in alongside this will vary from author to author as well as more generally between the two major EIPE variants. However, before we set out the two variants of EIPE, it makes sense to begin by outlining the essential characteristics of RIPE.

Regulatory IPE: who governs and who benefits?

In Table 18.1 we lay out three major variants of IPE. The first two we categorize under the heading of RIPE and distinguish them from EIPE.

RIPE's central organizing question in effect asks "who governs and how is international order regulated?" Such a question selects certain structures or institutions or particular elites as the object of study. And such a posture leads naturally on to the creation of a highly parsimonious framework, which in turn speaks directly to the ontological ordering principle of "parsimony" that has been made famous by such IR scholars as Kenneth Waltz (1979) and Robert Keohane (1984). The proclaimed advantage of ontological parsimony is that it simplifies the study of the international system, or the complex world economy, into discrete, manageable chunks.

It bears noting that the traditional focus on *order* is to a large extent a function of the birth of the discipline at a particular time and place, which in turn imbued RIPE with a specific identity. RIPE was born primarily in the USA during the early 1970s when the world economy was going into recession. As such, its mandate was to find ways of restoring world order and global economic growth. Moreover, in the process mainstream IPE and IR scholars implicitly draw on liberal political theory. Hobbes finds his

Table 18.1 Juxtaposing regulatory and everyday IPE

	Regulatory IPE (neorealism/neoliberalism/ systemic constructivism)	Regulatory IPE (e.g. world systems theory)	Everyday IPE (everyday life and everyday politics variants)(sociological)
Organizing question	Who governs?	Who rules/benefits?	Who acts and how do their actions enable change?
Unit of analysis	Hegemons/great powers, international regimes, ideational entrepreneurs	Capitalist world economy, structures of rule	Everyday actors interacting with elites and structures
Prime empirical focus	Supply of order and welfare maximization by elites	Maintenance of the powerful and the unequal distribution of benefits	Social transformative *and* disciplinary processes enacted, or informed, by everyday actions
Locus of agency	Top-down	Top-down	The bottom-up/top-down nexus
Level of analysis	Systemic	Systemic	Complex/holistic
Ontology	Structuralist	Structuralist	Agential or structurationist
Epistemology	Rationalist/positivist or interpretivist	Rationalist/positivist	Interpretivist/post-positivist and Rationalist
Conception of change	Coercion/mimetic conformity	Coercion/Resistance	Emancipatory/defiance/ mimetic challenge/ axiorationality

approximate manifestation in neorealist hegemonic stability theory (henceforth HST), where a dominant hegemonic power takes the form of a benign global leviathan that supplies order and all other states accept this as an unspoken social contract. Conversely, in the absence of a hegemon the world economy devolves into a war of all against all (Kindleberger 1973; Gilpin 1987). The Lockean equivalent is that of regime theory/ neoliberal institutionalism, wherein states in the international system, like individuals in society, come together and, through an informal social contract, set up a loose set of international institutions or regimes which enable cooperation and long-term welfare maximization (Keohane 1984). These remain in place only so long as they continue to enhance the interests of states, given that states can choose to opt out of the informal social contract that underpins a particular regime.

Most recently, at least in the mainstream of IR, the emergence of "systemic constructivism" has largely taken the form of a Kantian analogy, where international cooperation between states is envisaged as yet more deeply entrenched than that specified by neoliberalism (e.g. Finnemore 1996a; Wendt 1999). Indeed, systemic constructivists are primarily interested in revealing the positive ways in which states are socialized into cooperation within an increasingly tight international society. Thus if the neorealist/ neoliberal debate is a synonym for the "conflict versus cooperation debate," then we envisage systemic constructivism as located on the right-hand side of neoliberalism, so to speak (Hobson 2000: 154–55).

These approaches have a tendency to be purely top-down, if not structuralist. Neorealist HST invests ontological primacy in the presence or absence of a hegemon under strict conditions of international anarchy (Gilpin 1987). It is certainly true that relative consent for the hegemon that is issued by the non-hegemonic states is a factor here. But consent, or its withdrawal, does not ultimately affect the exercise of hegemony (John Ruggie's 1982 work on the social purposes underpinning embedded liberalism in the post-war period provides an important exception in this regard though, of course, he is no neorealist). In general, hegemony is simply assumed to be accepted and there is only a small role here for states that do not belong to the club of great powers let alone everyday actors (either within or without the United States). Similarly, Keohane's parsimonious approach seeks to reify states and black-boxes social actors, at both the domestic and international levels. Thus he, in effect, invests state elites with ontological primacy without "being distracted by the details and vagaries of domestic politics and other variables at the level of the acting unit" (Keohane 1991: 41). As such, clashes among non-elites within a domestic or international context are of little interest for understanding change in the world economy. And inter-state cooperation, which secures both prosperity and order, is achieved entirely in the absence of social actor influence.

It might be assumed that constructivism offers a way out from this structuralist and statist-orientated framework by offering up the role of social norms and social actors. Certainly it has a very strong potential to do so. But for the most part, *systemic constructivists* tend to operate almost exclusively within the regulatory problematic. As noted above, ultimately those constructivists who focus principally on social international structures seek to show how order (and cooperation) can be yet more entrenched than is envisaged by the rationalist neoliberal institutional framework. And surprisingly, domestic society is often explicitly bracketed, with ideational elites seemingly acting entirely independently of domestic interests (see, for example, the more general critique in Schmidt 2007).

Even in earlier work from more sociologically inclined constructivists who pay attention to domestic sensitivities, special emphasis is placed on elite actors or norm entrepreneurs who come to prominence in times of uncertainty or crisis, and who promulgate new ways of ordering economies (Blyth 2002). Here ideas are understood as weapons wielded by big and powerful actors, who are backed by their own political and material resources in helping to push them through. As Colin Hay aptly points out, constructivists require a prominent elite actor to provide an "ideational focus for the reconstruction of the perceived self-interest of the population at large" (Hay 2004c: 210). Thus while the social constructivist field has developed at a quick pace to include more non-elites actors, it often tends towards a top-down focus (cf. Blyth 2007a; Seabrooke 2007a; Widmaier 2007).

In a complementary move, a second organizing question has also guided the study of IPE: "Who benefits?" This was initiated by world systems theory (WST henceforth), which views the world economy's central dynamic as governed by the structure of capitalism (e.g. Wallerstein 1974). Focussing on the capitalist world structure, the theory suggests that the world economy operates in favor of the rich Northern core, which gains through unequal exchange at the expense of the poor Southern periphery. Accordingly, as a wealth of scholars have pointed out, the study of the world economy is conducted through a highly rarified focus, dealing at the aggregate level of regional conflicts (i.e. North versus South). Thus we learn little, if anything, about how the structure of the world economy impacts the everyday lives of ordinary people. Moreover, the approach is necessarily unable to provide a picture of either bottom-up agency or change in the world economy (see Cox 1986; Payne 1998)—though it is worth noting that more recent versions of world systems theory have sought to overcome some of the problems associated with the traditional approach (see Chase-Dunn and Hall 1991; Frank and Gills 1996; Denemark et al. 2000; Hobson and Seabrooke 2007b: 8). Thus in virtually exorcizing the process of change, the approach veers closely toward structural-functionalism, thereby contributing to the regulatory approach's privileging of order over change.

Finally, it is worth noting that although rational choice and public choice perspectives focus on individual agents and bottom-up processes (e.g. Frey 1986), they nevertheless fit squarely within the regulatory framework by seeking to provide a *better* account of the sources of regulation and order. Furthermore, their rationalist epistemology posits a self-maximizing individual regardless of time and place or social context. This diverges from an everyday approach, which envisages actors' choices as being informed by historically and socially contingent identities and interests. Perhaps the most fundamental of differences between rational choice and EIPE is that for the former, individuals often *bandwagon* with the dominant or seek to dominate others. This can blind us to revealing everyday contestations to the exercise of power by elites.

More generally, perhaps the key underlying problem with RIPE is that in creating parsimonious frameworks that effectively focus on the *small number of big and important things*, it necessarily delimits that which is to be studied. Thus a central focus on hegemony (HST) or states in international regimes (neoliberalism) or the structure of the world system (WST) or elite norm entrepreneurs (constructivism) may lead us to overlook the myriad social processes that exist at the everyday level, many of which also shape the world economy. The key problem with delimiting which information we want to select in order to tell us about the world economy is that it leads to a number of distortions (a problem that key figures behind RIPE have complained about; see Katzenstein et al. 1998: 684). Key among these is a pervasive problem of seeking to "select winners," reflected in the space that is devoted in textbooks to analyzing the actions of US hegemony-as-winner, Japan (1980s) or China (the present) as potential contenders to hegemony, or strategies by which states can win in trade wars, etc. (Murphy and Tooze

1991a). Indeed this bias, both in terms of IPE teaching and research, can be found in most of the standard textbooks (for references see Hobson and Seabrooke 2007b: 10). This point deserves elaboration.

The standard textbooks reel off an almost identical series of topics and issues, often in virtually the same order and all of which are situated within a winner/loser dichotomy. They typically begin in 1944 with the Bretton Woods agreement and the rise of US hegemony as the principal guarantor of world order and global welfare maximization. The next chapter might look at international monetary management and the regulation of the fixed exchange rate system by the IMF, while the following chapter might recount the story of the IMF alongside the GATT to account for the spread of free trade and the concomitant growth of world trade. North–South issues are usually dealt with, although, consistent with the privileged focus on the powerful North, the story is one of *Southern failure*. Thus the calls for a NIEO in the 1970s on the back of the successful economic coup that was delivered by oil cartel power end with the failure of non-oil cartel power, thereby ensuring that prime focus should remain upon the North. We then receive a deepening of the story of *Third World failure* and *Northern hegemony*, with a strong focus on the Third World debt crisis and the various Northern plans and IMF structural adjustment programs that were imposed on the failing economies of the Southern debtors. Finally, while there is often a chapter on Japan and the East Asian NICs, this focus weakened with Japan's recession after 1991 and was effectively terminated with the 1997 East Asian financial crisis, thereby returning the focus to the US-as-winner.

None of this is to say that these topics are unworthy of consideration. But the problematic within which they are analyzed severely delimits the picture of the world economy and, inter alia, obscures the many other bottom-up constitutive processes that inform the world economy. For example, let us consider the sub-prime crisis. In IPE much of the attention on international financial relations within the last decade has been on explaining international financial crises and how to repair the international financial architecture (e.g. Cartapanis and Herland 2002; Robertson 2007). Reasonably, these analyses consider the role of large institutions, executive ministries, and international institutions in explaining why financial crises occur. Why would international investors place their money in debt tied to housing for people with bad credit ratings? The answer is that the current predatory crisis piggy-backed on a US financial system in which mortgage-backed securities were mainly the preserve of quasi-public institutions that grew, in part, from progressive rights discourses for non-elites since the Great Depression (Seabrooke 2008). With the standard analytical tools found in IPE we know little about a market that is big enough to force events such as bank nationalizations in other states (as with Northern Rock in the UK). The point here is that the development of the most recent financial crisis is difficult to understand without a conception of everyday politics, since explaining the motivations for the common actors (states, elites, international organizations) in these markets, as well as their conformity to ideal-types (the presence of quasi-public institutions arguably rubs up against common perceptions of the US as the exemplar of a liberal market economy), is difficult without a more bottom-up sociological understanding of everyday politics.

Our central claim is that we need to consider more than just elite actors in the world economy. Not surprisingly, the elite suppliers of order constitute only a very small minority of the world's population. Indeed, one may be forgiven for thinking that RIPE provides the impression that the study of the world economy can be gleaned by examining the actions of elites, especially within rich industrialized states, or those within international organizations (both public and private), while the remainder are but power-takers whose actions are inconsequential for the making of the world economy (cf. Tétreault and Lipschutz 2005: 167). However, elites do not operate within a social vaccum but find that their power and policies are to a not insignificant extent often mediated and refracted through the actions of everyday agents in all manner of ways.

A range of scholars are now developing various approaches which rethink IPE so as to move beyond a conventional top-down view, some of which overlap with our theme on everyday agency (Amoore 2002; Davies and Neimann 2002; Tickner 2003; Davies 2005; Tétreault and Lipschutz 2005; Watson 2005; Antoniades 2007; Langley 2008). Furthermore, more attention is now being paid to challenging conventional understandings on political and economic change through work that seeks to understand IPE from the perspective of non-core economies (Dunn and Shaw 2001; Tickner 2003; Phillips 2005).

Most importantly, a functionalist privileging of order and regulation that is bequeathed by elite actors desensitizes us to revealing transformations in the world economy that are sometimes enabled or promoted by bottom-up processes informed by everyday politics and everyday life. Asking *who acts?* rather than simply *who governs?* enables Everyday IPE to reveal new sites of agency wherein bottom-up sources of change lie. There are currently two broad ways of achieving this alternative vision: one which generally stresses potential sites of agency from a normative/emanicaptory standpoint, while the other concentrates on analyzing different types of actions undertaken by everyday actors. Before setting out our own actions-based approach, it is useful to begin by considering the disciplinary wing of EIPE.

IPE as everyday life: the logic of discipline

There is little doubt that there has been a surge of interest in everyday approaches to understanding change in the world economy in recent years. We suggest that two main approaches to everyday IPE are beginning to emerge, which may be differentiated by the logics that they focus upon. The first concentrates on a *logic of discipline* in *everyday life*, while the second concentrates on the *logic of action* within *everyday politics*. We stress that while we prefer an approach that places greater emphasis on the logic of action, nevertheless the best insights into why everyday politics and everyday life matter for the transformation of the world economy can only be obtained by treating both logics seriously. In this section we outline the work on the logic of discipline in everyday life, including its aims, background, and foci, before providing a critique of its weak points. In the following section we provide similar treatment of our preferred everyday politics approach.

It is fair to state that much of the work associated with everyday life within IPE draws a great deal of inspiration from a range of European social theorists, philosophers, and sociologists. Key among these thinkers is Henri Lefebvre(1971, 1991b) for his work on everyday life (also de Certeau 1984), and Michel Foucault (1980), for his ideas about governmentality and technologies of the self that ordinary actors replicate in their own lives. An important aspect of the everyday life approaches is the point that in order to understand how our world is constructed, who holds power, and who transforms political and economic environments, common assumptions must be challenged and de-naturalized (Bratsis 2006). In such a way, the naturalized picture of order in the world that is bequeathed to us by RIPE becomes subjected to critique. In particular, it is important to reveal the logic of discipline that runs through, informs, and replicates the everyday experiences of non-elite actors (Langley 2007), as well as to consider how ordinary actors internalize risks (Beck 1992). That is, order is not natural but is constructed through the inculcation of a logic of discipline.

To reveal the way in which this is transmitted, much emphasis is accorded to relationships of production and marketing, understood in broader sociological terms, referring to the social reproduction of everyday spaces and families, the marketing of lifestyles to be administered, and the introduction and normalization of processes associated with the acceleration of modern capitalism (Lefebvre 1971: 23; cf. Peterson 2003). These processes provide what we understand as a new *logic of discipline* that non-elite actors translate into their everyday lives. At this point, everyday life theorists place strong emphasis on structures of exploitation and, above all, seek to reveal how they manifest and are played out at the everyday level of ordinary people. The initial emphasis is on questioning how changing work practices or financial practices, initiated by elites and their institutions, lead to new constraints or disciplinary behavior (primarily self-disciplinary) on non-elite actors that is expressed through the production of a new common sense in their everyday lives

For example, pioneering work by Louise Amoore (2002, 2004) discusses how changes in workplace environments by managers seek to provide superior risk management for the firm, but are coupled with increasing uncertainty over wages, work practices, and workplace social environments for ordinary workers (see also Davies and Niemann 2002; Davies 2005). Amoore details in her work how management consultants have established new practices for human capital risk management that embrace risk (in the case of the failed Andersen consultancy embroiled in the Enron scandal) and introduce new kinds of uncertainty for ordinary workers. This is done by tracing how consultancies, prominent business intellectuals, national political leaders, and international economic institutions propagate the notion of increased labor market risk as closely associated with entrepreneurship (Amoore 2004: 176). Here contingency and uncertainty are embraced by consultants while workers perceive changes in work practice as introducing uncertain pay, heightened surveillance, increased home-work, and exploitation (Amoore 2004: 182). But the workers may also question their opportunities here. Overall, from the new work practices it is "the ambiguity of relationship between taking risks and those reaping the rewards that operates as a disciplinary force—the message is that, in an uncertain world, the winners could become losers, and the losers, if sufficiently enterprising, could become winners" (Amoore 2004: 184). In short, new practices destabilize certainty in the workplace not simply through worse conditions but also through the provisions of incentives that encourage workers to discipline themselves, such as increasing the amount of work they do at home. Amoore traces this new logic of discipline through areas like outsourcing, seeking to highlight how conceptions of the risks associated with globalization are actually mediated through everyday life by "firms, communities, and families" (Amoore 2004: 192). The new logic of discipline is naturalized not only by management consultants, but also by international economic institutions (like the World Bank) who propagate a notion of labor market risk as an exogenous force of globalization (Amoore 2004: 177). Increased labor market risk and uncertainty over work therefore becomes the everyday *common sense*.

Similarly, important work by Paul Langley (2007, 2008) on the pension fund saving schemes and mortgage loan systems examines how practices of saving and borrowing have been transformed at the macro level, to then examine how such changes introduce new attitudes, routines, and practices within everyday life for non-elites. As with work practices, the key finding here is the introduction of greater uncertainties into the everyday lives of non-elites as new methods for calculating pension benefits become more performance-based, and how the assessment of mortgage credit becomes standardized, isolating many from systems of privilege and exposing them to greater social and financial uncertainties. For example, in Langley's work on changes in mass investment culture in the US and the UK, he details how changes from "defined benefit" to "defined contribution" occupational pension provisions has transformed attitudes, in that now the "everyday investor typically understands his or her calculative risk-taking practices in financial markets, and the returns that are expected to follow, as integral to a successful life as a 'free' subject" (Langley 2007: 104; see also Aitken 2005). New logics of discipline are encouraged by governments and elites and, akin to Amoore's work practices, produce a scenario where "neoliberal governmental programs demand a similarly entrepreneurial engagement with financial market risks [from workers] in order to provide for retirement ... [through] new forms of financial self-discipline that include investment as a technology of risk" (Langley 2008: 92). Similar to Amoore's work, much of the evidence for a new logic of discipline comes from pronouncements from economic and political elites, intellectuals, and business journalists, placed within the context of changing institutional structures and regulations for saving and borrowing.

Langley's work also places a premium on identity politics within everyday life. In his work on mortgage finance Langley is interested in how:

> Income and class are likely to be far from the only determinants in everyday experiences of financial inequality and, especially in terms of borrowing, representations of an increasingly "included" middle-class and an "excluded" poor and low-income other may well be highly problematic.
>
> (Langley 2008: 13)

The evidence for inclusion and exclusion is drawn from tracing the emergence of expanded credit and the internationalization of more predatory types of financing, such as pawnbrokers and, especially, sub-prime mortgages (Langley 2008: 164–82).

In most of the literature we categorize as everyday life, structures of power receive considerable emphasis and the analysis ultimately invokes a structurationism, insisting that structures and agency entwine in complex ways. In this way, elite exploitative power and non-elite agency are treated holistically. Another example of this can be found in Matthew Patterson's recent work, which speaks within a "cultural political economy" context with a strong emphasis on daily life. In particular, he examines the role of cars in daily life and the international political economy. Paterson seeks to challenge what he refers to as the notion of "automobility"—"the conjoining of 'autonomy' and 'mobility' in such a way as to legitimize the imperatives for movement that underpin modernity in general and globalization in particular" (Paterson 2007: 7)—of which the car is the principal artifact. Paterson traces how cars contribute to environmental degradation, the replication of late capitalism and global injustice, are a symbol of autonomy and modernization, and undermine the potential for a more sustainable future through their enmeshment with everyday life. This is achieved through discussions of critiques of car culture, backlashes that assert cars as a *natural* source of autonomy, and how "greening" the car is constrained by "political economy and cultural politics" (Paterson 2007: 28). Paterson draws on a wide array of sources, from autobiography to pro-car town planning reforms in Birmingham (also, in Ottawa he is known to bicycle to work in winter), to public intellectuals (for and against cars), popular culture, advertising, car resistance movements' activities and publications, government and corporate policies, and others. Paterson's work, like Amoore's and Langley's, is indicative here of the normative agenda in the work on everyday life. A strong element of the broader work is the view that everyday life is being homogenized or colonized by changes in modern capitalism. As such, and as seen above, scholars working on everyday life tend to emphasize the presence of "technologies of the self" through new logics of discipline (cf. Gill 1995).

The second stage of the everyday life approach seeks to reintroduce the agency of everyday actors, focusing on bottom-up processes that mediate the logic of discipline. This can take various forms. For example, it can be a call to arms, such as in Paterson's work, where he concludes his work by seeing his:

> central task as greening the economic strategies of contemporary societies ... and greening "daily life," the sorts of identity which give meaning to daily practices which engender particular sorts of environmental futures. How can we build an economic strategy without the car and to shape people (or more precisely, given the governmentality logic, work so that people shape themselves) for whom cycling, walking and the train become the "normal" daily practice?
>
> (Paterson 2007: 235)

Paterson explicitly wishes us to consider "alternative daily practices which might recognize and reinvigorate the sense of self which recognizes obligations to others, communality, and so on" (Paterson 2007: 18). He also documents actual resistance in daily life, including the actions of movements to "Reclaim the Streets," and particularly "radical" environmentalists who opposed road constructions and received the scorn of the pro-car media (Paterson 2007: 10, 166–84). Identity plays an important role in the protest movement here, including appearance, and, associated with their protests, demonstrates that "existing societies could be resisted and alternatives pursued" (Paterson 2007: 183).

In detailing agency from the bottom-up, Langley also traces forms of dissent to the common sense of the contemporary neoliberal order. He discusses "credit art," in which artists depict modern consumerism and may call people to question its role in everyday life, as well as credit unions that provide an "ambiguous mode of dissent in everyday borrowing" (Langley 2008: 218, 228). More importantly, perhaps, Langley hints at the capacity for "shareholder activism" to provide a means of resistance to the encroachment of a disciplinary logic of late financial capitalism (discussed below). The general story here is that while everyday subjects are deeply compromised by logics of discipline (much of which they self-impose), there is agency to resist. And this agency to resist can be emboldened through a critique of everyday life in order to clarify the normative agenda.

In general, the agential side of the approach seeks to reveal the potential for ordinary actors to transform their everyday lives for the greater good, where this is understood as sound economic, social, political, and environmental goals preferred by the scholar. As such, the everyday life approach is tied closely to an emancipatory program and to an ethic of liberation. To our minds, the everyday life literature continues within the tradition of critical IPE scholars who have a vision of scholarship as an emancipatory project (Cox 1997), in that there is a strong focus on the potential for resistance to what are commonly considered neoliberal trends, particularly by the act of critiquing the production or construction of everyday life.

In sum, the everyday life literature is largely a critical one that seeks not only to reveal the impact of structures of exploitation on the everyday lives of ordinary people, but is also interested in revealing potential sites of agency. And to pre-empt the following discussion, it is helpful here to differentiate two conceptions of everyday agency: analytical and normative. The stress within the everyday life literature is locating potential emancipatory sites of normative agency, primarily by tracing how ordinary people seek to resist or find ways to critique the situation that they find themselves in. The critique seeks to reveal possible worlds and emancipatory routes for agency by making ordinary people more self-aware about their daily behavior. While the everyday politics approach is also concerned with emancipatory logics of action, nevertheless the key focus is on what might be called *analytical agency*. This refers to the everyday actions that promote and enable change in the world economy, whether such actions challenge or reinforce certain structures of power. Thus agency here is not limited to emancipatory frameworks, but is important because it enables the analyst to provide the picture of bottom-up processes of change in the world economy; a vision that is entirely missing within the RIPE literature. Let us, therefore, turn to our own preferred everyday politics approach.

IPE as everyday politics: the logic of action

Taking further the point made above, we note that while the everyday life and the everyday politics approaches ultimately embrace structurationist ontologies, nevertheless the degrees of emphasis upon, and the conceptions of, agency differ in certain key respects. Thus while the everyday life approach places much emphasis on structures of exploitation coupled with a focus on normative agency, the everyday politics approach places much greater emphasis on analytical agency such that it is primarily concerned with revealing the manifold ways in which everyday actions shape and transform the world economy. In the everyday life approach agency is recognized to the extent that it transcends structures of power. The everyday politics approach, by contrast, has a much broader focus, seeking to reveal how agency can be exercised by social actors whether they are resisting power and power structures or whether they are simply going about their everyday life even if this reinforces structures of power. Moreover, this approach envisages a variety of forms of agency, ranging from subtle expressions of resistance to more dramatic exercises of defiance on the one hand, as well as subtle expressions of everyday actions that when aggregated can promote change even if this was never the original intention of the individuals concerned. The approach is also particularly interested in how the actions of powerful actors are mediated and even shaped through the actions of ordinary people whether this subverts or reinforces the powerful. Nevertheless, we do not envisage all developments in the world economy as but the product of bottom-up processes. Rather, we simply claim that dominant elites do not play the exclusive role in the world economy. Furthermore, we argue that we can learn a great deal more about the power as well as the limits of the legitimacy and authority of dominant elites by examining everyday contestations to their power.

Our emphasis on action/agency should by no means be taken to imply a belief on our part that everyday actors can behave entirely as they please or that they always succeed in getting what they want. As much as we reject overly voluntarist and liberal conceptions of agency, so we do not wish structures of power and repression out of existence. By definition, agents who are non-elites act within structurally repressive confines. But while at certain times the subordinate are indeed victims, nevertheless we wish to emphasize the point that at other times they attain agency. Indeed no agent is either entirely powerless or purely confined within a logic of discipline for there is always a space, however small, for the expression of agency. Thus a central purpose of EIPE is neither to marginalize the importance of the dominant nor to reify the agency of the weak. Rather, it is to analyze the interactive relationship between the two. While this can, of course, take the form of resistance by the weak, we are ultimately interested in how the weak can to a certain extent influence the agendas of the elites. It is, therefore, a two-way street that privileges neither but recognizes the agency of both.

Our IPE approach draws from, but is by no means limited to, the conceptions of agency found in the everyday politics literature that was pioneered by the likes of James C. Scott (1976, 1985, 1990) and Benedict J. Tria Kerkvliet (1990, 2005). From this literature, we draw a conception of agency that contests but does not necessarily undermine the power of elites. This occurs as subordinate actors challenge the legitimacy of elites and, in so doing, can pressurize them to change their policies. Challenging legitimacy is crucial to giving everyday actors a voice because it reminds us, at its most basic level, that even the subordinate have some capacity to change their own political, economic, and social environment. Legitimacy, after all, is not about how those in power command or proclaim the justice of their policies while the masses are conceived of as passive dopes that blindly accept this (Seabrooke 2006: ch. 2).

In the everyday politics literature, agency is generally expressed through subtle forms of defiance, which are conducted at the local level and are effected by everyday people in the form of verbal taunts, subversive stories, rumor, "sly civility," and so on. As Kerkvliet's work demonstrates, everyday politics is more subtle and more common than the more grandiose and dramatic forms of overt resistance that we often associate subordinate agency with. For example, in his study of collectivized agriculture in Vietnam, Kerkvliet illustrates how everyday acts such as cheating on rice stocks, local stories, and ignoring national government policies, developed in small incremental ways. But crucially, these aggregated into affecting national policy change with regard to collective agriculture, not because of a national ideological change but because the system had become so compromised that it could no longer be legitimately sustained. Thus while there were no overt protests or riots, economic policy was transformed nonetheless (Kerkvliet 2005).

The work on everyday politics also reminds us that one key reason why an actor may want to reject a claim to legitimacy by those who seek to govern is that it conflicts with her or his identity. RIPE places little importance on identity (with notable exceptions; see Abdelal 2001), and tends to views actors' preferences as aligned with their material self-interest. Even the systemic constructivists, who certainly discuss identity, analyze how identities are diffused by actors or norm-entrepreneurs and view them as the internalization of an obligation rather than as a well-spring for agency from everyday actors. Accordingly, to have a strong conception of legitimacy, EIPE also requires a strong conception of identity that draws from everyday actors and everyday experience.

In this regard we do not conceive of identity as simply interests plus social context, but as contestation over the meaning of who belongs within a domestic society, and how that society engages the international political economy. Viewing identity as contestation is important since social norms tend to "bind people to each other and at the same time turn people so bound against others" (Elias 1996: 160). Everyday contests among non-elites over the meaning of what it is to belong to an ethnicity, a nation, a gender, or a race are important because they inform the "thinkability" and "logicability" of how those groups should engage the world economy (cf. Hopf 2002: 13–15; Katzenstein 1996a). We also see no particular reason why fragmentation of identities should prevent us from recognizing everyday agency. We stress here that it is particularly important to recognize the potential for agency in everyday actors from peoples who have been marginalized, such as those who are repressed by discourses of Western dominance (Hobson 2004, 2007a, 2007b).

While our approach to EIPE borrows heavily from the everyday politics literature, we also seek to broaden the range of actors considered as non-elites. At the extreme, because we are particularly concerned with marginalized actors throughout the world economy, we extend "non-elites" to include peripheral states, since our objective is ultimately to demonstrate how actors who are not included in mainstream IPE accounts can deploy everyday actions to thereby shape and transform the world economy. This is, perhaps, inevitable when we move from a domestic or national focus toward an international or global one. Focusing only on actors such as peasants or workers or migrants would dilute the picture of the world economy that we seek to reveal, since there is more going on beyond the very local level. A further connotation flows from this: namely that we are most interested in how everyday actions promote change in the world economy. This, then, begs the questions: first, what do we include as everyday actions? And second, how do everyday actions promote change in the various spatial realms? We shall take each of these questions in turn.

We define everyday actions as *acts by those who are subordinate within a broader power relationship but, whether through negotiation, resistance or non-resistance—either incrementally or suddenly—shape, constitute, and transform the political and economic environments around and beyond them.* The strategic intention of these acts may be explicit or implicit, but, for our purposes, non-elite actors' behavior can be defined as politically oriented everyday action when it is informed by an actor's conception of social norms (i.e. action that is based on people's beliefs about how an economy or polity should be organized). This broad definition of everyday actions allows us to include a range of agents from individuals to meso-level groupings (e.g. peasants, migrant laborers, trade unions, small investors, low-income groups), and—where defensible—mega-scale aggregations (e.g. peripheral states and even non-Western peoples). The determination of who is non-elite within a system of power must, of course, be historically specified. We are inclusive in regard to which actors can be considered non-elites, in order to talk directly to IPE scholarship rather than restrict ourselves to providing only a critical anthropology or economic sociology of bottom-up processes. In other words, while most of the work on everyday politics discusses the micro- and meso-scales, our focus on everyday actions may also be applied to non-elite mega-scale aggregations within the international system.

Turning now to consider everyday forms of change, Table 18.2 juxtaposes our schema with that deployed by mainstream regulatory approaches. In the left-side column we envisage that *coercion, mimetic conformity,* and *radical uncertainty/crisis* are the typical ways of explaining change in RIPE. Coercion is often found as an explanation for change

Table 18.2 Juxtaposing types of change in regulatory and everyday IPE

Regulatory IPE (top-down change)	Everyday politics (IPE) (bottom-up change)
Coercion	Defiance
Mimetic conformity	Mimetic challenge
Radical uncertainty	Axiorational

in neorealism—where "might makes right"—and also in the exploitative North–South relationship highlighted by classical structuralism. What we have termed *mimetic conformity* is a common neoliberal institutionalist explanation for why states play the game according to a bounded rationality. Through bounded rationality actors learn that conformity is in their long-term self-interest and therefore persist in embracing the dominant structures in question. Finally, radical uncertainty/crisis has been embraced by systemic constructivists as an explanation and locale for the transformative power of ideas carried by elites (Parsons 2003). Most notably, all three types of change are top-down.

By contrast, in the right-hand column, we propose *defiance, mimetic challenge*, and *axiorationality* as three conceptions of bottom-up change within EIPE. Overt defiance is commonly stressed by those who seek to understand how everyday actors repel elite coercion through their overt resistance activities. Mimetic challenge—or "symbolic ju-jitsu" (Scott 1990)—is a common type of covert resistance strategy that is difficult to identify while it is occurring in private, but possible to trace once it has been employed in public. Change here is generated when everyday actors adopt the discourse and/or characteristics of the dominant to cloak their resistance-challenges to the legitimacy of the dominant. Here agents appeal to the normative discourse of the dominant in order to push through their own subversive agenda (e.g. the strategies of colonial resistance movements during decolonization). The key strategy here involves revealing how elite actions contradict their own self-referential discourses of appropriate behavior. In such a way, they become "rhetorically entrapped" (Schimmelfennig 2001), or, put more simply, they become hoisted upon their own discursive petard (Ford 2003; Sharman 2006). Thus by delegitimizing the policies of the dominant, the way is opened toward ending them. Revealing such strategies, therefore, moves us beyond the colonizer/colonized or the elite/marginalized dichotomies, entailing a dialogic or negotiative relationship (see also Hobson 2007a).

Finally, axiorationality provides a contrast with systemic constructivism's emphasis on temporary moments of radical uncertainty/crisis. Rather, axiorationality is habit-informed, reason-guided behavior within which an actor still retains a concept of interest. Axiorational behavior is aimed neither at purely instrumental goals nor purely value-oriented goals. Rather, it refers to a situation where an actor uses reason to reflect upon conventions and norms, as well as the interests they inform, and then chooses to act in ways which are in accordance with broader intersubjective understandings of what is socially legitimate.

It helps to understand axiorationality by contrasting it with rationalist understandings. The common materialist approach to political economy asserts that actors operate rationally according to pre-defined interests (i.e. prior to social interaction). In addition, Marxists insist that rational behavior is socially prescribed but that this is based on the materialist exigencies of the mode of production (the everyday life scholars discussed above provide a variation on this argument). Our claim, rather, is that actors often behave in economically rational ways, but that this is in part defined by norms and identities that prevail at any one point in time and which prescribe that which is rational in the first place.

Importantly, axiorational behavior is the most common form of everyday activity, allowing us to see how actors innovate by selecting new behavioral conventions that meet with their welfare-enhancing interests (not just economic, but also social). Actors do not, therefore, act according to an externally imposed logic of discipline, nor do they simply respond to market incentives. Rather, through an incremental process of selecting new conventions by a host of actors, so new social norms will emerge (Boudon 2001;

Seabrooke 2006: ch. 2). Crucially, such actions take place during normal times rather than only during periods of radical uncertainty. And because such actions are not subsumed under the category of resistance, it is often the case that the actors concerned may not know that they are contributing to change in the local, national, regional or global contexts. Thus axiorational agency is something that goes on much of the time rather than in selected moments of uncertainty and periodic economic crisis—*pace* systemic constructivism (see Seabrooke 2007a). Moreover, such change that occurs might reinforce existing patterns of power. Indeed, the aggregation of individual axiorational acts often serve to retrack the actions of the powerful rather than wholly subverting their power base.

For example, André Broome's (2009) work on international monetary crisis and currency reform in Central Asia highlights the difference between formal changes to international monetary systems that are typically discussed within the RIPE literature and broad social background changes in everyday practice in Central Asian states. The key here is that while the ordinary population is not overtly or covertly defying top-down policies, their actions (which seek to enhance their own welfare) nevertheless alter the calculus of elite interests, as well as how those interests are conceived. As such, Broome highlights the point that we cannot explain elite decisions simply by looking for strategic calculations and instrumental rationality because this fails to tell us why one option is chosen over another. Moreover, Broome points out that even when formal institutions are transformed with a high degree of consensus from elites, national governments, and international economic institutions in the *foreground* of politics, such reforms are unlikely to gain traction and public support if delinked from the *background* everyday politics of how people choose to barter and exchange, as well as what exchange system they view as legitimate. While there are a range of important studies in RIPE that tell us about the constraints the IMF imposes, or the domestic formal political limitations in place (Vreeland 2003), the EIPE value-added here is to focus on the limits of what is socially acceptable through how everyday actors respond. In short, axiorational behavior matters for RIPE because it places significant limitations on the pure exercise of power by elite actors, be they private interests, governments or international institutions. To further examine how everyday actions can be applied to empirical studies of the world economy, we take each form of agency in turn.

However, the discussion of defiance agency renders more scope for everyday challenges to the power of elites. For example, a number of scholars have sought to reveal how labor and labor movements can defy capital and in the process come to shape the world economy in various ways (O'Brien 2000; Herod 2007; cf. Morton 2007b). Andrew Herod, for example, develops the theme of defiance agency in the context of the US labor movement, and reveals how such agency constructs the global geography of capitalism. Critical of the focus on the capital-centrism of some Marxist approaches (e.g. Lefebvre 1976; Harvey 1982), he rejects viewing labor as a passive victim of capitalist globalization (see also Silver 2003). Drawing on Bruno Latour's (1996) "network" conception, he views each spatial realm as rope-like or capillary-like, thereby suggesting that each is inextricably linked rather than separate. In turn this helps reconceptualize workers' praxis. For in traditional or conventional accounts, each realm exists prior to workers' interaction, such that workers are thought to be confined to the national realm. Accordingly, workers are thought to suffer from spatial impotence, always facing the superior "trumping" power of capital that is allegedly derived from its unique spatial–global organization. But by resisting capital, workers' movements come to construct the

303

geography of global capitalism in ways that would ordinarily be obscured by top-down capital-centric analyses. How is this achieved?

One example that Herod provides concerns the resistance that was deployed by the United Steelworkers of America trade union (USWA) against the new owner of the Ravenswood aluminum smelting plant, Marc Rich. In the process they extended contacts with workers in countries where Rich already had business interests. They devised a strategy with other trade unions abroad (e.g. the International Metalworkers' Federation and various European-based TUs) to bring pressure to bear upon Rich. They also met with foreign banks and various governments (including a meeting with Czech president Vaclav Havel). The leverage used concerned the point that Rich was a fugitive from US justice, which enabled the unions to damage Rich's business interests through establishing such powerful connections. In the end the union managed to win major concessions from Rich. The upshot of this example is that "through their abilities to network transnationally ... USWA members ... also had a significant impact on the unfolding organisational geography of Rich's global investments, limiting his plans to expand into Eastern Europe and Latin America" (Herod 2007: 41). Herod is able to show through this example, and others like it, how workers and trade unions are able to reorganize the geography of global capitalism through such defiance (Herod 2007: 42–44).

Our second form of everyday change—mimetic challenge—can be illustrated empirically in a number of ways (see, e.g. Ford 2003; Sharman 2006, 2007b; Suzuki 2007). While regulatory approaches largely dismiss the agency of Southern states (e.g. Wallerstein 1974; Krasner 1985), J.C. Sharman's recent work reveals how the discursive/normative aspects of international regimes are autonomous sites of cultural contestation wherein peripheral states can not only resist the strong but can even push through their interests against those of the majority of the wealthy Northern states. This also brings into powerful focus the issue of a regime's legitimacy. He focuses on how tiny non-European offshore tax havens have challenged and battled the OECD's harmful tax practices regime. This story is not simply one of another Third World cartel from the Global South that can be picked apart by powerful states in the Global North. Nor is it an example of how peripheral states band together through cartel power to achieve their ends (as in the conventional framework for understanding North–South relations). Rather, the culture of regimes has a certain autonomy from the powerful states, even if they originally constructed the relevant discourse. By playing on the double-edged nature of regime discourse, so these weak tax havens are able rhetorically to challenge the Western states on their own discursive grounds in order to maintain their economic interests against those of the wealthy OECD (cf. Ford 2003). Thus while the OECD stands normatively for competition, so the tax havens are able to show that the harmful tax initiative is one that defies this discourse thereby weakening the legitimacy of the initiative. And as a result of their mimetic challenge strategies, the OECD has been unable to crack down on so-called "unfair" tax competition.

Turning now to the third type of agency—axiorationality—we emphasize the point that it is qualitatively different to the first two forms. For unlike overt defiance and mimetic challenge, axiorationality is not a form of resistance. Axiorational agency, which occurs as everyday agents go about their everyday business, can be seen to inform the policies of great power political economy (Seabrooke 2006, 2007b) or the rise and reproduction of globalization (Hobson 2007b; Wilson 2007).

With respect to great power political economy, Leonard Seabrooke emphasizes everyday domestic influences on the foreign financial policies of leading Western hegemonic states—Britain in the late nineteenth century and the United States after 1945

(Seabrooke 2006). He discusses how access to everyday social wants, such as credit, property, and lower tax burdens for lower income groupings, inform the domestic character of financial systems, which in turn inform a state's capacity to transform the international financial order. His key point is that the extent to which a state can work within legitimate social practices (according to the "moral economy" of lower income groupings) informs a state's foreign financial policy. Contestations to the legitimacy of a state's financial system do not take place only, or even primarily, in times of radical uncertainty and crisis, but instead through everyday incremental actions. Conventions concerning the capacity and, in particular, the *right* to access credit and property provide contestation on what is possible in policy for those governing. This is especially the case when negative feedback to ordinary people leads them to openly defy government policies through their individual actions or through the engagement of social movements. Such open defiance is rarer than the persistent incremental impulses provided by everyday actions.

Seabrooke's study of advanced industrial societies demonstrates that states which can change their everyday financial policies in line with changing conventions for the majority of the population (which often includes abandoning the poor) can thereby build a deeper and broader pool of capital to engage the international financial order. He contends that it is vital to recognize that while dominant actors claim legitimacy for their actions, active legitimation requires consent from the subordinates within the relationship. And without sufficient legitimacy a hegemon's financial power is ultimately undermined (also Seabrooke 2001). The sub-prime crisis may also be seen in these terms, since its emergence is in large part due to a failure in government oversight from the Bush administration, and the consequent exposure of lower-income and minority groups to predatory lending. In previous decades, through everyday politics, the same groups were able to access credit within a comparatively heavily regulated system built on rights discourses from the Great Depression and the Civil Rights Movement (Seabrooke 2008). And, in doing so, they unwittingly became a part of US financial power in the international political economy. The sub-prime crisis brings into sharp relief what happens to the world economy when these institutional forms, which are embedded within everyday desires and norms, are not protected.

All in all, these examples are provided to convey to the reader a flavor of how an everyday politics approach to IPE can be applied to understanding the world economy. These brief examples provide an alternative glimpse of the world economy; one that fills in many of the gaps that we have identified within RIPE. Such analyses ultimately serve to remind us that a focus on the small number of so-called big and important things is insufficient for grasping the bigger picture that requires revealing if we are to understand the world economy. For RIPE is ultimately problematic because its theoretical cogs are simply too large to get a grip on the minutiae of everyday life that significantly inform the way the world economy develops and is transformed over time. Everyday agency has an interstitial quality that, we believe, deserves further investigation if we wish to fully understand the world economy.

Conclusion

We have argued here that RIPE cannot provide us with all the information we need to understand change in the world economy, especially since it obscures how non-elites can transform the world economy, be it through defiance, mimicry or habit-informed

305

behavior. The recent work on everyday life provides new avenues for a critique of our daily actions so that we may seek to change them, while our own everyday politics approach seeks to actively isolate types of everyday agency that represent a social source of change in the world economy. In such ways, EIPE opens up new ways of studying the world economy beyond the limited parsimonious framework of mainstream regulatory approaches. Of course, the recent emergence of EIPE means that it is only in its formative stage and much work needs to be done in terms of theoretical and empirical development. But we believe that these new approaches offer up exciting new pathways into the study of the world economy and hope that others will be drawn into joining the project in order to drive it further.

Bibliography

Abbott, F. 2000. "The Legalization of World Politics: A Case Study." *International Organization* 54 (3): pp. 519–47.

Abdelal, R. 2001. *National Purpose in the World Economy: Post-Soviet States in Comparative Perspective*, Ithaca NY: Cornell University Press.

——2007. *Capital Rules: The Construction of Global Finance*, Cambridge, MA: Harvard University Press.

Abdelal, R., Blyth, M., and Parsons, C. [forthcoming]. *Constructivist International Political Economy*.

Abdelal, R., Herrera, Y., Johnston, A.I., and McDermott, R. 2006. "Identity as a variable." *Perspectives on Politics* 4(4): pp. 695–711.

Abdelal, R. and Kirshner, J. 1999–2000. "Strategy, economic relations, and the definition of national interests." *Security Studies* 9(1/2) (1999–2000): pp. 119–56.

Abdelal, R. and Segal, A. 2007. "Has globalization passed its peak?" *Foreign Affairs* (January/February): pp. 103–14.

Abegglen, J. C. 1994. *Sea Change: Pacific Asia as the New World Industrial Center*, New York: Macmillan.

Abu-Lughod, J. 1989. *Before European Hegemony: The World System A.D. 1250–1350*, New York, Oxford University Press.

Adas, M. 1989. *Machines as Measure of Men: Science, Technology and Ideologies of Western Dominance*, Ithaca NY: Cornell University Press.

Adcock, R. and Bevir, M. 2007. "The remaking of political theory." In Adcock, R., Bevir, M., and Stimson, S. C. eds. *Modern Political Science: Anglo-American Exchanges Since 1880*, Princeton, NJ: Princeton University Press: pp. 209–33.

Adler, E. 1997. "Seizing the middle ground: constructivism in world politics." *European Journal of International Relations* 3(3): pp. 319–63.

Adorno, T. 1951. *Minima Moralia: Reflections from Damaged Life*, Berlin: Suhrkamp Verlag, English translation by New Left Books.

Aglietta, M. 1976. *Régulation et Crises du Capitalisme*, Paris: Calmann-Lévy.

——2001. *A Theory of Capitalist Regulation: The US Experience*, London: Verso

Aglietta, M. and Orléan, A. 1982. *La Violence de la Monnaie*, Paris: Presses Universitaires de France.

Agnew, J. 1994. "The territorial trap: the geographical assumptions of international relations theory." *Review of International Political Economy* 1(1): pp. 53–80.

——2005. "Sovereignty regimes: territoriality and state authority in contemporary world politics." *Annals of the Association of American Geographers* 95: pp. 437–61.

Aitken, R. 2005. "'A direct personal stake': cultural economy, mass investment and the New York stock exchange." *Review of International Political Economy* 12(2): pp. 334–63.

——2007. *Performing Capital: Toward a Cultural Economy of Popular and Global Finance*, Basingstoke, UK: Palgrave Macmillan.

Akrasanee, A., Dapice, D., and Flatters, F. 1991. *Thailand's Export-Led Growth: Retrospect and Prospects*, Bangkok: Thailand Development Research Institute.

Aldcroft, D. H. and Oliver, M. J. 1998. *Exchange Rate Regimes in the Twentieth Century*, Cheltenham, UK: Edward Elgar.

Alderson, A. S. 1999. "Explaining deindustrialization: globalization, failure, or success?" *American Sociological Review* 64: pp. 701–21.

Amable, B. 2003. *The Diversity of Modern Capitalism*, Oxford: Oxford University Press.

Amenta, E., Bonastia, C., and Caren, N. 2001. "U.S. social policy in comparative and historical perspective: concepts, images, arguments, and research strategies." *Annual Review of Sociology*, 27: pp. 213–34.

Amin, A. and Palan, R. 2001. "Towards a non-rationalist international political economy." *Review of International Political Economy*, 8(4): pp. 559–77.

Amoore, L. 2002: *Globalization Contested*, Manchester, UK: Manchester University Press.

——2004. "Risk, reward and discipline at work." *Economy and Society* 33(2): pp. 174–96.

Amoore, L. and Langley, P. 2004. "Ambiguities of global civil society." *Review of International Studies* 30 (1): pp. 89–110.

Amsden, A. H. 1989. *Asia's Next Giant: South Korea and Late Industrialization*, New York: Oxford University Press.

Anchorduguy, M. 1997. "Japan at a technological crossroads: does change support convergence theory?" *Journal of Japanese Studies* 23 (Summer): pp. 363–97.

Anderson, P. 1964. "Origins of the present crisis." *New Left Review* 23: pp. 26–53.

——1976. *Considerations on Western Marxism*, London: New Left Books.

——1987. "The figures of descent." *New Left Review* 161: pp. 20–77.

Andrée, P. 2007. *Genetically-Modified Diplomacy: The Global Politics of Agricultural Biotechnology and the Environment*, Vancouver: University of British Columbia Press.

Andrews, D. M. ed. 2006. *International Monetary Power*, Ithaca, NY: Cornell University Press.

Antoniades, A. 2007. "Cave! Hic everyday life: repetition, hegemony and the social." paper presented at the Everyday Life in World Politics and Economics workshop, Centre for International Studies, London School of Economics (May).

Appadurai, A. 1999. "Globalization and the research imagination." *International Social Science Journal* 51 (2): pp. 229–38.

Appelbaum, R. P. 2000. "Moving up: industrial upgrading, social networks and buyer-driven commodity chains in East Asian Chinese business firms." *International Studies Review* 3(1): pp. 21–41.

Appelbaum, R. P. and Smith, D. A. 2001. "Governance and flexibility: the East Asian garment industry," in Deyo, F. C., Doner, R. F., and Hershberg, E. eds. *Economic Governance and the Challenge of Flexibility in East Asia*, Lanham, MD: Rowman & Littlefield: pp. 79–105.

Arantes, P. 2007. *Extinção*, São Paulo: Boitempo Editorial.

Aronica, R. and Randoo, M. 2006. *The World is Flat? A Critical Analysis of Thomas L. Friedman's New York Times Bestseller*. Tampa, FL: Meghan-Kiffer Press.

Arrighi, G. 1994. *The Long Twentieth Century: Money, Power and the Origins of Our Times*, London: Verso.

——1996. "The rise of East Asia: world systemic and regional aspects." *International Journal of Sociology and Social Policy* 16(7): pp. 6–44.

——2007. *Adam Smith in Beijing: Lineages of the Twenty-first Century*, London: Verso.

Arrighi, G., Hui, P., Hung, H. F., and Selden, M. 2003. "Historical capitalism, East and West," in Arrighi, G., Hamashita, T., and Selden, M. eds. *The Resurgence of East Asia. 500, 150 and 50 Year Perspectives*, London and New York: Routledge: pp. 259–333.

Arrighi, G., Ikeda, S., and Irwan, A. 1993. "The rise of East Asia: one miracle or many?" in Palat, R. A. ed. *Pacific Asia and the Future of the World-Economy*, Westport, CT: Greenwood Press: pp. 42–65.

Arrighi, G. and Silver, B. J. 1999. *Chaos and Governance in the Modern World System*, Minneapolis: University of Minnesota Press.

Asia Monitor Resource Center. 1987. *South Korea's New Trade Unions*, Hong Kong: Asia Monitor Resource Center.

Association Française de Science Politique. 2005. Program of the AFSP meeting, IPE workshop description.

——2007. Report of the Section d'Etudes Européennes after the AFSP meeting in Toulouse.

Atwell, W. S. 1986. "Some observations on the 'seventeenth-century crisis' in China and Japan." *Journal of Asian Studies* XLV: pp. 223–44

——1998. "Ming China and the emerging world economy *c*.1470–1650." In Twitchett, D. and Mote, F. W. eds. *The Cambridge History of China Vol. 8 (2), The Ming Dynasty*, Cambridge: Cambridge University Press: pp. 376–416.

Avant, D. 2005. *The Market for Force*, New York: Cambridge University Press.

Avi-Yonah, R. S. 2000. "World-class tax evasion: competition for investment capital is eroding the tax base of the advanced countries and making a safety net harder to finance." *The American Prospect* 11(13): pp. 28–30.

Axelrod, R. 1984. *The Evolution of Cooperation*, New York: BasicBooks.

Babb, S. 2001. *Managing Mexico: Economists from Nationalism to Neoliberalism*, Princeton, NJ: Princeton University Press.

——2007. "Embeddedness, inflation, and international regimes: The IMF in the early postwar period." *American Journal of Sociology* 113: pp. 128–64.

Backhouse, R. 2002. *The Penguin History of Economics*, London: Penguin.

Bagchi, A. K. 1982. *The Political Economy of Underdevelopment*, Cambridge: Cambridge University Press.

Baker, A. 1999. "Nebuleuse and the 'internationalization of the state' in the UK? The case of HM Treasury and the Bank of England." *Review of International Political Economy* 6(1): pp. 79–100.

Bakker, I. and Gill, S. R. eds. 2003. *Power, Production and Social Reproduction: Human In/Security in the Global Political Economy*, Basingstoke, UK: Palgrave.

Baldwin, D. A. 1993. *Neorealism and Neoliberalism: The Contemporary Debate*, New York: Columbia University Press.

Baran, P. 1957. *Political Economy of Growth*, New York: Monthly Review Press.

Barber, B. 2001. *Jihad vs. MacWorld*. New York: Ballantine Books.

Barber, W. 1991. *A History of Economic Thought*, London: Penguin.

Barkawi, T. and Laffey, M. 1999. "The imperial peace: democracy, force and globalization." *European Journal of International Relations* 5: pp. 403–34.

Barkin, J. S. 2003. *Social Construction and the Logic of Money: Financial Predominance and International Economic Leadership*, Albany, NY: State University of New York Press.

Barnett, C. 1972. *The Collapse of British Power*, London: Methuen.

——1986. *The Audit of War: the Illusion and Reality of Britain as a Great Power*, London: Macmillan.

Barnett, M. 2005. "Humanitarianism Transformed." *Perspectives on Politics* 3(4): pp. 723–40.

Barnett, M. N. 1998. *Dialogues in Arab Politics: Negotiations in Regional Order*, New York: Columbia University Press

Barnett, M. and Finnemore, M. 2004. *Rules for the World: International Organizations in World Politics*, Ithaca NY: Cornell University Press.

Barry, A., Osborne, T., and Rose, N. eds. 1996. *Foucault and Political Reason: Liberalism, Neo-liberalism and Rationalities of Government*, London: UCL Press.

Bartelson, J. 2001. *The Critique of the State*, Cambridge: Cambridge University Press.

Bartlett, B. S. 1991. *Monarchs and Ministers: The Grand Council in Mid-Ch'ing China, 1723–1820*, Berkeley: University of California Press.

Bartley, T. 2007. "Institutional emergence in an era of globalization: the rise of transnational private regulation of labor and environmental conditions." *American Journal of Sociology* 113: pp. 297–351.

Bartolini, L. and Drazen, A. 1997. "Capital account liberalization as a signal." *American Economic Review* 87 (March): pp. 138–54.

Battilossi, S. 2006. "Review." *Financial History Review* 13(2): pp. 314–17.

Bearce, D. H. 2007. *Monetary Divergence: Domestic Policy Autonomy in the Post-Bretton Woods Era*, Ann Arbor, MI: University of Michigan Press.

Beck, U. 1992. *Risk Society*, London: Sage.

Beckert, J. 1996. "What is sociological about economic sociology? Uncertainty and the embeddedness of economic action." *Theory and Society* 25(6): pp. 803–40.

——2002. *Beyond the Market: Social Foundations of Economic Efficiency*, Princeton, NJ: Princeton University Press.

——2007. "The social order of markets." MPlfG Discussion Paper, July 15, Max Planck Institute for the Study of Societies, Cologne, Germany.

Beinefeld, M. 2000. "Can global finance be regulated?" in Bello, W., Bullard, N., and Malhotra, K. eds. *Global Finance: New Thinking on Regulating Speculative Capital Markets*, London: Zed Books.

Belassa, B. 1979. "A 'stages' approach to comparative advantage." In Adelman, I. ed. *Economic Growth and Resources: Proceedings of the Fifth Congress of the International Economic Association, Tokyo 1977*, London: Macmillan: pp. 121–56.

Bell, S. 1995. "Between the market and the state: the role of business associations in public policy: evidence from Australia." *Comparative Politics* 28(1): pp. 25–53.

——2005. "How tight are the policy constraints? The policy convergence thesis, institutionally situated actors, and expansionary monetary policy in Australia." *New Political Economy* 10(1): pp. 65–89.

Bello, W. 1998. "East Asia: on the eve of the great transformation?" *Review of International Political Economy* 5(3): pp. 424–44.

——2005. *Dilemmas of Domination: The Unmaking of the American Empire*, New York: Metropolitan Books, Henry Holt and Company.

Bello, W., Kinley, W. F., and Elinson, E. 1982. *Development Debacle: the World Bank in the Philippines*, San Francisco, CA: Institute for Food and Development Policy (Food First).

Bello, W., Malig, M. L., Docena, H., and de Guzman, M. 2004. *The Anti-Development State: the Political Economy of Permanent Crisis in the Philippines*, London: Zed Books.

Bello, W. and Rivera, S. eds. 1977. *The Logistics of Repression*, Washington DC: Friends of the Filipino People.

Bello, W. and Rosenfeld, S. 1991. *Dragons in Distress: Asia's Miracle Economies in Crisis*, London: Penguin Books.

Bellow, S. 2001. *Ravelstein*, New York: Penguin Books.

Berger, P. L. and Luckmann, T. 1966. *The Social Construction of Reality: A Treatise in the Sociology of Knowledge*, Garden City, NY: Doubleday.

Berger, S. and Dore, R. eds. 1996. *National Diversity and Global Capitalism*, Ithaca, NY: Cornell University Press.

Berman, S. 1998. *The Social Democratic Moment: Ideas and Politics in the Making of Interwar Europe*, Cambridge, MA: Harvard University Press.

——2006. *The Primacy of Politics: Social Democracy and the Ideological Dynamics of the Twentieth Century*, New York: Cambridge University Press.

Berman, S. and K. McNamara. 1998. "Bank on Democracy: Why Central Banks Need Public Oversight," *Foreign Affairs* (3): pp. 2–8.

Bernstein, S. F. 2001. *The Compromise of Liberal Environmentalism*, New York: Columbia University Press.

Berrios, R. 2000. *Contracting for Development: The Role of For-Profit Contractors in U.S. Foreign Development Assistance*, Westport, CT: Praeger.

Bertolini, L. and Drazen, A. 1997. "Capital account liberalization as a signal." *American Economic Review* 87(1): 138–54.

Best, J. 2003. "From the top-down: the new financial architecture and the re-embedding of global finance." *New Political Economy* 8(3) (November): pp. 364–84.

——2004. "Hollowing out Keynesian norms: how the search for a technical fix undermined the Bretton Woods regime." *Review of International Studies* 30(3): pp. 383–404.

——2005. *The Limits of Transparency: Ambiguity and the History of International Finance*, Ithaca, NY: Cornell University Press.

Best, M. H. 1990. *The New Competition: Institutions of Industrial Restructuring*, Cambridge: Polity Press.

Betsill, M. M. 1999. "Changing the climate: NGOs, norms and the politics of global climate change," paper delivered at the Annual Convention of the International Studies Association, February 16–20, Washington DC.

Bevir, M. 2006. "Political studies as narrative and science, 1880–2000." *Political Studies* 54(3): pp. 583–606.

Bhagwati, J. 2004. *In Defense of Globalization*, New York: Oxford University Press.

Biernacki, R. 1995. *The Fabrication of Labor: Germany and Britain, 1640–1914*, Berkeley: University of California Press.

Biggart, N. W. and Guillén, M. 1999. "Developing difference: social organization and the rise of the auto industries of South Korea, Taiwan, Spain, and Argentina." *American Sociological Review* 65: pp. 722–47.

Black, D. R. and Swatuk, L. A. 1997. *Bridging the Rift: The New South Africa in Africa*, Boulder, CO: Westview Press.

Bland, A. E., Brown, P.A., and Tawney, R. H. eds. 1915. *English Economic History: Selected Documents*, London: G. Bell and Sons.

Blankenburg, S., Palma, J. G., and Tregenna, F. 2008. "Structuralism." *The New Palgrave Dictionary of Economics*, 2nd edition.

Blaug, M. 1990. *History of Economic Thought*, Cheltenham, UK: Edward Elgar.

——1992. *The Methodology of Economics, or How Economists Explain*, Cambridge: Cambridge University Press.

——1997. *Economic Theory in Retrospect*, Cambridge: Cambridge University Press, 5th edition.

Bleiker, R. 2000. *Popular Dissent, Human Agency and Global Politics*, Cambridge: Cambridge University Press.

Block, F. 1977. *The Origins of International Economic Disorder: A Study of United States International Monetary Policy from World War II to the Present*, Berkeley: University of California Press.

Blustein, P. 2001. *The Chastening*, New York: Public Affairs.

Blyth, M. 1997. "Any more bright ideas? The ideational turn of comparative political economy." *Comparative Politics* 29(1): pp. 229–50.

——2001. "The transformation of the Swedish model: economic ideas, distributional conflict and institutional change." *World Politics* 54(1) (October): pp. 1–26.

——2002. *Great Transformations: Economic Ideas and Institutional Change in the Twentieth Century*, New York: Cambridge University Press.

——2003. "Structures do not come with an instruction sheet: interests, ideas and progress in political science." *Perspectives on Politics* 1(4) (December): pp. 695–703.

——2006. "Great punctuations: prediction, randomness, and the evolution of comparative political science." *American Political Science Review* 100(4) (November): pp. 493–98.

——2007a. "When liberalisms change: comparing the politics of deflations and inflations." In Denzau, A., Roy, R. K., and Willett, T. eds. *Neoliberalism: National and Regional Experiments with Global Ideas*, London: Routledge.

——2007b: "Powering, puzzling, or persuading? The mechanisms of building institutional orders." *International Studies Quarterly* 51(4): pp. 761–77.

——2009. "An approach to comparative analysis, or a sub-field within a sub-field? Political economy." In Mark Lichbach and Alan Zuckerman, eds. *Comparative Politics: Rationality, Culture, and Structure*, Cambridge: Cambridge University Press.

Boli, J. and Meyer, J. W. 1987. "The ideology of childhood and the state: rules distinguishing children in national constitutions." In Thomas, G. M., Meyer, J. W., Ramirez, F. O., and Boli, J. *Institutional Structure: Constituting State, Society, and the Individual*, Beverly Hills: Sage: pp. 217–41.

Boli, J. and Thomas, G. M. eds. 1999a. *Constructing World Culture: International Nongovernmental Organizations Since 1875*, Stanford, CA: Stanford University Press.

——1999b. "Introduction." In Boli, J. and Thomas, G. M. eds. *Constructing World Culture: International Nongovernmental Organizations Since 1875*, Stanford CA: Stanford University Press: pp. 1–12.

Bönker, F. 2006. *The Political Economy of Fiscal Reform in Central-Eastern Europe: Hungary, Poland and the Czech Republic from 1989 to EU Accession*, Cheltenham, UK: Edward Elgar.

311

Bordo, M. D. and Eichengreen, B. 1998. "Implications of the Great Depression for the development of the international monetary system." In Bordo, M. D., Goldin, C., and White, E. N. eds. *The Defining Moment: The Great Depression and the American Economy in the Twentieth Century*, Chicago: University of Chicago Press: pp. 403–54.

Bordo, M. D., Simard, D., and White, E. N. 1998. "La stratégie française et le système monetaire de Bretton Woods." In Comité pour L'Histoire Economique et Financière de la France, *La France et les Institutions de Bretton Woods 1944–1994*, Paris: Ministère de l'Economie.

Borrus, M., Ernst, D., and Haggard, S. eds. 2000. *International Production Networks in Asia: Rivalry or Riches*, London: Routledge.

Boudon, R. 2001. *The Origin of Values*, New Brunswick NJ: Transaction Publishers.

Bourdieu, P. 1990. *Homo Academicus*, Stanford, CA: Stanford University Press.

Bourne, E. G. 1894. "Alexander Hamilton and Adam Smith." *Quarterly Journal of Economics* 8(3) (April): pp. 328–44.

Boyer, R. 1990. *The Regulation School: A Critical Introduction*, New York: Columbia University Press.

——2004. *Théorie de la Régulation, 1: Les Fondamentaux*, Paris: La Découverte.

——2007. "Capitalism strikes back: why and what consequences for the social sciences." *Revue de la Régulation* 1: pp. 1–25. http://regulation.revues.org/docannexe3353.html

Boyer, R. and Drache, D. eds. 1996. *States Against Markets: The Limits of Globalization*, London: Routledge.

Boyer, R. and Mistral, J. 1978. *Accumulation, Inflation, Crises*, Paris: Presses Universitaires de France.

Boyer, R. and Saillard, Y. 2002. *Regulation Theory: The State of the Art*, London: Routledge.

Braithwaite, J. and Drahos, P. 2000. *Global Business Regulation*, Cambridge: Cambridge University Press.

Bratsis, P. 2006. *Everyday Life and the State*, Boulder, CO: Paradigm Publishers.

Braudel, F. 1949. *La Méditerranée et le Monde Méditerranéen à l'Epoque de Philippe II*, Paris: Armand Colin.

——1958/1980. "History and the social sciences: the longue dureé." In *On History*, trans. Matthews, S., London: Weidenfeld & Nicolson.

——1982. *Civilization and Capitalism, 15th–18th Century, II: The Wheels of Commerce*, New York: Harper & Row.

Brawley, M. 1993. *Liberal Leadership: Great Powers and Their Challengers in Peace and War*, Ithaca, NY: Cornell University Press.

——1999. *Afterglow or Adjustment? Domestic Institutions and the Responses to Overstretch*, New York: Columbia University Press.

Brayton, S. 2002. "Outsourcing War: Mercenaries and the Privatization of Peacekeeping." *Journal of International Affairs* 55: pp. 303–29.

Breen, M. 2007. "Korea Inc. looks for a new CEO." *Far Eastern Economic Review* 170(10) (December): pp. 31–34.

Breslin, S. 2007. *China and the Global Political Economy*, Basingstoke, UK: Palgrave Macmillan.

Brewer, J. 1989. *The Sinews of Power: War, Money and the English State, 1688–1783*, London, Routledge.

Brittan, S. 1964. *The Treasury under the Tories*, Harmondsworth, UK: Penguin.

Britton, A. 2002. "Macroeconomics and history." *National Institute Economic Review* 179: pp. 104–18.

Britton, C. 2002. "Fundamentalism and idolatry." In Covington, C., Williams, P., Arundale, J., and Knox, J. eds. *Terrorism and War*, London: Karnac, pp. 175–84.

Broad, R. 1985. *Unequal Alliance*, Berkeley: University of California Press.

——1995. "The political economy of natural resources: case studies of the Indonesian and Philippine forest sectors." *The Journal of the Developing Areas* 29 (April): pp. 317–40.

Brodie, J. M. 1995. *Politics on the Margin: Restructuring and the Canadian Women's Movement*, Halifax, Nova Scotia: Fernwood.

Bromley, S. 1991. *American Hegemony and World Oil: The Industry, the State System and the World Economy*, Cambridge: Polity Press.

——2008. *American Power and the Prospects for International Order*, Cambridge: Polity Press.

Brooks, S. 2005. *Producing Security: Multinational Corporations, Globalization, and the Changing Calculus of Conflict*, Princeton, NJ: Princeton University Press.

——2009 [forthcoming]. *Social Protection and the Market in Latin America: The Transformation of Social Security Institutions*, Cambridge: Cambridge University Press.

Broome, A. 2009 [forthcoming]. "Money for nothing: everyday actors and monetary crises." *Journal of International Relations and Development* 12(1).

Broome, A. and Seabrooke, L. 2007. "Seeing like the IMF: institutional change in small open economies." *Review of International Political Economy* 14(4): pp. 576–601.

Brown, C. 1999. "Susan Strange: a critical appreciation." *Review of International Studies* 25(3): pp. 531–35.

Brown, D. L. 1985. *Weathering the Storm: Canada–U.S. Relations, 1980–83*, Toronto: C. D. Howe Institute.

Brown, M. ed. 2000. *The Rise of China*, Cambridge, MA: MIT Press.

Brubaker, R., Loveman, M., and Stamatov, P. 2004. "Ethnicity as Cognition." *Theory and Society* 33: pp. 31–64.

Brzezinski, Z. and Mearsheimer, J. J. 2005. "Clash of the Titans." *Foreign Policy* January/February: www.foreignpolicy.com.

Budd, A. 1978. *The Politics of Economic Planning*, Manchester, UK: Manchester University Press.

Bukovansky, M. 2002. *Legitimacy and Power Politics: The American and French Revolutions in International Political Culture*, Princeton, NJ: Princeton University Press.

Bulard, M. 2005. "China: Middle Kingdom, world centre." *Le Monde Diplomatique* (August).

Burchell, G., Gordon, C., and Miller, P. eds. 1991. *The Foucault Effect: Studies in Governmentality*, Hemel Hempstead, UK: Harvester Press.

Burn, G. 2006. *The Re-emergence of Global Finance*, London: Palgrave.

Burnham, P. 1990. *The Political Economy of Postwar Reconstruction*, London: Macmillan.

——1991. "Neo-Gramscian hegemony and international order." *Capital and Class* 45(1): pp. 73–93.

——1994. "The organisational view of the state." *Politics* 14(1): pp. 1–9.

——2003. *Remaking the Postwar World Economy*, Basingstoke, UK: Palgrave Macmillan.

Business World. 2003. "Government debt piling up." September 29.

Buthe, T. and W. Mattli. 2005. "Accountability in Accounting? The Politics of Private Rule-Making in the Public Interest," *Governance* 18 (3): pp. 399–429.

Butler, L. 2003. "Explaining Australia's share of ISI publications: the effects of a formula based on publication counts." *Research Policy* 32(1): pp. 143–55.

Byers, M. 2007. *Intent for Nation: what is Canada for?* Toronto: Douglas & McIntyre.

Byung-Nak, S. 1989. "The Korean economy." Unpublished manuscript, Seoul.

Cairncross, A. 1985. *Years of Recovery: British Economic Policy, 1945–1951*, London: Methuen.

——1995. *The British Economy Since 1945*, Oxford: Blackwell.

Calder, K. 1993. *Strategic Capitalism, Private Business, and Public Purpose in Japanese Industrial Finance*, Princeton, NJ: Princeton University Press.

Cameron, A. 2008. "Crisis? What crisis? Displacing the spatial imaginary of the fiscal state." *Geoforum* 39(3): 1145–54.

Cameron, A. and Palan, R. 2004. *The Imagined Economies of Globalization*, London: Sage.

Cameron, D. 1978. "The expansion of the public economy: a comparative analysis." *American Political Science Review* 72: pp. 1243–61.

Cameron, M. A. 1993. *The Political Economy of North American Free Trade*, Kingston, Ontario: McGill-Queen's University Press.

Cameron, M. A. and Tomlin, B. 2000. *The Making of NAFTA: How the Deal Was Done*, Ithaca, NY: Cornell University Press.

Cammack, P. 1989. "Bringing the state back in?" *British Journal of Political Science* 19(2): pp. 261–90.

——2007. "RIP IPE." Manchester Metropolitan Papers in the Politics of Global Competitiveness, no. 7 (May).

Campbell, D. 1993. *Politics without Principle: Sovereignty, Ethics, and the Narratives of the Gulf War*, Boulder, CO: Lynne Rienner.

Campbell, J. L. 1988. *Collapse of an Industry: Nuclear Power and the Contradictions of U.S. Policy*, Ithaca, NY: Cornell University Press.

313

——2001. "Convergence or divergence? Globalization, neoliberalism and fiscal policy in post-communist Europe." In Weber, S. ed. *Globalization and the European Political Economy*, New York: Columbia University Press: pp. 107–39.

——2003. "States, politics, and globalization: why institutions still matter." In Hall, J. A., Ikenberry, J., and Paul, T. V. eds. *The Nation State in Question*, Princeton, NJ: Princeton University Press: pp. 234–59.

——2004. *Institutional Change and Globalization*, Princeton, NJ: Princeton University Press.

——2005. "Fiscal sociology in an age of globalization: comparing tax regimes in advanced capitalist countries." In Nee, V. and Swedberg, R. eds. *The Economic Sociology of Capitalism*, Princeton, NJ: Princeton University Press: pp. 391–418.

Campbell, J. L. and Hall, J. A. 2006. "The state of Denmark." In Campbell, J. L., Hall, J. A., and Pedersen, O. K. *National Identity and the Varieties of Capitalism: The Danish Experience*, Montreal: McGill-Queen's University Press: pp. 3–49.

——2007. "The political economy of scale and nation." Paper presented at the American Sociological Association, New York.

Campbell, J. L. and Pedersen, O. K. 1996. "The evolutionary nature of revolutionary change in post-communist Europe." In Campbell, J. L. and Pedersen, O. K. eds. *Legacies of Change: Transformations of Postcommunist European Economies*, New York: Aldine de Gruyter: pp. 207–51.

——2001. "The second movement in institutional analysis." In Campbell, J. L. and Pedersen, O. K. eds. *The Rise of Neoliberalism and Institutional Analysis*, Princeton, NJ: Princeton University Press: pp. 249–83.

——2007. "The varieties of capitalism and hybrid success: Denmark in the global economy." *Comparative Political Studies* 40(3): pp. 307–32.

Campbell, J. L., Rogers Hollingsworth, J., and Lindberg, L. N. eds. 1991. *Governance of the American Economy*, New York: Cambridge University Press.

Capie, F. 2008. "Review." *Journal of Economic History* 68(2): pp. 628–29.

Capling, A. 2001. *Australia and the Global Trade System: From Havana to Seattle*, Cambridge: Cambridge University Press.

——2005. *All the Way with the USA: Australia, the US and Free Trade*, Sydney: University of New South Wales Press.

Caporaso, J. A. and Levine, D. P. 1992. *Theories of Political Economy*, Cambridge: Cambridge University Press.

Cardoso, F. H. 1974. "Notas sobre el estado actual de los estudios sobre la dependencia." In Serra, J. ed. *Desarrollo Latinoamericano*, Mexico: FCE.

——1977. "The originality of the copy: ECLA and the idea of development." *CEPAL Review* (2nd half 1977): pp. 7–24.

Cardoso, F. H. and Faletto, E. 1979. *Dependency and Development in Latin America*, Berkeley: University of California Press.

Carr, E. H. 1951 [1939]. *The Twenty Years' Crisis, 1919–1939: An Introduction to the Study of International Relations*, London: Macmillan.

Carruthers, B. G., Babb, S. L., and Halliday, T. C. 2001. "Institutionalizing Markets, or the Market for Institutions? Central Banks, Bankruptcy Law and the Globalization of Financial Markets." In Campbell, J. L. and Pedersen, O. K. eds. *The Rise of Neoliberalism and Institutional Analysis*, Princeton, NJ: Princeton University Press: pp. 94–126.

Cartapanis, A. and Herland, M. 2002. "The reconstruction of the international financial architecture: Keynes' revenge?" *Review of International Political Economy* 9(2): pp. 271–97.

Cerny, P.G. 1990. *The Changing Architecture of Politics: Structure, Agency, and the Future of the State*, Newbury Park, CA and London: Sage.

——1993. "Plurilateralism: structural differentiation and functional conflict in the post-Cold War world order." *Millennium: Journal of International Studies* 22(1) (Spring): pp. 27–51.

——1994a. "The infrastructure of the infrastructure? Towards embedded financial orthodoxy in the international political economy." In Palan, R. P. and Gills, B. eds. *Transcending the State-Global Divide: A Neostructuralist Agenda in International Relations*, Boulder, CO: Lynne Reinner: pp. 223–49.

——1994b. "The dynamics of financial globalization: technology, market structure and policy response." *Policy Sciences* 27(4) (November): pp. 319–42.

——1995. "Globalization and the changing logic of collective action." *International Organization* 49(4) (Autumn): pp. 595–625.

——1996. "International finance and the erosion of state policy capacity." In Gummett, P. ed. *Globalization and Public Policy*, Cheltenham, UK and Brookfield, VT: Edward Elgar: pp. 83–104.

——1997. "Paradoxes of the competition state: the dynamics of political globalization." *Government and Opposition* 32(2): pp. 251–74.

——1998. "Neomedievalism, civil wars and the new security dilemma." *Civil Wars* 1(1) (Spring): pp. 36–64.

——1999a. "Globalization, governance and complexity." In Prakash, A. and Hart, J. A. eds. *Globalization and Governance*, London: Routledge: pp. 184–208.

——2000a. "Embedding global finance: markets as governance structures." In Ronit, K. and Schneider, V. eds. *Private Organizations in Global Politics*, London: Routledge: pp. 59–82.

——2000b. "The new security dilemma: divisibility, defection and disorder in the global era." *Review of International Studies* 26(4) (October): pp. 623–46.

——2000c. "Restructuring the political arena: globalization and the paradoxes of the competition state." In Germain, R. ed. *Globalization and its Critics*, London: Macmillan: pp. 117–38.

——2000d. "Structuring the political arena: public goods, states and governance in a globalizing world." In Ronen Palan, ed. *Contemporary Theories in the Global Political Economy: Emerging Debates, Methodologies and Approaches*, London and New York: Routledge, pp. 21–35.

——2001. "From 'iron triangles' to 'golden pentangles'? Globalizing the policy process." *Global Governance* 7(4) (October): pp. 397–410.

——2003. "Globalization and other stories: paradigmatic selection in international politics." In Hülsemeyer, A. ed. *Globalization in the 21st Century: Convergence and Divergence*, London: Palgrave Macmillan: pp. 51–66.

——2006a. "Plurality, pluralism, and power: elements of pluralist analysis in an age of globalization." In Eisfeld, R. ed. *Pluralism: Developments in the Theory and Practice of Democracy*, Opladen, Germany: Barbara Budrich: pp. 81–111.

——2006b. "Restructuring the state in a globalizing world: capital accumulation, tangled hierarchies and the search for a new spatio-temporal fix." *Review of International Political Economy* 13(4): pp. 679–95.

——2008 [in press]. "Embedding neoliberalism: the evolution of a hegemonic paradigm." *Journal of International Trade and Diplomacy* (Spring).

de Certeau, M. 1984. *The Practice of Everyday Life*, Berkeley: University of California Press.

Chandler, A. D. 1977. *The Visible Hand: The Managerial Revolution in American Business*, Cambridge, MA: Harvard University Press.

Chandler, A. D. Jr. 1990. *Scale and Scope: The Dynamics of Industrial Capitalism*, Cambridge, MA: Harvard University Press.

Chase-Dunn, C. K. and Hall, T. D. 1991. *Core/Periphery Relations in Pre-Capitalist Worlds*, Boulder, CO: Westview Press.

Chase-Dunn, C., Kawano, Y., and Brewer, B. 2000. "Trade globalization since 1795: waves of integration in the world-system." *American Sociological Review* 65: pp. 77–95.

Checkel, J. 1998. "The constructivist turn in international relations." *World Politics* 50(2) (January): pp. 324–48.

Chen, C. 1984. "On the foreign trade of China in the 19th century and the China-India-Britain triangular trade." In *Essays in Chinese Maritime History*, Taipei: Sun Yat-Sen Institute for Social Sciences and Philosophy, Academia Sinica: pp. 131–73.

Chernow, R. 1997. *The Death of the Banker: The Decline and Fall of the Great Financial Dynasties and the Triumph of the Small Investor*, Toronto: Vintage Canada.

Chivvis, C. S. 2006. "Charles de Gaulle, Jacques Rueff and French international monetary policy under Bretton Woods." *Journal of Contemporary History* 41: pp. 701–20.

Christensen, T. 2006. "Fostering stability or creating a monster? The rise of China and U.S. policy toward East Asia." *International Security* 31(1) (Summer): pp. 81–126.

Chwieroth, J. 2007a. "Testing and measuring the role of ideas: the case of neoliberalism and the International Monetary Fund." *International Studies Quarterly* 51: pp. 5–30.

——2007b. "Neoliberal economists and capital account liberalization in emerging markets." *International Organization* 61(2) (Spring): pp. 443–63.

Clapp, J. 2001. *Toxic Exports: The Transfer of Hazardous Waste from Rich to Poor Countries*, Ithaca, NY: Cornell University Press.

Clark, A. M., Friedman, E. J., and Hochstetler, K. 1999. "Sovereignty, global civil society, and the social conferences: NGOs and states at the U.N. conferences on population, social development, and human settlements," paper presented at the Annual Convention of the International Studies Association, February 16–20, Washington DC.

Clarke, P. 1978. *Liberals and Social Democrats*, Cambridge: Cambridge University Press.

Clarkson, S. 2002. *Uncle Sam and Us: Globalization, Neoconservatism and the Canadian State*, Toronto: University of Toronto Press.

Clayton, R. and Pontusson, J. 1998. "Welfare state retrenchment revisited: entitlement cuts, public sector restructuring, and inegalitarian trends in advanced capitalist societies." *World Politics* 51(1) (October): pp. 67–98.

Clement, W. and Myles, J. 1994. *Relations of Ruling: Class and Gender in Postindustrial Societies*, Montreal: McGill-Queens University Press.

Clift, B. 2003. "The changing political economy of France: *dirigisme* under duress." In Ryner, M. and Cafruny, A. eds. *A Ruined Fortress? Neo-Liberal Hegemony and Transformation in Europe*, New York: Rowman and Littlefield: pp. 173–200.

——2007. "French corporate governance in the new global economy: mechanisms of change and hybridisation within models of capitalism." *Political Studies* 55(4): pp. 546–67.

Clift, B. and Tomlinson, J. 2004. "Fiscal policy and capital mobility: the construction of economic policy rectitude in Britain and France." *New Political Economy* 9(4) (December): pp. 515–38.

——2008. "Whatever happened to the balance of payments 'problem'? The contingent (re-) construction of British economic performance assessment." *British Journal of Politics and International Relations.* 10(4): pp. 607–29

Coates, D. 1994. *The Question of UK Decline*, Hemel Hempstead, UK: Harvester Wheatsheaf.

——2000. *Models of Capitalism*, Cambridge: Polity Press.

Coates, D. ed. 2005. *Varieties of Capitalism; Varieties of Approaches*, Basingstoke, UK: Palgrave.

Coates, D. and Hillard, J. 1986. "Introduction." In Coates, D. and Hillard, J. eds. *The Economic Decline of Modern Britain: The Debate Between Left and Right*, Brighton, UK: Wheatsheaf: pp. ix–xii.

Cobham, D. 2000. "Review." *Economic Journal* 110(461): pp. F259–61.

Coe, N., Hess, M., Yeung, H.-W., Dicken, P., and Henderson, J. 2004. "'Globalizing' regional development: a global production networks perspective." *Transactions of the Institute of British Geographers*, New Series 29(4): pp. 468–84.

Cohen, B. J. 1998. *The Geography of Money*, Ithaca, NY: Cornell University Press.

——2002. "Capital controls: why do governments hesitate?" In Armijo, L. E. ed. *Debating the Global Financial Architecture*, Albany, NY: SUNY Press.

——2003. "Capital controls: the neglected option." In Underhill, G. R. D. and Zhang, X. eds. *International Financial Governance under Stress: Global Structures versus National Imperatives*, New York: Cambridge University Press.

——2007. "The Transatlantic divide: why are American and British IPE so different?" *Review of International Political Economy* 14(2) (May): pp. 197–219.

——2008a. "The transatlantic divide: a rejoinder." *Review of International Political Economy* 15(1): pp. 30–34.

——2008b. *International Political Economy: An Intellectual History*, Princeton, NJ: Princeton University Press.

Cole, A. ed. 1928. *Industrial and Commercial Correspondence of Alexander Hamilton*, Chicago: A. W. Shaw.

Comim, F. 2000. "On the concept of applied economics: lessons from the history of growth theories." *History of Political Economy* 32 (Suppl. 1): pp. 145–76.

Commission on Global Governance. 1995. *Our Global Neighbourhood: The Report of the Commission on Global Governance*, Oxford: Oxford University Press.

Comor, E. A. 1998. *Communication, Commerce and Power*, London: Macmillan.

Conan, A. R. 1952. *The Sterling Area*, London: Macmillan.

——1961. *The Rationale of the Sterling Area*, London: Macmillan.

——1966. *The Problem of Sterling*, London: Macmillan.

Condliffe, J. B. 1950. *The Commerce of Nation*, New York: W. W. Norton and Co.

Considine, M. 2005. *Making Public Policy: Institutions, Actors, Strategies*, Cambridge: Polity Press.

Cooley, A. 2005. *Logics of Hierarchy: The Organization of Empires, States and Military Occupations*. Ithaca, NY: Cornell University Press.

—— 2008. *Base Politics: Democratic Change and the US Military Overseas*. Ithaca, NY: Cornell University Press.

Cooley, A. and Ron, J. 2002. "The NGO scramble: organizational insecurity and the political economy of transnational action." *International Security* 27(1): pp. 5–39.

Cooley, A. and H. Spruyt. 2009. *Contracting States: Sovereign Transfers in International Relations*, Princeton, NJ: Princeton University Press.

Cooney, K. and Sato, Y. eds. 2007. *The Rise of China and International Security: America and East Asia Respond to the Rising Power*, London: Routledge.

Cooper, A. F. 2004. *Tests of Global Governance: Canadian Diplomacy and the United Nations World Conferences*, Tokyo: United Nations University Press.

——2008. *Celebrity Diplomacy*, Boulder, CO: Paradigm Publishers.

Cooper, R. N. 1968. *The Economics of Interdependence: Economic Policy in the Atlantic Community*, New York: McGraw-Hill.

Coram, A. 2001. "Some political aspects of taxation and distribution in federal governments: an application of the theory of the core." *European Journal of Political Research* 39(4): pp. 417–29.

Cowhey, P. F. 1993. "Domestic Institutions and the Credibility of International Commitments: Japan and the United States," *International Organization* 50(2): pp. 109–39.

Cox, R. H. 2001. "The social construction of an imperative: why welfare reform happened in Denmark and the Netherlands but not in Germany." *World Politics* 53 (April): pp. 463–98.

Cox, R. W. 1972. "Labor and transnational relations," in Keohane, R. O. and Nye, J. S. eds. *Transnational Relations and World Politics*, Cambridge, MA: Harvard University Press.

——1977. "Labor and hegemony", *International Organization* 31(3): pp. 385–424.

——1981. "Social forces, states and world orders: beyond international relations theory." *Millennium* 10(2): pp. 126–55.

——1983. "Gramsci, hegemony and international relations: an essay in method." *Millennium* 12(2): pp. 162–75.

——1986. "Social forces, states and world orders: beyond international relations theory." In Keohane, R. O. ed. *Neorealism and its Critics*, New York: Columbia University Press: pp. 204–54.

——1987. *Production, Power and World Order: Social Forces in the Making of History*, New York: Columbia University Press.

——1992. "Multilateralism and world order." *Review of International Studies* 18(2): pp. 161–80.

——1996. "'Take six eggs': theory, finance and the real economy in the work of Susan Strange." In Cox, R. W. ed. *Approaches to World Order*, Cambridge: Cambridge University Press: pp. 174–90.

——1999. "Civil Society at the turn of the millennium: prospects for an alternative world order." *Review of International Studies* 25(1): pp. 3–28.

——2002. *The Political Economy of a Plural World: Critical Reflections on Power, Morals and Civilization*, London: Routledge.

——2004. "Beyond empire and terror: critical reflections on the political economy of world order." *New Political Economy* 9(3): pp. 307–23.

317

Cox, R. W. ed. 1997. *The New Realism: Perspectives on Multilateralism and World Order*, London: Macmillan for the United Nations University.

Cox, R. W. and Jacobson, H. K. 1973. *Anatomy of Influence: Decision-Making in International Organization*, New Haven, CT: Yale University Press.

Cox, R. W. with Sinclair, T. J. 1996. *Approaches to World Order*, Cambridge: Cambridge University Press.

Crafts, N. F. R. 1985. *British Economic Growth During the Industrial Revolution*, Oxford: Clarendon Press.

——1997. *Britain's Relative Economic Decline, 1870–1995*, London: Social Market Foundation.

Creighton, D. 1957. *Harold Adam Innis: Portrait of a Scholar*, Toronto: University of Toronto Press.

Crouch, C. 1977. *Class Conflict and the Industrial Relations Crisis: Compromise and Corporatism in the Policies of the British State*, London: Humanities Press, Heinemann Educational.

——2003. *Capitalist Diversity and Change*, Oxford: Oxford University Press.

——2005. *Capitalist Diversity and Change*, New York: Oxford University Press.

Crouch, C. ed. 1979. *The State and Economy in Contemporary Capitalism*, London: Croom Helm.

Crouch, C. and Streeck, W. eds. 1997. *Political Economy of Modern Capitalism: Mapping Convergence and Divergence*, London: Sage.

Crozier, M. and Friedberg, E. 1977. *L'Acteur et le système: les contraintes de l'action collective*, Paris: Editions du Seuil.

Culpepper, P. D. 2008. "The politics of common knowledge: ideas and institutional change in wage bargaining." *International Organization* 62(1) (Winter): pp.1–33.

Cumings, B. 1997. "Japan and Northeast Asia into the twenty-first century." In Katzenstein, P. J. and Shiraishi, T. eds. *Network Power. Japan and Asia*, Ithaca, NY: Cornell University Press: pp. 136–68.

——1999. "Webs with no spiders, spiders with no webs: the genealogy of the developmental state." In Woo-Cumings, M. ed. *The Developmental State*, Ithaca, NY: Cornell University Press: pp. 61–92.

Cushman, J. W. 1993. *Fields from the Sea: Chinese Junk Trade with Siam during the Late Eighteenth and Early Nineteenth Centuries*, Studies on Southeast Asia, Southeast Asia Program, Ithaca, NY: Cornell University Press.

Cusset, F. 2008. *French Theory: How Foucault, Derrida, Deleuze, & Co. Transformed the Intellectual Life of the United States*, Minneapolis: University of Minnesota Press.

Cutler, C. A. 2003. *Private Power and Global Authority: Transnational Merchant Law in the Global Political Economy*, Cambridge: Cambridge University Press.

Dahl, R. A. 1976. *Modern Political Analysis*. Englewood Cliffs, NJ: Prentice-Hall.

Darden, K. 2008. *Economic Liberalism and Its Rivals: The Formation of International Institutions among the Post-Soviet States*, New York: Cambridge University Press.

Davies, M. 2005. "The public spheres of unprotected workers?" *Global Society* 19(2): pp. 131–54.

Davies, M. and Neimann, M. 2002. "The everyday spaces of global politics: work, leisure, family." *New Political Science* 24(4): pp. 557–77.

Dean, M. 1999. *Governmentality: Power and Rule in Modern Society*, London: Sage.

Deleuze, G. 1991 [1953]. *Empiricism and Subjectivity: An Essay on Hume's Theory of Human Nature*, New York: Columbia University Press.

DeLong, J. B. 2005. "Sisyphus as social democrat: the life and legacy of John Kenneth Galbraith." *Foreign Affairs* 84(3) (May/June): pp. 126–30.

Denemark, R., Friedman, J., Gills, B. K., and Modelski, G. 2000. *World System History*, New York: Routledge.

Denemark, R. A. and O'Brien, R. 1997. "Contesting the canon: international political economy at UK and US universities." *Review of International Political Economy* 4(1): pp. 214–38.

Denzau, A. and North, D. 1994. "Shared mental models: ideologies and institutions." *Kyklos* 47: pp. 3–31.

Denzau, A. and Roy, R. K. 2007. "The neoliberal shift in US fiscal policy from the 1980s to the 1990s: a shared mental model approach to understanding coalition-driven policy shifts." In Denzau, A., Roy, R. K., and Willett, T. eds. *Neoliberalism: National and Regional Experiments with Global Ideas*, London: Routledge.

318

Denzau, A., Roy, R. K., and Willett, T. eds. 2007. *Neoliberalism: National and Regional Experiments with Global Ideas*, London: Routledge.

DerDerian, J. and Shapiro, M. J. eds. 1989. *International/Intertextual Relations: Postmodern Readings of World Politics*, Lexington, MA: Lexington Books.

de Soysa, I. and Oneal, J. R. 1999. "Boon or bane? Reassessing the productivity of foreign direct investment." *American Sociological Review* 64: pp. 766–82.

Dicken, P. 2007. *Global Shift: Mapping the Changing Contours of the World Economy*, London: Sage, 5th edition.

Dicken, P., Kelly, P., Olds, K., and Yeung, H. W. 2001. "Chains and networks, territories and scales: towards an analytical framework for the global economy." *Global Networks* 1(2): pp. 89–112.

Dickie, M., Mallet, V., and Sevastopulo, D. 2005. "Washington is turning its attention from the Middle East to contemplate a previously disregarded threat." *Financial Times*, April 7.

Dickins, A. 2006. "The evolution of international political economy." *International Affairs* 82(3): pp. 479–92.

DiMaggio, P. and Powell, W. 1983. "The iron cage revisited: institutional isomorphism and collective rationality in organizational fields." *American Sociological Review* 48: pp. 147–60.

DiMaggio, P. and Powell, W. eds. 1991. *The New Institutionalism in Organizational Analysis*, Chicago: University of Chicago Press.

Djelic, M.-L. 1998. *Exporting the American Model: The Postwar Transformation of European Business*, New York: Oxford University Press.

Djelic, M.-L. and Sahlin-Andersson, K. eds. 2006. *Transnational Governance: Institutional Dynamics of Regulation*, New York: Cambridge University Press.

Dobbin, F. 1993. "The social construction of the Great Depression: industrial policy during the 1930s in the United States, Britain, and France." *Theory and Society* 22: pp. 1–56.

——1994. *Forging Industrial Policy: The United States, Britain, and France in the Railway Age*, New York: Cambridge University Press.

Dobbin, F. ed. 2004a. *The New Economic Sociology: A Reader*, Princeton, NJ: Princeton University Press.

——2004b. *The Sociology of the Economy*, New York: Russell Sage Foundation.

Dobbin, F., Simmons, B., and Garrett, G. 2007. "The global diffusion of public policies: social construction, coercion, competition, or learning?" *Annual Review of Sociology* 33: pp. 449–72.

Dodgson, R. 1999. "Contesting neoliberal globalization at U.N. global conferences: the women's health movement and the International Conference on Population and Development." Paper presented at the Annual Convention of the International Studies Association, Washington DC, February 16–20.

Doner, R. F., Noble, G. W., and Ravenhill, J. 2004. "Production networks in East Asia's automobile parts industry." In Shahid, Y., Anjum Altaf, M., and Nabeshima, K. eds. *Global Production Networking and Technological Change in East Asia*, Washington DC: World Bank/Oxford University Press: pp. 159–208.

Doner, R. F., Ritchie, B. K., and Slater, D. 2005. "Systemic vulnerability and the origins of developmental states: Northeast and Southeast Asia in comparative perspective." *International Organization* 59 (2): pp. 327–61.

Dore, R. 2000. *Stock Market Capitalism: Welfare Capitalism*, New York: Oxford University Press.

Doremus, P. N., Keller, W. W., Pauly, L. W., and Reich, S. 1998. *The Myth of the Global Corporation*, Princeton, NJ: Princeton University Press.

Douglas, I. R. 1999. "Globalization as governance: toward an archaeology of contemporary political reason." In Prakash, A. and Hart, J. A. eds. *Globalization and Governance*, London: Routledge: pp. 134–60.

Douglas, M. 1986. *How Institutions Think*, Syracuse, NY: Syracuse University Press.

Dow, A., Dow, S., and Hutton, A. 2000. "Applied economics in a political economy tradition: the case of Scotland from the 1890s to the 1950s." *History of Political Economy* 32(Suppl. 1): pp. 177–98.

Drache, D. 2001. *The Market or the Public Domain: Global Governance and the Asymmetry of Power*, New York: Routledge.

Drezner, D. 2007. *All Politics is Global*. Princeton: Princeton University Press.

Duina, F. 1999. *Harmonizing Europe: Nation States Within the Common Market*, Albany: State University of New York Press.

——2004. "Regional market building as a social process: an analysis of cognitive strategies in NAFTA, the European Union, and Mercosur." *Economy and Society* 33(3): pp. 359–89.

——2006. *The Social Construction of Free Trade: The European Union, NAFTA, and Mercosur*, Princeton, NJ: Princeton University Press.

Dunleavy, P. J. 1994. "The globalization of public services production: can government be 'best in world'?" *Public Policy and Administration* 9(2) (Summer): pp. 36–64.

Dunn, K. C. and Shaw, T. M. eds. 2001. *Africa's Challenge to International Relations Theory*, Basingstoke, UK: Palgrave Macmillan.

Duus, P. 1984. "Economic dimensions of Meiji Imperialism: the case of Korea, 1895–1910." In Myers, R. H. and Peattie, M. R. eds. *The Japanese Colonial Empire, 1895–1945*, Princeton, NJ: Princeton University Press: pp. 128–71.

Eckersley, R. 2004. "The big chill: the WTO and multilateral environmental agreement." *Global Environmental Politics* 4(2): pp. 24–50.

——2007. "A green public sphere in the WTO? The *amicus curiae* interventions in the trans-atlantic biotech dispute." *European Journal of International Relations* 13(2): pp. 329–56.

Eckersley, R. ed. 1995. *Markets, the State and the Environment: Towards Integration*, Melbourne: Macmillan.

ECLAC. 1963. *The Economic Development of Latin America in the Post-War Period*, New York: United Nations.

The Economist. 2003. "Rating agencies; exclusion zone." February 8: p. 65.

Eichengreen, B. 1989. "Hegemonic stability theories of the international monetary system." In Cooper, R. ed. *Can Nations Agree? Issues in International Economic Cooperation*, Washington DC: Brookings Institution Press: pp. 285–86.

——1992. *Golden Fetters: The Gold Standard and the Great Depression, 1919–1939*, Oxford: Oxford University Press.

——1998. "Dental hygiene and nuclear war: how international relations look from economics." *International Organization* 52(4): pp. 993–1012.

——2002. "Capital account liberalization: what do the cross–country studies show us?" *World Bank Economic Review* 15(3): pp. 341–66.

——2004. "Review." *The American Historical Review* 109(5): pp. 1542–43.

——2007. *Global Imbalances and the Lessons of Bretton Woods*, Cambridge, MA: MIT Press.

Einstein, A. 1949. "Why socialism?" *Monthly Review* (May).

Elias, J. 2004. *Fashioning Inequality: The Multinational Company and Gendered Employment in a Globalizing World*, Aldershot, UK: Ashgate.

Elias, N. 1996. *The Germans*, New York: Columbia University Press.

Elisonas, J. 1991. "The inseparable trinity: Japan's relations with China and Korea," in Hall, J. ed. *The Cambridge History of Japan 4: Early Modern Japan*, Cambridge: Cambridge University Press: pp. 235–300.

Elkins, Z., Guzman A. and B. Simmons. 2006. "Competing for Capital: the Diffusion of Bilateral Investment Treaties, 1960–2000," *International Organization* 60(4): pp. 811–46.

Elms, D. K. 2008. "New directions for IPE: drawing from behavioral economics." *The International Studies Review* 10(2): pp. 239–65.

Emmott, B. 1989. *The Sun also Sets*, New York: Simon and Schuster.

Epstein, C. 2008a. *Producing Whales, Performing Power: A Study of Discourse in International Relations*, Cambridge, MA: MIT Press.

——2008b. *The Power of Words in International Relations: Birth of an Anti-Whaling Discourse*, Cambridge, MA: MIT Press.

Epstein, R. 2005. "Diverging effects of social learning and external incentives in Polish central banking and agriculture." In Schimmelfennig, F. and Sedelmeier, U. eds. *The Europeanization of Central and Eastern Europe*, Ithaca, NY: Cornell University Press.

——2006. "Cultivating consensus and creating conflict: international institutions and the (de)politicization of economic policy in postcommunist Europe." *Comparative Political Studies* 39(8) (October): pp. 1019–42.

Ernst, D. 2004. "Global production networks in East Asia's electronics industry and upgrading prospects in Malaysia." In Shahid Y., Anjum Altaf, M. and Nabeshima, K. eds. *Global Production Networking and Technological Change in East Asia*, Washington DC: World Bank/Oxford University Press: pp. 89–157.

Esherick, J. 1972. "Harvard on China: the apologetics of imperialism." *Bulletin of Concerned Asian Scholars* IV(4): pp. 9–16.

Esping-Andersen, G. 1990. *The Three Worlds of Welfare Capitalism*, Princeton, NJ: Princeton University Press.

——1999. *Social Foundations of Postindustrial Economies*, New York: Oxford University Press.

—— 2003. "Why no socialism anywhere? A reply to Alex Hicks and Lane Kenworthy." *Socio-Economic Review* 1: pp. 63–70.

EU. 2003. European Union budget website, as of February 2: http://europa.eu.int/comm/budget/abb/abb_2002/apb/relex_en.htm

Evans, P. 1979. *Dependent Development*, Berkeley: University of California Press.

——1995. *Embedded Autonomy: States and Industrial Transformation*, Princeton, NJ: Princeton University Press.

——2007. "Is it labor's turn to globalize? 21st century challenges and opportunities", paper presented to the Democracy and Development Seminar, Princeton Institute for International and Regional Studies (October 24).

Evans, P. and Rauch, J. E. 1999. "Bureaucracy and growth: a cross-national analysis of the effects of 'Weberian' state structures on economic growth." *American Sociological Review* 64: pp. 748–65.

Evans, P., Rueschemeyer, D., and Skocpol, T. eds. 1985. *Bringing the State Back In*, New York: Cambridge University Press.

Fairbank, J. K. 1983. *The United States and China*, Cambridge, MA: Harvard University Press.

Fallows, J. 1994. *Looking at the Sun*, New York: Pantheon Books.

Fearon, J. 1994. "Domestic Political Audiences and the Escalation of International Disputes," *American Political Science Review* 88: pp. 577–92.

Feigenbaum, H., Henig, J. and Hamnett, C. 1998 *Shrinking the State: the Political Underpinnings of Privatization*. Cambridge: Cambridge University Press.

Feis, H. 1930. *Europe: The World's Banker, 1870–1914*, New Haven, CT: Yale University Press.

——1965. *Europe: The World's Banker, 1870–1914*, New York: Norton.

Ferguson, B. 1993. *Remaking Liberalism: The Intellectual Legacy of Adam Shortt, O.D. Skelton, W.C. Clark and W.A. Mackintosh, 1890–1925*, Montreal and Kingston, Ontario: McGill-Queen's University Press.

Fernandez-Santamaria, J. A. 1977. *Reason of State and Statecraft in Spanish Political Thought, 1595–1640*, Cambridge: Cambridge University Press.

Feuerwerker, A. 1970. "Handicraft and manufactured cotton textiles in China, 1871–1910." *Journal of Economic History* 30(2): pp. 338–78.

Fine, B. 1980. *Economic Theory and Ideology*, London: Edward Arnold.

Finnemore, M. 1996a. *National Interests in International Society*, Ithaca, NY: Cornell University Press.

——1996b. "Norms, culture, and world politics: insights from sociology's institutionalism." *International Organization* 50(2): pp. 325–47.

——2003. *The Purpose of Intervention: Changing Beliefs about the Use of Force*, Ithaca, NY: Cornell University Press.

Fiori, J. 2008. "The 'New Left' in power: neo-liberal continuities with social safety nets in Lula's Brazil." M.Phil. dissertation, Cambridge University.

Firebaugh, G. 2006. *The New Geography of Global Income Inequality*, Cambridge, MA: Harvard University Press.

Fischer, S. 1997. "Capital account liberalization and the role of the IMF," paper presented at the Asia and IMF Seminar, Hong Kong, September 19.

Fligstein, N. 1990. *The Transformation of Corporate Control*, Cambridge, MA: Harvard University Press.

——2001. *The Architecture of Markets: An Economic Sociology of Twenty-First Century Capitalist Societies*, Princeton, NJ: Princeton University Press.

Florida, R. 2005. "The world is spiky." *Atlantic Monthly* 296(3): pp. 48–51.

Flynn, D. O. and Giraldez, A. 1995. "Born with 'silver spoon': the origin of world trade in 1571." *Journal of World History* 6(2): pp. 201–11.

FOLHAONLINE. 2008. www1.folha.uol.com.br/folha/brasil/ult96u87635.shtml

Ford, J. 2003. *A Social Theory of the WTO*, Houndmills, UK: Palgrave Macmillan.

Foucault, M. 1980. *Power/Knowledge: Selected Interviews and Other Writings, 1972–1977*, Gordon C. ed., Brighton UK: Harvester Press.

——1991. "Governmentality." In Burchell, G., Gordon, C., and Miller, P. eds. *The Foucault Effect: Studies in Governmentality*, Hemel Hempstead, UK: Harvester Press: pp. 87–104.

——2004. *Naissance de la biopolitique. Cours au Collège de France, 1978–1979*. Paris: Gallimard/Seuil.

Fourcade, M. 2006. "The construction of a global profession: the transnationalization of economics." *American Journal of Sociology* 112: pp. 145–94.

Fourcade-Gourinchas, M. and Babb, S. 2002. "The rebirth of the liberal creed: paths to neoliberalism in four countries." *American Journal of Sociology* 108: pp. 533–79.

Frank, A. G. 1967. *Capitalism and Underdevelopment in Latin America: Historical Studies of Chile and Brazil*, New York: Monthly Review Press.

Frank, A. G. and Gills, B. K. eds. 1996. *The World System*, London: Routledge.

Frangie, S. 2008. The Good Governance Agenda: Weak States and Economic Development., PhD Dissertation, Cambridge University, UK.

Freeden, M. ed. 1988. *J.A. Hobson: A Reader*, London: Unwin Hyman.

Freedom from Debt Coalition. 1997. *Primer on Philippine Debt*, Quezon City, Philippines: FDC.

——1997. "Revisiting Philippine Debt," paper presented at the National Debt Conference, Innotech, Commonwealth Avenue, Quezon City, October 9–10.

Freeman, L. 1997. *The Ambiguous Champion: Canada and South Africa in the Trudeau and Mulroney years*, Toronto: University of Toronto Press.

Freud, S. (1957). "Thoughts For the Times on War and Death." In J. Strachey, ed., *The Standard Edition of the Complete Psychological Works of Sigmund Freud, Volume XIV (1914–1916): On the History of the Psycho-Analytic Movement, Papers on Metapsychology and Other Works*, 273–300. London: Hogarth Press.

Frey, B. 1984. "The public choice view of international political economy." *International Organization* 38(1) (Winter): pp. 199–233.

——1986. *International Political Economics*, Oxford: Blackwell.

Friedberg, A. 1988. *The Weary Titan: Britain and the Experience of Relative Decline, 1895–1905*, Princeton, NJ: Princeton University Press.

——2005. "The future of U.S.–China relations: is conflict inevitable?" *International Security* 30(2) (Fall): pp. 7–45.

Frieden, J. 1991. "Invested interests: the politics of national economic policies in a world of global finance." *International Organization* 45(4) (Autumn): pp. 425–52.

——1994. International Investment and Colonial Control: A New Interpretation. *International Organization* 48 (4): pp. 559–93.

Frieden, J. and Lake, D. eds. 2000. *International Political Economy: Perspectives on Global Power and Wealth*, New York: St. Martin's Press.

Frieden, J. and Martin, J. 2003. "International political economy: global and domestic interactions." In Katznelson, I. and Milner, H. eds. *Political Science: The State of the Discipline*, New York: W.W. Norton.

Frieden, J. and Rogowski, R. 1996. "The impact of the international economy on national policies: an analytical overview." In Keohane, R. and Milner, H. eds. *Internationalization and Domestic Politics*, New York: Cambridge University Press.

Friedman, T. 1999. *The Lexus and the Olive Tree*, New York: Anchor Books.

——2005. *The World Is Flat: A Brief History of the 21st Century*. New York: Farrar, Straus and Giroux.

Funabashi, Y. 2003. "China is preparing a peaceful ascendancy." *International Herald Tribune*, December 30.

Furtado, C. 1970. *Obstacles to Development in Latin America*, New York: Anchor Books.

Gabriel, C. and Macdonald, L. 1994. "NAFTA, women and organising in Canada and Mexico: forging a feminist internationality." *Millennium* 23(3): pp. 535–62.

Galbraith, J. K. 1970. *Economics, Peace and Laughter*, Harmondsworth, UK: Penguin.

Gamble, A. 1974. *The Conservative Nation*, London: Routledge and Kegan Paul.

——1985. *Britain in Decline*, London: Macmillan.

——1986. "The political economy of freedom." In Levitas, R. ed. *The Ideology of the New Right*, Cambridge: Polity Press: pp. 25–54.

——1988. *The Free Economy and the Strong State: The Politics of Thatcherism*, Basingstoke, UK: Macmillan.

——1995. "New political economy." *Political Studies* 43(3): pp. 516–30.

——2000. "Theories and explanations of British decline." In English, R. and Kenny, M. eds. *Rethinking British Decline*, Basingstoke, UK: Macmillan: pp. 1–22.

——2003. *Between Europe and America*, Basingstoke, UK: Palgrave.

——2004. "British national capitalism since the war: declinism, Thatcherism and New Labour." In Perraton, J. and Clift, B. eds. *Where are National Capitalisms Now?* Basingstoke, UK: Palgrave: pp. 33–49.

Gamble, A. and Payne, A. eds. 1996. *Regionalism and World Order*, Basingstoke, UK: Macmillan.

Gamble, A., Payne, A. J., Hoogvelt, A., Dietrich, M., and Kenny, M. 1996. "Editorial: *New Political Economy*." *New Political Economy* 1(1): pp. 5–11.

Gao, W. 1993. *Zou xiang jinshi de Zhongguo yu 'chaogong' guo guanxi.* (The relation between China and its tributary states in modern times), Guangdong: Guangdong gaodeng jiaoyu chubanshe.

Garafolo, W., Albright, V., and Michaels, M. J. 2002. "IRS issues more summonses for offshore credit card data." *Journal of International Taxation* (November): pp. 44–45.

Garrett, G. 1998. *Partisan Politics in the Global Economy*, New York: Cambridge University Press.

——2000. "The causes of globalization." *Comparative Political Studies* 33(6/7): pp. 941–91.

Gavin, F. 2004. *Gold, Dollars, And Power: The Politics of International Monetary Relations, 1958–1971*, Chapel Hill: University of North Carolina Press.

Gellner, E. A. 1983. *Nations and Nationalism*, Oxford: Blackwell.

George, J. 1994. *Discourses of Global Politics: A Critical (Re)Introduction to International Relations*, Boulder, CO: Lynne Reinner.

Gereffi, G. 1996. "Global commodity chains: new forms of coordination and control among nations and firms in international industries." *Competition and Change* 1(4): pp. 427–39.

——2005. "The global economy: organization, governance, and development." In Smelser, N. and Swedberg, R. eds. *The Handbook of Economic Sociology*, 2nd edition, Princeton, NJ: Princeton University Press: pp. 160–82.

Gereffi, G., Humphrey, J., and Sturgeon, T. 2005. "The governance of global value chains." *Review of International Political Economy* 12(1): pp. 78–104.

Gereffi, G. and Korzeniewicz, M. eds. 1994. *Commodity Chains and Global Capitalism*, Westport, CT: Praeger.

Gereffi, G., Korzeniewicz, M., and Korzeniewicz, R. P. 1994. "Introduction: global commodity chains." In Gereffi, G. and Korzeniewicz, M. eds. *Commodity Chains and Global Capitalism*, Westport, CT: Praeger: pp.1–14.

Germain, R. D. 1991. *American Hegemony and the Trilateral Commission*, Cambridge: Cambridge University Press.

——1993. *Gramsci, Historical Materialism and International Relations*, Cambridge: Cambridge University Press.

——1996. "The worlds of finance: a Braudelian perspective on IPE."*European Journal of International Relations* 2(2): pp. 201–30.

——1997. *The International Organization of Credit*, Cambridge: Cambridge University Press.

——2001. "Institutional investors and Polanyi's double movement: a contemporary model of currency crises." *Review of International Political Economy* 8(3): pp. 389–437.

323

——2007. "'Critical' political economy, historical materialism and Adam Morton." *Politics* 27(2): pp. 127–31.

Germain, R. D. and Kenny, M. 1998. "Engaging Gramsci: international relations theory and the new Gramscians." *Review of International Studies* 24(1): pp. 3–21.

Gernier, J. 1852. "De l'origine du mot economie politique et des autres divers noms donnés à la science economique." *Journal des Economistes* XXXII(1) (July-August).

Gershman, J. and Bello, W. eds. 1993. *Reexamining and Renewing the Philippine Progressive Vision: Papers and Proceedings of the 1993 Conference of the Forum for Philippine Alternatives, San Francisco, California, April 2–4*, Manila: Forum for Philippine Alternatives.

Gertz, B. 2000. *The China Threat: How the People's Republic Targets America*, Washington DC: Regnery Publications.

GGDC. 2008. Gröningen Growth and Development Centre database: www.ggdc.net.

Ghemawat, P. 2007. "Why the World Isn't Flat," *Foreign Policy* 159: pp. 54–60.

Ghosh, J. 2007. "Whodunnit? Financial Crises and the End of the Developmental State," paper presented at the conference "A Decade after: Recovery and Adjustment since the East Asian Crisis," Bangkok, July 12–14.

Gibson-Graham, J. K. 1996. *The End of Capitalism (As We Knew It): A Feminist Critique of Political Economy*, Oxford: Blackwell.

——2006. *A Postcapitalist Politics*, Minneapolis: University of Minnesota Press.

Giddens, A. 1979. *Central Problems of Social Theory: Action, Structure and Contradiction in Social Analysis*, London: Macmillan.

——1985. *The Nation-State and Violence*, Berkeley: University of California Press.

Gill, S. 1991. *American Hegemony and the Trilateral Commission*, Cambridge: Cambridge University Press.

——1995. "Globalisation, market civilisation and disciplinary neoliberalism." *Millenium* 24(3): pp. 399–423.

——2002. *Power and Resistance in the New World Order*, Basingstoke, UK: Palgrave.

——2003. *Power and Resistance in the New World Order*, London: Palgrave Macmillan.

Gill, S. ed. 1993. *Gramsci, Historical Materialism and International Relations*, Cambridge: Cambridge University Press.

Gill, S. and Law, D. 1988a. *The Global Political Economy*, Baltimore, MD: Johns Hopkins University Press.

——1988b. *The Global Political Economy: Perspectives, Problems and Policies*, Hemel Hempstead: Harvester Wheatsheaf.

——1989. "Global hegemony and the structural power of capital." *International Studies Quarterly* 33(4): pp. 475–99.

Gill, S. R. and Mittelman, J. H. eds. 1997. *Innovation and Transformation in International Studies*, Cambridge: Cambridge University Press.

Gilpin, R. 1971. "The politics of transnational relations." *International Organization* 25(3) (Summer): pp. 398–419.

——1972. "The politics of transnational economic relations." In Keohane, R. O. and Nye, S. J. Jr. eds. *Transnational Relations and World Politics*, Cambridge, MA: Harvard University Press: pp. 48–69.

——1975a. *U.S. Power and the Multinational Corporation: The Political Economy of Foreign Direct Investment*, New York: Basic Books.

——1975b. "Three models of the future." *International Organization* 29(1) (Winter): pp. 37–60.

——1981. *War and Change in World Politics*, Cambridge: Cambridge University Press.

——1987. *The Political Economy of International Relations*, Princeton, NJ: Princeton University Press.

——2000. *The Challenge of Global Capitalism*, Princeton, NJ: Princeton University Press.

——2001. *Global Political Economy: Understanding the International Economic Order*, Princeton, NJ: Princeton University Press.

Glatzer, M. and Rueschemeyer, D. eds. 2005. *Globalization and the Future of the Welfare State*, Pittsburgh, PA: University of Pittsburgh Press.

Glyn, A. and Sutcliffe, B. 1972. *British Capitalism, Workers and the Profits Squeeze*, Harmondsworth, UK: Penguin.

de Goede, M. 2003. "Beyond economism in international political economy." *Review of International Studies* 29(1): pp. 79–98.

——2005. *Virtue, Fortune, and Faith: A Genealogy of Finance*, Minneapolis: University of Minnesota Press.

——2006. "International political economy and the promises of poststructuralism." In de Goede, M. ed. *International Political Economy and Poststructural Politics*, Basingstoke, UK: Palgrave Macmillan: pp. 1–20.

de Goede, M. ed. 2006. *International Political Economy and Poststructural Politics*, Basingstoke, UK: Palgrave Macmillan.

Goff, P. M. 2007. *Limits to Liberalization: Local Culture in a Global Marketplace*, Ithaca, NY: Cornell University Press.

Gold, T. 1986. *State and Society in the Taiwanese Miracle*, Armonk, NY: M. E. Sharpe.

Goldstein, A. 2005. *Rising to the Challenge: China's Grand Strategy and International Security*, Stanford, CA: Stanford University Press.

Goldstein, J. L. 1993. *Ideas, Interests, and American Trade Policy*, Ithaca, NY: Cornell University Press.

Goldstein, J. and Keohane, R. O. eds. 1993. *Ideas and Foreign Policy*, Ithaca, NY: Cornell University Press.

Goldstein, J. Kahler, M., Keohane, R. and Slaughter, A.M. 2000. "Introduction: Legalization and World Politics," *International Organization* 54 (3): pp. 385–99.

Goldsmith, B. 2007. "A liberal peace in Asia?" *Journal of Peace Research* 44(1): pp. 5–27.

Goldthorpe, J. H., Lockwood, D., Bechhofer, F., and Platt, J. 1968. *The Affluent Worker: Industrial Attitudes and Behavior*, Cambridge: Cambridge University Press.

Golob, S. 2003. "Beyond the policy frontier: Canada, Mexico, and the ideological origins of NAFTA." *World Politics* 55 (April): pp. 361–98.

Goodhart, C. and Xu, C. 1996. *The Rise of China as an Economic Power*, Cambridge, MA: Harvard Institute for International Development, Harvard University.

Goodman, J. B. and Pauly, L. W. 1993. "The obsolescence of capital controls? Economic management in an age of global markets." *World Politics* 46(1): pp. 50–82.

Goodman, N. 1978. *Ways of Worldmaking*, Indianapolis, IN: Hackett.

Gourevitch, P. 1986. *Politics in Hard Times: Comparative Responses to International Economic Crises*, Ithaca, NY: Cornell University Press.

Gowa, J. 1983. *Closing the Gold Window: Domestic Politics and the End of Bretton Woods*, Ithaca, NY: Cornell University Press.

——1984. "Bipolarity, multipolarity and free trade." *American Political Science Review* 85(4) (December): pp. 1245–56.

——1994. *Allies, Adversaries, and International Trade*, Princeton, NJ: Princeton University Press.

Grabel, I. 1997. "Creating 'credible' economic policies in developing and transitional economies." *Review of Radical Political Economics* 29(3): pp. 70–78.

——1999. "Rejecting exceptionalism." In Michie, M. and Grieve Smith, J. eds. *Global Instability: the Political Economy of World Economic Governance*, London: Routledge: pp. 37–67.

——2000. "The political economy of 'policy credibility': the new-classical macroeconomics and the remaking of emerging economies." *Cambridge Journal of Economics* 24(1): pp. 1–19.

——2003. "Ideology, power, and the rise of independent monetary institutions in emerging economies." In Kirshner, J. ed. *Monetary Orders: Ambiguous Economics, Ubiquitous Politics*, Ithaca, NY: Cornell University Press.

Granovetter, M. 1985. "Economic action and social structure: the problem of embeddedness." *American Journal of Sociology* 91(3): pp. 481–510.

Granovetter, M. and Swedberg, R. 1992. *The Sociology of Economic Life*, Boulder, CO: Westview Press.

Grant, W. 1982. *The Political Economy of Industrial Policy*, London: Butterworth.

Grant, W. ed. 1985. *The Political Economy of Corporatism*, London: Macmillan.

Gray, W. G. 2007. "Floating the system: Germany, the United States, and the breakdown of Bretton Woods, 1969–73." *Diplomatic History* 31(2): pp. 295–323.

Graz, J.-C. 1999. "L'économie politique internationale en France: une importation mal partie." *L'Economie Politique* 3(3).

Green, D. 1996. "Latin America: neoliberal failure and the search for alternatives." *Third World Quarterly* 17(1): pp. 109–22.

Greenberg, M. 1951. *British Trade and the Opening of China 1800–1842*, Cambridge: Cambridge University Press.

Greenfield, H. 2006. "After Thaksin: the CEO state, nationalism, and US imperialism." *Europe solidaire sans frontieres*, June 12. www.europe-solidaire.org/spip.php?article2587.

Grieco, J. 1988. "Anarchy and the limits of cooperation." *International Organization* 42(3) (Summer): pp. 485–507.

——1990. *Cooperation Among Nations: Europe, America, and Non-Tariff Barriers to Trade*, Ithaca, NY: Cornell University Press.

Griffin, P. 2007a. "Sexing the economy in a neo-liberal world order: neo-liberal discourse and the (re) production of heteronormative heterosexuality." *British Journal of Politics and International Relations* 9(2): pp. 220–38.

——2007b. "Refashioning IPE: what and how gender analysis teaches international (global) political economy." *Review of International Political Economy* 14(4): pp. 719–36.

Guillén, M. F. 1994. *Models of Management: Work, Authority and Organization in Comparative Perspective*, Chicago: University of Chicago Press.

——2001. *The Limits of Convergence: Globalization and Organizational Change in Argentina, South Korea, and Spain*, Princeton, NJ: Princeton University Press.

Gulati, R. 2007. *Managing Network Resources: Alliances, Affiliations, and Other Relational Assets*, New York: Oxford University Press.

Gunnell, J. C. 2005. "Political science on the cusp: rediscovering a discipline's past." *American Political Science Review* 99(4): pp. 597–609.

Gurowitz, A. 1999. "Mobilizing international norms: domestic actors, immigrants, and the Japanese state." *World Politics* 51(3) (April): pp. 413–45.

Guzzini, S. 2000. "Strange's oscillating realism: opposing the ideal—and the apparent." In Lawton, T. C., Rosenau, J. N., and Verdun, A.C. eds. *Strange Power: Shaping the Parameters of International Relations and International Political Economy*, Aldershot, UK: Ashgate: pp. 215–28.

Haas, P. M. 1992. "Introduction: epistemic communities and international policy coordination." *International Organization* 46(1) (Winter): pp. 187–224.

Haggard, S. 1990. *Pathways from the Periphery: The Politics of Growth in the Newly Industrializing Countries*, Ithaca, NY: Cornell University Press.

Haggard, S. and Kaufman, R. eds. 1992. *The Politics of Economic Adjustment*, Princeton, NJ: Princeton University Press.

Haggard, S. and MacIntyre, A. 1998. "The political economy of the Asian economic crisis." *Review of International Political Economy* 5(3): pp. 381–92.

Hall, R. B. 1999. *National Collective Identity: Social Constructs and International Systems.* New York: Columbia University Press.

Hall, D. 2002. "Environmental change, protest, and havens of environmental degradation: evidence from Japan-Southeast Asia relations." *Global Environmental Politics* 2(2): pp. 20–28.

Hall, P. A. ed. 1989. *The Political Power of Economic Ideas: Keynesianism across Countries*, Princeton, NJ: Princeton University Press.

Hall, P. A. 1992. "The movement from Keynesianism to monetarism: institutional analysis and British economic policy in the 1970s." In Steinmo, S., Thelen, K., and Longstreth, F. eds. *Structuring Politics*, New York: Cambridge University Press: pp. 90–113.

——1993. "Policy paradigms, social learning and the state." *Comparative Politics* 25: pp. 275–96.

Hall, P. A. and Gingerich, D. W. 2004. "Varieties of capitalism and institutional complementarities in the macroeconomy: an empirical analysis." Discussion paper, May 05, Max Planck Institute for the Study of Societies, Cologne, Germany: www.mpi-fg-koeln.mpg.de

Hall, P. A. and Soskice, D. 2001b. "An introduction to varieties of capitalism." In Hall, P. A. and Soskice, D. eds. *Varieties of Capitalism: The Institutional Foundations of Comparative Advantage*, New York: Oxford University Press: pp. 1–70.

Hall, P. A. and Soskice, D. eds. 2001a. *Varieties of Capitalism: The Institutional Foundations of Comparative Advantage*, Oxford: Oxford University Press.

Hall, R. B. 2003. "The discursive demolition of the Asian development model." *International Studies Quarterly* 47(1): pp. 71–99.

——[forthcoming]. *Central Banking as Global Governance: Constructing Financial Credibility*, New York: Cambridge University Press.

Halliday, T. and Carruthers, B. 2007. "The recursivity of law: global norm making and national lawmaking in the globalization of corporate insolvency regimes." *American Journal of Sociology* 112: pp. 1135–1202.

Hamashita, T. 1993. "Tribute and emigration: Japan and the Chinese administration of foreign affairs." *Senri Ethnological Studies* XXV: pp. 69–86.

——1994. "The tribute trade system and modern Asia." In Latham, A. J. H. and Kawakatsu, H. eds. *Japanese Industrialization and the Asian Economy*, London and New York: Routledge: pp. 91–107.

——1997. "The intra-regional system in East Asia in modern times." In Katzenstein, P. J. and Shiraishi, T. eds. *Network Power: Japan and Asia*, Ithaca, NY: Cornell University Press: pp. 113–35.

Hamilton, A. 2008. "Beyond the Sterling devaluation: the gold crisis of March 1968." *Contemporary European History* 17(1): pp. 73–95.

Hamilton, Alexander. 1928 [1791]. "Report on the subject of manufactures." In Cole, A. ed. *Industrial and Commercial Correspondence of Alexander Hamilton*, Chicago: A. W. Shaw.

——1966 [1775]. "The farmer refuted." In Street, H. C. ed. *The Papers of Alexander Hamilton*, vol. 1, New York: Columbia University Press.

Hamilton, G. G. 2006. *Commerce and Capitalism in Chinese Societies: The Organization of Chinese Economies*, London: RoutledgeCurzon.

Hamilton-Hart, N. 2006. "Consultants in the Indonesian state: modes of influence and institutional implications." *New Political Economy* 11(2): pp. 251–70.

Hardt, M. and Negri, A. 2001. *Empire*, Cambridge, MA: Harvard University Press.

Harley, C. K. 1982. "British industrialization before 1841: evidence of slower growth during the Industrial Revolution." *Journal of Economic History* 42(2): pp. 267–89.

Harmes, A. 2001a. *Unseen Power: How Mutual Funds Threaten the Political and Economic Wealth of Nations*, Toronto: Stoddart.

——2001b. "Institutional investors and Polanyi's double movement: a contemporary model of currency crises." *Review of International Political Economy* 8(3): pp. 389–437.

——2001c. "Mass investment culture." *New Left Review* 9: pp. 103–24.

Harris, N. 1986. *The End of the Third World*, Harmondsworth, UK: Penguin.

Hart, J. A. 1992. *Rival Capitalists: International Competitiveness in the United States, Japan, and Western Europe*, Ithaca, NY: Cornell University Press.

Hart, O. 1995. *Firms, Contracts and Financial Structure*. New York: Oxford University Press.

Hart-Landsberg, M. 1993. *Rush to Development*, New York: Monthly Review Press.

Harvey, D. 1982. *The Limits to Capital*, Oxford: Blackwell.

Hatch, W. 2000. "Regionalization trumps globalization: Japanese production networks in Asia." In Stubbs, S. and Underhill, G. R. D. eds. *Political Economy and the Changing Global Order*, New York: Oxford University Press: pp. 382–91.

Hatch, W. and Yamamura, K. 1996. *Asia in Japan's Embrace: Building a Regional Production Alliance*, Cambridge: Cambridge University Press.

Hawkins, D., Lake, D., Nelson, D. and Tierney, M. 2006. *Delegation and Agency in International Organizations*. New York: Cambridge University Press.

Hay, C. 1999. "Marxism and the state." In Gamble, A., Marsh, D., and Tant, T. eds. *Marxism and Social Science*, Basingstoke, UK: Macmillan: pp. 152–74.

——2001. "The 'crisis' in Keynesianism and the rise of neoliberalism in Britain: an ideational institutionalist approach." In Campbell, J. L. and Pedersen, O. K. eds. *The Rise of Neoliberalism and Institutional Analysis*, Princeton, NJ: Princeton University Press: pp. 193–218.

——2004a. "Taking ideas seriously in explanatory political analysis." *British Journal of Politics and International Relations* 6: pp. 142–49.

——2004b. "Common trajectories, variable paces, divergent outcomes? Models of European capitalism under conditions of complex economic interdependence." *Review of International Political Economy* 11(2): pp. 231–62.

——2004c. "Ideas, interests and institutions in the comparative political economy of great transformations." *Review of International Political Economy* 11(1): pp. 204–26.

Hay, C., Lister, M., and Marsh, D. eds. 2006. *The State: Theories and Issues*, Basingstoke, UK: Palgrave.

Hay, C. and Marsh, D. 1999. "Introduction: towards a new (international) political economy?" *New Political Economy* 4(1): pp. 5–23.

Hay, C. and Watson, M. 2003. "Diminishing expectations: the strategic discourse of globalization and the political economy of New Labour." In Ryner, M. and Cafruny, A. W. eds. *A Ruined Fortress?* Lanham, MD: Rowman and Littlefield: pp. 147–72.

Haydu, J. 1998. "Making use of the past: time periods as cases to compare and as sequences of problem solving." *American Journal of Sociology* 104: pp. 339–71.

Hayes, D. 2000. *Japan's Big Bang*, Boston, MA: Tuttle.

Hayward, J., Brown, A., and Barry, B. 1999. *The British Study of Politics in the Twentieth Century*, Oxford: Oxford University Press.

Heazle, M. 2006. *Scientific Uncertainly and the Politics of Whaling*, Seattle: University of Washington Press.

Heckscher, E. F. 1935. *Mercantilism* (two vols.) London: George Allen & Unwin.

Heclo, H. 1974. *Modern Social Politics in Britain and Sweden*, New Haven, CT: Yale University Press.

Heidegger, M. 1993. "Modern science, metaphysics and mathematics." In Krell, D. F. ed. *Basic Writings*, Routledge.

Held, D. 1995. *Democracy and the Global Order: From the Modern State to Democratic Governance*, Cambridge: Polity Press.

Held, D., McGrew, A., Goldblatt, D., and Perraton, J. 1999. *Global Transformations: Politics, Economics and Culture*, Cambridge: Polity Press.

Helleiner, E. N. 1994. *States and the Reemergence of Global Finance: From Bretton Woods to the 1990s*, Ithaca, NY: Cornell University Press.

——1997. "Braudelian reflections on economic globalization: the historian as pioneer." In Gill, S. R. and Mittelman, J. H. eds. *Innovation and Transformation in International Studies*, Cambridge: Cambridge University Press: ch. 6.

——2003. *The Making of National Money: Territorial Currencies in Historical Perspective*, Ithaca, NY: Cornell University Press.

——2006. *Towards North American Monetary Union? A Political History of Canada's Exchange Rate Regime*, Montreal: McGill-Queen's University Press.

Helleiner, E. N. and Pickel, A. eds. 2005. *Economic Nationalism and in a Globalizing World*, Ithaca, NY: Cornell University Press.

Hellman, J. A. 1999. *Mexican Lives*, New York: The New Press, 2nd edition.

Henderson, J., Dicken, P., Hess, M., Coe, N., and Yeung, H. W. 2002. "Global production networks and the analysis of economic development." *Review of International Political Economy* 9(3): pp. 436–64.

Herman, R. G. 1996. "Identity, norms, and national security: the Soviet foreign policy revolution and the end of the Cold War." In Katzenstein, P. J. ed. *Culture of National Security: Norms and Identity in World Politics*, New York: Columbia University Press.

Herod, A. 2007. "The agency of labour in global change: Reimagining the spaces and scales of trade union praxis within a global economy." In Hobson, J. M. and Seabrooke, L. eds. *Everyday Politics of the World Economy*, Cambridge: Cambridge University Press: pp. 27–44.

Herrera, Y. 2005. *Imagined Economies: The Sources of Russian Regionalism*, New York: Cambridge University Press.

Hess, M. and Yeung, H. W. 2006. "Whither global production networks in economic geography? Past, present and future." *Environment and Planning A* 38(7): pp. 1193–04.

Hettne, B. ed. 1995. *International Political Economy: Understanding Global Disorder*, London: Zed Books.

Hicks, A. 1999. *Social Democracy and Welfare Capitalism: A Century of Income Security Politics*, Ithaca, NY: Cornell University Press.

Hicks, A. and Kenworthy, L. 1998. "Cooperation and political economic performance in affluent democratic capitalism." *American Journal of Sociology* 103: pp. 1631–72.

——2003. "Varieties of welfare capitalism." *Socio-Economic Review* 1: pp. 27–61.

Higgott, R. 2007. "International political economy." In Pettit, P., Goodin, R., and Pogge, T. eds. *Companion to Political Philosophy*, 2nd edn., Oxford: Blackwell: pp. 153–82.

Higgott, R. and Watson, M. 2008. "All at sea in barbed wire canoe: Professor Cohen's transatlantic voyage in IPE." *Review of International Political Economy* 51(1): pp. 1–17.

Hindess, B. 1977. *Philosophy and Methodology in the Social Sciences*, Brighton, UK: Harvester.

Hirsch, F. 1965. *The Pound Sterling: A Polemic*, London: Penguin.

Hirschman, A. O. 1969 [1945]. *National Power and the Structure of Foreign Trade*, Berkeley and Los Angeles: University of California Press.

——1980 [1945]. *National Power and the Structure of Foreign Trade*, Berkeley and Los Angeles: University of California Press.

Hiscox, M. 2001. *International Trade and Political Conflict: Commerce, Coalitions and Mobility*. Princeton: Princeton University Press.

Hix, S. 2002. "Constitutional Agenda-Setting through Rule Interpretation: Why the European Parliament Won in Amsterdam," *British Journal of Political Science* 32(2): 259–80.

Hix, S. 2004. "A global ranking of political science departments." *Political Studies Review* 2: pp. 293–313.

Hobbes, T. 1968 [1651]. *Leviathan, or The Matter, Forme, and Power of a Commonwealth Ecclesiasticall and Civill*, Macpherson, C. B. ed., Harmondsworth, UK: Penguin Classics.

Hobday, M. 2001. "The electronics industries of the Asia-Pacific: exploiting international production networks for economic development." *Asian-Pacific Economic Literature* 15(1): pp. 13–29.

Hobsbawm, E. 1969. *Industry and Empire*, London: Weidenfeld and Nicolson.

Hobson, J. A. 1988 [1901]. "The social problem." In Freeden, M. ed. *J.A. Hobson: A Reader*, London: Unwin Hyman: pp. 33–40.

——1988 [1916]. "The new protectionism." In Freeden, M. ed. *J.A. Hobson: A Reader*, London: Unwin Hyman: pp. 168–72.

——1988 [1938a]. "Confessions of an economic heretic." In Freeden, M. ed. *J.A. Hobson: A Reader*, London: Unwin Hyman: pp. 29–33.

——1988 [1938b]. *Imperialism: A Study*, London: Unwin Hyman.

Hobson, J. M. 1997. *The Wealth of States: A Comparative Sociology of International Economic and Political Change*, Cambridge: Cambridge University Press.

——2000. *The State and International Relations*, Cambridge: Cambridge University Press.

——2004. *The Eastern Origins of Western Civilisation*, Cambridge: Cambridge University Press.

——2007a. "Is critical theory always *for* the white West and *for* Western imperialism? Beyond Westphalian, towards a post-racist, critical international relations." *Review of International Studies* 33(S1): pp. 91–116.

——2007b. "Eastern agents of globalisation: Oriental globalisation in the rise of Western capitalism." In Hobson, J. M. and Seabrooke, L. eds. *Everyday Politics of the World Economy*, Cambridge: Cambridge University Press: pp. 141–59.

Hobson, J. M. and Seabrooke, L. 2007b. "Everyday IPE: Revealing everyday forms of change in the world economy." In Hobson, J. M. and Seabrooke, L. eds. *Everyday Politics of the World Economy*, Cambridge: Cambridge University Press: pp. 1–23.

——2007c. "Conclusion: Everyday IPE puzzle sets, teaching and policy agendas." In Hobson, J. M. and Seabrooke, L. eds. *Everyday Politics of the World Economy*, Cambridge: Cambridge University Press: pp. 196–213.

Hobson, J. M. and Seabrooke, L. eds. 2007a. *Everyday Politics of the World Economy*, Cambridge: Cambridge University Press.

Hodgson, G. 1993. *Economics and Evolution: Bringing the Life back into Economics*, Ann Arbor and Cambridge: University of Michigan Press and Polity Press.

——2001. *How Economics Forgot History: The Problem of Historical Specificity in Social Science*, London: Routledge.

Hoffmann, S. 1965. *The State of War: Essays on the Theory and Practice of International Politics*, New York: Praeger.

——1974. *Decline or Renewal? France Since the 1930s*, New York: Viking Press.

——1977. "An American social science: international relations." *Daedalus* 106(3): pp. 41–60.

——2002. "Clash of globalizations." *Foreign Affairs* 81(4) (July/August): pp. 104–15.

Hollingsworth, J. R. and Boyer, R. eds. 1997. *Contemporary Capitalism: The Embeddedness of Institutions*, Cambridge: Cambridge University Press.

Hollis, M. and Smith, S. 1990. *Explaining and Understanding International Relations*, Oxford: Clarendon Press.

Holloway, J. and Picciotto, S. eds. 1978. *State and Capital: A Marxist Debate*, London: Edward Arnold.

Holsti, K. J. 2004. *Taming the Sovereigns: Institutional Change in International Politics*, New York: Cambridge University Press.

Hopf, T. 2002. *Social Construction of International Politics: Identities and Foreign Policies, Moscow, 1955 and 1999*, Ithaca, NY: Cornell University Press.

Huang, P. C. C. 1985. *The Peasant Economy and Social Change in North China*, Stanford, CA: Stanford University Press.

Hudson, A. C. 1998. "Reshaping the regulatory landscape: border skirmishes around the Bahamas and Cayman offshore centres." *Review of International Political Economy* 5: pp. 534–64.

Hui, P. 1995. "Overseas Chinese business networks: East Asian economic development in historical perspective." Ph.D. dissertation, Department of Sociology, State University of New York at Binghamton.

Hume, D. 1999 [1748]. *An Enquiry concerning Human Understanding*, Oxford: Oxford University Press.

Hung, H.-F. 2001a. "Imperial China and capitalist Europe in the eighteenth-century global economy." *Review* (Fernand Braudel Center) 24(4): pp. 473–513.

——2001b. "Maritime capitalism in seventeenth-century China: The rise and fall of Koxinga in comparative perspective." Unpublished manuscript, Department of Sociology, Johns Hopkins University.

——2003. "Orientalist knowledge and social theories: China and European conceptions of East-West differences from 1600 to 1900." *Sociological Theory* 21(3): pp. 254–80.

——2004. "Early modernities and contentious politics in mid-Qing China, *c*.1740–1839." *International Sociology* 19(4): pp. 478–503.

Huntington, S. P. 1996. *The Clash of Civilizations and the Remaking of World Order*, New York: Simon & Schuster.

Hutchcroft, P. 1998. *Booty Capitalism: The Politics of Banking in the Philippines*, Ithaca, NY: Cornell University Press.

Hutchison, T. 1994. *The Uses and Abuses of Economics: Contentious Essays on History and Method*, London: Routledge.

Hutton, W. 1995. *The State We're In*, London: Jonathan Cape.

Hülsemeyer, A. 2004. "Toward deeper North American integration: a customs union?" *Canadian-American Public Policy Occasional Paper no. 59*, Orono: University of Maine, Canadian-American Center.

Hyun-Chin Lim and Jin-Ho Jang 2006. "Between neoliberalism and democracy." *Development and Society* 35(1) (June).

Ikeda, S. 1996. "The history of the capitalist world-system vs. the history of East-Southeast Asia." *Review* (Fernand Braudel Center) 19(1): pp. 49–76.

Ingram, P., Robinson, J., and Busch, M. L. 2005. "The intergovernmental network of world trade: IGO connectedness, governance, and embeddedness." *American Journal of Sociology* 111: pp. 824–58.

Ip, G. and King, N. 2005. "Is China's rapid economic development good for U.S.?" *Wall Street Journal*, June 27.

Iriye, A. 1970. "Imperialism in East Asia." In Crowley, J. ed. *Modern East Asia*, New York: Harcourt: pp. 122–50.

Irondelle, B. 2006. "French political science and European integration: the state of the art." *French Politics* 4(2) (August): pp. 188–208.

330

Irwan, A. 1995. "Japanese and ethnic Chinese business networks in Indonesia and Malaysia." Ph.D. dissertation., Department of Sociology, State University of New York at Binghamton.

Jabko, N. 1999. "In the name of the market: how the European Commission paved the way for monetary union." *Journal of European Public Policy* 6(3) (September): pp. 475–95.

——2006. *Playing the Market: A Political Strategy for Uniting Europe*, Ithaca, NY: Cornell University Press.

——2007. *Playing the Market – Political Strategy for Uniting Europe, 1985*–2005, Ithaca, NY: Cornell University Press.

Jacoby, W. 2004. *The Enlargement of the European Union and NATO: Ordering from the Menu in Central Europe*, New York: Cambridge University Press.

Jang-Jip Choi 1983. "Interest control and political control in South Korea: a study of the labor unions in manufacturing industries, 1961–80." Ph.D. dissertation. Department of Political Science, University of Chicago, August.

Jensen, N. 2006. *Nation-States and the Multinational Corporations: A Political Economy of Foreign Direct Investment*. Princeton: Princeton University Press.

Jepperson, R. L., Wendt, A., and Katzenstein, P. J. 1996. "Norms, identity and culture in national security." In Katzenstein, P. J. ed. *The Culture of National Security*, New York: Columbia University Press: pp. 33–75.

Jervis, R. 1976. *Perception and Misperception in International Politics*, Princeton, NJ: Princeton University Press.

Jessop, B. 1974. *Traditionalism, Conservatism and British Political Culture*, London: Allen and Unwin.

——1982. *The Capitalist State*, Oxford: Martin Robertson.

——1990. *State Theory: Putting the Capitalist State in its Place*, Cambridge: Polity Press.

——1997. "The future of the national state: erosion or reorganization? Reflections on the West European case." paper presented at a conference on Globalization: Critical Perspectives, University of Birmingham, March 14–16.

——2002. *The Future of the Capitalist State*, Cambridge: Polity Press.

Jessop, B., Bonnet, K., Bromley, S., and Ling, T. 1988. *Thatcherism: A Tale of Two Nations*, Cambridge: Polity Press.

Jessop B. and Sum, N. L. 2001. "Pre-disciplinary and post-disciplinary perspectives in political economy." *New Political Economy* 6: pp. 89–101.

Jing, J. 1982. "Hierarchy in the Qing dynasty." *Social Science in China: A Quarterly Journal* 3(1): pp. 156–92.

Johnson, C. 1982. *M.I.T.I. and the Japanese Miracle: The Growth of Industrial Policy, 1925–1975*, Stanford, CA: Stanford University Press.

——1995. *Japan: Who Governs? The Rise of the Developmental State*, New York: W.W. Norton.

——1999. "The developmental state: odyssey of a concept." In Woo-Cumings, M. ed. *The Developmental State*, Ithaca, NY: Cornell University Press

——2000. *Blowback: the Costs and Consequences of American Empire*, New York: Henry Holt.

Johnson, H. G. 1971. "The Keynesian revolution and the monetarist counter-revolution." *American Economic Review* 61(2) (May): pp. 1–14.

Johnson, J. 2000 *A Fistful of Rubles: The Rise and Fall of the Russian Banking System*, Ithaca, NY: Cornell University Press.

Johnston, A. I. 1995. *Cultural Realism: Strategic Culture and Grand Strategy in Chinese History*, Princeton, NJ: Princeton University Press.

——1996. "Cultural realism and strategy in Maoist China." In P. J. Katzenstein, ed. *Culture of National Security: Norms and Identity in World Politics*, New York: Columbia University Press.

——2001. "Treating international institutions as social environments." *International Studies Quarterly* 45(3) (December): pp. 487–515.

——2008. *Social States: China in International Institutions, 1980–2000*, Princeton, NJ: Princeton University Press.

Jomo, K. S., Chung, C.Y., Folk, B. C., Ul-Haque, I., Phongpaichit, P., Simatupang, B., and Tateishi, M. 1997. *Southeast Asia's Misunderstood Miracle: Industrial Policy and Economic Development in Thailand, Malaysia, and Indonesia*, Boulder, CO: Westview Press.

Kahler, M. 1988. "External ambition and economic performance." *World Politics* 40(4) (July): pp. 419–51.

——1998. "Rationality in international relations." *International Organization* 52(4): pp. 919–41.

Kahler, M. and Lake, D. A. 2008. "Economic integration and global governance: why so little supranationalism?" paper to be presented to the annual convention of the International Studies Association, San Francisco, March 26–29.

Kaldor, M. 2001. *New and Old Wars: Organized Violence in a Global Era*, Stanford, CA: Stanford University Press.

Kane, J. and Patapan, H. 2006. "In search of prudence: the hidden problem of managerial reform." *Public Administration Review* 66(5): pp. 711–24.

Kaplan, R. D. 2005. "How we would fight China." *The Atlantic Monthly*, June: pp. 49–64.

Kasaba, R. 1993. "Treaties and friendships: British imperialism, the Ottoman empire, and China in the nineteenth century." *Journal of World History* 4(2): pp. 213–41.

Katzenstein, P. J. 1976. "International relations and domestic structures: foreign economic policies of advanced industrial states." *International Organization* 30(1) (Winter): pp. 1–45.

——1978. *Between Power and Plenty: Foreign Economic Policies of Advanced Industrial States*, Madison: University of Wisconsin Press.

——1985. *Small States in World Markets*, Ithaca, NY: Cornell University Press.

——1996a. *Cultural Norms and National Security: Police and Military in Postwar Japan*, Ithaca, NY: Cornell University Press.

——2005. *A World of Regions: Asia and Europe in the American Imperium*, Ithaca, NY: Cornell University Press.

——2006. *A World of Regions: Asia and Europe in the American Imperium*, Ithaca, NY: Cornell University Press, paperback edition.

Katzenstein, P. J. ed. 1996b. *Culture of National Security: Norms and Identity in World Politics*, New York: Columbia University Press.

——1997. *Tamed Power: Germany in Europe*, Ithaca, NY: Cornell University Press.

Katzenstein, P. J., Keohane, R. O., and Krasner, S. D. 1998. "*International Organization* and the study of world politics." *International Organization* 52(4): pp. 645–85.

——1999. "*International Organization* and the study of world politics." In Katzenstein, P. J., Keohane, R. O., and Krasner, S. D. eds. *Exploration and Contestation in the Study of World Politics*, Cambridge, MA: MIT Press: pp. 5–45.

Katzenstein, P. J. and Shiraishi, T. eds. 1996. *Network Power: Japan and Asia*, Ithaca, NY: Cornell University Press.

Katzenstein, P. J. and Sil, R. 2008. "The contributions of eclectic theorizing to the study and practice of international relations." In Reus-Smit, C. and Snidal, D. eds. *The Oxford Handbook of International Relations*, New York: Oxford University Press.

Kavanagh, D. 2003. "British political science in the inter-war years: the emergence of the founding fathers." *British Journal of Politics and International Relations* 5(4): pp. 594–613.

Kawakatsu, H. 1994. "Historical background." In Latham, A. J. H. and Kawakatsu, H. eds. *Japanese Industrialization and the Asian Economy*, London and New York: Routledge: pp. 4–8.

Kay, C. 1989. *Latin American Theories of Development and Underdevelopment*, London and New York: Routledge.

Kay, T. 2005. "Labor transnationalism and global governance: the impact of NAFTA on transnational labor relationships in North America." *American Journal of Sociology* 111: pp. 715–56.

Keal, P. 2003. *European Conquest and the Rights of Indigenous Peoples: The Moral Backwardness of International Society*, Cambridge: Cambridge University Press.

Keck, M. and Sikkink, K. 1998. *Activists beyond Borders: Advocacy Networks in International Politics*, Ithaca, NY: Cornell University Press.

Kelvin, Lord. 1900. Address to the BAAS: at www.physics.gla.ac.uk/Physics3/Kelvin_online.

Kennan, G. F. 1951. *American Diplomacy, 1900–1950*, Chicago: University of Chicago Press.

Kennedy, P. 1987. *The Rise and Fall of the Great Powers: Economic Change and Military Conflict from 1500 to 2000*, New York: Random House.

Kenny, M. 1995. *The First New Left: British Intellectuals After Stalin*, London: Lawrence and Wishart.

——2004. "The case for disciplinary history: political studies in the 1950s and 1960s." *British Journal of Politics and International Relations* 6(4): pp. 565–83.

——2007. "Birth of a discipline: interpreting British political studies in the 1950s and 1960s." In Adcock, R., Bevir, M., and Stimson, S. C. eds. *Modern Political Science: Anglo-American Exchanges Since 1880*, Princeton, NJ: Princeton University Press: pp. 158–79.

Kenny, M. and English, R. eds. 2000. *Rethinking British Decline*, Basingstoke, UK: Macmillan.

Kenworthy, L. 1997. "Globalization and economic convergence." *Competition and Change* 2: pp. 1–64.

——2004. *Egalitarian Capitalism*, New York: Russell Sage.

——2006. "Institutional coherence and macroeconomic performance." *Socio-Economic Review* 4: pp. 69–91.

Keohane, R. O. 1980. "The theory of hegemonic stability and changes in international economic regimes, 1967–77." In Holsti, O. R., Siverson, R. M., and George, A. L. eds. *Change in the International System*, Boulder, CO: Westview Press: pp. 131–62.

——1984. *After Hegemony: Cooperation and Discord in the World Political Economy*, Princeton, NJ: Princeton University Press.

——1986. "Theory of world politics: structural realism and beyond." In Keohane, R. O. ed. *Neorealism and its Critics*, New York: Columbia University Press.

——1991. *International Institutions and State Power*, Boulder, CO: Westview Press.

——2000. "Foreword." In Lawton, T. C., Rosenau, J. N., and Verdun, A. J. eds. *Strange Power: Shaping the Parameters of International Relations and International Political Economy*, Aldershot, UK: Ashgate: pp. ix–xvi.

——2001. "Governance in a partially globalized world." *American Political Science Review* 95(1): pp. 1–13.

Keohane, R. O. and Nye, J. S. Jr. eds. 1972. *Transnational Relations and World Politics*, Cambridge, MA: Harvard University Press.

——1977. *Power and Interdependence: World Politics in Transition*, Boston, MA: Little, Brown.

——1987. "*Power and Interdependence* revisited." *International Organization* 41(4) (Autumn), pp. 725–53.

Keohane, R. O. and Milner, H. V. eds. 1996. *Internationalization and Domestic Politics*, New York: Cambridge University Press.

Kerkvliet, B. J. T. 1990. *Everyday Politics in the Philippines*, Berkeley: University of California Press.

——2005. *The Power of Everyday Politics*, Ithaca, NY: Cornell University Press.

Kettell, S. 2004. *The Political Economy of Exchange Rate Policy-Making*, Basingstoke, UK: Palgrave.

Key, V.O. Jr. 1953. *Politics, Parties, and Pressure Groups*, New York: Thomas Y. Crowell.

Keynes, J. M. 1979/1945. *Collected Writings*, vol. 24, Basingstoke, UK: Macmillan.

——1937. "The General Theory of Employment." *Quarterly Journal of Economics* 51(2): 209–23.

——2007. "My early beliefs." In his *Two Memoirs*, London: Haus. 1st edition, London: Rupert Hart Davis, 1949.

Khan, M. 2000. "Rent-seeking as process." In Khan, M. and Jomo, K. S. eds. *Rents, Rent-Seeking and Economic Development: Theory and Evidence in Asia*, Cambridge: Cambridge University Press.

Kier, E. 1996. "Culture and French military doctrine before World War II." In Katzenstein, P. J. ed. *Culture of National Security: Norms and Identity in World Politics*, New York: Columbia University Press.

——1997. *Imagining War: French and British Military Doctrine between the Wars*, Princeton, NJ: Princeton University Press.

Kindleberger, C. P. 1970. *Power and Money: The Politics of International Economics and the Economics of International Politics*, New York: Basic Books.

——1973. *The World in Depression 1929–1939*, London: Allen Lane.

——1981. "Dominance and leadership in the international economy." *International Studies Quarterly* 25 (2) (June): 242–54.

——1986. "Review: hierarchy versus inertial cooperation." *International Organization* 40(4): pp. 841–47.

——1989a. *Manias, Panics, and Crashes: A History of Financial Crises*, New York: Basic Books.

———1989b. *Economic Laws and Economic History*, New York: Cambridge University Press.

King, M. R. 2005. "Epistemic communities and the diffusion of ideas: central bank reform in the United Kingdom." *West European Politics* 28(1): pp. 94–123.

Kirshner, J. 1995. *Currency and Coercion: The Political Economy of International Monetary Power*, Princeton, NJ: Princeton University Press.

———1998. "Political economy in security studies after the Cold War." *Review of International Political Economy* 5.

———1999. "Keynes, capital mobility, and the crisis of embedded liberalism." *Review of International Political Economy* 6(3) (Autumn): pp. 313–37.

———2000. "The study of money." *World Politics* 52: pp. 407–36.

———2007. *Appeasing Bankers: Financial Caution on the Road to War*, Princeton, NJ: Princeton University Press.

Kirshner, J. ed. 2003. *Monetary Orders: Ambiguous Economics, Ubiquitous Politics*, Ithaca, NY: Cornell University Press.

———2006. *Globalization and National Security*, New York: Routledge.

Kirshner, J., Gourevitch, P. A., and Eichengreen, B. 1997. "Crossing disciplines and charting new paths: the influence of Charles Kindleberger on international relations." *Mershon International Studies Review* 41(2): pp. 333–45.

Kitschelt, H. P., Lange, P., Marks, G., and Stephens, J. D. 1999. "Convergence and divergence in advanced capitalist democracies." In Kitschelt, H. P., Lange, P., Marks, G., and Stephens, J. D. eds. *Continuity and Change in Contemporary Capitalism*, New York: Cambridge University Press: pp. 427–60.

Kjaer, P. and Pedersen, O. K. 2001. "Translating liberalization: neoliberalism in the Danish negotiated economy." In Campbell, J. L. and Pedersen, O. K. eds. *The Rise of Neoliberalism and Institutional Analysis*, Princeton, NJ: Princeton University Press: pp. 219–48.

Klotz, A. 1995. *Norms in International Relations: The Struggle against Apartheid*, Ithaca, NY: Cornell University Press.

Knight, F. H. 1921. *Risk, Uncertainty, and Profit*, New York: Houghton Mifflin.

Knorr, K. 1975. *The Power of Nations*, New York: Basic Books.

Knorr, K. and Trager, F. eds. 1977. *Economic Issues and National Security*, Lawrence: University Press of Kansas.

Kohli, A. 2004. *State-directed Development: Political Power and Industrialization in the Global Periphery*, Cambridge: Cambridge University Press.

Koremenos, B. 2005. "Contracting Around International Uncertainty," *American Political Science Review* 99 (4): pp. 540–65.

Korpi, W. 2003. "Welfare-state regress in Western Europe: politics, institutions, globalization, and Europeanization." *Annual Review of Sociology* 29: pp. 589–609.

———2006. "Power resources and employer-centered approaches in explanations of welfare states and varieties of capitalism: protagonists, consenters, and antagonists." *World Politics* 58: pp. 167–206.

Krajnc, A. 1999. "Learning in British Columbia's Clayoquot and Great Bear rainforest campaigns: from public pressure to global civic politics," paper presented at the Annual Convention of the International Studies Association, Washington DC, February 16–20.

Krasner, S. D. 1976. "State power and the structure of international trade," *World Politics* 28(3): pp. 317–47.

———1978. *Defending the National Interest: Raw Materials Investments in U.S. Foreign Policy*, Princeton, NJ: Princeton University Press.

———1984. "Approaches to the state: alternative conceptions and historical dynamics." *Comparative Politics* 16(2): pp. 223–46.

———1985. *Structural Conflict*, Berkeley: University of California Press.

———1994. "International political economy: abiding discord." *Review of International Political Economy* 1(1): pp. 13–19.

Krasner, S. D. ed. 1983. *International Regimes*, Ithaca, NY: Cornell University Press.

Kratochwil, F. 1993. "The embarrassment of change" *Review of International Studies* 19(1): 63–81.

——1994. "The Limits of Contract," *European Journal of International Law* 5: 465–91.

Kratochwil, F. and Ruggie, J. G. 1986. "International organization: a state of the art on an art of the state." *International Organization* 40(4): pp. 753–75.

Kreisler, H. 2002. "Through the realist lens." *Conversations with History: Conversation with John Mearsheimer*, Institute of International Studies, UC Berkeley, April 8: http://globetrotter.berkeley.edu/.

Krieger, J. and Murphy, C. 1998. "Transnational opportunity structures and the evolving roles of movements for women, human rights, labor, development, and the environment: a proposal for research." Department of Political Science, Wellesley College.

Kristensen, P. H. and Zeitlin, J. 2005. *Local Players in Global Games*, New York: Oxford University Press.

Krueger, A. 1980. "Trade policy as an input to development." NBER Working Paper no. W0466 (November).

Krugman, P. 1994. "The myth of Asia's miracle." *Foreign Affairs* (November–December), HTTP: web.mit.edu/krugman/www/myth.html

Krugman, P. R. 1994. "Competitiveness—a dangerous obsession." *Foreign Affairs* 73(2): pp. 28–44.

Kuhn, T. 1962. *The Structure of Scientific Revolutions*, Chicago: University of Chicago Press.

Kurth Cronin, A. 2003. "Behind the curve: globalization and international terrorism." *International Security* 27(3) (Winter): pp. 30–58.

Kydd, A. 2001. "Trust Building, Trust Breaking: The Dilemma of NATO Expansion," *International Organization* 55(4): pp. 801–28.

Kyong-Dong Kim ed. 1987. *Dependency Issues in Korean Development*, Seoul: Seoul National University Press.

Laffey, M. 2004. "The red herring of economism: a reply to Marieke de Goede." *Review of International Studies* 30(3): pp. 459–68.

Lairson, T. D. and Skidmore, D. ed. 2003. *International Political Economy: The Struggle for Power and Wealth*, Belmont, CA: Wadsworth/Thomson Learning, 3rd edition.

Lake, D. A. 1993. "Leadership, hegemony, and the international economy: naked emperor or tattered monarch with potential?" *International Studies Quarterly* 37(4) (December): pp. 459–89.

——1996. Anarchy, Hierarchy, and the Variety of International Relations. *International Organization* 50 (1): pp. 1–33.

—— 1997. "The Rise, Fall, and Future of the Russian Empire: A Theoretical Interpretation." In Dawisha, K. and Parrott, B. eds. *The End of Empire? The Transformation of the USSR in Comparative Perspective*, Armonk, NY: M.E. Sharpe.

—— 1999. *Entangling Relations: American Foreign Policy in Its Century*. Princeton: Princeton University Press.

——1999. "Global governance: a relational contracting approach." in Prakash, A. and Hart, J. A. eds. *Globalization and Governance*, London: Routledge: pp. 31–53.

Lane, D. and Myant, M. eds. 2007. *Varieties of Capitalism in Post-Communist Countries*, Basingstoke, UK: Palgrave Macmillan.

Langley, P. 2002. *World Financial Orders: An Historical International Political Economy*, London: Routledge.

——2007. "Everyday investor subjects and global financial change: the rise of Anglo-American mass investment." In Hobson, J. M. and Seabrooke, L. eds. *Everyday Politics of the World Economy*, Cambridge: Cambridge University Press: pp. 103–19.

——2008. *The Everyday Life of Global Finance: Saving and Borrowing in Anglo-America*, Oxford: Oxford University Press.

Lanoszka, A. 2001. "The WTO accession process: negotiating participation in a globalizing economy." *Journal of World Trade* 35(4): pp. 575–602.

Laski, H. 1919. *Authority in the Modern State*, New Haven, CT: Yale University Press.

——1938. *Parliamentary Government in England*, London: Allen and Unwin.

Latour, B. 1987. *Science in Action: How to Follow Scientists and Engineers Through Society*, Milton Keynes, UK: Open University Press.

——1996. "On actor-network theory: a few clarifications." *Soziale Welt* 47: pp. 369–81.

Lawton, T.C, Rosenau, J. N., and Verdun, A.C. eds. 2000. *Strange Power: Shaping the Parameters of International Relations and International Political Economy*, Aldershot, UK: Ashgate.

Laxer, J. 1987. *Decline of the Superpowers: Winners and Losers in Today's Global Economy*, Toronto: James Lorimer & Co.

Lazonick, W. 1991. *Business Organization and the Myth of the Market Economy*, Cambridge: Cambridge University Press.

Leander, A. 2001. "Dependency today – finance, firms, mafias and the state: a review of Susan Strange's work from a developing country perspective." *Third World Quarterly*, 22(1): pp. 115–28.

Lefebvre, H. 1971. *Everyday Life in the Modern World*, New York: Harper and Row.

——1976. *The Survival of Capitalism*, London: St. Martin's Press.

——1991a. *The Production of Space*, Oxford: Blackwell.

——1991b. *Critique of Everyday Life*, London: Verso.

Leonard, M. 2005. "China's long and winding road." *Financial Times*, July 9–10.

Levitt, P. and Jaworsky, N. B. 2007. "Transnational migration studies." *Annual Review of Sociology* 33: pp. 129–56.

Leys, C. 1983. *Politics in Britain*, London: Heinemann.

——2001. *Market-Driven Politics: Neoliberal Democracy and the Public Interest*, London: Verso.

Liberman, P. 1996. "Trading with the enemy: security and relative economic gains." *International Security* 21(1) (Summer): pp. 147–75.

Lipietz, A. 1987. *Mirages and Miracles: The Crisis of Global Fordism*, London: Verso.

Lipson, C. 1986. "Bankers' Dilemmas: Private Cooperation in Rescheduling Sovereign Debts." In Oye, K. ed. *Cooperation Under Anarchy*, Princeton: Princeton University Press.

—— 2003. *Reliable Partners: How Democracies Have Made a Separate Peace*, Princeton: Princeton University Press.

Lipson, M., Maliniak, D., Oakes, A., Peterson, S., and Tierney, M. J. 2007. "Divided discipline? comparing views of US and Canadian IR scholars", *International Journal* 62(2): pp. 327–43.

Lischer, S. K..2005. *Dangerous Sanctuaries: Refugee Camps, Civil Wars and the Dilemmas of Humanitarian Aid*. Ithaca, NY: Cornell University Press.

Liska, G. 1957. *International Equilibrium*, Cambridge, MA: Harvard University Press.

List, F. 1885. *The National System of Political Economy*, London: Longmans, Green and Co.

Long, D. 1995. "The Harvard school of liberal international theory: a case for closure." *Millennium* 24 (3): pp. 489–505.

Lowi, T. J. 1964. "American business, public policy, case studies, and political theory." *World Politics* 16 (4) (July): pp. 677–715.

Lowry, S. T. 1974. "The archaeology of the circulation concept in economic theory." *Journal of the History of Ideas* 35(3): pp. 429–44.

Lukauskas, A. 1999. "Managing mobile capital: recent scholarship on the political economy of international finance." *Review of International Political Economy* 6(2): pp. 262–87.

Lukes, S. 1974/2005. *Power: A Radical View*, Basingstoke, UK: Palgrave Macmillan, 2nd edition.

Lyons, J. S., Cain, L. P., and Williamson, S. H. eds. 2007. *Reflections on the Cliometrics Revolution*, London: Routledge.

Lyotard, J-F. 1993. *Libidinal Economy*, London: Athlone Press.

Macdonald, L. 1997. *Supporting Civil Society: The Political Role of Non-Governmental Organizations in Central America*, London: Macmillan.

Machin, H. and Wright, V. eds. 1985. *Economic Policy and Policy-making Under the Mitterrand Presidency, 1981–1984*, London: Frances Pinter.

MacInnes, J. 1987. *Thatcherism at Work: Industrial Relations and Economic Change*, Milton Keynes, UK: Open University Press.

MacIntyre, A. 2001. "Institutions and investors: the politics of the economic crisis in Southeast Asia." *International Organization* 55(1): pp. 81–122.

——2002. *The Power of Institutions: Political Architecture and Governance*, Ithaca, NY: Cornell University Press.

MacIntyre, A. ed. 1995. *Business and Government in Industrialising Asia*, Ithaca, NY: Cornell University Press.

MacKenzie, D. 2003a. "Long term capital management and the sociology of arbitrage." *Economy and Society* 32: pp. 349–80.

——2003b. "The big, bad wolf and the rational market: portfolio insurance, the 1987 stock crash, and the performativity of economics." *Economy and Society* 33: pp. 303–34.

——2005. "Opening the black boxes of global finance." *Review of International Political Economy* 12: pp. 555–76.

——2006. *An Engine, Not a Camera: How Financial Models Shape Markets*, Cambridge, MA: MIT Press.

MacKenzie, D., Muniesa, F., and Siu, L. eds. 2007. *Do Economists Make Markets? On the Performativity of Economics*, Princeton, NJ: Princeton University Press.

Macrae, J. 2002. "The 'Bilateralisation' of Humanitarian Response: Trends in the Financial, Contractual and Managerial Environment of Official Humanitarian Aid." Background paper for UNHCR. London: Humanitarian Policy Group, Overseas Development Institute.

Mahon, R. 2002. *Childcare Policy at the Crossroads: Gender and Welfare State Restructuring*, New York: Routledge.

Mahoney, J. 2000. "Path dependence in historical sociology." *Theory and Society* 29: pp. 507–48.

Malhotra, D. and J. Keith Murninghan, 2002. "The Effects of Contracts on Interpersonal Trust." *Administrative Science Quarterly* 47(3): pp. 534–59.

Maliniak, D. and Tierney, M. J. 2007. "International political economy: a bridge too far or a bridge to nowhere?" paper prepared for the IPES meeting, Stanford University, November 9.

Mandelbaum, M. 2005. *The Case For Goliath: How America Acts As The World's Government in the Twenty-First Century*, New York: Public Affairs.

Mann, M. 1993. *The Sources of Social Power, Vol II: The Rise of Classes and Nation-States, 1976–1914*, New York: Cambridge University Press.

Mann, M. and Riley, D. 2007. "Explaining macro-regional trends in global income inequalities, 1950–2000." *Socio-Economic Review* 5: pp. 81–115.

Manser, W. A. P. 1971. *Britain in Balance: The Myth of Failure*, London: Penguin.

March, J. and Olsen, J. 1984. "The new institutionalism: organizational factors in political life." *American Political Science Review* 78: pp. 734–49.

Mariátegui, J. C. 1928. *Siete Ensayos de Interpretación de la Realidad Peruana*, Crítica. Lima, Peru: Biblioteca Amauta.

Marjoribanks, T. 2000. *News Corporation, Technology and the Workplace: Global Strategies, Local Change*, New York: Cambridge University Press.

Marquand, D. 1988. *The Unprincipled Society*, London: Jonathan Cape.

Marsden, R. 1999. *The Nature of Capital: Marx after Foucault*, London: Routledge.

Martin, L. 1993. *Coercive Cooperation: Explaining Multilateral Sanctions*, Princeton: Princeton University Press.

—— 2000. *Democratic Commitments*. Princeton: Princeton University Press.

Martin, L. and Simmons, B. 1998. "Theories and empirical studies of international institutions." *International Organization* 52(4) (Autumn): pp. 729–57.

Marx, K. 1973. *Grundrisse*, New York: Vintage.

Marx, K. and Engels, F. 1845. *The German Ideology*, London: Lawrence and Wishart.

Masina, P. ed. 2002. *Rethinking Developent in East Asia*, Richmond, Surrey, UK: Curzon Press.

Mastanduno, M. 1991. "Do Relative Gains Matter?" *International Security* 16:1 (Summer): pp. 73–113.

——1998. "Economics and security in statecraft and scholarship." *International Organization* 52(4) (Autumn): pp. 825–54.

Mathews, J. 1997. "Power shift." *Foreign Affairs* 76: pp. 50–76.

Mattli, W. 2001. "Private Justice in a Global Economy: From Literature to Arbitration." *International Organization* 55(4): pp. 919–47.

Maurer, B. 2006. "The anthropology of money." *Annual Review of Anthropology* 35: 15–36.

Maxfield, S. 1997. *Gatekeepers of Growth: The International Political Economy of Central Banking in Developing Countries*, Princeton, NJ: Princeton University Press.

337

May, C. 1996. "Strange fruit: Susan Strange's theory of structural power in the international political economy." *Global Society: Journal of Interdisciplinary International Relations* 10(2): pp. 167–90.

——2002. "An annotated bibliography of Susan Strange's academic publications 1949–99." 3rd Version, IPEG Papers in Global Political Economy no. 1: www.bisa.ac.uk/groups/18/papers/ChrisMay.pdf.

——2007. "The hypocrisy of forgetfulness: the contemporary significance of early innovations in intellectual property." *Review of International Political Economy* 14(1): pp. 1–25.

McBride, S. 2005. *Paradigm Shift: Globalization and the Canadian State*, Halifax, Nova Scotia: Fernwood, 2nd edition.

McCall Rosenbluth, F. 1989. *Financial Politics in Contemporary Japan*, Ithaca, NY: Cornell University Press.

McCormack, G. 1978. "The South Korean economy: GNP versus the people." In McCormack, G. and Selden, M. eds. *Korea North and South: The Deepening Crisis*, New York: Monthly Review Press: pp. 91–111.

McDermott, R. 2004. *Political Psychology in International Relations*, Ann Arbor: University of Michigan Press.

McFarland, A. S. 2004. *Neopluralism: The Evolution of Political Process Theory*, Lawrence: University of Kansas Press.

McKendrick, D. G., Doner, R. F., and Haggard, S. 2000. *From Silicon Valley to Singapore: Location and Competitive Advantage in the Hard Disk Drive Industry*, Stanford, CA: Stanford University Press.

McNally, C. A. ed. 2007. *China's Emergent Political Economy: Capitalism in the Dragon's Lair*, London: Routledge.

McNamara, K. 1998. *The Currency of Ideas: Monetary Politics in the European Union*, Ithaca, NY: Cornell University Press.

——2002. "Rational fictions: central bank independence and the social logic of delegation." *West European Politics* 25(1): pp. 47–76.

McNeill, W. 1982. *The Pursuit of Power: Technology, Armed Force, and Society since A.D. 1000*, Chicago: University of Chicago Press.

——1998. "World history and the rise and fall of the West." *Journal of World History* 9(2): pp. 215–37.

Mearsheimer, J. J. 1994. "The False Promise of International Institutions," *International Security* 19(3): pp. 5–49.

——2001. *The Tragedy of Great Power Politics*, New York: W.W. Norton.

Meier, G. 1989. *Leading Issues in Economic Development*, New York: Oxford University Press.

Meyer, J. W., Boli, J., and Thomas, G. M. 1987. "Ontology and rationalization in the Western cultural account." In *Institutional Structure: Constituting State, Society and the Individual*, Newbury Park, CA: Sage, pp. 12–28.

Meyer, J. W., Frank, D., Hironaka, A., Schofer, E., and Tuma, N. B. 1997. "The structuring of a world environmental regime, 1870–1990." *International Organization* 51: pp. 623–51.

Middlemas, K. 1986. *Power Competition and the State Volume 1: Britain in Search of Balance 1940–61*, London: Macmillan.

——1990. *Power Competition and the State Volume 2: Threats to the Postwar Settlement: Britain 1961–74*, London: Macmillan.

——1991. *Power Competition and the State Volume 3: The End of the Postwar Era: Britain since 1974*, London: Macmillan.

Middleton, R. 2002. "Struggling with the impossible: Sterling, the balance of payments and British economic policy, 1949–72." In Arnon, A. and Young, W. D. eds. *The Open Economy Macro-model: Past, Present and Future*, Boston, MA: Kluwer: pp. 103–54.

Mikler, J. 2005. "Institutional reasons for the effect of environmental regulations: passenger car CO_2 emissions in the EU, US and Japan." *Global Society* 19(4): pp. 409–44.

Miliband, R. 1969. *The State in Capitalist Society: An Analysis of the Western System of Power*, London: Weidenfeld and Nicolson.

Miller, C. T. 2006. *Blood Money: Wasted Billions, Lost Lives and Corporate Greed in Iraq*. New York: Little, Brown and Company.

——1970. "The capitalist state—a reply to Nicos Poulantzas." *New Left Review* 59: pp. 53–60.

Miller, G. 1992. *Managerial Dilemmas: The Political Economy of Hierarchy*, New York: Cambridge University Press.

Milner, H. V. 1997. *Interests, Institutions and Information: Domestic Politics and International Relations*, Princeton, NJ: Princeton University Press.

——1988. *Resisting Protectionism: Global Industries and the Politics of International Trade*, Princeton, NJ: Princeton University Press.

Mills, A. 1998. "To Contract or Not to Contract? Issues for Low and Middle Income Countries," *Health Policy and Planning*. 13(1): 32–40.

Minc, A. 1993. *Le nouveau Moyen Age*, Paris: Gallimard.

Mirowski, P. 1990. "The philosophical bases of institutionalist economics." In Lavoie, D. ed., *Economics and Hermeneutics*, London: Routledge.

Mitchell, T. 1998. "Fixing the economy." *Cultural Studies* 12(1): pp. 82–101.

Mittelman, J. H. 1998 "Coxian historicism as an alternative perspective in international studies." *Alternatives* 23(1): pp. 63–92.

——2000. *The Globalization Syndrome: Transformation and Resistance*, Princeton, NJ: Princeton University Press.

Momani, B. 2004. "American politicization of the International Monetary Fund." *Review of International Political Economy* 11(5): pp. 880–904.

Moravcsik, A. 1997. "Taking preferences seriously: a liberal theory of international politics," *International Organization* 51(4).

Morgenthau, H. J. 1951. *In Defense of the National Interest*, New York: Knopf.

——1960. *Politics among Nations: The Struggle for Power and Peace*, New York: Knopf.

——1978. *Politics among Nations: The Struggle for Power and Peace*, New York: Knopf, 5th revised edition.

Morton, A. D. 2006. "The grimly comic riddle of hegemony in IPE: where is class struggle?" *Politics* 26(1): pp. 62–72.

——2007a. *Unravelling Gramsci: hegemony and passive revolution in the global political economy*, London: Pluto Press.

——2007b. "Peasants as subaltern agents in Latin America: neoliberalism, resistance and the power of the powerless." In Hobson, J. M. and Seabrooke, L. eds. *Everyday Politics of the World Economy*, Cambridge: Cambridge University Press: pp. 120–38.

Mosley, L. 2003. *Global Capital and National Governments*, New York: Cambridge University Press.

Mügge, D. 2006. "Private-public puzzles: inter-firm competition and transnational private regulation." *New Political Economy* 1(2) (June): pp. 177–200.

Mun, T. 1949 [1664]. *England's Treasure by Forraign Trade*, Oxford: Blackwell.

Murphy, C. N. 1994. *International Organization and Industrial Change: Global Governance Since 1850*, Cambridge and New York: Polity Press and Oxford University Press.

——1998. "Egalitarian social movements and new world orders," paper presented at the annual conference of the British International Studies Association, University of Sussex, December 14–16.

——2000. "Global governance: poorly done and poorly understood." *International Affairs* 76(4) (October): pp. 789–803.

Murphy, C. N. and Nelson, D. R. 2001. "International political economy: a tale of two heterodoxies." *British Journal of Politics and International Relations* 3(3): pp. 393–412.

Murphy, C. N. and Tooze, R. 1991b. "Getting beyond the 'common sense' of the IPE orthodoxy." In Murphy, C. N. and Tooze, R. eds. *The New International Political Economy*, Boulder, CO: Lynne Rienner: pp. 11–31.

Murphy, C. N. and Tooze, R. eds. 1991a. *The New International Political Economy*, Boulder, CO: Lynne Rienner.

Mytelka, L. K. 2000. "Knowledge and structural power in the international political economy." In Lawton, T. C., Rosenau, J. N., and Verdun, A.C. eds. *Strange Power: Shaping the Parameters of International Relations and International Political Economy*, Aldershot, UK: Ashgate, pp. 39–56.

Nairn, T. 1964. "The British political elite." *New Left Review* 23: pp. 19–25.

——1976. "The twilight of the British state." *New Left Review* 101/2: pp. 3–61.

339

——1981a. "The crisis of the British state." *New Left Review* 130: pp. 37–44.

——1981b. *The Break-Up of Britain*, London: Verso, 2nd edition.

Nathan, A. J. 1972. "Imperialism's effects on China." *Bulletin of Concerned Asian Scholars* 4(4): pp. 3–8.

Nau, H. R. 1990. *The Myth of America's Decline: Leading the World Economy into the 1990s*, Oxford: Oxford University Press.

Naya, S. 1988. "The role of trade policies in the industrialization of rapidly growing asian developing countries." In Hughes, H. ed. *Achieving Industrialization in East Asia*, Cambridge: Cambridge University Press: pp. 64–94.

Naylor, R. T. 2002. *Wages of Crime: Black Markets, Illegal Finance, and the Underworld Economy*, Ithaca, NY: Cornell University Press.

Neocleous, M. 2004. "Bloody capital: cultural criticism of the critique of political economy?" Paper for the International Workshop on Cultural Political Economy, Lancaster University, June 4.

Newman, M. 2006. "Class, state and democracy: Laski, Miliband and the search for a synthesis." *Political Studies* 54(2): pp. 328–48.

Newton, S. 2004. "Keynesianism, sterling convertibility, and British reconstruction 1940–52." In Michie, R. and Williamson, P. eds. *The British Government and the City of London in the Twentieth Century*, Cambridge: Cambridge University Press: pp. 257–75.

New York Times. 1998. "Worsening financial flu lowers immunity to U.S. business." February 1.

Nexon, D. and T. Wright. 2007. "What's at Stake in the American Empire Debate." *American Political Science Review* 101(2): pp. 253–71.

Nielsen, F. 1994. "Income inequality and industrial development: dualism revisited." *American Sociological Review* 59: pp. 654–77.

Nielsen, F. and Alderson, A. 1995. "Income inequality, development, and dualism: results from an unbalanced cross-national panel." *American Sociological Review* 60: pp. 674–701.

Nitzan, J. 1998. "Differential accumulation: towards a new political economy of capital." *Review of International Political Economy* 5(2): pp. 169–217.

Nitzan, J. and Bichler, S. 2006. "New imperialism or new capitalism?" *Review* XXIX(1): pp. 1–86.

Nurkse, R. 1944. *International Currency Experience: Lessons of the Interwar Experience*, Geneva, Switzerland: League of Nations.

Nye, J. S. Jr. 1988. "Neorealism and neoliberalism." *World Politics* 40(2) (January): 235–51.

——1990a. "Soft power." *Foreign Policy* 80 (Fall): pp. 153–71.

——1990b. *Bound to Lead: The Changing Nature of American Power*, New York: Basic Books.

Oakeshott, M. 1976. "On misunderstanding human conduct: a reply to my critics." *Political Theory* 4(2) (August): pp. 353–67.

O'Brien, R. 1995. "International political economy and international relations: apprentice as teacher?" in Linklater, A. and Macmillan, J. eds. *Boundaries in Question: New Directions in International Relations*, London: Pinter: pp. 89–109.

——1997. *Subsidy Regulation and State Transformation in North America, the GATT and the EU*, London: Macmillan.

——2000. "Labour and IPE: rediscovering human agency." In Palan, R. ed. *Global Political Economy*, London: Routledge: pp. 89–99.

O'Brien, R., Goetz, A. M., Scholte, J. A., and Williams, M. 2000 *Contesting Global Governance: Multilateral Economic Institutions and Global Social Movements*, Cambridge: Cambridge University Press.

Ocampo, J. A. ed. 2005. *Beyond Reforms: Structural Dynamics and Macroeconomic Vulnerability*, Stanford, CA: Stanford University Press.

Odell, J. S. 1979. "The U.S. and the emergence of flexible exchange rates: an analysis of foreign policy change." *International Organization* 33(1) (Winter); pp. 57–81.

——1982. *U.S. International Monetary Policy: Markets, Power, and Ideas as Sources of Change*, Princeton, NJ: Princeton University Press.

——2000. *Negotiating the World Economy*, Ithaca, NY: Cornell University Press.

Okazaki, H. 1992. "New strategies toward super-Asian bloc." *This Is* (Tokyo) (August), reproduced in *Foreign Broadcast Information Service Daily Report: East Asia Supplement*, October 7, 1992.

Okimoto, D. I. and Rohlen, T. P. 1988. *Inside the Japanese System: Readings on Contemporary Society and Political Economy*, Stanford, CA: Stanford University Press.

Okuno-Fujiwara, M. 1991. "Industrial policy in Japan: a political economy view." In Krugman, P. ed. *Trade with Japan: Has the Door Opened Wider?* Chicago: University of Chicago Press: pp. 271–96.

de Oliveira, F. 2003. "The duckbilled platypus." *New Left Review* 24: pp. 40–58.

——2006. "Lula in the labyrinth." *New Left Review* 42: pp. 5–24.

Oliver, M. J. 2006. "Civilising international monetary systems." In Bowden, B. and Seabrooke, L. eds. *Global Standards Of Market Civilization*, London: Routledge.

Oliver, M. J. and Hamilton, A. 2007. "Downhill from devaluation: the battle for Sterling, 1968–72." *Economic History Review* 60(3): pp. 486–512

Olson, M. 1965. *The Logic of Collective Action*, Cambridge, MA: Harvard University Press.

——1982. *The Rise and Decline of Nations: Economic Growth, Stagflation, and Social Rigidities*. New Haven: Yale University Press.

Ong, A. 2000. "Graduated sovereignty in South-East Asia." *Theory, Culture and Society* 17(4): pp. 55–75.

Ong, A. and Nonini, D. M. eds. 1997. *Ungrounded Empires: The Cultural Politics of Modern Chinese Transnationalism*, New York: Routledge.

Onuf, N. 1989. *World of Our Making: Rules and Rule in Social Theory and International Relations*, Columbia: University of South Carolina Press.

Organski, A. F. K. 1968. *World Politics*, New York: Alfred A. Knopf, 2nd edition.

Ó Riain, S. 2000. "States and markets in an era of globalization." *Annual Review of Sociology* 26: pp. 187–213.

——2004. *The Politics of High-Tech Growth: Developmental Network States in the Global Economy*, New York: Cambridge University Press.

Orrù, M., Biggart, N., and Hamilton, G. G. 1997. *The Economic Organization of East Asian Capitalism*, London: Sage.

Osborne, D. and Gaebler, T. 1992. *Reinventing Government: How the Entrepreneurial Spirit is Transforming the Public Sector, from Schoolhouse to Statehouse, City Hall to the Pentagon*, Reading, MA: Addison-Wesley.

Ostrom, V. and Ostrom, E. 1977. "Public goods and public choices." In Savas, E. S. ed. *Alternatives for Delivering Public Services: Toward Improved Performance*, Boulder, CO: Westview Press: pp. 7–49.

Ostrom, V., Tiebout, C. M., and Warren, R. 1961. "The organization of government in metropolitan areas: a theoretical inquiry." *American Political Science Review* 55(3) (September): pp. 831–42.

Oye, K., ed. 1986. *Cooperation Under Anarchy*, Princeton: Princeton University Press.

Ozawa, T. 1993. "Foreign direct investment and structural transformation: Japan as a recycler of market and industry." *Business and the Contemporary World* 5(2): pp. 129–50.

Paish, F. 1956. "Britain's foreign investments the post-war record." *Lloyds Bank Review*, July.

Palan, R. 1999. "Susan Strange 1923–98: a great international relations theorist." *Review of International Political Economy* 6(2): pp. 121–32.

——2000. "The constructivist underpinnings of the new international political economy." In Palan, R. ed. *Global Political Economy: Contemporary Theories*, London: Routledge: pp. 215–28.

——2002. "Tax havens and the commercialization of state sovereignty." *International Organization* 56: pp. 151–66.

——2003. "Pragmatism and international relations in the age of banker's capitalism: Susan Strange's vision for a critical international political economy." In Bauer, H. and Brighi, E. eds. *75 Years of International Relations at LSE: A History*, London: Millennium Editions.

——2008. "Efficiency V. 'As long as it works': evolutionary institutionalism and the rise of American power." The International Studies Association Annual Convention, San Francisco, March 26–29.

Palan, R. ed. 2000. *Global Political Economy*, London: Routledge.

Palat, R. A. 1999. "Miracles of the day before? The great Asian meltdown and the changing world economy." *Development and Society* 28(1) (June): pp. 5–34.

Palma, J. G. 1978. "Dependency: a formal theory of underdevelopment, or a methodology for the analysis of concrete situations of underdevelopment?" *World Development*, 6(7/8): 881–924.

——2005a. "The seven main stylised facts of the Mexican economy since trade liberalisation and NAFTA." *Industrial and Corporate Change* 14(6): pp. 941–91.

——2005b. "Four sources of de-industrialisation and a new concept of the Dutch Disease." In Ocampo, J. A. ed. *Beyond Reforms: Structural Dynamics and Macroeconomic Vulnerability*, Stanford, CA: Stanford University Press.

——2006. "The 1999 financial crisis in Brazil: 'macho-monetarism' in action." *Economic and Political Weekly* 41(9): 727–38.

——2008a. "Raúl Prebisch." *The New Palgrave Dictionary of Economics*, London: Palgrave Macmillan, 2nd edition.

——2008b. "De-industrialisation, premature de-industrialisation and the Dutch Disease." *The New Palgrave Dictionary of Economics*, London: Palgrave Macmillan, 2nd edition.

Panitch, L. 1994. "Globalisation and the state." In Miliband, R. and Panitch, L. eds. *The Socialist Register 1994*, London: Merlin Press.

Park, S. 2005. "Norm diffusion within international organisations: a case study of the World Bank." *Journal of International Relations and Development* 8(2): pp. 114–41.

——2006. "Theorising norm diffusion within international organisations." *International Politics* 43(3): pp. 342–61.

Parker, G. 1989. "Taking up the gun." *MHQ: The Quarterly Journal of Military History* 1(4): pp. 88–101.

Parsons, C. 2003. *A Certain Idea of Europe*, Ithaca, NY: Cornell University Press.

Paterson, M. 1996. *Global Warming and Global Politics*, New York: Routledge.

——2007. *Automobile Politics: Ecology and Cultural Political Economy*, Cambridge: Cambridge University Press.

Pauly, L. W. 1988. *Opening Financial Markets: Banking Politics on the Pacific Rim*, Ithaca, NY: Cornell University Press.

——1997. *Who Elected the Bankers? Surveillance and Control in the World Economy*, Ithaca, NY: Cornell University Press.

Pauly, L. W. and Reich, S. 1997. "National structures and multinational corporate behavior: enduring differences in the age of globalization." *International Organization* 51(1) (Winter): pp. 1–30.

Payne, A. 1998. "The new political economy of area studies." *Millennium* 27(2): pp. 253–73.

Payne, A. J. and Gamble, A. 1996. "Introduction: the political economy of regionalism and world order." In Gamble and Payne, eds. *Regionalism and World Order*, Basingstoke, UK: Palgrave: pp. 1–20.

Peattie, M. 1984. "Introduction," to Myers, R. and Peattie, M. *The Japanese Colonial Empire, 1895–1945*, Princeton, NJ: Princeton University Press: pp. 3–26.

Peck, J. 2008 [in press]. "Remaking laissez-faire." *Progress in Human Geography*.

Peck, J. and Yeung, H. W. eds. 2003. *Remaking the Global Economy: Economic-Geographical Perspectives*, London: Sage.

Pelizzo, R. 2003. "Party positions or party direction? An analysis of party manifesto data." *West European Politics* 26(2): pp. 67–89.

Pellerin, H. 1999 "The cart before the horse? The coordination of migration policies in the Americas and the neoliberal economic project of integration." *Review of International Political Economy* 6(4) (Winter): pp. 468–93.

Pepper, G. T. and Oliver, M. J. 2006. *The Liquidity Theory of Asset Prices*, Chichester, UK: John Wiley.

Perdue, P. C. 1987. *Exhausting the Earth: State and Peasant in Hunan, 1500–1850*, Cambridge, MA: Harvard University Press.

——2003. "A frontier view of Chineseness." In Arrighi, G., Hamashita, T., and Selden, T. eds. *The Resurgence of East Asia. 500, 150 and 50 Year Perspectives*, London and New York: Routledge: pp. 51–77.

Perraton, J. and Clift, B. eds. 2004. *Where Are National Capitalisms Now?* Basingstoke, UK: Palgrave.

Perroux, F. 1939. "Pour un approfondissement de la notion de structure." In *Mélanges Economiques et Sociaux Offerts à Emile Witmeur*, Paris: Librairie du Recueuil Sirey: pp. 271–85.

Persaud, R. B. 2001. *Counter-Hegemony and Foreign Policy: The Dialectics of Marginalized and Global Forces in Jamaica*, Albany: State University of New York Press.

Peters, M. A. 2000. *Poststructuralism, Marxism, and Neoliberalism: Between Theory and Politics*, Oxford: Rowman and Littlefield.

342

Peterson, S., Tierney, M. J., and Maliniak, D. 2005. "Inside the ivory tower." *Foreign Policy* (November/December): pp. 58–64.

Peterson, V. S. 2003. *A Critical Rewriting of Global Political Economy*, London: Routledge.

Petras, J. and Veltmeyer, H. 2002. *Globalization Unmasked: Imperialism in the 21st Century*, New Jersey: Zed Books.

Petty, W. 1691. *The Political Anatomy of Ireland*, London: printed for Brown, D. and Rogers, W. at the Bible without Temple-Bar and at the Sun over-against St. Dunstan's Church, Fleet Street.

Phillips, N. ed. 2005. *Globalizing International Political Economy*, Houndmills, UK: Palgrave Macmillan.

Pierson, P. 1994. *Dismantling the Welfare State? Reagan, Thatcher, and the Politics of Retrenchment*, New York: Cambridge University Press.

Piore, M. J. and Sabel, C. F. 1984. *The Second Industrial Divide: Possibilities for Prosperity*, New York: Basic Books.

——1990 [1984]. *The Second Industrial Divide*, New York: Basic Books.

Pirie, I. 2005. "The new Korean state." *New Political Economy* 10(1): pp. 27–44.

——2008. *The Korean Developmental State: From Dirigism to Neo-Liberalism*, London, Routledge.

Piven, F. F. and Cloward, R. A. 1971. *Regulating the Poor*, New York: Vintage.

Poggi, G. 1978. *The Development of the Modern State*, Stanford, CA: Stanford University Press.

Polanyi, K. 1944. *The Great Transformation*, New York: Farrar & Rinehart, Inc.

——1957. *The Great Transformation: The Political and Economic Origins of Our Time*, Boston, MA: Beacon Press.

——1994. *The Great Transformation: The Political and Economic Origins of Our Times*, Boston, MA: Beacon Press.

Polillo, S. and Guillén, M. F. 2005. "Globalization pressures and the state: the global spread of central bank independence." *American Journal of Sociology* 110(6) (May): pp. 1764–802.

Pollard, S. 1982. *The Wasting of the British Economy: British Economic Policy, 1945 to the Present*, London: Croom Helm.

Poovey, M. 1998. *A History of the Modern Fact: Problems of Knowledge in the Sciences of Wealth and Society*, Chicago and London: University of Chicago Press.

Porter, M. E. 1990. *The Competitive Advantage of Nations*, London: Macmillan.

Porter, T. 1993. *States, Markets and Regimes in Global Finance*, London: Macmillan.

——2005. *Globalization and Finance*, Cambridge: Polity Press.

Poulantzas, N. 1969. "The problem of the capitalist state." *New Left Review* 58: pp. 67–78.

Powell, R. 1991. "Absolute and relative gains in international relations theory." *American Political Science Review* 85(4): pp. 1303–20.

Powell, W. W., Koput, K. W., and Smith-Doerr, L. 1996. "Interorganizational collaboration and the locus of innovation: networks of learning in biotechnology." *Administrative Science Quarterly* 41: pp. 116–45.

Prasad, M. 2005. "Why is France so French? Culture, institutions, and neoliberalism, 1974–81." *American Journal of Sociology* 111: pp. 357–407.

Pratt, J. and Zeckhauser, R. J. 1985. *Principals and Agents: The Structure of Business*, Cambridge, MA: Harvard Business School Press

Price, R. 1995. "A genealogy of the chemical weapons taboo." *International Organization* 49(1): pp. 73–104.

Price, R. and Reus-Smit, C. 1998. "Dangerous liaisons? Critical international theory and constructivism." *European Journal of International Relations* 4(3): pp. 259–94.

Putnam, R. D. 1988. "Diplomacy and domestic politics: the logic of two-level games." *International Organization* 42: pp. 427–60.

——2003. "APSA presidential address: The public role of political science." *Perspectives on Politics* 1(2): pp. 249–55.

Putzel, P. 2002. "Developmental states and crony capitalists," in Masina, P. ed. *Rethinking Development in East Asia*, Richmond, Surrey, UK: Curzon Press: pp. 161–88.

Radcliffe Report. 1958. *Report of the Committee on the Working of the Monetary System 1958–59*. Cmnd 827. London: HMSO.

343

Radice, H. 2004. "Comparing national capitalisms." In Perraton, J. and Clift, B. eds. *Where are National Capitalisms Now?* New York: Palgrave Macmillan: pp. 183–95.

Rae, H. 2002. *State Identities and the Homogenisation of Peoples*, Cambridge: Cambridge University Press.

Rajan, R. 2005. "Economic ship steady as she goes," *The Age* (Melbourne), September 23, www.imf. org/external/np/vc/2005/092305.htm.

Ravenhill, J. 2000. "APEC adrift: implications for economic regionalism in Asia and the Pacific." *Pacific Review* 13(2): pp. 319–33.

——2003. "The new bilateralism in the Asia Pacific." *Third World Quarterly* 24(2): pp. 299–317.

——2008b. "In search of the missing middle." *Review of International Political Economy* 15(1): pp. 18–29.

Ravenhill, J. ed. 2005. *Global Political Economy*, Oxford: Oxford University Press, 1st edition.

——2008a. *Global Political Economy*, Oxford: Oxford University Press, 2nd edition.

Redding, S. G. 1990. *The Spirit of Chinese Capitalism*, Berlin: De Gruyter.

Reich, R. B. 1991. *The Work of Nations: Preparing Ourselves for 21st Century Capitalism*, New York: Vintage Books.

——1983. *The Next American Frontier*, New York: Times Books.

Rekacewicz, P. 2001. "How the burden of the world's refugees falls on the South," *Le Monde Diplomatique* (English version), April.

Reus-Smith, C. 1999. *The Moral Purpose of the State: Culture, Social Identity, and Institutional Rationality in International Relations*, Princeton, NJ: Princeton University Press.

Reus-Smith, C. ed. 2004. *The Politics of International Law*, Cambridge: Cambridge University Press.

Riggs, F. W. 1964. *Administration in Developing Countries: The Theory of Prismatic Society*, Boston, MA: Houghton Mifflin.

Risse, T. 2000. "'Let's argue!': Communicative action in world politics." *International Organization* 54(1) (Winter): pp. 1–39.

Risse, T., Ropp, S. C., and Sikkink, K. eds. 1999. *The Power of Human Rights: International Norms and Domestic Change*, New York: Cambridge University Press.

Risse, T. and Sikkink, K. 1999. "The socialization of international human rights norms into domestic practices: introduction." In Risse, T., Ropp, S. C., and Sikkink, K. eds. *The Power of Human Rights: International Norms and Domestic Change*, New York: Cambridge University Press: pp. 1–38.

Robertson, J. 2007. "Reconsidering American interests in emerging market crises: an unanticipated outcome to the Asian financial crisis." *Review of International Political Economy*, 14(2): pp. 276–305.

Robinson, J. 1962. *Economic Philosophy*, Harmondsworth, UK: Penguin.

——1971. *Economic Heresies*, London: Macmillan.

Robinson, J. and Eatwell, J. 1973. *An Introduction to Modern Economics*, Maidenhead, UK: McGraw Hill.

Robison, R. and Hadiz, V. 2004. *Reorganizing Power in Indonesia*, London: RoutledgeCurzon.

Rocamora, J. and O'Connor, D. 1977. "The U.S., land reform, and rural development in the Philippines." In Bello, W. and Rivera, S. eds. *The Logistics of Repression*, Washington DC: Friends of the Filipino People: pp. 63–92.

Rodriguez, O. 2006. *El Estructuralismo Latinoamericano*, Mexico: FCE.

Rodrik, D. 1997. *Has Globalization Gone too Far?* Washington DC: Institute for International Economics.

——2000. "How far will international economic integration go?" *Journal of Economic Perspectives* 14(1): pp. 177–86.

Rogowski, R. 1989. *Commerce and Coalition: How Trade Affects Domestic Political Allignment*, Princeton, NJ: Princeton University Press.

Rojas, C. 2002. *Civilization and Violence: Regimes of Representation in Nineteenth-century Colombia*, Minneapolis: University of Minnesota Press.

Rollings, N. 2004. "Review." *Economic History Review* 57(2): pp. 427–28.

Rosamond, B. 2007. "European integration and the social science of EU studies: the disciplinary politics of a subfield." *International Affairs* 83(2): pp. 231–52.

Rose, N. 1999. *Powers of Freedom: Reframing Political Thought*, Cambridge: Cambridge University Press.

Rosecrance, R. 1986. *The Rise of the Trading State*, New York: Basic Books.

Rosser, A. 2002. *The Politics of Economic Liberalization in Indonesia*. Richmond, Surrey, UK: Curzon Press.

344

Rostow, W. W. 1961. *The Stages of Economic Growth: A Non-Communist Manifesto*, Cambridge: Cambridge University Press.

Rowe, W. 2001. *Saving the World: Chen Hongmou and Elite Consciousness in Eigteenth-Century China*. Stanford, CA: Stanford University Press

Rubinstein, W. D. 1993. *Capitalism, Culture and Decline in Britain, 1750–1990*, London: Routledge.

Ruccio, D. F. and Amariglio, J. 2003. *Postmodern Moments in Modern Economics*, Princeton, NJ: Princeton University Press.

Ruggie, J. G. 1982. "International regimes, transactions, and change: embedded liberalism in the postwar economic order." *International Organization* 36(2): pp. 379–415.

——1983. "International regimes, transactions, and change: embedded liberalism in the postwar economic order." In Krasner, S. D. ed. *International Regimes*, Ithaca, NY: Cornell University Press: pp. 195–231.

——1992. "Multilateralism: the anatomy of an institution." *International Organization* 46: pp. 561–98.

——1993. "Territoriality and beyond: problematizing modernity in international relations." *International Organization* 47(1) (Winter): pp. 139–74.

——1996. *Winning the Peace: America and World Order in the New Era*, New York: Columbia University Press.

——1998. *Constructing the World Polity*, London: Routledge

——1999a. "What Makes the World Hang Together: Neo-Utilitarianism and the Social Constructivist Challenge." *International Organization* 52: pp. 855–85.

——1999b. "What makes the world hang together? Neo-utilitarianism and the social constructivist challenge." In Katzenstein, P. J., Keohane, R. O., and Krasner, S. D. eds. *Exploration and Contestation in the Study of World Politics*, Cambridge, MA: MIT Press: pp. 215–45.

Rupert, M. 1995. *Producing Hegemony: The Politics of Mass Production and American Global Power*, Cambridge: Cambridge University Press.

Sabel, C. F. and Zeitlin, J. eds. 1996. *Worlds of Possibility: Flexibility and Mass Production in Western Industrialization*, Cambridge: Cambridge University Press.

Sader, E. 2005. "Taking Lula's measure." *New Left Review* 33: pp. 59–80.

Sakasakul, C. 1992. *Lessons from the World Bank's Experience of Structural Adjustment Loans (SALs): A Case Study of Thailand*, Bangkok: Thailand Development Research Institute.

Sako, M. 1992. *Prices, Quality and Trust: Inter-Firm Relations in Britain and Japan*, Cambridge: Cambridge University Press.

Sassen, S. 1999. *Guests and Aliens*, New York: New Press.

Sassen, S. ed. 2007. *Deciphering the Global: Its Scales, Spaces and Subjects*, London and New York: Routledge.

Sayer, A. 1995. *Radical Political Economy: A Critique*, Oxford: Blackwell.

——2004. "Seeking the geographies of power." *Economy and Society* 33: pp. 255–70.

Schechter, M. G. 2002. "Critiques of Coxian theory: background to a conversation." In Cox, R. W. and Schechter, M. G. eds. *The Political Economy of a Plural World: Critical Reflections on Power, Morals and Civilization*, London: Routledge: pp. 1–25.

Schenk, C. R. 1994. *Britain and the Sterling Area: From Devaluation to Convertibility*, London: Routledge.

——1995. "Review" *Economic History Review* 48(3): pp. 640–41.

Scherrer, C. 2005. "Internationale politisches Ökonomie." In Haug, W. F. ed. *Historisch-Kritisches Wörterbuch des Marxismus*, Hamburg, Germany: Argument.

Schimmelfennig, F. 2001. "The community trap: liberal norms, rhetorical action, and the eastern enlargement of the European Union." *International Organization* 55(1): pp. 47–80.

Schmidt, B. 1998. *The Political Discourse of Anarchy: A Disciplinary History of International Relations*, Albany: State University of New York Press.

Schmidt, V. A. 2002. *The Futures of European Capitalism*, New York: Oxford University Press.

——2003. "How, where and when does discourse matter in small states' welfare state adjustment?" *New Political Economy* 8(1) (March): pp. 127–46.

——2007. "Trapped by their ideas: French elites' discourses of European integration and globalization." *Journal of European Public Policy* 14(7): pp. 992–1009.

Schmoller, G. 1897. [1884] *The Mercantile System and Its Historical Significance*, English edition. New York and London: Macmillan, various reprints.

Schrank, A. 2004. "Ready-to-wear development? foreign investment, technology transfer, and learning by watching in the apparel trade." *Social Forces* 83: pp. 123–56.

—— 2005. "Entrepreneurship, export diversification, and economic reform: the birth of a 'developmental community' in the Dominican Republic." *Comparative Politics* 38(1): pp. 43–62.

Schrank, A. and Kurtz, M. 2005. "Credit where credit is due: open economy industrial policy and export diversification in Latin America and the Caribbean." *Politics and Society* 33: pp. 671–702.

Schurmann, F. 1974. *The Logic of World Power: An Inquiry into the Origins, Currents, and Contradictions of World Politics*, New York: Pantheon.

Schwartz, H. M. and Seabrooke, L. 2008. "Varieties of residential capitalism: a comparative and international political economy of housing." *Comparative European Politics* 6(3).

Scott, J. C. 1976. *The Moral Economy of the Peasant*, New Haven, CT: Yale University Press.

——1985: *Weapons of the Weak*, New Haven, CT: Yale University Press.

——1990: *Domination and the Arts of Resistance*, New Haven, CT: Yale University Press.

——1998. *Seeing Like a State: How Certain Schemes to Improve the Human Condition have Failed*, New Haven, CT: Yale University Press.

Seabrooke, L. 2001. *US Power in International Finance*, Basingstoke, UK: Palgrave.

——2006. *The Social Sources of Financial Power: Domestic Legitimacy and International Financial Orders*, Ithaca, NY: Cornell University Press.

——2007a. "The everyday social sources of economic crises: from 'great frustrations' to 'great revelations' in interwar Britain." *International Studies Quarterly* 51: pp. 795–810.

——2007b. "Everyday legitimacy and international financial orders: the social sources of imperialism and hegemony in global finance." *New Political Economy* 12(1): pp. 1–18.

——2008. "Sub-prime credit as a rights discourse: the progressive origins of a predatory market." mimeo, International Center for Business and Politics, Copenhagen Business School (March).

Searle, J. 1995. *Construction of Social Reality*, New York: Free Press.

Selden, M. 1997. "China, Japan and the regional political economy of East Asia, 1945–95." In Katzenstein, P. J. and Shiraishi, T. eds. *Network Power: Japan and Asia*, Ithaca, NY: Cornell University Press: pp. 306–40.

Semmel, B. 1970. *The Rise of Free Trade Imperialism*, Cambridge: Cambridge University Press.

Shafer, M. 1994. *Winners and Losers: How Sectors Shape the Developmental Prospects of States*, Ithaca, NY: Cornell University Press.

Shapcott, R. 2001. *Justice, Community and Dialogue in International Relations*, Cambridge: Cambridge University Press.

Shapiro, I. 2005. *The Flight from Reality in the Human Sciences*, Princeton, NJ: Princeton University Press.

Sharman, J. C. 2006. *Havens in a Storm: The Struggle for Global Tax Regulation*, Ithaca, NY: Cornell University Press.

——2007a. "Where do Australians publish?" Paper presented at Australian IPE Workshop, Adelaide, October 5.

——2007b. "The agency of peripheral actors: small state tax havens and international regimes as weapons of the weak." In Hobson, J. M. and Seabrooke, L. eds. *Everyday Politics of the World Economy*, Cambridge: Cambridge University Press: pp. 45–62.

Shaw, T. M. 1993. *Reformism and Revisionism in Africa's Political Economy in the 1990s: The Dialectic of Adjustment*, London: Macmillan.

Shonfield, A. 1958. *British Economic Policy Since the War*, London: Penguin.

——1969. *Modern Capitalism: The Changing Balance of Public and Private Power*, London: Oxford University Press.

Silberner, E. 1946. *The Problem of War in Nineteenth Century Economic Thought*, Princeton, NJ: Princeton University Press.

Silver, B. J. 2003. *Forces of Labor: Workers' Movements and Globalization since 1870*, Cambridge: Cambridge University Press.

346

Simmons, B. and Elkins, Z. 2004. "The globalization of liberalization: policy diffusion in the international political economy," *American Political Science Review* 98(1) (February): pp. 171–89.

Simon, H. A. 1997. *Models of Bounded Rationality, Vol. 3: Empirically Grounded Economic Reason*, Cambridge, MA: MIT Press.

Sinclair, T. 1994. "Passing judgment: credit rating processes as regulatory mechanisms of governance in the emerging world order." *Review of International Political Economy* 1: pp. 133–59.

——2005. *The New Masters of Capitalism: American Bond Rating Agencies and the Politics of Creditworthiness*, Ithaca, NY: Cornell University Press.

Singer, P. 2001. "Corporate warriors: the rise of the privatized military industry and its ramifications for international security." *International Security* 26: pp. 186–220.

Skinner, W. G. 1985. "The structure of Chinese History." *Journal of Asian Studies* 44(2): pp. 271–92.

Skocpol, T. ed. 1995. *Social Policy in the United States*, Princeton, NJ: Princeton University Press.

Skonieczny, A. 2001. "Constructing NAFTA: myth, representation, and the discursive construction of U.S. foreign policy." *International Studies Quarterly* 45: pp. 433–54.

Skrentny, J. D. 1996. *The Ironies of Affirmative Action: Politics, Culture, and Justice in America*, Chicago: University of Chicago Press.

——1998. "The effect of the Cold War on African-American civil rights: American and the world audience, 1945–68." *Theory and Society* 27: pp. 237–85.

Slaughter, A.-M. 2004. *A New World Order*, Princeton, NJ: Princeton University Press.

Smelser, N. and Swedberg, R. eds. 1994. *The Handbook of Economic Sociology*, Princeton, NJ: Princeton University Press.

——2005. *The Handbook of Economic Sociology*, Princeton, NJ: Princeton University Press, 2nd Edition.

Smillie, I. 1995. *The Alms Bazaar*, London: Intermediate Technology Press.

——2001. *Patronage or Partnership: Local Capacity Building in Humanitarian Crises*, Bloomfield, CT: Kumarian Press.

Smith, A. 1976 [1776]. *An Inquiry into the Nature and Causes of The Wealth of Nations*, Chicago: University of Chicago Press.

Smith, S. 1996 "The Canadian-Italian school of international theory." *Mershon International Studies review* 39(1): pp. 164–66.

——2000. "The discipline of international relations: still an American social science?" *British Journal of Politics and International Relations* 2(3): pp. 374–402.

So, A. Y. 1986. *The South China Silk District*, Albany: State University of New York Press.

So, A. Y. and Chiu, S. W. K. 1995. *East Asia and the World-Economy*, Newbury Park, CA: Sage.

Social Politics. 2005. Special issue on "Gender, Class, and Capitalism." 12(2): pp. 159–319.

Soederberg, S. 2004. *The Politics of the New Financial Architecture: Reimposing Neoliberal Dominance on the Global South*, London: Zed Books.

Soederberg, S., Menz, G., and Cerny, P. G. eds. 2005. *Internalizing Globalization: The Rise of Neoliberalism and the Erosion of National Varieties of Capitalism*, London and New York: Palgrave Macmillan.

Solomon, R. 1977. *The International Monetary System, 1945–1976*, New York: Harper and Row.

Soysal, Y. 1994. *Limits of Citizenship*, Chicago: University of Chicago Press.

Spero, J. E. 1977. *The Politics of International Economic Relations*, London: Allen and Unwin.

Spiro, D. 1999. *The Hidden Hand of American Hegemony: Petrodollar Recycling and International Markets*, Ithaca, NY: Cornell University Press.

Spruyt, H. 1994. *The Sovereign State and Its Competitors: An Analysis of Systems Change*, Princeton, NJ: Princeton University Press.

——2005. *Ending Empire*. Ithaca, NY: Cornell University Press.

Stark, D. and Bruszt, L. 1998. *Postsocialist Pathways: Transforming Politics and Property in East Central Europe*, New York: Cambridge University Press.

Steedman, I. 1977. *Marx After Straffa*, London: New Left Books.

Stephens, J. D., Huber, E., and Ray, L. 1999. "The Welfare State in Hard Times." In Kitschelt, H., Lange, P., Marks, G., and Stephens, J. D. eds. *Continuity and Change in Contemporary Capitalism*, New York: Cambridge University Press: pp. 164–93.

Stewart, J. 1966 [1767]. *An Inquiry into the Principles of Political Oeconomy*, Chicago: University of Chicago Press.

Stienstra, D. 1994. *Women's Movements and International Organizations*, London: Macmillan.

Stiglitz, J. 2002. *Globalization and its Discontents*, New York: W. W. Norton.

Stockton, N. 2005. "Preventing Corruption in Humanitarian Relief Operations." Paper Presented to the ADB/OECD Anti-Corruption Initiative for Asia and the Pacific. 28–30 September 2005, Beijing.

Stone, D. 1996. *Capturing the Political Imagination: Think Tanks and the Policy Process*, London: Frank Cass.

Stone, R. W. 2002. *Lending Credibility: The International Monetary Fund and the Post-Communist Transition*. Princeton: Princeton University Press.

—— 2004. "The Political Economy of IMF Lending in Africa," *American Political Science Review* 98 (4): pp. 577–91.

——2008. "Global public policy, transnational policy communities, and their networks." *The Policy Studies Journal* 36(1) (February): pp.19–38.

Stopford, J. and Strange, S. 1991. *Rival States, Rival Firms: Competition for World Market Shares*, Cambridge: Cambridge University Press.

Storing, H. J. ed. 1962. *Essays on the Scientific Study of Politics*, New York: Holt, Rinehart and Winston.

Strang, D. and Meyer, J. W. 1993. "Institutional conditions for diffusion." *Theory and Society* 22: pp. 487–511.

Strange, S. 1970a. "International money matters." *International Affairs* 46(4): pp. 737–43.

——1970b. "International economics and international relations: a case of mutual neglect." *International Affairs* 46(2): pp. 304–15.

——1971. *Sterling and British Policy: A Political Study of an International Currency in Decline*, New York: Oxford University Press.

——1972. "International Economic Relations I: The need for an interdisciplinary approach." In Morgan, R. ed. *The Study of International Affairs: Essays in Honour of Kenneth Younger*, London: RIIA/Oxford University Press: pp. 63–84.

——1983. "*Cave! Hic Dragones*: A Critique of Regime Analysis." In Krasner, S., ed. *International Regimes*, Ithaca, NY: Cornell University Press.

——1986. *Casino Capitalism*, Oxford: Blackwell.

——1987. "The persistent myth of lost hegemony." *International Organization* 41(4): pp. 551–74.

——1988. *States and Markets*, London: Pinter.

——1990. "Finance, information and power." *Review of International Studies* 16(3): pp. 259–74.

——1991. "An eclectic approach." In Murphy, C. N. and Tooze, R. eds. *The New International Political Economy*, Boulder, CO: Lynne Rienner, pp. 33–49.

——1994a. "Wake up, Krasner! The world has changed." *Review of International Political Economy* 1(2): pp. 209–20.

——1994b. *States and Markets*, London: Pinter, 2nd edition.

——1995. "ISA as a microcosm." *International Studies Quarterly* 39(3): pp. 289–96.

——1996. *The Retreat of the State: The Diffusion of Power in the World Economy*, Cambridge: Cambridge University Press.

——1998. *Mad Money*, Manchester, UK: Manchester University Press.

Sugihara, K. 1996. "The European miracle and the East Asian miracle. towards a new global economic history." *Sangyo to keizai* XI(12): pp. 27–48.

——2003. "The East Asian Path of Economic Development: A Long-term Perspective." In Arrighi, G., Hamashita, T., and Selden, M. eds. *The Resurgence of East Asia: 500, 150 and 50 Year Perspectives*, London and New York: Routledge: pp. 78–123.

Suleiman, E. 1974. *Power, Politics and Bureaucracy in France*, Princeton, NJ: Princeton University Press.

Summers, L. 1998. "The global economic situation and what it means for the United States." Remarks to the National Governors' Association, Milwaukee, Wisconsin, August 4.

Suzuki, S. 2007. "The agency of subordinate polities: Western hegemony in the East Asian mirror." In Hobson, J. M. and Seabrooke, L. eds. *Everyday Politics of the World Economy*, Cambridge: Cambridge University Press: pp. 177–95.

Swank, D. 2002. *Global Capital, Political Institutions and Policy Change in Developed Welfare States*, New York: Cambridge University Press.

Tabb, W. 1999. *Reconstructing Political Economy: The Great Divide in Economic Thought*, London: Routledge.

Taleb, N. N. 2007. *The Black Swan: The Impact of the Highly Improbable*, New York: Random House.

Tannenwald, N. 1999. "The nuclear taboo: The United States and the normative basis of nuclear non-use." *International Organization* 53(3) (Summer): pp. 433–68.

Tanzi, V. 2000. "Globalization, technological developments and the work of fiscal termites." International Monetary Fund Working Paper, WP/00/181, Geneva, Switzerland: IMF.

Taylor, L. 2004. *Reconstructing Macroeconomics. Structuralist Proposals and Critiques of the Mainstream*, Cambridge, MA: Harvard University Press.

Taylor, P. J. 1995. "Beyond containers: internationality, interstateness, interterritoriality." *Progress in Human Geography* 19(1): pp. 1–15.

——1996. "Embedded statism and the social sciences: opening up to new spaces." *Environment and Planning A* 28: pp. 1917–28.

——2007. "Problematizing city/state relations: towards a geohistorical understanding of contemporary globalization." *Transactions of the Institute of British Geographers* 32(2): pp. 133–50.

Tepperman, J. D. 2002. "This is not the job of soldiers for hire; the US military, not mercenaries should guard the Afghan president." *Los Angeles Times*, November 26: p. B13.

Tétreault, M. A. and Lipschutz, R. D. 2005. *Global Politics as if People Mattered*, Lanham MD: Rowman and Littlefield.

Thailand Development Research Institute (TDRI). 1992. *Thailand's Economic Structure: Summary Report*, Bangkok: TDRI.

Thatcher, M. 2007. *Internationalisation and Economic Institutions: Comparing the European Experience*, Oxford: Oxford University Press.

Thatcher, M., Hancké, B., and Rhodes, M. eds. 2007. *Beyond Varieties of Capitalism: Conflict, Contradictions, and Complementarities in the European Economy*, Oxford: Oxford University Press.

——2008. "Bolsa familia." July 2.

Thelen, K. 2003. "How institutions evolve: insights from comparative-historical analysis." In Mahoney, J. and Rueschemeyer, D. eds. *Comparative Historical Analysis in the Social Sciences*, New York: Cambridge University Press: pp. 208–41.

Thelen, K. and Steinmo, S. 1992. "Historical institutionalism in comparative politics." In *Structuring Politics: Historical Institutionalism in Comparative Analysis*, New York: Cambridge University Press: pp. 1–32.

Thomas, G. M., Meyer, J. W., Ramirez, F. O., and Boli, J. eds. 1987. *Institutional Structure: Constituting State, Society, and the Individual*, Newbury Park, CA: Sage.

Thompson, E. P. 1963. *The Making of the English Working Class*, London: Gollancz.

Thompson, G. 1986. *The Conservatives' Economic Policy*, London: Croom Helm.

——1990. *The Political Economy of the New Right*, London: Pinter.

——1999. "Strategy and tactics in the pedagogy of economics: what should be done about neoclassical economics?" in Garnett, R. ed. *What Do Economists Know? New Economics of Knowledge*, London: Routledge.

——2004. "The US economy in the 1990s: the 'new economy' assessed." In Perraton, J. and Clift, B. eds. *Where are National Capitalisms Now?* Basingstoke, UK: Palgrave: pp. 12–32.

Thompson, H. 1997. "The nation-state and international capital flows in historical perspective." *Government and Opposition* 32(1): pp. 84–113.

——2006. "The modern state and its adversaries." *Government and Opposition* 41(1): pp. 23–42.

——2007. "Debt and power: the United States' debt in historical perspective." *International Relations* 21(3): pp. 305–23.

Thompson, N. 1988. *The Market and its Critics*, London: Routledge.

——1994. "Hobson and the Fabians: two roads to socialism in the 1920s." *History of Political Economy* 26: pp. 203–20.

Tickner, A. B. 2003. "Seeing IR differently: notes from the Third World." *Millennium* 32(2): pp. 295–324.

349

Tilly, C. 1990. *Coercion, Capital, and European States, AD 990–1990*, New York: Blackwell.

Tiratsoo, N. and Tomlinson, J. 1998. *The Conservatives and Industrial Efficiency 1951–1964*, London: Routledge.

TNA 1952. "Straith to Brittain." 2 January, T236/3069, London: The National Archives, Kew.

——1955. "The market in transferable Sterling." 31 January, T236/3969, London: The National Archives, Kew.

——1975. "Treasury historical memorandum no. 20: The March gold crisis 1968." T267/21, London: The National Archives, Kew.

Tomlinson, J. 1990. *Public Policy and the Economy Since 1900*, Oxford: Clarendon Press.

——1996. "Inventing 'decline': the falling behind of the British economy in the postwar period." *Economic History Review* 49: pp. 731–57.

Tong, W. J. 1991. *Disorder Under Heaven: Collective Violence in the Ming Dynasty*, Stanford, CA: Stanford University Press.

Tooze, R. 1984. "Perspectives and theory: a consumers' guide." In Strange, S. ed. *Paths to International Political Economy*, London: George Allen and Unwin.

——1999. "Susan Strange, academic international relations and the study of international political economy." *New Political Economy*, 5(2): pp. 280–89.

——2000. "Ideology, knowledge and power in international relations and international political economy." In Lawton, T. C., Rosenau, J. N., and Verdun, A. C. eds. *Strange Power: Shaping the Parameters of International Relations and International Political Economy*, Aldershot, UK: Ashgate, pp. 175–94.

Tresize, P. 1983. "Industrial policy is not the major reason for Japan's success." *Brookings Review* 1(3): pp. 13–18.

Trevelyan, G. M. 1946. *English Social History*, London: Longmans, 2nd edition.

Tsiang, T.-F. 1967. "The English and the opium trade." In Schurmann, F. and Schell, O. eds. *Imperial China*, New York: Vintage Books: pp. 132–45.

Tsui-Auch, L. S. 1999. "Regional production relationship and developmental impacts: a comparative study of three regional networks." *International Journal of Urban and Regional Research* 23(2): pp. 345–60.

Tyson, L. d'Andrea. 1993. *Who's Bashing Whom? Trade Conflicts in High-Technology Industries*, Washington DC: Institute for International Economics.

Underhill, G. R. D. ed. 1997. *International Finance and the New World Order*, London: Macmillan.

US House of Representatives. 1998. Testimony of Charlene Barshefsky before the House Ways and Means Subcommittee, US House of Representatives, February 24.

Vachudova, M. 2005. "*Europe Undivided: Democracy, Leverage & Integration After Communism*. New York: Oxford University Press.

Van Harten, G. 2007 *Investment Treaty Arbitration and Public Law*, Oxford: Oxford University Press.

Verdun, A. and Jones, E. eds. 2005. *Political Economy of European Integration: Theory and Analysis*, New York: Routledge.

Verkuil, P. R. 2007. *Outsourcing Sovereignty*, New York: Cambridge University Press.

Vernon, R. 1971. *Sovereignty at Bay: The Multinational Spread of U.S. Enterprises*, New York: Basic Books.

——1989. "The foundations came last." In Kruzel, J. and Rosenau, J. N. eds. *Journeys Through World Politics: Autobiographical Reflections of Thirty-four Academic Travelers*, Lexington, MA: Lexington Books: pp. 437–45.

Viner, J. 1929. "International finance and balance of power diplomacy, 1880–1914." *Political and Social Science Quarterly* 9(4): pp. 408–51.

——1948. "Power versus plenty as objectives of foreign policy in the seventeenth and eighteenth centuries." *World Politics* 1(1) (October): pp. 1–29.

Vogel, E. F. 1979. *Japan as Number One: Lessons for America*, Cambridge, MA: Harvard University Press.

Vreeland, J. R. 2003. *The IMF and Economic Development*, New York: Cambridge University Press.

Wade, R. 1988. "The role of government in overcoming market failure: Taiwan, Republic of Korea, and Japan." In Hughes, H. ed., *Achieving Industrialization in Asia*, Cambridge: Cambridge University Press: pp. 129–63.

——1990. *Governing the Market: Economic Theory and the Role of Government in East Asian Industrialization*, Princeton, NJ: Princeton University Press.

——1998. "The Asian debt-and-development crisis of 1997–? Causes and consequences." *World Development* 26: pp. 1535–53.

——2002. "*US hegemony and the World Bank: the fight over people and ideas.*"Review of International Political Economy 9: pp. 215–43.

——2003. "Introduction: creating capitalisms." In his *Governing the Markett: Economic Theory and the Role of Government in East Asian Industrialization*, Princeton, NJ: Princeton University Press.

Wade, R. and Veneroso, F. 1998. "The Asian crisis: the high debt model versus the Wall Street-Treasury-IMF complex." *New Left Review,* 228: pp. 3–24.

Wæver, O. 1998. "The sociology of a not so international discipline: American and European developments in international relations." *International Organization* 52(4): pp. 687–72

Wakeman, F. 1985. *The Great Enterprise: The Manchu Reconstruction of Imperial Order in Seventeenth-Century China*, Berkeley: University of California Press.

Walker, P. and K. Pepper. 2007. "Follow the Money: A Review and Analysis of the State of Humanitarian Funding." Background paper prepared for the meeting of the Good Humanitarian Donorship and Interagency Standing Committee. Geneva, July 20, 2007.

Wallerstein, I. 1974. *The Modern World System I: Capitalist Agriculture and the Origins of the European World Economy in the Sixteenth Century*, New York: Academic Press.

——1980. *The Modern World-System II: Mercantilism and the Consolidation of the European World-Economy, 1600–1750*, New York: Academic Press.

——1999. "States? Sovereignty? The dilemmas of capitalists in an age of transition." In Smith, D. A., Solinger, D. J., and Topik, S. C. eds. *States and Sovereignty in the Global Economy*, London: Routledge: pp. 20–33.

Wallerstein, I. ed. 2004. *The Modern World-System in the Longue Durée*, Boulder, CO: Paradigm Publishers.

Waltz, K. 1959. *Man, the State, and War*, New York: Columbia University Press.

——1970. "The myth of national interdependence." In Charles Kindleberger, ed. *The International Corporation*, Cambridge, MA: MIT Press.

——1979. *Theory of International Politics*, Reading, MA: Addison-Wesley.

——1999. "Globalization and governance." *PS: Political Science and Politics* 32(4) (December): pp. 639–700.

——2001. *Man, the State and War: A Theoretical Analysis*, New York: Columbia University Press, 2nd edition.

Wang, G. 1991. *China and the Chinese Overseas*, Singapore: Times Academic Press.

——1998. "Ming foreign relations: Southeast Asia." In Twitchett, D. and Mote, F. W. eds. *The Cambridge History of China Vol. 8 (2), The Ming Dynasty*, Cambridge: Cambridge University Press: pp. 301–32.

——2000. *The Chinese Overseas: From Earthbound China to the Quest for Autonomy*, Cambridge, MA: Harvard University Press.

Wan-Soon Kim and You-Il Lee 2005. "The chill wind of Korean xenophobia." *Far Eastern Economic Review* 168(11) (December): pp. 41–46.

Watson, M. 1999. "Rethinking capital mobility, re-regulating financial markets." *New Political Economy* 4(1): pp. 55–76.

——2002. "The institutional paradoxes of monetary orthodoxy: reflections on the political economy of central bank independence." *Review of International Political Economy* 9(1): pp. 183–96.

——2003. "Ricardian political economy and the 'varieties of capitalism' approach: specialisation, trade and comparative institutional advantage." *Comparative European Politics* 1(2): pp. 227–40.

——2005. *Foundations of International Political Economy*, Basingstoke, UK: Palgrave Macmillan.

——2008. "Theoretical traditions in global political economy." In Ravenhill, J. ed. *Global Political Economy*, 2nd edition, Oxford: Oxford University Press: pp. 27–66.

Webb, M. C. 1995. *The Political Economy of Policy Coordination: International Adjustment Since 1945*, Ithaca, NY: Cornell University Press.

——2004. "Defining the boundaries of legitimate state practice: norms, transnational actors and the OECD's project on harmful tax competition." *Review of International Political Economy* 11(4): pp. 787–827.

Weber, H. 2004. "Reconstituting the 'Third World'? Poverty reduction and territoriality in the global politics of development." *Third World Quarterly* 25(1): pp. 187–206.

——2006. "A political analysis of the PRSP initiative: social struggles and the organization of persistent relations of inequality." *Globalizations* 3(2): pp. 187–206.

Weber, M. 1979. *Economy and Society*, Berkeley: University of California Press.

Weber, S. 2001. "Introduction." In Weber, S. ed. *Globalization and the European Political Economy*, New York: Columbia University Press: pp. 1–28.

Wechsler, W. 2001. "Follow the money." *Foreign Affairs* 80: pp. 47–50.

Weingast, B. R. and Witttman, D. A. 2006. *The Oxford Handbook of Political Economy*, Oxford: Oxford University Press.

Weiss, L. 1998. *The Myth of the Powerless State*, Ithaca, NY: Cornell University Press.

Weiss, L. ed. 2003. *States in the Global Economy: Bringing Domestic Institutions Back In*, Cambridge: Cambridge University Press.

Weiss, L. and Thurbon, E. 2006. "The business of buying American: public procurement as a trade strategy in the USA." *Review of International Political Economy* 13 (5): pp. 701–24.

Weiss, L., Thurbon, E., and Mathews, J. 2004. *How to Kill a Country: Australia's Devastating Trade Deal with the United States*, Sydney: Allen & Unwin.

Weller, P. and Xu, Y-C. 2004. *The Governance of World Trade: International Civil Servants in the GATT/WTO*, Cheltenham, UK: Edward Elgar.

Wendt, A. 1987. "The agent-structure problem in international relations theory." *International Organization* 41(3): pp. 335–70.

——1992. "Anarchy is what states make of it: the social construction of power politics." *International Organization* 46(2): pp. 391–425.

——1994. "Collective identity formation and the international state." *American Political Science Review* 88(2): pp. 384–96.

——1999. *Social Theory of International Politics*, Cambridge: Cambridge University Press.

——2001. "Driving with the Rearview Mirror: On the Rational Science of Institutional Design," *International Organization* 55(4): pp. 1019–49.

Western, B. 2001. "Institutions, investment and the rise in unemployment." In Campbell, J. L. and Pedersen, O. K. eds. *The Rise of Neoliberalism and Institutional Analysis*, Princeton, NJ: Princeton University Press: pp. 71–93.

Western, B. and Beckett, K. 1999. "How unregulated is the U.S. labor market? The penal system as a labor market institution." *American Journal of Sociology* 104: pp. 1030–60.

Wheeler, J. C. 2000. *Cosmic Catastrophes: Supernovae, Gamma-ray Bursts, and Adventures in Hyperspace*, Cambridge: Cambridge University Press.

White, L. H. 2000. "Review." *Journal of Economic Literature* 38(4): pp. 951–53.

Whitford, J. 2005. *The New Old Economy: Networks, Institutions, and the Organizational Transformation of American Manufacturing*, New York: Oxford University Press.

Whitley, R. 1992. *Business Systems in East Asia: Firms, Markets and Societies*, London: Sage.

——1998. "Internationalization and varieties of capitalism: the limited effects of cross-national coordination of economic activities on the nature of business systems." *Review of International Political Economy* 5(3): pp. 445–81.

——1999. *Divergent Capitalisms: The Social Structuring and Change of Business Systems*, New York: Oxford University Press.

Whitley, R. and Kristensen, P. H. eds. 1996. *The Changing European Firm: Limits to Convergence*, London: Routledge.

——1997. *Governance at Work: The Social Regulation of Economic Relations*, Oxford: Oxford University Press.

Whitworth, S. 1994. *Feminism and International Relations*, London: Macmillan.

Widmaier, W. 2003. "Constructing monetary crises: new Keynesian understandings and monetary cooperation in the 1990s." *Review of International Studies* 29: pp. 61–78.

——2004. "The social construction of the 'impossible trinity': the intersubjective bases of monetary cooperation." *International Studies Quarterly* 48(2): pp. 433–53.

——2007. "Where you stand depends on how you think: economic ideas, the decline of the Council of Economic Advisers, and the rise of the Federal Reserve." *New Political Economy* 12(1) (March): pp. 43–59.

Widmaier, W. W., Blyth, M., and Seabrooke, L. 2007. "Exogenous shocks or endogenous constructions? The meanings of wars and crises." *International Studies Quarterly* 51(4): pp. 747–59.

Wiener, M. J. 1981. *English Culture and the Decline of the Industrial Spirit, 1850–1980*, Cambridge: Cambridge University Press.

Wilden, A. 1972. *System and Structure: Essays in Communication and Exchange*, London: Tavistock Publications.

Will, P-E. and Wong, R. B. 1991. *Nourish the People: The State Civilian Granary System in China, 1650–1850*, Ann Arbor: University of Michigan Press.

Willett, T. D. ed. 1988. *Political Business Cycles: The Politics of Money, Inflation, and Unemployment*, Durham, NC: Duke University Press.

Willett, T. D. and Vaubel, R. eds. 1991. *The Political Economy of International Organizations*, Boulder, CO: Westview Press.

Willetts, P. ed. 1982. *Pressure Groups in the Global System: The Transnational Relations of Issue-Orientated Non-Governmental Organizations*, New York: St. Martin's Press.

Williamson, O. 1975. *Markets and Hierarchies*. New York: Free Press.

——1985. *The Economic Institutions of Capitalism*. New York: Free Press.

Wills, J. E. Jr. 1979. "Maritime China from Wang Chih to Shih Lang: themes in peripheral history." In Spence, J. D. and Wills, J. E. Jr. eds. *Conquest, Region, and Continuity in Seventeenth Century China*, New Haven, CT and London: Yale University Press: 203–38.

——1998. "Relations with maritime Europeans." In Twitchett, D. and Mote, F. W. eds. *The Cambridge History of China Vol. 8 (2), The Ming Dynasty*, Cambridge: Cambridge University Press, pp. 333–75.

Wilson, A. 2007. "Diasporic agents and Trans-Asian flows in the making of Asian modernity: the case of Thailand." In Hobson, J. M. and Seabrooke, L. eds. *Everyday Politics of the World Economy*, Cambridge: Cambridge University Press: pp. 160–76.

Winch, D. 1969. *Economics and Policy: A Historical Survey*, London: Fontana/Collins.

Winham, G. R. 1986. *International Trade and the Tokyo Round Negotiations*, Princeton, NJ: Princeton University Press.

Wolf, E. 1982. *Europe and the People without History*, Berkeley: University of California Press.

Wolfe, R. 1998 *Farm Wars: The Political Economy of Agriculture and the International Trading Regime*, London: Macmillan.

Wolfers, A. 1962. "The goals of foreign policy." In Wolfers, A. *Discord and Collaboration*, Baltimore, MD: Johns Hopkins University Press.

Wolin, S. S. 1968. "Paradigms and political theories." In King, P. and Parekh, B. C. eds. *Politics and Experience: Essays Presented to Professor Michael Oakeshott on the Occasion of His Retirement*, Cambridge: Cambridge University Press: pp. 125–52.

Woll, C. 2008. "Lecture critique de Pierre Berthaud et Gérard Kébabdjian (dir.) La question politique en économie internationale." *Critique Internationale* 38, (janvier-mars): pp. 201–5.

Womack, J. P., Jones, D. T., and Roos, D. 1990. *The Machines That Changed the World*, New York: Rawson Associates.

Wong, R. B. 1997. *China Transformed: Historical Change and the Limits of European Experience*, Ithaca, NY: Cornell University Press.

Woo-Cumings, M. 1991. *Race to the Swift*, New York: Columbia University Press.

——2005. "Back to basics: ideology, nationalism, and Asian values in East Asia," in Helleiner, E. and Pickel, A. eds. *Economic Nationalism in a Globalizing World*, Ithaca, NY: Cornell University Press: pp. 91–117.

Woo-Cumings, M. ed. 1999. *The Developmental State*, Ithaca, NY: Cornell University Press.

Woods, N. 2006. *The Globalizers: The IMF, the World Bank, and Their Borrowers*, Ithaca, NY: Cornell University Press.

World Bank. 1993. *The East Asian Miracle*, Oxford: Oxford University Press.

Xu, Y-C. 2004. *Electricity Reform in China, India and Russia: The World Bank Template and the Politics of Power*, Cheltenham, UK: Edward Elgar.

Yang, C. 2007. "Divergent practices of capitalisms in China: Hong Kong and Taiwan-invested electronics clusters in Dongguan." *Economic Geography* 83(4): pp. 395–420.

Yang, Y.-R. and Hsia, C.-J. 2007. "Spatial clustering and organizational dynamics of trans-border production networks: a case study of Taiwanese IT companies in the Greater Suzhou area, China." *Environment and Planning A* 39(6): pp. 1382–1402.

Yarbrough, B. V. and R. M. Yarbrough. 1992. *Cooperation and Governance in International Trade: The Strategic Organizational Approach*. Princeton, NJ: Princeton University Press

Yeung, H. W. 2000. "The dynamics of Asian business systems in a globalising era." *Review of International Political Economy* 7(3): pp. 399–433.

——2001. "Organising regional production networks in Southeast Asia: implications for production fragmentation, trade and rules of origin." *Journal of Economic Geography* 1(3): pp. 299–321.

——2004. *Chinese Capitalism in a Global Era: Towards Hybrid Capitalism*, London: Routledge.

——2007a. "Remaking economic geography: insights from East Asia." *Economic Geography* 83(4): pp. 339–48.

——2007b. "From followers to market leaders: Asian electronics firms in the global economy." *Asia Pacific Viewpoint* 48(1): pp. 1–25.

——[forthcoming]. "Regional development and the competitive dynamics of global production networks: an East Asian perspective." *Regional Studies* 42.

Yeung, H. W. and Lin, G. C. S. 2003. "Theorizing economic geographies of Asia." *Economic Geography* 79(2): pp. 107–28.

Yonay, Y. P. 1998. *The Struggle Over the Soul of Economics: Institutionalist and Neoclassical Economists in America Between the Wars*, Princeton, NJ: Princeton University Press.

Yoshihara, K. 1994. *The Nation and Economic Growth*, Kuala Lumpur, Malaysia: Oxford University Press.

Yusuf, S., Altaf, M. Anjum, and Nabeshima, K. eds. 2004. *Global Production Networking and Technological Change in East Asia*, Washington DC: Oxford University Press for World Bank.

Zacher, M. W. 1992. *Canadian Foreign Policy and International Economic Regimes*, Vancouver: UBC Press.

Zacher, M. W. and Sutton, B. A. 1996. *Governing Global Networks: international regimes for transportation and communications*, Cambridge: Cambridge University Press.

Zeitlin, J. 2003. "Introduction." In Zeitlin, J. and Trubek, D. eds. *Governing Work and Welfare in a New Economy: European and American Experiments*, New York: Oxford University Press: pp. 1–32.

Zizek, S. 2008. *Violence*, London: Picador.

Zweig, D. 2002. *Internationalizing China: Domestic Interests and Global Linkages*, Ithaca, NY: Cornell University Press.

Zweig, D. and Chen, Z. eds. 2007. *China's Reforms and International Political Economy*, London: Routledge.

Zysman, J. 1983. *Governments, Markets, and Growth: Financial Systems and the Politics of Industrial Change*, Ithaca, NY: Cornell University Press.

Zysman, J. and Tyson, L. d'Andrea eds. 1983. *American Industry in International Competition*, Ithaca, NY: Cornell University Press.

Index

currency markets 25; European Central Bank 68; European IPE 4, 113, 234; European monetary integration 34, 233, 278; extroversion of the European power struggle/developmental path 169–70, 173, 183; inflation 68; IR 232; lack of IPE in continental Europe 15, 18, 231–42; Marxism 235; model of European state formation and behavior 12, 167–70, 183; Netherlands 238; scientific turn 159; territorial expansion 168–69, 170, 173, 174; Treaties of Westphalia (1648) 30, 31, 169, 205; warfare 168, 169, 171, 173, 174, 183; welfare state 67, 277–78; *see also* European Union; France; Germany
European Union 234; capital mobility 69; European Community Humanitarian aid Office (ECHO) 59; European Economic Community (EEC) 285, 288; liberal rules 69
everyday IPE (EIPE) 17–18, 290–306; agency 290, 291, 295, 298–306 (analytical 295, 299; axiorational agency 301, 302–3, 304–6; defiance agency 18, 301, 302, 303–4, 305–6; mimetic challenge 18, 301, 302, 304, 305–6; normative 295, 299); central purpose of 300; a critical trend 295, 298–99; elite actors 292, 294–95, 297, 299, 300, 302, 303; everyday actions 291, 299, 301, 303, 305; everyday forms of change 301–2; *everyday life* approach: the logic of discipline 18, 290, 295–99, 306 (Amoore, Louise 296, 297, 298; Langley, Paul 296–97, 298; Patterson, Matthew 297–98); *everyday politics* approach: the logic of action 18, 290, 294, 295, 299–305, 306 (Broome, André 303; Herod, Andrew 303–4; Seabrooke, Leonard 304–5; Sharman, J.C. 304); housing finance/global financial power 18, 304–5; interdisciplinary way of studying IPE 18; juxtaposing regulatory/everyday IPE 17–18, 291, 293, 295, 300; juxtaposing types of change in regulatory/everyday IPE 301–2; Kerkvliet, Benedict J. Tria 290, 300; Lefebvre, Henri 290, 295; legitimacy 18, 300, 305; microstate tax havens 18, 304; non-elite actors 18, 290–91, 292, 296, 298, 299–300, 301, 302, 303–6; norms, normative agenda 295, 298, 299, 301, 302, 304; order 291–96, 295, 305; pension reform 18, 20, 296–97; power 299, 300, 301, 303; regulatory IPE (RIPE): who governs and who benefits? 17–18, 290, 291–95, 301–2; resistance to neoliberal trends 298; risk 20, 296, 297; risks of being an 'interdiscipline' 19, 20; Scott, James 290, 300; sociology 17, 18, 291–93, 295, 296; structure/agency relationship 297–98, 299; structures of power 299; 'technologies of the self' 295, 298; *see also* constructivism; Foucault, Michel; neoliberalism; neorealism; sociology

feminism 14, 81, 84, 223, 224, 226
Finnemore, Martha 32, 222, 268; security studies 64; *see also* constructivism
Foreign Direct Investment (FDI): democracy/autocracy credibility 56, 57
foreign policy 142; American IPE 25, 28, 29, 36–37, 44; Australia 217; Britain 106; Canada 81, 83; China 45, 46; *Foreign Policy* 91; globalization 28; imperialism 102–3; international politics/international economic relationship 36–37; Kennan, George F. 44; mercantilism 47; Morgenthau, Hans 44, 64; United States 54, 102, 126, 164; Viner, Jacob 25; *see also* policy; realism
foreign trade: China 171, 172; Hobson, J.A. 103; international cooperation 39; mercantilism 45, 47; *see also* globalization; trade; transnationalism
Foucault, Michel 11, 131, 236, 290, 295; governmentality 137, 295; neoliberalism 258; *normalization* 123; post-structuralism 128, 133; power-knowledge 132, 134, 137, 244; *see also* post-structuralism
France 15, 231–42, 269–70; American IPE 231, 232, 234, 238, 241–42; *Annales* school 231, 232, 235; Braudel, Fernand 232–33; British IPE 234, 238, 241–42; comparative political economy 233–34, 238, 241; Cournot, A.A. 15, 235; difficult transition in political economy 236–38; economic structuralism 245, 253; empiricism 237; France as one extreme pole of a European dilemma 238–41; Gold Pool 286, 287; *Grandes Ecoles* 236, 240; heterodox economists 15, 232, 233; imported/endogenously generated theory 15, 234, 237, 238, 239; institutionalism 236–37; IPE in France and Europe: a brief inventory 232–34; IR 232, 234, 238, 241; Marxism 15, 232, 234–36, 237, 238, 241; neoliberalism 231; political economy 15, 231, 232, 233, 235–38, 240, 241; political science 234, 235, 236, 238, 239, 240; *politiques publiques* 234, 237; post-structuralism 237–38; reasons why IPE remains underdeveloped 15, 16, 231–32, 234; Regulation School 15, 208, 215, 231, 233, 235, 236, 241 (Fordism/post-Fordism 15, 233, 235); Sciences Po 236, 240; social science 235, 236, 240, 241; Walras, M.E.L. 15, 235; *see also* Braudel, Fernand; Europe; Germany
Frieden, Jeffrey 1–2; consensus on theories, methods and analytical frameworks 1–2, 3, 4; *International Political Economy: Perspectives on Global Power and Wealth* 1; relational contracting 53; *see also* United States

gains: absolute 51, 107; relative 6, 39–40, 47, 51, 107; security issues 40

275; embedded autonomy 274, 275;
institutional heterogeneity: liberal-coordinated
market economies 275, 279;
interorganizational, interpersonal networks
275, 279; social effects of political-economic
institutions 274); constructivism 17; dependency
theory 272–73; developed/developing
countries 274; everyday IPE (EIPE) 17, 18,
291–93, 295, 296 (*everyday politics* approach
18, 290, 299–305, 306); globalization 266,
272–73, 274, 277, 279; ideas, ideational
approach 17, 266, 279, 292–93; international
diffusion 267–70, 271, 279; international
division of labor 17, 266, 272–73; international
relations 266–67; internationalization and
globalization 70; neoliberalism 16–17, 266,
270–72, 277, 279; new IPE 281; norms,
normative approach 16, 84, 266, 267–70, 271,
278, 279; regulatory IPE (RIPE): who
governs and who benefits? 291–93; United
States 17, 279; welfare state reform 276–78,
279; why sociology has been side-lined in IPE
279; world systems theory 272–73; *see also*
constructivism; social science
sovereignty 223; East Asia 175, 186, 213, 222;
graduated sovereignty 213; rights 6;
semisovereign states 176, 184, 198; sovereign
transfers among states 54–55; *Sovereignty at Bay*
25; *see also* globalization; state
Spruyt, Hendrik: relational contracting 53–54, 55
state 9, 11, 43, 71, 281; American IPE 5, 28, 30,
31–32, 36, 38–39, 41–44, 51–53, 71, 82, 107,
125; anarchy 40, 50; Aristotle 108, 109;
autonomy 40, 41; balance of power between
states 41; balance of power: from market to
state 129, 130; 'billiard-balls' model 12, 29,
98, 116; British IPE 9, 103–9, 110, 123, 129,
130, 142–43, 147–48; capacity 41; capitalism
173, 181; competition 142–43, 147–48,
213–14; constructivism 71, 72; contractualism
48; core/peripheral/semi-peripheral states 167,
175, 245–46, 248–52, 253, 272; credibility 56;
developmental states and the IPE 180–200;
East Asia/European interstate system
comparison 167–70, 173, 174; East Asian IPE
205; empiricism 114–15, 123, 125; financial
system 304–5; globalization 28, 41, 220–21,
277; hegemonic stability theory (HST) 5,
31–32; international diffusion 267–70; IPE
and state behavior 23; Japan 177, 181;
liberalism 36, 38, 71; List, Friedrich 39;
market vs. state debate 13, 184–86, 189, 199,
206; Marxism 36, 108; mercantilism 38–39;
microeconomic analogy 43; model of
European state formation 12; nation-state 12,
142–43, 152, 153, 166–67, 213–14, 267–70,
272; national industrial welfare state/

competition state 142–43, 147–48, 213–14;
nationalism 44; neoliberalism 51–53, 107, 258;
neorealism 42–44, 82, 107; new roles for the
state 147–48; outsourcing 57–60; rational
institutional design 51–53; rationalism 48;
realism 28, 30, 36, 38, 41, 44, 71, 213–14;
regime theory 5, 31; 'retreat of the state' 129,
156, 195, 233; the rise of East Asia 13–14,
177, 180–200, 201–15; security 36, 39; state
actors 151–53; state behavior 12, 23, 29, 33,
37, 43, 44, 63, 71, 123, 284; state-centric
paradigm 28, 29, 34, 41, 60, 81, 82, 142, 213,
234; state/market relation 82, 129, 130, 137,
180–200, 258; 'states as billiard-balls' model
12, 29, 98, 116; Strange, Susan 129, 130, 213;
structural analysis 43–44; structural change,
public goods, and the role of the state 142,
145–47; structural power 129; structurational
approach to IPE 142, 145–48; systemic
governance 31; transnational corporations
(TNCs) and states 134–35; wealth/power
relationship 37; welfare state 66–67, 69, 85,
142–43, 147, 148, 157, 276–77; welfare state
reform 276–78, 279; *see also* Asia, East Asia;
developmental state; globalization; hegemony;
international relations; neoliberalism; policy;
realism; security issues; transnationalism
state interests 268, 286, 292; Canada 82; China
164, 166, 173; European monetary integration
34; globalization 42, 47; liberalism 36; List,
Friedrich 38, 39; Marxism 36; mercantilism
39; realism 29, 36, 41, 46, 47, 50, 71, 215;
United States 129, 164
Strange, Susan 62, 79, 99, 102, 103, 126–39,
241, 284; *1970 as year zero* for British IPE
95–96, 111; American/British schools'
differences 130; American/British schools'
similarities 10, 130; American IPE 126, 127,
130, 132, 215; agenda setting 128, 130, 131;
agents 129, 130–32, 133, 134 (self-interested
agents 129, 130); authority 129, 130; balance
of power 129, 130; British International
Studies Association (BISA) 111, 126; Canadian
IPE 90, 132; career 126; champion of a
power-materialist discipline of IPE 131;
control of knowledge 131; corporation 129;
eclecticism 127; economics 280; empiricism
122, 132; finance structure 127, 129, 130,
131, 132; Foucault, Michel 128, 131, 132;
Gramsci, Antonio 132; international
organization 129; International Political
Economy Group (IPEG) 111, 126; IR 132,
215; key individual in British IPE 8, 10, 82,
95, 102, 126, 130, 138; knowledge structure
127, 129, 130–32, 135, 138; Lukes, Steven
130; markets 129, 130; post-structuralism 10,
127–39; 'power-knowledge' 10, 127–28, 132,

133; production structure 129, 131, 132; *Qui bono?* (who benefits?) 10, 129–30; regime theory 50; relational power 10, 11, 128–29; relational/structural power differences 129; security structure 129, 131, 132; soft power 130; state 129, 130, 213; *States and Markets* 131, 132, 135; structural power 10, 11, 122, 127, 128–32, 134, 138; US hegemonic power, and decline 127, 129, 130, 132; *Wake up Krasner, the world has changed* 99, 125; *see also* Britain; neorealism; post-structuralism

structuralism 141, 291, 292; change 301–2; distribution of power 42, 43, 46; Economic Commission for Latin America and the Caribbean (ECLAC) 245–47, 248, 250; French economic structuralism 245, 253; Japanese economic stagnation 193–94; Latin America 16, 244–47, 248, 253–54; Mearsheimer, John 45, 46; realism 6, 7, 42–44, 45, 46; structural realism 45, 46

structurational approach to IPE 10–11, 140–59; actors 141–42, 143, 144–45, 148–55, 156–58 (economic agents: workers, managers, financiers 150–51, 155, 156–57, 158; political agents: politicians and bureaucrats 151–53, 155, 156, 158; social agents: social movements, interest groups, ordinary people 150, 153–55, 156, 158, 159); constructing a new world order 148–50; globalization 141, 142, 143, 145–50 (internationalization, transnationalization, translocalization 143); methodology 158; multi-actor, multi-nodal, global politics 10–11, 13, 141, 142, 155, 158; multiple equilibria 142, 143, 145, 148, 150; national industrial welfare state/competition state 142–43, 147–48; 'neomedievalism' 157; new roles for the state 147–48; path dependency 143; pluralism 141, 142; political structuration 11, 141; process of structuration 11, 143–45, 155–58; process matters 11; public/private goods 142; scenarios of change 155–58; structural change, public goods, and the role of the state 142, 145–47 (categories of collective goods 146–47; structure of consumption 145–46; structure of production 145–46); structuration 141; structure/agency relationship 10–11, 141, 143, 144–58; *see also* Britain; globalization; transnationalism

Taiwan 176, 179, 187, 260; China 163, 178; developmental state 182, 206, 212; export orientation 190–91; hegemonic web: US, Japan, Korea and Taiwan 183–84; industrialization 183–84, 187–88, 212; Japan 182; land reform 186, 187–88, 193; security and land reform 187–88; United States 179, 183–84, 187–88, 199; Vietnam War 183–84;

Wade, Robert 13, 182, 185, 205; Why Korea and Taiwan? The Japanese connection 182–83, 199; *see also* Asia, East Asia; developmental state

terrorism 20, 41, 227; US war on terror 166

Thailand 167, 189, 192, 194, 260; anti-IMF nationalism 197, 200; Asian financial crisis 196, 221; developmental state 197, 199–200; interventionism 189–90; Japanese direct investment 191, 192–93; neoliberal reform 197, 222; Shinawatra, Thaksin 197; veto power 221; *see also* Asia, East Asia; developmental state

trade 48, 281, 290; American IPE 28, 38, 69–70, 122, 127; Asia Pacific Economic Co-operation (APEC) 221–22; Association of Southeast Asian Nations (ASEAN) 222; China-centered tribute trade system 167, 168, 171, 176; free trade 38, 65, 70, 73, 81, 107, 122, 123, 146, 222, 294; General Agreement on Tariffs and Trade (GATT) 53, 222, 294; German inter-war trading relations 37; global trade 60; international trade 38, 39, 70, 85, 142, 170, 224, 278; internationalizing markets for goods and services 69–70; liberalization 28, 70; Mexico 56; neo-classical trade theory 122; North American Free Trade Agreement (NAFTA) 56, 86; policy 66, 148; politics 29; US Cold War regime/China-centered tribute trade system comparison 176–77; *see also* economy; foreign trade; liberalism; market; mercantilism; neoliberalism; policy; World Trade Organization (WTO)

transnationalism 13, 28, 29; actors 28, 29, 30, 57, 59, 148–55; 198, 268; American IPE 28, 29–30, 81; Canada 81; constructing a new world order 148–50; economic transnationalization 151; Gilpin, Robert 30; global governance 57–60; global production networks (GPN) 207; historical materialism 84; international diffusion 267–70; multinational corporations 81, 82, 145, 150–51, 177, 250, 272; power-knowledge 134–35; scenarios of change 155–58; systemic governance 31; transnational advocacy coalitions/networks 154–55; transnational corporations (TNCs) 207; transnational corporations (TNCs) and states 134–35; transnational 'cosmopolitan democracy' 156; *Transnational Relations and World Politics* 30; *see also* contractualism; globalization; state; structurational approach to IPE

United Nations (UN) 58, 268; Canada 77; transnational advocacy coalitions/networks 159; UN High Commissioner for Refugees (UNHCR) 59

World Bank 85, 224, 260, 267; *The East Asian Miracle* 185–86, 189–90, 194; environmental sustainability 222–23; gender 223; neoliberal ideology 223; Philippines 192, 193; rational institutional design 52

world economy 18, 23, 62, 63, 66, 73, 281; Asia 12, 188, 202, 204, 210; British IPE 100, 148; constitution 60, 73; constructivism 7, 73, 74, 75, 76; everyday IPE (EIPE) 290–95, 299, 300–301, 305–6; interdependence 29, 49, 210; Latin America 16, 245, 247, 249; liberal 31; material facts/social facts 73; United States 24; *see also* globalization; transnationalism

world systems theory 213, 266, 272–73, 291, 293; core/peripheral/semi-peripheral states 167, 175, 245–46, 248–52, 253, 272, 293; globalization 272–73; hegemonic power 273; regulatory IPE (RIPE): who governs and who benefits? 291, 293; state 273; Wallerstein, Immanuel 111, 232, 272, 293; *see also* Braudel, Fernand; capitalism

World Trade Organization (WTO) 60, 69–70, 73, 151; Asia Pacific Economic Co-operation (APEC) 222; Australian IPE 219; relational contracting 53; Trade Related Investment Measures Agreement (TRIMs) 190; *see also* trade